THE COMPLETE OFFICIAL
1275 cc
SPRITE/MIDGET

Model Years 1967–1974

Selected Titles From Bentley Publishers

Engineering

Robert Bentley's Repair Manual for British Cars
John Organ
ISBN 978-0-8376-0041-3

Vintage Racing British Sports Cars *Terry Jackson*
ISBN 978-0-8376-0153-3

Scientific Design of Exhaust & Intake Systems *Philip H. Smith and John C. Morrison*
ISBN 978-0-8376-0309-4

The Design and Tuning of Competition Engines *Philip H. Smith* ISBN 978-0-8376-0140-3

New Directions in Suspension Design: Making the Car Faster
Colin Campbell
ISBN 978-0-8376-0150-2

Racing Car Design and Development *Len Terry with Alan Baker* ISBN 978-0-8376-0080-2

Austin-Healey

Austin-Healey 100/6 NS 3000 Workshop Manual: 1956-1968
British Leyland Motors
ISBN 978-0-8376-0133-5
Softcover, 416 pages
Includes: Workshop Manual

The Complete Official 1275 cc Sprite/Midget: 1967-1974
British Leyland Motors
ISBN 978-0-8376-0127-4
Softcover, 400 pages

MG

The Complete Official MGB: 1962-1974 *British Leyland Motors*
ISBN 978-0-8376-0115-1
Softcover, 480 pages
Includes: Driver's Handbook, Workshop Manual, Special Tuning Manual

The Complete Official MGB: 1975-1980 *British Leyland Motors*
ISBN 978-0-8376-0112-0
Softcover, 304 pages
Includes: Driver's Handbook, Workshop Manual

The Complete Official MG Midget 1500: 1975-1979
British Leyland Motors
ISBN 978-0-8376-0131-1
Softcover, 384 pages
Includes: Driver's Handbook, Workshop Manual

The MG Workshop Manual: 1929-1955 *W.E. Blower*
ISBN 978-0-8376-0117-5
Softcover, 608 pages

Triumph

The Complete Official Triumph GT6, GT6+ & GT6 MK III: 1967-1973 *British Leyland Motors*
ISBN 978-0-8376-0120-5
Softcover, 480 pages
Includes: Driver's Handbook, Workshop Manual

The Complete Official Triumph TR6 & TR250: 1967-1976
British Leyland Motors
ISBN 978-0-8376-0108-3
Softcover, 608 pages
Includes: Driver's Handbook, Workshop Manual

The Complete Official Triumph Spitfire MK III, MK IV & 1500: 1968-1974 *British Leyland Motors*
ISBN 978-0-8376-0123-6
Softcover, 480 pages
Includes: Driver's Handbook, Workshop Manual

The Complete Official Triumph Spitfire 1500: 1975-1980
British Leyland Motors
ISBN 978-0-8376-0122-9
Softcover, 520 pages
Includes: Driver's Handbook, Workshop Manual

The Complete Official Triumph TR7: 1975-1981
British Leyland Motors
ISBN 978-0-8376-0116-8
Softcover, 544 pages
Includes: Driving Manual, Workshop Manual

The Complete Official Triumph TR4 & TR4A: 1961-1968
British Leyland Motors
ISBN 978-0-8376-0121-2
Softcover, 404 pages
Includes: Driving Manual, Workshop Manual, Competition Preparation Manual by R.W. "Kas" Kastner

The Complete Official Triumph TR2 & TR3: 1953-1961
British Leyland Motors
ISBN 978-0-8376-0125-0
Softcover, 454 pages
Includes: Driver's Instruction Book, Service Instruction Manual

Jaguar

The Complete Official Jaguar "E" Series 1 & Series 2: 1961-1971
British Leyland Motors
ISBN 978-0-8376-0115-1
Softcover, 790 pages
Includes: Driver's Handbook, Workshop Manual, Special Tuning Manual

Bentley Publishers®
Automotive Reference

Bentley Publishers has published service manuals and automobile books since 1950. For more information, please contact Bentley Publishers at 1734 Massachusetts Avenue, Cambridge, MA 02138 USA, or visit our web site at **BentleyPublishers.com**

THE COMPLETE OFFICIAL
1275 cc
SPRITE/MIDGET
1967–1974

Comprising the official

Driver's Handbook

Workshop Manual

Emission Control Supplement

B BentleyPublishers®
.com

BENTLEY PUBLISHERS® | Automotive Reference™

Bentley Publishers, a division of Robert Bentley, Inc.
1734 Massachusetts Avenue
Cambridge, MA 02138 USA
800-423-4595 / 617-547-4170

Information that makes
the difference®

BentleyPublishers®
.com

Technical contact information
We welcome your feedback. Please submit corrections and additions to our technical
discussion forum at:

`http://www.BentleyPublishers.com`

Updates and corrections
We will evaluate submissions and post appropriate editorial changes online as updates or
tech discussion. Appropriate updates and corrections will be added to the book in future
printings. Check for updates and corrections for this book before beginning work on
your vehicle. See the following web address for additional information:

`http://www.BentleyPublishers.com/updates/`

WARNING—Important Safety Notice

In this book we have attempted to describe repairs, modifications and accessories which may be used with Sprite or Midget vehicles, using examples and instructions which we believe to be accurate. However, the examples, instructions, and other information are intended solely as illustrations and should be used in any particular application only by personnel who are experienced in the repair and modification of Sprite or Midget vehicles and who have independently evaluated the repair, modification or accessory. Implementation of a modification or attachment of an accessory described in this book may render the vehicle, attachment, or accessory unsafe for use in certain circumstances. **REPAIR AND MODIFICATION OF MOTOR VEHICLES CAN BE DANGEROUS UNLESS UNDERTAKEN WITH FULL KNOWLEDGE OF THE CONSEQUENCES.**

Do not use this book unless you are familiar with basic automotive repair procedures and safe workshop practices. This book illustrates procedures required for some service and modification work; it is not a substitute for full and up-to-date information from the vehicle manufacturer or aftermarket supplier, or for proper training as an automotive technician. Note that it is not possible for us to anticipate all of the ways or conditions under which vehicles may be serviced or modified or to provide cautions as to all of the possible hazards that may result.

The vehicle manufacturer and aftermarket suppliers will continue to issue service information updates and parts retrofits after the editorial closing of this book. Some of these updates and retrofits will apply to procedures and specifications in this book. We regret that we cannot supply updates to purchasers of this book.

We have endeavored to ensure the accuracy of the information in this book. Please note, however, that considering the vast quantity and the complexity of the information involved, we cannot warrant the accuracy or completeness of the information contained in this book.

FOR THESE REASONS, NEITHER THE PUBLISHER NOR THE AUTHOR MAKES ANY WARRANTIES, EXPRESS OR IMPLIED, THAT THE EXAMPLES, INSTRUCTIONS OR OTHER INFORMATION IN THIS BOOK ARE FREE OF ERRORS OR OMISSIONS, ARE CONSISTENT WITH INDUSTRY STANDARDS, OR THAT THEY WILL MEET THE REQUIREMENTS FOR A PARTICULAR APPLICATION, AND WE EXPRESSLY DISCLAIM THE IMPLIED WARRANTIES OF MERCHANTABILITY AND OF FITNESS FOR A PARTICULAR PURPOSE, EVEN IF THE PUBLISHER OR AUTHOR HAVE BEEN ADVISED OF A PARTICULAR PURPOSE, AND EVEN IF A PARTICULAR PURPOSE IS INDICATED IN THE BOOK. THE PUBLISHER AND AUTHOR ALSO DISCLAIM ALL LIABILITY FOR DIRECT, INDIRECT, INCIDENTAL OR CONSEQUENTIAL DAMAGES THAT RESULT FROM ANY USE OF THE EXAMPLES, INSTRUCTIONS OR OTHER INFORMATION IN THIS BOOK. IN NO EVENT SHALL OUR LIABILITY WHETHER IN TORT, CONTRACT OR OTHERWISE EXCEED THE COST OF THIS BOOK.

Your common sense and good judgment are crucial to safe and successful automotive work. Read procedures through before starting them. Think about how alert you are feeling, and whether the condition of your vehicle, your level of mechanical skill or your level of reading comprehension might result in or contribute in some way to an occurrence which might cause you injury, damage your vehicle, or result in an unsafe repair or modification. If you have doubts for these or other reasons about your ability to perform safe work on your vehicle, have the work done at an authorized Sprite or Midget dealer or other qualified shop.

Before attempting any work on your Sprite or Midget, read the Cautions on page xii and any warning or caution that accompanies a procedure or description in the book. Review the Cautions each time you prepare to work on your Sprite or Midget.

This book is prepared, published and distributed by Bentley Publishers, 1734 Massachusetts Avenue, Cambridge, Massachusetts 02138 USA.

The Complete Official 1275 cc Sprite/Midget: 1967–1974
© 1975 Robert Bentley, Inc. Bentley Publishers is a registered trademark of Robert Bentley, Inc.

 is a registered trademark of Bentley Publishers and Robert Bentley, Inc.

ISBN 978-0-8376-1748-0
Job Code: X027-04

Library of Congress Catalog Card No. 75-37232

The paper used in this publication is acid free and meets the requirements of the National Standard for Information Sciences-Permanence of Paper for Printed Library Materials. ∞

Manufactured in the United States of America.

Preface

This was assembled with the sports car enthusiast in mind. However, the appeal of this manual is not confined to such a limited group; anyone who owns a Sprite or Midget will derive great benefit from the material presented here. The *Driver's Handbook* is the same manual provided with every new Sprite and Midget. It includes lubrication instructions as well as minor tune up and maintenance procedures. The *Workshop Manual* is the official factory service manual and was intended primarily for use by dealer service departments. This explains the liberal reference to special service tools, although the instructions start at quite a basic level and presuppose only limited knowledge of the subject. Included here are descriptions of how each part of the car functions. The *Engine Emission Control Supplement* is an important adjunct to the *Workshop Manual*. All tuning adjustments that have an influence on exhaust content are described here, as are repairs related to the carburetors or to the various components of the emission control system.

There are several reasons why a person will work on his own car. To begin with, a great deal of money can be saved, although often at the expense of an equal amount of time and effort. The automobile enthusiast takes pride in and derives pleasure from driving a well-tuned machine and will go to great lengths to keep his car in such condition. He is quite often extremely knowledgeable about the workings of his car and firmly believes that the care and attention he can provide far outweigh the experience of a professional mechanic who is merely doing his job. Furthermore, he realizes that an intimate knowledge of his car's behavior helps to make him a better driver.

What follows is intended to provide some useful information and hints for the less experienced individual who would like to work on his own car. The most important thing to keep in mind is that there is nothing mysterious about the functioning of a car. Even though some cars have been known to exhibit a definite personality, a fault becomes quite logical once its cause has been found.

Maintenance and General Care

An automobile, like any piece of machinery, responds well to regular maintenance and careful use. There is much to be gained by conscientiously following the manufacturer's recommendations concerning lubrication and adjustments, as described in the *Driver's Handbook*. This is one area where an ounce of prevention is really worth a pound of cure. Whether or not this maintenance is carried out by the individual owner, it is essential that attention be given at periodic intervals. It is worthwhile to keep an accurate record of all maintenance and repairs performed. Several sheets at the end of this manual are available for this purpose, with space provided for the mileage and date. In addition to allowing the owner to keep careful track of service intervals, such records are useful at the time of resale.

Although simple maintenance procedures can be carried out with a minimum of tools, the car owner will sooner or later find it desirable to obtain a fairly complete set. The basic tools include an assortment of open and box end wrenches and a selection of screwdrivers, pliers, one or two adjustable wrenches and other assorted items like feeler gauges, spark plug socket, etc. If any extensive work is contemplated, a ⅜″ or ½″ drive socket set will be most useful. Also, a torque wrench is a very worthwhile purchase. A good set of tools can be a good investment; they will last a lifetime if properly used and cared for. Avoid buying cheaply made tools as they will break or wear out quickly and will often damage bolts, fittings, etc.

Whenever possible, use the wrench correctly suited for the job; excessive use of pliers and adjustable wrenches will roughen and deform the parts they are removing, making later use of the correct tool impossible. It is important that all bolts, nuts and spark plugs be tightened correctly. A fastener that is too tight can be worse than one which is too loose. Broken bolts and distorted parts are the trademarks of the musclebound mechanic. An experienced mechanic knows by feel how to tighten things and he develops this knowledge by long use of a torque wrench. If you have one, by all means use it. It is a good idea to refrain from purchasing specialized tools, such as gear pullers, bushing and seal drivers and odd wrenches, until the need actually arises. In this way the initial expense is reduced and one is always certain of getting the correct sized tool for his needs.

It is appropriate to mention here that the bolts and nuts used on the Sprite and Midget are for the most part fitted by standard American wrenches, although in certain instances the older Whitworth pattern wrenches are called for. However, these instances are rare, usually involving some accessory component such as the fuel pump, and careful use of adjustable wrenches will almost always get the job done.

In any work done on a car, it is of the utmost importance to keep everything as clean as possible. Dirt will cause endless trouble if not kept out.

In many cases, there are several ways of doing a job in addition to that suggested by the factory. For example, a commercially available timing light, triggered by the spark to no. 1 cylinder, can be used to set the timing with equal or better accuracy. Also, any of the presently available "ignition analyzers" as used in garages and service stations can be used to test the electrical system.

A final note in this section concerns the oil and gas to be used. Although certain brands of oil are recommended by the factory, any premium grade oil of the recommended weight will prove satisfactory. Do not attempt to use a racing oil on the street as it is not designed for prolonged use. As regards the grade of gasoline to be used, it should be realized that this car, and all imported cars for that matter, was designed to use locally available fuels. Since American gasolines are somewhat superior in octane rating (knock resistance), there is no reason why the car cannot use a Regular grade of fuel. If this is to be done successfully, however, the engine will have to be kept in careful tune.

The presence of knocking or detonation, commonly called "pinging" and sounding like loose marbles in the crankcase, indicates the need for a spark adjustment or the presence of too much carbon in the combustion chambers. Carbon is a normal by-product of combustion and, under prolonged city driving conditions, can build up to the point where the compression ratio is significantly raised. This increase in compression will raise the octane required of the fuel, making the engine more likely to ping. This condition is remedied by removing the cylinder head and scraping out the carbon, described in the *Workshop Manual* under the heading of "decarbonizing". An alternative to the above procedure is simply to use a fuel of higher octane rating. This is the approach used by American car manufacturers and decarbonizing is practically unheard of in this country. In addition, the spark can be advanced slightly with Premium fuel resulting in more power and often better fuel economy. Occasional fast driving or highway use will keep the carbon buildup below a troublesome level; and for a car that is principally driven in such a manner, there is no reason why a Regular grade of gasoline cannot be used.

Major Repairs

When the need to make a major repair arises, there are several factors to consider before deciding whether or not to undertake the job. The most important point is to understand exactly what the repair entails. This can best be done by reading thoroughly the appropriate section or sections in the *Workshop Manual* and by talking with experts to resolve any unanswered questions. When such an understanding has been reached, the problem can be expressed in terms of the amount of money to be saved vs. the labor and equipment involved.

Most repairs involve the use of a series of special tools to make the job easier, more efficient or even possible. Without a doubt, to achieve the best results the procedures should be carried out exactly as described, using all the special tools. However, in many instances similar or alternate methods can be used which will remove the need to purchase the factory tools. For example, seals can often be installed by the careful use of an arbor press or a hammer and drift punch; most of the commercially available gear and bearing pullers will work quite satisfactorily.

There are, however, certain jobs which should only be attempted by experienced people using the correct equipment. There is no other way to adjust properly a differential; and engine boring, bushing reaming, etc., require the services of a competent machine shop. One, therefore, needs to distinguish between what can and cannot be done. It is usually not worthwhile to purchase expensive equipment to do a job only once.

One will find that a majority of the major repairs involve only one or two operations which require skilled personnel or special equipment. It is well within the abilities of the average

v

person to perform all operations up to this point, go to an expert for the required steps, and to continue from there. For example, one can save a great deal of money in an engine overhaul by performing the disassembly, assembly and cleaning operations himself.

In repairs of this sort, cleanliness is very important. Any time an engine block or gear case is disassembled, it and its contents should be cleaned thoroughly inside and out, including all oil passages. It is common practice to have an engine block "boiled" in a weak acid solution. This process results in a very clean block but also destroys the pressed-in camshaft bearings. As the fitting of new camshaft bearings involves the fairly expensive process of align boring, it is often advisable to use a cold solvent instead.

The importance of clearly understanding every step of the job cannot be overemphasized. Always read and understand the entire procedure before starting. It is also generally advisable to use only genuine replacement parts when making repairs of a major nature.

Engine Emissions

The emission control systems, their maintenance, repair, and adjustment are covered with exacting thoroughness in the third part of this book. It is exceedingly important for the car owner to understand that the control of undesirable engine emissions is not achieved by the mere addition of equipment to the engine. Fundamental design differences exist between older, uncontrolled engines and the engines covered by this book.

Removing any part of the emission control system can have a serious and detrimental effect on overall engine operation. In the mistaken belief that doing so will improve performance or economy, car owners sometimes try to remove or deactivate emission controls. They are invariably disappointed. Any performance gains are largely imaginary and a *loss* of performance and economy is not unusual. Worse yet, improper spark timing and overheating can result. Eventually, these conditions may lead to burned valves, damaged pistons, general unreliability, and expensive repairs.

If you use your Sprite or Midget on the public roads, you will enjoy good performance and long service by maintaining the engine emission controls in perfect condition and adjustment. If you intend to modify the car for racing, you will need to replace many of the normal parts with special parts from the official competition parts lists. It is important to note that the presence of parts in the competition parts listings does not mean that they are legal for either public roads or for all types of racing. It's up to the individual to determine just what is allowed when planning the car, not after being protested at the track or arrested on the road.

In non-sanctioned racing, such as gymkhanas and autocrosses, almost anything goes. But club racing and events regulated by national organizations generally have very strict limits concerning which equipment is permissible. An intelligent thing to do is to talk to others running your make in the type of racing you wish to enter. They will be able to tell you not only what is legal, but also which modifications produce the best results. There is no substitute for experience.

Massachusetts Institute of Technology
Cambridge, Massachusetts

Richard Roberts, S.M.
Mechanical Engineering

Special Note

Although the *Workshop Manual* (Part 2 of this book) includes some material applicable to earlier models, this collection of manuals explicitly covers only the Sprite Mark IV and Midget Mark III equipped with the 1275 cc engine and sold from 1967 through 1974. All necessary and pertinent information regarding these models is presented here.

The owners of earlier models are advised to purchase our earlier edition, **The Complete Official 948 cc & 1098 cc Sprite/Midget** book, which has recently been reprinted for the convenience of those who wish to preserve Mark I, II, and III Sprites and Mark I and II Midgets in serviceable or competition condition. The 1975 and later MG Midgets, which have 1500 cc engines, are to be covered in a separate publication.

Editor's Notes are provided throughout this book when additional information is helpful to the reader's understanding of the material. These notes are found at the end of Part I and at the end of individual sections in the *Workshop Manual*.

> Sprite and Midget cars before 1967 were designated by Mark number only. Model year designations were introduced in 1967.

Special thanks are due David G. Head

New England Parts Representative

Leyland Motor Sales

Leonia, N.J.

English-American Equivalents

English	American
GENERAL	
L.H.S.	left hand side
R.H.S.	right hand side
L.H.D.	left hand drive
R.H.D.	right hand drive

(viewed from drivers seat)

English	American
bush	bushing (bronze, rubber, etc.)
circlip	snap ring
distance piece	spacer
end float	end clearance
engine revolution counter	tachometer
extractor	gear or bearing puller
fraze	burr from cutting, drilling, etc.
grub screw	dog screw, locating screw
joint washer	gasket
jointing compound	gasket cement, sealing compound
laden	loaded
methylated spirits	denatured alcohol
paraffin	kerosene
perished	rotted (from oil, etc.)
petrol	gasoline
renew	replace
set screw	bolt
spanner	end wrench
spigot	pilot
split pin	cotter pin
spring washer	lock washer
swarf	chips from cutting, drilling, etc.
ENGINE	
choke tube	venturi
cotters	split valve locks
float chamber	carburetor bowl
gudgeon pin	piston pin, wrist pin
oil sump	oil pan
silencer	muffler
valve crash speed	valve float rpm, redline
welch plug	water jacket plug, core plug, freeze plug
CLUTCH	
clutch housing	bell housing
clutch release bearing	throwout bearing
clutch withdrawal fork	throwout arm
spigot bearing	pilot bearing
GEARBOX	
bulk ring	synchronizing ring, synchro cone
first motion shaft	input shaft
laygear	counter gear, cluster gear
layshaft	countershaft, cluster gear shaft
propeller shaft	driveshaft
third motion shaft	output shaft
REAR AXLE	
crown wheel	ring gear

ELECTRICAL

control box	voltage regulator
distributor suction advance	vacuum advance
dynamo	generator
earth	ground (positive earth = positive ground)
H.T.	high tension
Megger	ohm meter
micro adjuster	octane selector (changes vacuum advance)

SUSPENSION AND STEERING

hydraulic damper	shock absorber
swivel axle	spindle, stub axle
swivel pin	pivot pin, king pin

BODY

bonnet	hood, engine compartment cover
boot	trunk compartment
bulkhead	firewall
fascia	dashboard
hood	top, roof
mono construction body	unit construction body (no frame)
over rider	bumperette
seat squab	seat back, upright portion of seat
wing	fender

Contents

1 OFFICIAL SPRITE/MIDGET DRIVER'S HANDBOOK

2 OFFICIAL SPRITE/MIDGET WORKSHOP MANUAL

X

3 OFFICIAL SPRITE/MIDGET WORKSHOP MANUAL SUPPLEMENT (ENGINE EMISSION CONTROL)

Please read these warnings and cautions before proceeding with maintenance and repair work.

WARNING –

• Never work under a lifted car unless it is solidly supported on stands intended for the purpose. Do not support a car on cinder blocks, hollow tiles, or other props that may crumble under continuous load. Do not work under a car that is supported solely by a jack.

• If you are going to work under a car on the ground, make sure that the ground is level. Block the wheels to keep the car from rolling. Disconnect the battery ground strap to prevent others from starting the car while you are under it.

• Never run the engine unless the work area is well ventilated. Carbon monoxide kills.

• Friction materials such as brake and clutch linings or brake pads may contain asbestos fibers. Do not create dust by grinding, sanding or by cleaning with compressed air. Avoid breathing asbestos fibers and asbestos dust. Breathing asbestos may result in serious diseases, such as asbestosis or cancer, and cause severe injury and death.

• Tie long hair behind your head. Do not wear a necktie, scarf, loose clothing, or necklace when you work near machine tools or running engines. If your hair, clothing, or jewelry were to get caught in the machinery, severe injury could result.

• Disconnect the battery ground strap whenever you work on the fuel system or the electrical system. When you work around fuel, do not smoke or work near heaters or other fire hazards. Keep an approved fire extinguisher handy.

• Illuminate your work area adequately but safely. Use a portable safety light for working inside or under the car. Make sure its bulb is enclosed by a wire cage. The hot filament of an accidentally broken bulb can ignite spilled fuel or oil.

• Catch draining fuel, oil, or brake fluid in suitable containers. Do not use food or beverage containers that might mislead someone into drinking from them. Store flammable fluids away from fire hazards. Wipe up spills at once, but do not store the oily rags, which can ignite and burn spontaneously.

• Finger rings should be removed so that they cannot cause electrical shorts, get caught in running machinery, or be crushed by heavy parts.

• Keep sparks, lighted matches, and open flame away from the top of the battery. If hydrogen gas escaping from the cap vents is ignited, it will ignite gas trapped in the cells and cause the battery to explode.

• Always observe good workshop practices. Wear goggles when you operate machine tools or work with battery acid. Gloves or other protective clothing should be worn whenever the job requires it.

CAUTION –

• If you lack the skills, tools, and equipment, or a suitable workshop for any procedure described in this manual, we suggest you leave such repairs to an Authorized Dealer or other qualified shop. We especially urge you to consult your Authorized Dealer before attempting any repairs on a car still covered by the new-car warranty.

• British Leyland Motors is constantly improving its cars and sometimes these changes, both in parts and specifications, are made applicable to earlier models. Therefore part numbers listed in this manual are for reference only. Always check with your Authorized Parts Department for the latest information.

• Before starting a job, make certain that you have all necessary tools and parts on hand. Read all instructions thoroughly; do not attempt shortcuts. Use tools appropriate to the work and use only replacement parts meeting specifications. Makeshift tools, parts, and procedures will not make good repairs.

• Use pneumatic and electrical tools only to loosen threaded parts and fasteners. Never use such tools to tighten fasteners, especially on light alloy parts.

• Be mindful of the environment and ecology. Before you drain the crankcase, find out the proper way to dispose of the oil. Do not pour oil onto the ground, down a drain, or into a stream, pond, or lake. Consult local ordinances that govern the disposal of wastes.

SPRITE/MIDGET

1275 cc

DRIVER'S HANDBOOK

Part 1

© BRITISH LEYLAND UK LIMITED, 1972

FOREWORD

This Handbook provides an introduction to your car, together with information on the care and periodic maintenance required to combine trouble-free motoring with minimal running costs.

Claims for the replacement of parts under warranty must be submitted to the supplying Distributor or Dealer, or when this is not possible, to the nearest Distributor or Dealer, informing them of the vendor's name and address. Except in emergency, warranty work should always be carried out by an appointed Distributor or Dealer.

By keeping the Passport to Service, signed by the Distributor, Dealer, or vendor in the vehicle, you can quickly establish the date of purchase and provide the necessary details if adjustments are required to be carried out under warranty.

Regular use of the Passport to Service Maintenance Scheme is the best safeguard against the possibility of abnormal repair bills at a later date. Failure to have your car correctly maintained could invalidate the terms of the Warranty and may result in unsatisfactory operation of the emission control systems.

Safety features embodied in the car may be impaired if other than genuine parts are fitted. In certain territories, legislation prohibits the fitting of parts not to the vehicle manufacturer's specification. Owners purchasing accessories while travelling abroad should ensure that the accessory and its fitted location on the car conform to mandatory requirements existing in their country of origin.

Your Distributor or Dealer is provided with the latest information concerning special service tools and workshop techniques. This enables him to undertake your service and repairs in the most efficient and economic manner. The operations carried out by your Distributor or Dealer will be in accordance with current recommendations and may be subject to revision from time to time.

Further details on Service Parts will be found under 'SERVICE' on page 61. **Please note that references to right- or left-hand in this Handbook are made when viewing the car from the rear.**

Specification details set out in this Handbook apply to a range of vehicles and not to any particular vehicle. For the specification of any particular vehicle owners should consult their Distributor or Dealer.

The Manufacturers reserve the right to vary their specifications with or without notice, and at such times and in such manner as they think fit. Major as well as minor changes may be involved in accordance with the Manufacturer's policy of constant product improvement.

Whilst every effort is made to ensure the accuracy of the particulars contained in this Handbook, neither the Manufacturer nor the Distributor or Dealer, by whom this Handbook is supplied, shall in any circumstances be held liable for any inaccuracy or the consequences thereof.

Emission Controls

Your car is fitted with emission controls and devices required by the United States Clean Air Act and the Canadian Federal Motor Vehicle Safety Act.

Please read carefully the 'EMISSION CONTROL SYSTEMS' section of the Handbook which contains information on the emission control systems fitted to your car and recognition of symptoms of malfunctions which could affect emissions.

It is imperative that you familiarize yourself with the contents of this section, and ensure that the car you have purchased will remain in compliance with the intentions of the above act.

[The procedures for carrying out all emission control maintenance checks and adjustments are given in Part 3 of this Manual.]

CONTROLS

Fig. 1
CONTROLS

Pedals
(1) (2) (3)

The pedals are arranged in the conventional positions.

The brake pedal operates the dual hydraulic braking system applying the brakes on all four wheels, also when the ignition is switched on bringing the stop warning lights into operation.*

Hand brake
(4)

The hand brake is of the pull-up lever type, operating mechanically on the rear wheels only. To release the hand brake pull the lever upwards slightly, depress the button on the end of the lever and push the lever down.

Gear lever
(5)

The gear positions are indicated on the lever knob. To engage reverse gear move the lever to the right in the neutral position until resistance is felt, apply further side pressure to overcome the resistance and then move it backwards to engage the gear. Synchromesh is provided on second, third, and fourth gears.

The reverse lights operate automatically when reverse is selected with the ignition switched on.

Mixture control (choke)
(6)

Pull out the control to enrich the fuel/air mixture to assist starting when the engine is cold. Turn the control knob a quarter of a turn clockwise to lock the control in the position selected.

To release the control turn it in an anti-clockwise direction.

Notes on setting the control are given on page 6.

*Also see 'RUNNING INSTRUCTIONS'

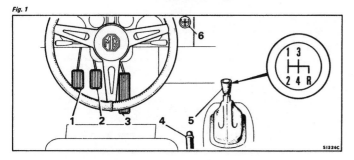

Fig. 1

WARNING SYSTEMS

Anti-theft

Warning buzzer. A combined ignition and steering lock with warning buzzer is fitted to the car. The warning buzzer will sound if the driver's door is opened while the key is in the steering lock. The buzzer will not operate if the key is removed from the lock.

Recommended procedure. When leaving the car unattended:

Set the hand brake.

Lock the steering by removing the key from the ignition steering lock.

Lock the car doors and remove the key.

Brakes
Fig. 1

Pressure failure warning. The lamp (1) in the switch will glow, when the brake pedal is pressed, if any part of the hydraulic system is inoperative or on considerable adjustment of the rear brakes is required. If this occurs and in your judgement you can drive safely with braking on two wheels only, proceed at reduced speed to the nearest service facility for immediate repairs. The vehicle should not be driven in this condition except in cases of real emergency and when in your judgement you can proceed safely at reduced speed. Extreme care must be taken and heavy braking avoided.

To test the warning lamp, press the switch (1). If the bulb is functioning the lamp will glow and will go out as the switch is released. To test the hydraulic system, apply normal foot pressure to the brake pedal. The lamp will remain off if the hydraulic system is functioning satisfactorily. Check the bulb and the system frequently.

If the warning lamp glows at any time except when the bulb is being tested the cause must be investigated **IMMEDIATELY.**

Seat Belt Warning
Fig. 2

The seat belt warning system fitted to the car consists of a warning lamp (1) on the control console illuminating the words 'FASTEN BELTS', and a warning buzzer.

Fig. 1

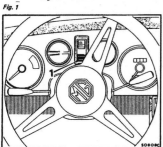

Fig. 2

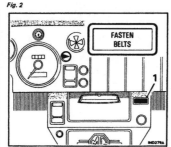

The warning system operates when the ignition is switched on (position 'II' on the ignition switch), a forward or reverse gear selected and either the driver's or passenger's seat belt is not fastened by the wearer.

PRECAUTION: A heavy parcel placed on the passenger's seat may operate the warning system. To prevent this happening fasten the passenger's seat belt.

LOCKS

It is most important that owners **MAKE A NOTE OF THE KEY NUMBERS IMMEDIATELY** on taking delivery of the car and at the same time consult their Distributor or Dealer regarding steering lock key replacements.

Keys

Identification. To reduce the possibility of theft, locks are not marked with a number. Owners are advised to make a note of the numbers stamped on the keys, on the numbered tag supplied, or on a label stuck to the windscreen. The driver and passenger door locks use a common key. The luggage compartment and steering locks are operated by separate keys.

Steering
Fig. 1

The lock face is marked 'O' (off), 'I' (auxiliary), 'II' (ignition), 'III' (start). To lock the car steering the key must be removed from the lock (4).

To lock the steering, turn the key to position 'I', press the key in and while maintaining pressure turn the key anti-clockwise to position 'O' and withdraw the key. The steering lock is set during withdrawal of the key and rotation of the steering-wheel engages the lock. When unlocking, turn the steering to assist disengagement of the locking plunger.

Under no circumstances must the key be moved from the 'I' position towards the 'O' position. **WHEN THE CAR IS IN MOTION.** The car may be towed for recovery with the key in the lock at position 'I'.

WARNING.—The lock fitted to the steering-column works in conjunction and is integral with the ignition starter switch. The designed operating sequence prevents the engine being started with the steering LOCKED. Serious consequences may result from alterations or substitution of the ignition start switch which would permit the engine to be started with the LOCK ENGAGED. **Under no circumstances must the ignition switch or the ignition engine start function be separated from the steering lock.**

Fig. 1

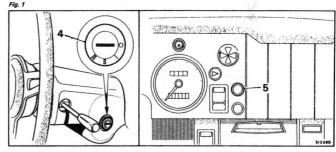

Ignition and starter
Fig. 1

Insert the key in the lock, and turn to position 'I'. In this position the ignition is off but electrical items not wired through the ignition switch may be operated, viz. radio. Turn the key to position 'II' to switch on the ignition; further movement to 'III' operates the starter.

The fuel gauge or direction indicators will not operate unless the ignition switch is at position 'II'.

To remove the key from the lock, turn the key to position 'I', press the key in, and while maintaining pressure turn anti-clockwise to position 'O' and withdraw the key.

(5) Ignition warning light (red). The ignition warning light serves the dual purpose of reminding the driver to switch off the ignition and of acting as a no-charge indicator. The light should glow when the ignition is switched on, and go out and stay out at all times while the engine is running above normal idling speed.

Doors
Fig. 2

The door key can only be inserted or withdrawn when the key and key slot (1) are vertical. Forward key movement locks, opposite unlocks. To lock the doors from inside the car, turn the locking lever (2), downwards.

Luggage compartment
Fig. 3

The luggage compartment lid is locked by turning the key (3) clockwise one half turn.

Fig. 2

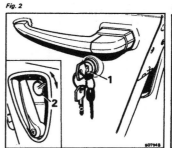

Fig. 3

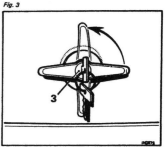

INSTRUMENTS AND SWITCHES

Instruments
Fig. 1

(1) **Speedometer.** In addition to recording the road speed this instrument also records the total distance (3), and the distance travelled for any particular trip (2). To reset the trip recorder, push the knob (4) upwards and turn it clockwise, ensuring that all the counters are returned to zero.

(5) **Tachometer.** The instrument indicates the revolutions per minute of the engine and assists the driver to use the most effective engine speed range for maximum performance in any gear.*

(6) **Oil.** The gauge indicates the pressure of the oil in the engine lubrication system.*

(7) **Water.** The gauge is marked 'C' (cold), 'N' (normal), and 'H' (hot), indicating the temperature of the coolant as it leaves the cylinder head.*

(8) **Fuel.** When the ignition is switched on the gauge indicates approximately the amount of fuel in the tank.*

* Also see 'RUNNING INSTRUCTIONS

Fig. 1

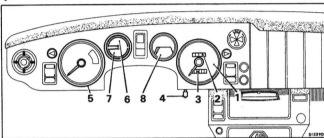

Switches
Fig. 2

(1) **Lighting switch.** Press the lower end of the switch rocker to the first position to operate the parking and tail lamps and to the second position to operate the headlamps. The marking on the switch is illuminated when the panel lamps are switched on.

(2) **Headlamp low beam**—(4) **Flasher.** With the headlamps switched on at the lighting switch, move the lever down away from the steering-wheel to operate the high beam (3), lifting the lever towards the steering-wheel from the low-beam position will flash (4), the headlamp high-beams irrespective of whether the lighting switch is on or off.

(5) **Headlamp high-beam warning lamp (blue).** The warning lamp glows when the headlamps are switched on and the beam is in the raised position. The lamp goes out when the beam is lowered.

(6) **Panel lamp switch.** With the parking lamps switched on, illumination of the instruments and switches may be varied by rotating the panel lamp switch knob. Turning the switch knob clockwise from the off position illuminates the panel lamps; further clockwise movement will increase the light brilliance.

Fig. 2

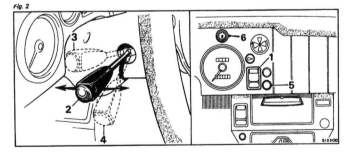

Switches
Fig. 3

(1) **Direction indicators.** The switch is self-cancelling and operates the indicators only when the ignition is switched on. A visual warning of a front or rear bulb failure is given by the warning lamp and the serviceable bulb on the affected side giving a continuous light when the indicator is switched on.

(2) **Direction indicator warning lamp (green).** The arrow-shaped lamps show the direction selected and operates with the flashing direction indicators.

(3) **Hazard warning.** To use the direction indicators as hazard warning lights, press the lower end of the switch rocker; all direction indicators and the warning lamp (4), will operate together, irrespective of whether the ignition is switched on or off. The marking on the switch will be illuminated when the panel lamps are switched on.

(5) **Horn.** The horn is sounded by pressing the centre disc of the steering-wheel.

(6) **Windscreen wiper.** Move the switch lever down to operate the windscreen wipers at slow speed; further movement in the same direction will operate the wipers at fast speed. The wiper blades park automatically when the switch lever is returned to the off position.

(7) **Windscreen washer.** Press the knob on the end of the switch lever to operate the windscreen washer. When the windscreen is dirty, operate the washer before setting the wipers in motion.

In cold weather the washer reservoir should be filled with a mixture of water and a recommended washer solvent to prevent the water freezing. On no account should radiator anti-freeze or methylated spirits (denatured alcohol) be used in the windscreen washer.

(8) **Cigar-lighter (if fitted).** To operate, press the cigar-lighter fully in; when ready for use it will partially eject itself and may then be withdrawn. The rim of the cigar-lighter is illuminated when the panel lamps are switched on.

Radio (if fitted). Full operating instructions are supplied with the radio.

Fig. 3

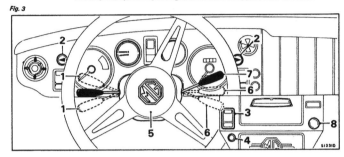

BODY FITTINGS

DRIVING MIRRORS

External
Fig. 1

The mirror head is adjustable from the driving position when the window is open. To obtain the maximum rear vision the mirror and arm must be retained in the position shown.

Interior
Fig. 2

The mirror stem with anti-dazzle head is designed to break away from the mounting bracket on impact. The stem may be refitted in the mounting bracket as follows. Align the stem ball (1) with the bracket cup (2), ensuring that the small protrusion (3) on the stem aligns with the indent of the mounting bracket. Give the stem a smart tap with a soft instrument to join the two components.

Anti-dazzle. To reduce mirror dazzle, pull the lever (4) away from the windscreen.

Windows and ventilators

Rotate the handle on each door to open and close the windows. The ventilation panels adjacent to each window may be opened after releasing the catch.

Luggage compartment

To open, turn the handle anti-clockwise and raise the lid. When fully raised the support stay will automatically spring into engagement and the lid will be held in the open position. Opening the lid automatically switches on the courtesy light.

To close, raise the lid slightly, push the catch on the support stay forward to release the locking mechanism and lower the lid. Closing the lid automatically switches off the courtesy light.

Head restraint

The vertical position of the head restraint may be adjusted.

To lower, push the head restraint down towards the seat.

To raise, place both hands under the restraint pad and lift the head restraint up away from the seat.

Fig. 1 **Fig. 2**

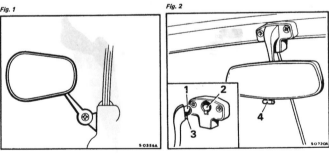

Cubby box

To open. Press the button (1) and lower the flap.
To lock. Insert the key and turn clockwise.
To unlock. Turn the key anti-clockwise.

Hard top

Fitting. Lower the hood.

Fig. 3 and 4

Position the hard top on the car and engage the toggle fastener tongues in their sockets on the windscreen rail. Check that the rubber sealing strip is correctly positioned forward of the rail. Fasten the toggle links and lock them with the securing brackets (inset, Fig. 3). Fit the bolts into both side-fixing brackets and tighten them down gently and evenly until the hard top seals at both sides and the rear. Do not tighten the bolts hard down.

4

Check the width of the gap between the flanges of the side-fixing brackets (see Fig. 4), remove the bolts and fit packing washers between the flanges to the thickness of the gap.

Refit and tighten the securing bolts.

Bonnet
Fig. 5
To raise the bonnet, pull the knob (1) located inside the car on the left-hand side below the fascia panel.

Press the safety catch (2) under the front of the bonnet and raise the bonnet. When fully raised the support stay will automatically spring into engagement and the bonnet will be held in the open position.

To close, raise the bonnet slightly, push the catch (3) on the bonnet stay rearwards to release the locking mechanism and lower the bonnet. Apply light pressure with the palms of the hands at the front corners of the bonnet and press down quickly; undue force is not necessary and may cause damage. The safety catch and lock will be heard to engage.

Fig. 3

Fig. 4

 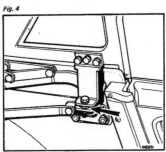

Drain points
Fig. 6
The body and doors are provided with drain holes to allow rain-water and condensation to flow freely from the panels, thus preventing accumulated water from causing rust and corrosion. It is essential that the drain holes are kept clear and are not inadvertently blocked. When painting or applying underseal to the body underpanels or doors, temporarily seal or mask the drain holes to prevent the ingress of sealant. Periodically inspect the drain holes and clear any obstruction using a piece of stiff wire or a suitable tool.

Jacking up beneath the underfloor may deform the drain apertures; always use the jacking points provided.

Fig. 5

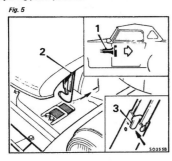

Fig. 6

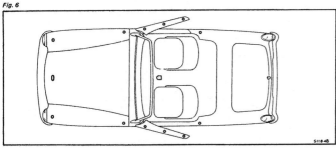

Hood (Soft top)
It is most important that the instructions for raising, lowering, and folding the hood are carried out in the sequence given. Do not apply pressure to the frame-members other than the header rail; undue force is not necessary and should be avoided. Do not fold or stow the hood when it is wet or damp.

Lowering
(1) Unclip the sun visors and move to one side. Release the press studs on the windscreen frame and hood frame links (Fig. 7).
(2) Release the hood from the self-fastening strip and the three fasteners on each rear quarter panel.
(3) Open the toggle catches on the windscreen rail (inset, Fig. 7).
(4) Press the header rail rearwards to collapse the hinge links, at the same time keeping the hood material pulled out towards the rear away from the frame (Fig. 8).
(5) Collapse the frame into its stowage position in the rear compartment and lay the hood material on the luggage compartment lid.
(6) Fold the quarter-light inwards, on a line between the quarter-light and back-light (Fig. 9).

Fig. 7   *Fig. 8*

Fig. 9   *Fig. 10*

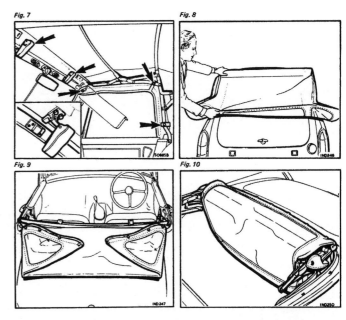

(7) Fold the hood over the frame into the rear compartment (Fig. 10).
(8) Lay the hood cover over the hood and secure the rear edge with the fasteners (Fig. 11).
(9) Arrange the cover and secure it at the sides with the fasteners provided at each quarter; secure the front edge to the cockpit rear panel with the four press studs (Fig. 11). Reposition the sun visors.

Raising
(1) Remove the hood cover and open both doors.
(2) Lift the hood over the frame and lay it on the luggage compartment lid.
(3) Unfold the quarter-lights and pull the header rail forward and upwards at the point indicated by the label. Ensure that the hood material takes up its correct position as the frame is erected.
(4) Engage the hood toggle fastener tongues in their sockets on the windscreen rail, check that the rubber sealing strip is correctly positioned forward of the rail, and fasten the toggle links.
(5) Secure the hood with the fasteners on the rear quarters, windscreen side-posts, and frame hinge links.
(6) Stow the hood cover.

Tonneau cover
Fitting. Lay the cover over the cockpit and secure the rear edge and sides with the fasteners on the tonneau and quarter-panels.

Extend the cover forward and secure the front edge to the fasteners on the fascia panel top and windscreen pillars.

Usage. The centre zip allows the cover to be folded down to give access to the driving seat or both seats. Fold the cover down behind the seat and secure it with the fasteners to the heelboard (see Fig. 12). The short side zips permit the use of seat belts when the cover is folded down.

Removing. Reverse the fitting procedure.

Fig. 11   *Fig. 12*

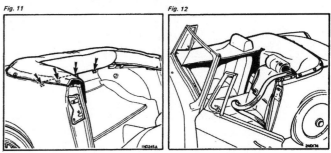

SEATS AND SEAT BELTS

SEATS *Fig. 1*

Seat adjustment
Driving position. Both seats are adjustable and can be moved easily into the most comfortable position. Move the lever (1) located beneath the front of the seat outwards; hold the lever in this position while the seat position is adjusted. The locking pin is spring-loaded and will automatically lock the seat in the required position when the lever is released.

Seat back adjustment. The rake of the back or squab of the seats can also be adjusted. Ease the body weight from the seat back and move the lever (2), in the direction of the arrow. Release the lever and ensure that the seat back is fully locked in position; check by applying back pressure on the seat.

Head restraint The head restraint (3) may be raised or lowered as desired.

SEAT BELTS *Fig. 2*

Warning system See page 5 for details of the seat belt warning system which provides an audible and visual warning reminder.

To fasten Lift the engagement tongue (1) and draw the belt from the reel over the shoulder and across the chest, and push it into the locking clip (2) of the short belt nearest the wearer.

To release Press the release button (3) on the short belt.

To stow After releasing the belt, hook the tongue (1) onto the parking device (5).

Fig. 1

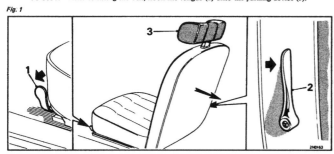

Wearing Never attempt to wear the belt other than as a complete diagonal and lap assembly. Do not try to use the belt for more than one person at any one time, even small children.

Ensure that the belt webbing is not twisted when in use, and that the belt is adjusted to the correct tightness.

Care of the belts After releasing the belt allow the webbing to retract into the automatic reel. Ensure that while the belt is retracted the engagement tongue has not moved on the belt to a point near the sill mounting; this can be remedied by moving the tongue (1) and belt clip (4) towards the reel.

Do not attempt to bleach the belt webbing or re-dye it. If the belts become soiled, sponge with warm water using a non-detergent soap and allow to dry naturally. **Do not use caustic soap, chemical cleaners or detergents for cleaning; do not dry with artificial heat or by direct exposure to the sun.**

No unauthorized alterations or additions to the belts should be made. Inspect the webbing periodically for signs of abrasion, cuts, fraying, and general wear; pay particular attention to the fixing points and adjusters. Replace belts that are defective or have been subjected to severe strain in an accident.

Fig. 2

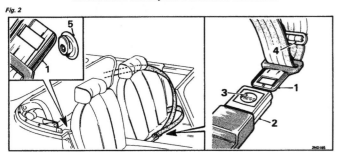

HEATING AND VENTILATING

HEATER The heating and ventilating system is designed to provide fresh air either heated by the engine cooling system or at outside temperature to the car at floor level and for demisting and defrosting to the windscreen.

Air distribution Two doors, located one at each side of the gearbox tunnel, control distribution of air between screen and car interior. To supply air to the car, open the doors; to boost the flow of air to the screen, close the doors.

Controls Heater (Fig. 1). A valve controlling the flow of coolant through the heater unit is fitted at the rear of the cylinder head. The valve is opened by turning it in an anti-clockwise direction when heating is required or shut off by turning clockwise when the system is to be used for cool air ventilation.

Air flow (Fig. 2). The knob (1) operates a valve in the air intake and controls the flow of air to the car interior. Turn the knob anti-clockwise from the 'OFF' position to open the valve, the valve is fully open when the knob is turned to the 'ON' position.

Booster. Press the lower end of the switch rocker (2) to boost the air flow.

Fig. 1   *F. 2*

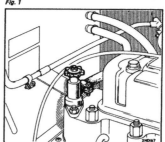 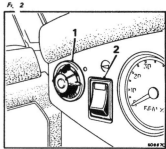

Illumination The markings on the booster switch, the control dial and the position indicator on the rotary control knob are illuminated when the panel lamps are switched on.

Usage By varying the settings of the air flow control, opening or closing the air distribution doors, and utilizing the booster blower, a wide range of settings can be obtained for heating, when the heater valve is open, or for ventilating when the valve is shut, to suit prevailing conditions.

RUNNING INSTRUCTIONS

The following instructions are a guide for starting, running and loading the car, and include notes on the use of the controls and the indications of the instruments.

Choice of fuel Our MG engines have been designed to operate on fuels of 91 octane rating or above and have not been developed for the regular use of unleaded or low lead gasolines. The use of such fuels cannot be recommended as they could have a detrimental effect on engine components, resulting in loss of performance, excess exhaust emissions and, possibly, complete engine failure.

Starting Check that the gear lever is in the neutral position.

Pull out the **mixture control (choke)**.

Switch on the ignition (page 3) and check:
    That the **ignition warning lamp** glows
    That the fuel gauge registers

Operate the **starter**.

After the engine has started, check:
    That the **oil pressure gauge** registers
    That the **ignition warning light** has gone out.

Push the mixture control (choke) in to the minimum setting.

Check the **temperature** gauge reading.

Mixture control (choke) The function of this control is to enrich the air/fuel mixture for cold engine starting and to provide a faster idle speed without enrichment during the warm-up period.

The amount which the control knob must be pulled out to achieve easy starting will be dependent on engine temperature and prevailing conditions.

To lock the control in the required position, turn the control knob a quarter of a turn clockwise.

After the engine has been started with the aid of the choke, unlock the control and push it in gradually as the engine warms, until only about ¼ in of travel remains. With the control in this position the engine will run at a faster idle speed and attain its correct working temperature as quickly as possible.

Do not warm up the engine by allowing it to idle slowly or by leaving it to idle with the control pulled out. Driving the car onto the road while the engine is cold with the control partly pulled out is preferable to allowing the engine to idle, or run with the control pulled out, in the garage or on the driveway prior to moving off.

Ignition warning lamp The lamp should glow when the ignition is switched on, and go out and stay out at all times while the engine is running above normal idling speed. Failure to do so indicates a fault in the battery charging system. Check that the fan belt is correctly tensioned before consulting your Distributor or Dealer.

Starter Do not operate the starter for longer than five to six seconds.

To prevent damage the starter cannot be operated while the engine is running.

If after a reasonable number of attempts the engine should fail to start, switch off the ignition and investigate the cause. Continued use of the starter when the engine will not start, not only discharges the battery but may also damage the starter.

If the starter pinion fails to engage with the flywheel ring, or fails to disengage when the engine starts, the starter will emit a high-pitched whine; release the ignition key immediately. Should the starter pinion become jammed in mesh with the flywheel ring, turn the squared end of the armature spindle with a spanner.

6

| Oil pressure gauge | The gauge should register a pressure as soon as the engine is started up. The pressure may rise above 70 lb./sq. in. (4·92 kg./cm.²) when the engine is started from cold and as the oil is circulated and warmed the pressure should then drop to between 40 and 70 lb./sq. in. (2·81 to 4·92 kg./cm.²) at normal running speeds and to approximately 20 lb./sq. in. (1·4 kg./cm.²) at idling speed.

Should the gauge fail to register any pressure, stop the engine immediately and investigate the cause. Start by checking the oil level. |
| --- | --- |
| Temperature gauge | Normal operating temperature is reached when the pointer is in the 'N' sector.

Overheating may cause serious damage. Investigate any upward change in the temperature gauge reading immediately. Check coolant level and fan belt tension. |
| Tachometer | For normal road work, and to obtain the most satisfactory service from your engine, select the appropriate gear to maintain engine speeds of between 2,000 and 4,500 r.p.m.

When maximum acceleration is required upward gear selections should be made when the needle reaches the yellow sector (5,500–6,300 r.p.m.). Prolonged or excessive use of the highest engine speeds will tend to shorten the life of the engine. Allowing the engine to pull hard at low engine speeds must be avoided as this also has a detrimental effect on the engine.

The beginning of the red sector (6,300 r.p.m.) indicates the maximum safe speed for the engine.

Never allow the needle to enter the red sector. |
| Running in | The treatment given to a new car will have an important bearing on its subsequent life, and engine speeds during this early period must be limited. The following instructions should be strictly adhered to.

During the first 500 miles (800 km.):
DO NOT exceed 45 m.p.h. (72 km.p.h.).
DO NOT operate at full throttle in any gear.
DO NOT allow the engine to labour in any gear. |
Wet brakes	If the car has been washed, driven through water, or over wet roads for prolonged periods full braking power may not be available. Dry the brakes by applying the foot brake lightly several times, while the car is in motion. Keep the hand brake applied while using high pressure washing equipment.
Vehicle loading	Due consideration must be given to the overall weight carried when fully loading the car. Any loads carried on a luggage rack or downward load from a towing hitch must also be included in the maximum loading.
Towing	**The towing weight of 1,344 lb. (610 kg.) is the maximum that is permissible.** When using bottom gear a gradient of up to 1 in 8 can be ascended while towing a weight not exceeding this figure. It may be necessary to adjust the maximum towing weight to comply with local conditions and regulations. The recommended downward load of a trailer or caravan on the towing hitch is 75 to 100 lb. (34 to 45 kg.), but this may be reduced or exceeded at the discretion of the driver. Any load carried on the luggage rack or downward load from a towing hitch must also be included in the maximum loading of the vehicle.
Towing for recovery	Should it become necessary to tow the car, use the towing eyes provided.

The ignition/steering lock key must be at positions 'I' or 'II' and must not be removed during the tow. For tow starting the key must be at position 'II'. |

CLEANING

| Interior | Clean the carpets with a semi-stiff brush or a vacuum cleaner preferably before washing the outside of the car. The most satisfactory way to give carpets and nylon faced upholstery a thorough cleaning is with **UNIPART Upholstery Cleaner**, diluted one part with eight parts warm water. Apply vigorously with a semi-stiff brush, and remove the surplus with a damp cloth or sponge. Carpets should not be cleaned by the 'dry-clean' process. The plastic faced upholstery and roof lining may be treated with undiluted **UNIPART Upholstery Cleaner** spread thinly over the surface to be cleaned with a brush or cloth. Leave for five minutes, then wipe off with a moist sponge or cloth.

UNIPART Upholstery Cleaner can be used for cleaning and renovating all the usual upholstery materials, and rubber, but it should not be used on painted surfaces. |
| --- | --- |
| Body | Regular care of the body finish is necessary if the new appearance of the car exterior is to be maintained against the effects of air pollution, rain, and mud.

Wash the bodywork frequently, using a soft sponge and plenty of water containing **UNIPART Car Shampoo**. Large deposits of mud must be softened with water before using the sponge. Smears should be removed by a second wash in clean water, and with the sponge if necessary. When dry, clean the surface of the car with a damp chamois-leather. In addition to the regular maintenance, special attention is required if the car is driven in extreme conditions such as sea spray or on salted roads. In these conditions and with other forms of severe contamination an additional washing operation is necessary which should include under-body hosing. Any damaged areas should be immediately covered with paint and a complete repair effected as soon as possible. Before touching-in light scratches and abrasions with paint, thoroughly clean the surface. Use petrol/white spirit (gasoline/hydrocarbon solvent) to remove spots of grease or tar.

The application of **UNIPART Car Polish** is all that is required to remove traffic film and to ensure the retention of the new appearance. |
| Bright trim | Never use an abrasive on stainless, chromium, aluminium, or plastic bright parts and on no account clean them with metal polish. Remove spots of grease or tar with petrol/white spirit (gasoline/hydrocarbon solvent) and wash frequently |

with water containing **UNIPART Car Shampoo**. When the dirt has been removed polish with a clean dry cloth or chamois-leather until bright. Any slight tarnish found on stainless or plated components which have not received regular attention may be removed with **UNIPART Chrome Cleaner**. An occasional application of light mineral oil or grease will help to preserve the finish, particularly during winter, when salt may be used on the roads, but these protectives must not be applied to plastic finishes.

Windscreen	If windscreen smearing has occurred it can be removed with **UNIPART Screen Cleaner**.
Hood	To clean the hood it is only necessary to use soap and water, with a soft brush to remove any ingrained dirt. Frequent washing with soap and water considerably improves the appearance and wearing qualities of the hood, and it should be washed at least as often as the rest of the car.

Do not use caustic soaps, detergents, or spirit cleaners to clean the hood or the hood back-light.

UNIPART products mentioned above are obtainable from your Distributor or Dealer. |

Cooling System

| Frost precautions | Anti-freeze can remain in the cooling system for two years provided that the specific gravity of the coolant is checked periodically and anti-freeze added as necessary. The specific gravity check should be carried out by an authorized Distributor or Dealer.

Only top up when the cooling system is at its normal running temperature in order to avoid losing anti-freeze due to expansion.

After the second winter the system should be drained and flushed. Refer to the instructions given for draining the cooling system, then clean out the system thoroughly by flushing water through the radiator passages using a hose inserted in the radiator filler orifice. (See Editor's Note at end of Part I)

Before adding the recommended anti-freeze make sure that the cooling system is watertight; examine all joints and renew any defective hose.

We recommend owners to use **UNIPART Frostbeat** or **Bluecol Anti-freeze** to protect the cooling system during frosty weather and reduce corrosion to the minimum. We also approve the use of anti-freeze which conforms to specification B.S.3151 or B.S.3152.

The correct quantities of anti-freeze for different degrees of frost protection are: |
| --- | --- |

Anti freeze	Commences to freeze		Frozen solid		Amount of anti-freeze		
%	°C.	°F.	°C.	°F.	Pts.	U.S. Pts.	Litres
25	−13	9	−26	−15	1½	2	·85
33⅓	−19	−2	−36	−33	2	2½	1·14
50	−36	−33	−48	−53	3	3½	1·17

WHEELS AND TYRES

| Jacking up *Fig. 1* | The jack is designed to lift one side of the car at a time. Apply the hand brake, and place a wedge against each side of one of the wheels on the opposite side of the car to the one being jacked.

Remove the plug from the jacking socket located in the door sill panel and insert the lifting arm of the jack into the socket. **Make certain that the jack lifting arm is pushed fully into the socket and that the base of the jack is on firm ground.** The jack will lean slightly outwards at the top to allow for the radial movement of the car as it is raised. |
| --- | --- |
| Jack maintenance | If the jack is neglected it may be difficult to use in a roadside emergency. Examine it occasionally, clean off accumulated dust, and lightly oil the thread to prevent the formation of rust. |
| **WHEELS** Preventive maintenance | Owners are recommended to check wheel nuts on pressed type wheels for tightness each week. Take care not to overtighten (torque wrench setting 44 to 46 lb. ft. (6·08 to 6·36 kg. m.). |

Fig. 1

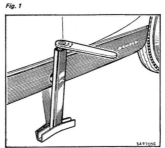

Fig. 2

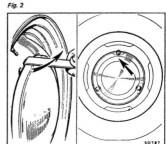

Pressed type
Removing the wheel discs
Fig. 2

Insert the wheel disc lever in the recess provided in the road wheel and lever off the disc, using a sideways motion.

To refit the hub disc, place the disc rim over two of the three retaining shoulders of the wheel. Position the disc on the third retaining shoulder and snap the rim into the locked position by striking the disc a quick blow with a clenched hand in the position shown (Fig. 2).

Removing and refitting
Fig. 3
(1)
and
Fig. 4

Slacken the four nuts securing the road wheel to the hub; turn anti-clockwise to loosen and clockwise to tighten. Raise the car with the jack to lift the wheel clear of the ground and remove the nuts. Withdraw the road wheel from the hub. When refitting the road wheel locate the wheel on the hub, lightly tighten the nuts with the wheel nut spanner (securing nuts must be fitted with the **taper side towards the wheel**), and lower the jack. Fully tighten the wheel nuts, tightening them diagonally and progressively, at the same time avoid over-tightening.

Replace the wheel disc and jack socket plug.

Wire type
Removing and refitting
Fig. 3
(2)

Use the spanner to slacken the octagonal hub nuts.

Always jack up a wheel before using the hammer, and always hammer the nuts tight.

Locknuts are marked 'LEFT' or 'RIGHT' to show to which side of the car they must be fitted, and also with the word 'UNDO' and an arrow.

Before replacing a wheel wipe all serrations, threads, and cones of the wheel and hub and then lightly coat them with grease. If a forced change is made on the road, remove, clean, and grease as soon as convenient.

Maintenance

When the car is new, after the first long run or after 50 miles of short runs, jack up the wheels and hammer the nuts to make sure that they are tight.

Once a year remove the wheels for examination and regreasing.

TYRES
Tyre markings

Tyres are marked with the maximum load and inflation pressure figures. When fitting replacement tyres ensure that they are to the same specification and marking. **The permissible load and tyre pressures are shown on page 15 of this handbook.**

Radial-ply tyres (SP)

Radial-ply tyres (SP) should only be fitted in sets of four, although in certain circumstances it is permissible to fit a pair on the rear wheels; tyres of different construction must not be used on the same axle. A pair must never be fitted to the front wheels with conventional tyres at the rear. Consult your Distributor or Dealer before changing to radial-ply tyres.

The positional changing of wheels must not be undertaken if radial-ply tyres have been fitted to the rear wheels only.

Fig. 3

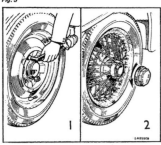

Fig 4

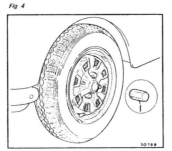

Wear indicator. Tyres fitted as original equipment have wear indicators incorporated in their tread pattern. When the tyre tread has worn down until 0·06 in. of the tread is remaining the wear indicator bar will appear across the full width of the tread pattern.

Tyre pressure

Spare wheel. The spare wheel supplied with new cars is inflated above the recommended running pressure. The pressure must be checked and adjusted before use.

Tyre maintenance

Tyres, including the spare, must be maintained at the pressures recommended (see 'GENERAL DATA'); check with an accurate tyre gauge at least once a week, and regulate as necessary. Pressures should be checked when the tyres are cold; do not reduce the pressure in warm tyres where the increase above the normal pressure is due to temperature. See that the valve caps are screwed down firmly by hand. The cap prevents the entry of dirt into the valve mechanism and forms an additional seal on the valve, preventing any leakage if the valve core is damaged. The spare wheel supplied with new cars is inflated above the recommended running pressure. The pressure must be checked and adjusted before use.

Excessive local distortion can cause the casing of a tyre to fracture and may lead to premature tyre failure. Tyres should be examined, especially for cracked walls, exposed cords, etc. Flints and other sharp objects should be removed from the tyre tread; if neglected, they may work through the cover. Any oil or grease which may get onto the tyres should be cleaned off by using fuel sparingly. Do not use paraffin (kerosene), which has a detrimental effect on rubber.

Repairs

When repairing tubes, have punctures or injuries vulcanized. Ordinary patches should only be used for emergencies. Vulcanizing is absolutely essential for tubes manufactured from synthetic rubber. (See Editor's Note at end of Part 1)

Replacement

Radial-ply tyres are standard equipment and **replacements must be of the radial-ply type.**

Wheel and tyre balancing

Unbalanced wheel and tyre assemblies may be responsible for abnormal wear of the tyres and vibration in the steering. Consult your Distributor/Dealer.

BRAKES

Brake and clutch master cylinder
Fig. 1

The level of the fluid in the brake master cylinder reservoir is visible through the plastic reservoir (1); the level must be maintained up to the position marked (2) on the side of the reservoir.

To check the level of the fluid in the clutch master cylinder reservoir (3), remove the plastic filler cap. The fluid level must be maintained at the bottom of the filler neck.

Use only **Lockheed Universal Brake Fluid (Series 329S) or Castrol Girling Brake Fluid**; alternatively, use a brake fluid conforming to F.M.V.S.S. D.O.T.3 **specification with a minimum boiling-point of 260° C. (500° F.).** Before refitting the filler caps check that the breather holes (indicated by the arrows) in the caps are clear. The centre disc (4) of the brake reservoir cap may be removed for cleaning. **(See Editor's Note at end of Part 1)**

Brake pedal
Fig. 2

A free movement of ⅛ in. (3·2 mm.) (A), measured at the pedal pad must be maintained on the pedal. To adjust the free movement, slacken the stop light switch locknut (1) and turn the switch (2) clockwise to decrease or anti-clockwise to increase the clearance. Tighten the stop light switch locknut.

Fig. 1

Fig. 2

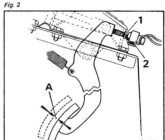

Front brakes
Fig. 3

Adjustment of the disc brakes to compensate for friction pad wear is automatic and manual adjustment is therefore not required. Before the lining material (arrowed) has worn down to the minimum permissible thickness of 1/16 in. (1·6 mm.) or will have done so before the next inspection is due, the brake pads must be renewed. Special equipment is required, and new pads should be fitted by an authorized Distributor or Dealer.

Rear brakes

Excessive brake pedal travel is an indication that the rear brake-shoes require adjusting. The brakes on both rear wheels must be adjusted to regain even and efficient braking.

Adjusting
Fig. 4

Block the front wheels, fully release the hand brake and jack up each rear wheel in turn. Turn the adjuster (arrowed) in a clockwise direction (viewed from the centre of the car) until the wheel is locked, then turn the adjuster back until the wheel is free to rotate without the shoes rubbing. Repeat the adjustment on the other rear brake.

Inspecting rear brake linings

Block the front wheels, release the hand brake, and jack up each rear wheel in turn. Remove the road wheel and slacken off the brake-shoe adjuster fully. Remove the two countersunk screws (pressed wheels) or the four nuts (wire wheels) and withdraw the brake-drum.

Inspect the linings for wear, and clean out the dust from the backplate assembly and drum.

Refit the drum and road wheel and adjust the brake-shoes.

Replacing brake-shoes or pads

When it becomes necessary to renew the brake-shoes or pads it is essential that only genuine shoes or pads, with the correct grade of lining, are used. Always fit new shoes or pads as complete axle sets, never individually or as a single wheel set. Serious consequences could result from out-of-balance braking due to mixing of linings.

Replacement brake-shoes or pads are obtainable from your Distributor or Dealer.

Fig. 3

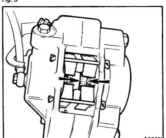

Fig. 4

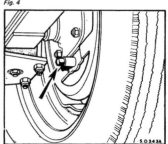

Hand brake

The hand brake is automatically adjusted with the rear brakes. If there is excessive movement of the hand brake lever, consult your Distributor or Dealer.

Lubrication
Fig. 5

Charge the nipples on the hand brake balance lever (2) and hand brake cable (1) with one of the recommended greases.

8

Preventive maintenance   In addition to the recommended periodical inspection of brake components it is advisable as the car ages, and as a precaution against the effects of wear and deterioration, to make a more searching inspection and renew parts as necessary.

It is recommended that:

(1) Disc brake pads, drum brake linings, hoses, and pipes should be examined at intervals no greater than those laid down in the Passport to Service.

(2) Brake fluid should be changed completely every 18 months or 18,000 miles whichever is the sooner.

(3) All fluid seals in the hydraulic system should be renewed, and all flexible hoses should be examined and renewed if necessary every 3 years or 36,000 miles (60000 km.) whichever is the sooner. At the same time the working surface of the piston and of the bores of the master cylinder, wheel cylinders, and other slave cylinders should be examined and new parts fitted where necessary.

Care must be taken always to observe the following points:

(a) At all times use the recommended brake fluid.

(b) Never leave fluid in unsealed containers. It absorbs moisture quickly and this can be dangerous if used in the braking system.

(c) Fluid drained from the system or used for bleeding is best discarded.

(d) The necessity for absolute cleanliness throughout cannot be over-emphasized.

Fig. 5

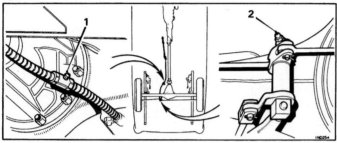

ELECTRICAL

POLARITY   The electrical installation on this car is **NEGATIVE** (−) earth return and the correct polarity must be maintained at all times. Reversed polarity will permanently damage semi-conductor devices in the alternator and tachometer, and the radio transistors (when fitted).

Before fitting a radio or any other electrical equipment, make certain that it has the correct polarity for installation in this vehicle.

Battery
Fig. 1   The battery must be kept clean and dry, and the terminals should be smeared with petroleum jelly. The vehicle must be level when the electrolyte in the cells is being checked.

More frequent topping-up of the electrolyte levels may be necessary in hot weather or when long journeys are made.

DO NOT USE A NAKED LIGHT WHEN CHECKING THE LEVELS.
(See Editor's Notes at end of Part 1)
NOTE.—Do not leave the battery in a discharged state for any length of time. When not in regular use have the battery fully charged, and every fortnight give a short refresher charge to prevent permanent damage to the battery plates.

'Pacemaker' (Type A9, AZ9, A11, AZ11). The electrolyte levels (1) are visible through the transluscent battery case or may be checked by fully raising the vent cover (2) and tilting it to one side. The electrolyte level in each cell must be maintained so that the separator plates (3) are just covered. To avoid flooding, the battery must not be topped up within half an hour of it having been charged from any source other than the generating system fitted to the car.

To top up the levels raise the vent cover and pour distilled water into the trough (4) until all the rectangular filling slots (5) are full and the bottom of the trough is just covered. Press the cover firmly into position; the correct quantity of distilled water will automatically be distributed into each cell. In extremely cold conditions, run the engine immediately after topping-up to mix the electrolyte.

Fig. 1

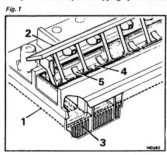

FUSES
Fig. 2   The fuses are housed under the fuse cover (1) mounted in the engine compartment adjacent to the battery.

Fuse connecting 1–2. The fuse (2) protects one parking lamp, one tail lamp, one number-plate lamp, and one front and rear side marker lamp.

Fuse connecting 3–4. The fuse (3) protects one parking lamp, one tail lamp, one number-plate lamp, and one front and rear side marker lamp.

Fuse connecting 5–6. The fuse (4) protects the circuits which operate only when the ignition is switched on. These circuits are for the direction indicators, brake stop lamps, reverse lamps and seat belt warning.

Fuse connecting 7–8. The fuse (5) protects the equipment which operates independently of the ignition switch, namely horns, interior and luggage compartment lamps, headlamp flasher, brake failure warning lamp, door and seat belt audible warning, and the cigar-lighter (if fitted).

Two spare fuses (6) are provided and it is important to use the correct replacement fuse. The fusing value, current rated 17 amp. (35 amp. blow rated), is marked on a coloured slip of paper inside the glass tube of the fuse.

Line fuses
Fig. 2   **Auxiliary equipment.** The 35 amp. line fuse (7) protects the windscreen wiper, windscreen washer, heater blower motor and radio circuits when the ignition is switched off and the ignition switch is in position 'I'.

Hazard warning. The 35 amp. line fuse (8) protects the hazard warning lamps and is located behind the hazard warning switch. It is accessible only when the centre console is withdrawn (see page 10).

Radio (if fitted). A separate additional line fuse protects the radio. See the instructions supplied with the radio for the correct fuse ratings.

To change a line fuse, hold one end of the cylindrical fuse holder (9), push in, and twist the other end (10). Remove the fuse (11) from the cylindrical holder.

Fig. 2

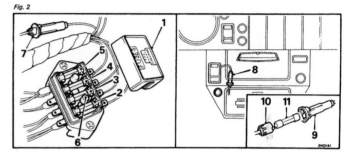

Blown fuses   The units which are protected by the fuses can be identified from the wiring diagram. A blown fuse is indicated by the failure of all the units protected by it, and is confirmed by examination of the fuse when withdrawn.

Before renewing a blown fuse inspect the wiring of the units that have failed for evidence of a short-circuit or other fault.

Accessories   If an electrical accessory is being fitted and it is required to operate independently of the ignition circuit it should be connected to terminal '8' on the fuse block; if it is required to operate only when the ignition is switched on, connect it to terminal '6'. The terminal numbers are marked on the fuse block.

HEADLAMPS
Light unit
Fig. 3   To remove a light unit, remove the outer rim retaining screw (1) and withdraw the outer rim (2). Unscrew the three inner rim retaining screws (3), remove the inner rim (4), withdraw the light unit (5), and disconnect the three-pin plug (6).

To fit a light unit, connect the three-pin plug, position the light unit in the headlamp body ensuring that the three lugs formed on the outer edge of the light unit engage in the slots formed in the body, and fit the inner retaining rim. Refit the outer rim.

Beam setting   Two adjusting screws are provided on each headlamp for setting the main beams. The screw (7) is for adjusting the beam in the vertical plane, and the screw (8) is for horizontal adjustment. The beams must be set in accordance with local regulations; resetting and checking should be entrusted to your Distributor or Dealer, who will have special equipment available for this purpose.

Fig. 3

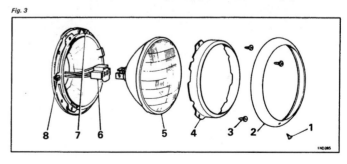

LAMPS
Parking and direction indicator lamps
Fig. 4   To gain access to the parking and direction indicator bulb, unscrew the two retaining screws (1) and withdraw the rim (2) and lens (3).

9

Stop, tail, and direction indicator lamps
Fig. 5

Remove the lens retaining screws (1) and slide the lens upwards to gain access to the direction indicator and stop/tail bulbs.

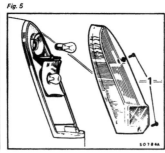

Fig. 4

Fig. 5

Number-plate lamp
Fig. 6

To renew a bulb, remove the two securing screws and lift off the lamp hood (1) and lens (2). When refitting, ensure that the lamp lens seal (3) is correctly positioned. Tighten the screws evenly and progressively to compress the seal.

Side marker lamps
Fig. 7

(1) **Front (amber)**. To renew a bulb, remove the securing screw (1) and lift off the lamp lens, noting that one end is secured by a locating tab (2). When refitting, ensure that the sealing rubber is positioned correctly and that the lens tab (2) is located beneath the lamp body rim before refitting the securing screw.

(2) **Rear (red)**. To gain access to the bulb (3), the rubber lips retaining the chrome bezel and lamp lens should be eased open with a screwdriver and the bezel (1), and lens (2), removed. When refitting ensure that the thick end of the wedge-shaped lens faces rearwards.

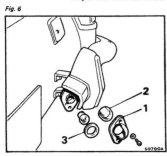

Fig. 6

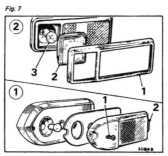

Fig. 7

Reverse lamps
Fig. 8 (A)

To renew a bulb, remove the two securing screws and withdraw the lens. Press the bulb down towards the lower contact and withdraw it from the lamp. Fit one end of the new bulb into the hole in the lower contact, then press the top of the bulb into the lamp until the point of the cap engages in the hole in the upper contact.

Interior courtesy lamp
Fig. 8 (B)

To replace a defective bulb, remove the two screws securing the lamp lens. Withdraw the festoon-type bulb from the retaining clips.

Luggage compartment lamp
Fig. 8 (C)

The lens is held in the lamp by four locating lugs. To gain access to the bulb, gently squeeze the sides of the lens together and withdraw it from the lamp. The bulb may then be withdrawn from its contacts.

Fig. 8

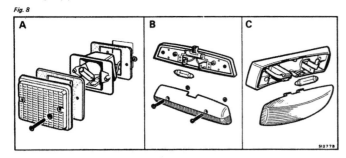

A

B

C

Warning, panel and illumination lamps
Figs. 9 and 10

Access to the bulbs is gained from the back of the fascia and/or by removing the centre console.

Centre console. Remove the four screws (12) securing the centre console. Withdraw the console, tilting the top forward slightly to clear the under edge of the fascia.

Heater control lamp bulb. Remove the push-fit bulb holder (1) from the control and remove the bayonet fixing type bulb (2).

Instrument panel lamp bulbs. Remove the push-fit bulb holders (3) from the instruments and unscrew the bulb (4).

Warning lamp bulbs. Remove the push-fit bulb holders (5) from the lamps and remove the bayonet type fixing bulbs (6). To remove the ignition and high beam warning bulbs the centre console must also be withdrawn.

Lights and heater booster switch bulbs. Remove the push-fit bulb holders (7) from the switches and remove the bayonet type fixing bulbs (8). To remove the lights switch bulb the centre console must also be withdrawn.

Brake failure warning lamp. Remove the retaining spring clip (9) and withdraw the holder/test-push assembly from the fascia. Through the two pivot holes in the holder depress the pivot legs (10) and remove the test-push rocker from its holder. Unscrew and remove the bulb (11).

Fig. 9

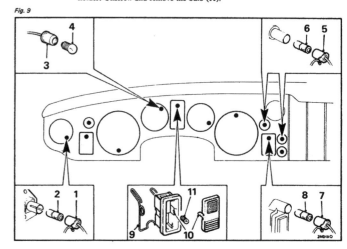

Hazard switch bulb. Withdraw the centre console. Remove the push-fit bulb holder (13) from the switch, and remove the bayonet fixing type bulbs (14).

Hazard warning lamp bulb. Withdraw the centre console. Remove the push-fit bulb holder (15) from the lamp and remove the bayonet fixing type bulb (16).

Seat belt warning lamp bulb. Withdraw the centre console. Remove the push-fit bulb holder (17) from the lamp and remove the bayonet fixing type bulb (18).

Cigar-lighter (if fitted) illumination bulb. Withdraw the centre console. Squeeze the sides of the bulb hood (19) and remove the hood. Remove the bulb holder (20) from the hood clip and remove the bayonet fixing type bulb (21).

Fig. 10

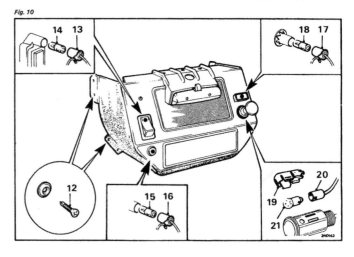

Replacement bulbs		Volts	Watts	Part No.
Headlamp—sealed beam	.. .. ..	12	50/40	—
Sidelamp (with flasher)	.. ..	12	5/21	GLB 380
Stop/tail	.. ..	12	5/21	GLB 380
Reverse	.. ..	12	18	BFS 273
Number-plate lamp	.. ..	12	6	GLB 989
Direction indicator	.. ..	12	21	GLB 382
Side marker lamp, front and rear		12	5	BFS 501
Ignition warning	.. .. ..	12	2	GLB 281
Main beam	.. ..	12	2	GLB 281
Direction indicator warning lamp		12	2	GLB 987
Brake warning lamp	.. ..	12	1·5	GLB 280
Panel illumination lamp	..	12	2·2	GLB 987
Cigar-lighter illumination	..	12	2·2	BFS 643
Luggage compartment lamp	..	12	6	GLB 254
Courtesy lamp	.. .. ..	12	6	GLB 254
Hazard warning lamp	.. ..	12	2	GLB 987
Seat belt warning lamp	.. ..	12	2	GLB 281
Switch illumination	.. ..	12	2	GLB 281
Heater rotary control illumination		12	2	GLB 281

10

WINDSCREEN WIPER

Arms
Fig. 11

To reposition a wiper arm, hold the spring clip (1) clear of the retaining groove in the spindle (2) and withdraw the arm. Place the arm in the required position and press it onto the spindle until it is secured by the clip.

Blades
Fig. 11

To renew a wiper blade, pull the wiper arm (4) away from the windscreen, press down the arm against the spring fastener (3) and pull the blade from the arm. Insert the end of the wiper arm into the spring fastener of the new blade and push the blade into engagement with the arm.

Washer
Fig. 12

The electric pump for the windscreen washer is mounted on the left-hand side of the engine compartment bulkhead. The fluid flow is indicated on the pump just above the fluid connections.

FUEL PUMP

Fuel is delivered to the carburetters by an S.U. electric fuel pump. The pump is situated beneath the luggage compartment on the right-hand side.

Alternator

The following precautions must be observed to prevent inadvertent damage to the alternator and its control equipment.

Polarity. Ensure that the correct battery polarity (**negative ground**) is maintained at all times; reversed battery or charger connections will damage the alternator rectifiers.

Battery connections. The battery must never be disconnected while the engine is running.

Contact set renewing. Remove the nut (8) and lift the top insulating bush and both leads from the stud. Remove the securing screw (6) with its spring and plain washer, and lift off the one-piece contact set. If removal of the moving contact only is required leave the securing screw (6) in position.

Fitting. Before fitting a new contact set, wipe the points clean with fuel or spirit. Lubricate the pivot post (2) and check that the insulating bush (9) is correctly positioned below the spring loop. Position the contact set on the distributor plate and lightly tighten the securing screw (6). Locate the lead terminals around the insulating bush so that they make contact with the spring and tighten the nut (8). Set the contact gap.

Whenever a new contact set has been fitted, recheck the gap after the first 500 miles (800 km.). During this period, the heel of the contact will have bedded in and reduced the gap.

Spark plugs
Fig. 2

The spark plugs should be cleaned, preferably with an air-blast service unit.

Check the plug gaps, and reset if necessary to the recommended gap (see 'GENERAL DATA'). To reset, use a special Champion spark plug gauge and setting tool; move the side electrode, never the centre one.

When refitting the plugs make sure that the washers are not defective in any way.

Screw the plug down by hand as far as possible, then use a spanner for tightening only. Always use a tubular box spanner to avoid possible damage to the insulator, and do not under any circumstances use a movable wrench. Never overtighten a plug, but ensure that a good joint is made between the plug body, washer, and cylinder head. Wipe clean the outside of the plugs before reconnecting the H.T. leads.

When fitting new spark plugs ensure that only the recommended type and grade are used (see 'GENERAL DATA').

Fig. 2

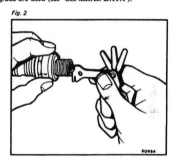

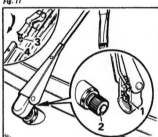
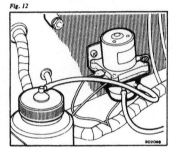

Fig. 11   *Fig. 12*

IGNITION

Ignition timing

The ignition timing is set dynamically to give optimum engine performance with efficient engine emission control. Electronic test equipment must be used to check the ignition timing setting and the automatic advance (see 'GENERAL DATA'). Checking and adjustment to the ignition timing setting should be carried out by your Austin MG Dealer control service station.

The dynamic ignition timing must be checked after cleaning, resetting, or renewing of the distributor contacts. (See Editor's Note at end of Part 1)

Basic tuning data will be found on the Vehicle Emission Control Information Label located in the engine compartment.

Distributor
Fig. 1

Cleaning contacts. Inspect the contact points (1) and, if burned, clean with fine emery cloth or fine carborundum stone. Wipe the contacts clean with a fuel-moistened cloth. Renew pitted or worn points.

Lubrication. Very lightly smear the pivot post (2) and around the cam (3) with grease. Add a few drops of oil through the hole in the contact breaker plate to lubricate the centrifugal weights and around the screw (5) in the centre of the cam spindle (do not remove this screw as clearance is provided for oil to pass). **Avoid over-lubricating.** Carefully wipe away all surplus lubricant and see that the contact breaker points are perfectly clean and dry.

Contact breaker gap. Turn the crankshaft until the points are fully open. Check the contact gap (1) with a feeler gauge (see 'GENERAL DATA'); the gauge should be a sliding fit in the gap.

If the gap varies appreciably from the gauge thickness, slacken the contact plate securing screw (6) and adjust the gap by inserting a screwdriver in the notched hole (7) at the end of the plate and turning clockwise to decrease and anti-clockwise to increase the gap. Tighten the securing screw. Turn the crankshaft and recheck the gap. Refit the rotor, wipe the inside of the distributor cover clean and refit.

Fig. 1

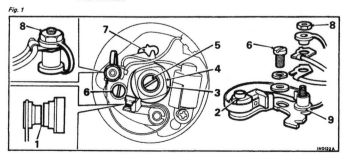

ENGINE

LUBRICATION

Checking
Fig. 1

The level of the oil in the engine sump is indicated by the dipstick (3) on the right-hand side of the engine. Maintain the level at the 'MAX' mark on the dipstick and never allow it to fall below the 'MIN' mark. The oil level should always be checked before a long journey.

The filler (2) is on the forward end of the rocker cover and is provided with a quick-action cap. The filler cap also incorporates a filter for the crankcase emission control system.

Draining

To drain the engine oil, remove the drain plug (1) located on the right-hand side at the rear of the sump. This operation should be carried out while the engine is warm.

Clean the drain plug; check that its copper sealing washer is in a satisfactory condition, and refit.

Filling

Fill the engine with the correct quantity of recommended oil. Run the engine for a short while then allow it to stand for a few minutes before checking the level with the dipstick.

Oil filter changing
Fig. 1

The oil filter is a disposable cartridge type.

To renew, unscrew the cartridge (4) from the filter head (5) and discard the cartridge.

NOTE. If difficulty in unscrewing the cartridge is experienced, consult your Distributor or Dealer.

Fig. 1

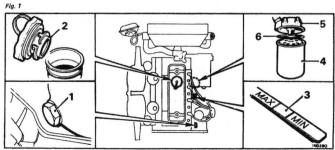

11

Smear the new seal (6) with engine oil and fit it into its groove in the new cartridge. Screw the cartridge to the filter head using hand force only.

Refill the engine with the correct quantity of a recommended lubricant, start the engine and check for oil leakage.

Oil filter changing (early cars)
Fig. 1a
The external oil filter is of the renewable-element type and is located on the right-hand side of the cylinder block. The filter is released by undoing the central bolt securing the filter body to the filter head. Wash out the casing with petrol (gasoline) and dry it before fitting a new element. Check that the sealing rings (1) and (3) and the rubber washer (2) are in a satisfactory condition. Reassemble the filter, ensuring that the components are correctly positioned.

Fig. 1a

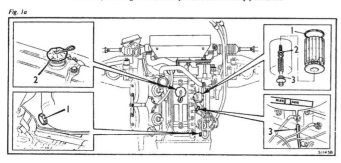

Dynamo lubrication
To lubricate the dynamo add a few drops of oil through the central hole (arrowed, Fig. 2) in the rear bearing housing. Avoid overlubrication.

DRIVE BELTS
Belt tension
When correctly tensioned, a total deflection of ½ in., under moderate hand pressure, should be possible at the midway point of the longest belt run between the pulleys on the fan belt and the air pump drive belt.

Adjusting
Fan belt
Fig. 3
Slacken the three dynamo securing bolts (1) and adjusting link nut (2), move the dynamo to the required position using hand pressure only; avoid over-tensioning. Tighten the securing bolts and adjusting link nut.

Alternator
Fig. 4
Tension. When correctly tensioned, a total deflection of ½ in. (13 mm) under moderate hand pressure, should be possible at the midway point of the longest belt run between the pulleys.

Adjusting. To adjust the belt tension, slacken the securing bolts (1) and adjusting link nuts (2), and move the alternator to the required position. Apply any leverage necessary to the alternator end bracket (3) only and not to any other part; to avoid damaging the drive-end bracket the lever should preferably be of wood or soft metal. Tighten the bolts and re-check the belt tension. **DO NOT OVERTIGHTEN** as this will impose an excess loading on the drive bearings.

VALVE ROCKER CLEARANCE
Checking
Fig. 5
Remove the rocker cover and insert a ·012 in. feeler gauge between the valve rocker arms and valve stems (inset). The gauge should be a sliding fit when the engine is cold. Check each clearance in the following order:

Adjusting
Check No. 1 valve with No. 8 fully open. Check No. 8 valve with No. 1 fully open.
" " 3 " " 6 " " " " 6 " " 3 " "
" " 5 " " 4 " " " " 4 " " 5 " "
" " 2 " " 7 " " " " 7 " " 2 " "

Slacken the adjusting screw locknut on the opposite end of the rocker arm and rotate the screw clockwise to reduce the clearance or anti-clockwise to increase it. Retighten the locknut when the clearance is correct, holding the screw against rotation with a screwdriver.

Fig. 2

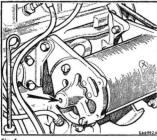

Fig. 3

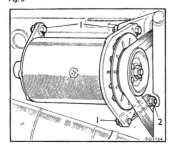

Fig. 4

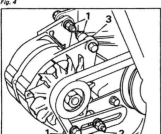

Fig. 5

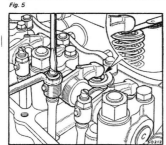

EMISSION CONTROL SYSTEMS

You and each subsequent owner of the car are urged to make sure that the recommended maintenance procedures are carried out at the intervals specified. For the emission controls to continue to function effectively, it is strongly recommended that you arrange for regular maintenance inspections to be carried out by your Austin MG Dealer or by any other qualified service outlet which regularly performs such service on British Leyland cars.

You have been provided with a Passport to Service which contains an inspection and maintenance schedule up to 50,000 miles or 5 years.

You should have the maintenance record completed by your Austin MG Dealer (or by other dealer or station equipped to render such service) at the regular mileage intervals indicated in the Schedule. The Handbook and Passport to Service should be handed to subsequent purchasers of the vehicle at the time of sale so that the maintenance instructions are available and that the record of maintenance can be continued.

You are also urged to study with care the section covering 'MALFUNCTION IDENTIFICATION'. Study of this section will be of aid to you in detecting possible malfunctions of the emission controls so that necessary service measures can immediately be taken.

IMPORTANT
Your attention is particularly drawn to the following:
1. Maintenance and service charges applicable to the emission control system are **not** covered by the warranty and are not reimbursable, unless shown to have been caused by defects in materials and workmanship covered by the warranty.

2. Our MG engines have not been designed for regular use of unleaded or low lead gasoline and use of such fuels cannot be recommended as they could have a detrimental effect on engine components, resulting in loss of performance, excess exhaust emissions and possibly complete engine failure.

General description
This section gives a general description of the crankcase, exhaust and fuel evaporative emission control systems fitted to this vehicle and the function of their individual components. It must be emphasized that correct carburetter adjustment and ignition timing which have been pre-set at the factory are essential for the efficient functioning of the exhaust emission controls. Should it become necessary to check these settings this work should be carried out by an Austin MG or British Leyland Dealer who has the specialist equipment and training to undertake these adjustments.

The basic engine tuning data will be found on the emission control information label located in the front of the engine compartment.

Crankcase Emission Control
The engine crankcase breather outlet incorporates an oil separator flame-trap which is connected by hoses to the controlled depression chamber between the piston and the throttle disc valve of the carburetter(s). Piston blowby fumes are drawn into the chamber where they combine with the engine inlet charge for combustion in the engine cylinders in the normal way. Fresh filtered air is supplied to the engine crankcase through a hose connected between the engine valve rocker cover and the charcoal canister of the fuel evaporative emission control system.

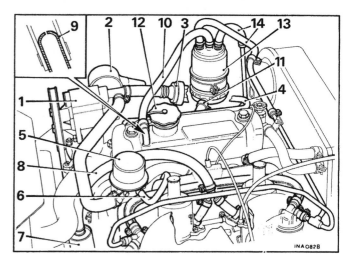

Fig. 1   The emission control components

1. Air pump
2. Air pump air cleaner
3. Check valve
4. Air manifold
5. Gulp valve
6. Sensing pipe
7. Oil separator/flame trap
8. Breather pipe
9. Restrictor connection
10. Purge line
11. Air vent pipe
12. Sealed oil filler cap
13. Charcoal absorption canister
14. Vapour lines

Exhaust Emission Control
The exhaust emission control system is designed to give the required degree of control of the carbon monoxide, unburnt hydrocarbons and oxides of nitrogen content of exhaust gases.

The main feature of the exhaust emission control system is a combination of the engine modification and air injection techniques and consists of modified carburetters, modified ignition timing, and air injection into the exhaust ports.

The quantity of air-polluting elements in the gases leaving the exhaust pipe is reduced by adding air to the hot gases immediately they leave the combustion chambers of the engine. The injection of air into the exhaust gases promotes a continued conversion of the undesirable hydrocarbon and carbon monoxide components of the exhaust gases to relatively harmless carbon dioxide and water.

An air pump mounted on the front of the engine, and belt driven from the water pump pulley, supplies air under pressure through hoses and a check valve and distribution manifold to injectors in each exhaust port in the engine cylinder head. The check valve prevents high pressure exhaust gases from blowing back into the air pump due to, for example, pump drive failure.

Air from the pump is also supplied to a gulp valve, the outlet of which is connected to the engine inlet manifold. A small bore sensing pipe connected between the inlet manifold and the diaphragm chamber of the gulp valve relays changes in manifold depression to the valve which will open under certain conditions such as those created by deceleration or engine overrun.

When the gulp valve opens a small quantity of air is admitted directly into the inlet manifold to lean off the rich air/fuel mixture which is present in the manifold under conditions immediately following throttle closure. This mixture, having been reduced to a burnable condition, combines with engine inlet charge for combustion in the engine cylinders in the normal way.

The carburetters are manufactured to a special exhaust emission specification and are tuned to give the maximum emission control consistent with retaining vehicle performance and driveability. The metering needle is arranged in such a manner that it is always lightly spring loaded against the side of the jet to ensure consistency of fuel metering. A spring loaded valve incorporated in the throttle disc limits the inlet manifold depression and ensures that during conditions of engine overrun the air/fuel mixture enters the engine cylinders in a burnable condition consistent with low emission levels.

The ignition distributor is tuned with slightly retarded ignition at low engine r.p.m. compared with non-emission equipped vehicles, and the timing is balanced between mechanical and vacuum characteristics to give optimum timing consistent with low emissions.

Fuel Evaporative Loss Control To prevent air pollution by vapours from the fuel tank and carburetter vents, the control equipment stores the vapour in a charcoal filled canister while the engine is stopped and disposes of it via the engine crankcase emission control system when the engine is running.

The fuel tank venting is designed to ensure that vapours are vented through the control system even when the car is parked on an inclined surface.

A capacity limiting device in the fuel tank ensures sufficient free capacity is available after filling to accommodate fuel which would otherwise be displaced as a result of a high temperature rise. The inclusion of a small separation tank in the vapour line prevents liquid fuel from being carried with the vapour to the storage canister.

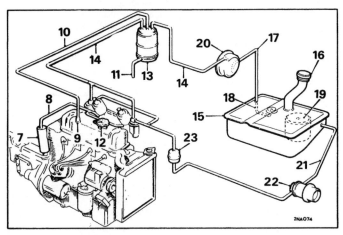

Fig. 2 The layout of the fuel evaporative loss control system

7. Oil separator/flame trap	16. Sealed fuel filler cap
8. Breather pipe	17. Vapour line
9. Restrictor connection	18. Vapour tube
10. Purge line	19. Capacity limiting tank
11. Air vent pipe	20. Separation tank
12. Sealed oil filler cap	21. Fuel pipe
13. Charcoal adsorption canister	22. Fuel pump
14. Vapour lines	23. Fuel line filter
15. Fuel tank	

MALFUNCTION IDENTIFICATION

Check the following items regularly for visual signs of a malfunction and also if any of the Driving Symptoms listed should persistently occur. If you are unable to locate and/or correct the malfunction you are advised to contact your Austin MG Dealer immediately.

Visual Checks
1. Condition and adjustment of drive belts.
2. Baked or overheated hose between air pump and check valve.
3. All hoses for security, damage and deterioration.
4. Fuel leakage.
5. Oil filler cap for sealing.
6. Fuel filler cap for sealing.

Driving Symptoms
1. Violent backfire in exhaust system.
2. Hesitation to accelerate on re-opening the throttle after sudden throttle closure.
3. Engine surges (erratic operation at varying throttle openings).
4. Engine idles erratically or stalls.
5. Noisy air pump.
6. Ignition warning light on above idle speed (slack or broken fan belt).
7. Smell of fuel vapours.
8. Engine stops after short running periods (fuel starvation).
9. Lack of power.
10. High fuel consumption.
11. Engine misfires (engine jerks on cruise and acceleration).
12. High temperature indicated (overheating of coolant).

MAINTENANCE OPERATIONS

All items marked † in the 'MAINTENANCE SUMMARY' given on pages 15 and 16 are emission control related.

Adsorption canister *Fig. 3* The charcoal adsorption canister must be renewed every 24,000 miles or 24 months.

To renew the canister, disconnect the air vent pipe (1), vapour pipes (2) and purge pipe (3) from their connections on the canister. Remove the securing bracket nut and bolt (4), collecting the spacer, and remove the canister.

When refitting, ensure that all connections to the canister are tightened securely.

Gulp valve *Fig. 4* To renew, disconnect the hoses (1) and sensing pipe (1) from the gulp valve. Unscrew the mounting screws and nuts (2) and remove the gulp valve (3). Fit the new valve, re-connect the hoses and sensing pipe, ensuring that all joints are made secure and airtight.

Fuel line filter The filter must be renewed every 12,000 miles or 12 months.

Purge line restrictor To check, disconnect the purge line from the rocker cover elbow. Examine the orifice of the restriction formed in the elbow for obstruction. Clear any dirt or deposits from the restrictor orifice, using a length of wire.

Fig. 3 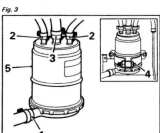   *Fig. 4*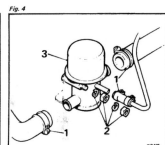

AIR PUMP The air pump should be checked for correct functioning every 24,000 miles or 24 months.

Drive belt *Fig. 5* Tension. When correctly tensioned, a total deflection of ½ in. (13 mm.) under moderate hand pressure, should be possible at the midway point of the longest belt run between the pulleys.

Adjusting. To adjust the belt tension, slacken the securing bolts (1) and adjusting link nuts (2), and move the air pump to the required position. Tighten the bolts and re-check the belt tension. **DO NOT OVERTIGHTEN** as this will impose an excess loading on the drive bearings.

Air cleaner *Fig. 6* The element of the air pump air cleaner must be renewed every 12,000 miles (20000 km.) or 12 months; more frequent changes may be necessary in dusty operating conditions.

Unscrew the self-locking nut (1), withdraw the cover (2) and discard the element (3). Clean the inside of the cover thoroughly and re-assemble using a new element.

Fig. 5 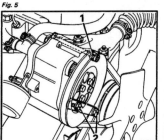   *Fig. 6*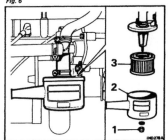

Filler caps Both the engine oil filler cap and the fuel tank filler cap are non-venting and form a seal on the filling apertures.

IT IS ESSENTIAL TO THE SATISFACTORY OPERATION OF THE EVAPORATIVE LOSS SYSTEM THAT BOTH CAPS ARE ALWAYS REFITTED CORRECTLY AND TIGHTENED FULLY. A DEFECTIVE CAP OR CAP SEAL MUST BE REPLACED.

FUEL SYSTEM

AIR CLEANERS The elements of the carburetter air cleaners must be renewed every 12,000 miles (20000 km.) or 12 months; more frequent changes may be necessary in dusty operating conditions.

Carburetter The air cleaner covers and elements should only be removed when the elements
Fig. 2 are being renewed. To fit new elements, remove the interconnecting bracket securing nut (1) and unscrew the air cleaner bolts (2) from the mounting plate (3). Lift off the assembly, remove the cover (5) and extract the element (4) and the distance pieces (6) for the air cleaner bolts.

CARBURETTERS
Air pollution The carburetter incorporates features which assist in reducing exhaust emissions.
control
Maladjustment or the fitting of parts not to the required specification may render these features ineffective.

Lubrication **Carburetter.** Unscrew the damper cap at the top of the carburetter and withdraw
Fig. 2 the damper. Top up with clean engine oil to bring the oil level 1 inch below the top of the carburetter damper tube. Push the damper assembly back into position and screw in the cap. Under no circumstances should heavy bodied lubricant be used. Failure to lubricate the piston damper may cause the piston to flutter and reduce acceleration and have an adverse effect on exhaust emission.

Throttle. Lubricate the carburetter throttle and choke control linkages and cables, and the accelerator pedal fulcrum.

Fig. 1   Fig. 2

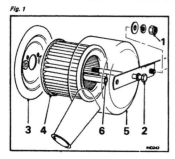
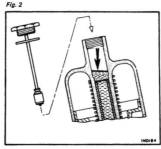

Tuning The efficient operation of the engine and exhaust emission control equipment
Fig. 3 depends not only on correct carburetter settings but also on correct ignition timing, contact breaker and spark plugs and valve rocker clearances. It is essential that these items are checked before adjusting the carburetters. Tuning of the carburetters is confined to setting the idle and fast idle speeds and the mixture setting at idle speed. Adjustments should only be undertaken on cars required to conform with exhaust emission control regulations if the use of a reliable tachometer, carburetter balance meter and an exhaust gas analyser (CO meter) is available.

1. Remove the air cleaners.
2. Top up the carburetter piston dampers with recommended engine oil to the correct level.
3. Check the throttle control for correct functioning.
4. Ensure that the mixture control (choke) will return fully, that the cable has 1/16 in. (2 mm.) free play (1) before it starts to pull on the lever and a small clearance exists between the fast idle screws (2) and their cams.
5. Raise each carburetter lifting pin (3), release the pin and check that the piston falls freely onto the bridge of the carburetter, indicated by a distinct metallic click. Consult your Distributor/Dealer if the piston fails to fall freely.
6. Connect a reliable tachometer.
7. Start the engine and run it at a fast idle speed until it attains normal running temperature then run it for a further five minutes.
8. Increase the engine speed to 2,500 rev./min. for 30 seconds.

NOTE.—Tuning can now be commenced. If delay prevents the adjustment being completed within three minutes, increase the engine speed to 2,500 rev./min. for 30 seconds and then continue tuning. Repeat this clearing procedure at three minute intervals until tuning is completed.

Fig. 3   Fig. 4

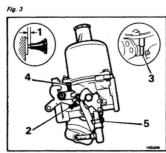
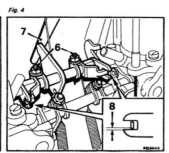

9. Check the idle speed (tachometer), see 'GENERAL DATA' and check the carburetters for balanced air intake using a balance meter.
10. If the balance is not correct, adjust as follows: release a throttle connector (6) between the carburetters and adjust by turning the throttle adjusting screw (4) on one of the carburetters until the balance is correct. Then adjust the idle speed by turning the throttle adjusting screw (4) on each carburetter by the same amount. Re-check the carburetter balance.
Check the throttle shaft pin clearance and adjust if necessary—see paragraph 17.

If a smooth idle at the correct speed and balance is not obtainable adjust the idle speed mixture setting as follows:

11. Stop the engine. Remove each suction chamber and piston, and screw the jets (5) up until they are flush with the bridge of the carburetter or up as far as possible. Turn down the jet adjusting nut (5) on each carburetter two complete turns. Refit the piston and suction chambers and top up the piston damper oil levels.
NOTE.—This operation need not be carried out if it is known that the jets are in the same relative position.
12. Start the engine. Turn the jet adjusting nut (5) on both carburetters in the same direction, one flat at a time, up to weaken or down to richen, within the limits of the adjustment restrictor until the fastest speed is recorded on the tachometer. Now turn the nuts up slowly until the speed just commences to fall. Turn the nuts down very slowly by the **minimum amount** until the maximum speed is regained.
13. Using the exhaust gas analyser check that the percentage CO reading is within the prescribed limits. If the reading falls outside the limits reset both jet adjusting screws equally by the minimum amount necessary to bring the reading just within the limits. If a smooth idle at the correct speed or the prescribed CO reading cannot be obtained you should consult your Austin MG Dealer.
14. Recheck the idle speed and carburetter balance and adjust as necessary with the throttle adjusting screws.
15. Set the throttle interconnection clamping levers so that the link pin is 0·012 in. (0·31 mm.) away from the lower edge of the forks (see inset 8) as follows:
16. Stop the engine and slacken both clamping bolts (6) on the throttle spindle interconnection.
17. Insert a 0·012 in. (0·3 mm.) feeler gauge (7) between the throttle shaft stop and the carburetter heat shield. Move each throttle spindle interconnection lever downwards until the lever pin rests on the lower arm of the carburetter throttle fork. Tighten the clamping bolts (6) on each fork, ensuring that there is approximately 1/32 in. (0·79 mm.) end float on the interconnection rod. Remove the feeler gauge. The pins on the throttle spindle lever should then have clearance in the throttle fork.
18. Ensure that 1/16 in. (2 mm.) free movement exists before the cable starts to pull on the lever.
19. Run the engine at 1,500 r.p.m. and check the carburetters for balance.
20. Pull out the mixture control knob until the linkage is about to move the carburetter jets. Lock the knob in position.
21. Using the balance meter to ensure equal adjustment, turn the fast idle adjusting screws equally to give the fast idle speed—see 'GENERAL DATA'. Stop the engine.
22. Refit the air cleaners.

GEARBOX AND REAR AXLE

Gearbox To gain access to the gearbox combined oil filler and level plug, lift the floor
Fig. 1 covering on the left-hand side of the gearbox cover and remove the rubber plug. Clean around the filler plug before removing it.

The oil level should be maintained at the bottom of the filler plug aperture threads.

Rear axle A combined oil filler and level plug is located on the rear of the axle. The oil
Fig. 2 level should be maintained at the bottom of the plug aperture; ensure that the car is standing level when checking. After topping up the oil level, allow sufficient time for any surplus oil, which may have been added accidentally, to run out of the aperture before replacing the plug.

Ensure that the rear axle oil is not drained when the After-sales Service is carried out.

Fig. 1   Fig. 2

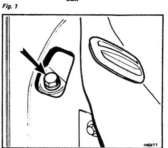
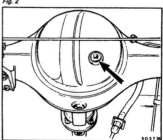

STEERING AND SUSPENSION

Lubrication A lubrication nipple for the steering rack is located on the right-hand side of the
Steering rack rack housing, which is accessible when the bonnet is raised. When lubricating
Fig. 1 give a maximum of 10 strokes with an oil gun filled with one of the recommended oils.

14

Swivel axle pins *Fig. 2*	Two lubricating nipples (1) and (2) are provided on each swivel pin. To lubricate, charge the nipples with one of the recommended greases. To ensure full penetration of the lubricant, this operation is best carried out with the car partly jacked up.	

Swivel axle pins
Fig. 2
Two lubricating nipples (1) and (2) are provided on each swivel pin. To lubricate, charge the nipples with one of the recommended greases. To ensure full penetration of the lubricant, this operation is best carried out with the car partly jacked up.

Steering connections
Fig. 2
The steering tie-rod ball joint at each side is provided with a lubrication nipple (3). To lubricate, charge the nipples with one of the recommended greases.

Front suspension outer fulcrum pins
Fig. 2
A lubricating nipple (4) is provided on each of the outer fulcrum pins. To lubricate, charge the nipples with one of the recommended greases.

Front wheel alignment
Incorrect front wheel alignment can cause excessive and uneven tyre wear. The front wheels must be set parallel or toe-in $\frac{1}{8}$ in. (3.2 mm.) to each other when the steering is in the straight-ahead position.

To set the wheel alignment correctly requires the use of a special gauge; this work should be entrusted to your Distributor or Dealer.

Fig. 1

Fig. 2

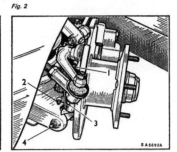

GENERAL DATA

Engine	Engine type	12CC 12CD (4-cylinder overhead valve)
	Engine type (evaporative loss) ..	12CJ, 12V
	Bore	2.78 in. (70.61 mm)
	Stroke	3.2 in. (81.28 mm)
	Cubic capacity	77.8 cu. in. (1274.86 c.c.)
	Compression ratio	8.8:1—Late U.S.A., 8.0:1
	Firing order	1,3,4,2
	Valve rocker clearance (cold) .	.012 in. (.3 mm)
	Idle speed (12CC)	700 r.p.m. (hot)
	Idle speed (other)	1,000 r.p.m.
	Fast idle speed	1,100 r.p.m. to 1,200 r.p.m.
	Oil pressure:	
	Normal (approx.)	40 to 70 lb./sq. in. (2.81 to 4.92 kg./cm.²)
	Idling (approx.)	20 lb./sq. in. (1.4 kg./cm.²)
Ignition	Spark plugs (12CC)	Champion UN12Y
	Spark plugs (other)	Champion N.9.Y
	Spark plug gap	.024 to .026 in. (.62 to .66 mm)
	Static ignition timing (12CC): ..	
	High compression	7° B.T.D.C.
	Low compression	7° B.T.D.C.
	Stroboscopic ignition timing: ..	
	. (12CC)	22° at 1,000 r.p.m.
	(12CD, 12CJ)	10° B.T.D.C. at 1,000 r.p.m.
	Stroboscopic ignition timing (12V) ..	9° B.T.D.C. at 1,500 r.p.m.
	(vacuum disconnected) ..	
Fuel system	Carburetors	Twin S.U. type HS2
	Carburetor needle	ABC (spring-loaded type)
	Early cars	AN, AAC
	Pump (12V)	S.U. type AUF 305 electric
	(other)	S.U. (Electric) type AUF 206
Transmission	Rear axle ratio	3.9 : 1
	Overall gear ratios: First ..	12.48 : 1
	With	Second	7.472 : 1
	synchromesh	Third ..	5.292 : 1
		Fourth ..	3.9 : 1
	Reverse ..	16.044 : 1

Dimensions		*Pressed spoked*	*Pressed disc*	*Wire*
	Track: Front ..	3 ft. 10$\frac{7}{16}$ in. (118.27 cm.)	3 ft. 10$\frac{5}{16}$ in. (117.63 cm.)	3 ft. 10$\frac{5}{16}$ in. (117.63 cm.)
	Rear ..	3 ft. 10 in. (116.84 cm.)	3 ft. 8$\frac{3}{4}$ in. (113.66 cm.)	3 ft. 9$\frac{1}{4}$ in. (114.93 cm.)
	Turning circle: Left lock ..	32 ft. 1$\frac{1}{2}$ in. (9.79 m.)		
	Right lock ..	31 ft. 2$\frac{1}{4}$ in. (9.51 m.)		
	Front wheel alignment ..	Parallel to $\frac{1}{8}$ in. toe-in (0 to 3.2 mm)		
	Wheelbase	6 ft. 8 in. (2.03 m.)		
	Overall length	11 ft. 5$\frac{3}{4}$ in. (3.49 m.)		
	Overall width	4 ft. 6$\frac{7}{8}$ in. (1.4 m.)		
	Overall height	4 ft. $\frac{3}{4}$ in. (1.22 m.)		
	Ground clearance ..	5 in. (12.7 cm.)		
Capacities	Fuel tank	6 gallons (7.2 U.S. gallons, 27.3 litres)		
	Fuel tank (evaporative loss) ..	5 gallons (6 U.S. gallons, 22.7 litres)		
	1974 Fuel tank (evaporative loss) ..	6½ gallons (7.7 U.S. gallons, 29 litres)		
	Engine sump (including filter) ..	6½ pints (7.8 U.S. pints, 3.7 litres)		
	Gearbox	2¼ pints (2.7 U.S. pints, 1.3 litres)		
	Rear axle	1¾ pints (2.1 U.S. pints, .99 litre)		
	Cooling system (with heater) ..	6 pints (7 U.S. pints, 3.4 litres)		

Wheels and tyres	Wheel size: Pressed spoked.. ..	4½J SL × 13
	Pressed disc	3.5D × 13
	Wire	4J × 13

Tyres:	*Size*	*Type*
	5.20 × 13S ..	Cross ply
	145SR × 13 ..	Radial ply

Tyre pressures

	5.20—13S		145SR—13	
	Cross-ply tyres		**Radial-ply tyres**	
	Front	*Rear*	*Front*	*Rear*
Normal car weight	18 lb./sq. in. (1.27 kg./cm.²)	20 lb./sq. in. (1.4 kg./cm.²)	22 lb./sq. in. (1.55 kg./cm.²)	24 lb./sq. in. (1.69 kg./cm.²)
Maximum weight	18 lb./sq. in. (1.27 kg./cm.²)	24 lb./sq. in. (1.69 kg./cm.²)	22 lb./sq. in. (1.55 kg./cm.²)	26 lb./sq. in. (1.83 kg./cm.²)

It is recommended that for sustained speeds at near the maximum the above tyre pressures are increased by 4 lb./sq. in. (.28 kg./cm.²).

Weights

	Including	*Total weight*	*Distribution*	
			Front	*Rear*
Kerbside	Full fuel tank, all optional extras and accessories	1,701 lb. (772 kg.) 1974: 1,746 lb. (792 kg.)	861 lb. (391 kg.) 1974: 868 lb. (394 kg.)	840 lb. (381 kg.) 1974: 878 lb. (398 kg.)
Normal	Kerbside weight, driver, passenger, and 50 lb. luggage	2,051 lb. (930 kg.) 1974: 2,046 lb. (928 kg.)	948 lb. (429 kg.) 1974: 966 lb. (438 kg.)	1,103 lb. (500 kg.) 1974: 1,080 lb. (500 kg.)
Maximum	Normal weight and towbar hitch load	2,151 lb. (975 kg.) 1974: 2,196 lb. (996 kg.)	913 lb. (413 kg.) 1974: 933 lb. (423 kg.)	1,238 lb. (561 kg.) 1974: 1,263 lb. (573 kg.)
Maximum permissible towing weight		1,344 lb. (610 kg.) 1974: 1,344 lb. (610 kg.)		
Towbar hitch load		Maximum 100 lb. (45.4 kg.)		

MAINTENANCE SUMMARY

[NOTE—See page 382 for Maintenance Summary issued in 1975.]
Basic tuning data will be found on the Vehicle Emission Control Information Label located in the engine compartment.

Weekly or before a long journey

Check oil level in engine and top up if necessary
Check battery and top up to correct level if necessary
Check coolant level and top up if necessary
Check windscreen washer and top up if necessary
Check tyre pressures including spare and adjust if necessary

Maintenance Intervals
†These items are emission related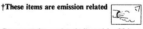

Carry out the services indicated by **X** in column

The lubrication service at 3,000-mile or 3-month intervals
A at 6,000-mile or 6-month intervals
B at 12,000-mile or 12-month intervals

	Lubrication Service	**A**	**B**
LUBRICATION			
Change engine oil	X	X	X
Fit new oil filter		X	X
Check level of all fluid reservoirs, brake, clutch, rear axle, transmission, battery, windscreen washer	X	X	X
Check all tyre pressures, including spare	X	X	X
Lubricate all grease fittings	X	X	X
Lubricate all locks and hinges	X	X	X
†Lubricate all throttle and choke controls and cables ..	X	X	X
†Lubricate steering rack and pinion	At 30,000 miles or 36 months		
ENGINE			
†Check all drive belts. Adjust if required		X	X
†(Renew all belts at 24,000 miles or 24 months)			
†Check all hoses, vacuum, air and water for condition and tightness		X	X
†Renew all air filter cleaner elements (air pump and carburetter)			X
†Adjust valve rocker clearances		X	X
†Tighten all manifold nuts		X	X
†Visually check exhaust and intake systems for leaks ..		X	X
†Check heating and cooling system for leaks		X	X
†Check resistor in rocker cover purge line for obstruction			X
†Check air injection manifold for damage, leaks and security			X
†Inspect the check and gulp valves and renew if necessary			X
†Inspect air pump, correct or renew if necessary	At 24,000 miles or 24 months		

	A	B
IGNITION		
†Renew spark plugs		x
†Renew breaker points		x
†Lubricate distributor cam, breaker pivots and advance mechanism	x	x
†Wipe clean and examine distributor cap for cracks and tracking, and the carbon brush for sticking and wear	x	x
†(Renew distributor cap every 24,000 miles or 24 months)		
†Wipe clean and examine high tension leads for damage, deterioration and security		x
†(Renew high tension leads every 24,000 miles or 24 months)		
FUEL SYSTEM		
†Top up carburetter piston damper	x	x
†Renew fuel line filter		x
†Renew charcoal canister		At 24,000 miles or 24 month intervals
†Check condition of fuel filler cap seal and renew if necessary		x
OSCILLOSCOPE CHECK		
†Check/adjust breaker points, resistance and dwell	x	x
†Check/adjust ignition timing and distributor advance characteristics (vacuum disconnected)	x	x
†Check distributor vacuum advance at idle	x	x
†Check/adjust idle speed and mixture setting	x	x
†Check/adjust choke and carburetter fast idle speed setting	x	x
†Power check, engine cylinder comparison	x	x
†Check spark plugs (cruise and unload condition); clean and adjust if necessary	x	
Check charging system output	x	x
STEERING AND SUSPENSION		
Check for leaks	x	x
Check steering joints for security, backlash and gaiter condition	x	x
Check/adjust front wheel alignment	x	x
BRAKES		
Check visually hydraulic pipes and unions for chafing, leaks and corrosion	x	x
Check/adjust brake pedal travel, check hand brake operation	x	x
Inspect brake pads for wear and discs for condition	x	
Inspect brake linings and pads for wear, drums and discs for condition		
ELECTRICAL		
Check function of lamps, horns, indicators and windscreen wipers	x	x
Grease battery connections		x
Check headlamp beam alignment and adjust if necessary		x
Check windscreen wiper blades; if necessary replace	x	x
EXHAUST, FUEL AND CLUTCH PIPES		
†Check visually fuel and clutch pipes and unions for chafing, leaks and corrosion	x	x
†Check exhaust for leakage and security	x	x
WHEELS AND TYRES		
Check that tyres comply with manufacturer's specification		x
Check visually and report depth of tread, cuts in tyre fabric, exposure of ply or cord structure, lumps or bulges	x	x
Check tightness of road wheel nuts	x	x
BODY		
Check condition and security of seats and seat belts	x	x
Check rear view mirror for looseness, cracks or crazing	x	x

The schedule on the preceding pages is the minimum service required to maintain your vehicle under normal driving conditions. For other than normal driving conditions, and those caused by seasonal changes, we recommend that you consult your Distributor or Dealer.

SERVICE

Service Your Distributor or Dealer is provided with the latest information concerning special service tools and workshop techniques. This enables him to undertake your service and repairs in the most efficient and economic manner.

Service parts and accessories Genuine BRITISH LEYLAND and UNIPART parts and accessories are designed and tested for your vehicle and have the full backing of the British Leyland Factory Warranty. ONLY WHEN GENUINE BRITISH LEYLAND AND UNIPART PARTS ARE USED CAN RESPONSIBILITY BE CONSIDERED UNDER THE TERMS OF THE WARRANTY.

For more information on UNIPART, see your British Leyland Distributor or Dealer.

Genuine British Leyland and UNIPART parts and accessories are supplied in cartons and packs bearing either or both of these symbols.

Safety features embodied in the car may be impaired if other than genuine parts are fitted. In certain territories, legislation prohibits the fitting of parts not to the vehicle manufacturer's specification. Owners purchasing accessories while travelling abroad should ensure that the accessory and its fitted location on the car conform to mandatory requirements existing in their country of origin.

Identification When communicating with your Distributor or Dealer always quote the commission and engine numbers. When the communication concerns the transmission units or body details it is necessary to quote also the transmission casing and body numbers.

Commission number. Stamped on a plate secured to the left-hand side of the bonnet lock platform.

Engine number. Stamped on a plate secured to the right-hand side of the cylinder block.

Gearbox number. Stamped on the left-hand side of the gearbox casing.

Rear axle number. Stamped on the front of the left-hand rear axle tube near the spring seating.

Supplementary tool kit To supplement the tool kit a waterproof canvas roll containing the following is obtainable from all Distributors. Part No. AKF 1596 should be quoted.

6 spanners:
$\frac{3}{16}$ in. × $\frac{1}{4}$ in. A.F.
$\frac{7}{16}$ in. × $\frac{1}{2}$ in. A.F.
$\frac{1}{2}$ in. × $\frac{9}{16}$ in. A.F.
$\frac{5}{16}$ in. × $\frac{3}{8}$ in. A.F.
$\frac{11}{16}$ in. × $\frac{13}{16}$ in. A.F.
$\frac{1}{4}$ in. × $\frac{7}{32}$ in. A.F.

1 pair 6 in. pliers.
1 7 in. × $\frac{3}{8}$ in. diameter tommy-bar.
1 $\frac{1}{2}$ in. × $\frac{9}{16}$ in. A.F. tubular spanner.
2 screwdrivers.

British Leyland Motors Inc.
600 Willowtree Road, Leonia
New Jersey 07605
Telephone: (201) 461/7300 *Telex:* 135491

British Leyland Motors Canada Limited
4445 Fairview Street
P.O. Box 5033
Burlington · Ontario · Canada
Telephone: (416) 632/3040 *Telex:* 021678

TUNING MODIFICATIONS

Tuning modifications For competition, circuit racing, and speed trials a wide range of MG Factory Special Tuning parts are available through your Distributor or Dealer. Full details of the varying stages of tune and the fitting of the parts listed below are given in Tuning Booklet C-AKD 5098.

> **Warning:** The car is delivered from the factory in its standard form tuned to give maximum performance with complete reliability, and meeting any U.S. legal requirements as to emission control and safety regulations.
>
> Super-tuned cars should be utilized only in off-road competition driving. Super-tuning, modifications, alterations to the car from its factory-delivered standard form may prohibit its use on public roads.
>
> **REMINDER:** The warranty provides that it is invalidated if the car is used for racing.

Engine Half-race and full-race camshafts. Lightened timing gears. Competition cylinder head. Competition pistons, competition inlet and exhaust valves. Competition valve spring sets. Competition valve gear. Large capacity, deep sump. Competition oil cooler. Competition large bore manifold. Lightened flywheel.

Carburetter Twin 1½ in. or 1¾ in. S.U. carburetters and full installation kit. Weber twin-choke carburetters and full installation kit.

Ignition Competition distributor with a special advance curve. Racing sparking plugs.

Transmission Competition clutch assembly and driven plate. Range of axle ratios. Front and rear road springs. Limited slip differential. Heavy-duty axle shafts. Close-ratio gears.

Suspension Front anti-roll bar and installation kit. Competition setting shock absorbers. Front suspension lowering kit.

Wheels and brakes Wide-rim wire wheels. Competition brake pads.

Miscellaneous Lightweight bucket seats. Leather bonnet straps. Alternator pulleys for reduced speed.

For further details see your Distributor or Dealer or write to:

Special Tuning Department
Austin Morris Group BRITISH LEYLAND UK LIMITED
Body and Assembly Division MG Plant
ABINGDON-ON-THAMES BERKSHIRE ENGLAND
Telephone: Abingdon 251 *Telex:* 83128 *Telegrams:* Emgee, Abingdon

RECOMMENDED LUBRICANTS

Component	Engine, Synchromesh Gearbox, Overdrive, Distributor, Carburetter, and Oil-can			Rear Axle and Steering Gear		Grease Points	Upper Cylinder Lubrication
Climatic conditions	All temperatures above −10° C. (10° F.)	Temperatures −15° to −5° C. (0° to 20° F.)	All temperatures below −15° C. (0° F.)	All temperatures above −10° C. (10° F.)	All temperatures below −5° C. (20° F.)	All conditions	All conditions
Viscosity requirement	S.A.E. 10W/50 S.A.E. 10W/40 S.A.E. 20W/50 or S.A.E. 20W/40	S.A.E. 10W/50 S.A.E. 10W/40 or S.A.E. 10W/30	S.A.E. 5W/30 or S.A.E. 5W/20	S.A.E. 90 Hypoid	S.A.E. 80 Hypoid		
Minimum performance level		MIL-L-2104B	MIL-L-2104B	MIL-L-2104B	MIL-L-2105B	Multipurpose Lithium Grease N.L.G.I. Consistency No. 2	Upper Cylinder Lubricant
BP	BP Super Visco-Static	BP Super Visco-Static 10W/30 or 10W/40	BP Super Visco-Static	BP Hypogear 90 EP	BP Hypogear 80 EP	BP Energrease MP	BP Power Lube
SHELL	Super Shell Motor Oil	Super Shell Motor Oil	Shell Super Motor Oil 5W/30	Shell Spirax Heavy Duty 90	Shell Spirax Heavy Duty 80	Shell Darina AX	Shell Upper Cylinder Lubricant
FILTRATE	Filtrate Super 20W/50	Filtrate Super 10W/30	Filtrate 5W/20	Filtrate Epex 90	Filtrate Epex 80	Filtrate Super Lithium Grease	Filtrate Petroyle
STERNOL	Sternol Super W.W. Motor Oil	Sternol W.W. Multigrade 10W/40	Sternol W.W. Multigrade 5W/20	Sternol Ambroleum HD 90	Sternol Ambroleum HD 80	Sternol Ambroline Grease LHT 2	Sternol Magikoyl
DUCKHAMS	Duckhams Q. 20–50	Duckhams Q. 5500	Duckhams Q5–30	Duckhams Hypoid 90S	Duckhams Hypoid 80S	Duckhams L.B. 10 Grease	Duckhams Adcoid Liquid
CASTROL	Castrol GTX or Castrol XL 20/50	Castrolite or Castrol Super	Castrol CRI 5W/20	Castrol Hypoy B. 90	Castrol Hypoy B. 80	Castrol L.M. Grease	Castrollo
ESSO	Uniflo or Esso Extra Motor Oil 20W/50	Uniflo or Esso Extra Motor Oil 10W/30	Esso Extra Motor Oil 5W/20	Gear Oil G.X. 90	Gear Oil G.X. 80	Esso Multi-purpose Grease H	Esso Upper Cylinder Lubricant
MOBIL	Mobiloil Special 20W/50 or Super 10W/50	Mobiloil Super 10W/50	Mobiloil 5W/20	Mobilube HD 90	Mobilube HD 80	Mobilgrease MP	Mobil Upperlube

LUBRICATION

NOTE:—Ensure that the vehicle is standing on a level surface when checking the oil levels.

WEEKLY

(1) ENGINE. Check oil level and top up if necessary.

Every 6,000 miles or 6 months

(2) ENGINE. Drain and refill with new oil.

(3) ENGINE OIL FILTER. Remove disposable cartridge, fit new.

(4) CARBURETTERS. Top up carburetter piston damper.

(5) THROTTLE AND CHOKE. Lubricate throttle and choke control linkages, cables, and accelerator pedal fulcrum.

(6) DISTRIBUTOR. Lubricate all parts as necessary.

(7) REAR AXLE. Check oil level, and top up if necessary.

(8) GEARBOX. Check oil level and top up if necessary.

(9) STEERING TIE-ROD BALL JOINT (2 nipples)

(10) FRONT SUSPENSION (6 nipples)

(11) HAND BRAKE CABLE (1 nipple)

(12) HAND BRAKE COMPENSATING LEVER

    Give three or four strokes with a grease gun.

Lubricate all door, bonnet, boot locks, and hinges, and hand brake mechanical linkage.

Every 30,000 miles or 36 months

(13) STEERING RACK. Lubricate steering rack—this work must be entrusted to your Distributor or Dealer.

Lubrication service at 3,000 miles or 3 months

(2) ENGINE. Drain and refill with new oil.

(5) THROTTLE AND CHOKE. Lubricate throttle and choke control linkages, cables, and accelerator pedal fulcrum.

(7) REAR AXLE. Check oil level, and top up if necessary.

(8) GEARBOX. Check oil level, and top up if necessary.

(9) STEERING TIE-ROD BALL JOINT (2 nipples)

(10) FRONT SUSPENSION (6 nipples)

(11) HAND BRAKE CABLE (1 nipple)

(12) HAND BRAKE COMPENSATING LEVER (1 nipple)

    Give three or four strokes with a grease gun.

Lubricate all door, bonnet, boot locks, and hinges and hand brake mechanical linkage.

Recommended oils and greases are given above.

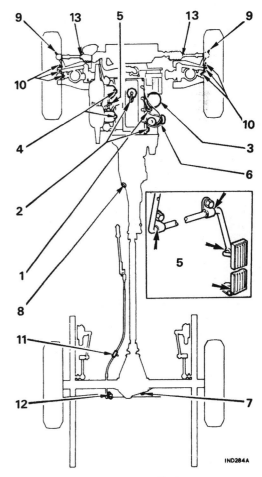

IND284A

17

EDITOR'S NOTES

Cooling System

Anti-freeze solutions

You can check the specific gravity of the coolant solution by using an anti-freeze hydrometer. With this instrument, a quantity of coolant is sucked in and the position of a glass float indicates the specific gravity of the solution, usually in terms of the temperature at which ice begins to form.

A more thorough job of flushing can be done if the thermostat is removed from its housing and the housing reinstalled before flushing.

Wheels and Tires

Tire Maintenance

"Vulcanizing" is a process of tire repair in which a patch is applied under heat and pressure.

Brakes

Brake and clutch master cylinder

Only the brake fluids specified should be used. Other brake fluids may have a lower boiling point and will boil in disc brake systems under hard usage. This can cause temporary malfunction until the fluid has cooled (pedal will feel spongy).

Electrical

Battery

Do not use a naked light, or open flame, when examining the condition of the cells. The reason for this is that hydrogen and oxygen gases are produced under normal charging conditions and the mixture of these two gases in the proper proportions is explosive.

Checking the specific gravity

When checking the specific gravity of a battery be sure to use a battery hydrometer, not an anti-freeze hydrometer.

Ignition

Checking ignition timing

The spark timing may be set with a commercially available timing light. A flash occurs every time the No. 1 cylinder fires, illuminating the timing marks at the crankshaft pulley. The engine should be run at the rpm specified in "General Data" and the knurled nut adjusted until the setting corresponds to that listed in "General Data" for the engine type you are working with.

SPRITE/MIDGET
WORKSHOP MANUAL

Part 2

INTRODUCTION

DESCRIPTION

This Manual is intended to assist the skilled mechanic in carrying out repairs and replacements in a minimum of time.

References to left- or right-hand side in this Manual are made when viewing the car from the rear.

MANUAL ARRANGEMENT

The first part of the Manual includes the General Data, and Engine Tuning Data.

A Service Tools section and the Recommended Lubricants Chart are featured at the end of the Manual.

The remainder of the Manual is divided into sections and each section carries a reference letter that identifies the section with an assembly or a major component. Each section is preceded by a contents page and is sub-divided numerically. The pages and illustrations are numbered consecutively within each section and the section title and letter are shown at the top of each page.

Maintenance items within the Sections should be carried out at the intervals specified in the Passport to Service or Driver's Handbook.

IMPORTANT

On cars fitted with emission control equipment service operations and adjustments showing this symbol must be followed by an exhaust emission check.

Servicing and adjusting vehicle control equipment must be carried out in accordance with the instructions given in **Workshop Manual Supplement AKD 4957** [Part 3 of this Manual].

REPAIRS AND REPLACEMENTS

When replacements are required it is essential that only genuine **British Leyland** parts and **Unipart** replacements are used.

Attention is particularly drawn to the following points concerning repairs and the fitting of replacement parts and accessories:

Safety features embodied in the car may be impaired if other than genuine parts are fitted. In certain territories, legislation prohibits the fitting of parts not to the vehicle manufacturers specification.

Torque wrench setting figures given in the Manual must be strictly adhered to.

Locking devices, where specified, must be fitted. If the efficiency of a locking device is impaired during removal it must be renewed.

Owners purchasing accessories while travelling abroad should ensure that the accessory and its fitted location on the car conform to mandatory requirements existing in their country of origin. **The terms of the Owner's Service Statement may be invalidated by the fitting of other than genuine British Leyland parts and Uniparts.**

All **British Leyland** parts and **Unipart** replacements have the full backing of the Owner's Service Statement.

Genuine parts are supplied in cartons bearing one or both of these symbols.

COPYRIGHT

© **British Leyland UK Limited, 1973.**

Sprite and Midget. Issue 8. 82790

SPECIFICATION

Purchasers are advised that the specification details set out in this Manual apply to a range of vehicles and not to any particular vehicle. For the specification of any particular vehicle Purchasers should consult their Distributor or Dealer.

The Manufacturers reserve the right to vary their specifications with or without notice, and at such times and in such manner as they think fit. Major as well as minor changes may be involved in accordance with the Manufacturer's policy of constant product improvement.

Whilst every effort is made to ensure the accuracy of the particulars contained in this Manual, neither the Manufacturer nor the Distributor or Dealer, by whom this Manual is supplied, shall in any circumstances be held liable for any inaccuracy or the consequences thereof.

Getting the Best from your Car

Compression ratios 8·8 : 1 and 8·9 : 1

The high-compression engine is a highly developed unit, and it is essential that you should know something about the specialized maintenance it requires if you are to maintain it at the peak of its mechanical efficiency. Special recommendations on the sparking plugs, ignition settings, and fuel to be used are given by the manufacturers, and it is stressed that failures are bound to occur if these are not strictly adhered to. Particular care is needed with this engine owing to its high compression ratio, which makes it extremely sensitive to variations in fuel, ignition timing, and the heat range of the sparking plugs.

In lower compression engines a much wider range of fuels can be tolerated without causing serious damage to the engine, and ignition settings will stand variations of a reasonable amount. Also, even if the incorrect sparking plugs are used, no more damage may be incurred than burnt-out plugs or leaky valves. But with an engine having a very high compression ratio the range of fuels, sparking plugs, and ignition settings is much narrower and it is essential that the mixture should always be correct, and particularly never overweak at maximum load or power.

High-compression engines are very sensitive to variations in spark advance (over-advance) and to fuel/air ratio (mixture). Variations in these settings will increase the combustion temperature, and if the variation is excessive pre-ignition will cause high shock waves, resulting in damage to the engine.

The engine should be decarbonized at regular intervals as excessive deposits of ash from the combustion of lubricating oil and fuel can cause pre-ignition difficulties.

Choice of fuel

Compression ratio 8·9 : 1

The octane number of a motor fuel is an indication given by the fuel technicians of its knock resistance. High-octane fuels have been produced to improve the efficiency of engines by allowing them to operate on high compression ratios, resulting in better fuel economy and greater power. Owing to the high compression ratio of this engine, fuels with an octane rating below 98 are **not** suitable; should it be necessary to use a fuel with a lower octane number, the car must be used very carefully until the correct fuel can be obtained.

It is necessary to use Super grade fuels in the 100-octane range unless Premium fuels of minimum 98-octane Research are available.

Compression ratio 8·8 : 1

Fuels with an octane rating below 94 are **not** suitable.

Premium grade fuels with octane ratings of 97 to 99 must be used when optimum performance is required.

Sparking plugs

The correct grade of sparking plug for use under normal driving conditions is given in 'GENERAL DATA'. Plugs of a lower heat range (hotter running) should not be used, otherwise pre-ignition will occur, with consequent rise in combustion temperature and resulting engine damage. For competition work or hard driving where high output is consistently sustained refer to Tuning Booklet C–AKD 5098. Accumulated deposits of carbon, leaking or cracked insulators, and thin electrodes are all causes of pre-ignition. The plugs should therefore be examined, cleaned, and adjusted at the specified intervals and defective ones renewed. New plugs should be fitted at regular intervals.

Ignition setting

It is of the utmost importance that the correct setting should always be maintained. It will be appreciated that any variation in the contact breaker gap will affect the ignition setting, and your particular attention is called to the check and adjustment of the distributor points specified in Section B. After adjusting the contact breaker gap to the correct setting (see 'GENERAL DATA') it is advisable to check the ignition timing, and to correct it if necessary.

An accurate static check can be carried out by a very simple electrical method. To do this, connect a 12-volt lamp between the low-tension terminal on the side of the distributor and a good earth point on the engine. With the ignition switched on and the sparking plugs removed, turn the crankshaft until the crankshaft pulley T.D.C. pointer is exactly at the correct number of degrees as stated under 'GENERAL DATA'. If the ignition timing is correct the lamp will light at exactly this point. Any discrepancy in the ignition setting can be rectified by turning the vernier adjusting nut on the distributor until the test lamp lights at exactly the correct setting. If pinking should occur due to the use of a fuel of a lower range than our recommendations, retarding the ignition 2 to 3° can be tolerated. Under no circumstances should the ignition be advanced beyond the correct setting.

Sprite and Midget. Issue 9. 82790

22

CONTENTS

GENERAL DATA
(948 c.c.)

ENGINE

Type	9CG.
Number of cylinders	4.
Bore	2·478 in. (62·94 mm.).
Stroke	3·00 in. (76·2 mm.).
Capacity	57·87 cu. in. (948 c.c.).
Firing order	1, 3, 4, 2.
Compression ratio: High	9 : 1.
Low	8·3 : 1.
Capacity of combustion chamber (valves fitted) ..	24·5 c.c.
Valve operation	Overhead, by push-rod.
Oversize bore: 1st	·010 in. (·254 mm.).
Max.	·040 in. (1·016 mm.).
Torque (H.C.)	52·8 lb. ft. (7·3 kg. m.) at 3,000 r.p.m.

Crankshaft

Main journal diameter	1·7505 to 1·7510 in. (44·46 to 44·47 mm.).
Minimum regrind diameter	1·7105 in. (43·45 mm.).
Crankpin journal diameter	1·6254 to 1·6259 in. (41·28 to 41·30 mm.).
Crankpin minimum regrind diameter	1·5854 in. (40·27 mm.).

Main bearings

Number and type	3 shell type.
Material: Bottom half	Steel-backed, lead-indium-lined.
Top half	Steel-backed, lead-indium-lined.
Length	1·1875 in. (30·16 mm.).
End-clearance	·002 to ·003 in. (·051 to ·076 mm.).
End-thrust	Taken by thrust washers at centre main bearing.
Diametrical clearance	·001 to ·0025 in. (·025 to ·063 mm.).
Undersizes	− ·010 in., − ·020 in., − ·030 in., − ·040 in.
	(− ·254 mm., − ·508 mm., − ·762 mm., −1·02 mm.).

Connecting rods

Length between centres	5·75 in. (14·605 cm.).

Big-end bearings

Material: Bottom half	Steel-backed, lead-indium-lined.
Top half	Steel-backed, lead-indium-lined.
Bearing side clearance	·008 to ·012 in. (·203 to ·305 mm.).
Bearing diametrical clearance	·001 to ·0025 in. (·025 to ·063 mm.).

Pistons

Type	Flat crown, aluminium alloy, anodized.
Clearances: Bottom of skirt	·0016 to ·0022 in. (·040 to ·056 mm.).
Top of skirt	·0036 to ·0042 in. (·0914 to ·1067 mm.).
Oversizes	+ ·010 in., + ·020 in., + ·030 in., + ·040 in.
	(+ ·254 mm., + ·508 mm., + ·762 mm., +1·02 mm.).

Piston rings

Compression: Plain	Top ring.
Tapered	Second and third rings.
Width (plain)	·069 to ·070 in. (1·75 to 1·78 mm.).
Thickness	·103 to ·109 in. (2·62 to 2·78 mm.).
Fitted gap	·007 to ·012 in. (·178 to ·30 mm.).
Clearance in groove	·0015 to ·0035 in. (·038 to ·089 mm.).
Oil control type	Slotted scraper.
Width	·124 to ·125 in. (3·15 to 3·175 mm.).
Thickness	·103 to ·109 in. (2·62 to 2·78 mm.).
Fitted gap	·007 to ·012 in. (·178 to ·30 mm.).
Clearance in groove	·0015 to ·0035 in. (·038 to ·089 mm.).

Gudgeon pin

Type	Semi-floating.
Fit in piston	·0001 to ·00035 in. (·0025 to ·009 mm.).
Fit in connecting rod	·0001 to ·0006 in. (·0025 to ·015 mm.).
Diameter (outer)	·6244 to ·6246 in. (15·86 to 15·865 mm.).

Valves

Seat angle: Inlet and exhaust	45°.
Head diameter: Inlet	1·151 to 1·156 in. (29·23 to 29·36 mm.).
Exhaust	1·000 to 1·005 in. (25·4 to 25·53 mm.).
Stem diameter: Inlet	·2793 to ·2798 in. (7·094 to 7·107 mm.).
Exhaust	·2788 to ·2793 in. (7·081 to 7·094 mm.).
Valve lift	·312 in. (7·925 mm.).
Valve stem to guide clearance: Inlet	·0015 to ·0025 in. (·038 to ·063 mm.).
Exhaust	·002 to ·003 in. (·051 to ·076 mm.).
Valve rocker clearance: Running (cold)	·012 in. (·305 mm.); ·015 in. (·381 mm.) for competition work.
Valve rocker bush bore (reamed)	·5630 to ·5635 in. (14·30 to 14·31 mm.).

Valve timing

Timing markings	Dimples on timing wheels.
Chain pitch and number of pitches	⅜ in. (9·52 mm.). 52 pitches.
Inlet valve: Opens	5° B.T.D.C.
Closes	45° A.B.D.C.
Exhaust valve: Opens	51° B.B.D.C.
Closes	21° A.T.D.C.
Valve rocker clearance: timing check	·021 in. (·74 mm.).

Valve guides

Length: Inlet and exhaust	1·687 in. (42·86 mm.).
Diameter—inlet and exhaust: Outside	·4695 to ·470 in. (11·92 to 11·94 mm.).
Inside	·2813 to ·2818 in. (7·145 to 7·177 mm.).
Fitted height above head	1⁹⁄₃₂ in. (15·1 mm.).

Valve springs

Free length: Inner	1·672 in. (42·47 mm.).
Outer	1·75 in. (44·45 mm.).
Fitted length: Inner	1·179 in. (29·95 mm.).
Outer	1·291 in. (32·79 mm.).
Number of working coils: Inner	6½.
Outer	4½.
Pressure: Valve open: Inner	30 lb. (13·6 kg.).
Outer	88 lb. (39·9 kg.).
Valve closed: Inner	18 lb. (8·17 kg.).
Outer	52 lb. (23·6 kg.).

Tappets

Type	Bucket.
Diameter	·8120 in. (20·62 mm.).
Length	1·505 in. (38·23 mm.).

Camshaft

Journal diameters: Front	1·6655 to 1·666 in. (42·304 to 42·316 mm.).
Centre	1·62275 to 1·62325 in. (41·218 to 41·231 mm.).
Rear	1·3725 to 1·3735 in. (34·862 to 34·887 mm.).
End-float	·003 to ·007 in. (·076 to ·178 mm.).
Bearing: number and type	3. Steel-backed white metal.
Inside diameter (reamed in position): Front	1·667 to 1·6675 in. (42·342 to 42·355 mm.).
Centre	1·62425 to 1·62475 in. (41·256 to 41·369 mm.).
Rear	1·3745 to 1·3750 in. (34·912 to 34·925 mm.).
Clearance	·001 to ·002 in. (·025 to ·051 mm.).

General Data 2   Sprite and Midget. Issue 5. 65317

26

ENGINE LUBRICATION SYSTEM

Oil pump

Type	Eccentric rotor or vane type.
Relief pressure valve operates	60 lb./sq. in. (4·2 kg./cm.²).
Relief valve spring: Free length	2·859 in. (72·63 mm.).
Fitted length	2·156 in. (54·77 mm.).

Oil filter

Type	Full-flow.
Capacity	1 pint (1·2 U.S. pints, ·57 litre).

Oil pressure

Normal running	30 to 60 lb./sq. in. (2·1 to 4·22 kg./cm.²).
Idling (minimum)	10 to 25 lb./sq. in. (·7 to 1·7 kg./cm.²).

FUEL SYSTEM

Carburetters

Make and type	S.U. twin HS2 semi-downdraught.
Diameter	1¼ in. (31·75 mm.).
Jet	·090 in. (2·29 mm.).
Needles	Standard V3. Rich V2. Weak GX.
Piston spring	Light blue.

Fuel pump

Make and type	A.C. 'Y' type. Mechanical.
Delivery rate	40 pints/hr. (48 U.S. pints/hr., 22·8 litres/hr.).
Delivery pressure	1·5 to 2·5 lb./sq. in. (·105 to ·175 kg./cm.²).

Air cleaners

Type	Paper element.

COOLING SYSTEM

Type	Pressurized radiator. Thermo-siphon, pump- and fan-assisted.
Thermostat setting	65 to 70° C. (149 to 158° F.).
Blow-off pressure	7 lb./sq. in. (·49 kg./cm.²).

IGNITION SYSTEM

Sparking plugs	Champion N5.
Size	14 mm.
Plug gap	·024 to ·026 in. (·625 to ·660 mm.).
Coil	Lucas Type LA12.
Distributor	Lucas Type DM2P4.
Distributor contact points gap	·014 to ·016 in. (·36 to ·40 mm.).
Static ignition setting: High compression	4° B.T.D.C.
Low compression	1° B.T.D.C.

CLUTCH

Type	Single dry plate.
Diameter	6¼ in. (16 cm.).
Facing material	Wound yarn.
Pressure springs	6.
Colour	Yellow and dark green.
Damper springs	4.
Colour	Light grey.
Clutch fluid	Lockheed Super Heavy Duty.

Sprite and Midget. Issue 6. 17826   General Data 3

27

GEARBOX

Number of forward speeds	4.
Synchromesh	Second, third, and top gears.
Ratios: Top	1·0 : 1.
Third	1·357 : 1.
Second	1·916 : 1.
First	3·200 : 1.
Reverse	4·114 : 1.
Overall ratios: Top	4·22 : 1.
Third	5·726 : 1.
Second	8·085 : 1.
First	13·504 : 1.
Reverse	17·361 : 1.
Speedometer gear ratio	5/13.

STEERING

Type	Rack and pinion.
Steering-wheel turns—lock to lock	2¼.
Steering-wheel diameter	16 in. (40·6 cm.).
Camber angle	¾°.
Castor angle	3°.
King pin inclination	6¾°.
Toe-in	0 to ⅛ in. (0 to 3·17 mm.).

Static unladen condition.

Steering lock angle of outer wheel with inner wheel at 20° ..	18½°.

FRONT SUSPENSION

Type	Independent. Coil springs.
Free length	9·4 in. (23·8 cm.).
Mean coil diameter	3·625 in. (9·2 cm.).
Number of effective coils	7.
Working load	750 lb. (340 kg.).
Spring rate	271 lb. in. (3·127 kg. m.).
Dampers (front)	Lever arm type.

REAR SUSPENSION

Type	Quarter-elliptic.
Spring details: Number of leaves	15.
Thickness of leaves	5 at $\frac{5}{32}$ in. (3·97 mm.), 10 at ⅛ in. (3·18 mm.).
Width of leaves	1¾ in. (44·45 mm.).
Working load	375 lb. (170 kg.).
Free camber	$3\frac{7}{32}$ in. (81·76 mm.).
Dampers (rear)	Lever arm type.

PROPELLER SHAFT

Type	Tubular. Reverse spline.
Make and type of joints	Hardy Spicer. Needle-roller.
Propeller shaft length (between centres of joints) ..	26¼ in. (66·6 cm.).
Diameter	1¾ in. (44·45 mm.).

REAR AXLE

Type	Three-quarter-floating.
Ratio	9/38 (4·22 : 1).
(Later cars)	3·9 : 1

ELECTRICAL EQUIPMENT

System	12-volt. Positive earth.
Charging system	Compensated voltage control.
Battery	Lucas BT7A (BTZ7A Export).
Capacity	43 amp.-hr. (at 20-hour rate).
Electrolyte to fill one cell	¾ pint (430 c.c., ⅞ U.S. pint).
Starter motor	Lucas 4-brush M35G/1.
Dynamo	Lucas C39.
Maximum output	19 amps.
Field coil resistance	6·1 ohms±5%.
Control box	Lucas RB106.
Cut-out: Cut-in voltage	12·7 to 13·3.
Drop-off voltage	8·5 to 11·0.
Reverse current	5·0 amps. (max.).

Regulator RB106/2 (at 3,000 r.p.m. dynamo speed):

Open-circuit setting at 20° C. (68° F.)	16·0 to 16·6 volts.

For ambient temperatures other than 20° C. (68° F.) the
following allowances should be made to the above setting:
For every 10° C. (18° F.) above 20° C. (68° F.) subtract
·1 volt.
For every 10° C. (18° F.) below 20° C. (68° F.) add
·1 volt.

BRAKES

Type	Lockheed hydraulic.
Front	Two leading shoes.
Rear	Single leading shoe.
Drum size	7 in. (17·78 cm.).
Lining dimensions: Front and rear	6¾ in. × 1¼ in. (17·14 cm. × 3·175 cm.).
Total lining area	67·5 sq. in. (435·37 cm.²).
Brake fluid	Lockheed Super Heavy Duty.

WHEELS

Type	Ventilated disc. 4-stud fixing.

TYRES

Size	5·20—13.
Tyre pressures—normal and fully loaded: Front	18 lb./sq. in. (1·27 kg./cm.²).
Rear ..	20 lb./sq. in. (1·41 kg./cm.²).

Tyre pressures—for sustained speeds in excess of 80–85 m.p.h.

(129–136 km.p.h.) increase pressure to: Front	24 lb./sq. in. (1·69 kg./cm.²).
Rear	26 lb./sq. in. (1·83 kg./cm.²).

CAPACITIES

	Imp.	*U.S*	*Litres*
Engine sump (including filter)	6·5 pts.	7·8 pts.	3·7
Gearbox	2·25 pts.	2·7 pts.	1·3
Rear axle	1·75 pts.	2·1 pts.	·99
Cooling system (without heater)	10 pts.	12 pts.	5·68
Heater	·5 pt.	·6 pt.	·25
Fuel tank	6 gal.	7·2 gal.	27·3

GENERAL DIMENSIONS

Wheelbase	6 ft. 8 in. (2·03 m.).
Overall length	11 ft. 5⅜ in. (3·49 m.).
Overall width	4 ft. 5 in. (1·35 m.).
Overall height	4 ft. 1¾ in. (1·25 m.).
Ground clearance..	5 in. (12·7 cm.).
Turning circle: Left lock	32 ft. 1½ in. (9·79 m.).
Right lock	31 ft. 2½ in. (9·51 m.).
Track: Front	3 ft. 9¾ in. (1·16 m.) (static unladen condition).
Rear	3 ft. 8¾ in. (1·14 m.).
Vehicle weight (dry)	1,400 lb. (635 kg.).

Sprite and Midget. Issue 6. 4780   General Data 5

29

WEIGHTS OF COMPONENTS

Engine	246 lb. (111·5 kg.).
Gearbox	44 lb. (19·95 kg.).
Axle	83 lb. (37·64 kg.).

TORQUE WRENCH SETTINGS

Cylinder head nuts	40 lb. ft. (5·5 kg. m.).
Main bearing set screws	60 lb. ft. (8·3 kg. m.).
Connecting rod bolts	35 lb. ft. (4·8 kg. m.).
Flywheel securing bolts	40 lb. ft. (5·5 kg. m.).
Steering-wheel nut	40 lb. ft. (5·5 kg. m.).
Road wheel nuts	45 lb. ft. (6·22 kg. m.).
Rear damper bolts	25 lb. ft. (3·4 kg. m.).
Front hub nuts	25 to 65 lb. ft. (3·4 to 8·9 kg. m.).

GENERAL DATA
(1098 c.c.)

The following information is applicable to the 1098-c.c.-engined car and should be used in conjunction with the preceding specification for the 948-c.c.-engined car.

ENGINE

Type	10CG.
Bore	2·543 in. (64·58 mm.).
Stroke	3·296 in. (83·72 mm.).
Capacity	67 cu. in. (1098 c.c.).
Compression ratio	8·9 : 1 (or 8·1 : 1).
Capacity of combustion chamber (valves fitted)	1·8 cu. in. (28·2 c.c.).
Valve operation	Overhead by push-rod.
Oversize bore: 1st	+·010 in. (·254 mm.).
Max.	+·020 in. (·508 mm.).
Torque	H.C. 62 lb. ft. (8·6 kg. m.) 3,250 r.p.m.
	L.C. 61 lb. ft. (8·4 kg. m.) 3,250 r.p.m.

Main bearings
Length	1$\frac{1}{16}$ in. (27 mm.).

Pistons
Type	Solid skirt.
Clearances: Bottom of skirt	·0005 to ·0011 in. (·013 to ·028 mm.).
Top of skirt	·0021 to ·0037 in. (·053 to ·094 mm.).
Oversizes	+·010 in., +·020 in. (+·254 mm., +·508 mm.).

Piston rings
Compression: Type: Top ring	Plain, internally chamfered (chrome-faced).
Second and third rings	Tapered.
Width: Top ring	·062 to ·0625 in. (1·575 to 1·587 mm.).
Second and third rings	·0615 to ·0625 in. (1·558 to 1·587 mm.).
Thickness	·106 to ·112 in. (2·69 to 2·84 mm.).
Clearance in groove	·002 to ·004 in. (·051 to ·102 mm.).
Oil control: Type: Early engines	Slotted scraper.
Thickness	·106 to ·112 in. (2·69 to 2·84 mm.).
Type: Later engines	Wellworthy-Duraflex 61.
Fitted gap: Rails	·012 to ·028 in. (·31 to ·7 mm.).
Side spring	·10 to ·15 in. (2·54 to 3·81 mm.).

Gudgeon pin
Type	Fully floating.
Fit in piston	Hand push fit.

Valves
Head diameter: Inlet	1·213 to 1·218 in. (30·81 to 30·94 mm.).

FUEL SYSTEM
Carburetters
Needles: Standard	GY.
Weak	GG.
Rich	M.
Piston spring	Blue.

COOLING SYSTEM
Thermostat setting
Standard	82° C. (180° F.).
Hot climates	74° C. (165° F.).
Cold climates	88° C. (190° F.).

IGNITION SYSTEM

Distributor

Type	25D4.
Serial number	40919.
Rotation of rotor	Anti-clockwise.
Cam closed period	60°±3°.
Cam open period	30°±3°.
Automatic advance	Centrifugal and vacuum.
Automatic advance commences	400 r.p.m.
Maximum advance (crankshaft degrees)	32° at 5,500 r.p.m.
Vacuum advance (crankshaft degrees)	20° at 13 in. (33·3 cm.) Hg.
Decelerating check (crankshaft degrees, engine r.p.m.) ..	32° at 5,500 r.p.m.
	28° at 4,400 r.p.m.
	16° at 1,800 r.p.m.
	4° at 1,200 r.p.m.
	1° at 800 r.p.m.
Contact point gap setting	·014 to ·016 in. (·35 to ·4 mm.).
Breaker spring tension	18 to 24 oz. (510 to 680 gm.).
Condenser capacity	·22 mF.
Timing marks	Pointer on timing chain case and notch on crank-shaft pulley.
Static ignition setting: High compression	5° B.T.D.C.
Low compression	3 to 5° B.T.D.C.
Stroboscopic timing	8° B.T.D.C. at 600 r.p.m. (engine).

CLUTCH

Diameter	7¼ in. (184 mm.).
Pressure springs	6.
Colour	Red.
Damper springs	4.
Colour	Black/light green.
Clutch fluid	Lockheed Disc Brake Fluid (Series II).

GEARBOX

Ratios: Reverse	4·120 : 1.
Overall ratios: Reverse	17·32 : 1.

ELECTRICAL EQUIPMENT

Battery	Lucas N9 or NZ9.
Capacity	43 amp.-hr. (at 20-hour rate).
Electrolyte to fill one cell	¾ pint (430 c.c., ⅞ U.S. pint).
Dynamo	Lucas C40/1.
Maximum output	22 amps.
Field coil resistance	6·0 ohms.
Control box	Lucas RB 106/2.

BRAKES

Type	Lockheed hydraulic; disc front, drum rear; leading and trailing shoes.
Brake fluid	Lockheed Disc Brake Fluid (Series II).

Front

Disc diameter	8·25 in. (209·5 mm.).
Pad area (total)	18 sq. in. (116·1 cm.²).
Swept area (total)	135·28 sq. in. (871 cm.²).
Lining material	Ferodo DA3.
Minimum pad thickness	$\frac{1}{16}$ in. (1·59 mm.).

General Data 8   Sprite and Midget. Issue 3. 4780

32

Rear

Drum diameter	7 in. (177·8 mm.).
Lining dimensions	6·68 in. × 1·25 in. × ·187 in. (169·8 mm. × 37·5 mm. × 4·75 mm.).
Swept area (total)	55 sq. in. (342 cm.²).
Lining material	Ferodo AM8.

GENERAL DIMENSIONS

Track: Front	3 ft. 10$\frac{1}{16}$ (1·16 m.) (static unladen condition).
Rear	3 ft. 8$\frac{3}{4}$ in. (1·14 m.).
Vehicle weight (dry)	1,466 lb. (665 kg.).

WEIGHTS OF COMPONENTS

Engine	253 lb. (114·7 kg.).

TORQUE WRENCH SETTINGS

Rocker bracket nuts	25 lb. ft. (3·4 kg. m.).
Sump to crankcase	6 lb. ft. (·8 kg. m.).
Cylinder side covers	2 lb. ft. (·28 kg. m.).
Timing cover—$\frac{1}{4}$ in. UNF. bolt	6 lb. ft. (·8 kg. m.).
Timing cover—$\frac{5}{16}$ in. UNF. bolt	14 lb. ft. (1·9 kg. m.).
Water pump	17 lb. ft. (2·3 kg. m.).
Water outlet elbow	8 lb. ft. (1·1 kg. m.).
Oil filter	16 lb. ft. (2·2 kg. m.).
Oil pump	9 lb. ft. (1·2 kg. m.).
Manifold to cylinder head	15 lb. ft. (2·1 kg. m.).
Rocker cover	4 lb. ft. (·56 kg. m.).
Crankshaft pulley nut	70 lb. ft. (9·6 kg. m.).
Distributor clamp bolt: Fixed nut type	50 lb. in. (·576 kg. m.).
Fixed bolt type	30 lb. in. (·345 kg. m.).

Suspension and steering

Steering lever ball joint nut	32·3 to 34·3 lb. ft. (4·4 to 4·7 kg. m.).
Steering-wheel nut	41 to 43 lb. ft. (5·6 to 5·9 kg. m.).
Road wheel nuts	44 to 46 lb. ft. (6·0 to 6·3 kg. m.).
Disc to hub	40 to 45 lb. ft. (5·5 to 6·2 kg. m.).
Front swivel hub to calliper	45 to 50 lb. ft. (6·2 to 7·0 kg. m.).
Front shock absorber bolts	25 to 30 lb. ft. (3·4 to 4·1 kg. m.).

Sprite and Midget. Issue 3. 17826   General Data 9

33

GENERAL DATA
SPRITE (Mk. III) and MIDGET (Mk. II)

The following information is applicable to the Sprite (Mk. III) and Midget (Mk. II) and should be used in conjunction with the preceding specifications.

ENGINE

Type	10CC.
Torque	H.C. 65 lb. ft. (8·9 kg. m.) at 3,500 r.p.m.
	L.C. 64 lb. ft. (8·8 kg. m.) at 3,250 r.p.m.

Crankshaft

Main journal diameter	2·0005 to 2·0010 in. (50·79 to 50·80 mm.).

FUEL SYSTEM

Carburetters

Needles	Standard AN. Rich H6. Weak GG.

Fuel pump

Make and type	S.U. (electrical) Type AUF200.
Delivery rate	56 pints/hr. (67 U.S. pints/hr., 32 litres/hr.).
Delivery pressure	2·5 to 3·0 lb./sq. in. (·17 to ·21 kg./cm.²).

FRONT SUSPENSION

Spring free length	9·59 in. (24·4 cm.).

REAR SUSPENSION

Type	Semi-elliptic.
Spring details: Number of leaves	5.
Thickness of leaves	₁₁ in. (4·37 mm.).
Width of leaves	1½ in. (38·10 mm.).
Working load	375 lb. (170 kg.).
Free camber	4·437 (112·7 mm.).

TYRES

Tyre pressures—for sustained speeds in excess of 80–85 m.p.h.

(129–136 km.p.h.) increase pressure to: Front	22 lb./sq. in. (1·55 kg./cm.²).
Rear	24 lb./sq. in. (1·69 kg./cm.²).

WEIGHTS

Vehicle weight (dry)..	1,490 lb. (676 kg.).

TORQUE WRENCH SETTINGS

Cylinder side cover (deep pressed type)	5 lb. ft. (·7 kg. m.).

GENERAL DATA
SPRITE (Mk. IV) and MIDGET (Mk. III)

The following information is applicable to the Sprite (Mk. IV) and Midget (Mk. III) and should be used in conjunction with the preceding specifications.

ENGINE

Type: Early cars	12CC, 12CE.
Midget Mk. III from Car No. G–AN5–105501 ..	12V.
Number of cylinders	4.
Bore	2·78 in. (70·61 mm.).
Stroke	3·2 in. (81·28 mm.).
Capacity	77·8 cu. in. (1274·86 c.c.).
Firing order	1, 3, 4, 2.
Valve operation	Overhead by push-rod.
Compression ratio: H.C.	8·8 : 1.
L.C.	8·0 : 1.
B.M.E.P.: H.C. (Standard)	139 lb./sq. in. (9·77 kg./cm.²) at 3,000 r.p.m.
L.C. (Standard)	127 lb./sq. in. (8·93 kg./cm.²) at 3,000 r.p.m.
Torque: H.C. (Standard)	72 lb. ft. (9·96 kg. m.) at 3,000 r.p.m.
L.C. (Standard)	64·5 lb. ft. (8·91 kg. m.) at 3,000 r.p.m.
Cranking pressure: H.C.	120 lb./sq. in. (8·44 kg./cm.²) at 350 r.p.m.
Engine idle speed	650 to 700 r.p.m.
Oversize bore: 1st	·010 in. (·254 mm.).
Max.	·020 in. (·508 mm.).

Crankshaft

Main journal diameter	2·0005 to 2·0010 in. (50·813 to 50·825 mm.).
Crankpin journal diameter	1·6252 to 1·6259 in. (41·28 to 41·29 mm.).
Regrind—Main and crankpin journals	Maximum permissible, without heat treatment: 0·010 in. (·254 mm.) below the standard diameter.
Crankshaft end-thrust	Taken by thrust washers at centre main bearing.
Crankshaft end-float	·002 to ·003 in. (·051 to ·076 mm.).

Main bearings

Number and type	3 thin-wall; split shells, steel backed: copper-lead-indium.
Material	VP3 lead-indium or NFM/3B.
Length	·975 to ·985 in. (24·765 to 25·019 mm.).
Diametrical clearance	·0010 to ·0027 in. (·0254 to ·067 mm.).

Connecting rods

Type	Horizontally split big-end, plain small-end.
Length between centres	5·748 to 5·792 in. (145·99 to 145·101 mm.).

Big-end bearings

Type and material	Steel-backed lead-indium plated.
Length	·840 to ·850 in. (21·336 to 21·590 mm.).
Diametrical clearance	·0010 to ·0025 in. (·0254 to ·063 mm.).
End-float on crankpin	·006 to ·010 in. (·15 to ·254 mm.).

Pistons

Type	Aluminium solid skirt dished crown.
Clearance in cylinder: Top of skirt	·0029 to ·0037 in. (·074 to ·095 mm.).
Bottom of skirt	·0015 to ·0021 in. (·038 to ·054 mm.).
Number of rings	4 (3 compression, 1 oil control).
Width of ring grooves: Top, second, and third ..	·0484 to ·0494 in. (1·229 to 1·255 mm.).
Oil control	·1578 to ·1588 in. (4·008 to 4·033 mm.).
Gudgeon pin bore	·8125 to ·8129 in. (20·638 to 29·647 mm.).

Sprite and Midget. Issue 4. 82963   General Data 13

35

Piston rings

Compression:

Type: Top .. .. Internally chamfered chrome.

    Second and third .. .. Tapered cast iron.

Width: Top .. .. } ·0615 to ·0625 in. (1·558 to 1·583 mm.).

    Second and third .. .. .. }

Fitted gap: Top .. .. ·011 to ·016 in. (·279 to ·406 mm.).

    Second and third .. .. .. ·008 to ·013 in. (·203 to ·330 mm.).

Ring to groove clearance: Top .. .. } ·0015 to ·0035 in. (·038 to ·088 mm.).

    Second and third .. }

Oil control

Type .. .. Duaflex 61.

Fitted gap: Rails .. .. } ·012 to ·028 in. (·305 to ·70 mm.).

    Side spring .. .. .. }

Gudgeon pin

Type .. .. Pressed in connecting rod.

Fit in piston .. .. Hand push-fit.

Diameter (outer) .. .. ·8123 to ·8125 in. (20·63 to 20·64 mm.).

Fit to connecting rod .. .. ·0008 to ·0015 in. (·020 to ·038 mm.) interference.

Camshaft

Journal diameters: Front .. .. .. 1·6655 to 1·6660 in. (42·304 to 42·316 mm.).

    Centre .. .. .. 1·62275 to 1·62325 in. (41·218 to 41·231 mm.).

    Rear .. .. .. 1·37275 to 1·37350 in. (34·866 to 34·889 mm.).

Bearing liner inside diameter (reamed after fitting): Front 1·6670 to 1·6675 in. (42·342 to 42·355 mm.).

    Centre 1·62425 to 1·62475 in. (41·256 to 41·369 mm.).

    Rear 1·3745 to 1·3750 in. (34·912 to 34·925 mm.).

Bearings: Type .. .. White-metal lined, steel backed.

Diametrical clearance .. .. ·001 to ·002 in. (·0254 to ·0508 mm.).

End-thrust .. .. Taken on locating plate.

End-float .. .. ·003 to ·007 in. (·076 to ·178 mm.).

Cam lift .. .. ·250 in. (6·35 mm.).

Drive .. .. Duplex chain and gear from crankshaft.

Timing chain .. .. ⅜ in. (9·52 mm.) pitch × 52 pitches.

Tappets

Type .. .. Bucket.

Outside diameter .. .. ·81175 to ·812 in. (20·618 to 20·64 mm.).

Length .. .. 1·495 to 1·505 in. (37·973 to 38·23 mm.).

Rocker gear

Rocker shaft:

    Diameter .. .. ·5615 to ·5625 in. (14·262 to 14·287 mm.).

Rocker arm:

    Bore .. .. ·686 to ·687 in. (17·424 to 17·449 mm.).

    Rocker arm bush inside diameter .. .. .. ·5630 to ·5635 in. (14·3 to 14·313 mm.).

Valves

Seat angle: Inlet and exhaust .. .. .. 45°.

Head diameter: Inlet .. .. 1·307 to 1·312 in. (33·198 to 33·21 mm.).

    Exhaust .. .. 1·1515 to 1·1565 in. (29·243 to 29·373 mm.).

Stem diameter: Inlet .. .. ·2793 to ·2798 in. (7·094 to 7·107 mm.).

    Exhaust .. .. ·2788 to ·2793 in. (7·081 to 7·094 mm.).

Stem to guide clearance: Inlet and exhaust .. .. ·0015 to ·0025 in. (·0381 to ·0778 mm.).

Valve lift: Inlet and exhaust .. .. .. ·318 in. (8·076 mm.).

Valve guides

Length: Inlet .. .. }	1·6875 in. (42·87 mm.).
Exhaust	
Fitted height above seat: Exhaust .. .. }	·540 in. (13·72 mm.).
Inlet	

Valve springs

	Outer	*Inner*
Free length	1·828 in. (46·47 mm.).	1·703 in. (43·26 mm.).
Fitted length	1·383 in. (35·13 mm.).	1·270 in. (32·26 mm.).
Load at fitted length	51 lb. (23·1 kg.).	25 lb. (11·3 kg.).
Load at top of lift	87 lb. (39·5 kg.).	44 lb. (20 kg.).
Valve crash speed	6,750 r.p.m.	

Valve timing

Timing marks	Dimples on timing gears.
Rocker clearance: Running (Standard)	·012 in. (·30 mm.) cold.
(Competition work) ..	·015 in. (·38 mm.) cold.
Timing	·029 in. (·72 mm.).
Inlet valve: Opens	5° B.T.D.C.
Closes	45° A.B.D.C.
Exhaust valve: Opens	51° B.B.D.C.
Closes	21° A.T.D.C.

Lubrication

System pressure: Running	40 to 70 lb./sq. in. (2·81 to 4·92 kg./cm.²).
Idling	20 lb./sq. in. (1·4 kg./cm.²).
Oil pump	Eccentric rotor: splined drive from camshaft.
Oil filter	Full-flow type; renewable element: differential pressure switch. Later cars: disposable cartridge type.
Oil pressure relief valve	50 lb./sq. in. (5·3 kg./cm.²).
Relief valve spring: Free length	2·86 in. (72·64 mm.).
Fitted length	2·156 in. (54·77 mm.).
Load at fitted length	13 to 14 lb. (5·90 to 6·35 kg.).

IGNITION SYSTEM

Coil

Coil	Lucas 11C 12.
Resistance at 20° C. (68° F.) primary winding ..	3 to 3·4 ohms.
Consumption: Ignition switch on	3·5 to 4 amps.
At 2,000 r.p.m.	1 amp.

Distributor

Distributor	Lucas 23D4.	
Rotation of rotor arm	Anti-clockwise.	
Cam closed period	60°±3°.	
Cam open period	30°±3°.	
Serial number	40819.	41198.
Type	23D4.	25D4.
Automatic advance	Centrifugal.	Centrifugal and vacuum.
Centrifugal advance		
Crankshaft degrees—(vacuum pipe disconnected) ..	0°–3° at 600 r.p.m. 6°–12° at 1,000 r.p.m. 11°–15° at 2,000 r.p.m. 22°–26° at 5,200 r.p.m. 28°–32° at 7,000 r.p.m.	0°–1° at 600 r.p.m. 2°–6° at 800 r.p.m. 4°–8° at 1,000 r.p.m. 10°–14° at 2,000 r.p.m. 20°–24° at 5,600 r.p.m.
Vacuum advance		
Starts		5 in. Hg.
Finishes		8 in. Hg.
Total crankshaft degrees		6°±2°.
Contact point gap setting	·014 to ·016 in. (·35 to ·40 mm.).	
Breaker spring tension	18 to 24 oz. (510 to 680 gm.).	
Condenser capacity	·18 to ·24 mF.	
Timing marks	Pointer on timing chain case and notch in crankshaft pulley.	

Sprite and Midget. Issue 6. 82963   General Data 15

37

Static ignition timing: H.C. .. .. 7° B.T.D.C.

L.C. .. .. 7° B.T.D.C.

Stroboscopic ignition timing .. .. 22° at 1,200 r.p.m. (23D4 distributor).

13° at 1,000 r.p.m. (25D4 distributor).

Sparking plugs .. .. Champion N9Y.

Size .. .. 14 mm.

Gap .. .. ·024 to ·026 in. (·62 to ·66 mm.).

COOLING SYSTEM

Thermostat settings: Standard .. .. 82° C. (180° F.).

Hot countries .. .. .. 74° C. (165° F.).

Cold countries .. .. .. 88° C. (190° F.).

Pressure cap: Early cars .. .. 7 lb./sq. in. (·49 kg./cm.²).

Later cars .. .. 15 lb./sq. in. (1·05 kg./cm.²).

Capacity with heater .. .. 6 pints (3·4 litres, 7 U S. pints).

FUEL SYSTEM

Carburetter .. .. Twin S.U. Type H.S.2.

Choke diameter .. .. 1·25 in. (31·75 mm.).

Jet size .. .. ·090 in. (2·29 mm.).

Needles .. .. Standard AN; Weak GG; Rich H6.

Piston spring .. .. Light blue.

CLUTCH

Make and type .. .. Borg & Beck; diaphragm-spring type.

Clutch plate diameter .. .. 6·5 in. (165 mm.).

Facing material: Early cars .. .. .. Wound yarn.

Later cars .. .. .. Thermoid 11046

Number of damper springs .. .. 4.

Damper spring colour .. .. 2 lavender, 2 white and violet.

Later cars: 2 violet and white, 1 pale blue, 1 maroon and cream.

Clutch release bearing .. .. Carbon pad.

Later cars: carbon pad, Schunke and Ebe ref. U.5671.

Clutch fluid .. .. Lockheed Disc brake (Series II).

STEERING

Type .. .. Rack and pinion.

Steering-wheel turns lock to lock:

Early cars .. .. 2·25.

Midget Mk. III from Car No. G–AN5–114643 .. .. 2·8.

Steering-wheel diameter .. .. 15½ in. (39·4 cm.).

Toe-in .. .. 0 to ⅛ in. (0 to 3·17 mm.).

Camber angle .. .. ¾°.

Caster angle .. .. 3°.

Pinion end-float:

Midget Mk. III from Car No. G–AN5–114643 .. .. ·010 in. (·25 mm.).

King pin inclination:

Early cars .. .. $6\frac{3}{4}° \pm 1\frac{1}{4}°$.

Later cars: Laden .. .. 6° 30'

Unladen .. .. 6° 45' } ±1° 15'.

Steering lock angle of outer wheel with inner wheel at 20°:

Early cars .. .. $19\frac{3}{4}° \pm 1\frac{1}{4}°$.

Later cars .. .. $19° \ 30'^{+30'}_{-1°}$.

BRAKES

Lining material: front .. .. Ferodo 2424F–GG.

rear .. .. Ferodo AM8–FF.

Brake fluid .. .. Lockheed Disc Brake (Series II).

Front brake disc size: Standard width .. .. .. ·300 to ·305 in. (7·62 to 7·75 mm.).

Minimum permissible width .. .. ·29 in. (7·37 mm.).

WHEELS

Size and type (Pressed spoked) ..	..	..	..	..	..	4½J SL × 13.
(Pressed disc)	..	..	..	..	..	3·5D × 13.
(Wire)	..	..	..	..	..	4J × 13.

GEARBOX

Number of forward speeds ..	..	..	..	..	..	4.
Synchromesh ..	..	..	..	..	..	Second, third, and top gears.
Ratios: Top ..	..	..	..	..	..	1·0 : 1.
Third ..	..	..	..	..	..	1·357 : 1.
Second	..	..	..	..	..	1·916 : 1.
First ..	..	..	..	..	..	3·200 : 1.
Reverse	..	..	..	..	..	4·114 : 1.
Overall ratios: Top ..	..	..	..	..	..	3·9 : 1.
Third ..	..	..	..	..	..	5·292 : 1.
Second..	..	..	..	..	..	7·472 : 1.
First ..	..	..	..	..	..	12·480 : 1.
Reverse	..	..	..	..	..	16·044 : 1.
Speedometer gear ratio	..	..	..	..	..	5/13.

TYRE PRESSURES

	5·20—13S Cross-ply tyres		145SR—13 Radial-ply tyres	
	Front	*Rear*	*Front*	*Rear*
Normal car weight	18 lb./sq. in. (1·27 kg./cm.²)	20 lb./sq. in. (1·4 kg./cm.²)	22 lb./sq. in. (1·55 kg./cm.²)	24 lb./sq. in. (1·69 kg./cm.²)
Maximum weight	18 lb./sq. in. (1·27 kg./cm.²)	24 lb./sq. in. (1·69 kg./cm.²)	22 lb./sq. in. (1·55 kg./cm.²)	26 lb./sq. in. (1·83 kg./cm.²)

It is recommended that for sustained speeds at near the maximum the above tyre pressures are increased by 4 lb./sq. in. (·28 kg./cm.²).

WEIGHTS

	Including	*Total weight*	*Distribution*	
			Front	*Rear*
Kerbside	Full fuel tank, all optional extras and accessories	1,701 lb. (772 kg.)	861 lb. (391 kg.)	840 lb. (381 kg.)
Normal	Kerbside weight, driver, passenger, and 50 lb. (22·7 kg.) luggage	2,001 lb. (908 kg.)	959 lb. (435 kg.)	1,042 lb. (473 kg.)
Maximum	Normal weight and towbar hitch load	2,151 lb. (975 kg.)	926 lb. (420 kg.)	1,225 lb. (556 kg.)
Maximum permissible towing weight		1,344 lb. (610 kg.)		
Towbar hitch load		Maximum 100 lb. (45·4 kg.)		

Sprite and Midget. Issue 6. 82963   General Data 17

39

CAPACITIES

Fuel tank: Midget Mk. III from Car No. G–AN5–105501 ..   7 gallons (32 litres).

DIMENSIONS

	Pressed spoked wheels	Wire wheels	Pressed disc wheels
Turning circle: Later cars		32 ft. 5 in. (9·88 m.).	
Track: Front	3 ft. 10 9/16 in. (1·18 m.).	3 ft 10 9/16 in. (1·18 m.).	3 ft. 10 9/16 (1·18 m.).
Rear	3 ft. 10 in. (1·17 m.).	3 ft. 9¼ in. (1·15 m.).	3 ft. 8¾ in. (1·14 m.).
Overall width		4 ft. 8½ in. (1·5 m.).	4 ft. 6⅞ in. (1·4 m.).
Overall height		4 ft. ⅞ in. (1·22 m.).	

DIMENSIONS (1974 U.S.A. cars)

	Pressed spoked wheels	Wire wheels	Pressed disc wheels
Overall width	4 ft. 5⅝ in. (1·36 m.).	4 ft. 8⅛ in. (1·44 m.)	4 ft. 6⅞ in. (1·39 m.).
Overall height:			
Cross-ply tyres	4 ft. ⅝ in. (1·24 m.).	4 ft. ⅝ in. (1·24 m.)	4 ft. ⅝ in. (1·24 m.).
Radial-ply tyres	4 ft. ¼ in. (1·23 m.).	4 ft. ¼ in. (1·23 m.)	4 ft. ¼ in. (1·23 m.).
Overall length (Midget Mk. III from Car No. G–AN5–138801)	11 ft. 4½ in. (3·47 m.).	11 ft. 4½ in. (3·47 m.)	11 ft. 4½ in. (3·47 m.).

TORQUE WRENCH SETTINGS

Oil pump securing bolts	12 lb. ft. (1·66 kg. m.).
Cylinder head nuts:	
Plain studs	42 lb. ft. (5·81 kg. m.).
Studs stamped 22 or with small drill point	50 lb. ft. (6·91 kg. m.).
Connecting rod nuts	40 lb. ft. (5·53 kg. m.).
	Nyloc nut: 32 to 34 lb. ft. (4·43 to 4·70 kg. m.).
Fan securing bolts	100 lb. in. (1·15 kg. m.).
Road wheel nuts	45 lb. ft. (6·22 kg. m.).
Steering-column pinch bolt	9 to 11 lb. ft. (1·2 to 1·5 kg. m.).
Oil filter	10 to 15 lb. ft. (1·38 to 2 kg. m.).
Petrol tank drain plug	100 to 120 lb. in. (1·15 to 1·38 kg. m.).
Oil pipe union adaptor—oil filter head	19 to 21 lb. ft. (2·63 to 2·9 kg. m.).
Clutch bolts	18 to 22 lb. ft. (2·49 to 3·04 kg. m.).
Midget Mk. III from Car No. G–AN5–114643:	
Steering rack clamp bolts	20 to 22 lb. ft. (2·77 to 3·04 kg. m.).
Steering rack mounting bracket retaining bolts ..	23 to 25 lb. ft. (3·18 to 3·46 kg. m.).
Tie-rod end assembly locknut	30 to 35 lb. ft. (4·15 to 4·84 kg. m.).
Tie-rod end assembly ball joint nut	28 to 32 lb. ft. (3·87 to 4·48 kg. m.).
Tie-rod inner ball joint assembly locknut	80 lb. ft. (11·06 kg. m.).

ELECTRICAL

Regulator

Make/type	Lucas RB340.
Setting at 20° C. (68° F.), 3,000 r.p.m. dynamo ..	14·5 to 15·5 volts.
Cut-in voltage	12·7 to 13·3 volts.
Drop-off voltage	9·5 to 11·0 volts.

Starter

Make/type	Lucas M35J.
Brush spring tension	28 oz. (·8 kg.).
Minimum brush length	⅜ in. (9·5 mm.).
Minimum commutator thickness	·08 in. (2·05 mm.).
Lock torque	7 lb. ft. (·97 kg. m.) at 250–375 amps.
Light running current	65 amps. at 8,000 to 10,000 r.p.m.
Maximum armature end-float	·010 in. (·25 mm.).
Torque at 1,000 r.p.m.	4·4 lb. ft. (·61 kg. m.) at 260 to 275 amps.

General Data 18

Sprite and Midget. Issue 6. 82963
MG Midget. AKM 2092/1

40

Battery

Make/type	Lucas A9/AZ9–A11/AZ11.
Capacity at 20-hr. rate	A9/AZ9: 40 amp. hr.
	A11/AZ11: 50 amp. hr.

Fusebox

Make/type	Lucas 7FJ.

Alternator (Later Midget Mk. III cars)

Type	Lucas 16ACR.
Brush length—new	·5 in. (12·6 mm.).
Brush length—minimum	·2 in. (5 mm.) protruding beyond brush box moulding.
Brush spring pressure	9 to 13 oz. (255 to 369 gm.) when brush is pushed in flush with brush box face.

Field winding:

Resistance at 20° C. (68° F.):	
Rotor with forged claw	4·3 ohms±5%.
Rotor with pressed claw	3·3 ohms±5%.
Current flow at 12 volts	3 amperes.
Insulation test equipment	110-volt A.C. supply and 15-watt test lamp.

Stator windings:

Continuity test equipment	12-volt D.C. supply and 36-watt test lamp.
Insulation test equipment	110-volt A.C. supply and 15-watt test lamp.
Diode current test equipment	12-volt D.C. supply and 1·5-watt test lamp.
Alternator output at 14 volts	34 amperes at 6,000 alternator r.p.m.

FRONT SUSPENSION (Later Midget Mk. III from Car No. G–AN5–123837)

Spring coil diameter (mean)	3·575 to 3·625 in. (9·1 to 9·2 cm.).
Free height	9·85 in. (25 cm.).
Fitted length at load of 750±15 lb. (337±6·8 kg.) ..	7·08 in. (18 cm.).
Number of effective coils	7.

Sprite and Midget. Issue 4. 83942
MG Midget. AKM 2092/1

41

General Data 19

The data given in this section refers specifically to equipment fitted to the Sprite Mk. IV and Midget Mk. III in conformity with local and territorial requirements, and must be used in conjunction with the standard data given.

ENGINE

Type (1969–70)	12CD (EEC).
Type (1970–71)	12CJ (EEC, ELC).
Type (1971–72)	12V 587Z (EEC, ELC).
Type (1972-74)	12V 671Z (EEC, ELC).

Abbreviations: EEC, Exhaust Emission Controls   ELC, Evaporative Loss Control.

Valve guides .. .. ·5 molybdenum added.
Only valve guides having a ·025×·010 in. (·635×·254 mm.) identification groove machined ·187 in. (4·76 mm). from the top of the valve guide should be used on engines 12CD, 12CJ, and 12V.

Servicing, adjusting and tuning the above type engines and cars fitted with vehicle emission control equipment must be carried out in accordance with the instructions given in Workshop Manual Supplement AKD 4957.   [Part 3 of this Manual].

FUEL SYSTEM

Fuel tank capacity:

Early cars	6 U.S. gallons (22·7 litres).
Midget Mk. III from Car No. G–AN5–105501 ..	7 U.S. gallons (27·3 litres).

Fuel pump (later cars):

Type	S.U. electric AUF 300.
Minimum flow	18 U.S. gal./hr. (68·2 litres/hr.).
Suction head	18 in. (·457 mm.).
Delivery head	4 ft. (122 cm.).

Fuel pump (1974 cars):

Type	S.U. electric AUF 305.
Delivery pressure	2·8 to 3·8 lb./sq. in. (0·2 to 0·27 kg./m.²).

BRAKES

Lining material: front	Ferodo 2424F-GG.
rear	Ferodo AM8-FF.
Brake fluid	Lockheed Disc Brake (Series 329).

ELECTRICAL

Alternator (Midget Mk. III from Car No. G–AN5–105501)

Type	Lucas 16ACR.
Brush length—new	0·5 in. (12·6 mm.).
Brush length—minimum	0·2 in. (5 mm.) protruding beyond brush box moulding.
Brush spring pressure	9 to 13 oz. (255 to 369 gm.) when brush is pushed in flush with brush box face.

Field winding:

Resistance	4·33 ohms.
Current flow at 12 volts	3 amperes.
Insulation test equipment	110-volt A.C. supply and 15-watt test lamp.

Stator windings:

Continuity test equipment	12-volt D.C. supply and 36-watt test lamp.
Insulation test equipment	110-volt A.C. supply and 15-watt test lamp.
Diode current test equipment	12-volt D.C. supply and 1·5-watt test lamp.
Alternator output at 14 volts	34 amperes at 6,000 alternator r.p.m.

General Data 20

Sprite and Midget. Issue 4. 83942
MG Midget. AKM 2092/1

42

ENGINE TUNING DATA 1
MODEL: SPRITE Mk. II/MIDGET Mk. I (948-c.c. ENGINE)

ENGINE

Type	9CG.
Displacement	57·87 cu. in. (948 c.c.).
Compression ratio	9 : 1.
Compression pressure	168 lb./sq. in. (11·82 kg./cm.²).
Firing order	1, 4, 3, 2.
Static ignition timing	4° B.T.D.C.
Stroboscopic ignition timing	6° B.T.D.C. at 600 r.p.m. (engine).
Timing mark location	Pointer on timing chain cover and notch on crankshaft pulley.

DISTRIBUTOR

Make/Type	Lucas/DM2P4.
Serial No.	40561.
Contact breaker gap	·014 to ·016 in. (·36 to ·40 mm.).
Contact spring tension	18 to 24 oz. (510 to 680 gm.).
Rotation at rotor	Anti-clockwise.
Dwell angle	60°±3°.

Centrifugal advance

Crankshaft degrees/speed (vacuum pipe disconnected) ..	0°–4° at 1,200 r.p.m.
	10°–15° at 2,000 r.p.m.
	24°–28° at 4,600 r.p.m.
	24°–28° at 5,600 r.p.m. (max.).

Vacuum advance

Starts	5 in. Hg.
Finishes	12 in. Hg.
Total crankshaft degrees	12°.

IGNITION COIL

Make/Type	Lucas/LA12.
Resistance	3·2 to 3·4 ohms.

SPARKING PLUGS

Make/Type	Champion/N5.
Gap	·024 to ·026 in. (·61 to ·66 mm.).

ELECTRICAL

Dynamo	Lucas/C39.
Battery	Lucas/BT7A or BT27A.
Volts/Polarity	12 volt/Positive earth.
Starter	Lucas/N35G/1.
Control unit	Lucas/RB106/2.

CARBURETTERS

Make/Type	S.U./HS2.
Jet	·090 in. (2·29 mm.).
Needle	Standard V3; Rich V2; Weak GX.
Piston spring	Light blue

ENGINE

Type	10CG.
Displacement	67 cu. in. (1098 c.c.).
Compression ratio	8·9 : 1.
Compression pressure	165 lb./sq. in. (11·6 kg./cm.²).
Firing order	1, 3, 4, 2.
Static ignition timing	5° B.T.D.C.
Stroboscopic ignition timing	8° B.T.D.C. at 600 r.p.m. (engine).
Timing mark location	Pointer on timing chain case and notch on crankshaft pulley.
Engine idle speed	1,000 r.p.m.

DISTRIBUTOR

Make/Type	Lucas/25D4.
Serial No.	40919.
Contact breaker gap	·014 to ·016 in. (·36 to ·40 mm.).
Contact spring tension	18 to 24 oz. (510 to 680 gm.).
Rotation at rotor	Anti-clockwise.
Condenser capacity	·22 mF.
Dwell angle	60°±3°.

Centrifugal advance

Crankshaft degrees/speed (vacuum pipe disconnected) ..	1° at 800 r.p.m.
	4° at 1,200 r.p.m.
	16° at 1,800 r.p.m.
	28° at 4,400 r.p.m.
	32° at 5,500 r.p.m.

Vacuum advance

Starts	4 in. Hg.
Finishes	13 in. Hg.
Total crankshaft degrees	20°.

IGNITION COIL

Make/Type	Lucas/LA12.
Resistance	3·2 to 3·4 ohms.

SPARKING PLUGS

Make/Type	Champion/N5.
Gap	·024 to ·026 (·610 to ·660 mm.).

ELECTRICAL

Dynamo	Lucas/C40.
Battery	Lucas/N9 or NZ9.
Volts/Polarity	12 volt/Positive earth.
Starter	Lucas/M35G.
Control unit	Lucas/RB106/2.

CARBURETTER

Make/Type	S.U./HS2.
Jet	·090 in. (2·29 mm.).
Needle	Standard GY; Rich M; Weak GG.
Piston spring	Blue.

ENGINE

Type	10CG.
Displacement	67 cu. in. (1098 c.c.).
Compression ratio	8·9 : 1.
Compression pressure	165 lb./sq. in. (11·6 kg./cm.²).
Firing order	1, 3, 4, 2.
Static ignition timing	5° B.T.D.C.
Stroboscopic ignition timing	8° B.T.D.C. at 600 r.p.m. (engine).
Timing mark location	Pointer on timing chain case and notch on crankshaft pulley.
Engine idle speed	1,000 r.p.m.

DISTRIBUTOR

Make/Type	Lucas/25D4.
Serial No.	40919.
Contact breaker gap	·014 to ·016 in. (·36 to ·40 mm.).
Contact spring tension	18 to 24 oz. (510 to 680 gm.).
Rotation at rotor	Anti-clockwise.
Dwell angle	60°±3°.

Centrifugal advance

Crankshaft degrees/speed (vacuum pipe disconnected) ..	0°–1° at 800 r.p.m.
	2°–6° at 1,200 r.p.m.
	17°–21° at 2,000 r.p.m.
	19°–23° at 2,400 r.p.m.
	26°–30° at 4,400 r.p.m.
	30°–34° at 6,000 r.p.m.

Vacuum advance

Starts	4 in. Hg.
Finishes	13 in. Hg.
Total crankshaft degrees	20°.

IGNITION COIL

Make/Type	Lucas/LA.12.
Resistance	3·2 to 3·4 ohms.

SPARKING PLUGS

Make/Type	Champion/N5.
Gap	·024 to ·026 in. (·610 to ·660 mm.).

ELECTRICAL

Dynamo	Lucas/C40.
Battery	Lucas/N9 or NZ9.
Volts/Polarity	12 volt/Positive earth.
Starter	Lucas/M35G.
Control unit	Lucas/RB106/2.

CARBURETTER

Make/Type	S.U./HS2.
Jet	·090 in. (2·29 mm.).
Needle	Standard AN; Rich H6; Weak GG.
Piston spring	Blue.

ENGINE TUNING DATA 4

MODEL: SPRITE Mk. IV/MIDGET Mk. III (1275-c.c. ENGINE) TO ENGINE No. 12CC/Da/H16300

ENGINE

Type	12CC.
Displacement	77·8 cu. in. (1274·86 c.c.).
Compression ratio	8·8 : 1.
Compression pressure	120 lb./sq. in. (8·4 kg./cm.²) at 350 r.p.m.
Firing order	1, 3, 4, 2.
Static ignition timing	7° B.T.D.C.
Stroboscopic ignition timing (vacuum pipe disconnected) ..	22° B.T.D.C. at 1,200 r.p.m. (23D4), 13° B.T.D.C. at 1,000 r.p.m. (25D4).
Timing mark location	Pointer on timing chain case and notch on crankshaft pulley.
Engine idle speed	700 r.p.m. (hot).

DISTRIBUTOR

Make	Lucas.	
Contact breaker gap	·014 to ·016 in. (·36 to ·40 mm.).	
Contact spring tension	18 to 24 oz. (510 to 680 gm.).	
Rotation at rotor	Anti-clockwise.	
Dwell angle	60°±3°.	
Condenser capacity	·18 to ·24 mF.	
Type	**23D4**	**25D4**
Automatic advance	Centrifugal	Centrifugal and vacuum
Serial number	40819	41198 or 41270.
Centrifugal advance		
Crankshaft degrees speed (vacuum pipe disconnected) ..	0°–3° at 600 r.p.m.	0°–2° at 600 r.p.m.
	6°–12° at 1,000 r.p.m.	2°–6° at 800 r.p.m.
	11°–15° at 2,000 r.p.m.	4°–8° at 1,000 r.p.m.
	22°–26° at 5,200 r.p.m.	10°–14° at 2,000 r.p.m.
	28°–32° at 7,000 r.p.m.	20°–24° at 3,600 r.p.m.
Vacuum advance (25D4 Distributor only)		
Starts		5 in. Hg.
Finishes		8 in. Hg.
Total crankshaft degrees		6°±2°.

IGNITION COIL

Make/Type	Lucas/11C12.
Resistance	3·0 to 3·4 ohms.

SPARKING PLUGS

Make/Type	Champion/N9Y.
Gap	·024 to ·026 in. (·610 to ·660 mm.).

ELECTRICAL

Dynamo	Lucas/C40.
Battery	Lucas/N9 or NZ9.
Volts/Polarity	12 volt/Positive earth.
Starter	Lucas/M35G.
Control unit	Lucas/RB106.

CARBURETTER

Make/Type	S.U./HS2.
Jet	·090 in.
Needle	Standard AN; Rich H6; Weak GG.
Piston spring	Blue.

Sprite and Midget. Issue 2. 29459
MG Midget. AKM 2092/1

MODEL: SPRITE Mk. IV/MIDGET Mk. III (1275-c.c. ENGINE) FROM ENGINE No. 12CE/Da/H101

ENGINE

Type	12CE and 12CD.
Displacement	77·8 cu. in. (1274·86 c.c.).
Compression ratio	8·8 : 1.
Compression pressure	120 lb./sq. in. (8·4 kg./cm.²) at 350 r.p.m.
Firing order	1, 3, 4, 2.
Static ignition timing	7° B.T.D.C.
Stroboscopic ignition timing (vacuum line disconnected)	13° B.T.D.C. at 1,000 r.p.m.
Timing mark location	Pointer on timing chain case and notch on crankshaft pulley.
Engine idle speed	700 r.p.m. (hot).

DISTRIBUTOR

Make/Type	Lucas/25D4.
Serial No.	41198 or 41270.
Contact breaker gap	·014 to ·016 in. (·36 to ·40 mm.).
Contact spring tension	18 to 24 oz. (510 to 680 gm.).
Rotation at rotor	Anti-clockwise.
Dwell angle	60°±3°.

Centrifugal advance

Crankshaft degrees/speed (vacuum pipe disconnected) ..	0°–2° at 600 r.p.m.
	2°–6° at 800 r.p.m.
	4°–8° at 1,000 r.p.m.
	10°–14° at 2,000 r.p.m.
	20°–24 at 3,600 r.p.m.

Vacuum advance

Starts	5 in. Hg.
Finishes	8 in. Hg.
Total crankshaft degrees	6°±2°.

IGNITION COIL

Make/Type	Lucas/HA12.
Resistance	3·0 to 3·4 ohms.

SPARKING PLUGS

Make/Type	Champion/N9Y.
Gap	·024 to ·026 in. (·610 to ·660 mm.).

ELECTRICAL

Dynamo	Lucas/C40.
Battery	Lucas/N9 or NZ9. Later cars Lucas A9/AZ9 or A11/AZ11.
Volts/Polarity	12 volt/**Negative** earth.
Starter	Lucas/M35G. Later cars Lucas M35J.
Control unit	Lucas/RB106. Later cars Lucas RB340.

CARBURETTER

Make/Type	S.U./HS2.
Jet	·090 in.
Needle	Standard AN; Rich H6; Weak GG.
Piston spring	Blue.

Sprite and Midget. Issue 5. 83942
MG Midget. AKM 2092/1

Engine Tuning Data 5

47

ENGINE TUNING DATA 6, 7 AND 8

MODEL: MIDGET Mk. III (1275-c.c. ENGINE) FROM ENGINE No. 12V/586F/H101 and 12V/586F/L101
MODEL: MIDGET Mk. III (1275-c.c. ENGINE) FROM ENGINE No. 12V/588F/H101 and 12V/588F/L101
MODEL: MIDGET Mk. III (1275-c.c. ENGINE) FROM ENGINE No. 12V/778F/H101

ENGINE

Type	12V 586F, 12V 588F, and 12V 778F.
Displacement	77·8 cu. in. (1274·86 c.c.).
Compression ratio	8·8 : 1.
Compression pressure	Nominal 170 lb./sq. in. (12 kg./cm.²) at 350 r.p.m.
Firing order	1, 3, 4, 2.
Static ignition timing	7° B.T.D.C.
Stroboscopic ignition timing (vacuum pipe disconnected) ..	16° B.T.D.C. at 1,000 r.p.m.
Timing mark location	Pointer on timing chain case and notch on crankshaft pulley.
Engine idle speed	700 r.p.m. (hot).

DISTRIBUTOR

Make/Type	Lucas/25D4.
Serial No.	41270.
Contact breaker gap	·014 to ·016 in. (·36 to ·40 mm.).
Contact spring tension	18 to 24 oz. (510 to 680 gm.).
Rotation at rotor	Anti-clockwise.
Dwell angle	60°±3°.

Centrifugal advance

Crankshaft degrees/speed (vacuum pipe disconnected) ..	0°−1° at 600 r.p.m. (0°−2° at 600 r.p.m. on 12V 588F and 12V 778F engines)
	2°−6° at 800 r.p.m.
	4°−8° at 1,000 r.p.m.
	10°−14° at 2,000 r.p.m.
	20°−24° at 3,600 r.p.m.

Vacuum advance

Starts	5 in. Hg.
Finishes	8 in. Hg.
Total crankshaft degrees	6°±2°.

IGNITION COIL

Make/Type	Lucas/HA12 (Lucas 11C12 on 12V 778F engines).
Resistance	3·0 to 3·4 ohms (2· to 3·1 ohms on 11 C12 coils).

SPARKING PLUGS

Make/Type	Champion/N9Y.
Gap	·024 to ·026 in. (·610 to ·660 mm.).

ELECTRICAL

Dynamo/Alternator	Lucas/C40 (Lucas/16 ACR alternator on 12V 588F and 12V 778F engines).
Battery	Lucas A9/AZ9, A11/AZ11 or A98.
Volts/Polarity	12 volt/Negative earth.
Starter	Lucas M35J.
Control unit	Lucas RB340 (C40 dynamo only).

CARBURETTER

Make/Type	S.U./HS2.
Jet	·090 in.
Needle	Standard AN; Rich H6; Weak GG (AAC on 12V 778F engines only).
Piston spring	Blue.

Engine Tuning Data 6

Sprite and Midget. Issue 5. 83942

SECTION A

THE ENGINE

† These operations must be followed by an exhaust emission check

THE POWER UNIT

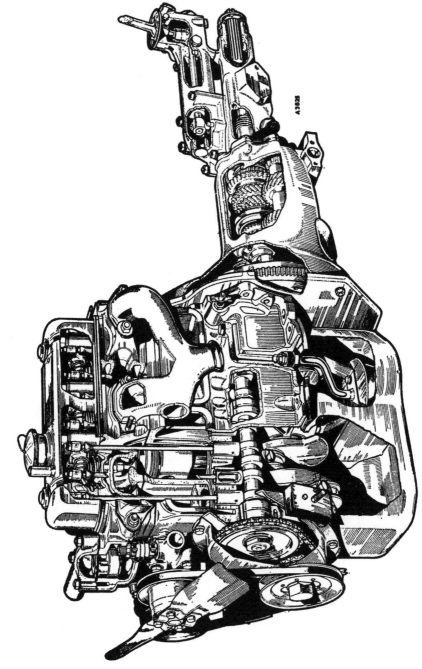

A.3525

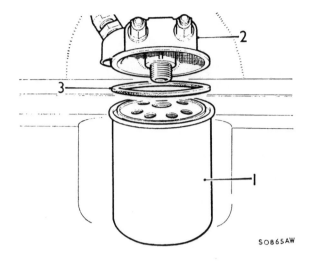

SO865AW

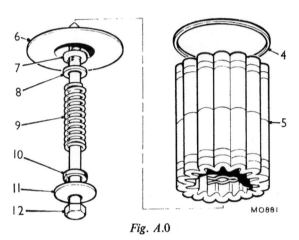

MO881

Fig. A.0

The disposable cartridge (1) and renewable element
(2) engine oil filters

1. Disposable cartridge.
2. Filter head.
3. Seal.
4. Filter head seal.
5. Filter element.
6. Pressure plate.
7. Felt or rubber washer.
8. Plain washer.
9. Spring.
10. Rubber seal.
11. Body washer.
12. Bolt.

Section A.1

LUBRICATION

Checking the engine oil level

Inspect the oil level in the engine, and top up if necessary to the 'MAX' or 'FULL' mark on the dipstick. The oil filler cap is on the top of the engine valve cover and is released by turning it anti-clockwise.

Changing the engine oil

Drain the oil from the engine by removing the drain plug on the right-hand side of the engine sump.

The oil will flow more readily if drained when the engine is hot; allow at least 10 minutes for draining before replacing the plug.

NOTE.—Disconnect the battery cable from its terminal on the starter before commencing work on the filter.

Disposable cartridge type

Unscrew the cartridge (1) from the filter head (2) and discard the cartridge.

NOTE.—Consult your Distributor or Dealer if the cartridge is difficult to unscrew. Smear the new seal (3) with engine oil and fit it in the groove in the new cartridge. Screw the cartridge to the filter head using hand force only. **DO NOT OVERTIGHTEN.**

Renewable element type

Unscrew the centre bolt securing the filter to the filter head. Discard the filter element and wash the filter bowl in fuel. Remove the old sealing washer (4) from the filter head and fit the new washer. Assemble the filter in the order shown, ensuring that the seals are serviceable and that the rubber seal (10) is under the bolt head and the washer (7) is a tight fit on the bolt.

Section A.2

OIL PRESSURE

The oil gauge is combined with the thermometer on the instrument panel.

The normal operating and idling oil pressures are given in the appropriate engine section of 'GENERAL DATA'.

If no pressure is registered by the gauge, stop the engine at once and investigate the cause.

NOTE.—The automatic relief valve in the lubrication system deals with any excessive oil pressure when starting from cold.

Checking for low oil pressure

Check the level of the oil in the sump by means of the dipstick, and top up if necessary. Ascertain that the gauze strainer in the sump is clean and not choked with sludge, also that there is no leakage at the strainer union on the suction side of the pump. In the unlikely event of the oil pump being defective, remove the unit and rectify the fault. The oil relief valve should also be examined.

Section A.3

OIL PRESSURE RELIEF VALVE

The non-adjustable oil pressure relief valve is situated at the rear right-hand side of the cylinder block and is held in position by a domed hexagon nut sealed by two fibre washers or one copper washer.

A

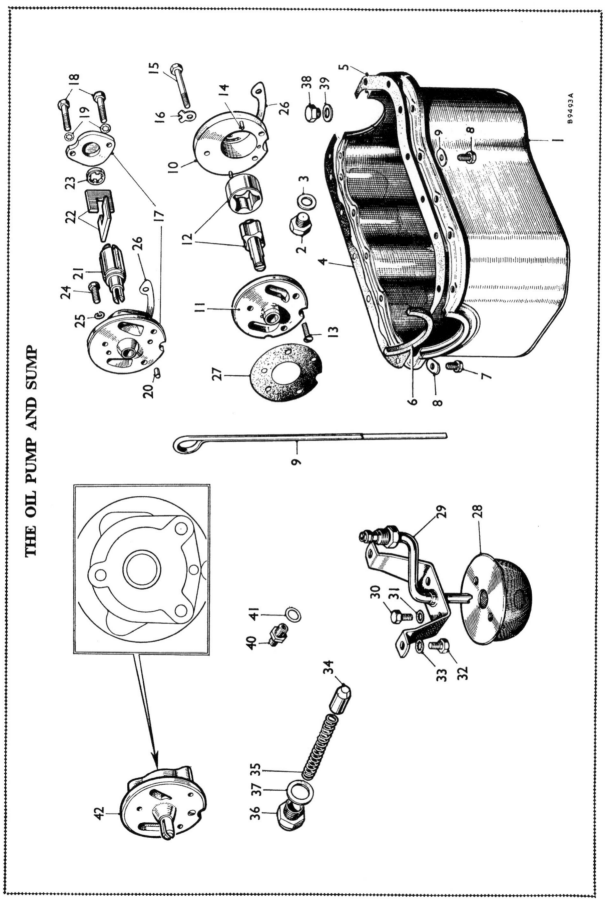

THE OIL PUMP AND SUMP

B9493A

KEY TO THE OIL PUMP AND SUMP

No.	Description	
1.	Sump.	
2.	Sump drain plug.	
3.	Washer.	
4.	Sump to crankcase joint—R.H.	
5.	Sump to crankcase joint—L.H.	
6.	Main bearing cap oil seal.	
7.	Screw and captive washer.	
8.	Washer.	
9.	Dipper rod.	
10.	Oil pump body.	
11.	Cover (plain hole).	
12.	Driving shaft with inner and outer rotors.	Hobourn-Eaton Type.
13.	Cover to body screws.	
14.	Dowel.	

No.	Description	
15.	Pump to crankcase screw.	Hobourn-Eaton Type.
16.	Lock washer.	
17.	Body and cover assembly.	
18.	Screw.	
19.	Shakeproof washer.	
20.	Dowel.	
21.	Rotor.	Burman Type.
22.	Vane.	
23.	Sleeve.	
24.	Pump to crankcase screw.	
25.	Spring washer.	
26.	Lock plate (for all pumps).	
27.	Pump to crankcase joint.	
28.	Oil strainer.	

No.	Description
29.	Suction pipe with oil strainer bracket.
30.	Screw.
31.	Shakeproof washer.
32.	Screw (bracket to bearing cap).
33.	Shakeproof washer.
34.	Oil relief valve.
35.	Spring for oil relief valve.
36.	Cap nut.
37.	Washer.
38.	Oil priming plug.
39.	Washer (copper).
40.	Oil pressure union.
41.	Washer (fibre).
42.	Pump assembly—Concentric Type.

53

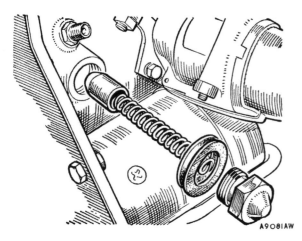

Fig. A.1

The location of the oil pressure relief valve

The relief valve spring maintains a pressure on the valve cup, which in turn seats on the machined face in the cylinder block to provide an extra oil return passage should the pressure become excessive.

The valve cup should be examined to ensure that it is seating correctly and that the spring has not lost its tension. The cup can be removed and ground into its seating with Service tool 18G 69 and the spring checked by measuring its length; to give the required relief pressure see 'GENERAL DATA'.

A new cup and spring should be fitted if required.

Section A.4

SUMP AND GAUZE STRAINER

Removing

Drain the oil into a suitable container. Remove the set screws and spring washers and lower the sump.

Unscrew the oil suction pipe at its connection with the crankcase. Remove the two set screws securing the strainer support bracket to the main bearing cap. Remove the strainer and support bracket from the engine. Clean the strainer in petrol (gasoline) and dry thoroughly with a non-fluffy rag.

Refitting

Refit the strainer and its securing bracket, ascertaining that the oil suction pipe is located in its connection to the crankcase.

Secure the suction pipe connection and the two strainer support bracket set screws.

Clean the sump thoroughly inside and out, paying particular attention to the joint faces. Remove all traces of cleaning fluid.

Refit the sump by reversing the sequence of operations for removal, using a new joint washer if necessary.

Section A.5

OIL PUMP

Removing

Remove the engine as detailed in Section A.31.

Remove the flywheel, clutch assembly, and engine back plate as detailed in Section A.20.

Unscrew the oil pump retaining screws and withdraw the pump.

Concentric type

This pump is serviced as a complete assembly only.

Burman type
Dismantling

Unscrew the cover securing screws, remove the cover and withdraw the rotor and vane assembly.

Remove the retaining sleeve from the end of the rotor and extract the vanes.

Reassembling

Reverse the dismantling procedure.

Hobourn-Eaton type
Dismantling

Remove the cover securing screw and withdraw the cover from the dowels in the pump body. Remove the outer and inner rotors complete with the drive shaft.

Inspection

Clean all the parts thoroughly and inspect them for excessive wear.

Check the diametrical clearance between the outer rotor and the pump body. If the clearance exceeds ·010 in. (·254 mm.) the rotors, pump body, or the complete assembly must be renewed.

Lay a straight-edge across the joint face of the pump body and measure the clearance between the underside of the straight-edge and the face of the rotors. If the clearance exceeds ·005 in. (·127 mm.) the cover locating dowels can be removed and the joint face carefully lapped.

Check the clearance between the rotor lobes as shown in Fig. A.2. If the clearance exceeds ·006 (·152 mm.) the rotors must be renewed.

Reassembling

Reverse the dismantling procedure.

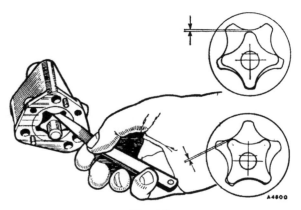

Fig. A.2

The positions of the lobes when checking the clearance

Sprite and Midget. Issue 4. 4780

Refitting

The refitting of the pump to the cylinder block is the reverse of the removal procedure; particular attention must, however, be given to the fitting of the paper joint washer to ensure that the intake and delivery ports are not obstructed. Use a new paper joint washer if the old one is damaged in any way.

Section A.6

ROCKER SHAFT ASSEMBLY

Removing

Drain the cooling system, using a clean container for the coolant if it contains anti-freeze intended for further use.

Remove the securing screws and lift off the rocker cover, care being taken not to damage the cork gasket.

Release the rocker shaft bracket securing nuts and the external cylinder head stud nuts gradually, a turn at a time, in the order shown in Fig. A.6, until all the load is released.

It is of great importance that the external cylinder head fixing nuts should be released at the same time in order to eliminate any distortion that might take place and result in water finding its way into the cylinder bores and the engine sump.

Remove the rocker shaft bracket nuts and lift off the rocker assembly together with the brackets.

Withdraw the push-rods, at the same time marking them for replacement in their original positions.

Dismantling

Remove the grub screw locating the rocker shaft in the front rocker mounting bracket. Withdraw the split pins, flat washer, and spring washer from the end of the shaft and slide the rockers, brackets, and springs from the shaft. Remove the screwed plug fitted to one end of the shaft and clean out the oilway.

Reassembling

When reassembling commence with the front mounting bracket, securing it with the grub screw. Follow up with

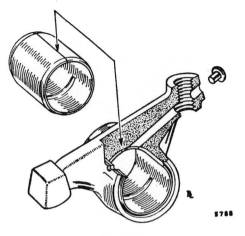

Fig. A.4

When rebushing the forged-type rocker make certain that the joint in the bush is in the position indicated

the remaining brackets and springs, replacing them in their original positions on the shaft. The screwed plug end of the shaft should be positioned to the front of the engine.

Refitting

Refitting is the reverse of the removal procedure, with special emphasis on the tightening of the rocker bracket and cylinder head stud nuts; these must be tightened in the order shown in Fig. A.6 and to the torque wrench figure given under 'GENERAL DATA'.

Refer to Section A.18 for details of valve rocker adjustment.

Section A.7

TAPPETS

Removing

Remove the carburetters and manifold and the rocker cover.

Remove the rocker assembly and withdraw the push-rods, keeping them in their respective positions to ensure their replacement onto the same tappets. Remove the tappet covers and lift out the tappets, also keeping them in their correct order to assist in replacing them in their original locations.

Refitting

Refitting is the reverse of the removal sequence.

New tappets should be fitted by selective assembly so that they just fall into their guides under their own weight when lubricated.

Assembly is the reverse of the above procedure, but care should be taken to see that the tappet cover joints are oil-tight and that the rockers are adjusted to give the correct valve clearance.

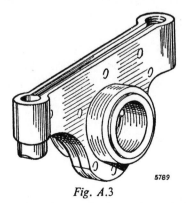

Fig. A.3

The pressed-steel type of valve rocker, which must not be rebushed

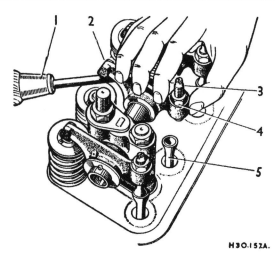

H3O.152A.

Fig. A.5

Push-rod removal

1. Screwdriver.   3. Adjusting screw.
2. Valve rocker.   4. Locknut.
           5. Push-rod.

Section A.8

ROCKER BUSHES

Pressed-steel type

Remove and dismantle the rocker shaft assembly as detailed in Section A.6.

Rebushing is not practicable and must not be undertaken. When bushes become worn new rocker assemblies must be fitted.

Forged type (See Editor's note at end of Section A.)

To rebush, the use of special Service tools 18G 226 and 18G 226 A comprising a drift and anvil is recommended. Bushes and rockers are very easily damaged by the use of improvised drifts.

The anvil is recessed to hold the rocker in position while the worn bush is driven or pressed out.

Press the new bush into the rocker bore with the butt joint of the bush positioned at the top of the bore as in Fig. A.4. The drift is recessed to prevent the bush opening when being driven into position.

It will be necessary to drill the oil holes in the bush to coincide with the oilways in the rocker. Should the oil hole to the adjuster end be drilled before the bush is fitted, extra care must be taken to keep the holes in the bush and rocker in line during the pressing-in operation. If the holes are drilled after fitting, the following procedure must be adopted. Remove the adjuster screw and use a No. 43 drill (·089 in. [2·26 mm.] diameter) to drill out the end plug and to continue the oilway through the bush. Replug the end after the operation with a rivet (Part No. 5C 2436) and weld it in position.

The hole in the top of the rocker barrel must be continued through the bush with a No. 47 (·0785 in. [1·98 mm.] diameter) drill. Finally, burnish-ream the bush to the dimensions given under 'GENERAL DATA'.

Section A.9

CARBURETTERS AND AIR CLEANERS

Removing

Remove the air cleaners as detailed in Section D.6. Disconnect the mixture and throttle control cables, the suction advance pipe, and the fuel delivery hose from their respective positions on the carburetters.

Release the interconnecting coupling tension springs and the throttle stop return spring.

Remove the nuts and spring washers securing the carburetters to the manifold flanges. Lift off the carburetter assemblies as one unit. The carburetter interconnecting couplings are fitted in sleeved nuts, and when the carburetter assemblies are removed the couplings can be lifted away from both carburetters.

It should be noted that the heat shield fitted between the carburetters and the manifold flanges has gaskets, which should be renewed if the shield has been removed.

Refitting

Reverse the removal procedure when refitting.

Section A.10

EXHAUST SYSTEM

Removing

Release the securing clip and disconnect the down pipe from its fixing point on the clutch housing and from the two locations on the rear body section.

Refitting

Refitting is the reverse of the removal procedure.

Section A.11

INLET AND EXHAUST MANIFOLD

Removing

Remove the carburetters and air cleaners as detailed in Section A.9. Slacken off and release the exhaust pipe clamp. Remove the nuts and washers securing the manifold to the cylinder head; withdraw the manifold.

When a heater is fitted remove the water pipe brackets from the induction manifold.

Refitting

Reverse the above order, but thoroughly clean the joint faces and fit a new gasket, placing the perforated metal face of the gasket towards the manifold.

Section A.12

CYLINDER HEAD

Removing

Remove the bonnet.

Drain the cooling system by means of the drain tap on the radiator bottom tank and the tap or plug (later cars) at the rear left-hand side of the cylinder block.

A.8   Sprite and Midget. Issue 6.   10858

56

Disconnect the negative cable from the battery. Slacken the retaining clip on the hose connecting the radiator to the thermostat housing and pull the hose clear of the housing.

Remove the carburetters and air cleaners as described in Section A.9. Take out the rocker cover retaining screws and rubber cups and remove the cover.

Detach the high-tension cables and remove the sparking plugs, taking care not to damage the porcelain insulators.

Remove the suction pipe clip from its fixture on the hot water control valve. If a heater is fitted release the retaining clip and detach the inlet hose.

Slacken the top clip on the water by-pass hose.

has been completely reassembled and run for a short period.

Replace the inlet and exhaust manifold.

If a heater is fitted attach the hose to the heater inlet pipe.

Replace the rocker cover, being careful to fit its cork gasket correctly into position and securing it by its nuts, washers, and rubber cups.

Replace the carburetters and air cleaners (as in Section A.9).

Connect the negative cable to the battery terminal; close the water drain taps and refill the cooling system.

Check, adjust, and replace the sparking plugs, and clip on the high-tension leads.

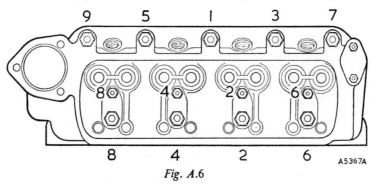

Fig. A.6

The order of loosening and tightening the cylinder head nuts

When a heater is fitted remove the water pipe from the induction manifold.

Remove the inlet and exhaust manifold as described in Section A.11.

Remove the rocker assembly as described in Section A.6, not forgetting to slacken the external cylinder head holding nuts at the same time. Withdraw the push-rods, keeping them in order of removal.

The cylinder head may now be removed.

NOTE.—To facilitate breaking the cylinder head joint tap each side of the head with a hammer, using a piece of wood interposed to take the blow. Lift the head squarely to prevent the studs binding in their holes.

Refitting

Make sure that the surfaces of both the cylinder block and the cylinder head are clean; it is not necessary to use jointing compound or grease for the gasket. It will be noticed that the cylinder head gasket is marked 'FRONT' and 'TOP' so that it will be replaced correctly. Having slipped the gasket over the studs, lower the cylinder head into position and fit the five cylinder head securing nuts finger-tight.

Insert the push-rods, replacing them in the positions from which they were taken. Replace the rocker assembly and securing nuts and fit the nuts finger-tight. Tighten all the nuts gradually, a turn at a time, in the order given in Fig. A.6

Whenever the head has been moved or the valves have been ground in or otherwise disturbed it is necessary to check the valve clearances as in Section A.18. These, of course, will be finally adjusted after the engine

Switch on and check the fuel system for leaks.

Start the engine and run it until the normal working temperature is reached. Remove the rocker cover and check the valve clearances (see Section A.18). Replace the rocker cover.

Refit the bonnet.

Section A.13

DECARBONIZING

Remove the cylinder head as described in Section A.12. Withdraw the valves as described in Section A.14.

Remove the cylinder head gasket and plug the waterways with clean rag.

If special equipment is not available scrape the carbon deposit from the piston crowns, cylinder block, and cylinder head, using a blunt scraper.

A ring of carbon should be left round the periphery of the piston crown and the rim of carbon round the top of the cylinder bore should not be touched. To facilitate this an old piston ring can be sprung into the bore so that it rests on top of the piston.

The cylinder head is next given attention. The sparking plugs must be cleaned and adjusted. Clean off the carbon deposit from the valve stems, valve ports, and combustion spaces of the cylinder head. Remove all traces of carbon dust with compressed air, then thoroughly clean with paraffin and dry off.

Fit a new gasket when replacing the head if the old one has been damaged, noting that the gasket is marked to indicate the top face and the front end.

Sprite and Midget. Issue 3. 10858   *A.9*

57

THE CYLINDER HEAD AND VALVE GEAR

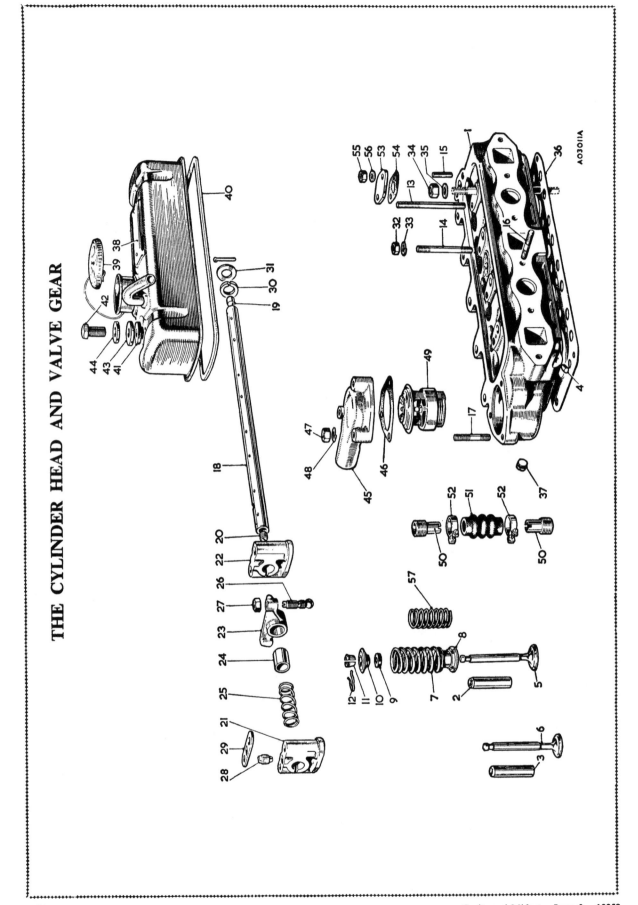

KEY TO THE CYLINDER HEAD AND VALVE GEAR

No.	Description
1.	Cylinder head with valve guides.
2.	Inlet valve guide.
3.	Exhaust valve guide.
4.	Oil hole plug.
5.	Inlet valve.
6.	Exhaust valve.
7.	Outer valve spring.
8.	Shroud for valve guide.
9.	Valve packing ring.
10.	Valve spring cup.
11.	Valve cotter.
12.	Valve cotter circlip.
13.	Rocker bracket stud (long).
14.	Rocker bracket stud (short).
15.	Cover-plate stud.
16.	Manifold stud.
17.	Water outlet elbow stud.
18.	Valve rocker shaft (plugged).
19.	Rocker shaft plug (plain).

No.	Description
20.	Rocker shaft plug (screwed).
21.	Rocker shaft bracket (tapped).
22.	Rocker shaft bracket (plain).
23.	Rocker (bushed).
24.	Rocker bush.
25.	Rocker spacing spring.
26.	Tappet adjusting screw.
27.	Locknut.
28.	Rocker shaft locating screw.
29.	Rocker shaft bracket plate.
30.	Spring washer.
31.	Washer.
32.	Nut.
33.	Spring washer.
34.	Cylinder head nut.
35.	Washer.
36.	Cylinder head gasket.
37.	Thermal indicator boss screwed plug.
38.	Valve rocker cover.

No.	Description
39.	Oil filler cap.
40.	Cover joint.
41.	Cover bush.
42.	Nut.
43.	Distance piece.
44.	Cup washer.
45.	Water outlet elbow.
46.	Joint.
47.	Nut.
48.	Spring washer.
49.	Thermostat.
50.	By-pass adaptor.
51.	By-pass connector (rubber).
52.	By-pass clip.
53.	Cover-plate.
54.	Joint (plate to cylinder head).
55.	Cover nut.
56.	Spring washer.
57.	Inner valve spring.

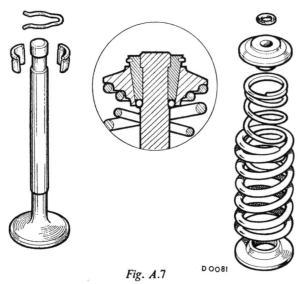

Fig. A.7

The component parts of the valve assembly. The inset shows the valve seal fitted correctly at the bottom of the cotter groove below the cotters

Section A.14

VALVES

Removing (See Editor's note at end of Section A.)

Remove the cylinder head as detailed in Section A.12.

Before removing the valves stamp the head of each with a number to indicate its position. Commence with No. 1 at the front of the engine.

Remove the cotter clip, compress the valve springs and remove the split cotters.

Release the valve springs and remove the compressor.

Remove the retaining cap, valve springs, spring locating cup, and rubber seal. Withdraw the valve from the guide.

Keep the valves in their relative positions when removed from the cylinder head to ensure replacement in their original valve guides. The exhaust valve heads are concave and are smaller than the inlet valves.

Refitting

Place each valve in its respective guide and fit the spring locating cup, springs, and the retaining cap. Compress the springs and fit a new sealing rubber to the valve stem, push the seal against the bottom shoulder of the cotter recess, and refit the cotters. Ensure that the rubber seal is not pushed out of the cotter recess onto the larger diameter of the stem, release the compressing tool, and fit the split cotter retaining clip.

Section A.15

VALVE-GRINDING

Remove the valves as in Section A.14.

Clean each valve thoroughly and examine for pitting. Valves in a pitted condition should be refaced or new valves should be fitted. Stamp any new valve with the number of the port to which it is fitted.

If the valve seats show signs of pitting or unevenness they should be trued by the use of the Service cutting

tools. When using a cutting tool take care to remove only as much metal as necessary to ensure a true surface. Worn valve seats usually have a glass-hard surface, and the glaze breaker should be used to prepare the valve seat surface for any recutting that may be necessary. Narrowing cutters should be used to restore the valve seats to the original standard.

When grinding a valve the face should be smeared lightly with fine- or medium-grade carborundum paste and then lapped in with a suction grinder. Avoid the use of excessive quantities of grinding paste and see that it remains in the region of the valve seating only.

A light coil spring placed under the valve head will assist considerably in the process of grinding. The valve should be ground to its seat with a semi-rotary motion and occasionally allowed to rise by the pressure of the light coil spring. This assists in spreading the paste evenly over the valve face and seat. Carry out the grinding operation until a dull, even, mat surface free from blemish is produced on the valve seat and valve face.

On completion, the valve seat and ports should be cleaned with a rag soaked in paraffin (kerosene), dried, and then thoroughly cleaned by compressed air. The valves should be washed in paraffin (kerosene) and all traces of grinding paste removed.

Refer to Section A.14 for details of valve refitting.

Section A.16

VALVE SEAT INSERTS

Should the valve seatings become so badly worn or pitted that the normal workshop cutting and refacing tools cannot restore them to their original standard of efficiency, special valve seat inserts can be fitted.

The seatings in the cylinder head must be machined to the dimensions given in Fig. A.9. Each insert should have an interference fit of ·0025 to ·0045 in. (·063 to ·11 mm.) and must be pressed and not driven into the cylinder head.

After fitting, grind or machine the new seating to the dimensions given in Fig. A.9. Normal valve-grinding may be necessary to ensure efficient valve-seating.

(See Editor's note at end of Section A.)

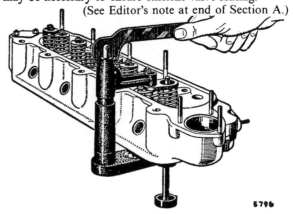

Fig. A.8

Compressing a valve spring, using the special compressing tool 18G 45

*A.*12

Sprite and Midget.   Issue 4.   4780

Section A.17

VALVE GUIDES

Removing

Remove the cylinder head as shown in Section A.12.

Remove the appropriate valve and spring as in Section A.14. Rest the cylinder head with its machined face downwards on a clean surface and drive the valve guide downwards into the combustion space with a suitably sized drift. This should take the form of a hardened-steel punch $\frac{7}{16}$ in. (11 mm.) in diameter and not less than 4 in. (10 cm.) in length, with a locating spigot $\frac{9}{32}$ in. (7·14 mm.) diameter machined on one end for a length of 1 in. (2·5 cm.) to engage the bore of the guide.

Refitting

When fitting new valve guides they should be driven in from the top of the cylinder head. The inlet valve guides must be inserted with the largest chamfer at the top, and the exhaust valve guides should have their counterbored ends at the bottom. The valve guides should be driven into the combustion spaces until they are $\frac{19}{32}$ in. (15·1 mm.) above the machined surface of the valve spring seating (see Fig. A.11).

Section A.18

VALVE ROCKER CLEARANCE

Check the clearance between the valve stem and the valve rocker, using a feeler gauge, when the valve is in

Fig. A.10

Checking and adjusting the valve rocker clearance

the fully closed position. The clearance must be to the dimensions given in **'GENERAL DATA'**.

To adjust, hold the rocker adjusting screw with a screwdriver and slacken the locknut. Rotate the adjusting screw until the correct clearance is obtained. Hold the adjusting screw against rotation and lock it in position with the locknut, then recheck the clearance.

To avoid unnecessary turning of the crankshaft and to ensure that the valve being checked is in the fully closed position, check the valve rocker clearances in the following order.

Adjust No. 1 rocker with No. 8 valve fully open.

,,	,,	3	,,	,,	,,	6	,,	,,	,,
,,	,,	5	,,	,,	,,	4	,,	,,	,,
,,	,,	2	,,	,,	,,	7	,,	,,	,,
,,	,,	8	,,	,,	,,	1	,,	,,	,,
,,	,,	6	,,	,,	,,	3	,,	,,	,,
,,	,,	4	,,	,,	,,	5	,,	,,	,,
,,	,,	7	,,	,,	,,	2	,,	,,	,,

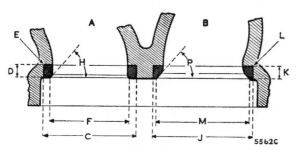

Fig. A.9

Valve seat machining dimensions

948-c.c. Engines

	Exhaust (A)		Inlet (B)
C.	1·124 to 1·125 in. (28·55 to 28·58 mm.).	J.	1·187 to 1·188 in. (30·16 to 30·17 mm.).
D.	·186 to ·188 in. (4·72 to 4·77 mm.).	K.	·186 to ·188 in. (4·72 to 4·77 mm.).
E.	Maximum radius ·015 in. (·38 mm.).	L.	Maximum radius ·015 in. (·38 mm.).
F.	1·0235 to 1·0435 in. (25·99 to 26·50 mm.).	M.	1·0855 to 1·1055 in. (27·58 to 28·07 mm.).
H.	45°.	P.	45°.

1098-c.c. Engines

Cylinder Head 12G 206 as above except.
J.   1·3075 to 1·3085 in. (33·178 to 33·203 mm.).
M.   1·1435 to 1·1635 in. (29·045 to 29·553 mm.).

Cylinder Head 12G 295 as above except:
J.   1·3745 to 1·3755 in. (34·90 to 34·95 mm.).
M.   1·206 to 1·226 in. (30·60 to 31·15 mm.).

Section A.19

DISTRIBUTOR DRIVING SPINDLE

Removing

Remove the distributor as detailed in Section B.7.

Take out the screw securing the distributor housing to the cylinder block and withdraw the housing.

Screw a $\frac{5}{16}$ in. UNF. bolt approximately 3½ in. (89 mm.) long into the tapped end of the distributor drive spindle and withdraw the spindle.

Refitting

Turn the crankshaft until No. 1 piston is at T.D.C. on its compression stroke. When the valves on No. 4 cylinder are 'rocking' (i.e. exhaust just closing and inlet just

Fig. A.11

When fitting valve guides they must be driven in until they are $\frac{19}{32}$ in. (15·1 mm.) above the machined face of the valve spring seat

opening) No. 1 piston is at the top of its compression stroke. If the engine is set so that the groove in the crankshaft pulley is in line with the largest pointer on the timing cover, or the dimples in the crankshaft and camshaft gears are in line, the piston is exactly at T.D.C.

Screw the $\frac{5}{16}$ in. by $3\frac{1}{2}$ in. UNF. bolt into the threaded end of the distributor drive gear and, holding the drive gear with the slot just below the horizontal and the large offset uppermost, enter the gear. As the gear engages with the camshaft the slot will turn in an anti-clockwise direction until it is approximately in the two o'clock position.

Remove the bolt from the gear, insert the distributor housing, and secure it with the special bolt and washer.

Ensure that the correct bolt is used and that the head does not protrude above the face of the housing.

Refit the distributor, referring to Section B.7 if the clamp plate has been released.

Section A.20

CLUTCH, FLYWHEEL, AND ENGINE REAR PLATE

Removing (See Editor's note at end of Section A.)

Remove the engine as detailed in Section A.31. If the engine complete with gearbox has been removed, see Section F for gearbox removal.

Release the clutch cover screws, a turn at a time, by diagonal selection until the spring pressure is relieved. Two dowels locate the clutch cover on the flywheel.

Tap back the tabs on the lock plates, release the securing bolts, and remove the flywheel.

Remove the set screws and withdraw the engine rear plate.

Refitting (See Editor's note at end of Section A.)

Before reassembling, the engine rear plate should be checked for distortion, and a new joint washer fitted if necessary.

Care must also be taken when refitting the flywheel. All bolts and set screws should be fitted to the torque wrench settings given under 'GENERAL DATA'.

Refitting is the reverse of the removal procedure.

NOTE.—Use pilot shaft 18G 139 for driving plate centralization.

A.14

Section A.21

FITTING FLYWHEEL STARTER RINGS

To remove the old starter ring from the flywheel flange split the ring gear with a cold chisel, taking care not to damage the flywheel. Make certain that the bore of the new ring and its mating surface on the flywheel are free from burrs and are perfectly clean.

The new ring must be heated to a temperature of 300 to 400° C. (572 to 752° F.), the strip of scarlet paint on the ring will turn grey/brown when this temperature is reached. The temper of the teeth will be affected if the specified temperature is exceeded. The use of a thermostatically controlled furnace is recommended. Place the heated ring on the flywheel with the lead of the ring teeth towards the flywheel register. The expansion will allow the ring to be fitted without force by pressing or tapping lightly until the ring is hard against its register.

This operation should be followed by natural cooling, when the 'shrink fit' will be permanently established and no further treatment required.

Section A.22

TIMING COVER

Removing (See Editor's note at end of Section A.)

Drain the cooling system as described in Section C. Remove the radiator (see Section C). Release but do not remove the dynamo attachment bolts and lift off the fan belt. Tap back the tab on the crankshaft pulley nut locking washer. Remove the pulley nut, using Service tool 18G 98, and carefully lever the pulley from the crankshaft.

Remove the set screws securing the timing cover to the front engine plate and lift off the cover.

Refitting (See Editor's note at end of Section A.)

Reverse the removal procedure when refitting the cover.

The oil seal in the cover must be renewed if it shows signs of damage or deterioration, using Service tool 18G 134 together with adaptor 18G 134 BD. A new cover gasket should also be fitted.

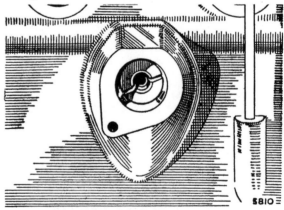

Fig. A.12

The distributor drive with the slot in the correct position and the large offset uppermost

Sprite and Midget. Issue 6. 10858

Ensure the oil thrower behind the crankshaft pulley is fitted with the face marked 'F' away from the engine.

Fill the annular groove between the lips of the oil seal with grease and use Service tool 18G 1044 to centralize the oil seal on the crankshaft.

NOTE.—The early type front cover and oil thrower must be used together. When refitting; ensure the oil thrower is fitted with its concave side facing away from the engine. Use Service tool 18G 138 to centralize the rubber seal on the crankshaft or use the crankshaft pulley as follows:

The crankshaft pulley should be assembled to the cover before the cover is fitted and used to ensure correct centralization of the oil seal. Lubricate the hub of the pulley and insert it into the oil seal, turning the pulley in a clockwise direction to avoid damaging the lip of the seal. Push the pulley and cover onto the crankshaft, making sure that the keyway on the pulley bore is lined up with the Woodruff key fitted to the crankshaft before finally drifting the pulley into position. Replace the cover set screws and tighten them evenly.

Section A.23

TIMING GEARS

Removing

Remove the timing cover and oil thrower as in Section A.22.

Unlock and remove the camshaft chain wheel nut and remove the nut and lock washer. Note that the locating tag on the lock washer fits into the keyway of the camshaft chain wheel.

The camshaft and crankshaft chain wheels may now be removed together with the timing chain, by easing each wheel forward a fraction at a time with suitable small levers. Note the packing washers immediately behind the crankshaft gear.

Refitting (See Editor's note at end of Section A.)

When reassembling, replace the same number of washers as was found when dismantling unless new

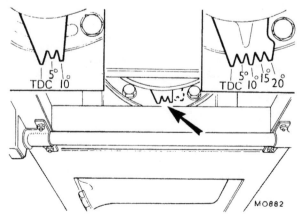

Fig. A.13

The notch in the pulley approaching the T.D.C. position for pistons 1 and 4. The pointers are provided to assist in accurate ignition timing

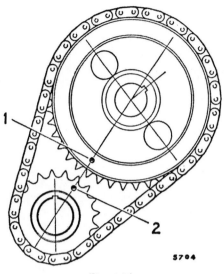

Fig. A.14

The timing gears assembled into the timing chain with the two marks on the gears opposite each other

camshaft or crankshaft components have been fitted which will disturb the alignment of the two gear wheels. To determine the thickness of washers required place a straight-edge across the sides of the camshaft wheel teeth and measure with a feeler gauge the gap between the straight-edge and the crankshaft gear.

When replacing the timing chain and gears set the crankshaft with its keyway at T.D.C. and the camshaft with its keyway approximately at the one o'clock position as seen from the front. Assemble the gears into the timing chain with the two marks on the gear wheels opposite to each other, as in Fig. A.14. Keeping the gears in this position, engage the crankshaft gear keyway with the key on the crankshaft and rotate the camshaft until the camshaft gear keyway and key are aligned. Push the gears onto the shafts as far as they will go and secure the camshaft gear with the lock washer and nut.

Replace the oil thrower; with the face marked 'F' or the concave side (early type) away from the engine, and the remaining components as detailed in Section A.22.

Section A.24

VALVE TIMING

Set No. 1 cylinder inlet valve clearance to ·021 in. with the engine cold, and then turn the crankshaft until the valve is about to open. The indicator groove in the flange of the crankshaft pulley should then be opposite the centre pointer (this indicates 5° B.T.D.C. of No. 1 and No. 4 pistons) on the indicator bracket, situated beneath the crankshaft pulley.

NOTE.—It is not possible to check the valve timing accurately with the valve rockers set at their normal running rocker clearance. Reset the inlet valve rocker clearance to ·012 in. (·305 mm.) when the timing check is completed (engine cold).

THE ENGINE INTERNAL COMPONENTS

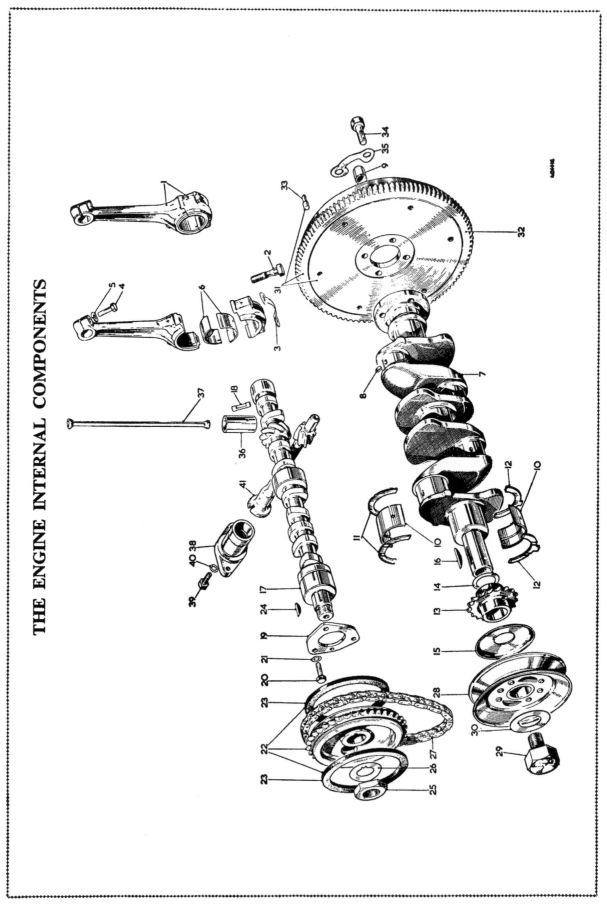

KEY TO THE ENGINE INTERNAL COMPONENTS

No.	Description
1.	Connecting rod cap.
2.	Cap bolt.
3.	Lock washer for bolt.
4.	Clamping screw.
5.	Spring washer for clamping screw.
6.	Big-end bearing.
7.	Crankshaft with oil restrictors and bush.
8.	Oil restrictor.
9.	First motion shaft bush.
10.	Main bearing.
11.	Upper thrust washer.
12.	Lower thrust washer.
13.	Crankshaft gear.
14.	Packing washer.

No.	Description
15.	Oil thrower.
16.	Gear and crankshaft key.
17.	Camshaft with oil pump driving pin.
18.	Oil pump driving pin.
19.	Locking plate.
20.	Plate to crankcase screw.
21.	Shakeproof washer.
22.	Camshaft gear with tensioner rings.
23.	Tensioner ring.
24.	Gear key.
25.	Gear nut.
26.	Lock washer.
27.	Camshaft driving chain
28.	Crankshaft pulley.

No.	Description
29.	Pulley retaining bolt.
30.	Lock washer.
31.	Flywheel with starter ring and dowels.
32.	Starter ring.
33.	Dowel.
34.	Flywheel to crankshaft screw.
35.	Lock washer.
36.	Tappet.
37.	Push-rod.
38.	Distributor housing.
39.	Screw.
40.	Shakeproof washer.
41.	Distributor driving spindle.

Section A.25

CAMSHAFT

Drain the sump and remove it from the engine.

Remove the rocker assembly, push-rods, and tappets (Sections A.6 and A.7), the timing cover and gears (Sections A.22 and A.23), and the oil pump (Section A.5).

Remove the distributor assembly (Section A.19).

Remove the set screws securing the camshaft locating plate to the cylinder block, and withdraw the camshaft forward, rotating it slowly to assist this operation.

Camshaft bearings (See Editor's note at end of Section A.)

If the camshaft bearing clearances are excessive new bearings must be fitted. Steel-backed white-metal bearings are used, and removing and refitting are facilitated by the use of a special camshaft liner removing and replacing tool. New bearings must be reamed to give the correct running clearance (see 'GENERAL DATA').

Removing the liners

Centre

Insert the pilot adaptor 18G 124 K into the camshaft liner front bore from the inside of the block and the adaptor 18G 124 B into the centre liner from the rear, small end first.

With the body of the tool positioned on the centre screw, pass the screw through the pilot adaptor and the adaptor in the centre liner.

Place the slotted washer on the flat at the rear of the centre screw and insert the tommy-bar into the screw behind the slotted washer.

Tighten up the wing nut to withdraw the liner.

Front and rear

Insert the small end of the adaptor 18G 124 K into the camshaft front liner from the inside of the cylinder block, thread the body of the tool onto the centre screw, and pass the screw through the adaptor from the front of the block. Place the slotted washer on the flat at the rear of the centre screw and insert the tommy-bar into the centre screw behind the slotted washer.

Tighten up the wing nut to withdraw the worn liner.

The rear liner is withdrawn by the same method, using the adaptor 18G 124 M and withdrawing the liner from the rear of the block.

Replacing the liners

Line up the oil holes in the liners and the cylinder block and make certain that they remain correctly positioned during the whole operation.

Front and rear

Place the new liner on the smallest diameter of the adaptor 18G 124 K and insert the adaptor into the camshaft front liner bore from the inside of the block, largest diameter first.

Thread the body of the tool onto the centre screw and pass the screw through the adaptor located in the front liner from the front of the block.

Position the larger of the two 'D' washers on the centre screw with the cut-away portion turned away from the butt joint of the liner: this joint **must** be covered by the washer.

Place the slotted washer on the flat at the rear of the centre screw and insert the tommy-bar into the screw behind the slotted washer.

Tighten the wing nut to pull the liner squarely into position.

The rear liner is replaced by the same method, using the adaptor 18G 124 M and pulling the liner into position from the rear of the block. The 'D' washer **is not** to be used when refitting a rear liner.

Centre

Insert the pilot adaptor 18G 124 K into the camshaft front liner from the inside of the block.

Place a new liner on the small end of the adaptor 18G 124 B and position the adaptor in the centre liner bore from the rear, largest diameter first.

With the body of the tool positioned on the centre screw insert the screw through the pilot adaptor and the adaptor in the centre liner bore.

Position the larger 'D' washer on the centre screw with the cut-away portion turned away from the butt joints of the liner; this joint must be covered by the washer.

Place the slotted washer and the tommy-bar in the centre screw and tighten up the wing nut to pull the liner into position.

Reaming the liners

It is essential that the cutter flutes are kept clear of swarf at all times during the cutting operation, preferably with air-blast equipment. The cutter should be withdrawn from the liner half-way through the cut and the swarf removed from the cutter and the liner.

Feed the reamer very slowly and keep the cutters dry.

The arbor should be lightly lubricated before assembling the cutters and pilots. All oilways should be thoroughly cleaned when the cutting operations have been completed.

Front and rear

Insert the taper pilots 18G 123 AT and 18G 123 BA into the centre and rear liners respectively.

Place the parallel pilot 18G 123 AQ on the arbor, followed by the cutter 18G 123 AN.

Thread the arbor through the front and centre liners, fit the cutter 18G 123 AP on the arbor, and thread the arbor through the taper pilot in the rear liner.

Secure the cutters and pilots in their respective positions; 18G 123 AN is located in No. 10 and 18G 123 AP is located in No. 7 on the arbor.

The cutter for the front liner will cut first with the arbor piloting in the centre and rear liners. The cutter for the rear liner will follow with the arbor piloting in the front and centre liners. Clear away all the swarf before the plain pilot is allowed to enter the front liner.

When the cut in the rear liner is finished, free the cutters and withdraw the arbor.

Centre

Set up for the second part of the operation by inserting the pilots 18G 123 BC and 18G 123 BB in the front and rear liners.

Thread the arbor through the pilot in the front liner and place the cutter for the centre liner on the arbor. Thread the arbor through the centre liner and the pilot located in the rear liner. Secure the cutter and pilots in position; 18G 123 B is located in No. 7 position on the arbor.

Ream the centre liner, release the cutter, and withdraw the arbor.

Refitting

Refitting is the reverse of the removal procedure.

Section A.26

PISTONS AND CONNECTING RODS
(Early Cars)

Removing (See Editor's note at end of Section A.)

Remove the cylinder head assembly (Section A.12), and drain and remove the sump. Tap back the two locking plate tabs and remove the big-end securing bolts. Remove the bearing cap and release the connecting rod from the crankshaft.

Dismantling

The gudgeon pin is rigidly held in the split little-end of the connecting rod by a clamp bolt engaging the central groove of the gudgeon pin.

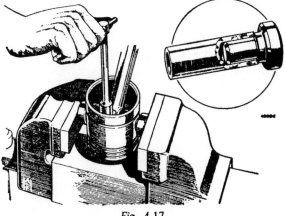

Fig. A.17

The use of special gudgeon pin plugs to hold the connecting rod and piston assembly while the gudgeon pin clamp screw is tightened or loosened is essential

Before the piston and gudgeon pin can be dismantled from the connecting rod it is necessary to remove the clamp screw. To hold the assembly in a vice for this operation without damage special holding plugs should be inserted in each end of the gudgeon pin.

Unscrew the gudgeon pin clamp screw and remove it completely. Push out the gudgeon pin.

Reassembling

A certain amount of selective assembly must be used when fitting new gudgeon pins. They must be a thumb-push fit for three-quarters of their travel, to be finally tapped home with a rawhide mallet. This operation must be carried out with the piston and gudgeon pin cold.

When reassembling, particular attention must be given to the following points:

(1) That the piston is fitted the same way round on the connecting rod. The connecting rod is fitted with the gudgeon pin clamp screw on the camshaft side.

(2) That the gudgeon pin is positioned in the connecting rod so that its groove is in line with the clamp screw hole.

(3) That the clamp screw spring washer has sufficient tension.

(4) That the clamp screw will pass readily into its hole and screw freely into the threaded portion of the little-end, and also that it will hold firmly onto the spring washer.

Refitting

Replacement of the piston and connecting rod is a direct reversal of removal, but the piston ring gaps should be staggered at 90° to each other.

It is essential that each connecting rod and piston assembly should be replaced in its own bore and fitted the same way round, the gudgeon pin clamp screw on the camshaft side of the engine.

Refit the big-end bearings in their original positions.

The top and bottom halves of new bearings are, however, interchangeable, each being drilled for cylinder wall lubrication.

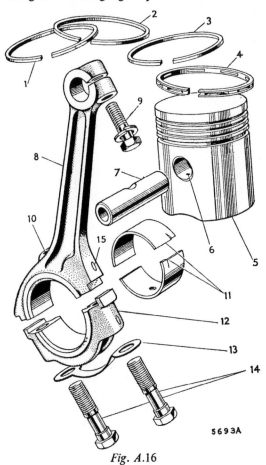

5693A

Fig. A.16

A piston and connecting rod assembly

1.	Piston ring—parallel.	10.	Cylinder wall lubricating jet.
2.	Piston ring—taper.		
3.	Piston ring—taper.	11.	Connecting rod bearings.
4.	Piston ring—scraper.		
5.	Piston.	12.	Connecting rod cap.
6.	Gudgeon pin lubricating hole.	13.	Lock washer.
7.	Gudgeon pin.	14.	Bolts.
8.	Connecting rod.	15.	Connecting rod and cap marking.
9.	Clamping screw and washer.		

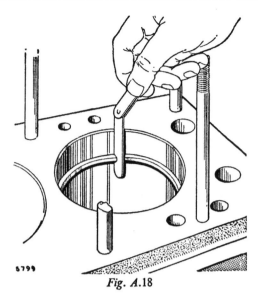

Fig. A.18

Checking the piston ring gap

Section A.27

PISTON RINGS

Removing

If no special piston ring expander is available use a piece of thin steel such as a smoothly ground hacksaw blade or disused ·020 in. (·50 mm.) feeler gauge.

Raise one end of the ring out of its groove. Insert the steel strip between the ring and the piston. Rotate the strip round the piston, applying slight upward pressure to the raised portion of the ring until it rests on the land above the ring grooves. It can then be eased off the piston.

Do not remove or replace the rings over the piston skirt, but always over the top of the piston.

Refitting

Before fitting new rings clean the grooves in the piston to remove any carbon deposit. Take care not to remove any metal, or side-play between the ring and the groove will result, with consequent excessive oil consumption and gas leakage.

Test new rings in the cylinder bore to ensure that the ends do not butt together. The best way to do this is to insert the piston approximately 1 in. (2·54 cm.) into the cylinder bore and push the ring down onto the top of the piston and hold it there in order to keep the ring square with the bore. The correct ring gap is given in 'GENERAL DATA'.

The second and third rings are tapered and must be fitted with the narrow taper upwards. A letter 'T' is stamped on the narrow face to facilitate identification.

The cylinder bore glazing should be removed before fitting new rings to a worn cylinder bore.

Section A.28

PISTON SIZES AND CYLINDER BORES
(Early Cars)

In addition to the standard pistons there is a range of four oversize pistons available for Service purposes.

Oversize pistons are marked with the actual oversize dimensions enclosed in an ellipse. A piston stamped ·020 is suitable only for a bore ·020 in. (·508 mm.) larger than the standard bore and, similarly, pistons with other markings are suitable only for the oversize bore indicated.

The piston markings indicate the actual bore size to which they must be fitted, the requisite running clearance being allowed for in the machining.

After reboring an engine, or whenever fitting pistons differing in size from those removed during dismantling, ensure that the size of the piston fitted is stamped clearly on the top of the cylinder block alongside the appropriate cylinder bore.

Pistons are supplied in the sizes indicated in the following table:

Piston marking	Suitable bore size	Metric equivalent
STANDARD	2·4778 to 2·4781 in.	62·935 to 62·940 mm.
OVERSIZE		
+·010 in. (·254 mm.)	2·4878 to 2·4881 in.	63·189 to 63·194 mm.
+·020 in. (·508 mm.)	2·4978 to 2·4981 in.	63·443 to 63·448 mm.
+·030 in. (·762 mm.)	2·5078 to 2·5081 in.	63·697 to 63·702 mm.
+·040 in. (1·016 mm.)	2·5178 to 2·5181 in.	63·951 to 63·956 mm.

Section A.29

CRANKSHAFT AND MAIN BEARINGS

The crankshaft is statically and dynamically balanced and is supported in the crankcase by three renewable

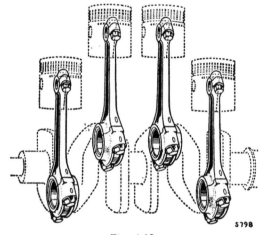

Fig. A.19

The correct assembly of connecting rods to the pistons and crankshaft

A.20

Sprite and Midget **Issue 5. 65173**

main bearings. The end-float is controlled by a thrust washer fitted on each side of the centre main bearing.

Removing

Drain the sump. Remove the engine (Section A.31) and place upside-down in a dismantling fixture.

Remove the oil strainer, timing chain and gears, and the flywheel and engine rear plate. Remove the sparking plugs to facilitate turning the crankshaft.

Check the crankshaft end-float to determine whether renewal of the thrust washers is necessary.

Remove the connecting rod bearing caps and shells, keeping the shells with their respective caps for correct replacement, and release the connecting rods from the crankshaft.

Withdraw the main bearing caps complete with the bottom bearing shells; caps and their respective shells must be kept together.

Remove the screwed plug from the rear bearing cap oil return pipe and withdraw the pipe. Note that each main bearing cap is stamped with a number, this number being repeated on the web of the crankcase near the bearing cap. The bottom halves of the two thrust washers will be removed with the centre main bearing cap.

Remove the crankshaft, the two remaining halves of the thrust washers, and the top half-shells of the main bearings from the crankshaft.

Inspecting (See Editor's note at end of Section A.)

Inspect the crankcase main journals and crankpins for wear, scores, scratches, and ovality. If necessary, the crankshaft may be reground to the minimum limits shown under **'GENERAL DATA'**. Main bearings for reground crankshafts are available in sizes shown under **'GENERAL DATA'**.

Clean the crankshaft thoroughly, ensuring that the connecting oilways between the journals and crankpins are perfectly clear. They can be cleaned out by applying a pressure gun containing petrol or paraffin. When clean inject engine oil in the same manner.

Thoroughly clean the bearing shells, caps, and housings above the crankshaft.

Examine the bearing shells for wear and pitting, and look for evidence of breaking away or picking up. Renew the shells if necessary.

Bearings are prefinished with the correct diametral clearance, and do not require bedding in. New bearings should be marked to match up with the marking on the caps, and **on no account should the caps be filed to take up wear or to reduce running clearance.**

Check the thrust washers for wear on their bearing

surfaces, and renew if necessary to obtain the **correct** end-float.

Refitting

Installation of the crankshaft and bearings is a reversal of the removal procedure, particular attention, however, being given to the following points:

(1) Ensure that the thrust washers are replaced the correct way round (the oil grooves should face outwards) and locate the bottom half tab in the slot in the bearing cap.

(2) The bearing shells are notched to fit the recesses machined in the housing cap.

(3) Remember to fit the packing washers behind the crankshaft timing chain wheel.

(4) Lubricate the bearings freely with engine oil.

(5) The rear main bearing cap horizontal joint surfaces should be thoroughly cleaned and lightly covered with Hylomar Jointing Compound before the cap is fitted to the cylinder block. This ensures a perfect oil seal when the cap is bolted down to the block.

(6) Lubricate the rear main bearing cap joint seal liberally with oil before refitting.

(7) Tighten the main bearing bolts (see **'GENERAL DATA'** for torque spanner settings).

Section A.30

CYLINDER LINERS

Should the condition of the cylinder bores be such that they cannot be cleaned up to accept standard oversize pistons, dry cylinder liners can be fitted. This operation may be carried out by the use of specialized proprietary equipment or with a power press using pilot adaptors to the dimensions shown in Fig. A.20. The press must be capable of 3 tons (3048 kg.) pressure to fit new liners and 5 to 8 tons (5080 to 8128 kg.) to remove old liners.

Remove the engine from the vehicle as detailed in Section A.31. Dismantle the engine and remove the cylinder head studs. If liners have not previously been fitted the bores must be machined and honed to the dimensions given in the table below.

Removing worn liners

Place the cylinder block face downwards on suitable wooden supports on the bed of the press, making sure that there is sufficient space between the block and the bed of the press to allow the worn liner to pass down. Insert the pilot in the bottom of the liner and carefully press the liner from the bore.

Engine type	Liner Part No.	Machine bores of cylinder block to this dimension before fitting liner	Outside diameter of liner	Interference fit of liner in cylinder block bore	Machine liner bore to this dimension after fitting
'A' (948 c.c.)	2A 784	2·6035 to 2·604 in. (66·128 to 66·14 mm.)	2·606 to 2·60675 in. (66·19 to 66·21 mm.)	·002 to ·00325 in. (·05 to ·08 mm.)	2·477 to 2·4785 in. (62·915 to 62·954 mm.)
'A' (1098 c.c.)	12G 164	2·64075 to 2·64125 in. (67·076 to 67·088 mm.)	2·64325 to 2·64400 in. (67·139 to 67·158 mm.)	·002 to ·00325 in. (·05 to ·08 mm.)	2·542 to 2·5435 in. (64·566 to 64·605 mm.)

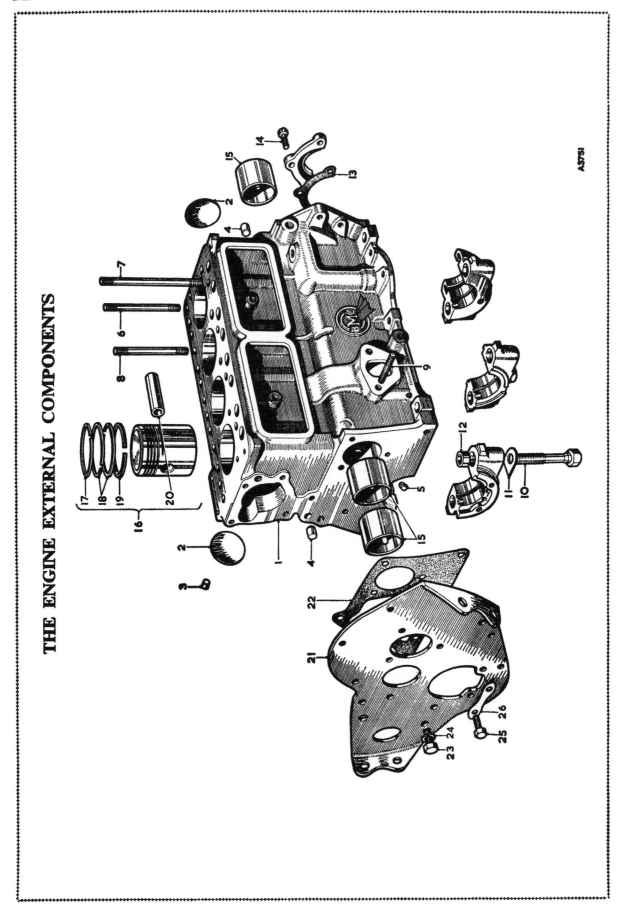

A

THE ENGINE EXTERNAL COMPONENTS

A.22

KEY TO THE ENGINE EXTERNAL COMPONENTS

No.	Description
1.	Block assembly.
2.	Welch plug.
3.	Oil pressure relief valve passage plug.
4.	Oil gallery plug.
5.	Camshaft bearing oil feed restrictor.
6.	Cylinder head stud.
7.	Cylinder head stud (long).
8.	Cylinder head stud (short).
9.	Fuel pump stud.

No.	Description
10.	Main bearing cap set screw.
11.	Lock washer.
12.	Main bearing cap dowel.
13.	Rear cover joint.
14.	Rear cover set screw.
15.	Camshaft bearing liners.
16.	Piston assembly.
17.	Compression ring (plain).
18.	Compression ring (taper).

No.	Description
19.	Scraper ring.
20.	Gudgeon pin.
21.	Engine mounting plate (front).
22.	Mounting plate joint.
23.	Mounting plate screw to crankcase.
24.	Washer.
25.	Mounting plate to bearing cap screw.
26.	Locking plate.

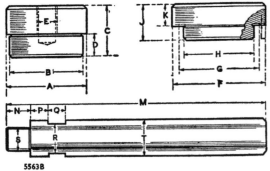

5563B

Fig. A.20

Cylinder liner pilots should be made to the above dimensions from case-hardening steel and case-hardened. The pilot extension should be made from 55-ton hardening and tempering steel hardened in oil and then tempered at 550° C. (1,020° F.)

948-c.c. engine	1098-c.c. engine
Pressing-out pilot	**Pressing-out pilot**
A. $2\frac{17}{64}{}^{+\cdot005}_{-\cdot000}$ in.	A. $2\frac{5}{8}{}^{+\cdot005}_{-\cdot000}$ in.
(65·48 ${}^{+\cdot127}_{-\cdot000}$ mm.).	(66·68 ${}^{+\cdot127}_{-\cdot000}$ mm.).
B. $2\cdot465{}^{+\cdot000}_{-\cdot005}$ in.	B. $2\cdot537{}^{+\cdot000}_{-\cdot005}$ in.
(62·61 ${}^{+\cdot000}_{-\cdot127}$ mm.).	(64·44${}^{+\cdot000}_{-\cdot127}$ mm.).
C. $1\frac{3}{4}$ in. (44·45 mm.).	C. $1\frac{3}{4}$ in. (44·45 mm.).
D. $\frac{3}{4}$ in. (19·05 mm.).	D. $\frac{3}{4}$ in. (19·05 mm.).
E. $\frac{3}{4}$ in. B.S.W. thread.	E. $\frac{3}{4}$ in. B.S.W. thread.
Pressing-in pilot	**Pressing-in pilot**
F. 3 in. (76·20 mm.).	F. $3\frac{1}{16}$ in. (77·79 mm.).
G. $2\frac{5}{8}$ in. (66·68 mm.).	G. $2\frac{11}{16}$ in. (67·26 mm.).
H. $2\cdot455{}^{+\cdot000}_{-\cdot005}$ in.	H. $2\cdot515{}^{+\cdot000}_{-\cdot005}$ in.
(62·35${}^{+\cdot000}_{-\cdot127}$ mm.).	(63·88${}^{+\cdot000}_{-\cdot127}$ mm.).
J. $1\frac{1}{4}$ in. (31·75 mm.).	J. $1\frac{1}{4}$ in. (31·75 mm.).
K. $\frac{3}{4}$ in. (19·05 mm.).	K. $\frac{3}{4}$ in. (19·05 mm.).
L. ·015 in. (·38 mm.).	L. ·015 in. (·38 mm.).
Pilot extension	**Pilot extension**
M. $14\frac{1}{2}$ in. (36·83 cm.).	M. $10\frac{1}{2}$ in. (26·67 cm.).
N. $\frac{7}{8}$ in. (22·22 mm.).	N. $\frac{7}{8}$ in. (22·22 mm.).
P. $\frac{5}{8}$ in. (15·87 mm.).	P. $\frac{5}{8}$ in. (15·87 mm.).
Q. $\frac{5}{8}$ in. (15·87 mm.).	Q. $\frac{5}{8}$ in. (15·87 mm.).
R. 1 in. (25·4 mm.) flats.	R. 1 in. (25·4 mm.) flats.
S. $\frac{3}{4}$ in. B.S.W. thread.	S. $\frac{3}{4}$ in. B.S.W. thread.
T. $1\frac{1}{4}$ in. (31·75 mm.).	T. $1\frac{1}{4}$ in. (31·75 mm.).

Pressing in new liners

Thoroughly clean the inside of the bores and the outside of the liners. Stand the cylinder block upright on the bed of the press, insert the pilot guide in the top of the liner, and position the liner with its chamfered end in the top of the bore. Make certain that the liner is square with the top of the block and that the ram of the press is over the centre of the pilot. Press the liner into the bore.

Each liner must be machined to the dimensions given on page A.21 after pressing into position.

Section A.31

ENGINE

Removing

Disconnect the earth lead from the battery and remove the bonnet from the bonnet hinges.

Remove the radiator as in Section C, and if a heater is fitted disconnect the inlet and outlet hoses at the heater unit.

Disconnect the control cables from the carburetters and the oil pressure gauge pipe and oil cooler pipes (if fitted) from their engine connections. If the vehicle is fitted with a drive type tachometer, remove the drive cable and reduction gear assembly from the rear of the dynamo.

All Lucar connectors fitted to the generator, coil, and distributor low-tension cables should be disconnected.

Detach the high-tension cables from their connections at the coil and the sparking plugs and remove the distributor cap.

Remove the starter cable from its connection on the front end of the starter motor and disconnect the fuel inlet pipe at the fuel pump union. Release the clamp attaching the exhaust manifold to the down pipe and lower the down pipe from the manifold.

With gearbox

NOTE.—The following operations apply only when the engine is removed complete with the gearbox assembly.

Working from within the vehicle, remove the self-tapping screws securing the gear lever aperture cover to the gearbox surround and lift off the cover. Remove the anti-rattle cap, spring, and plunger. Remove the gear change lever retaining plate set screws and extract the gear change lever complete with the retaining plate. Turn back the carpet and remove the gearbox rear mounting screws. From beneath the car, disconnect the speedometer drive cable and release it from its clip; disconnect the wires from the reverse light switch (if fitted). Detach the slave cylinder from the gearbox bell housing by removing the securing set screws and withdrawing the push-rod from the rear of the cylinder. Disconnect the propeller shaft from the rear axle and remove it from the vehicle over the axle assembly and to the left-hand side of the differential casing. Remove the remaining gearbox mounting set screws.

Without gearbox

NOTE.—The following operations apply only when the engine is removed as a single unit.

Remove the filter bowl and the starter motor from the right-hand rear of the cylinder block. Take the weight of the gearbox on a suitable jack and remove the set screws securing the gearbox to the engine crankcase.

Remove the left-hand front engine mounting complete with its bracket and the right-hand front engine mounting rubber together with the front exhaust down pipe support bracket from its fixing on the gearbox bell housing.

Take the weight of the assembly or assemblies with suitable lifting equipment and remove the engine from the vehicle.

Refitting

Refit the engine by reversing the sequence of operations detailed for removal.

Section A.32

ENGINE MOUNTINGS

Removing

Support the engine assembly with suitable lifting equipment and remove both the left- and right-hand mounting rubber securing nuts and mounting rubber bracket-to-body securing set screws. Release the exhaust down pipe manifold clamp and remove the front down pipe strap from the support bracket. Lift the engine approximately ¾ in. (19 mm.), ensuring that the fan assembly will not foul the radiator fan cowling. Swing the engine to the left as far as possible and remove the right-hand rubber mounting together with its body bracket.

The left-hand front rubber mounting and bracket assembly can now be easily removed.

Refitting

When refitting, the right-hand front rubber mounting and bracket should be positioned first. Both mounting rubbers and brackets should be fitted before any set screws or nuts are replaced.

Section A.33

PISTONS AND CONNECTING RODS
(Later Cars)

The piston/gudgeon pin and connecting rod/small-end bush can only be obtained as assemblies. Therefore, under no circumstances should the small-end bush or gudgeon pin be renewed separately.

Removing and refitting

See Section A.26.

(See Editor's note at end of Section A.)

Dismantling

The gudgeon pins are fully floating; remove the two circlips locating each pin and press the pins out. It is essential that the piston assemblies should be replaced in their own bores and fitted the same way round: they should be marked to facilitate this.

Reassembling

Assemble the pistons to the connecting rods with the gudgeon pin, which should be a hand push fit at a room temperature of 20° C. (68° F.). Secure each pin in its piston with two circlips, ensuring that they fit well into their grooves.

Section A.34

PISTON SIZES AND CYLINDER BORES
(Later Cars)

In production, pistons are fitted by selective assembly, to facilitate this the piston crowns are marked with an identifying figure. The figure enclosed in a diamond

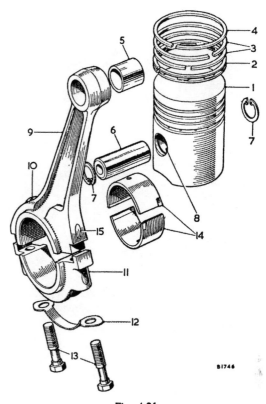

Fig. A.21

Piston and connecting rod

1. Piston.	9. Connecting rod.
2. Piston ring—scraper.	10. Cylinder wall lubricating jet.
3. Piston rings—taper.	11. Connecting rod cap.
4. Piston ring—parallel.	12. Lock washer.
5. Small-end bush.	13. Bolts.
6. Gudgeon pin.	14. Connecting rod bearings.
7. Circlip.	15. Connecting rod and cap marking.
8. Gudgeon pin lubricating hole.	

corresponds with a similar marking on the cylinder block adjacent to the bore.

In addition to the standard pistons, two oversize pistons are available for service purposes, the oversize is stamped on the piston crown enclosed in an ellipse. The markings indicate the actual bore size to which they must be fitted, the requisite clearance being allowed for in the machining.

Piston marking	Suitable bore size	Metric equivalent
STANDARD	2·5424 to 2·5447 in.	64·576 to 64·635 mm.
OVERSIZE +·010 in. (·254 mm.)	2·5524 to 2·5547 in.	64·830 to 64·889 mm.
+·020 in. (·508 mm.)	2·5624 to 2·5647 in.	65·084 to 65·143 mm.

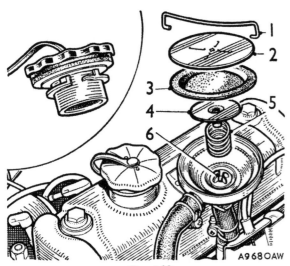

Fig. A.22

Closed-circuit breathing arrangement: (Inset) oil filler cap with combined air filter and the breather control valve

1. Retaining clip.   4. Metering valve.
2. Cover.   5. Spring.
3. Diaphragm.   6. Cruciform guides.

Section A.35

OIL CONTROL PISTON RINGS—DUAFLEX 61
(Later Cars)

When fitting this later type of oil control ring, the following points should be carefully noted.

(a) Gap the rails and side spring to the dimension given in **'GENERAL DATA'**.

(b) The lugs of the expander must be butted together (not crossed), and inserted into one

of the holes in the scraper ring groove on the non-thrust side of the piston.

(c) Stagger the gaps of the twin rails and side spring on the non-thrust side of the piston.

(d) When compressing the rings prior to refitting the pistons ensure that the ends of the rings are fully home in the groove.

(e) Remove any glaze from the cylinder bores before refitting the pistons.

Section A.36

CRANKCASE CLOSED-CIRCUIT BREATHING

Oil filler cap

An air filter is incorporated in the oil filler cap. The cap and filter are renewed only as a complete assembly.

Breather control valve

Testing

With the engine at normal operating temperature, run it at idling speed. Remove the oil filler cap. If the valve is functioning correctly the engine speed will rise by approximately 200 r.p.m. as the cap is removed, the change in speed being audibly noticeable. If no change in speed occurs the valve must be serviced.

Servicing

Remove the spring clip and dismantle the valve.

Clean all metal parts with a solvent (trichlorethylene, fuel, etc.). If deposits are difficult to remove, immerse in boiling water before applying the solvent. Do not use an abrasive. Clean the diaphragm with detergent or methylated spirits.

Replace components showing signs of wear or damage.

Reassemble the valve, making sure the metering needle is in the cruciform guides and the diaphragm is seated correctly.

EDITOR'S NOTES

A. The Engine

Rocker bushes, forged type

Unless the proper equipment is available, it is advised that an automotive machine shop handle the pressing, drilling and reaming operations. It is essential that the rocker arms be re-assembled on the rocker shaft with the proper clearance.

Valves, removing

Stamp or otherwise mark the valves to ensure their being replaced in the same guide during reassembly. Merely keeping them placed in the correct order is usually sufficient.

Any commercially available C-type valve spring compressor may be used to remove the valves.

Unless the specialized tools are available, the cutting and refacing of badly worn valve seats and valves should be left to a professional machine shop.

When the valves are only lightly worn or when the mating surfaces have been newly cut and refaced, the valves should be lapped in as described. A suction cup type valve grinder and a commercially available grinding compound should be used. Grinding should proceed until a dull, even, light-gray ring is produced on the seat and valve face. It is essential that all traces of grinding paste be removed before replacing the valves.

Valve seat inserts

This is an expensive process and should only be attempted by a competent machinist.

Removing Clutch, flywheel, and engine rear plate

If possible, mark the position of the flywheel on the crankshaft so that the flywheel can be reinstalled in its original position. Alternately, place pistons No. 1 and No. 4 at the top of their strokes, then install the flywheel with the mark "1/4" at the top.

Refitting clutch, flywheel and engine rear plate

A used first motion shaft (input shaft) may be used in place of tool 18G139 or a commercially available pilot tool may be used. It is essential that the driven plate (clutch disc) be aligned correctly or it will be impossible to install the transmission.

Timing cover, removing

Service tool 18G98 may be replaced by a large box type wrench and hammer. The shock loading is necessary to remove the bolt.

Timing cover, refitting

The oil seal may be reinstalled by careful use of a drift punch and hammer.

Timing Gears, refitting

The packing washers behind the crankshaft gear are used to obtain proper alignment of the timing wheels. The straight edge-feeler gauge method should be used to check alignment or to determine what thickness of shims is needed to regain proper alignment. The crankshaft gear should be pushed firmly onto the crankshaft while measuring. If the straightedge bears on the crankshaft gear, shims must be removed; if a space exists between the straightedge and the crankshaft gear, shims must be added equal to the thickness of the largest feeler gauge that can be easily inserted into the gap. Shim thickness may be measured with a micrometer.

Camshaft, camshaft bearings

As the replacing and reaming of the camshaft bearings is an extensive (as well as expensive) process, it should only be done when absolutely necessary. For this reason anything that will damage good bearings, such as chemical degreasing, should be avoided. When needed, this job is best left to a professional machine shop unless the correct tools are available.

Pistons and connecting rods

If there is a substantial ridge at the top of the cylinder bore, it must be removed with a ridge reamer before removing the piston. Otherwise damage may occur to the rings and ring grooves. The forward edge of the piston top should be marked to ensure correct replacement.

It is essential that a piston ring compressor be used when replacing a piston in its cylinder (see tools in Section S). Severe damage to the rings and piston may otherwise occur.

Crankshaft and main bearings, inspecting

Although the bearings come correctly prefinished from the manufacturer, it is highly recommended that the actual clearances be checked during assembly to see how well they conform to those listed in the General Data.

The best way to check is to use Plastigage, a thin soft plastic ribbon designed for the purpose. The procedure is as follows

1. The bearing is installed and the cap is correctly torqued down.
2. The cap is loosened and a small piece of Plastigage is inserted between the crankshaft and the bearing.
3. The bearing cap is again brought up to the correct torque readings and again removed.
4. The bearing clearance is indicated by the width of the flattened strip of Plastigage.
5. All traces of plastic are removed, the bearing is oiled, and the cap is reinstalled to the correct torque readings.

Do not turn the engine while the Plastigage is being used. Incorrect clearances indicate either excessive wear or incorrect assembly.

Any commercially available gasket compound may be substituted for the jointing compound referred to.

BentleyPublishers.com
BentleyPublishers.com—All Rights Reserved

Section Aa

THE ENGINE

The information given in this Section refers specifically to the Sprite (Mk. IV) and Midget (Mk. III) and must be used in conjunction with Section A.

† These operations must be followed by an exhaust emission check

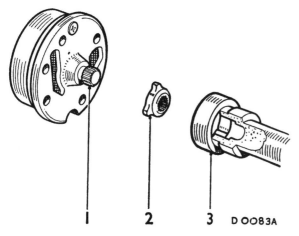

Fig. Aa.1

The oil pump drive, showing the correct position for the early-type driving flange

1.   Oil pump drive shaft.   **2.**   Driving flange.
3.   Camshaft.

Section Aa.1

OIL PUMP

Removing

(1) Remove the engine (Section Aa.9).
(2) Remove the clutch assembly, flywheel, and the engine back plate (Section A.20).
(3) Unscrew the oil pump retaining screws and withdraw the pump.

Dismantling

(4) Refer to Section A.5 for the instruction covering the Concentric or Hobourn-Eaton pumps.

Refitting

(5) Follow the instructions given in Section A.5, noting that the early-type oil pump driving flange, which has offset drive lugs, is fitted with these lugs facing the oil pump. The driving lugs are centralized on later types.

Section Aa.2

ROCKER SHAFT ASSEMBLY

Removing and refitting

(1) Follow the instructions in Section A.6.

Dismantling and reassembling

(2) Carry out the instructions in Section A.6, noting that the six distance pieces are fitted; one to each side of the two outer rockers, and one to the bracket side of the two middle rockers.

Section Aa.3

VALVES

Removing

(1) Remove the cylinder head (Section A.12).
(2) Using tool 18G 45 compress the valve springs,

Aa.2

remove the cotters, valve spring cups, springs, and valve spring seats.

(3) Remove the valve oil seal (inlet valves only—later engines), and withdraw the valves, marking them for reassembly in their original positions.

Refitting

(4) Fit each valve into its respective guide, followed by the spring seat (where fitted); then slide an oil seal down each inlet valve stem and fit it over the valve guide. Do not refit an oil seal to any of the exhaust valves, even if seals had originally been fitted.

(5) Fit the spring seat, springs, and spring cups.

(6) Compress the springs using tool 18G 45 and fit the cotters.

Section Aa.4

VALVE SEAT INSERTS

If the valve seats cannot be restored by the recutting process (Section A.15), machine out the seatings to the dimensions given in Fig. Aa.3 and press special inserts into the cylinder head. Each insert must have an interference fit of ·0025 to ·0045 in. (·063 to ·11 mm.).

After fitting, grind or machine the new seating to the dimensions given in Fig. Aa.3, and rifle out the insert to the contour of the port. Normal valve-grinding may be necessary to ensure efficient valve seating.

NOTE.—It is not possible to fit both an inlet and an exhaust valve seat insert in any one cylinder.

Section Aa.5

CAMSHAFT

Removing

(1) Drain the sump and remove the engine (Section Aa.9).

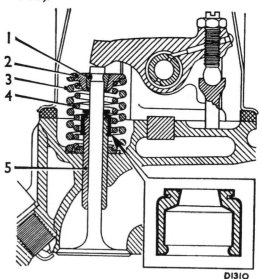

Fig. Aa.2

The valve components assembled. (The inlet valve oil seal is shown inset)

1.   Split cotters.   2.   Retaining cup.   3.   Outer spring.
4.   Inner spring.   5.   Valve guide.

Sprite and Midget.   Issue 3.   29459

(2) Remove the rocker shaft assembly and the push-rods (Section A.6).

(3) Remove the timing cover and gears (Section A.22 and A.23).

(4) Remove the distributor assembly (Section A.19).

(5) Remove the sump.

(6) Remove the camshaft locating plate.

(7) Invert the engine, to allow the tappets to fall clear of the camshaft, withdraw the camshaft rotating it slowly to assist disengagement of the distributor drive. The oil pump drive flange may come away with the camshaft as it is withdrawn, if so it must be refitted (drive lug side towards the oil pump) to the oil pump drive shaft.

Refitting

(8) Reverse the removal procedure in (1) to (9) noting the following points:

   (a) Ensure that the oil pump driving flange is correctly positioned on the pump drive shaft.

   (b) Rotate the camshaft slowly when refitting to assist engagement of the oil pump drive flange.

   (c) Fit the camshaft locating plate with its white-metal side towards the camshaft.

Camshaft bearing liners

(9) Refer to Section A.25 for removal, refitting, and reaming instructions.

Section Aa.6

TAPPETS

Removing

(1) Remove the camshaft (Section Aa.5).

(2) With the camshaft removed the tappets may be withdrawn from the cylinder block using a magnet or alternatively, turn the engine upright and allow the tappets to slide out under their own weight. Label the tappets to ensure correct reassembly in their original positions.

Section Aa.7

PISTONS AND CONNECTING RODS

Removing

Connecting rods

(1) Remove the cylinder head (Section A.12).

(2) Drain and remove the sump.

(3) Unscrew the connecting rod cap bolts, remove the caps with their bearing halves, and withdraw the connecting rods and pistons from the top of the cylinder bores. The connecting rods and caps should be marked to ensure refitting in their original positions.

Pistons

The gudgeon pin is a press fit to the connecting rod small-end. The interference fit of the pin in the small-end retains the gudgeon pin in its correct relative position and

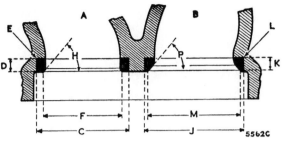

Fig. Aa.3

Valve seat machining dimensions

	Exhaust (A)		Inlet (B)
C.	1·2505 to 1·2515 in. (26·048 to 26·073 mm.).	J.	1·3805 to 1·3815 in. (35·063 to 35·088 mm.).
D.	·186 to ·188 in. (4·72 to 4·77 mm.).	K.	·186 to ·188 in. (4·72 to 4·77 mm.).
E.	Maximum radius ·015 in. (·38 mm.).	L.	Maximum radius ·015 in. (·38 mm.).
F.	1·144 to 1·164 in. (29·046 to 29·554 mm.).	M.	1·2995 to 1·3195 in. (32·89 to 33·38 mm.).
H.	45°.	P.	45°.

the piston bosses form the pin bearing surfaces. It is therefore essential that the specified interference fit (see **'GENERAL DATA'**) is maintained.

To remove the gudgeon pin Service tool 18G 1002 must be used to avoid crushing or distorting the piston.

(4) Retain the hexagonal body (8) of Service tool 18G 1002 in a vice with the cut-out (10) uppermost (see Fig. Aa.4).

(5) Screw the large nut (1) back until it is flush with the end of the centre screw (9), push the screw and nut forward until the nut contacts the thrust race (2).

(6) Slide the parallel sleeve (3), short length diameter first, on to the centre screw up to the shoulder.

(7) Place the piston assembly on the centre screw, then fit the remove/replacer bush (5), longest diameter portion towards the piston.

(8) Screw the stop nut (6) onto the centre screw and adjust it until there is approximately $\frac{1}{32}$ in. (·8 mm.) end-play in the whole assembly, ensuring that the parallel sleeve and the remover/replacer bush are correctly located in the gudgeon pin bores on both sides of the piston.

(9) Lock the stop nut securely in position with the lock screw (7).

(10) Check that the curved face of the body is clean, then slide the piston assembly carefully into position against the curved face. Check that the piston rings are over the cut-out in the tool body.

(11) Screw the large nut (1) up to the thrust race (2).

(12) Hold the lock screw (7), not the stop nut, with a spanner, and turn the large nut (1) until the gudgeon pin is withdrawn from the piston.

Refitting

Pistons

(13) Remove the large nut (1) of Service tool 18G 1002, and pull the centre screw out a few inches as shown in Fig. Aa.5.

(14) Slide the parallel sleeve (3), longest length diameter portion first, on to the centre screw up to the shoulder.

(15) Place the piston on the connecting rod small end up to the undercut (11).

(16) Smear the gudgeon pin with thin oil and slide it over the centre screw and into the piston bore up to the face of the connecting rod.

(17) Slide the remover/replacer brush, short spigot towards the gudgeon pin, on to the centre screw.

(18) Screw the stop nut (6) onto the centre screw, adjust the nut to give 1/32 in. (·8 mm.) end-play, and lock the nut securely in position with the lock screw (7).

the piston skirt. Under no circumstances must the flange be allowed to contact the piston.

If the torque wrench has not broken throughout the pull the fit of the gudgeon pin to the connecting rod is not acceptable and necessitates the renewal of components.

It is essential that the large nut and the centre screw of the tool is kept well lubricated with thin engine oil, to avoid excessive friction which may result in a false torque wrench reaction.

(23) Check that the piston pivots freely on the pin, and is also free to slide sideways. Should this not be so, wash the assembly in fuel or paraffin (kerosene), lubricate the gudgeon pin with neat Acheson's

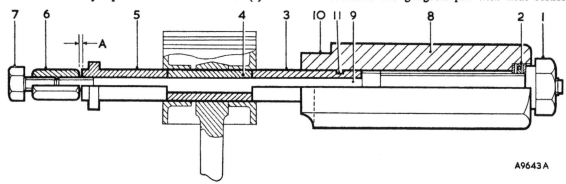

Fig. Aa.4

Service tool 18G 1002 in position to remove the gudgeon pin

1. Large nut.	7. Lock screw.
2. Thrust race.	8. Body.
3. Parallel sleeve.	9. Centre screw.
4. Gudgeon pin.	10. Cut-out.
5. Remover/replacer bush.	11. Undercut.
6. Stop nut.	'A' = 1/32 in. (·8 mm.).

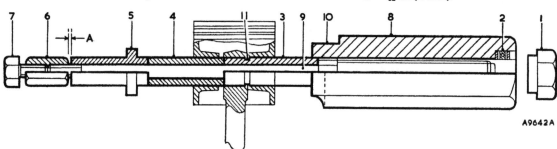

Fig. Aa.5

Service tool 18G 1002 in position to refit the gudgeon pin

(19) Check that the curved face of the body is clean, then slide the piston into position against the curved face. Check that the piston rings are over the cut-out in the tool body.

(20) Screw the large nut onto the centre screw until it contacts the thrust race (2).

(21) Set the torque wrench 18G 537 to 16 lb. ft. (2·21 kg. m.). This represents the minimum load for an acceptable fit.

(22) Using Service tool 18G 587 with the torque wrench on the large nut (1), and holding the lock screw (7) with a suitable spanner, turn the large nut to pull the gudgeon pin until the flange of the remover/replacer bush (5) is 1/32 in. (·8 mm.) from

Colloids 'oil dag' and recheck. If stiffness persists, dismantle the assembly and check for ingrained dirt or damage.

(24) When the assembly is satisfactory, check the piston and connecting rod for alignment and, lubricate the gudgeon pin with Acheson's Colloids 'oil dag' before refitting to the engine.

Connecting rods

(25) Reverse the removal procedure in (1) to (3) noting the following points.

   (a) Stagger the piston ring gaps at 90° to each other. For oil control rings see Section A.35. Compress the piston rings using Service tool 18G 55A.

Aa.4

(*b*) Ensure that each connecting rod and piston is refitted in to original bore, the correct way round.

(*c*) Check that the big-end bearings are correctly located in the connecting rods and caps. Check that the self-locking nuts lock to the stud threads efficiently. If in doubt fit new nuts. Tighten the bearing cap nuts to the torque figure given in 'GENERAL DATA'.

NOTE.—The big-end bearings are offset on the connecting rods, the rods should be fitted so that the bearings of Nos. 1 and 3 are offset towards the rear of the engine, and the bearings of Nos. 2 and 4 are offset towards the front (see Fig. Aa.6).

Section Aa.8

PISTON SIZES AND CYLINDER BORES

In addition to the standard pistons there are also two oversize pistons available for service purposes.

Oversize pistons are marked with the actual oversize dimension enclosed in an ellipse, and are suitable for a bore oversize to standard by the same dimension.

The piston markings indicate the actual bore size to which they must be fitted, the requisite running clearance being allowed for in the machining.

Pistons are available in the sizes indicated in the table.

Piston marking	Suitable bore size	Metric equivalent
STANDARD	2·7803 to 2·7800 in.	70·622 to 70·615 mm.
OVERSIZE +·010 in. (·254 mm.)	2·7903 to 2·7900 in.	70·876 to 70·869 mm.
+·020 in. (·508 mm.)	2·8003 to 2·8000 in.	71·13 to 71·123 mm.

Section Aa.9

ENGINE

Removing

(1) Remove the bonnet (Section R.2).

(2) Disconnect the earth lead from the battery.

(3) Drain the cooling system (Section C.3), the engine sump (Section A.1), and the gearbox (Section F.1).

(4) Remove the radiator (Section C.5).

(5) Unscrew the two through-bolts from both air cleaners and remove the air cleaners.

(6) Disconnect the inlet and outlet heater hoses from the heater unit.

(7) Disconnect the petrol feed pipe from its connection on the front carburetter, and disconnect the choke cable from the mixture control lever.

(8) Release the clamp securing the exhaust pipe to the manifold and lower the pipe.

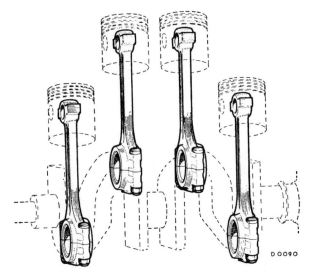

Fig. Aa.6

The correct assembly of the connecting rods and pistons to the crankshaft

(9) Disconnect the throttle cable from the accelerator pedal cross-shaft and pull the cable through the engine bulkhead.

(10) Disconnect the cables from the dynamo and oil filter and the low-tension cables from the coil and distributor.

(11) Detach the high-tension cables from the sparking plugs and coil and remove the distributor cap.

(12) Disconnect the cable from its connection on the starter, and disconnect the oil pressure gauge pipe from the cylinder block union.

(13) Remove the carpet covering the gearbox tunnel, remove the screws securing the gear lever aperture cover and remove the cover.

(14) Unscrew the plug in the change speed tower and withdraw the damper spring and plunger.

(15) Unscrew the three screws securing the gear lever retaining plate and lift out the lever complete with retaining plate.

(16) Remove the gearbox rear mounting bolts from the sides of the gearbox tunnel.

(17) Remove the clutch slave cylinder securing bolts, and withdraw the cylinder from its push-rod.

(18) Disconnect the speedometer cable from the gearbox.

(19) Remove the two gearbox mounting bolts fitted through the under frame.

(20) Mark the propeller shaft rear universal joint flange and the rear axle flange, to assist correct reassembly, remove the flange securing bolts, disconnect the propeller shaft, and withdraw it rearwards out of engagement with the gearbox shaft.

(21) Take the weight of the engine on a crane, remove the three bolts securing the left-hand engine mounting to the body and the two nuts securing the right-hand engine mounting to the engine front plate.

Sprite and Midget. Issue 3. 29459

*Aa.*5

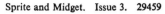

(22) Ease the engine and gearbox assembly forward until the gearbox remote control is clear of the tunnel and then tilt the assembly and lift it from the car.

Refitting

(23) Lower the assembly into the car with the lifting sling positioned at the front of the engine. Transfer the sling position to the rear of the engine, raise the gearbox and enter the remote control into the tunnel.

(24) With access through the gear lever aperture in the tunnel, enter the propeller shaft coupling onto the gearbox shaft splines.

(25) Push the assembly back into its correct position and fit the two gearbox rear mounting bolts.

(26) Reverse the operations in (1) to (15) and (17) to (21), then refill the engine and gearbox with a recommended oil. Refill the cooling system.

Section Aa.10

CYLINDER LINERS

Follow the instructions given in Section A.30, using pilot adaptors to the dimensions given in Fig. Aa.7, and machining the bores of the cylinder block and the cylinder liners to the dimensions given in the table below.

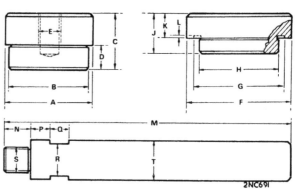

Fig. Aa.7

Cylinder liner pilots should be made to the above dimensions from case-hardening steel, and case hardened. The pilot extension should be made from 55-ton hardening and tempering steel, hardened in oil and then tempered at 550° C. (1,020° F.)

Pressing-out pilot:
A. 2·778 in. ± $^{·005}_{·000}$ in. (70·55 ± $^{·13}_{·00}$ mm.).
B. 2·859 ± $^{·000}_{·005}$ in. (72·63 ± $^{·00}_{·13}$ mm.).
C. 1·75 in. (44·5 mm.).
D. ·75 in. (19 mm.).
E. ¼ in. B.S.W. thread.

Pressing-in pilot:
F. 3·312 in. (84·14 mm.).
G. 2·906 in. (73·8 mm.).
H. 2·753 ± $^{·000}_{·005}$ in. (69·93 ± $^{·00}_{·13}$ mm.).
J. 1·25 in. (31·75 mm.).
K. ·75 in. (19 mm.).
L. ·015 in. (·38 mm.).

Pilot extension: Dimensions as given in Fig. A.20.

Engine type	Liner Part No.	Machine bores of cylinder block to this dimension before fitting liner	Outside diameter of liner	Interference fit of liner in cylinder block bore	Machine liner bore to this dimension after fitting
1275 c.c.	AEG 428	2·8750 to 2·8755 in. (73·025 to 73·038 mm.)	2·8775 to 2·87825 in. (73·088 to 73·108 mm.)	·002 to ·00325 in. (·05 to ·08 mm.)	2·7800 to 2·7815 in. (70·612 to 70·650 mm.)

Aa.6

82

Sprite and Midget. Issue 3. 29459
MG Midget. AKM 2092/1

Section Ab

THE ENGINE (EMISSION CONTROL)

The information given in this Section refers specifically to service operations on, or affected by equipment fitted to the Sprite Mk. IV and Midget Mk. III in conformity with local and territorial requirements, and must be used in conjunction with Section A and Section Aa.

Section Ab.1

CRANKSHAFT PULLEY

Removing

(1) Remove the radiator and return pipe as described in Section C.5.

(2) Slacken the air pump mounting bolts and remove the air pump drive belt.

(3) Slacken the dynamo mounting bolts and remove the fan belt.

(4) Unscrew the four fan and pulley retaining screws and remove the fan and pulley.

(5) Remove the three bolts securing the right-hand engine mounting to the body.

(6) Remove the two mounting stud nuts from the left-hand engine mounting.

(7) Unscrew the three exhaust pipe flange bolts and detach the pipe from the manifold.

(8) Raise the front of the engine just sufficiently to allow the crankshaft pulley to be withdrawn over the body cross-member.

(9) Knock back the lock washer tag on the pulley retaining bolt.

(10) Using tool 18G 98 A remove the pulley retaining bolt.

(11) Carefully withdraw the pulley from the crankshaft.

Refitting

(12) Reverse the removing procedure in (1) to (11), refill the cooling system.

Section Ab.2

TIMING COVER

Removing

(1) Remove the crankshaft pulley as described in Section Ab.1.

(2) Disconnect the crankcase breather pipe from the oil separator.

(3) Remove the timing cover securing screws and withdraw the cover.

Inspection

(4) Inspect the oil seal in the cover; renew the seal if there are signs of wear or deterioration using tool 18G 134 with adaptor 18G 134 BD.

Refitting

(5) Reverse the removing procedure in (1) to (3) using tool 18G 1044 to centralize the oil seal on the crankshaft, refill the cooling system.

Section Ab.3

ENGINE

Removing

(1) Remove the bonnet (Section R.2).

(2) Disconnect the battery.

(3) Drain the cooling system (Section C.3) and the gearbox (Section F.1).

(4) Remove the radiator and bottom return pipe (Section C.5).

(5) Remove both carburetter air cleaners.

(6) Disconnect the petrol feed pipe and choke cable from the carburetters.

(7) Disconnect the inlet and outlet hoses from the heater unit, and the carbon canister hoses from the carburetter and the rocker cover.

(8) Unscrew the three exhaust pipe flange bolts and detach the pipe from the manifold.

(9) Disconnect the throttle cable from the accelerator pedal cross-shaft and pull the cable through the engine bulkhead.

(10) Disconnect the cables from the dynamo/alternator, and the low tension cable from the distributor.

(11) Detach the high tension cables from the sparking plugs and coil and remove the distributor cap.

(12) Disconnect the cable from the starter.

(13) Disconnect the oil pressure gauge pipe from the cylinder block union.

(14) Unscrew the gland nut and withdraw the temperature gauge sensing bulb from the cylinder head.

(15) Remove the carpet covering the gearbox tunnel, remove the screws securing the gear lever aperture cover and remove the cover.

(16) Unscrew the plug in the change speed tower and withdraw the damper spring and plunger.

(17) Unscrew the three screws securing the gear lever retaining plate and lift out the lever complete with retaining plate.

(18) Remove the gearbox rear mounting bolts from the sides of the gearbox tunnel.

(19) Disconnect the reverse light switch wiring at the snap connectors on the side of the gearbox.

(20) Remove the clutch slave cylinder securing bolts and withdraw the cylinder from its push-rod. Note that the earthing strap is fitted under the head of the lower slave cylinder bolt.

(21) Disconnect the speedometer cable from the gearbox and release the cable from its clip on the engine rear plate.

(22) Remove the two gearbox mounting bolts fitted through the under frame.

(23) Mark the propeller shaft rear universal joint and the rear axle flange to assist correct refitting, remove the flange securing bolts, disconnect the propeller shaft, and withdraw it rearwards out of engagement with the gearbox.

(24) Take the weight of the engine on a crane, remove the three bolts securing the right-hand engine mounting to the body and the two nuts securing the left-hand engine mounting to the engine front plate.

(25) Ease the engine and gearbox forward until the gearbox remote control is clear of the tunnel, then tilt the assembly and lift it from the car.

Refitting

(26) Lower the assembly into the car with the lifting sling positioned at the front of the engine.

(27) Transfer the sling position to the rear of the engine, raise the gearbox and enter the remote control into the tunnel.

(28) With access through the gear lever aperture, enter the propeller shaft coupling onto the gearbox shaft splines.

(29) Push the assembly back into its correct position and fit the two gearbox rear mounting bolts.

(20) Reverse the operations in (1) to (17) and (19) to (24), refill the gearbox with a recommended lubricant and refill the cooling system.

Section Ab.4

INLET AND EXHAUST MANIFOLD

Removing

(1) Disconnect the battery.

(2) Remove the air cleaners as detailed in Section D.6.

(3) Disconnect the mixture control, fuel delivery hose, engine breather pipe and the float chamber vent pipe from the carburetters.

(4) Release the three throttle return springs from the levers on the carburetter linkage.

(5) Remove the four nuts securing the carburetters to the inlet manifold and withdraw the carburetters, at the same time disconnecting the throttle interconnecting spindle from the carburetter linkage.

(6) Remove the two bolts and nuts securing the carburetter heat shield to its steady clips. Withdraw the carburetter distance pieces, and the heat shield complete with accelerator cable from the manifold.

(7) Disconnect the ignition vacuum advance pipe from the union on the inlet manifold and unscrew the union from the manifold to release the heater water pipe.

(8) Disconnect the sensing hose from the gulp valve and the gulp valve hose from the inlet manifold.

(9) Remove the nuts securing the exhaust pipe to the manifold flange.

(10) Remove the nuts securing the inlet and exhaust manifold to the cylinder head. Withdraw the gulp valve, inlet manifold and exhaust manifold.

Refitting

(11) Reverse the procedure in (1) to (10), ensuring that the mixture control has $\frac{1}{16}$ in. (1·5 mm.) free movement before it commences to operate the carburetter cam levers.

Section Ab.5

ENGINE RESTRAINT

(Midget Mk. III from Car No. G–AN5–146370)

Removing

(1) Slacken the restraint tube front nut.

(2) Remove the restraint tube rear nut and withdraw the rear plate and buffer.

(3) Remove the nut and bolt securing the restraint tube to the gearbox bracket and withdraw the restraint tube from the bracket on the rear engine mounting cross-member.

(4) Remove the distance tube, front buffer and plate from the restraint tube.

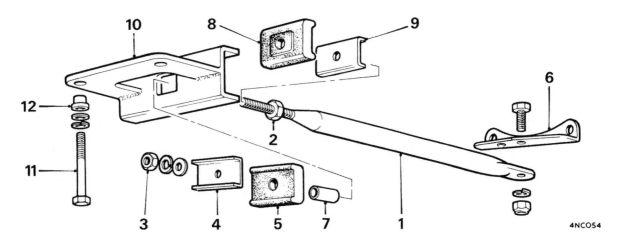

4NCO54

*Fig. Ab.*1

The engine restraint (Midget Mk. III from Car No. G–AN5–146370)

1. Engine restraint tube.
2. Front nut.
3. Rear nut.
4. Rear plate.
5. Rear buffer.
6. Gearbox bracket.
7. Distance tube.
8. Front buffer.
9. Front plate.
10. Engine mounting rear cross-member bracket.

Sprite and Midget. Issue 1. 10858
MG Midget. AKM 2092/1

85

*Ab.*3

Refitting

  (5) Reverse the procedure in 1 to 4, noting the following:

    (*a*) Inspect the buffers for damage and deterioration, and renew if necessary.

    (*b*) Tighten the restraint tube rear nut first, then tighten the front nut.

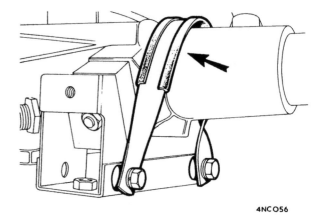

4NC056

*Fig. Ab.*2

Showing the gearbox steady strap
(*Midget Mk. III from Car No. G–AN5–146370*)

SECTION B

THE IGNITION SYSTEM

GENERAL DESCRIPTION

The ignition system consists of two circuits—primary and secondary. The primary circuit includes the battery, the ignition switch, the primary or low-tension circuit of the coil, and the distributor contact breaker and capacitor. The secondary circuit includes the secondary or high-tension circuit of the coil, the distributor rotor and cover segments, the high-tension cables, and the sparking plugs.

The ignition coil, which is mounted to the right-hand side of the engine, consists of a soft-iron core around which is wound the primary and secondary windings. The coil carries at one end a centre high-tension terminal and two low-tension terminals marked 'SW' (switch) and 'CB' (contact breaker) respectively.

The ends of the primary windings are connected to the 'SW' and 'CB' terminals and the secondary winding to the 'CB' terminal and the high tension terminal.

The distributor is mounted on the right-hand side of the engine and is driven by a shaft and helical gear from the camshaft. Automatic timing control of the distributor is by a centrifugal mechanism and a vacuum-operated unit each operating entirely independently of the other. The centrifugal mechanism regulates the ignition advance according to engine speed, while the vacuum control varies the timing according to engine load. The combined effect of the two mechanisms gives added efficiency over the full operating range of the engine. An adjuster is provided, giving a fine manual timing adjustment to allow for the engine condition and the grade of fuel used.

A moulded rotor with a metal electrode is mounted on top of the cam. Attached to the distributor body above the centrifugal advance mechanism is a contact breaker plate carrying the contact breaker points and a capacitor connected in parallel. A cover is fitted over the distributor body and retained by two spring clips attached to the body.

Inside the cover is a centre electrode and spring-loaded carbon brush which makes contact with the rotor electrode. The brush is of composite construction, the top portion being made of a resistive compound, while the lower portion is made of softer carbon to prevent wear of the rotor electrode. Under no circumstances must a short, non-resistive brush be used to replace this long, resistive type. A measure of radio interference suppression is given by this brush.

Spaced circumferentially around the distributor cover are the sparking plug high-tension cable segments.

The distributor is secured in position on the cylinder block by a clamp plate.

Section B.1

LUBRICATION

Distributor

Cam bearing

Lift the rotor off the top of the spindle by pulling it squarely and add a few drops of oil to the cam bearing. Do not remove the screw which is exposed. There is a clearance between the screw and the inner face of the spindle for the oil to pass.

Cam

Lightly smear the cam with a very small amount of grease; if this is not available, clean engine oil may be used.

Automatic timing control

Carefully add a few drops of oil through the hole in the contact breaker base through which the cam passes.

Do not allow the oil to get on or near the contacts. Do not over-oil.

Section B.2

LOCATING THE CAUSE OF UNEVEN FIRING

Start the engine and set it to run at a fairly fast idling speed.

Short-circuit each plug in turn by pulling the insulator sleeve up the cable and placing a hammer head or the blade of a screwdriver with a wooden or insulated handle between the terminal and the cylinder head. No difference in the engine performance will be noted when short-circuiting the plug in the defective cylinder. Shorting the other plugs will make uneven running more pronounced.

Having located the cylinder which is at fault, stop the engine and remove the cable from the terminal of the sparking plug. Restart the engine and hold the end of the cable about $\frac{3}{16}$ in. (4·8 mm.) from the cylinder head.

If the sparking is strong and regular, the fault probably lies in the sparking plug. Remove the plug, clean it, and adjust the gap to the correct setting (see 'GENERAL DATA'), or alternatively fit a new plug.

If there is no spark or if it is weak and irregular examine the cable from the sparking plug to the distributor. After a long period of service the insulation may be cracked or perished, in which case the cable should be renewed.

Finally, examine the distributor moulded cap, wipe the inside and outside with a clean, dry cloth, see that the carbon brush moves freely in its holder, and examine the moulding closely for signs of breakdown. After long service it may become tracked—that is, a conducting path may have formed between two or more of the electrodes or between one of the electrodes and some part of the distributor in contact with the cap. Evidence of a tracked cap is shown by the presence of a thin black line. A replacement distributor cap must be fitted in place of one that has become tracked.

Section B.3

TESTING THE LOW-TENSION CIRCUIT

Spring back the securing clips on the distributor and remove the moulded cap and rotor. If the rotor is a tight fit it can be levered off carefully with a screwdriver.

Check that the contacts are clean and free from pits, burns, oil, or grease. Turn the crankshaft and check that the contact points are opening and closing correctly and that the clearance between them is correct when they are fully opened.

Reset the gap if necessary (see 'GENERAL DATA').

Disconnect the cable at the contact breaker terminal of the coil and at the low-tension terminal of the distributor, and connect a test lamp between these terminals. If the lamp lights when the contacts close and goes out when the contacts open the low-tension circuit is in order. Should the lamp fail to light, the contacts are dirty or there is a broken or loose connection in the low-tension wiring.

Locating a fault

Having determined, by testing as previously described, that the fault lies in the low-tension circuit, switch on the ignition and turn the crankshaft until the contact breaker points are fully opened.

Refer to the wiring diagram and check the circuit with a voltmeter (0–20 volts) as follows.

NOTE.—If the circuit is in order the reading on the voltmeter should be approximately 12 volts.

(1) *Battery to control box terminal 'A'* (brown lead). Connect a voltmeter between the control box terminal 'A' and earth. No reading indicates a damaged cable or loose connections.

(2) *Control box.* Connect a voltmeter between the control box auxiliary terminal and earth. No reading indicates a broken or loose connection.

(3) *Control box auxiliary terminal to terminal on ignition switch* (brown with blue lead). Connect a voltmeter between the ignition switch terminal and earth. No reading indicates a damaged cable or loose connections.

(4) *Ignition switch.* Connect a voltmeter between the other ignition switch terminal and earth. No reading indicates a fault in the ignition switch.

(5) *Ignition switch to fusebox terminal 'A3'* (white lead). Connect the voltmeter between the fusebox terminal 'A3' and earth. No reading indicates a damaged cable or loose connections.

(6) *Fusebox terminal 'A3' to ignition coil terminal 'SW'* (white lead). Connect a voltmeter between the

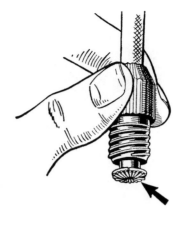

O825HW

Fig. B.2

The correct method of fitting a high-tension cable to the ignition terminal nut

ignition coil terminal 'SW' and earth. No reading indicates a damaged cable or loose connections.

(7) *Ignition coil.* Disconnect the cable from the 'CB' terminal of the ignition coil and connect a voltmeter between this terminal and earth. No reading indicates a fault in the primary winding of the coil and a replacement coil must be fitted. If the correct reading is given, remake the connections to the coil terminal.

(8) *Ignition coil to distributor* (white with black lead). Disconnect the cable from the low-tension terminal on the distributor and connect the voltmeter between the end of this cable and earth. No reading indicates a damaged cable or loose connections.

(9) *Contact breaker and capacitor.* Connect the voltmeter across the contact breaker points. No reading indicates a fault in the capacitor.

Section B.4

HIGH-TENSION CABLES

The high-tension cables must be examined carefully and any which have the insulation cracked, perished, or damaged in any way must be renewed.

To fit the cables to the terminal of the ignition coil thread the knurled moulded terminal nut over the lead, bare the end of the cable for about $\frac{1}{4}$ in. (6 mm.), thread the wire through the brass washer removed from the original cable, and bend back the strands over the washer. Finally, screw the terminal into the coil.

If the leads are at any time removed from the cap, the holes which receive them should be filled with Silicone grease. Cut the new cables to the required length, push them completely home, and tighten the securing screws, watching in the process that the displaced surplus grease exudes evenly all round the leads to form a perfect seal. Care should be taken to leave an adequate surplus on the surface of the cap at the lead entry point.

Wipe the inside and outside of the moulded distributor cap with a soft dry cloth, taking care not to disturb the

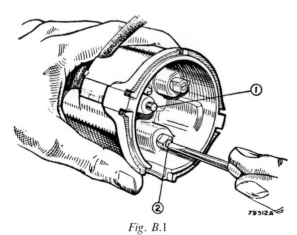

Fig. B.1

The method of connecting high-tension leads

1. Carbon brush.   2. Cable-securing screw.

Sprite and Midget.   Issue 4.   51576

B.3

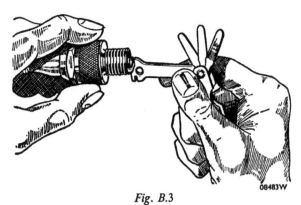

Fig. B.3

*Reset the plug gap, using the Champion special
gap-setting tool shown above*

seals of water-repellent Silicone grease at the points of
entry of the ignition cable leads into the cap. Adequate
sealing is vital since otherwise water may in extreme
circumstances penetrate into the cap down the outside
of the leads and cause ignition failure.

Section B.5

SPARKING PLUGS

Service procedure

To maintain peak sparking plug performance plugs
should be inspected, cleaned, and adjusted at regular
intervals. Under certain fuel and operating conditions,
particularly extended slow-speed town driving, sparking
plugs may have to be serviced at shorter intervals.

Disconnect the ignition cables from all sparking plugs.
Loosen the sparking plugs about two turns anti-clockwise, using the correct socket or box spanner.

Blow away the dirt from around the base of each
plug. If compressed air is not available blow out the dirt
with a tyre pump.

Remove the sparking plugs and place them in a suitable
holder, preferably in the order that they were installed
in the engine.

Analysing service conditions

Examine the gaskets to see if the sparking plugs were
properly installed. If the gaskets were excessively compressed, installed on dirty seats, or distorted, leakage
has probably occurred during service which would tend
to cause overheating of the sparking plugs. Gaskets
properly installed will have flat, clean surfaces. Gaskets
which are approximately one-half their original thickness
will be satisfactory but thinner ones should be renewed.

Examine the firing ends of the sparking plugs, noting
the type of deposit and the degree of electrode erosion.
Remember that if insufficient voltage is delivered to the
sparking plug, no type of plug can fire the mixture in the
cylinder properly.

Normal condition—look for powdery deposits ranging
from brown to greyish tan. Electrodes may be worn
slightly. These are signs of a sparking plug of the correct

heat range used under normal conditions—that is, mixed
periods of high-speed and low-speed driving. Cleaning
the plugs and resetting the gaps are all that is required.
Watch for white to yellowish powdery deposits. These
usually indicate long periods of constant-speed driving
or a lot of slow-speed city driving. These deposits have
no effect on performance if the sparking plugs are cleaned
thoroughly at regular intervals. Remember to 'wobble'
the plug during abrasive blasting in the Champion
service unit. Then file the sparking surfaces to expose
bright, clean metal.

Oil fouling is usually indicated by wet, sludgy deposits
traceable to excessive oil entering the combustion chamber
through worn cylinders, rings, and pistons, excessive
clearances between intake valve guides and stems, or
worn and loose bearings, etc. Hotter-type sparking plugs
may alleviate oil fouling temporarily, but in severe cases
engine overhaul is called for.

Petrol fouling is usually indicated by dry, black, fluffy
deposits which result from incomplete combustion. Too
rich an air/fuel mixture or excessive use of the mixture
control can cause incomplete burning. In addition, a
defective coil, contact breaker points, or ignition cable
can reduce the voltage supplied to the sparking plug and
cause misfiring. If fouling is evident in only a few cylinders
sticking valves may be the cause. Excessive idling or slow
speeds can also keep the plug temperatures so low that
normal combustion deposits are not burned off. In the
latter case hotter-type plugs may be installed.

Burned or overheated sparking plugs are usually
identified by a white, burned or blistered insulator nose
and badly eroded electrodes. Inefficient engine cooling
and incorrect ignition timing can cause general overheating. Severe service, such as sustained high speed and
heavy loads, can also produce abnormally high temperatures in the combustion chamber which necessitate the
use of colder-type sparking plugs.

File the sparking surfaces of the electrodes with a
points file until they are bright, clean, and parallel. For
best results hold the plug in a vice and, if necessary,
enlarge the gaps slightly.

Reset the gaps, using the bending fixture of the
Champion gap-setting tool. Do not apply pressure on the
centre electrode as insulator fracture may result. Use the
bending fixture to obtain parallel sparking surfaces for
maximum gap life.

Visually inspect all sparking plugs for cracked or
chipped insulators. Discard all plugs with insulator
fractures.

Test the sparking ability of a used sparking plug on a
comparator.

Clean the threads by means of a hand or power-driven
wire brush. If the latter type is used the wire diameter
should not exceed ·005 in. (·127 mm.). Do not wire-brush
the insulator or the electrodes.

Clean the gasket seats on the cylinder head before
installing sparking plugs to ensure proper seating of the
sparking plug gaskets. Then, using a new gasket, screw
in each plug by hand finger tight.

B.4

Sprite and Midget. Issue 4. 51576

NOTE.—If the sparking plug cannot be seated on its gasket by hand clean out the cylinder head threads with a clean-out tap or with another used sparking plug having three or four vertical flutes filed in its threads.

Finally, tighten the sparking plugs to the following values:

Size	C.I. head	Turns
14 mm.	30 lb.ft.	$\frac{1}{2}$
	(4·15 kg. m.)	

The number of turns listed approximate to the proper torque values and should be used if a torque wrench is not available or cannot be used because of limited accessibility.

Connect the H.T. terminals after the plugs are installed.

Standard gap setting

The sparking plug gap settings recommended and listed under 'GENERAL DATA' have been found to give the best overall performance under all service conditions. They are based on extensive dynamometer testing and experience on the road and are generally a compromise between the wide gaps necessary for best idling performance and the small gaps required for the best high-speed performance.

All plugs should be reset to the specified gap by bending the side electrode only, using the special tool available from the Champion Sparking Plug Company.

Section B.6

CONTACT BREAKER

The distributor has a pretilted contact breaker unit. The moving contact breaker plate is balanced on two nylon studs and the angle through which the plate may be tilted is controlled by a stud riveted to the moving contact breaker plate locating in a slot in the base plate. The plate carrying the fixed contact is secured by one screw only.

Turn the crankshaft until the contact breaker points are fully opened and check the gap with a gauge (see 'GENERAL DATA'). If the gap is correct the gauge should be a sliding fit. Do not alter the setting unless the gap varies considerably from the gauge thickness.

To adjust the setting keep the crankshaft in the position which gives maximum opening of the contacts. Slacken the fixed contact plate securing screw and adjust the contact gap by inserting a screwdriver in the notched hole and turn clockwise to reduce the gap and anti-clockwise to increase it. Tighten the securing screw.

If the contacts are dirty or pitted they must be cleaned by polishing them with a fine carborundum stone and afterwards wiping them with a cloth moistened with fuel. The moving contact can be removed from its mounting in order to assist cleaning. Check and adjust the contact breaker setting after cleaning the contacts.

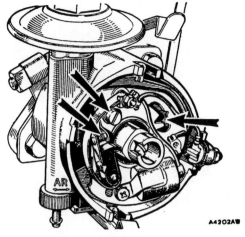

A4202A

Fig. B.4

The distributor with the moulded cap and rotor removed, showing the contact breaker adjustment

Check that the moving arm is free on its pivot. If it is sluggish remove the arm and polish the pivot pin with a strip of fine emery-cloth. Afterwards clean off all traces of emery dust and apply a spot of clean engine oil to the top of the pivot. The contact breaker spring tension should be between 20 and 24 oz. (567 and 680 gm.) measured at the contacts.

Section B.7

DISTRIBUTOR

Removing

Before removing the distributor turn the crankshaft until the rotor arm is pointing to the segment in the cover for No. 1 cylinder plug lead. This is to provide a datum for replacement.

The distributor can be removed and replaced without interfering with the ignition timing, provided the clamp plate pinch-bolt is not disturbed.

Remove the distributor cover and disconnect the low-tension lead from the terminal on the distributor. Disconnect the suction advance pipe at the union on the distributor.

Unscrew the tachometer drive (if fitted) from its connection at the rear of the dynamo.

Extract the two bolts securing the distributor clamp plate to the distributor housing and withdraw the distributor.

Dismantling

The contact breaker plate may be removed as an assembly to give access to the centrifugal weights without completely dismantling the distributor. To do this first remove the rotor arm and then withdraw the slotted nylon low-tension terminal insulator from the distributor body.

Take out the two screws which secure the plate assembly to the distributor body, ease up the plate, and

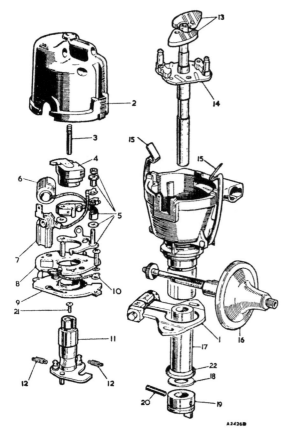

Fig. B.5

The components of the distributor

1.	Clamping plate.	
2.	Moulded cap.	
3.	Brush and spring.	
4.	Rotor arm.	
5.	Contacts (set).	
6.	Capacitor.	
7.	Terminal and lead (low-tension).	
8.	Moving contact breaker plate.	
9.	Contact breaker base plate.	
10.	Earth lead.	
11.	Cam.	

12.	Automatic advance springs.
13.	Weight assembly.
14.	Shaft and action plate.
15.	Cap-retaining clips.
16.	Vacuum unit.
17.	Bush.
18.	Thrust washer.
19.	Driving dog.
20.	Parallel pin.
21.	Cam screw.
22.	'O' ring oil seal.

unhook the flexible actuating link connected to the contact breaker plate.

The following procedure is necessary if the distributor is to be completely stripped.

Before dismantling, make a careful note of the positions in which the various components are fitted in order that they may be replaced correctly.

Spring back the clips and remove the moulded cap.

Lift the rotor off the top of the spindle. If it is a tight fit it must be levered off carefully with a screwdriver.

Remove the nut from the moving contact anchor pin. Withdraw the insulating sleeve from the capacitor lead and low-tension lead connectors, noting the order in

which they are fitted. Lift the moving contact from the pivot pin.

Take out the screw and spring and flat washers securing the fixed contact plate and remove the plate.

Take out the securing screw and remove the capacitor.

Extract the two screws securing the base plate to the distributor body, noting that one also secures the earthing lead, and lift out the base plate.

Unhook the flexible actuating link connecting the diaphragm in the vacuum unit with the moving contact breaker plate.

IMPORTANT.—Note the relative positions of the rotor arm drive slot in the cam and the offset drive dog at the driving end of the spindle to ensure that the timing is not 180° out when the cam is reassembled.

Take out the cam retaining screw, remove the automatic advance springs, and remove the cam.

Take out the centrifugal weights.

To release the suction advance unit remove the circlip, adjusting nut, and spring. Withdraw the unit.

Clean the distributor cover and examine it for signs of cracks and evidence of 'tracking', i.e. conducting paths which may have formed between adjacent segments. This is indicated by thin black lines between the segments; when this has occurred the cover should be renewed.

Ensure that the carbon brush moves freely in the distributor cover.

Examine the attachment of the metal electrode to the rotor moulding. If slack or abnormally burned, renew the rotor.

The contact faces of the contact breaker points should present a clean, greyish, frosted appearance. If burned or blackened, renew the contact set or polish the contact face of each point with a fine oil-stone, working with a rotary motion. Care should be taken to maintain the faces of the points flat and square, so that when reassembled full contact is obtained. Clean the points thoroughly in fuel.

Check that the movable contact arm is free on its pivot without slackness.

Check the centrifugal timing control balance weights and pivot pins for wear, and renew the cam assembly or weights if necessary. Examine the 'O' ring oil seal (if fitted) on the body shank, and renew if necessary.

The cam assembly should be a free sliding fit on the driving shaft. If the clearance is excessive, or the cam face is worn, renew the cam assembly or shaft as necessary.

Check the fit of the shaft in the body bearing bushes. If slack, renew the bushes and shaft as necessary.

To release the spindle from the body drive out the parallel driving pin passing through the collar of the driving tongue member at the lower end of the spindle.

Press out the old bush. The new bush should be allowed to stand completely immersed in thin engine oil for 24 hours, or alternatively for two hours in oil which has been heated to 100° C. (212° F.), before pressing it into the distributor body.

B.6

Sprite and Midget. Issue 6. 4780

Reassembling

Reassembly is a direct reversal of the dismantling procedure, although careful attention must be given to the following points.

As they are assembled, lubricate the components of the automatic advance mechanism, the distributor shaft, and the portion of the shaft on which the cam fits with thin, clean engine oil.

Turn the vacuum control adjusting nut until it is in the half-way position when replacing the control unit.

When engaging the cam driving pins with the centrifugal weights make sure that they are in the original position. When seen from above, the small offset of the driving dog must be on the right and the driving slot for the rotor arm must be in the six o'clock position.

Adjust the contact breaker to give a maximum opening (see **'ENGINE TUNING DATA'**).

Refitting

To replace the distributor insert it into the distributor housing until the driving dog rests on the distributor drive shaft. Rotate the rotor arm slowly until the driving dog lugs engage with the drive shaft slots, both of which are offset to ensure correct replacement. Turn the distributor body to align the clamping plate holes with those in the housing. The remainder of the assembling is now in the reverse order of that of removal.

Provided that the crankshaft has not been turned, the rotor arm will be opposite the segment for No. 1 plug lead. The high-tension leads can then be replaced on their respective plug terminals in the order of firing, i.e. 1, 3, 4, 2, remembering that the distributor rotation is anti-clockwise when viewed from above.

Static ignition timing is given under **'ENGINE TUNING DATA'**.

NOTE.—If the clamping plate has been removed, or even slackened, resulting in lost timing, the procedure given in Section B.8 should be undertaken to reset the distributor.

Section B.8

TIMING THE IGNITION

Where the ignition timing has been lost the following procedure should be undertaken to reset the distributor to its correct firing position.

Remove the distributor and make quite certain that the distributor driving spindle has been refitted correctly as in Section A.19.

Remove the valve rocker cover so that the valve action can be observed. Rotate the crankshaft, using a spanner on the crankshaft pulley securing nut until No. 1 piston is at the top of its compression stroke (i.e. the exhaust valve of No. 4 cylinder is just closing and the inlet valve just opening). Turn the crankshaft until the recess in the crankshaft pulley flange is in line with the largest pointer (T.D.C.) on the timing case cover (Fig. B.6). If the timing cover has been removed, align the timing marks on the

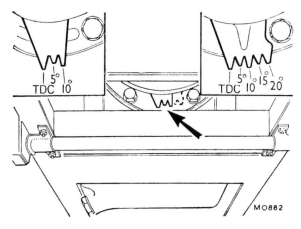

Fig. B.6

The timing pointer and the groove in the crankshaft pulley are provided to assist in accurate ignition timing

camshaft and crankshaft wheels. Nos. 1 and 4 pistons are now at T.D.C. Set the micrometer adjustment on the distributor in its central position. The crankshaft should now be rotated to obtain its correct position.

Set the contact breaker points (see **'ENGINE TUNING DATA'**) when in their position of maximum opening. Insert the distributor into its housing, and engage the driving dog lug with the slot in the driving spindle (both of which are offset) by slowly rotating the rotor arm.

Screw in the two set screws to secure the distributor clamp plate to the distributor housing. Tighten up the clamp plate pinch-bolt to the correct torque tightness (see **'GENERAL DATA'**) in order to ensure correct alignment before tightening the set screws down in the centre of the elongated holes of the clamp plate.

To obtain an accurate setting the electrical method should be used in determining the actual position at which the points must break, and the following procedure should be adopted.

Slacken the clamp pinch-bolt and rotate the distributor body in an anti-clockwise direction until the points are fully closed.

With the low-tension lead connected to the distributor turn on the ignition switch, connect a 12-volt lamp in parallel with the contact breaker points (i.e. one lead from the distributor low-tension terminal and the other to earth), and rotate the distributor clockwise until the lamp lights, indicating that the points have just opened. Secure the distributor body in this position by tightening up the clamp plate pinch-bolt.

Finally, check that the rotor arm is opposite the correct segment in the distributor cap for the No. 1 cylinder.

Reconnect the suction advance pipe and refit the distributor cover and valve rocker cover.

When using a stroboscopic lamp, do not allow the engine r.p.m. to rise high enough to operate the centrifugal advance weights. If the vacuum advance take-off is direct from the induction manifold this should be disconnected before attempting the timing check, otherwise engine timing will be set retarded.

Section B.9

IGNITION ADJUSTMENT

Manual adjustment is provided for the ignition point to enable the best setting to be attained for varying grades of fuel. The adjustment nut is indicated by the lower arrow in Fig. B.7; turning the nut clockwise retards and anti-clockwise advances the ignition. Each graduation on the adjusting spindle barrel represents approximately 5° timing movement and is equal to 55 clicks on the knurled adjuster nut. The range of adjustment provided by this micrometer adjuster is normally ample to deal with any variation encountered.

Do not disturb the pinch-bolt unless absolutely necessary. Should the ignition timing have been lost, retiming should be undertaken as given in Section B.8.

Section B.10

CAPACITOR

The best method of testing the capacitor is by substitution. Disconnect the original capacitor and connect a new one between the low-tension terminal of the distributor and earth.

Should a new capacitor be necessary, it is advisable to fit a complete capacitor and bracket, but should a

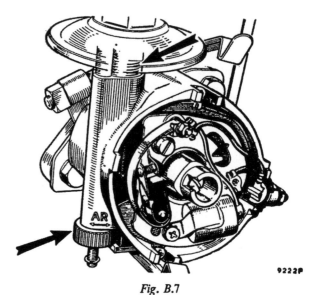

92220

Fig. B.7

Showing the adjustment nut and the vernier scale

capacitor only be available, use a hot iron to soften the solder securing the defective capacitor to the bracket. Care must be taken not to overheat the new capacitor when soldering it in position. The capacity of the capacitor is ·18 to ·22 microfarad.

Section Ba

THE IGNITION SYSTEM

The information contained in this Section refers specifically to the Sprite (Mk. IV) and Midget (Mk. III) and must be used in conjunction with Section B.

† These operations must be followed by an exhaust emission check

Section Ba.1

DISTRIBUTOR

The information given in Section B.7 applies to the distributor fitted to the Sprite (Mk. IV) and Midget (Mk. III) with the exception that there was no vacuum advance unit or moving contact plate fitted to the distributors on early cars. The instructions for removing, dismantling, and reassembling may be followed but references to these components where not fitted should be ignored.

Section Ba.2

IGNITION ADJUSTMENT

Early cars

To adjust the ignition setting, slacken the distributor clamp screw and turn the distributor body clockwise to advance or anti-clockwise to retard.

The correct static ignition timing is given in 'GENERAL DATA'.

Later cars

Follow the instructions given in Section B.9.

Section Ba.3

HIGH TENSION CABLES

Radio-frequency suppressed high-tension cables are used on later cars. In this cable, a graphite-impregnated core replaces the metallic conductor of the earlier type of cable. Connectors used with metal-cored cable are unsuitable for use and new-type cable connectors have been introduced; these are a push-fit to the coil and distributor covers.

Ignition waterproofing

When fitting new high tension cables waterproof the coil and distributor cable entry points by sealing all gaps with a silicon-based grease. On cars exported to certain markets and fitted with coil and distributor covers the cable entry point to the cover should also be greased.

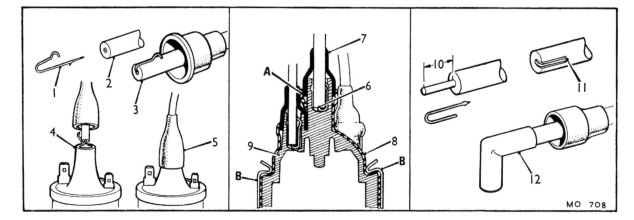

Fig. Ba.1

The correct assembly method for later-type suppressed high tension cables

COIL

1. Spiked connector.
2. Flush cable end.
3. Assembly of spiked connector and lead cover.
4. Push cable into coil chimney until connector clicks into the insert groove.
5. Pull terminal cover down over coil chimney.

DISTRIBUTOR

6. Prepared cable end.
7. Locate terminal covers onto the distributor outlets.
8. Fit distributor cover and pull firmly into place, ensure that lip (a) of the terminal cover is entered into the distributor cover as shown.
9. When fitting the distributor cap to the distributor, the spring clips (b) should be assembled over the distributor cover as shown.

PLUGS

10. Insulation removed for ½ in. (12·7 mm.).
11. Inner core folded onto cable, staple pushed into the centre of the cord as far as possible.
12. Cord and staple must make a good contact with the body of the connector.

Ba.2   Sprite and Midget. Issue 3. 29459

96

Section Ba.4

IGNITION CIRCUIT TESTING

Testing

Equipment: 0–20 volt moving-coil voltmeter.

Before testing the ignition circuit check that the battery is in a fully-charged state.

Wiring—ignition switch to coil

(1) Connect the voltmeter between the cable connected to the + (positive) terminal of the ignition coil and a good earth point.

(2) Switch on the ignition and note the voltmeter reading:

    (*a*) A voltmeter reading of approximately battery voltage indicates that the wiring between the ignition switch and ignition coil is satisfactory.

    (*b*) No voltmeter reading indicates an open circuit between the ignition switch and the coil.

Coil primary winding

(3) Disconnect the cable from the coil — (negative) terminal.

(4) Connect the voltmeter between the — (negative) terminal and a good earth point.

(5) Switch on the ignition and note the voltmeter reading:

    (*a*) A voltmeter reading of approximately battery voltage indicates that the coil primary winding is satisfactory.

    (*b*) No voltmeter reading indicates an open circuit of the primary winding.

Distributor points, L.T. wiring and earth

(6) With the original connections restored to the coil, connect the voltmeter between the — (negative) terminal and a good earth.

(7) Remove the distributor cap.

(8) Switch on the ignition, and whilst observing the voltmeter reading open the distributor points.

    (*a*) With the points open a voltmeter reading of approximately the battery voltage should be registered, indicating that the distributor low tension wiring, earth connection, and the contact breaker points are satisfactory.

    (*b*) If no reading is registered when the points are open, check that the distributor is correctly earthed; check the L.T. cable between the distributor and coil for continuity; check the contact breaker capacitor by substitution.

Coil secondary winding and capacitor

(9) Withdraw the coil H.T. lead from the distributor cap.

(10) Remove the distributor cap.

(11) Switch on the ignition.

(12) Hold the end of the H.T. lead $\frac{1}{4}$ in. (6 mm.) away from the engine block and 'flick' the points open.

    (*a*) With each flick of the points a spark should occur between the end of the H.T. lead and the block.

    (*b*) If the spark is weak or no spark occurs, check the capacitor by substitution as in 13 to 15.

Capacitor—by substitution

(13) Disconnect the existing capacitor at the contact breaker.

(14) Connect a test capacitor between the distributor L.T. terminal and earth.

(15) Switch on the ignition, hold the coil H.T. lead $\frac{1}{4}$ in. (6 mm.) away from the engine block and flick the points open.

    (*a*) If a good spark occurs the original capacitor is faulty.

    (*b*) If no spark occurs the secondary winding of the coil is faulty.

Rotor arm insulation

(16) Switch on the ignition, hold the coil H.T. lead $\frac{1}{8}$ in. (3 mm.) away from the rotor electrode, and flick the points open.

    (*a*) If no spark occurs the rotor arm insulation is satisfactory.

    (*b*) If a spark occurs the rotor arm must be renewed.

Sprite and Midget. Issue 1. 29459   *Ba*.3

97

SECTION C

THE COOLING SYSTEM

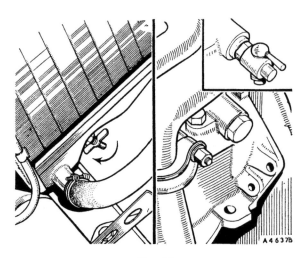

Fig. C.1

(Left) Access to the radiator drain tap is gained from beneath the front of the car. (Early cars only)

(Right) The drain tap or plug (later models) for the cylinder block is located on the right-hand side of the block at the rear

Section C.1

LUBRICATION

Early cars

Remove the plug from the water pump body and add a small quantity of one of the recommended greases. Do not pressure lubricate the water pump, or the seal may be damaged.

Later cars

The greasing plug has been deleted from the water pump as no lubrication is required.

Section C.2

RADIATOR FILLER CAP

The cooling system is under appreciable pressure while the engine is hot, and the radiator filler cap must be removed very carefully or left in position until the water has cooled.

If it is necessary to remove the filler cap when the engine is hot it is absolutely essential to remove it gradually, and the filler spout is provided with a specially shaped cam to enable this to be done easily.

Unscrew the cap slowly till the retaining tongues are felt to engage the small lobes on the end of the filler spout cam, and wait until the pressure in the radiator is fully released before finally removing the cap.

It is advisable to protect the hand against escaping steam when removing the cap.

C.2

Section C.3

DRAINING AND FLUSHING THE SYSTEM

Early cars

Draining

Remove the radiator header tank filler cap.

Open both drain points (see Fig. C.1) and the heater tap.

Flushing (See Editor's note at end of Section C.)

To ensure efficient circulation of the coolant and to reduce the formation of scale and sediment in the radiator the system should be periodically flushed with clean running water. The water should be allowed to run through until it comes out clear from the drain tap. This service is preferably carried out before adding anti-freeze in the autumn, and again when the anti-freeze is drained off for the summer.

If furring is excessive, remove the radiator as in Section C.5 and flush through in the reverse way to the flow, i.e. turn the radiator upside-down and let the water flow in through the bottom hose connection and out through the top. The use of radiator reverse-flush adaptor 18G 187 with a 1 in. (25·4 mm.) diameter water hose is recommended for this purpose.

Refilling

Close the drain points but leave the heater tap open.

Ensure that the water hose clips are tightened.

Fill the system through the filler in the radiator header tank until the water is up to the level indicator strip.

Check that the heater unit is completely full by disconnecting the heater outlet pipe.

Avoid overfilling when anti-freeze is in use to prevent unnecessary loss on expansion.

Screw the filler cap firmly into position.

The cooling system is unsuitable for use with anti-freeze mixtures having an alcohol base owing to the high temperatures attained in the top tank. Only anti-freeze mixtures of the ethylene glycol or glycerine type should be employed.

Later cars

Draining

(1) Remove the radiator filler plug.

(2) Remove drain plug from the radiator return pipe. To drain the cooling system on cars not fitted with drain taps or plugs, slacken the hose clip and remove the bottom hose at its connection to the radiator.

(3) Remove cylinder block drain plug.

Flushing

(4) Carry out operations (1) to (3).

(5) Insert a hose pipe into the radiator filler plug orifice and allow water to pass through the system until clean water flows from both drain points.

Filling

(6) Refit both drain plugs.

(7) Open the heater water valve.

(8) Fill the system through the radiator filler orifice and fit the filler plug.

Sprite and Midget. Issue 5. 82963

(9) Top up the expansion tank to the half-full point and refit the expansion tank cap.

(10) Run the engine at a fast idle speed for approximately 30 seconds.

(11) Stop the engine and top up the system through the radiator filler.

(12) Refit the filler plug and run the engine until normal operating temperature is reached.

(13) Stop the engine and allow the system to cool.

(14) When the system has cooled, remove the expansion tank cap, and top up the tank to the half-full point.

(15) Refit the expansion tank cap.

Section C.4

THERMOSTAT

Removing

Drain the cooling system (Section C.3). Disconnect the outlet hose from the outlet elbow. Remove the securing nuts and spring washers from the thermostat cover and lift the cover away from its studs. Remove the paper joint washer and lift out the thermostat.

Examine the thermostat for damage and check that the valve is in the closed position. If the thermostat is damaged or the valve is in the open position, renew the thermostat.

To test the thermostat, immerse it in water heated to the temperature marked on the thermostat, the valve will open if the thermostat is functioning correctly. If the valve fails to open renew the thermostat.

IMPORTANT. In warm climates where the thermostat is removed as a permanent measure, it is essential that a thermostat blanking sleeve is fitted. Failure to fit a sleeve will result in higher operating temperatures and possible damage.

Refitting

Installation of the thermostat assembly is the reverse of the removal procedure. Fit a new paper joint washer if the existing one is damaged.

Section C.5

RADIATOR AND EXPANSION TANK

Radiator—early cars

Removing

Drain the cooling system (see Section C.3). Release the hose clip on the thermostat housing and remove the hose from the housing extension. Remove the radiator bottom hose by releasing the clips on the bottom radiator connection. Remove the fresh air induction pipe from its connection on the front cowling. Remove the temperature gauge thermal element from the right-hand side of the radiator. Remove the bolts which secure the radiator to the support brackets and remove the radiator.

Refitting

Reverse the removal procedure.

Radiator—later cars

Removing

(1) Drain the cooling system (Section C.3).

(2) Remove the radiator grille (Section R.3).

(3) Disconnect the top, bottom, and expansion hoses from the radiator connections.

(4) Remove the two nuts and screws securing the top radiator cowl plate to the body.

(5) Slacken the two nuts and screws securing the bottom radiator cowl plate to the body.

(6) Remove the four radiator side securing bolts.

(7) Lift out the radiator complete with cowl.

(8) Disconnect the return hose from the cylinder block.

(9) Remove the two bolts securing the radiator bottom return pipe and remove the pipe complete with hoses.

Refitting

(10) Reverse the removing procedure then refill the cooling system.

Expansion tank

Removing

(1) Remove the filler cap.

(2) Disconnect the spill hose from the radiator connection.

(3) Unscrew the tank mounting screws and remove the expansion tank complete with spill hose.

Refitting

(4) Reverse the removing procedure in (2) and (3), half fill the tank with coolant and refit the filler cap.

Section C.6

FAN BELT

Adjusting

To adjust the dynamo and fan belt tension slacken the two dynamo pivot bolts, release the bolt on the slotted adjusting link, and raise the dynamo bodily until the belt tension is correct. Tighten the bolts with the dynamo held in this position. A gentle hand-pull only must be exerted on the dynamo, otherwise the tension will be excessive and undue strain will be thrown on the dynamo bearings.

The belt should be sufficiently tight to prevent slip, yet it must be possible to move it laterally about 1 in. (2·54 cm.) at the centre of its longest run.

Removing

Slacken the dynamo pivot and adjusting link bolts. Push the dynamo down, release the belt from the crankshaft pulley, and remove the belt.

Section C.7

WATER PUMP

Removing

(1) Remove the radiator (Section C.5).
(2) Remove the fan retaining screws and withdraw the fan.
(3) Slacken the air pump mounting screws and remove the pump drive belt.
(4) Remove the air pump adjusting link bolt, raise the air pump as high as the hoses will allow, then tighten the mounting bolts to retain the pump.
(5) Slacken the dynamo mounting bolts and remove the fan belt.
(6) Remove the two dynamo top mounting bolts and swing the dynamo down so that it rests on the wing valance.
(7) Disconnect the by-pass hose from the water pump.
(8) Disconnect the radiator bottom hose from the water pump and heater tube.
(9) Remove the four water pump retaining screws and withdraw the pump from the cylinder block.

Dismantling

(10) Withdraw the bearing locating wire.
(11) Pull the fan hub from the pump spindle.
(12) Tap the spindle rearwards to remove the spindle and bearing assembly from the pump.
(13) Pull the impeller from the spindle and then remove the seal.

Inspection

(14) Check the bearing and spindle for signs of wear and damage, the complete assembly must be renewed if worn or damaged.
(15) Renew the seal if the pump was leaking or if the seal shows signs of wear or damage.
(16) Check that the fan hub has retained its interference fit to the spindle, renew the hub if the correct fit has been lost.

Reassembling (Fig. C.2).

(17) Check the fit of the hub to the spindle, and renew the hub if necessary. The hub must be fitted with its face flush with the end of the spindle B.
(18) Press the spindle bearing assembly into the case and take measurement E; adjust the position of the spindle bearing assembly to obtain the correct measurement.
   (a) On pumps fitted with the early-type seal and thrower check the bearing to thrower clearance D, before fitting the spindle.
   (b) On pumps fitted with a greaser plug, align the holes in the bearing and body A.
(19) Fit a new seal, lubricate the seal with a mineral-based oil immediately prior to assembly.
(20) Press the impeller onto the spindle, ensuring that the correct running clearance C is maintained between the impeller vanes and the pump body.

1

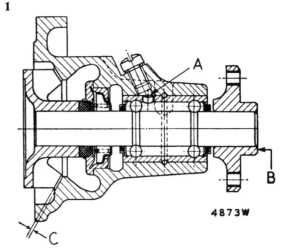

4873W

2

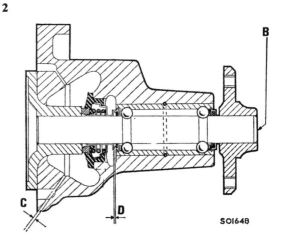

SO1648

3

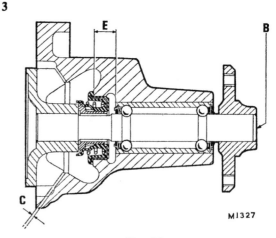

M1327

Fig. C.2

Section through the water pumps

1. With grease plug.   2. Sealed type.
3. Sealed type, bearing thrower deleted, pressure-balanced seal.
A. Bearing lubricating hole.
B. Hub face flush with spindle.
C. ·020 to ·030 in. (·51 to ·76 mm.) clearance.
D. ·042 to ·062 in. (1·1 to 1·6 mm.) clearance.
E. Distance from rear face of spindle bearing (outer track) to seal housing shoulder should be ·534 in. (13·56 mm.).

C.4

Sprite and Midget. Issue 8. 82963

Section C.8

TEMPERATURE GAUGE

A temperature gauge unit, consisting of a thermal element and dial indicator, is fitted to the vehicle. The thermal element is held in the radiator header tank by a gland nut. The dial indicator is situated in the instrument panel and is connected to the element by a capillary tube filled with mercury.

Damage to any of the above-mentioned parts will necessitate the renewal of the complete temperature gauge unit.

The combined water temperature and oil pressure gauges are of integral construction, and should one of these instruments fail, both will have to be renewed.

Section C.9 (See Editor's note at end of Section C.)

FROST PRECAUTIONS

Water, when it freezes, expands, and if precautions are not taken there is considerable risk of bursting the radiator, cylinder block, or heater (where fitted). Such damage may be avoided by draining the cooling system when the vehicle is left for any length of time in frosty weather, or by adding anti-freeze to the water.

As the cooling system of the vehicle is pressurized relatively high temperatures are developed in the radiator upper tank. For this reason anti-freeze solutions having an alcohol base are unsuitable owing to their high evaporation rate producing rapid loss of coolant and a consequent interruption of the circulation of coolant.

Only anti-freeze of the ethylene glycol or glycerine type is suitable for use in the cooling system. We recommend owners to use Bluecol Anti-freeze (non-corrosive)

in order to protect the cooling system during frosty weather and reduce corrosion to a minimum. We also approve the use of any anti-freeze which conforms to Specification B.S.3151 or B.S.3152.

Before adding anti-freeze mixture to the radiator it is advisable to clean out the cooling system thoroughly by swilling out the passages with a hose inserted in the filler cap while keeping the drain taps open.

Anti-freeze can remain in the cooling system for two years provided that the specific gravity of the coolant is checked periodically and anti-freeze added as required. Specialized equipment is necessary to check the specific gravity, which can be obtained from the anti-freeze manufacturer.

After the second winter, drain the system and flush out. Refill with fresh water or the recommended anti-freeze solution.

Only top up when the cooling system is at its normal running temperature, in order to avoid losing anti-freeze due to expansion.

Make sure that the cooling system is water-tight, examine all joints, and replace any defective rubber hose with new.

The correct quantities of anti-freeze for different degrees of frost resistance are given in the table above.

No provision is made for draining the heater or expansion tank and it is therefore essential that the cooling system is filled with an anti-freeze solution when the vehicle is operating in freezing conditions.

Refer below for the percentage of approved anti-freeze necessary for the required protection.

After adding the required amount of anti-freeze to the system, add a ¼ pint of neat anti-freeze to the coolant in the expansion tank.

Anti-freeze	Commences to freeze		Frozen solid		Amounts of anti-freeze					
					Pts.		U.S. Pts.		Litres	
%	°C.	°F.	°C.	°F.	Mk. I & II	Mk. III	Mk. I & II	Mk. III	Mk. I & II	Mk. III
25	—13	9	—26	—15	2¾	1½	3	2	1·5	·85
33⅓	—19	—2	—36	—33	3½	2	4	2½	2	1·15
50	—36	—33	—48	—53	5½	3	6	3½	3	1·17

EDITOR'S NOTES

C. The Cooling System

Flushing the system

A more thorough job of flushing can be done if the thermostat is removed, allowing water to flow in the block as well as the radiator.

Frost precaution

An anti-freeze hydrometer is used to check the specific gravity of the coolant solution. With this device, a small quantity of coolant is drawn into a tube and the position of a glass float indicates the specific gravity of the solution, usually in terms of the temperature at which ice begins to form.

SECTION D

THE FUEL SYSTEM

† These operations must be followed by an exhaust emission check

GENERAL DESCRIPTION

The fuel system comprises a fuel tank mounted below the luggage compartment, an A.C. 'Y' type mechanically operated fuel pump, and twin S.U. HS2 semi-down-draught automatic expanding choke-type carburetters.

The level of the fuel in the tank is registered electrically by a meter on the instrument panel.

The air cleaner fitted to the carburetters has a renewable paper-element filter to trap road dust and other harmful matter from the air before it reaches the carburetters.

Section D.1

LUBRICATION

Carburetter dampers

Unscrew the cap from the top of each suction chamber and refill the hollow piston rod with thin engine oil until the level is $\frac{1}{2}$ in. (13 mm.) from the top. Under no circumstances must heavy-bodied lubricant be used. Failure to lubricant the piston damper will cause piston flutter and reduce acceleration.

Section D.2

FUEL TANK

Removing

From within the luggage compartment release the securing clips and draw back the hose from the fuel tank inlet. Raise the vehicle to a workable height, remove the drain plug, and drain the petrol into a container.

Disconnect the fuel outlet pipe at its union with the tank. Remove the nuts and washers securing the tank to the under side of the body; at the same time steady the tank with a jack.

Lower the tank sufficiently to allow access to the fuel tank gauge unit and remove the Lucar connector.

The fuel tank can now be removed.

Refitting

Reverse the removal procedure when refitting.

Section D.3

FUEL TANK GAUGE UNIT

Remove the fuel tank as described in Section D.2.

Remove the screws securing the gauge unit to the tank and withdraw the complete assembly, taking care not to strain or bend the float lever.

When replacing the gauge unit a new joint washer must be fitted and a suitable sealing compound employed to make a fuel-tight joint.

D.2

Section D.4

FUEL PUMP

Removing

Disconnect the pipe unions, remove the set screws securing the petrol pump to the engine crankcase, and remove the pump.

Dismantling

Remove the securing bolt and lift off the top cover. Remove the filter gauze and cork sealing washer.

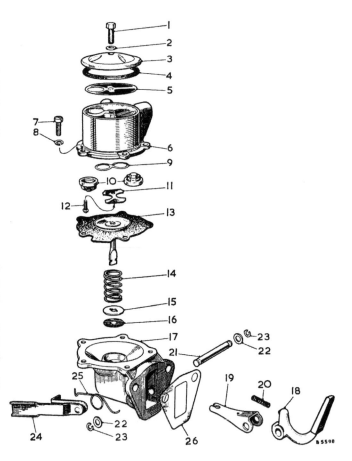

Fig. D.1

The A.C. 'Y' type fuel pump components

1.	Cover screw.	14.	Spring.
2.	Gasket.	15.	Metal washer.
3.	Filter cover.	16.	Fabric washer.
4.	Filter cover gasket.	17.	Pump body.
5.	Filter gauze.	18.	Rocker arm.
6.	Upper casting.	19.	Rocker arm link.
7.	Screw.	20.	Rocker arm spring.
8.	Lock washer.	21.	Rocker arm pin.
9.	Valve gasket.	22.	Washer.
10.	Valve assembly.	23.	Clip.
11.	Valve retainer.	24.	Priming lever.
12.	Screw.	25.	Spring.
13.	Diaphragm.	26.	Gasket.

Sprite and Midget.   Issue 5.   10858

106

Remove the upper chamber securing screws and separate the two halves of the pump body. To assist when reassembling, it is advisable to mark the two halves of the pump body before dismantling.

Remove the securing screws, valve plate, inlet and delivery valve assemblies, and gasket.

Remove the diaphragm and pull-rod assembly by rotating it through 90°. The diaphragm spring, metal washer, and fibre washer can now be removed.

Removal of the retaining circlip and washer from either side permits the rocker arm pivot pin to be drawn out, which in turn will release the rocker arm, connecting link, washers, and anti-rattle spring.

Reassembling

Reassembly is the reverse of the removal procedure, with attention being paid to the following.

The fitting of the rocker arm pin can be simplified by first inserting a piece of ·240 in. (6·1 mm.) diameter rod through the pin hole in one side of the body far enough to engage the rocker arm washers and link, then pushing in the rocker arm pin from the opposite side, removing the guide rod as the pin takes up its proper position. Under certain conditions it is possible to insert the diaphragm pull rod too far through the slot in the operating link, with the result that the connecting link, instead of engaging the two small slots in the pull rod, rides on the pull rod shoulder.

Correct assembly can be checked by measuring the distance from the top of the pump body to the upper diaphragm protector when the diaphragm is held at the top of its stroke by the return spring. A measurement

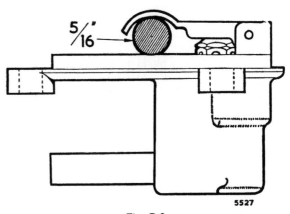

Fig. D.3

The method of checking the correct adjustment of the hinged lever (early cars)

of approximately $\frac{9}{16}$ in. (14·3 mm.) indicates correct assembly, whereas one of $\frac{3}{16}$ in. (4·8 mm.) proves that the assembly is unsatisfactory.

Push the rocker arm towards the pump until the diaphragm is level with the body flanges.

Place the upper half of the pump into the proper position, as shown by the marks made on the flanges before dismantling, and refit.

Refitting

Reverse the procedure outlined for the removal from the engine. Ensure that the rocker arm is correctly positioned against the eccentric on the camshaft, as there is a possibility of inadvertently getting the rocker arm under the eccentric or to one side, when damage will result on tightening the bolts. After refitting, the engine should be run for a short time and pipe unions and pump examined for fuel leakage.

Section D.5

CARBURETTERS

IMPORTANT. The instructions given in **this section** for adjusting, dismantling and reassembling the carburetters applies only to **cars not fitted with exhaust emission control equipment.** Carburetters fitted to **cars with exhaust emission control equipment** must be tuned and serviced in accordance with the instructions given in **Workshop Manual Supplement AKD 4957.**

Piston sticking

The piston assembly comprises the suction disc and the piston forming the choke, into which is inserted the hardened and ground piston rod which engages in a bearing in the centre of the suction chamber and in which is inserted the jet needle. The suction disc, piston, and needle all have suitable clearances to prevent sticking; if sticking does occur the whole assembly should be cleaned carefully and the piston rod lubricated with a spot of thin oil. No oil must be applied to any part

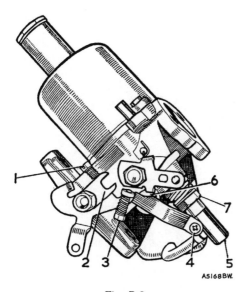

Fig. D.2

The HS2-type carburetter

1. Throttle adjusting screw.
2. Butterfly operating fork.
3. Fast-idle adjusting screw.
4. Jet link securing screw.
5. Jet head.
6. Float-chamber securing nut.
7. Jet adjusting nut.

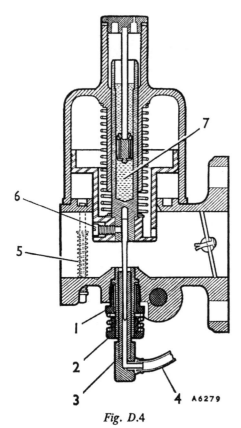

Fig. D.4

A section through the carburetter showing:

1. Jet locking nut.   4. Nylon fuel pipe.
2. Jet adjusting nut.   5. Piston lifting pin.
3. Jet head.   6. Needle securing screw.
     7. Piston damper oil well.

except the piston rod. A sticking piston can be ascertained by removing the piston damper and lifting the piston with a pencil or similar instrument; the piston should come up quite freely and fall back smartly onto the jet bridge when released. On no account should the piston return spring be stretched or its tension be altered in an attempt to improve its rate of return.

Water and dirt in one of the carburetters

Should this be suspected, start the engine, open the throttle, and block up the air inlet momentarily, keeping the throttle open until the engine starts to race.

If the jet is completely blocked and the engine will not run, the jet must be removed and thoroughly cleaned.

Float-chamber flooding

This is indicated by fuel flowing from the breather hole in the top of the float-chamber lid below the main fuel feed pipe, and is generally caused by grit between the float-chamber needle and its guide. The float-chamber lid should be removed and the needle and its guide thoroughly cleaned.

Float needle sticking

If the engine stops, apparently through lack of fuel when there is plenty in the tank and the pump is working

properly, the probable cause is a sticking float needle. An easy test for this is to disconnect the pipe from the pump to the carburetters and turn the crankshaft by operating the starter while the end of the pipe is directed onto a pad of cloth or into a container.

If fuel is delivered, starvation is almost certainly being caused by a float needle sticking to its seating, and the float-chamber lid should therefore be removed and the needle and seating cleaned and refitted.

At the same time it will be advisable to clean out the entire fuel feed system as this trouble is caused by foreign matter in the fuel, and unless this is removed it is likely to recur. It is of no use whatever renewing any of the component parts of the carburetters, and the only cure is to make sure that the fuel tank and pipe lines are entirely free from any kind of foreign matter or sticky substance capable of causing trouble.

Adjustments

Slow-running is governed by the setting of the jet adjusting nuts and the throttle adjusting screws, both of which must be correctly set and synchronized if satisfactory results are to be obtained.

Before blaming the carburetter settings for bad slow-running make certain that the trouble is not caused by badly adjusted distributor contact points, faulty plugs, incorrect valve clearance, or faulty valves and springs.

Slow-running adjustment and synchronization

When the engine is fully run in the slow running may require adjustment. This must only be carried out when the engine has reached its normal running temperature.

As the needle size is determined during engine development, tuning of the carburetters is confined to correct idling setting. Slacken the actuating arms on the throttle spindle interconnection. Close both throttles fully by unscrewing the throttle adjusting screws, then open each throttle by screwing down each idling adjustment screw one turn.

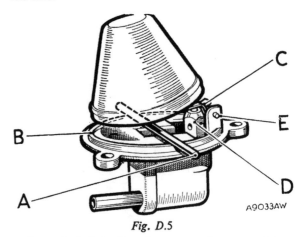

Fig. D.5

The method of checking the correct adjustment of the float lever (later cars)

A. $\frac{1}{8}$ to $\frac{3}{16}$ in. (3·18 to   C. Angle of float lever.
     4·76 mm.).   D. Float needle and seat assembly.
B. Machined lip.   E. Lever hinge pin.

Sprite and Midget. Issue 5. 10858

Remove the pistons and suction chambers and disconnect the choke control cable. Screw the jet adjusting nuts until each jet is flush with the bridge of its carburetter, or as near to this as possible (both jets being in the same relative position to the bridge of their respective carburetters). Replace the pistons and suction chamber assemblies and check that the pistons fall freely onto the bridge of the carburetters (by means of the piston lifting pins). Turn down the jet adjusting nut two complete turns (12 flats).

Restart the engine, and adjust the throttle adjusting screws to give the desired idling speed by moving each throttle adjusting screw an equal amount. By listening to the hiss in the intakes, adjust the throttle adjusting screws until the intensity of the hiss is similar on both intakes. This will synchronize the throttles.

When this is satisfactory the mixture should be adjusted by screwing each jet adjusting nut up or down by the same amount until the fastest idling speed is obtained consistent with even firing. During this adjustment it is necessary that the jets are pressed upwards to ensure that they are in contact with the adjusting nuts.

As the mixture is adjusted the engine will probably run faster, and it may therefore be necessary to unscrew the throttle adjusting screws a little, each by the same amount, to reduce the speed.

Now check the mixture strength by lifting the piston of the front carburetter by approximately $\frac{1}{32}$ in. (1 mm.), when:

(1) If the engine speed increases, this indicates that the mixture strength of the front carburetter is too rich.

(2) If the engine speed immediately decreases, this indicates that the mixture strength of the front carburetter is too weak.

(3) If the engine speed momentarily increases very slightly, then the mixture strength of the front carburetter is correct.

Repeat the operation at the rear carburetter, and after adjustment re-check the front carburetter, since both carburetters are interdependent.

When the mixture is correct the exhaust note should be regular and even. If it is irregular, with a splashy type of misfire and colourless exhaust, the mixture is too weak. If there is a regular or rhythmical type of misfire in the exhaust beat, together with a blackish exhaust, then the mixture is too rich.

Throttle linkage

The throttle on each carburetter is operated by a lever and pin, with the pin working in a forked lever attached to the throttle spindle. A clearance between the pin and fork must be maintained when the throttle is closed and the engine at rest to prevent any load from the accelerator linkage and return springs being transferred to the throttle butterfly and spindle.

To set this clearance: with the throttle shaft levers free on the throttle shaft, put a ·012 in. (·3 mm.) feeler between the throttle shaft stop at the top and the car-

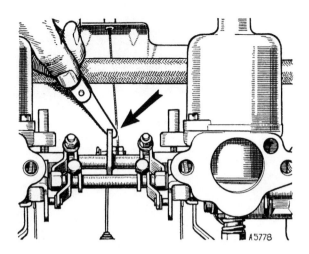

Fig. D.6

The feeler between the throttle shaft stop and the carburetter heat shield

buretter heat shield. Move the throttle shaft lever downwards until the lever pin rests lightly on the lower arm of the fork in the carburetter throttle lever. Tighten the clamp bolt of the throttle shaft lever at this position. When both carburetters have been dealt with, remove the feeler. The pins on the throttle shaft levers should then have clearance in the forks.

Reconnect the choke cable, ensuring that the jet heads return against the lower face of the jet adjusting nuts when the choke control is pushed fully in.

Pull out the mixture control knob on the dash panel until the linkage is about to move the carburetter jets (a minimum of $\frac{1}{4}$ in. or 6 mm.) and adjust the fast idle adjusting screws to give an engine speed of about 1,000 r.p.m. when hot.

Float-chambers

The position of the hinged lever in the float-chamber must be such that the level of the float (and therefore the height of the fuel at the jet) is correct.

This is checked by inserting a round bar between the hinged lever and the machined lip of the float-chamber lid. The end of the lever should just rest on the bar (see Fig. D3. or D.5) when the needle is on its seating. If this is not so, the lever should be reset at the point where the end meets the shank.

Do not bend the shank, which must be perfectly flat and at right angles to the needle when it is on its seating.

Centring the jet

When the suction piston is lifted by the spring-loaded piston lifting pin it should fall freely and hit the inside jet bridge with a soft, metallic click— that is, with the jet adjusting nut (2, Fig. D4.) in its topmost position.

If this click is not audible, but is so when the test is repeated with the jet in the fully lowered position, then the jet unit requires recentring on the needle.

Sprite and Midget. Issue 5. 65317   *D.5*

109

D

THE CARBURETTER COMPONENTS

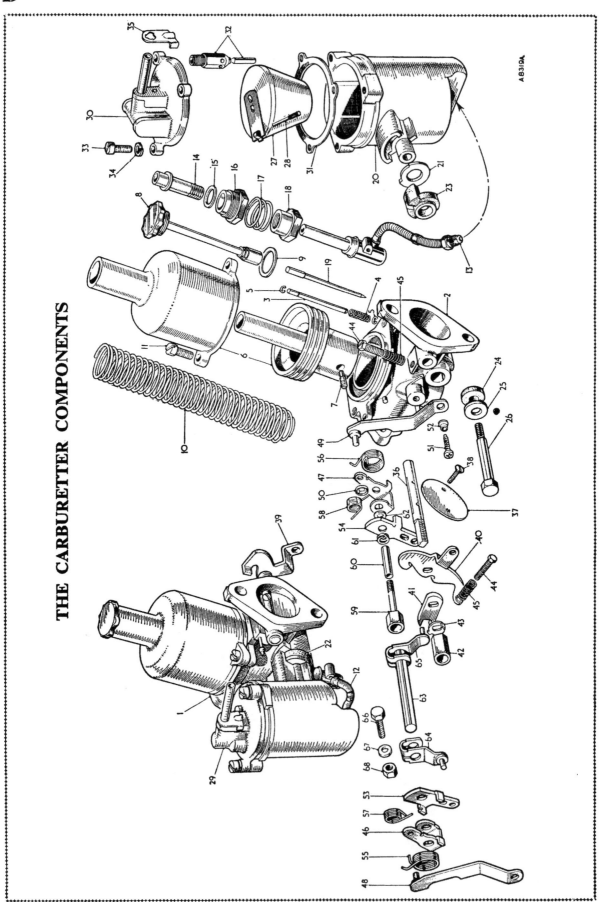

110

KEY TO THE CARBURETTER COMPONENTS

No.	Description	No.	Description	No.	Description
1.	Carburetter body (left).	24.	Washer (rubber).	46.	Pick-up lever (left carburetter).
2.	Carburetter body (right).	25.	Washer (steel).	47.	Pick-up lever (right carburetter).
3.	Piston lifting pin.	26.	Bolt.	48.	Link (left carburetter).
4.	Spring.	27.	Float assembly.	49.	Link (right carburetter).
5.	Circlip.	28.	Lever pin.	50.	Washer.
6.	Piston chamber assembly.	29.	Float-chamber lid (left carburetter).	51.	Screw.
7.	Screw.	30.	Float-chamber lid (right carburetter).	52.	Bush.
8.	Cap and damper assembly.	31.	Washer.	53.	Cam lever (left carburetter).
9.	Fibre washer.	32.	Needle and seat assembly.	54.	Cam lever (right carburetter).
10.	Piston spring.	33.	Screw.	55.	Pick-up lever spring (left carburetter).
11.	Screw.	34.	Spring washer.	56.	Pick-up lever spring (right carburetter).
12.	Jet assembly (left carburetter).	35.	Baffle plate.	57.	Cam lever spring (left carburetter).
13.	Jet assembly (right carburetter).	36.	Throttle spindle.	58.	Cam lever spring (right carburetter).
14.	Bearing.	37.	Throttle disc.	59.	Bolt.
15.	Washer.	38.	Screw.	60.	Tube.
16.	Screw.	39.	Throttle return lever (left carburetter).	61.	Spring washer.
17.	Spring.	40.	Throttle return lever (right carburetter).	62.	Distance piece.
18.	Screw.	41.	Lost motion lever.	63.	Jet rod.
19.	Needle.	42.	Nut.	64.	Lever and pin assembly (left carburetter).
20.	Float-chamber.	43.	Tab washer.	65.	Lever and pin assembly (right carburetter).
21.	Support washer.	44.	Throttle screw stop.	66.	Bolt.
22.	Rubber grommet (left carburetter).	45.	Spring.	67.	Washer.
23.	Rubber grommet (right carburetter).			68.	Nut.

Sprite and Midget. Issue 2. 65317   D.7

111

Disconnect the rod between the jet lever and the jet head.

Unscrew the union holding the nylon feed tube into the base of the float-chamber, and withdraw the tube and jet together. Unscrew the jet adjusting nut and remove the lock spring. Replace the adjusting nut and screw it right up to its topmost position, then replace the jet and feed tube.

Slacken off the large jet locking nut (1, Fig. D.4) until the jet bearing is just free to rotate by finger pressure.

With the damper removed and using a pencil on top of the piston rod, gently press the piston and needle down onto the jet bridge.

Tighten the jet locking nut, observing that the jet head is still in its correct angular position.

Lift the piston and check that it falls freely and evenly, hitting the jet bridge with a soft, metallic click. Then fully lower the jet and re-check to see if there is any difference in the sound of the impact; if there is and the second test produces a sharper impact sound, the centring operation will have to be repeated until successful. Remove the adjusting nut and replace the lock spring after the conclusion of the operation.

Needles

Remove the piston and suction chamber assembly. Slacken the needle clamping screw, extract the needle and check its identifying mark (see GENERAL DATA). Refit the correct needle ensuring that the shoulder on the shank is flush with the piston base.

Removing

Remove the air cleaners as detailed in Section D.6. Disconnect the mixture and throttle control cables, the suction advance pipe, and the fuel delivery hose from their respective positions on the carburetters.

Release the interconnecting coupling tension springs and the throttle stop return spring.

Remove the nuts and spring washers securing the carburetters to the manifold flanges. Lift off the carburetter assemblies as one unit. The carburetter interconnecting couplings are fitted in sleeved nuts, and when the carburetter assemblies are removed the couplings can be lifted away from both carburetters.

Refitting

Reverse the removal procedure when refitting. It should be noted that the heat shield fitted between the carburetters and the manifold flanges has gaskets, which should be renewed if the shield has been removed.

Section D.6

AIR CLEANERS

Removing

Disconnect the breather pipe from the front air cleaner.

Remove the centre-securing nut and washer on the tie bracket.

Remove the through-bolts and lift away the air cleaners from the carburetter assemblies.

NOTE.—Servicing of the paper-element-type air cleaners should be carried out at regular intervals.

In countries where dusty operating conditions exist this operation should be carried out at more frequent intervals.

Refitting

Refitting is a reversal of the removal procedure.

D.8   Sprite and Midget. Issue 2. 65317

112

Section Da

THE FUEL SYSTEM

The information given in this Section refers specifically to the Sprite (Mk. III and IV) and Midget (Mk. II and III) and must be used in conjunction with Section D

GENERAL DESCRIPTION

The fuel system is the same as that used on earlier cars, with the exception of the pump which is an S.U. AUF 200 [or AUF 216. The fuel pump S.U. Type AUF 305, used on some late models is covered in the Appendix on page 364.]

Section Da.1

FUEL PUMP

Removing and refitting

The pump is situated beneath the luggage compartment on the right-hand side. For removal: disconnect the battery earth lead and detach the earth and supply leads from the terminals on the pump.

Disconnect the inlet, outlet, and vent pipe connections.

Remove the two bolts securing the pump bracket to the rear foot-well panel.

When replacing, ensure that the outlet is vertically above the inlet port, i.e. the inlet and outlet nozzles are horizontal.

Also ensure a good earth connection.

Dismantling

Contact breaker

(1) Remove the insulated sleeve, terminal nut, and connector together with its shakeproof washer. Remove the tape seal (if fitted) and take off the end-cover.

(2) Remove the condenser (if fitted) from its clip, unscrew the 5 B.A. screw which holds the contact blade to the pedestal. This will allow the washer, the long-coil lead, and the contact blade to be removed.

Coil housing and diaphragm

(3) Unscrew the coil housing securing screws, using a thick-bladed screwdriver to avoid damaging the screw heads.

(4) Remove the earthing screw.

(5) *Roller type.* Hold the coil housing over a bench or receptacle to prevent the 11 brass rollers from being damaged or lost as they come free, unscrew the diaphragm assembly anti-clockwise until the armature spring pushes it free of the housing.
Guide plate type. Turn back the edge of the diaphragm and carefully lever the two end lobes of the armature guide plate from the recess in the coil housing, unscrew the diaphragm assembly anti-clockwise until the armature spring pushes it free of the housing. Remove the armature guide from the diaphragm assembly.

Pedestal and rocker

(6) Remove the end-cover seal washer, unscrew the terminal nut, and remove the lead washer; this will have flattened on the terminal tag and thread, and is best cut away with cutting pliers or a knife. Unscrew the two 2 B.A. screws, holding the pedestal to the coil housing, remove the earth terminal tag together with the condenser clip (if fitted). Tip the

pedestal and withdraw the terminal stud from the terminal tag. The pedestal may now be removed with the rocker mechanism attached.

(7) Push out the hardened steel pin which holds the rocker mechanism to the pedestal.

Body and valves

(8) Unscrew the two 2 B.A. screws securing the spring clamp plate holding the inlet and outlet nozzles. Remove the nozzles, filter, and valve assemblies.

Inspection

If gum formation has occurred in the fuel used in the pump, the parts in contact with the fuel will have become coated with a substance similar to varnish. This has a strong stale smell and may attack the neoprene diaphragm. Brass and steel parts so affected can be cleaned by being boiled in a 20 per cent. solution of caustic soda, dipped in a strong nitric acid solution, and finally washed in boiling water. Light alloy parts must be well-soaked in methylated spirit and then cleaned.

(1) Clean the pump and inspect for cracks, damaged joint faces, and threads.

(2) Examine the plastic valve assemblies for kinks or damage to the valve plates. They can best be checked by blowing and sucking with the mouth.

(3) Check that the narrow tongue on the valve cage, which is bent over to retain the valve and to prevent it being forced out of position, has not been distorted but allows a valve lift of approximately $\frac{1}{16}$ in. (1·6 mm.).

(4) Examine the valve recesses in the body for damage and corrosion; if it is impossible to remove the corrosion, or if the seat is pitted, the body must be discarded.

(5) Ensure that the coil housing vent tube is not blocked.

(6) Clean the filter with a brush and examine for fractures, renew if necessary.

(7) Examine the coil lead tag for security and the lead insulation for damage.

(8) Examine the contact breaker points for signs of burning and pitting; if this is evident, the rocker assembly and spring blade must be renewed.

(9) Examine the pedestal for cracks or other damage, particularly to the narrow ridge in the edge of the rectangular hole on which the contact blade rests.

(10) Examine the non-return vent valve in the end-cover (if fitted) for damage, ensure that the small ball valve is free to move.

(11) Examine the diaphragm for signs of deterioration.

(12) Renew the following parts: all fibre and cork washers, gaskets and 'O' section sealing rings, rollers showing signs of wear on periphery, damaged bolts and unions.

Reassembling

Pedestal and rocker

NOTE.—The steel pin which secures the rocker mechanism to the pedestal is specially hardened and must not be replaced by other than a genuine S.U. part.

Sprite and Midget. Issue 5. 82324

THE FUEL PUMP COMPONENTS

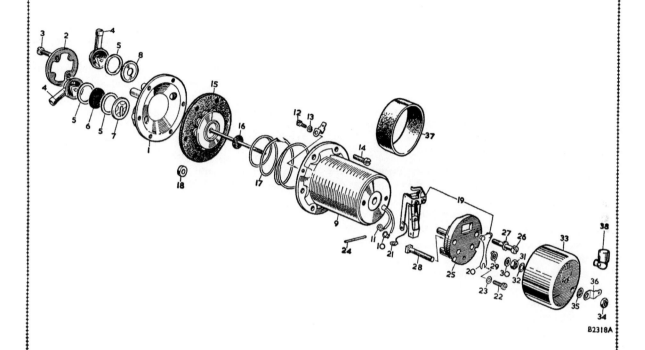

B2318A

No.	Description	No.	Description	No.	Description
1.	Body.	14.	Screw—housing to body.	27.	Washer—spring.
2.	Spring clamp plate.	15.	Diaphragm assembly.	28.	Screw for terminal.
3.	Screw.	16.	Impact washer.	29.	Washer—spring.
4.	Nozzle—inlet/outlet.	17.	Spring.	30.	Washer—lead—for screw.
5.	Sealing washer.	18.	Roller.	31.	Nut for screw.
6.	Filter.	19.	Rocker and blade.	32.	Spacer—nut to cover.
7.	Valve—inlet.	20.	Blade.	33.	Cover—end.
8.	Valve—outlet.	21.	Tag—2 B.A. terminal.	34.	Nut for cover.
9.	Housing—coil.	22.	Screw for blade.	35.	Washer—shakeproof.
10.	Tag—5 B.A. terminal.	23.	Washer—dished.	36.	Connector—Lucar.
11.	Tag—2 B.A. terminal.	24.	Spindle for contact breaker.	37.	Packing sleeve.
12.	Screw—earth.	25.	Pedestal.	38.	Non-return valve.
13.	Washer—spring.	26.	Screw—pedestal to housing.		

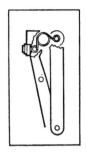 

A.9309A

*Fig. Da.*1

Fitting the rocker assembly to the pedestal: (inset) the correct position of the centre toggle spring after assembly

(1) Invert the pedestal and fit the rocker assembly to it by pushing the steel pin through the small holes in the rockers and pedestal struts. Then position the centre toggle so that, with the inner rocker spindle in tension against the rear of the contact point, the centre toggle spring is above the spindle on which the white rollers run.

This positioning is important to obtain the correct 'throw-over' action; it is also essential that the rockers are perfectly free to swing on the pivot pin and that the arms are not binding on the legs of the pedestal. If necessary, rockers can be squared-up with a pair of long-nosed pliers.

(2) Assemble the square-headed 2 B.A. terminal stud to the pedestal, the back of which is recessed to take the square head.

(3) Assemble the 2 B.A. spring washer and put the terminal stud through the 2 B.A. terminal tag, then fit the lead washer and the coned nut with its coned face to the lead washer. (This makes better contact than an ordinary flat washer and nut.) Tighten the 2 B.A. nut, and finally add the end-cover seal washer.

(4) Assemble the pedestal to the coil housing by fitting the two 2 B.A. pedestal screws, ensuring that the spring washer on the left-hand screw (9 o'clock position) is between the pedestal and the earthing tag.

(5) Tighten the screws, taking care to prevent the earthing tag from turning, as this will strain or break the earthing flex. Do not overtighten the screws or the pedestal will crack. **Do not fit the contact blade at this stage.**

Diaphragm assembly

(6) Place the armature spring into the coil housing with its larger diameter towards the coil.

(7) Before fitting the diaphragm, make sure that the impact washer is fitted to the armature (this is a small neoprene washer that fits in the armature

recess). Do not use jointing compound or dope on the diaphragm.

(8) Fit the diaphragm by inserting the spindle in the hole in the coil and screwing it into the threaded trunnion in the centre of the rocker assembly.

(9) Screw in the diaphragm until the rocker will not throw over; this must not be confused with jamming the armature on the coil housing internal steps.

(10) *Roller type.* With the pump held with the rocker end downwards, turn back the edge of the diaphragm and fit the 11 brass rollers into the recess in the coil housing.

On later-type rocker mechanisms with adjustable fingers fit the contact blade and adjust the finger settings as described under those headings, then carefully remove the contact blade.

(11) With the pump held horizontally, slowly unscrew the diaphragm while at the same time actuating it, until the rocker just throws over. Unscrew the diaphragm until the holes are aligned, then unscrew it a further quarter of a turn (four holes).

(12) *Roller type.* Press the centre of the armature and fit the retaining fork at the back of the rocker assembly.

Body components

(13) *Guide plate type.* Turn back the edge of the diaphragm and insert one end lobe of the armature guide plate into the recess between the armature and the coil housing. Progressively position all four lobes, then commencing in the centre and finishing with the two end ones, press the lobes firmly into the recess.

(14) Place the outlet valve assembly, tongue side uppermost, in the recess marked 'outlet', place a joint washer on top of the valve assembly, and complete by adding the outlet nozzle.

(15) Place the inlet valve assembly, tongue side downwards, in the recess marked 'inlet', follow this with a joint washer, then the filter, dome side upwards, then another joint washer, completing the assembly with the inlet nozzle.

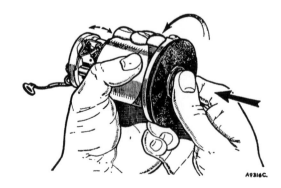

A9316C.

*Fig. Da.*2

Unscrew the diaphragm until the rocker just throws over

*Da.*4

Sprite and Midget. Issue 3. 10858

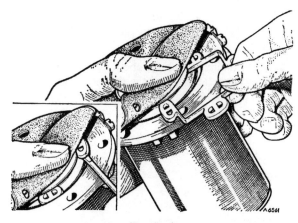

Fig. Da.3

Fitting the armature guide plate. (Inset), levering one of the end lobes from the recess

(16) Take care that both assemblies rest down evenly into their respective recesses. Position the nozzles as required, place the clamp plate on top, and tighten down firmly on to the body with the two 2 B.A. screws.

Body attachment
(19) Offer up the coil housing to the body—ensure correct seating between them.
(20) Line up the six securing holes, making sure that the cast lugs on the coil housing are at the bottom, insert the six 2 B.A. screws finger-tight. Fit the earthing screw with its Lucar connector.
(21) *Roller type.* Carefully remove the retaining fork from the rocker assembly and check that the rollers are correctly positioned.
(22) Tighten the securing screws in diagonal sequence.

Contact blade
(23) Fit the contact blade and coil lead to the pedestal with the 5 B.A. washer and screw.
(24) Adjust the contact blade so that the contact points on it are a little above the contact points on the rocker when the points are closed; also, that

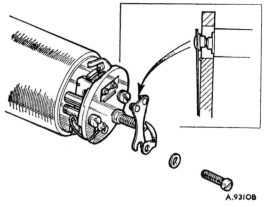

Fig. Da.4

Setting the correct relative position of blade and rocker contact points

when the contact points make or break, one pair of points wipe over the centre-line of the other in a symmetrical manner. As the contact blade is provided with a slot for the attachment screw, some degree of adjustment is possible.
(25) Tighten the contact blade attachment screw when the correct setting is obtained.

Contact gap setting
(26) Check that when the outer rocker is pressed on to the coil housing, the contact blade rests on the narrow rib or ridge which projects slightly above the main face of the pedestal. If it does not, slacken the contact blade attachment screw, swing the blade clear of the pedestal, and bend it downwards a sufficient amount so that when repositioned it rests against the rib lightly; over-tensioning of the blade will restrict the rocker travel.

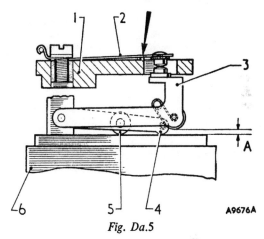

Fig. Da.5

The contact gap setting on earlier-type rocker assemblies

1. Pedestal.	4. Inner rocker.
2. Contact blade.	5. Trunnion.
3. Outer rocker.	6. Coil housing.

A = ·030 in. (·8 mm.).

Earlier-type rocker assemblies
(27) Check the gap between the points indirectly by carefully holding the contact blade against the rib on the pedestal without pressing against the tip. Then check if a ·030 in. (·8 mm.) feeler will pass between the fibre rollers and the face of the coil housing (A) (Fig. Da.5). If necessary, the tip of the blade can be set to correct the gap.

Modified rocker assemblies
(28) Check the lift of the contact blade tip above the top of the pedestal (A) (Fig. Da.6) with a feeler gauge, bend the stop finger beneath the pedestal, if necessary, to obtain a lift of ·035±·005 in. (·9±·13 mm.).
(29) Check the gap between the rocker finger and the coil housing with a feeler gauge (B) (Fig. Da.6), bend the stop finger, if necessary, to obtain a gap of ·070±·005 in. (1·8±1·3 mm.).

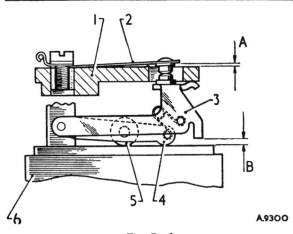

Fig. Da.6

The rocker finger settings on modified rocker assemblies

1. Pedestal.
2. Contact blade.
3. Outer rocker.
4. Inner rocker.
5. Trunnion.
6. Coil housing.

A = ·035 in. (·9 mm.).   B = ·070 in. (1·8 mm.).

End-cover

(30) Ensure that the end-cover seal washer is in position on the terminal stud, fit the bakelite end-cover, secure with the brass nut, fit the terminal tag or connector, and insulated sleeve.

(31) The pump is now ready for test.

Testing on a test stand

Preparation

(1) Churchill test rig:

Secure the pump in the clamping ring with the outlet connection uppermost. Connect to a 12-volt battery, and with the switch in the 'OFF' position, clip the connector to the pump. Connect the delivery and return of the correct bore to the pump.

S.U. test rig:

Mount the pump on the test stand, using the appropriate adaptor set according to the type of pump. Connect the feed and earth terminals to the test battery and check the contact gap setting as described under that heading. Replace the end cover with a cut-away one which allows observation of the rocker assembly while retaining the pivot pin. Use paraffin (kerosene) in the test tank. Ensure an adequate supply.

Priming

(2) Unscrew the regulator valve (Churchill rig only) and switch on: the pump should prime from dry in 10 to 15 seconds. Allow the pump to run for a minute to stabilize the flow.

Air leak check

(3) When the pump is first started air bubbles will be mixed with the liquid discharged from the pipe projecting downwards into the flow-meter; these bubbles should cease after a minute or so. If they

do not, an air leak is indicated either in the pump or the connecting unions, and this must be rectified.

Valve seat check

(4) Let the pump run for about 10 minutes and then test as follows: With the regulator valve (delivery tap) turned completely off the pump should stand without repeating for a minimum of 20 seconds at the correct delivery head. If it repeats, the inlet valve is not seating correctly and the cause must be investigated.

Delivery check

(5) Churchill: Obtain a delivery head reading of 4 feet (1220 mm.) on the gauge by adjusting the regulator valve on top of the flow glass. When correct, the pump flow rate may be read directly from the appropriate colour scale on the flow glass.

S.U.: The paraffin (kerosene) should rise in the glass tube until it flows over the top of the pipe in which a side hole is drilled; if the output is not up to specification, the side hole will carry off all paraffin (kerosene) pumped and none will flow over the top.

The delivery rate should be 56 pints (67 U.S. pts., 32 litres) per hour.

Minimum delivery check

(6) With the tap turned on only slightly, and by pressing gradually inwards on the tip of the contact blade, so as to reduce the effective stroke, check that the pump continues to work with an

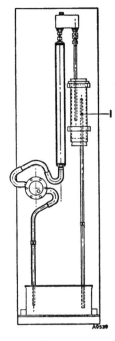

Fig. Da.7

A checking rig for the fuel pump is obtainable from the S.U. Carburetter Co. Ltd.

(1) The ⅛ in. (4 mm.) dia. hole is 2 in. (50 mm.) below the top of the pipe.

increasing frequency until it eventually stops because there is no gap left between the points.

Reduced voltage

(7) Connect a resistance and voltmeter in circuit and test the pump at 9·5 volts with regulator valve open (tap full on); the pump should work satisfactorily although with reduced output.

Sparking check

(8) Check for excessive sparking at the contact points. A moderate degree is permissible; excessive sparking would indicate that the special leak wire incorporated in the coil winding has fractured, necessitating a new coil unit, or that the condenser is faulty.

Fault diagnosis

1. *Suspected fuel feed failure*

Disconnect the fuel line at the carburetter and check for flow.

(*a*) If normal, examine for obstructed float-chamber needle seating or gummed needle.

(*b*) If normal initially, but diminishing rapidly and accompanied by slow pump operation, check for correct tank venting by removing the filler cap. Inadequate venting causes a slow power stroke, with resultant excessive burning of contact points.

(*c*) If reduced flow is accompanied by slow operation of the pump, check for any restriction on the inlet side of the pump, such as a clogged filter, which should be removed and cleaned. In the case of reduced flow with rapid operation of the pump, check for an air leak on the suction side, dirt under the valves, or faulty valve sealing washers.

(*d*) If no flow, check for:

(i) *Electrical supply*

Disconnect the lead from the terminal and test for an electrical supply.

(ii) *Faulty contact points*

If electrical supply is satisfactory the bakelite cover should be removed to check that the tungsten points are in contact. The lead should then be replaced on the terminal and a short piece of bared wire put across the contacts. If the pump then performs a stroke the fault is due to dirt, corrosion, or maladjustment of the tungsten points.

(iii) *Obstructed pipeline between fuel tank and pump*

The inlet pipe should be disconnected; if the pump then operates, trouble is due to a restriction in the pipeline between the pump and the tank. This may be cleared by the use of compressed air after removing the fuel tank filler cap. It should be noted, however, that compressed air should not be passed through the pump, as this will cause serious damage to the valves.

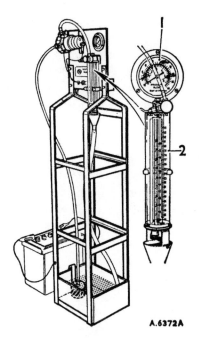

A.6372A

Fig. Da.8

A checking rig for S.U. fuel pumps available from V. L. Churchill and Co. Ltd. The rig measures output in gallons of paraffin (kerosene) per hour, against the required suction and delivery head

1. Pressure gauge.   2. Flow glass.

(iv) *Faulty diaphragm action*

If the previous operations fail to locate the trouble, stiffening of the diaphragm fabric or abnormal friction in the rocker 'throw-over' mechanism is to be suspected. To remedy these faults, the coil housing should be removed and the diaphragm flexed a few times, taking care not to lose any of the 11 rollers under it. Prior to reassembly, it is advisable to apply a little thin oil to the 'throw-over' spring spindles at a point where they pivot in the brass rockers. The diaphragm armature assembly should then be assembled and set in accordance with the instructions given under that heading.

2. *Noisy pump*

Air leaks. If the pump is noisy in operation, an **air** leak at one or other of the suction lines may be the cause. Such a leak may be checked by disconnecting the fuel pipe from the carburetter and allowing the pump to discharge into a suitable container with the end of the pipe submerged. The emission of continuous bubbles at this point will confirm the existence of an air leak. The fault should be rectified by carrying out the following procedure:

(*a*) Check that all connections from the fuel tank to the pump are in good order.

(*b*) Check that the inlet union is tight.

Sprite and Midget. Issue 4. 82324   **Da.7**

119

(*c*) Check that the coil housing securing screws are well and evenly tightened. Air leaks on the suction side cause rapid operation of the pump and are the most frequent cause of premature failure.

3. *Pump operates without delivering fuel*

If the pump operates without delivering fuel the most likely causes are:

(*a*) A serious air leak on the suction side, or,

(*b*) Foreign matter lodged under one of the valves, particularly under the inlet valve.

To remedy (*a*) see para. 2 above.

To remove any foreign matter lodged under the valves these should be removed for cleaning.

Section Da.2

FUEL TANK

(Midget Mk. III from Car No. G–AN5–105501)

Removing

(1) Disconnect the earth cable from the battery.

(2) Drain the fuel tank.

(3) Unscrew the spare wheel retaining screw and move the spare wheel away from the fuel tank filler hose.

(4) Slacken the two clips securing the filler hose to the inlet tube and the fuel tank inlet pipe.

[NOTE: The carburetters used with Engine Type 12V 778F are covered in the Appendix on page 362.]

(5) Disconnect the filler hose from the fuel tank inlet pipe.

(6) Disconnect the fuel gauge tank unit electrical connection.

(7) Disconnect the harness clips from the fuel tank.

(8) Disconnect the feed pipe from the fuel tank.

(9) Remove the six nuts securing the fuel tank, noting that the front nut on the right-hand side retains the large wiring harness clip.

(10) Remove the fuel tank.

Refitting

(11) Reverse the removing procedure in (1) to (10), ensuring that the sealing ring is fitted to the fuel tank filler neck before the tank is fitted.

Section Da.3

FUEL TANK GAUGE UNIT

Removing

(1) Remove the fuel tank.

(2) Remove the gauge unit locking ring, using 18G 1001.

(3) Remove the tank unit and the rubber sealing washer.

Refitting

(4) Reverse the removing procedure in (1) to (3).

Section Db

THE FUEL SYSTEM (EVAPORATIVE LOSS)

The information given in this Section refers specifically to service operations on, or affected by, equipment fitted to the MG Midget (GAN5) in conformity with local and territorial requirements.

Section Db.1

FUEL TANK

Removing

(1) Remove the spare wheel.

(2) Disconnect the battery (negative earth) and drain the fuel tank.

(3) Slacken the two hose clips securing the rubber hose to the tank fuel inlet pipe and filler tube.

(4) Remove the screw, large plain washers and sealing washers securing the tank inside the boot.

(5) Underneath the car, disconnect the petrol feed pipe and gauge unit electrical connections.

(6) Remove the nuts and washer retaining the tank lip to the four studs. Release the two vapour pipe clips and move the pipe to one side.

(7) Remove the tank unit.

Refitting

(8) Reverse the removing procedure (1) to (7).

Section Db.2

VAPOUR SEPARATOR TANK

Removing

(1) Disconnect the battery.

(2) Remove the two flexible pipe connections from the tank. Remove the screw, nut and washer retaining the tank.

(3) Remove the tank. Under extreme operating conditions the tank may contain fuel.

Refitting

(4) Reverse the removing procedure (1) to (3).

Section Db.3

LEAK TESTING

If a fault in the operation of the Evaporative Loss Control System is suspected or components of the system other than the filters or canister have been removed and refitted, the system must be pressure-tested in accordance with the test procedure given in **Workshop Manual Supplement AKD 4957.**

Section Db.4

FUEL TANK
(From Commission No. 105501)

Removing

(1) Disconnect the earth cable from the battery.

(2) Drain the fuel tank.

(3) Unscrew the spare wheel retaining screw and move the wheel away from the fuel tank filler hose.

(4) Slacken the two clips securing the filler hose to the inlet tube and fuel tank inlet pipe.

(5) Disconnect the filler hose from the fuel tank inlet pipe.

(6) Disconnect the fuel gauge tank unit electrical connections.

(7) Disconnect the harness clips from the fuel tank.

(8) Disconnect the feed pipe from the fuel tank.

(9) Release the two vapour pipe clips and move the pipe to one side.

(10) Remove the six nuts securing the fuel tank noting that the front nut on the right-hand side retains the large wiring harness clip.

(11) Remove the fuel tank.

Refitting

(12) Reverse the removing procedure in (1) to (11), ensuring that the sealing ring is fitted to the fuel tank filler neck before the tank is fitted.

SECTION E

THE CLUTCH

THE CLUTCH COMPONENTS
(Early Cars)

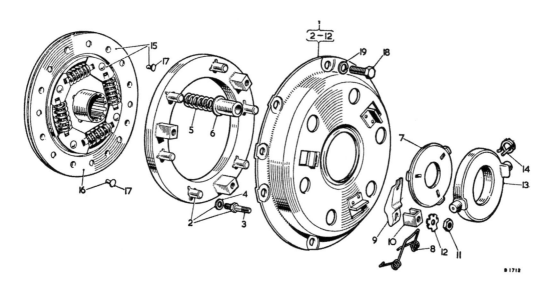

No.	Description	No.	Description
1.	Cover assembly.	11.	Nut.
2.	Pressure plate.	12.	Tab washer.
3.	Pressure plate stud.	13.	Release bearing and cap assembly.
4.	Washer.	14.	Bearing retainer.
5.	Thrust spring.	15.	Driven plate.
6.	Thrust spring cup.	16.	Linings.
7.	Thrust plate.	17.	Rivets.
8.	Thrust plate retainer.	18.	Set screw.
9.	Release lever.	19.	Washer.
10.	Release lever bearing plate.		

GENERAL DESCRIPTION

The clutch is a Borg & Beck single dry-plate type operated hydraulically. A steel cover bolted to the flywheel encloses the driven plate, the pressure plate, the pressure springs, and the release levers. The driven plate, to which the friction linings are riveted, incorporates springs assembled around the hub to absorb power shocks and torsional vibration. The pressure springs force the pressure plate against the friction linings, gripping the driven plate between the pressure plate and the engine flywheel. When the clutch pedal is depressed the release bearing is moved forward against the release plate, which bears against the three release levers. The outer or shorter ends of the release levers engage the pressure plate lugs; pressure applied by the release bearing causes the pressure plate to be pulled away from the driven plate, compressing the pressure springs which are assembled between the pressure plate and the clutch cover. As the friction linings wear, the pressure plate moves closer to the fly-wheel face and the outer or shorter ends of the release levers follow. This causes the inner or longer ends of the levers to travel farther towards the gearbox and decreases the clearance between the release lever plate and the release bearing. This is automatically compensated unless the master cylinder has been disturbed.

When the clutch pedal is depressed, fluid pressure is transmitted through the master cylinder to the slave cylinder mounted on the clutch housing, moving the slave cylinder piston and push-rod. As the push-rod is connected to the lower arm of the clutch withdrawal lever, thereby the clutch is released. The push-rod is non-adjustable.

The correct amount of free movement between the master cylinder push-rod and piston is set during erection of the vehicle and should never need alteration.

In the event of the adjustment having been disturbed reset the effective length of the rod connecting the piston to the pedal until the pedal pad can be depressed approximately $\frac{5}{32}$ in. (4 mm.) before the piston begins to move. The clearance can be felt if the pedal is depressed by hand. It is very important that the push-rod should have a minimum free movement of $\frac{1}{32}$ in. (·8 mm.) before the piston starts to move.

Section E.1

CLUTCH
(Early Cars)

Removing

Remove the gearbox and the clutch assembly as described in Sections F and A respectively.

Dismantling (See Editor's note at end of Section E.)

The clutch tool 18G 99 A provides an efficient and speedy means of dismantling, reassembling, and adjusting the clutch with a high degree of accuracy. The tool is universal, and a chart detailing the sizes of spacing washers and distance pieces for particular types of clutch is provided on the inside of the metal container lid.

Detach the retaining springs from the release lever plate and remove the springs and plate. Place the tool base plate on a flat surface. Select three spacing washers for the particular clutch and place them in position on the base plate.

Position the clutch on the three spacing washers so that the holes in the clutch cover align with the tapped holes in the base plate with the release levers as close to the spacing washers as possible. Insert the tool set screws, tightening them a little at a time in a diagonal pattern until the cover is firmly and evenly secured to the base plate. This is most important if the best results are to be achieved.

Knock back the tab washers and remove the shoulder stud adjusting nuts. Lift off the washers, bearing plates, and release levers.

Unscrew the set screws securing the clutch cover to the base plate in a diagonal pattern, releasing the pressure on the clutch springs gradually and evenly. Lift off the cover and remove the pressure springs.

Clean the clutch parts carefully. If the linings are to be used again they should not be allowed to come in contact with cleaning fluids.

Examine the friction linings for wear or loose rivets and check the driven plate for uneven or worn splines, distortion, or signs of fatigue cracks.

It is essential to install a complete driven plate assembly when renewal of the friction surfaces is required. If the facings have worn to such an extent as to warrant renewal, then slight wear will have taken place on the splines and also on the torque reaction springs and their seatings. The question of balance and concentricity is also involved. Under no circumstances is it satisfactory to repair or rectify faults in clutch driven plate centres, and we do not countenance this as manufacturers.

Examine the machined face of the pressure plate; if this is badly grooved and rough, the surface may be reground until the grooves disappear.

Examine the machined surface of the release lever plate. If this is badly grooved, renew the plate. A new plate will also be necessary if the surfaces on the reverse side of the plate, which are in contact with the tips of the release levers, are worn down.

Examine the tips of the release levers which bear on the back of the release lever plate. A small amount of worn flat surface is permissible, but if this is excessive the lever should be renewed. Check for excessive wear in the groove in which the fulcrum bears. If the metal here has worn at all thin, the lever must be renewed as there is a danger of it breaking under load, with disastrous results to the whole clutch mechanism.

Examine the release bearing for cracks or bad pitting, also measure the amount of bearing standing proud of the metal cup. If the bearing is cracked or badly pitted, or there is $\frac{1}{16}$ in. (1·6 mm.) or less of bearing standing proud of the cup, the cup and bearing must be renewed.

Examine the pressure springs for weakness or distortion, and renew if necessary. Renew in sets only.

Examine the clutch withdrawal shaft for slackness in the bushes. Renew the bushes if necessary.

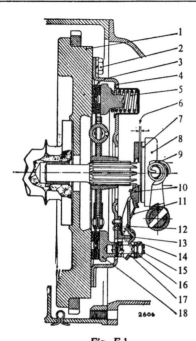

Fig. E.1

The clutch unit in section (early cars)

1. Flywheel.
2. Holding screw.
3. Driven plate.
4. Cover.
5. Thrust spring.
6. Clearance ·0625 in. (1·58 mm.).
7. Graphite release bearing.
8. Release bearing cup.
9. Release bearing carrier.
10. Release lever plate.
11. Lever retainer and anti-rattle spring.
12. Release lever.
13. Knife-edge fulcrum.
14. Tag lock washer.
15. Stud.
16. Adjusting nut.
17. Bearing plate.
18. Pressure plate.

Reassembling

Parts not being replaced by new ones must be refitted in their original positions.

Reassembly is the reverse of the dismantling procedure.

Adjusting the clutch

The clutch must now be adjusted, still using the clutch assembly tool. With the clutch bolted to the tool base plate, as on completion of assembly, proceed as follows. Screw the actuator into the base plate and pump the handle a dozen times to settle the clutch mechanism. Remove the actuator. Screw the tool centre pillar into the base plate and select a distance piece, as shown on the chart. Place the distance piece over the centre pillar with its recessed face downwards. Place the gauge height finger over the centre pillar. Adjust the height of the release levers by tightening or loosening the adjusting nuts until the height finger, when rotated, just contacts the highest point on the tip of each release lever. Press downwards on the height finger to ensure that it bears squarely on the adaptor while rotating. Remove the height finger and pillar, and screw the actuator into the base plate. Operate the clutch several times to enable the components to settle on their knife-edges. Remove the actuator and replace the centre pillar, distance piece, and height finger. Readjust the release levers if necessary.

Repeat the procedure to ensure that the release levers are finally seated, and gauge once more. Remove the centre pillar, distance piece, and height finger and secure the adjusting nuts. Fit the release lever plate on the tips of the release levers and secure it by the three retaining springs. Release the tool set screws in diagonal sequence a little at a time, relieving pressure slowly and evenly. Remove the clutch assembly from the base plate.

Refitting (See Editor's note at end of Section E.)

Refitting is a reverse of the removal procedure. Use Service tool 18G 139 for clutch centralization.

Section E.2

CLUTCH PEDAL

Removing

Working beneath the bonnet, disconnect the clutch and brake pedal levers from the master cylinder push-rods by removing the spring clips and withdrawing the clevis pins. From within the car, remove the nut and spring washer and withdraw the fulcrum pin; note that a distance piece separates the two pedals. The pedals can now be removed.

The pedals together with the master cylinder assembly can be removed as one unit. This operation is described in the master cylinder removal section.

Refitting

When refitting reverse the removal procedure.

Section E.3

MASTER CYLINDER

Construction

The master cylinder caters for operation of both brakes and clutch. It has two bores side by side and, except for the fact that one has no check valve, each bore accommodates normal master cylinder parts. The bore with the check valve serves the brakes, the other serves the clutch slave cylinder.

Removing

The following removal procedure allows the withdrawal of the master cylinder unit complete with clutch and brake pedals.

NOTE.—Before disconnecting the master cylinder ascertain, for assembly purposes, which bore communicates with the clutch slave cylinder.

Remove the heater blower unit (if fitted) by first releasing the two electrical connections. Remove the set screws securing the heater blower bracket to the bulkhead. Remove the set screws securing the master cylinder mounting plate to the engine bulkhead. Disconnect the two hydraulic pipes at their unions with the rear of the master cylinder unit.

Withdraw the master cylinder unit upwards and at the same time manipulate the clutch and brake pedals through the aperture in the bulkhead.

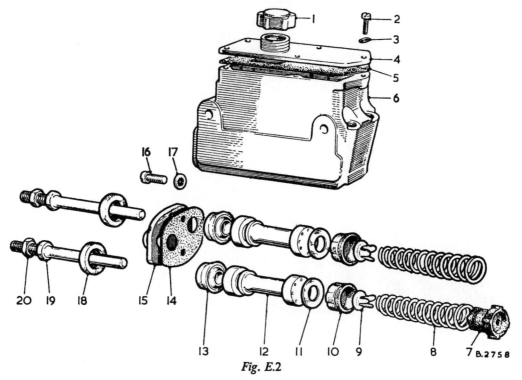

Fig. E.2

Master cylinder (exploded)

1. Filler cap.	8. Return spring.	14. Gasket.
2. Fixing screw.	9. Spring retainer.	15. Boot fixing plate.
3. Shakeproof washer.	10. Main cup.	16. Fixing washer.
4. Tank cover.	11. Piston washer.	17. Shakeproof washer.
5. Tank cover gasket.	12. Piston.	18. Boot.
6. Cylinder barrel and tank.	13. Secondary cup.	19. Push rod.
7. Valve (brake bore only).		20. Push rod adjuster.

Dismantling

Disconnect each pedal from its master cylinder push-rod by removing the spring clips and withdrawing the clevis pins.

Remove the bolts securing the master cylinder unit to its mounting plate and withdraw the complete unit.

Remove the set screws securing the boot fixing plate to the master cylinder body.

Detach the fixing plate from the master cylinder, and remove the boots and push-rods.

Remove the common filler cap and drain the fluid into a clean container.

Withdraw the piston, piston washer, main cup, spring retainer, and the return spring.

Remove the secondary cup by stretching it over the end flange of the piston.

Examine all parts, especially the washers, for wear or distortion, and replace with new parts where necessary.

Reassembling

Reassembly is the reverse of the removal procedure, with particular attention being paid to the fitting of the rubber boots. The vent hole in each boot should be at the bottom when the cylinder is mounted on the vehicle.

Refitting

The installation of the master cylinder unit is the reversal of the removal procedure.

If no further maintenance is necessary, remember to bleed the system.

Section E.4

SLAVE CYLINDER

Construction

The cylinder is bolted to the under side of the clutch housing and comprises a piston, rubber cup, cup filler, spring, push-rod, and bleeder screw.

Removing

Place a receptacle to catch the fluid and remove the pipe union on the slave cylinder. Remove the split pin and clevis pin from the clutch withdrawal lever yoke. Remove the bolts securing the cylinder to the clutch housing and lift off the slave cylinder assembly.

Dismantling

Remove the rubber cover, push-rod, and circlip, and if a compressed-air line is available blow out the piston and seal. The spring can also be removed. The main casting can be cleaned with any of the normal cleansing fluids, but slave cylinder components should be cleaned in hydraulic fluid. All traces of cleansing fluid should be removed before reassembly. Lubricate the slave cylinder bore and components with hydraulic fluid and renew any rubbers before assembling the slave cylinders.

E

THE CLUTCH COMPONENTS
(Later Cars)

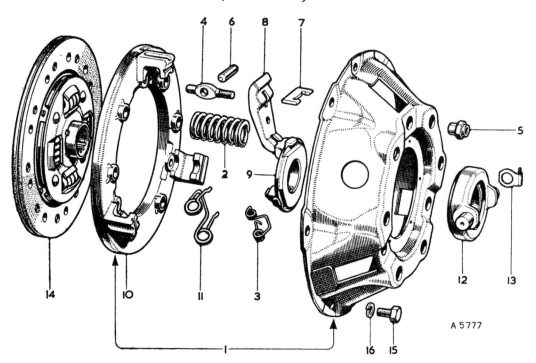

A 5777

No.	Description	No.	Description	No.	Description
1.	Clutch assembly.	7.	Strut.	12.	Release bearing.
2.	Thrust spring.	8.	Release lever.	13.	Retainer.
3.	Release lever retainer.	9.	Bearing thrust plate.	14.	Driven plate assembly.
4.	Eyebolt.	10.	Pressure plate.	15.	Clutch to flywheel screw.
5.	Eyebolt nut.	11.	Anti-rattle spring.	16.	Spring washer.
6.	Release lever pin.				

Sprite and Midget. Issue 4. 65317

Reassembling

Reassembling is the reverse of the removal procedure.

Refitting

For refitting reverse the removal procedure. The clutch hydraulic system should always be bled after an overhaul operation.

Bleeding

Fill the master cylinder reservoir with the recommended fluid and attach a rubber tube to the slave cylinder bleed valve; immerse the open end of the tube in a clean receptacle containing a small amount of fluid. With a second operator to pump the clutch pedal, open the bleed screw on the slave cylinder approximately three-quarters of a turn; at the end of the down stroke on the clutch pedal close the bleed screw before allowing the pedal to return to the 'off' position.

Continue this series of operation until clear fluid free from air bubbles is delivered into the container.

Section E.5

CLUTCH
(Later Cars)

Removing

Remove the gearbox and the clutch assembly as described in Sections F and A respectively.

Dismantling (See Editor's note at end of Section E.)

The clutch tool 18G 99 A proves an efficient and speedy means of dismantling, reassembling, and adjusting the clutch with a high degree of accuracy. The tool is universal and a chart detailing the sizes of spacing washers and distance pieces for particular types of clutch is provided on the inside of the metal container lid.

Consult the code card to determine the correct spacers for the particular clutch. Place the spacers on the base plate in the positions indicated on the code card and place the clutch on the spacers. Screw the actuator into

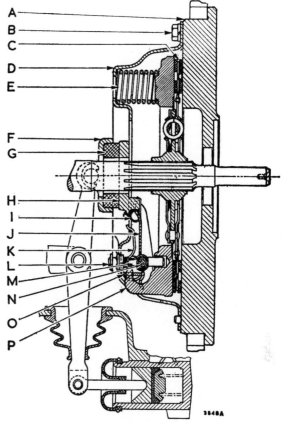

Fig. E.4

A section through the clutch (later cars)

A. Flywheel.	I. Lever retainer spring.
B. Securing bolt.	J. Release lever.
C. Driven plate.	K. Anti-rattle spring.
D. Clutch cover.	L. Adjusting nut.
E. Thrust coil spring.	M. Eyebolt.
F. Release bearing cup.	N. Floating pin (release lever).
G. Graphite release bearing.	O. Strut.
H. Release plate.	P. Pressure plate.

the central hole in the base plate and press the handle to clamp the clutch. Screw the set bolts firmly into the base plate. The clutch can now be compressed or released as required.

Compress the clutch with the actuator and remove the adjusting nuts gradually to relieve the load of the thrust springs. Lift the cover off the clutch and carry out whatever additional dismantling may be necessary.

Reassembling

Parts not being replaced by new ones must be refitted in their original positions.

Reassembly is the reverse of the dismantling procedure.

Adjusting the clutch

See end of Section E.1.

Refitting

Refitting is a reverse of the removal procedure. Use Service tool 18G 139 for clutch centralization.

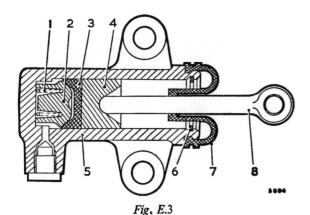

Fig. E.3

A section through a clutch slave cylinder

1. Spring.		5. Body.
2. Cup filler.		6. Circlip.
3. Cup.		7. Rubber boot.
4. Piston.		8. Push-rod.

E. The Clutch

Clutch, dismantling

Generally speaking, a worn clutch is replaced as an assembly, with a rebuilt or new unit. If it is desirable for some reason to disassemble the clutch (stiffer springs for racing, etc.), a clutch assembly table equivalent to Service tool 18G99A may be found at any well equipped clutch and brake shop, which will be able to perform the operations described here.

It is unwise to attempt to reassemble and adjust a clutch assembly without the proper equipment.

Clutch, refitting

A transmission first motion (input) shaft or other suitable pilot may be used instead of Service tool 18G139.

SECTION Ea

THE CLUTCH

The information given in this Section refers specifically to the Sprite (Mk. IV) and Midget (Mk. III) and must be used in conjunction with Section E.

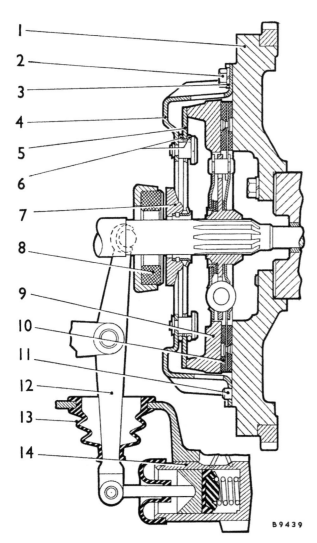

1
2
3
4
5
6
7
8
9
10
11
12
13
14

B9439

Fig. Ea.1

A section through the clutch

1. Flywheel.	8. Release bearing.
2. Clutch securing bolt.	9. Pressure plate.
3. Spring washer.	10. Driven plate.
4. Cover.	11. Dowel.
5. Diaphragm/spring.	12. Release lever.
6. Annular rings.	13. Rubber boot.
7. Release plate.	14. Slave cylinder.

Section Ea.1

CLUTCH

Removing

(1) Remove the engine and gearbox assembly as described in Section Aa.9 (1) to (22).

(2) Remove the starter motor.

(3) Remove the bolts retaining the gearbox to the engine and withdraw the gearbox.

(4) Unscrew the bolts securing the clutch assembly to the flywheel in diagonal sequence, to allow the diaphragm spring pressure to be released evenly, and remove the clutch assembly.

(5) Rotate the release bearing spring retainers through 90° and withdraw the bearing from the withdrawal lever fork.

Inspection

(6) Examine the clutch driven plate facings for wear and discoloration. If the facings are worn or are darkened to the extent that the grain of the facing material cannot be clearly distinguished the driven plate must be renewed.

(7) Inspect the splines, springs, and spring pockets in the drive plate for wear, and renew the driven plate if necessary, do not attempt to repair or rectify faults in the driven plate centre. Excessive wear of the driven plate splines may be due to misalignment and the flywheel should be checked for true using a dial indicator; the reading should not vary more than ·003 in. (·07 mm.) anywhere on the flywheel face.

(8) Examine the pressure plate and diaphragm spring for signs of overheating, if there is evidence of overheating the complete clutch cover assembly must be renewed.

(9) Check the release bearing for excessive wear, and renew if necessary.

Refitting

(10) Position the driven plate assembly on the flywheel with the long side of the hub towards the flywheel.

(11) Centralize the driven plate by inserting tool 18G 139 through the splined hub and entering the pilot end of the tool into the spigot bearing of the crankshaft.

(12) Locate the clutch cover assembly on the flywheel dowels, screw in the securing bolts, and tighten the bolts a turn at a time in diagonal sequence to the torque figure given in 'GENERAL DATA'.

(13) Remove the clutch centralizing tool.

(14) Fit the release bearing to the withdrawal lever fork and ensure that the spring retainers are correctly located.

(15) Refit the gearbox to the engine taking care that the gearbox is supported during the refitting, to avoid strain on the first motion shaft, and distortion or displacement of the clutch components.

(16) Fit the starter motor.

(17) Refit the engine and gearbox assembly (Section Aa.9 (23) to (26)).

Section Ea.2

MASTER CYLINDER

Removing

(1) Raise the bonnet and remove the pedal box lid.

(2) Disconnect the hydraulic pipe from the clutch master cylinder.

(3) Withdraw the split pin from the clevis pin connecting the push-rod to the clutch pedal and remove the clevis pin.

Ea.2   **Sprite and Midget. Issue 1.   4870**

132

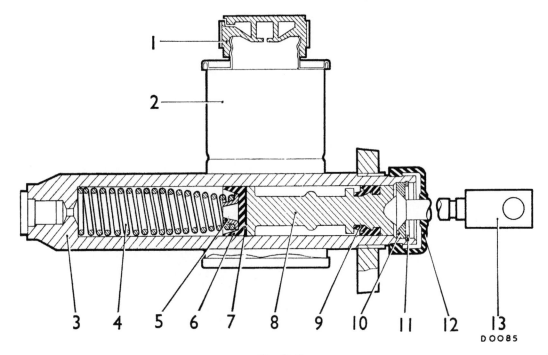

Fig. Ea.2

A section through the master cylinder

1. Filler cap.	5. Spring retainer.	9. Secondary cup.
2. Reservoir.	6. Main cup.	10. Dished washer.
3. Body.	7. Piston washer.	11. Circlips.
4. Spring.	8. Piston.	12. Rubber boot.
		13. Push-rod.

(4) Unscrew the two bolts securing the master cylinder to the pedal box and remove the master cylinder.

Dismantling

(5) Remove the filler cap and drain the fluid.

(6) Detach the rubber boot from the body and slide it up the push-rod.

(7) Remove the circlip retaining the push-rod, and withdraw the push-rod complete with the rubber boot and dished washer.

(8) Withdraw the piston complete with the secondary cup, the piston washer, main cup, spring retainer, and spring from the body.

(9) Remove the secondary cup from the piston by carefully stretching it over the end of the piston using only the fingers.

Inspection

(10) Clean all the parts thoroughly using the recommended clutch fluid and dry them with a clean, non-fluffy cloth.

(11) Examine the metal parts for wear and damage, inspect the rubber cups for swelling, perishing,

distortion, or any other signs of deterioration. Renew all worn, damaged, or suspect parts.

Reassembling

(12) Dip all the internal components in the recommended clutch fluid and assemble them while wet.

(13) Stretch the secondary cup over the piston with the lip of the cup facing towards the head of the piston. When the cup is in its groove work round it gently with the fingers to ensure that it is correctly seated.

(14) Fit the spring retainer into the small diameter end of the spring and insert the spring into the body, large diameter end first.

(15) Fit the main cup, cup washer, piston, and push-rod. When fitting the cups carefully enter the lip edge of the cups into the barrel first.

(16) Fit the circlip and rubber boot.

Refitting

(17) Reverse the removal procedure in (1) to (4) then fill the master cylinder with the recommended clutch fluid (see 'GENERAL DATA') and bleed the system (see Section E.4).

SECTION F

THE GEARBOX

THE GEARBOX COMPONENTS

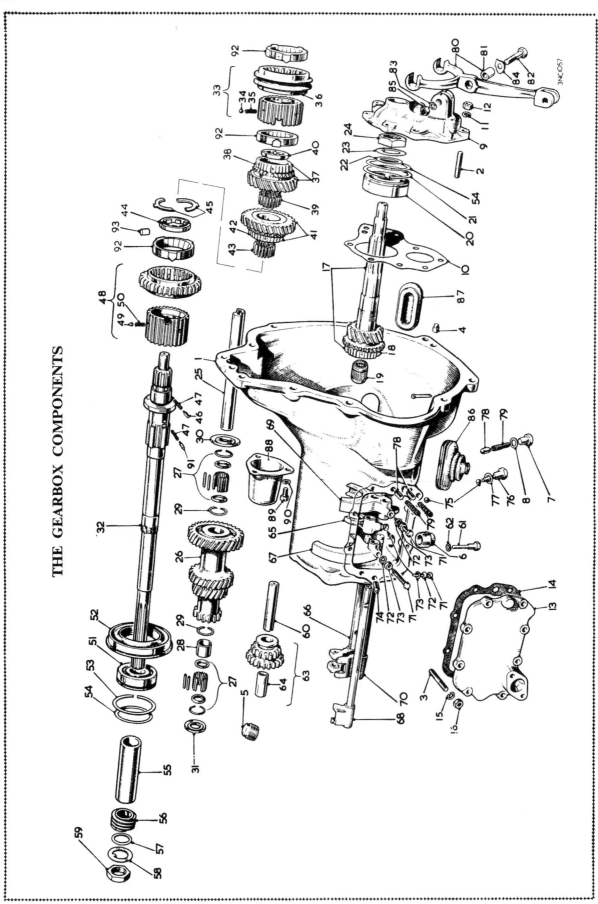

Sprite and Midget. Issue 5. 29459
MG Midget. AKM 2092/1

KEY TO THE GEARBOX COMPONENTS

No.	Description	No.	Description
1.	Case assembly.	32.	Third motion shaft.
2.	Stud for front cover.	33.	Third and fourth speed synchronizer.
3.	Stud for side cover.	34.	Ball.
4.	Dowel.	35.	Spring.
5.	Filler plug.	36.	Sleeve.
6.	Drain plug.	37.	Third speed gear with cone.
7.	Plug for reverse plunger spring.	38.	Synchronizing cone.
8.	Washer.	39.	Needle roller.
9.	Front cover.	40.	Third speed gear locking collar.
10.	Front cover joint.	41.	Second speed gear with cone.
11.	Spring washer.	42.	Synchronizing cone.
12.	Nut.	43.	Needle roller.
13.	Side cover.	44.	Second speed locking collar.
14.	Joint for side cover.	45.	Washer.
15.	Spring washer.	46.	Peg for locking collar.
16.	Nut.	47.	Springs for pegs.
17.	First motion shaft with cone.	48.	First speed gear assembly.
18.	Synchronizing cone.	49.	Ball.
19.	Needle-roller bearing.	50.	Spring for ball.
20.	First motion shaft journal ball bearing.	51.	Third motion shaft journal ball bearing.
21.	Spring ring.	52.	Bearing housing.
22.	Washer.	53.	Spring ring.
23.	Lock washer.	54.	Bearing packing washer.
24.	Nut.	55.	Third motion shaft distance piece.
25.	Layshaft.	56.	Speedometer gear.
26.	Laygear.	57.	Plain washer.
27.	Needle-roller bearing with spring ring.	58.	Locking washer.
28.	Distance piece.	59.	Third motion shaft nut.
29.	Spring ring.	60.	Reverse shaft.
30.	Thrust washer (front).	61.	Screw.
31.	Thrust washer (rear).	62.	Spring washer.

No.	Description
63.	Reverse wheel and bush.
64.	Bush.
65.	Reverse fork.
66.	Reverse fork rod.
67.	First and second speed fork.
68.	First and second speed fork rod.
69.	Third and fourth speed fork.
70.	Third and fourth speed fork rod.
71.	Fork locating screw.
72.	Shakeproof washer.
73.	Nut.
74.	Interlock plunger.
75.	Interlock ball.
76.	Plug.
77.	Washer.
78.	Plunger for fork rod.
79.	Spring.
80.	Clutch withdrawal lever with bush.
81.	Bush.
82.	Bolt.
83.	Spring washer.
84.	Locking washer.
85.	Nut.
86.	Dust cover.
87.	Dust cover for bell housing.
88.	Starter pinion cover.
89.	Screw.
90.	Washer.
91.	Peg for locking collar.
92.	Baulk ring (later gearboxes).
93.	Second speed synchronizer plunger [later gearboxes].

Sprite and Midget. Issue 4. 51576
MG Midget. AKM 2092/1

137

F.3

F

GENERAL DESCRIPTION

The gearbox has four forward speeds and one reverse, and synchromesh is incorporated on second, third, and top gears.

Top gear is a direct drive; third and second are in constant mesh; first and reverse are obtained by sliding spur pinions.

Section F.1

LUBRICATION

The combined lubrication filler and level plug situated on the gearbox extension is reached by lifting the floor covering from inside the car and removing the rubber plug on the left-hand side of the gearbox cover. The oil must be level with the bottom of the filler hole. The drain plug is situated on the bottom of the gearbox casing.

Section F.2

GEARBOX

Removing

The engine and gearbox may be removed from the vehicle as a complete unit as described in Section A.31 and then separated. The alternative method is first to remove the engine as detailed in Section A.31 and then withdraw the gearbox after completing the following operations.

Remove the self-tapping screws from the change speed lever cover and withdraw the cover from the lever.

Remove the anti-rattle plunger spring and cap from the side of the change speed lever turret. Remove the change speed lever cover set screws and the lever.

Turn back the carpet surrounding the gearbox cover to expose the gearbox rear mountings and remove the securing set screws.

Working beneath the vehicle, remove the speedometer drive cable at its union with the gearbox rear extension.

Remove the clutch slave cylinder as detailed in Section E.4. Disconnect the propeller shaft from the rear axle (see Section G.2). Remove the remaining gearbox rear mounting set screws and lift the gearbox clear of the vehicle.

Dismantling

Unscrew the filler plug. Drain the oil by removing the plug from the bottom of the gearbox. Unscrew and remove the speedometer pinion sleeve with a box spanner from the left-hand side of the gearbox rear extension, and withdraw the speedometer pinion.

Remove the nuts securing the remote control housing and lift the housing off the rear cover.

Unscrew the set screws and spring washers securing the rear cover to the gearbox.

Pull the rear cover back slightly and turn it in an anti-clockwise direction, as viewed from the rear, to enable the control lever to clear the fork rod ends, and then remove the rear cover from the gearbox.

Remove the control shaft locating screw, and screw it into the tapped front end of the control shaft. Slight pressure on the screw will facilitate the removal of the control shaft, which is a push fit in the rear cover. The control lever will slip off the end of the shaft as the shaft is removed.

Remove the one-piece nylon control lever bush from the control lever.

Unscrew the set screws securing the bottom cover to the change speed lever tower. Retain the paper joint washer if undamaged.

Unscrew and remove the change speed lever locating peg and the anti-rattle springs. The latter are removed by unscrewing the caps and then tilting the remote control housing so that the springs and plungers drop out.

Unscrew the set screws securing the change speed lever cover to the top of the change speed lever tower and remove the lever, taking care to retain the thrust button and thrust button spring.

Unscrew the set screws in the front and rear selector levers, remove the core plugs at either end of the remote control housing, and, using a suitable drift, tap out the remote control shaft. The front and rear selector levers can then be removed.

To remove the reverse selector plunger first unscrew the reverse plunger cap and remove the detent spring and ball, then remove the locating pin.

Remove the clutch release bearing by levering out the two retaining springs.

To remove the clutch withdrawal lever tap back the locking washer and remove the nut and washer. The bolt may then be unscrewed. Do not attempt to knock the bolt out, as it is threaded into the support bracket. Unscrew and remove the bolt and lock washer.

Remove from the front cover the nuts and washers situated within the clutch bell housing. The front cover may then be withdrawn by gripping the clutch with-drawal lever brackets with the finger and thumb and pulling. Remove the paper joints and packing shim.

Release the set screws in the side cover. Remove the side cover and joint washer. Remove the two springs from the front edge of the side cover joining face. Turn the gearbox on its side so that the two plungers fall out of the holes from which the springs were removed.

Remove the plugs situated near the clutch bell housing on the side cover side of the gearbox casing. They each have a fibre washer, and the lower of the plugs covers the reverse plunger and springs, which may be removed by tilting the gearbox on its side. The other plug, which has a long shank, blocks the hole through which the interlock ball between the first and second and third and fourth selector rods is inserted.

Select neutral by aligning the slots in the rear ends of the selector rods. Working on the gearbox, with the side cover facing upwards, unlock and remove the reverse fork locating screw, locknut, and shakeproof washer through the drain plug hole. Similarly, remove the locating screw locknut and shakeproof washer from the first and second and third and fourth speed forks.

Tap the third and fourth speed selector rod from the

Sprite and Midget. Issue 4. 51576

front end and draw it out through the back of the gearbox. Similarly, remove the first and second speed selector rod (nearest side cover) and then the reverse selector rod.

As the selector rods are being drawn out take care to remove the two interlock balls from the front end of the gearbox casing. Also the double-ended interlock plunger should be removed from the back end of the gearbox casing. The three selector forks may now be lifted out of the gearbox.

Tap the layshaft out of the front of the gearbox with a bronze drift. On removing the drift the laygear cluster and thrust washers will drop into the bottom of the gearbox. On later cars the front thrust washer is located by four springs.

Draw the third motion shaft assembly rearwards out of the gearbox case.

Insert a long, soft-metal drift through the mainshaft opening in the rear of the casing and drive the first motion shaft forwards out of the gearbox. The laygear cluster and thrust washers may now be removed.

Remove the reverse shaft locking screw. Place a screwdriver on the slotted end of the reverse shaft and push it into the gearbox with a turning motion. The reverse shaft and gear may now be removed.

Reassembling (See Editor's note at end of Section F.)

Reverse the sequence of operations detailed for dismantling, but note the following important points:

(1) If a new front or rear cover washer is to be fitted, compress it by bolting the cover and washer in position before any other component is fitted; remove the cover and washer.

(2) When refitting the laygear use 18G 471 for shaft alignment, see Section F.5, subsection '**Laygear thrust washers**'.

(3) To ensure oil-tight joints and the correct fitting of the end covers shims are fitted. The method of determining their thickness is as follows.

End cover shims

Although a ·006 in. (·15 mm.) shim is usually found to be sufficient, use the following method to shim the front and rear covers. Measure the depth of the front
(See Editor's note at end of Section F.)

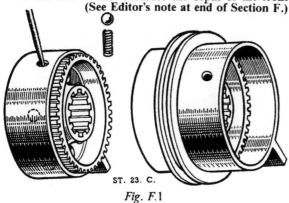

ST. 23. C.

Fig. F.1

Using Service tool 18G 144 to assemble the spring-loaded balls to a coupling sleeve and synchronizer

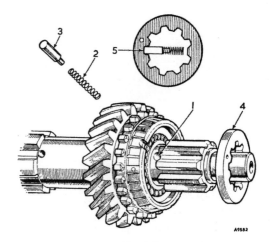

Fig. F.2

Securing the third motion shaft gears

1. Hole in shaft for locking plunger.
2. Spring.
3. Locking plunger.
4. Locking washer.
5. Locking washer with plunger engaged.

cover recess and the amount by which the bearing outer race protrudes from the casing, and tighten the cover with only the paper joint washer in position to allow it to be compressed. Take off the cover and remove the paper joint washer and measure its thickness. Add the thickness of the joint washer to the depth of the cover recess and subtract the amount by which the bearing protrudes from the casing. The result gives the thickness of shims to be used. Use the least possible number of shims to arrive at the correct thickness.

Shims are also available in thicknesses of ·004 in. (·10 mm.) and ·010 in. (·25 mm.). Tighten the rear cover (evenly by diametrical selection) with the nine long set pins and spring washers. Correct shimming is done in exactly the same way as for the front cover.

Refitting

Refitting is the reverse of the dismantling procedure.

Section F.3

THIRD MOTION SHAFT

Dismantling

Remove the third and fourth speed synchronizer assemblies. Depress the spring-loaded plunger which locks the front splined ring at the end of the third motion shaft. Turn the ring so that one of its splines covers the plunger (a peg spanner is useful for turning the splined ring). Slide the splined ring and third speed gear off the end of the shaft and remove the plunger and spring. The third speed gear has needle-roller bearings.

At the other end of the shaft knock back the locking washer and unscrew the securing nut. The lock washer, washer, speedometer wheel, and distance piece may now be removed. Draw the ball journal bearing off the end of the shaft with its housing, and then drift the bearing out of the housing. Draw the first speed gear and

THE REAR EXTENSION COMPONENTS

EI 3 4 5B

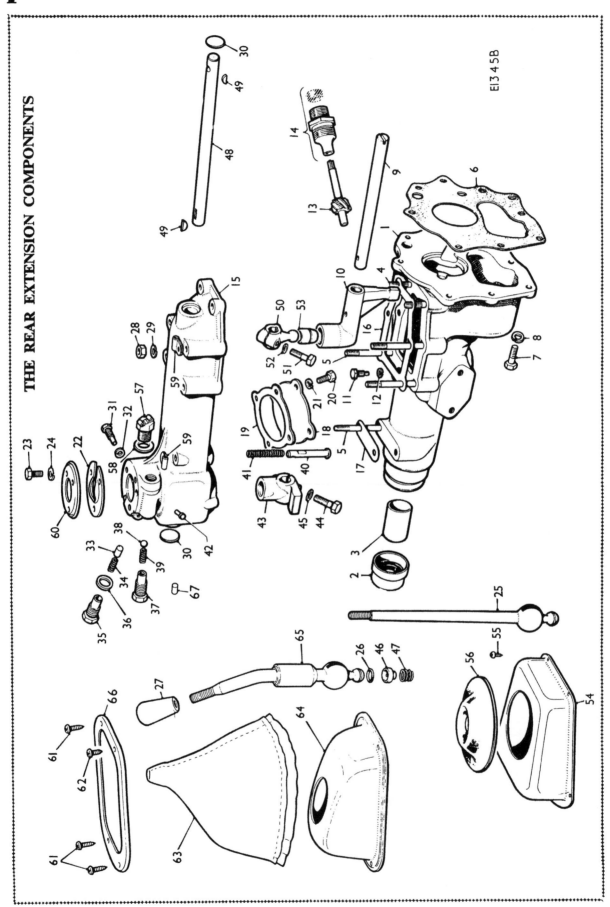

Sprite and Midget. Issue 7. 80661
MG Midget. AKM 2092/1

KEY TO THE REAR EXTENSION COMPONENTS

No.	Description
1.	Rear extension.
2.	Oil seal.
3.	Sliding joint bush.
4.	Extension short stud.
5.	Extension long stud.
6.	Joint washer.
7.	Screw.
8.	Spring washer.
9.	Control shaft.
10.	Control lever.
11.	Control lever locating peg.
12.	Spring washer.
13.	Speedometer pinion.
14.	Speedometer pinion oil seal assembly.
15.	Remote control casing.
16.	Extension front joint.
17.	Extension rear joint.
18.	Lever tower bottom cover.
19.	Joint washer.
20.	Screw.
21.	Spring washer.
22.	Lever seat cover.
23.	Screw.
24.	Spring washer.

No.	Description
25.	Change speed lever.
26.	Ring (rubber).
27.	Knob.
28.	Stud nut.
29.	Spring washer.
30.	Welch plug.
31.	Lever locating peg.
32.	Spring washer.
33.	Control shaft damper plunger.
34.	Spring.
35.	Spring retaining cap.
36.	Washer.
37.	Reverse selector detent plug.
38.	Ball (early cars).
39.	Spring.
40.	Reverse selector plunger.
41.	Spring.
42.	Reverse selector plunger locating pin.
43.	Rear selector lever.
44.	Screw.
45.	Spring washer.
46.	Thrust button.

No.	Description
47.	Spring.
48.	Remote control shaft.
49.	Key.
50.	Front selector lever.
51.	Screw.
52.	Spring washer.
53.	Front selector lever bush.
54.	Remote control cover.
55.	Screw.
56.	Grommet.
57.	Reverse lamp switch.
58.	Washer for switch.
59.	Clip, reverse lamp switch lead.
60.	Retaining plate, gaiter support.
61.	Self-tapping screw (long).
62.	Self-tapping screw (short).
63.	Gaiter.
64.	Gaiter support.
65.	Change speed lever.
66.	Retainer—gaiter support.
67.	Reverse detent plunger (later cars).

Midget Mk. III (GAN5) and Sprite Mk. IV (HAN10) cars.

Sprite and Midget.   Issue 2.   80661
MG Midget.   AKM 2092/1

141

F.7

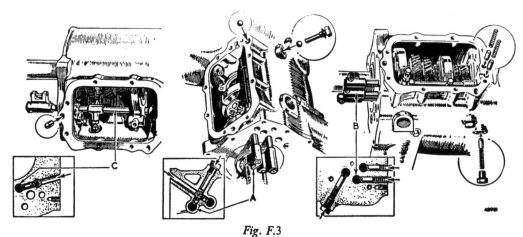

Fig. F.3

The location and correct assembly of the selector locking balls, plungers, and springs

A. First and second gear fork rod in place (gearbox upside-down).   B. Third and fourth gear fork rod in place.

C. Reverse gear fork rod in place.

synchronizer assembly off the shaft. Depress the spring-loaded plunger which locks the rear splined ring at the end of the third motion shaft. Turn the ring so that one of its splines covers the plunger and slide the splined ring off the shaft. Remove the plunger and spring and lift the two halves of the washer for the splined ring off the shaft. Slide the second speed gear off the shaft, taking care to retain the needle rollers.

Reassembling

The third motion shaft ball journal bearing outer race is grooved to take a spring ring. This spring ring registers in a recess in the bearing housing. Press the bearing into the flanged end of the housing so that the spring ring end of the bearing is trailing. Assemble the needle rollers on the shaft and fit the second speed gear. Place the two halves of the washer for the splined ring on the shaft behind the second speed gear. Ensure that the two halves of the washer are assembled with the locking pegs registered in the correct position in the splined ring. Assemble the spring and plunger in the hole in the shaft and refit the splined ring. Slide the first speed gear and synchronizer assembly onto the shaft with the protruding end of the synchronizer towards the bearing. Press the bearing and its housing onto the shaft so that the flange of the bearing housing (when fitted) is towards the rear of the shaft. Refit the distance piece, speedometer drive, plain washer, lock washer, and locknut in position.

From the opposite end of the shaft assemble the needle-roller bearing and refit the third speed gear assembly. Place the spring and plunger in the hole in the shaft and refit the splined ring. Slide the third and fourth speed synchronizer onto the shaft with the boss on the synchronizer hub, away from the splined ring.

Section F.4

FIRST MOTION SHAFT

Dismantling

Unlock and remove the securing nut and withdraw the lock washer and packing shim.

Press the bearing from the shaft and remove the circlip from the bearing.

Reassembling

Reverse the dismantling procedure, ensuring that the inner tag of the lock washer, which engages the keyway in the shaft, is turned away from the bearing.

Section F.5

LAYGEAR ASSEMBLY

Dismantling

Needle-roller bearings are fitted in each end of the laygear. The needles are held in position in their races (one at each end) by spring rings.

Remove the spring rings from their locating grooves and extract the outer race needle rollers and the inner race. Remove the inner spring ring from its groove in the large end of the laygear and the distance piece and spring ring from the small end of the laygear.

Laygear thrust washers

These washers are designed to permit a laygear end-float of ·001 to ·003 in. (·025 to ·076 mm.) (Sprite Mk. II, III and Midget Mk. I, II) and ·003 to ·005 in. (·076 to ·127 mm.) (Sprite Mk. IV and Midget Mk. III). If the end-float exceeds this amount, the thrust washers must be renewed. On later cars the front thrust washer is located by four springs which are housed in drillings in the gearbox case. The smaller thrust washer at the rear is available in four thicknesses from ·123 to ·131 in. (3·124 to 3·327 mm.) to allow for end-float adjustment.

Reassembling

Reverse the dismantling procedure. Use Service tool 18G 471 for layshaft gear alignment.

Section F.6

GEAR SYNCHRONIZING CONES
(Early Cars)

These cones are 'shrunk on' to the second, third, and fourth speed gears and are normally supplied as a complete unit for spares purposes. Where facilities exist for shrinking on and finally machining the cones, they can be supplied separately. If the gear is to operate satisfactorily, however, care must be taken in fitting them.

The internal machining of the cone is calculated to allow for a shrinkage fit onto the gear, and the cone must be heat-expanded before it can be fitted.

When heated in oil to approximately 121·1° C. (250° F.) expansion will allow the cone to be pressed home onto the gear without damage.

NOTE.—The six large recesses on the perimeter of the cone must line up with the hole in the boss of the gear.

After shrinking on, the unit should be immediately quenched in water to prevent the gear itself being softened. Punch-mark the cone in each of the six recesses. This ensures resistance to displacement when changing gear.

When the cone is in position the final machining can be done in accordance with the dimensions given in Fig. F.4.

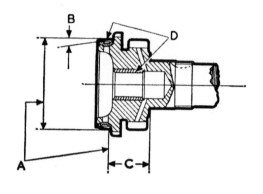

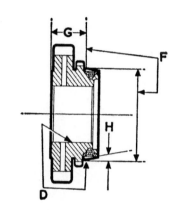

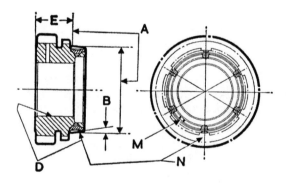

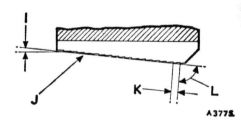

Fig. F.4

Top left: First motion shaft. Lower left: Third speed mainshaft gear. Top right: Second speed mainshaft gear. Lower right: Cone

Dimensions

A. Taper 1·997 in. (50·72 mm.) dia. at this line to gauge.

B. Taper 10° 10′, to be true and concentric with bore to ·001 in. (·025 mm.).

C. ·909/·912 in. (23·09/23·16 mm.).

D. Taper to be true and concentric with bore to ·001 in. (·025 mm.).

E. ·862/·865 in. (21·8/21·9 mm.).

F. Taper 1·966 in. (49·9 mm.) dia. at this line to gauge.

G. ·810/·813 in. (20·57/20·65 mm.).

H. 8° 20′.

I. 6°.

J. Coarse turning may be either right- or left-hand.

K. ·015 in. (·38 mm.).

L. 90°.

M. One notch to be ground in position shown relative to grooves with indentations.

N. Synchronizing cone to be heated in oil, shrunk onto gear, and punched into holes as shown with centre line of holes and spaces in cone in line.

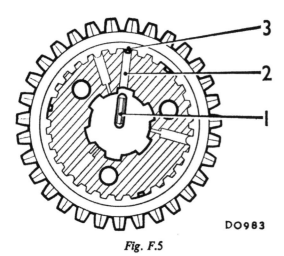

DO983

Fig. F.5

The three-speed synchromesh first and second speed gear assembly, showing the plunger (1) in its drilling in the hub (2) aligned with the cut-away tooth (3) in the gear assembly

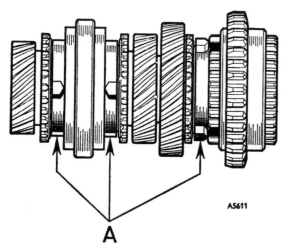

A5611

Fig. F.6

The mainshaft, showing (A) the baulk rings (later cars)

Section F.7

REVERSE LAMP SWITCH

To prevent the cables fraying away from the reverse lamp switch soldered connections, two cable clips should be fitted as shown in the rear extension components illustration. Allow a short length of slack cable between the switch connections and the first retaining clip.

Section F.8

THIRD MOTION SHAFT
(Later Cars)

Dismantling and reassembling

The dismantling and reassembling sequences are the same as detailed in Section F.3 except that the second and third/top gear synchronizers are fitted with baulk rings (see Fig. F.6).

NOTE.—Should the first and second speed gear assembly have been dismantled, the correct position of the gear on the hub when reassembling is most important. Should the gear be incorrectly assembled on the hub, selection of second gear will be impossible.

When reassembling the gear to the hub ensure that the plunger in the hub aligns with the cut-away tooth in the gear assembly (see Fig. F.5), and that the cone end of the hub and the tapered side of the gear teeth are on opposite sides of the assembly.

Section F.9

CHANGE SPEED LEVER
(Flexible Type)

Removing

(1) Unscrew and remove the gear knob.

(2) Turn back the carpet and remove the self-tapping screws securing the gaiter support clamp ring. Remove the gaiter and clamp ring.

(3) Remove the three screws with washers securing the gaiter support retaining plate. Remove the gaiter support and retaining plate.

(4) Remove the change speed lever damper plunger nut and washer, remove the damper spring and plunger. Remove the lever locating peg and spring washer from the side of the extension box casing.

(5) Remove the change speed lever plate and the lever assembly.

Reassembling

Remove the sequence (1) to (5).

EDITOR'S NOTES

F. The Gearbox
Gearbox, reassembling
Service tool 18G471 is very helpful when reinstalling the laygear but is not absolutely necessary.

Figure F.1
Service tool 18G144 is designed to assist in the assembly of the synchronizer but is not absolutely necessary. For this operation, an extra pair of hands will often suffice.

SECTION G

THE PROPELLER SHAFT

GENERAL DESCRIPTION

The propeller shaft and universal joints are of unit construction, the latter being of the non-constant-velocity type.

The fore-and-aft movement of the rear axle and other components is allowed for by a sliding spline between the propeller shaft and gearbox unit. Each universal joint consists of a centre spider, four needle-roller bearings, and two yokes.

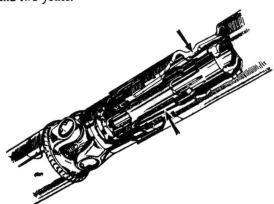

Fig. G.1

The propeller shaft sliding joint, showing the oilways which conduct oil from the gearbox

Section G.1

LUBRICATION

Lubrication nipples are provided on the front and rear universal joints on the propeller shafts fitted to early cars. Lift the floor covering and remove the rubber plug in the left-hand side of the propeller shaft tunnel to gain access to the front nipple.

The universal joints on later cars are pre-packed with lubricant and sealed.

The sliding joint is automatically lubricated from the gearbox.

Section G.2

PROPELLER SHAFT
(Early cars)

Removing

Mark the flange and disconnect the propeller shaft from the rear axle. Remove it from the vehicle over the axle assembly and to the left-hand side of the differential casing.

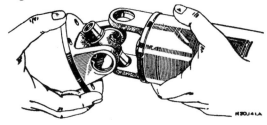

Fig. G.2

Separating the joint

Dismantling

Remove the enamel and any road dirt from the snap rings and bearing faces. Remove the snap rings. If the ring does not come out, tap the bearing face lightly to relieve the pressure against the ring. Hold the splined end of the shaft in one hand and tap the radius of the yoke with a lead or copper hammer; the bearing will then begin to emerge. If difficulty is experienced, use a small bar to tap the bearing from the inside, taking care not to damage the race itself. Turn the yoke over and extract the bearing with the fingers, being careful not to lose any of the needles. Repeat this operation for the other bearings.

Examination

When the propeller shaft has been in use for a long time the parts most likely to show signs of wear are the bearing races and the spider journals.

The complete assembly should be renewed if looseness or stress marks are observed, as no oversize journals or bearings are provided.

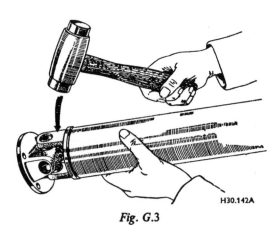

H30.142A

Fig. G.3

Tapping the joint to extract the bearing

It is essential that bearing races should be a light drive fit in the yoke trunnions. Any ovality in the trunnion bearing holes indicates the necessity of fitting new yokes.

Reassembling

Ensure that the holes in the journals of the universal joints are cleaned out. Assemble the needle rollers in the bearing races. Should difficulty be experienced in assembly, smear the walls of the races with light grease to retain the needle rollers in place. It is advisable to renew, if necessary, the cork washer and the washer retainers on the spider journals. Continue assembling in the reverse of the dismantling procedure.

Refitting

When refitting the propeller shaft a second operator is required. With the aid of a screwdriver approximately 8 in. (20 cm.) long inserted through the front universal joint lubricating hole in the propeller shaft tunnel, lift the shaft and guide it onto the splines of the third motion shaft and into the gearbox rear extension.

Section G.3

PROPELLER SHAFT
(Later cars)

Removing and dismantling

(1) Carry out the operations detailed in Section G.2.

Inspection

(2) Wash all the parts thoroughly in petrol (fuel) to remove old grease, and carry out the examination detailed in Section G.2.

Reassembling

It is of extreme importance that the assembly of the journals be carried out under absolutely clean, dust-free conditions.

(3) Fill the reservoir holes in the journal spider with the recommended grease taking care to exclude all air pockets. Fill each bearing assembly with grease to a depth of ⅛ in. (3 mm.).

(4) Fit new seals to the spider journals and insert the spider into the flange yoke, tilting it to engage in the yoke bores.

(5) Fit a bearing assembly into the yoke bore in the bottom position, and using a soft-nosed drift slightly smaller in diameter than the hole in the yoke, tap it into the yoke bore until it is possible to fit the circlip. Repeat this operation for the other three bearings starting opposite the bearing first fitted.

(6) After assembly, carefully remove all surplus grease with a soft cloth. If the bearing appears to bind, tap lightly with a wooden mallet; this will relieve any pressure of the bearing on the ends of the journals.

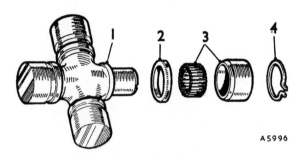

A5996

Fig. G.4

A universal joint bearing—sealed type

1. Journal spider.
2. Rubber seal.
3. Needle rollers and bearings.
4. Circlip.

SECTION H

THE REAR AXLE AND REAR SUSPENSION

THE REAR AXLE COMPONENTS

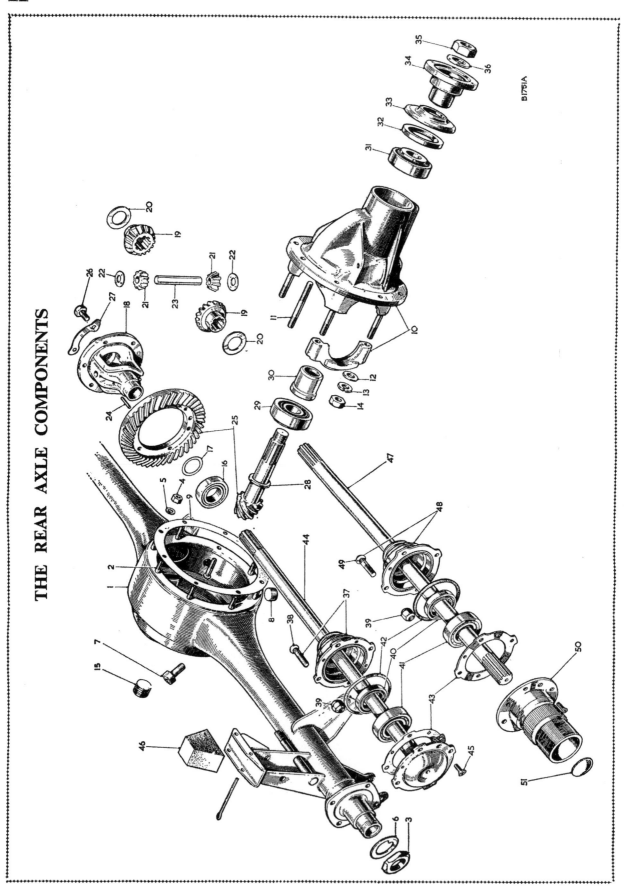

B1751A

KEY TO THE REAR AXLE COMPONENTS

No.	Description
1.	Case assembly.
2.	Gear carrier stud.
3.	Bearing retaining nut.
4.	Gear carrier to axle case nut.
5.	Spring washer.
6.	Washer.
7.	Breather assembly.
8.	Drain plug.
9.	Gear carrier joint.
10.	Carrier assembly.
11.	Bearing cap stud.
12.	Plain washer.
13.	Spring washer.
14.	Nut.
15.	Filler plug.
16.	Differential bearing.
17.	Bearing packing washer.

No.	Description
18.	Differential cage.
19.	Differential wheel.
20.	Thrust washer.
21.	Differential pinion.
22.	Thrust washer.
23.	Pinion pin.
24.	Pinion peg.
25.	Crown wheel and pinion.
26.	Bolt.
27.	Lock washer.
28.	Pinion thrust washer.
29.	Inner pinion bearing.
30.	Bearing spacer.
31.	Pinion outer bearing.
32.	Oil seal.
33.	Dust cover.
34.	Universal joint flange.

No.	Description	
35.	Pinion nut.	
36.	Spring washer.	
37.	Hub assembly.	
38.	Wheel stud.	
39.	Nut.	
40.	Oil seal.	
41.	Hub bearing.	
42.	Oil seal ring.	
43.	Hub shaft joint.	
44.	Axle shaft.	
45.	Screw.	
46.	Bump rubber.	
47.	Axle shaft.	
48.	Hub assembly.	Wire wheels only.
49.	Wheel stud.	
50.	Hub extension.	
51.	Welch plug.	

GENERAL DESCRIPTION

The rear axle is of the three-quarter-floating type incorporating hypoid final drive reduction gears. The axle shafts, pinion, and differential assemblies can be withdrawn without removing the axle from the vehicle. The rear wheel bearing outer races are located in the hubs, and the inner races are mounted on the axle tube and secured by nuts and lock washers. Wheel studs in the hubs pass through the brake-drums and axle shaft driving flanges. Brake-drums are located on the hub flanges by two countersunk screws in each.

The differential and pinion shaft bearings are preloaded, the amount of preload being adjustable. The position of the pinion in relation to the crown wheel when being adjusted must be kept within the maker's figure limits. The backlash between the gears is adjustable by shims. Suspension is by rubber-mounted quarter-elliptic leaf springs and the shackles are fitted with rubber bushes of the flexing type.

Section H.1

LUBRICATION

The combined filler and level plug situated on the rear axle casing is reached from beneath the rear of the car. The oil must be level with the bottom of the filler hole. The drain plug is situated on the bottom of the rear axle casing.

Section H.2

AXLE UNIT

Removing

Raise the vehicle by placing a jack under the differential housing and support the body. Remove the wheels.

The down pipe, silencer, and exhaust pipe should be withdrawn from the car as described in Section A.

Keeping the jack in position, release each check strap by unscrewing the nut and bolt at its body connection.

Release each damper arm from its connecting linkage.

Disconnect each suspension upper link from the rear axle bracket by unscrewing the nut and bolt and tapping the bolt from its housing.

Disconnect the brake cable at the cable adjustment.

Working beneath the car, unscrew the self-locking nuts and remove the bolts securing the propeller shaft flange to the axle pinion flange.

Disconnect the hydraulic brake pipe at the main union just forward of the differential housing.

After ascertaining that the weight of the axle is fully on the jack, unscrew and remove the shackle pins.

Lower the axle and withdraw it from the car.

Refitting

The refitting of the rear axle is a reversal of the removal procedure, with attention to the following. If for any reason it has been necessary to remove the suspension upper link and at the same time the rear axle has been withdrawn from the car, do not tighten the shackle pins until the upper link is mounted in position.

Section H.3

AXLE SHAFTS

Removing

Raise the vehicle by placing a jack under the differential housing. Place supports under the rear springs and remove the wheels.

Release the handbrake and back off the brake shoes adjusters.

Disc wheels

Remove the brake drum locating screws and tap the drums off the hubs.

Remove the axle shaft retaining screw and withdraw the shaft from the hub assembly. Should the paper washer be damaged, it must be renewed when reassembling.

Wire wheels

Remove the nuts securing the drum to the hub and tap the drums off the hub. Remove the retaining screws securing the hub extension flanges to the hubs. Withdraw the hubs extensions and axle shaft. Should the paper washer or 'O' ring be damaged, it must be renewed when re-assembling.

Refitting

Reverse the removal procedure when refitting.

Section H.4

HUBS

Removing (See Editor's note at end of Section Ha.)

(1) Remove the brake drum and axle shaft as described in Section H.3.

(2) Using tool 18G 152 remove the nut and lock washer.

(3) Withdraw the hub complete with bearing and seal using tool 18G 146, or 18G 304 (Z) with adaptors 18G 304 F and 18G 304 H.

Refitting

Before refitting, repack the hub bearings with grease.

The hub bearing is non-adjustable and is replaced in one operation by pressing it into position.

It is essential when fitting the differential shaft that the paper joint washer between its flange and the hub is compressed before the abutment shoulder of the shaft pulls up against the bearing races. If in an emergency a paper joint washer is hand-made, ensure that it is about ·010 in. (·2 mm.) thick. An oil leak will invariably result if the washer is too thin.

It is advisable to use joint washers supplied by BMC Service Ltd. to ensure correct assembly.

If the seal has been removed, drift it into position with the bearing (lip towards the bearing) using tool 18G 134 with adaptor 18G 134 Q.

The hub is then drifted onto the axle casing with Service tools 18G 134 and 18G 134 Q. Continue to assemble to the reverse of the removal procedure.

Section H.5

RENEWING THE PINION OIL SEAL

Mark the propeller shaft and pinion shaft driving flanges so that they can be replaced in the same relative positions, and disconnect the propeller shaft.

Unscrew the nut in the centre of the driving flange, using Service tool 18G 34 A to prevent the flange from turning. Remove the nut and washer and withdraw the flange and pressed end cover from the pinion shaft.

Extract the oil seal from the casing.

Press a new seal into the casing with the edge of the sealing ring facing inwards.

Replace the driving flange and end cover, taking care not to damage the edge of the oil seal, and tighten the nut with a torque wrench (Service tool 18G 372) to a reading of 140 lb. ft. (19·4 kg. m.).

Reconnect the propeller shaft, taking care to fit the two flanges with the locating marks in alignment.

Section H.6

DIFFERENTIAL ASSEMBLY

Removing

Drain the rear axle.

Remove the axle shafts as detailed in Section H.3.

Mark the propeller shaft and pinion shaft driving flanges to ensure correct assembly. Remove the self-locking nuts and disconnect the joint.

Remove the nuts securing the differential assembly to the axle banjo and withdraw the complete unit.

Dismantling (See Editor's note at end of Section Ha.)

Check to ensure that the differential housing caps are marked to ensure correct replacement, then remove the bearing cap securing nuts and spring washers. Remove the bearing caps and withdraw the differential cage.

Remove the differential bearings from the cage, using Service tool 18G 47 C together with 18G 47 M. Note that the thrust face of each bearing is marked with the word 'THRUST', and that shims are fitted between the inner ring of each bearing and differential cage.

Knock back the tabs of the locking washers, unscrew the bolts securing the crown wheel to the differential, and remove the crown wheel from the differential cage.

Tap out the dowel pin locating the differential pinion shaft. The diameter of the pin is ⅛ in. (3·18 mm.) and it must be tapped out from the crown wheel side of the differential cage as the hole into which it fits has a smaller diameter at the crown wheel end to prevent the pin

Fig. H.1

Refitting the inner race of the pinion rear bearing, using tool 18G 285. This tool is also used to remove the race

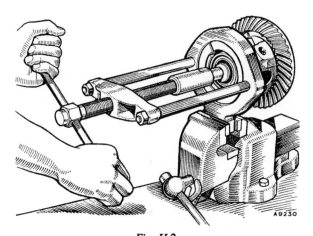

Fig. H.2

Remove the differential bearings, using remover 18G 47 C with adaptor 18G 47 M

passing right through. It may be necessary to clean out the metal peened over the entry hole with a ⅛ in. drill in order to facilitate removal of the dowel pin. Drive out the differential pinion shaft and remove the pinions and thrust washers from the differential cage.

Remove the pinion nut, driving flange, and pressed end cover.

Drive the pinion shaft towards the rear through the carrier; it will carry with it the inner race and the rollers of the rear bearing, leaving the outer race and the complete front bearing in position.

Tap out the inner race of the front bearing and the oil seal. The outer races should be withdrawn with Service tool 18G 264 with adaptors 18G 264 D and 18G 264 E.

Slide off the pinion sleeve and the shims; withdraw the rear bearing inner race from the pinion shaft with Service tool 18G 285, noting the spacing washer against the pinion head. Withdraw the rear bearing outer race with Service tool 18G 264 and adaptor 18G 264 E.

Reassembling

Where it is only necessary to fit a replacement oil seal the axle may be reassembled in the reverse order of dismantling, assuming that the original shim thicknesses are retained. Where any part is renewed, such as a crown wheel and pinion, pinion bearings, etc., the setting of the pinion (i.e. its position relative to the crown wheel) must be checked. This work should be carried out with the aid of Service tools 18G 191 and 18G 191 A.

Examine the crown wheel teeth. If a new crown wheel is needed **a mated pair—pinion and crown wheel—must be fitted.**

1. SETTING THE PINION POSITION

Fit the bearing outer races to the gear carrier, using Service tools 18G 134 and 18G 134 Q.

Smooth off the pinion head with an oil-stone, but do not erase any markings that may be etched on the pinion head.

Assemble the pinion and rear bearing with a washer of known thickness behind the pinion head.

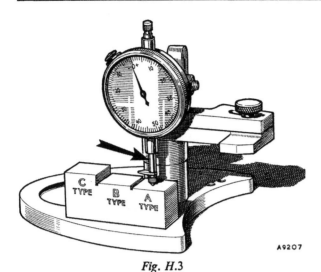

Fig. H.3

Setting the dial gauge to zero on the gauge block pinion position setting. The arrow indicates the extension foot

Position the pinion in the gear carrier without the bearing spacer and oil seal.

Fit the inner ring of the front bearing and the driving flange and tighten the nut gradually until a bearing preload of 8 to 10 lb. in. (·09 to ·12 kg. m.) is obtained.

Remove the keep disc from the base of the magnet. Adjust the dial indicator to zero on the machined step 'A' of the setting block.

Clean the pinion head and place the magnet and dial indicator in position. Move the indicator arm until the foot of the gauge rests on the centre of the differential bearing bore at one side and tighten the knurled locking screw. Obtain the maximum depth reading and note any variation from zero setting. Repeat the check in the opposite bearing bore. Add the two variations together and divide by two to obtain a mean reading.

Take into consideration any variation in pinion head thickness. This will be shown as an unbracketed figure etched on the pinion head and will always be minus (−). If no unbracketed figure is shown, the pinion head is of nominal thickness.

Using the mean clock gauge reading obtained and the unbracketed pinion head figure (if any), the following calculation can be made.

(*a*) **If the clock reading is minus** add the clock reading to the pinion head marking, the resulting sum being minus. **Reduce the washer thickness** by this amount.

Example

Clock reading	..	..	..	− ·002 in.
Pinion marking	..	..	..	− ·005 in.
Variation from nominal	..	..		− ·007 in.

Reduce the washer thickness by this amount.

(*b*) **If the clock reading is plus and numerically less** than the pinion marking **reduce** the washer thickness by the difference.

Example

Pinion marking	..	..	..	− ·005 in.
Clock reading	..	..	..	+ ·003 in.
Variation from nominal	..	..		− ·002 in.

Reduce the washer thickness by this amount.

(*c*) **If the clock reading is plus and numerically greater** than the pinion marking **increase** the washer thickness by the difference.

Example

Clock reading	..	..	..	+ ·008 in.
Pinion marking	..	..	..	− ·003 in.
Variation from nominal	..	..		+ ·005 in.

Increase the washer thickness by this amount.

The only cases where no alterations are required to the washer thickness are when the clock reading **is plus** and **numerically equal** to the unbracketed pinion marking, or the clock reading is zero and there is no unbracketed marking on the pinion head.

Allowance should then finally be made as follows for the mounting distance marked on the pinion head in a rectangular bracket.

If the marking is a **plus** figure **reduce** the washer thickness by an equal amount.

If the marking is a **minus** figure **increase** the washer thickness by an equal amount.

A tolerance of ·001 in. is allowed in the thickness of the washer finally fitted.

2. PINION BEARING PRELOAD

A washer of the thickness indicated by the use of the tool and calculations should now be fitted under the pinion head and the pinion assembled with bearings, pinion bearing distance piece, oil seal, universal joint flange, and nut. (See Editor's note at end of Section Ha.)

NOTE.—The pinion bearing distance piece is of the collapsible type. That is to say, when the pinion nut is tightened to the correct torque spanner reading of 135 to 140 lb. ft. (18·69 to 19·4 kg. m.) the distance piece collapses to give the correct bearing preload of 11 to 13 lb. in. (·126 to ·149 kg. m.). It will only perform this function

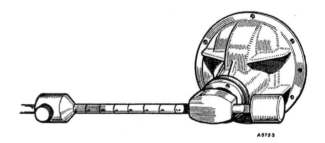

Fig. H.4

Checking the bevel pinion bearing preload (Service tool 18G 207)

H.6

Sprite and Midget. Issue 4. 4780

once. Thus, when the pinion is reassembled a new distance piece must be fitted.

Prevent the universal joint flange from turning and tighten the pinion nut gradually to a torque spanner reading of 140 lb. ft. (19·4 kg. m.). Checks should be made during the tightening, using Service tool 18G 207, to ensure the pinion bearing preload does not exceed 13 lb. in. (·15 kg. m.). When the nut is correctly tightened it should provide a pinion bearing preload of 11 to 13 lb. in. (·13 to ·15 kg. m.). When the correct preload is obtained no further attention is needed so far as the pinion is concerned.

3. SETTING THE CROWN WHEEL POSITION

The method of setting the position of the crown wheel assembly depends upon the markings given on the differential gear carrier and differential gear cage.

To assist in the calculation of the thickness of shims to be fitted behind each differential cage bearing variations are indicated by stamped numbers on the carrier adjacent to the bearing bores. The dimensions to be considered are shown in Fig. H.6. (A) being the distance from the centre-line to the bearing register of the carrier on the left-hand side and (B) the distance from the centre-line to the bearing register of the carrier on the right-hand side. The (C) dimension is from the bearing register on one side of the cage to the register on the other side, while the (D) dimension is from the rear face of the crown wheel to the bearing register on the opposite side. Any variation on the (A) dimension will be found stamped on

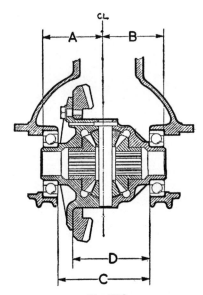

Fig. H.6

Illustrates the points from which the calculations must be made to determine the shim thickness for the bearings on each side of the carrier

the carrier adjacent to the bearing bore, and similarly with the (B) dimension. Variations on the (C) and (D) dimensions are stamped on the machined face of the differential cage.

It is possible to calculate the shim thickness required on the left-hand side by the use of the following formula:

$$A + D - C + \cdot 002 \text{ in.}$$

Substituting the actual variations shown, this formula gives the shim thickness required to compensate for the variations in machining plus the extra ·002 in. (·05 mm.) to give the necessary bearing pinch. In addition, allowance must be made for variations in bearing thickness in the following manner.

Rest the bearing, with the inner race over the recess and outer ring thrust face downwards, on the small surface plate of Service tool 18G 191 A. Drop the magnet on the surface plate and zero the clock gauge to the small gauge block on its step marked 'A'. (This is the thickness of the standard bearing.) Swing over the indicator until it rests on the plain surface of the inner race, and, holding the inner race down against the balls, take a reading (Fig. H.7). Normally the bearing will be standard to −·003 in., though in some cases tolerances may be from standard to −·005 in. A negative variation shown by this test indicates the additional thickness of shimming to be added to that side of the differential.

The formula for the right-hand side is:

$$B - D + \cdot 006 \text{ in.}$$

and here again final allowance must be made for variation in bearing thickness.

When a framed number is marked on the back of the crown wheel, e.g. +2, it must be taken into account before assembling the shims and bearings to the differential cage. This mark assists in relating the crown wheel with the pinion.

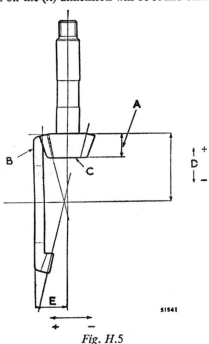

Fig. H.5

Crown wheel and pinion markings

A. Pinion head thickness. Max. −·007 in. (−·178 mm.).
B. Crown wheel marked here.
C. Pinion marked here.
D. Pinion mounting distance. Max. ±·004 in. (±·102 mm.).
E. Crown wheel mounting distance. Max. ±·005 in. (±·127 mm.).

A9232

Fig. H.7

Checking crown wheel to pinion backlash (Service tools 18G 191 and 18G 191 A)

If, for example, the mark is +2, then shims to the value of ·002 in. (·05 mm.) must be transferred from the left-hand side (the crown wheel side) to the right-hand side. If the marking is —2, then shims to the value of ·002 in. (·05 mm.) must be moved from the right-hand side to the left-hand side.

4. ADJUSTING THE BACKLASH

Assemble the bearings (thrust faces outwards) and shims as calculated to the differential cage.

Bolt the crown wheel to the differential cage but do not knock over the locking tabs. Tighten the bolts to a torque wrench reading of 60 lb. ft. (8·30 kg. m.).

Mount the assembly on two 'V' blocks and check the amount of run-out of the crown wheel, as it is rotated, by means of a suitably mounted dial indicator. The maximum permissible run-out is ·002 in. (·05 mm.) and any greater irregularity must be corrected. If there is excessive run-out detach the crown wheel and examine the joint faces on the flange of the differential cage and on the crown wheel for any particles of dirt.

When the parts are thoroughly cleaned it is unlikely that the crown wheel will not run true.

Tighten the bolts to the correct torque wrench reading and knock over the locking washers.

Fit the differential to the gear carrier. Replace the bearing caps and tighten the nuts to a torque wrench reading of 65 lb. ft. (8·99 kg. m.). Bolt the special tool surface plate to the gear carrier flange and mount the clock gauge on the magnet bracket in such a way that an accurate backlash figure may be obtained (see Fig. H.8).

H.8

The correct figure for the backlash to be used with any particular crown wheel and pinion is etched on the rear face of the crown wheel concerned and must be adhered to strictly.

A movement of ·002 in. (·05 mm.) shim thickness from one side of the differential cage to the other will produce a variation in backlash of approximately ·002 in. (·05 mm.).

Great care must be taken to ensure absolute cleanliness during the above operations, as any discrepancies resulting from dirty assembly would affect the setting of the crown wheel or pinion.

Refitting is a reversal of the removal procedure.

Section H.7

SPRINGS

Removing

Raise the vehicle by placing a jack under the differential housing and support the body. After ascertaining that the weight of the axle is fully on the jack and that the springs are in the fully unloaded position remove the shackle pins.

The spring can now be removed simply by extracting the bolts which pass upwards at the forward end of the spring into the spring attachment plate. The 'U' bolt must also be removed when the spring can be pulled out of its mounting.

Refitting

Reverse the removal procedure when refitting the spring assemblies.

NOTE.—Tighten the spring bolts when the normal working load has been applied to the springs.

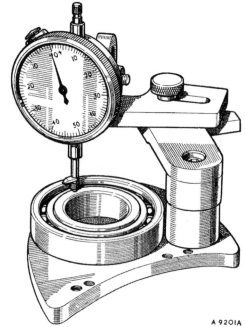

A 9201A

Fig. H.8

Checking differential bearing width with Service tools 18G 191 and 18G 191 A

Sprite and Midget. Issue 3. 65317

SECTION Ha

THE REAR AXLE AND REAR SUSPENSION

The information given in this Section refers specifically to the Sprite (Mk. III and IV) and Midget (Mk. II and III) and must be used in conjunction with Section H

GENERAL DESCRIPTION

The rear axle is the same as that used on earlier cars. Suspension is by rubber-mounted semi-elliptic leaf springs and the shackles are fitted with rubber bushes of the flexing type.

Section Ha.1

AXLE UNIT

Removing

Raise the vehicle by placing a jack under the differential housing and support the body. Remove the wheels.

Remove the down pipe, silencer, and exhaust pipe (see Section A).

Keeping the jack in this position, release each check strap at its axle location.

Release each damper arm from its connecting linkage. Disconnect the brake cable at the cable adjuster. Unscrew the nuts and remove the bolts securing the propeller shaft flange to the axle pinion flange (see Section G). Disconnect the hydraulic brake pipe at the main union just forward of the differential housing. Remove the 'U' bolt securing nuts. Ascertain that the weight of the axle is fully on the jack, unscrew and remove the rear shackle pins.

Refitting

Reverse the removal procedure.

NOTE.—Before tightening the spring bolts it is essential that the normal working load be applied to the springs so that the flexing rubber bushes are deflected to an equal extent in both directions during service. Failure to take this precaution will inevitably lead to early deterioration of the bushes.

Section Ha.2

SPRINGS

Removing

Raise the vehicle by placing a jack under the differential housing and support the body. Ascertain that the weight of the axle is fully on the jack and that the springs are in the fully unloaded position. Remove the wheels. From within the car remove the set screws securing the front anchor bracket to the rear of the body foot-well.

From beneath the car remove the two front bracket securing set screws. Remove the four 'U' bolt securing nuts and the damper anchorage plate. Remove the rear shackle nuts, pins, and plates and lift out the spring assembly.

Refitting

Remove the axle check strap to assist fitting the 'U' bolts. Tighten the spring bolt when the normal working load has been applied to the spring.

Reverse the removal procedure.

EDITOR'S NOTES

H. The Rear Axle and Rear Suspension

Hubs

Appropriate hub and gear pullers may be substituted if the suggested service tools are not available. The object is to remove or install the part in question without damaging it.

Careful use of a soft-faced hammer and appropriate drifts can be very often substituted for suggested driving tools.

Differential assembly, dismantling

Any disassembly of the differential unit involving the replacement of parts will require that the necessary clearances be reset. This job requires very specialized tools and the ability to use them in the manner indicated. Unless the proper equipment is available, it is advisable to leave this work to a properly equipped shop. An improperly set differential assembly will be noisy and will wear quickly.

An arbor press and suitable adaptors may be used in place of the recommended bearing removal and installation tools.

Pinion bearing preload

An inch-pound torque wrench may be used in place of Service tool 18G207 for measuring the pinion bearing preload.

Ha.2   Sprite and Midget. Issue 2. 4780

158

SECTION J

THE STEERING GEAR

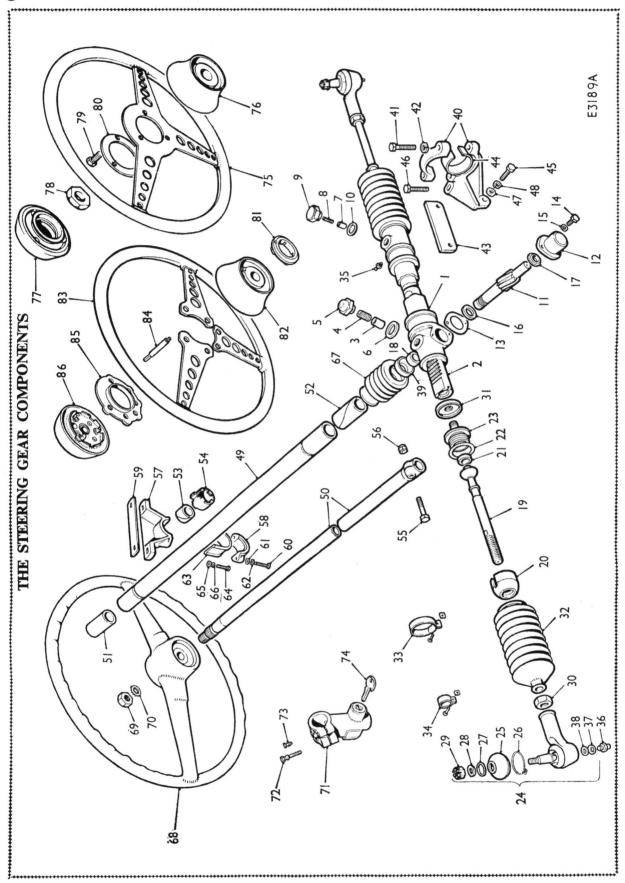

THE STEERING GEAR COMPONENTS

E3189A

KEY TO THE STEERING GEAR COMPONENTS

No.	Description	No.	Description	No.	Description
1.	Rack housing.	28.	Plain washer.	57.	Bracket.
2.	Rack.	29.	Nut.	58.	Bracket cap.
3.	Damper pad.	30.	Locknut.	59.	Shim.
4.	Damper pad spring.	31.	Lock washer.	60.	Set screw.
5.	Damper pad housing.	32.	Seal.	61.	Plain washer.
6.	Shim.	33.	Clip (inner).	62.	Spring washer.
7.	Secondary damper pad.	34.	Clip (outer).	63.	Seating.
8.	Secondary damper spring.	35.	Lubricator.	64.	Set screw.
9.	Secondary damper housing.	36.	Lubricator.	65.	Plain washer.
10.	Housing washer.	37.	Dished washer.	66.	Spring washer.
11.	Pinion.	38.	Fibre washer.	67.	Draught excluder.
12.	Pinion tail bearing.	39.	Retainer.	68.	Steering-wheel.
13.	Shim.	40.	Bracket and cap assembly.	69.	Nut.
14.	Set screw.	41.	Set screw.	70.	Shakeproof washer.
15.	Spring washer.	42.	Spring washer.	71.	Steering-column lock.
16.	Pinion thrust washer (top).	43.	Seating.	72.	Shear bolt.
17.	Pinion thrust washer (bottom).	44.	Packing.	73.	Locating screw.
18.	Pinion seal.	45.	Set screw.	74.	Lock key.
19.	Tie-rod.	46.	Set screw.	75.	Steering-wheel.
20.	Ball housing (female).	47.	Plain washer.	76.	Steering-wheel nut.
21.	Ball seat.	48.	Spring washer.	77.	Motif.
22.	Shim.	49.	Outer column.	78.	Nut.
23.	Ball housing (male).	50.	Inner column tube.	79.	Set screw.
24.	Ball socket assembly.	51.	Felt bearing (top).	80.	Locking ring.
25.	Boot.	52.	Felt bearing (bottom).	81.	Slip ring.
26.	Clip.	53.	Felt bearing (bottom).	82.	Steering wheel boss.
27.	Ring.	54.	Clip.	83.	Steering wheel.
		55.	Bolt.	84.	Horn contact.
		56.	Nut.	85.	Lock ring.
				86.	Horn push.

Items 75–80: Midget Mk. III (GAN5). Sprite Mk. IV (HAN10).

Items 81–86: From car number Midget Mk. III (GAN5) 89515. Sprite Mk. IV (HAN10) 86303.

GENERAL DESCRIPTION

The steering gear is of the rack and pinion type and is secured above the front frame cross-member immediately behind the radiator. Tie-rods, operating the swivel arms, are attached to each end of the steering-rack by ball joints enclosed in rubber gaiters.

The steering-column engages the splined end of a helical-toothed pinion to which it is secured by a clamp bolt.

End-play of the pinion is eliminated by adjustment of the shims fitted beneath the pinion tail end bearings. A damper pad inserted in the steering rack controls the backlash between the pinion and the rack.

Section J.1

LUBRICATION

(Early cars)

The lubrication nipple provided at the left-hand side of the rack housing (right-hand side on left-hand-drive cars) is accessible when the bonnet is raised. Apply a gun filled with lubricant and give 10 strokes only at regular intervals.

CAUTION: If the vehicle is hoisted with its front wheels clear of the ground care should be taken to avoid forceful movement of the wheels from lock to lock, as damage may occur within the steering mechanism.

Section J.2

FRONT WHEEL ALIGNMENT

When correctly adjusted the front wheels should toe in 0 to ⅛ in. (0 to 3 mm.). To carry out the necessary adjustment first check that all tyres are inflated to the recommended pressures (see 'GENERAL DATA').

Turn the wheels to the straight-ahead position. [Roll the vehicle backwards and forwards and bounce the suspension to relieve suspension and tyre stresses.] With conventional base-bar-type alignment gauges measurements in front of and behind the wheel centres should be taken at the same points on tyres or rim flanges. This is achieved by marking the tyres where the first reading is taken and moving the car forward approximately half a road wheel revolution before taking the second reading at the same points.

If the wheel alignment is incorrect adjust the track by slackening the locknut for each tie-rod ball joint and the clips securing the rubber gaiters to the tie-rods, then rotate each tie-rod equally in the necessary direction. Both tie-rods have right-hand threads.

NOTE.—To ensure that the steering-rack is in the central position and that the steering geometry is correct it is important to adjust the tie-rods to exactly equal lengths.

After adjustment tighten the ball joint locknuts.

Section J.3

STEERING-COLUMN ASSEMBLY

Removing

Remove the connector from the negative battery terminal. Release and remove the clamp bolt nut from the splined lower end of the steering-column. Disconnect the horn wire at its snap connection beneath the fascia. Remove the steering-column surround situated between the fascia panel and the steering-wheel, after removing its securing set screws located behind the fascia. Release the bolts securing the column bracket beneath the fascia panel. The steering-wheel may now be withdrawn. The inner and outer columns can be separated once the steering-wheel motif, steering-wheel securing nut, and steering-wheel have been removed. (See Section J.6 for later cars.) To avoid damage to the horn switch contact use Service tool 18G 562 to unscrew the nut.

Refitting

Refitting of the steering-column assembly is the reverse of the removal procedure. Use Service tool 18G 562 when tightening the steering-wheel nut.

Section J.4

STEERING-RACK AND PINION

(Early cars)

Removing

Remove the clamp nut and bolt from the splined lower end of the steering-column and disengage the column from the splines.

Remove the split pins and slotted nuts from the ball pins and detach the tie-rod ball joint from the swivel arm, using Service tool 18G 1063.

Remove the set screws securing the steering-rack clamp mounting brackets to the front cross-member. The rack assembly complete with tie-rods and brackets can now be removed.

Dismantling

Measure and record the distance from the spanner flats on the tie-rods to each of the ball joint locknuts; this will be of great assistance when reassembling.

Slacken the ball joint locknuts and unscrew the ball joint assemblies.

Position the rack housing over a receptacle to catch the oil, release the gaiter clips from the rack housing and tie-rods, and remove the rubber gaiters.

Remove the hexagonal cap adjacent to the oil nipple on the housing and withdraw it complete with sealing washer, pressure pad, and spring.

Remove the damper pad housing fitted at the pinion end of the rack housing and withdraw it complete with plunger, spring, and shims.

Extract the bolts securing the pinion shaft tail bearing and remove the bearing and shims. Withdraw the pinion complete with the bottom thrust washer. The top thrust washer (the thickest one) is trapped behind the rack teeth and may be removed after the rack is withdrawn.

Secure the rack housing between suitable clamps in a vice and tap back the washers locking the tie-rod ball housing. Remove the ball joint cap, using Service tool 18G 313.

NOTE.—In some cases the latter operation releases the ball seat housing from the ball joint cap; in this case difficulty will be experienced in removing the ball housing from the rack. It is therefore essential to release the ball housing from the rack before the ball seat housing and joint cap are separated.

Remove the lock washer and withdraw the steering-rack from the housing.

Remove the ball seat housing from the ball joint caps, using Service tool 18G 313 together with 18G 312. The shims and ball seats are now free to be removed: ensure that the shims are kept to their respective sides.

Thoroughly clean and examine all parts of the dismantled assembly for wear, and renew if necessary.

Reassembly

Reassemble by reversing the dismantling procedure and pay special attention to the following points.

The ball joints linking the tie-rods to the rack must be a reasonably tight sliding fit without play. Any adjustment required is carried out by varying the thickness of shims fitted beneath the ball joint cap seating. The shims are available in thicknesses of ·002, ·003, ·005, and ·010 in. (·05, ·08, ·13, and ·25 mm.). When correctly adjusted, the ball housing must be locked in three places with the flange of the lock washers.

Place the thickest of the pinion thrust washers in position in the rack housing with its chamfered edge towards the rack. Replace the smaller thrust washer on the plain end of the pinion shaft with the chamfered edge towards the pinion teeth.

Ensure also that the centre tooth on the rack is in line with the mark on the splined end of the pinion shaft when replacing the pinion. Excessive end-float of the pinion is rectified by the fitting of shims. By means of a dial

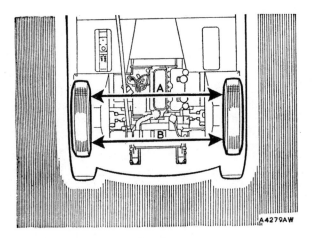

Fig. J.1

The toe-in must be adjusted so that (A) *is 0 to ⅛ in.*
(0 to 3 mm.) greater than (B)

gauge placed at the end of the pinion shaft, check the end-float of the shaft, which should be between ·002 and ·005 in. (·05 and ·13 mm.). The shims are available in thicknesses of ·003, ·005, and ·010 in. (·08, ·13, and ·25 mm.). Replace the ball joint locknuts and joint assem-

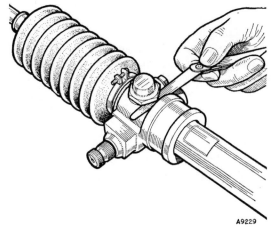

Fig. J.2

Checking the adjustment of the damper cap

blies in approximately their original positions, referring to the figures recorded when the rack was dismantled. To replace and adjust the rack damper, position the plunger in the cap and replace the cap. Screw down the cap until it is just possible to rotate the pinion shaft by drawing the rack through its housing. With a feeler gauge measure the clearance between the hexagon of the damper cap and its seating in the rack housing (Fig. J.2). After obtaining a figure, add ·002 to ·005 in. (·05 to ·13 mm.) to arrive at the correct thickness of shims which must be placed beneath the damper cap. Shims are available in thicknesses of ·003 and ·010 in. (·08 and ·25 mm.). Remove the damper cap and plunger. Fit the spring beneath the plunger and assembly with the required number of shims to give the stated clearance. Fit a new pinion shaft oil seal and pump 10 fl. oz. (·28 litre) approximately of oil into the rack housing through the nipple provided.

Refitting

Refitting is the reverse of the removal procedure, except that the bolts securing the housing to its mounting brackets should not be fully tightened until the assembly has been replaced. This method of assembly will ensure that the steering-rack pinion is in correct alignment with the column. Finally, tighten the rack housing bolts.

Section J.5

STEERING LOCK IGNITION SWITCH

Cars exported to certain markets are fitted with a combined ignition/starter switch and steering-column lock mounted on the steering-column.

On cars fitted with the lock a sleeve integral with the inner column is slotted to permit engagement of the lock tongue; the outer column is also slotted to allow the lock tongue to pass through. A hole drilled in the upper surface of the outer column locates the steering lock bracket. The bracket is secured by two bolts each waisted below the head to permit removal of the heads by shear action during assembly.

To remove the lock, disconnect the battery and the ignition/starter switch connections and turn the lock setting to 'GARAGE' to unlock the steering. Free the steering-column assembly as described in Section J.3 and remove the lock securing bolts with a suitable tool.

Section J.6

STEERING-WHEEL AND HUB
(Midget GAN5, Sprite HAN10)

Removing

(1) Remove the steering-wheel motif assembly; it is a press-fit.

(2) Turn back the lock tabs on the centre boss retainer, and remove bolts, centre boss retainer and the steering-wheel.
NOTE.—From Car No. G–AN5–105501 the lock tabs have been deleted from the centre boss retainer.

Hub

(3) Slacken the steering-wheel nut and fit Service tool 18G 1181 to the hub using the special bolts. Mark the hub and column to assist correct re-alignment and pull the hub until it is a loose fit on the steering-column. Remove 18G 1181, the steering-wheel nut and hub.

(4) When refitting the hub, position it on the column splines in the original position. Fit the nut and tighten to the torque wrench setting given in **'GENERAL DATA'**.

Section J.7

STEERING COLUMN ASSEMBLY
(Midget Mk. III from Car No. G–AN5–105501)

Removing

NOTE.—From Car No. G–AN5–114643 a new type of steering rack is fitted; making it unnecessary to carry out operations 2, 3 and 4 when removing the column from the steering rack.

(1) Disconnect the battery.

(2) Turn the steering until the pinch bolt nut is upper-most and remove the nut.

(3) Using a soft drift, push the bolt until the threaded end is flush with the column.

(4) Turn the steering until the bolt head is uppermost, taking care that the bolt does not foul the brake pipe as the steering is turned.

(5) Remove the pinch bolt.

(6) Disconnect the multi-connector block.

(7) Disconnect the wiring from the ignition/steering lock switch.

(8) Turn the steering to the straight-ahead position.

(9) Remove the bolts retaining the steering-column support bracket.

(10) Remove the steering-column complete with steering-wheel and direction indicator switch.

Refitting

(11) Check that the steering rack is in the straight-ahead position.

(10) Check that the column is in the straight-ahead position with the pinch bolt split uppermost.

(11) Reverse the removing procedure in (1) to (10).

Section J.8

STEERING LOCK IGNITION SWITCH
(Midget Mk. III from Car No. G–AN5–105501)

Removing

(1) Remove the steering-column (Section J.3).

(2) Remove the steering-wheel and hub (Section J.6).

(3) Remove the direction indicator/headlight flasher/low-high beam switch.

(4) Turn the ingition key to position '1' to ensure that the steering lock is disengaged.

(5) Drill out, or remove with a suitable proprietary tool, the retaining shear bolts.

(6) Unscrew the steering lock locating grub screw.

(7) Remove the steering lock and ignition starter switch.

Refitting

(8) Reverse the removing procedure in (1) to (7), using new shear bolts and ensuring that the shear bolts are tightened until the bolt heads shear at the waisted point giving a torque tightness of 12 lbf. ft. (1·66 kgf. m.).

Section J.9

LUBRICATION
(Midget Mk. III from Car No. G–AN5–114643)

It is recommended that after every 30,000 miles (50000 km.) or 3 years the steering rack is inspected and lubricated.

(1) Clean the bellows and the ends of the rack housing.

(2) Inspect the bellows for cracks, splits, signs of deterioration, or leakage of lubricant. If a bellows is damaged, or there are signs of lubricant leakage, the bellows must be renewed as described in Section J.13.

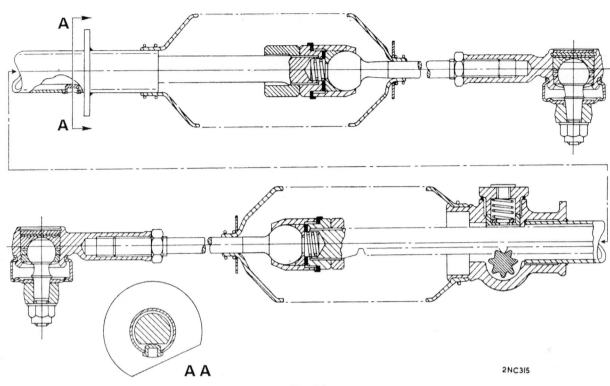

AA

2NC315

Fig. J.3

A section through the steering rack and tie-rods. Inset AA: the correct position of the flat on the rack in relation to the plug

(3) Release the bellows fixings from both ends of the rack housing.

(4) Roll the bellows back to expose the rack and inner ball joints.

(5) Examine the existing grease around the inner ball joint and the rack for ingress of water or dirt; if this is evident, the steering rack must be removed for dismantling and inspection of the components as described in Section J.11.

(6) If the inner ball joint and the rack are in a satisfactory condition, apply approximately 2 oz. (57 gm.) of a recommended grease around each inner ball joint and the rack including the teeth.

(7) Unroll the bellows and secure to the rack housing.

CAUTION: If the vehicle is hoisted with its front wheels clear of the ground, care should be taken to avoid forceful movement of the wheels from lock to lock as damage may occur within the steering mechanism.

Section J.10

STEERING RACK AND PINION
(Midget Mk. III from Car No. G–AN5–114643)

Removing

CAUTION.—Should a rubber bellows become damaged, with a subsequent loss of lubricant, it is necessary to remove the steering rack assembly for dismantling and inspection of the components. If a rubber bellows has

been damaged in the workshop and dirt has not entered the steering rack assembly, a new bellows may be fitted and the inner ball joint and rack lubricated with a recommended grease (see Section J.9).

(1) Remove the radiator.

(2) Turn the steering to the straight-ahead position.

(3) Remove the road wheels.

(4) Remove the nuts from the tie-rod end assemblies.

(5) Using tool 18G 1063, detach the tie-rod end assemblies from the steering levers.

(6) Remove the steering-column pinch bolt.

(7) Remove the bolts retaining the steering-column support bracket.

(8) Withdraw the steering-column from the pinion.

(9) Mark the steering rack housing in relation to the mounting bracket clamp to assist when refitting.

(10) Remove the clamp bolts and clamps from the mounting brackets.

(11) Withdraw the steering rack assembly.

Dismantling

(12) Slacken the tie-rod end assembly locknuts and remove the tie-rod end assemblies and locknuts from the tie-rods.

(13) Slacken the bellows retaining clips and remove the bellows wire from the pinion end of the steering rack.

Sprite and Midget. Issue 1. 82963

J.7

165

THE STEERING RACK COMPONENTS
(Midget Mk. III from Car No. G–AN5–114643)

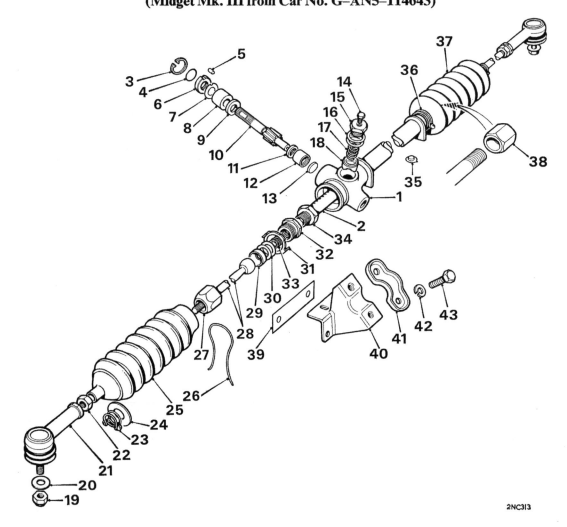

2NC3I3

No.	Description	No.	Description
1.	Rack housing.	23.	Small retaining clip.
2.	Rack.	24.	Protective shield.
3.	Circlip.	25.	Bellows for rack housing—pinion end.
4.	'O' ring.	26.	Bellows tie-wire.
5.	Dowel.	27.	Cup nut.
6.	Retaining ring.	28.	Tie-rod.
7.	Shims.	29.	Cup.
8.	Pinion shaft bush.	30.	Shims.
9.	Thrust washer.	31.	Tab washer.
10.	Pinion.	32.	Sleeve nut.
11.	Thrust washer.	33.	Spring.
12.	Pinion spigot bush.	34.	Locknut for sleeve nut—pinion end.
13.	End cover.	35.	Plug.
14.	Grease plug.	36.	Large retaining clip.
15.	Screwed cap.	37.	Bellows for rack housing
16.	Shims.	38.	Locknut for sleeve nut } Non-pinion end.
17.	Spring.	39.	Packing for rack mounting bracket—pinion end.
18.	Plunger.	40.	Rack mounting bracket.
19.	Nut.	41.	Rack mounting clamp.
20.	Washer.	42.	Spring washer.
21.	Tie-rod end assembly.	43.	Setscrew.
22.	Locknut.		

(14) Remove the bellows together with their protective shields fitted behind the outer retaining clips.

(15) Slacken the locknuts and unscrew the tie-rod inner ball joint assemblies.

(16) Withdraw the coil springs and unscrew the locknuts from each end of the rack.

(17) Remove the bellows retaining clip from the rack housing.

(18) Unlock the tab washer and unscrew the sleeved nut from the cup nut and remove the tab washer, shims and cup to dismantle the tie-rod inner ball joint assembly.

(19) Remove the grease plug from the screwed cap.

(20) Remove the screwed cap and shims.

(21) Withdraw the spring and plunger from the rack housing.

(22) Remove the circlip retaining the pinion assembly.

(23) Withdraw the pinion assembly and dowel.
       CAUTION.—Take care not to lose the dowel.

(24) Remove the retaining ring, shims and thrust washer from the pinion shaft.

(25) Remove the 'O' ring from the annular groove in the retaining ring.

(26) Withdraw the rack from the pinion end of the housing.

(27) Remove the thrust washer from the pinion housing bore.

(28) Turn the rack housing over and, with the base of the pinion bore uppermost, drift out the lower bush and end plug.

Inspection

(29) Thoroughly clean all components.

(30) Inspect the rack and pinion for wear, cracks or damage, with particular attention to the condition of the teeth.

(31) Thoroughly examine the bellows for cracks, splits or signs of deterioration.

(32) Renew all damaged or excessively worn components.

Reassembling

(33) Immerse the pinion bushes and the plunger in S.A.E. 20 engine oil, and heat the oil to 100° C. (212° F.) for two hours, then allow the oil to cool before removing the bushes and plunger from the oil and fitting to the rack; this allows the pores of the bushes and plunger to be filled with lubricant.

(34) Fit the bottom bush into the pinion housing as follows:

   (*a*) Fit the large bush on the pinion shaft and then stand the splined end of the shaft on the press base-plate.

   (*b*) Place the end plug into the recess in the lower bush and position the bush on the pinion spigot.

(*c*) Position the pinion housing over the pinion, and press the housing over the bush, ensuring that the splined pinion shaft is centralized in the pinion housing bore with its bush.

(35) Fit the thrust washer, chamfered bore uppermost, into the pinion housing.

(36) Insert the rack into the housing from the pinion end, noting the following:

   (*a*) Liberally smear the rack and its teeth with grease.

   (*b*) Insert the rack into the housing with $3\frac{1}{2}$ in. (88·90 mm.) of the teeth end protruding from the 'travel' abutment face of the pinion housing (see dimension 'E' of Fig. J.6).

   (*c*) The flat on the rack registers against the locating plug (which must be taped in position), noting that the plug will be retained in position by the mounting bracket when the rack is fitted.

(See Editor's note at end of Section J.)

Pinion end-float

(37) Assemble the thrust washer, bush and retaining ring to the splined end of the pinion shaft, ensuring that the face of the bush with the lubricating groove butts against the thrust washer.

(38) Insert the pinion assembly into the pinion housing, ensuring that the flat on the pinion is facing towards the plunger boss.

(39) Fit the retaining circlip.

(40) Mount a dial gauge on the rack housing.

(41) Push the pinion down and zero the dial gauge.

(42) Lift the pinion until the retaining ring contacts the circlip and note the dial gauge reading which represents the pinion shaft end-float.

(43) Remove the dial gauge.

(44) Remove the circlip and withdraw the pinion assembly.

(45) Withdraw the retaining ring and fit a new 'O' ring to its annular groove.

(46) From the reading obtained in (42) select shims that will give a maximum of ·010 in. (·25 mm.) end-float.
       Shims are available in the following thicknesses:
       ·005 in. (·13 mm.).
       ·010 in. (·25 mm.).

(47) Fit the shims and retainer to the pinion shaft.

(48) Insert the pinion assembly into the pinion housing (with the pinch bolt flat towards the plunger boss), ensuring that the cut-away on the shims and retaining ring are aligned with the dowel hole in the pinion housing.

(49) Fit the dowel and retaining circlip, with the points of the circlip opposite the dowel to prevent the circlip becoming dislodged.

Plunger pre-load

(50) Fit the plunger and screwed cap to the rack housing, tightening the screwed cap until all end-float has been eliminated.

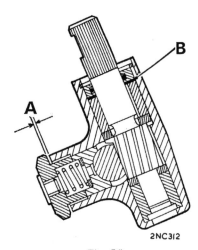

Fig. J.4

A section through the pinion housing

A. The gap between the screwed cap and the housing when the plunger and screwed cap are fitted and all end-float eliminated.

B. Shims fitted to produce a maximum pinion end-float of ·010 in. (·25 mm.).

(51) Measure the clearance between the screwed cap and the rack housing using a feeler gauge. Ensure that the housing is free from burrs.

(52) Remove the screwed cap and plunger.

(53) Smear the plunger with grease and fit the plunger and spring into the rack housing.

(54) Make up a shim pack equal to that measured in (51) plus and additional ·004 in. (·1 mm.).

    CAUTION: It is important that at least one ·004 in. (·1 mm.) shim is used.

    Shims are available in the following thicknesses:
      ·002 in. (·05 mm.).
      ·004 in. (·1 mm.).
      ·010 in. (·25 mm.).

(55) Assemble the shims to the screwed cap; fit and tighten the cap.

(56) Fit a grease nipple to the screwed cap and inject ½ to ¾ oz. (14 to 21 gm.) of a recommended grease into the unit; remove the grease nipple.

(57) Fit the grease plug to the screwed cap.

(58) Check that the screwed cap is correctly adjusted. If correct a force of 2 lb. (·91 kg.) acting at a radius of 8 in. (20·3 cm.) will rotate the pinion shaft through three-quarters of a turn in either direction of the rack centre tooth position.

    Re-adjust if necessary by adding or subtracting shims beneath the screwed cap.

Tie-rod inner ball joint

(59) Smear the tie-rod ball with graphite grease.

(60) Slide the cup nut over the tie-rod and position the cup over the tie-rod ball.

(61) Position a new tab washer on the sleeve nut followed by a shim pack of known thickness and screw the sleeve nut into the cup nut.

    Shims are available in the following thicknesses:
      ·002 in. (·05 mm.).
      ·010 in. (·25 mm.).

(62) Measure the clearance between the tab washer and the cup nut, using a feeler gauge. This dimension plus ·002 in. (·05 mm.) is the amount by which the shim pack must be reduced to give the correct ball end movement.

(63) Dismantle the ball joint and reassemble it with the correct shim pack as determined in (62).

(64) Check the pre-load on the tie-rod ball spheres. When the adjustment is correct the following torque is required on a tie-rod to produce articulation 35 degrees either side of the centre plane.
    Steel cup: Articulation torque 40 lb. in. (·46 kg. m.).
    Nylon cup: Articulation torque 15 to 50 lb. in. (·17 to ·57 kg. m.).
    CAUTION.—If a nylon cup is replacing a steel cup the thrust spring must be discarded.

(65) Lock the tab washer over the cup nut and sleeve nut.

(66) Repeat (59) to (65) for the remaining tie-rod inner ball joint assembly.

(67) Position the bellows retaining clip on the rack housing at the bearing end.

(68) Screw the locknuts on to each end of the rack, ensuring that there is 23·20 in. (589·28 mm.) between their inside faces.
    CAUTION.—The locknut at the pinion end of the rack is smaller than the locknut at the bearing end of the rack.

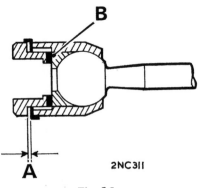

Fig. J.5

A section through the inner ball joint assembly

A. The gap between the tab washer and cup nut when shims of known thickness are fitted.

B. These shims must be reduced by ·002 in. (·05 mm.) and the width of gap 'A'.

J.10   Sprite and Midget. Issue 1. 82963

168

(69) Insert the thrust springs into the ends of the rack if steel cups are used in the inner ball joint assemblies.

(70) Screw each tie-rod assembly as far as possible up to the locknut.

(71) Tighten each locknut to the torque figure given in **'GENERAL DATA'**.

(72) **Push the bellows onto the tie-rods, ensuring that the protective shields are fitted on the outer end of the bellows behind the small clips.**

(73) Lubricate around each inner ball joint and the rack including the teeth with approximately 2 oz. (57 gm.) of a recommended grease.

(74) Secure the bellows to the rack housing and tie-rods with the clips and wire.

(75) Screw the tie-rod end assembly locknuts onto the tie-rods.

(76) Screw the tie-rod end assemblies onto the tie-rods, ensuring there is 42·68 in. (1084·1 mm.) between the ball pin centres.

(77) Tighten the locknuts to the torque figure given in **'GENERAL DATA'**.

Refitting

(78) Position the rack into the mounting brackets and fit the clamps but do not tighten the clamp fixing bolts.

(79) Check that the rack is in the straight-ahead position with the pinch bolt flat on the pinion shaft uppermost.

(80) Check that the steering-column is in the straight-ahead position with the slot of the clamp uppermost.

(81) Slide the column over the pinion shaft as far as it will go.

(82) Fit the steering-column support bracket securing bolts.

(83) Turn the steering-wheel one complete turn to the left and back, then one complete turn to the right and back.

(84) Check that the marks made in (9) are aligned, and tighten the clamp bolts to the torque figures given in **'GENERAL DATA'**.
   CAUTION.—If the marks made in (9) are not aligned or new mounting brackets are being fitted the steering rack must be aligned as described in Section J.11.

(85) Tighten the steering-column pinch bolt to the torque figure given in **'GENERAL DATA'**.

(86) Reverse the removing procedure in (1) to (5), noting:

   (*a*) Tighten the tie-rod end assembly ball joint nut to the torque figure given in **'GENERAL DATA'**.

   (*b*) Check the front wheel alignment (Section J.2.).

Section J.11
(See Editor's note at end of Section J.)
STEERING RACK MOUNTING BRACKETS
(Midget Mk. III from Car No. G–AN5–114643)

Removing

(1) Remove the radiator (Section C.5).

(2) Remove the steering rack (Section J.10).

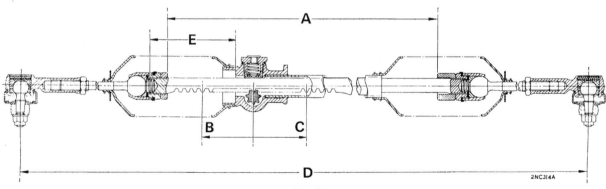

Fig. J.6

Steering rack assembly dimensions

A. 23·20 in. (589·28 mm.).
B. Rack travel from centre tooth position 2·72 in. (69·09 mm.).
C. Rack travel from centre tooth position 2·72 in. (69·09 mm.).
D. 42·68 in. (1084·1 mm.).
E. 3½ in. (88·90 mm.) fitting dimension – end of rack to 'travel' abutment face of pinion housing.

(3) Remove the securing bolt from each mounting bracket and remove the radiator lower tube assembly.

(4) Remove the front bolts securing the mounting brackets to the cross-member, collecting any packing fitted between the mounting bracket on the pinion end of the rack and the cross-member.

> **CAUTION.**—It is important that this packing is retained for refitting the mounting brackets. If they are mislaid or their thicknesses have not been recorded, the steering rack must be realigned as described in Section J.12.

Refitting

CAUTION.—If new mounting brackets are being fitted or the steering rack is being refitted after an accident damage repair to the front end, the steering rack must be aligned as described in Section J.12.

(5) Reverse the removing procedure in (1) to (4), ensuring that:

(a) The thickness of packing removed from between the mounting bracket on the pinion end of the rack and the cross-member are refitted.

(b) Each mounting bracket front and top fixing bolts are tightened to the torque figure given in **'GENERAL DATA'**.

Section J.12

STEERING RACK ALIGNMENT
(Midget Mk. III from Car No. G–AN5–114643)

When fitting new mounting brackets

(1) Fit the mounting brackets to the rack assembly, tightening the clamp bolts and then slackening off one full turn.

(2) Fit the rack assembly into the car.

(3) Screw in the two front bolts and the top bolt securing the mounting bracket farthest from the steering pinion to the cross-member, noting:

(a) The radiator lower tube assembly is retained in position by the mounting bracket top securing bolt.

(b) The mounting bracket securing bolts are not tightened at this stage.

(4) Check that the rack is in the straight-ahead position, with the flat on the pinion shaft uppermost.

(5) Check that the steering-column is in the straight-ahead position, with the slot of the clamp uppermost.

(6) Slide the steering-column sleeve over the pinion shaft as far as it will go.

(7) Fit the steering-column support bracket securing bolts.

(8) Fit and tighten the pinion pinch bolt to the torque figure given in **'GENERAL DATA'**.

(9) Turn the steering-wheel one complete turn to the left and back, then one complete turn to the right and back, noting any movement of the rack assembly in relation to the body cross-member; slowly turn the rack in both directions until the neutral point (i.e. where no movement of the rack assembly is visible) is found.

(10) Measure the gap between the mounting bracket on the pinion end of the rack and the cross-member, fit packing to the thickness of the gap and insert the two front and top fixing bolts, noting:
   (a) Packing is available in thicknesses of $\frac{1}{32}$ in. (·79 mm.) only.
   (b) The radiator lower tube assembly is retained in position by the top bolt.

(11) Tighten the mounting bracket top and front securing bolts to the torque figure given in **'GENERAL DATA'**.

(12) Commence at the pinion end and tighten the mounting bracket clamp bolts to the torque figure given in **'GENERAL DATA'**.

(13) Fit the tie-rod end assembly ball joints, tightening the nuts to the torque figure given in **'GENERAL DATA'**.

(14) Fit the road wheels.

(15) Fit the radiator (Section C.5).

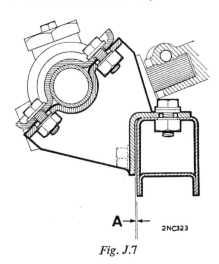

2NC323

Fig. J.7

The rack mounting bracket on the pinion side showing (A) the face of the bracket to be measured for packing

J.12

Section J. 13

STEERING RACK BELLOWS

(Midget Mk. III from Car No. G–AN5–114643)

Removing

(1) Remove the road wheel.

(2) Mark the position of the tie-rod end assembly locknut, for when refitting.

(3) Slacken the tie-rod end assembly locknut.

(4) Remove the nut securing the tie-rod end assembly to the steering lever.

(5) Using tool 18G 1063, detach the tie-rod end assembly from the steering lever.

(6) Remove the tie-rod end assembly and locknut from the tie-rod.

(7) Slacken the bellows retaining clips/wire.

(8) Detach the large clip from the bellows and allow it to hang on the end of the rack housing. Withdraw the bellows from the rack housing and the tie-rod.

(9) Remove the small clip and protective shield from the bellows.

Inspection

(10) Examine the existing grease around the inner ball joint and the rack for ingress of water or dirt; if this is evident, the steering rack must be removed for dismantling and inspection of the components as described in Section J.11.

(11) If the inner ball joint and the rack are in a satisfactory condition, apply around each inner ball joint and the rack including the teeth approximately 2 oz. (57 gm.) of a recommended grease.

Refitting

(12) Fit a new bellows.

(13) Secure the bellows to the rack housing with the clip or wire.

(14) Fit the protective shield and small clip to the outer end of the bellows.

(15) Reverse the procedure in (1) to (6).

(16) Check the front wheel alignment as described in Section J.2.

CAUTION: If the vehicle is hoisted with its front wheels clear of the ground, care should be taken to avoid forceful movement of the wheels from lock to lock as damage may occur within the steering mechanism.

EDITOR'S NOTES

J. The Steering Gear

Steering Rack and Pinion–Reassembling
When the steering rack is in the straight-ahead position, the flat on the pinion must be positioned 30° to either side of the pinion housing's center line on the plunger cap side of the rack housing. Before you reinstall the steering rack assembly, be sure to lubricate it as described in Section J.9.

Steering Rack Mounting Brackets
When you remove the front bolts that hold the mounting brackets to the crossmember, make mental note of the positions of the brake pipe clips.

Section Ja

THE STEERING GEAR (Energy Absorbing Column)

The information given in this Section refers specifically to service operations on, or affected by equipment fitted to the Sprite Mk. IV and Midget Mk. III in conformity with local and territorial requirements, and must be used in conjunction with Section J.

Section Ja.1

STEERING-COLUMN

Removing
(1) Disconnect the battery.
(2) Remove the pinion pinch bolt
(3) Remove the three toe-plate to column securing bolts, fixing ring, and washer.
(4) Note the location, quantity, and thickness of the packing washers between the column upper fixing flanges and the body brackets, remove the three securing bolts and nuts and collect the packing washers. **If the packing washers are mislaid or their fitting positions are not recorded the steering-column must be aligned as described in Section Ja.3 when refitted.**
(5) Disconnect the steering-column switch wiring at the snap connectors and multi-snap connectors below the fascia.
(6) Withdraw the steering-column assembly complete with steering-wheel and switches from the car.

Dismantling
(7) Withdraw the motif disc from the centre of the steering-wheel, unscrew the wheel retaining nut and remove the steering-wheel (See Section J.6).
(8) Unscrew the switch cowl retaining screws and remove the cowl.
(9) Unscrew the two windscreen wiper/washer switch retaining screws and remove the switch assembly complete with wiring.
(10) Unscrew the two direction indicator/horn switch retaining screws and remove the switch assembly complete with wiring.
(11) Unscrew the four ignition switch retaining screws and remove the switch complete with wiring.

Reassembling
(12) Reverse the dismantling procedure in (7) to (11).

Refitting
NOTE—**If a new steering-column is being fitted it must be aligned as described under the appropriate heading in Section Ja.3.**
(13) Fit the column assembly into the car and enter the pinion into the inner column sleeve.
(14) Fit the packing washers in their original positions between the column fixing flanges and the body brackets; fit the three securing bolts and nuts, tightening them by hand until the packing washers are just pinched.
(15) Fit the sealing washer and fixing ring to the toe-plate, then screw in and tighten the three toe-plate bolts.
(16) Tighten the three upper fixing bolts to the torque figure given in 'GENERAL DATA'.
(17) Fit and tighten the pinion pinch bolt to the torque figure given in 'GENERAL DATA'.

Section Ja.2

STEERING RACK AND PINION
(Early cars)

Removing
(1) Remove the radiator (Section C.5).
(2) Remove the split pins and slotted nuts from the ball pins.
(3) Using tool 18G 1063 detach the tie-rod ball joints from the steering levers.
(4) Remove the steering-column pinch bolt.
(5) Remove the six bolts securing the rack assembly to the body cross-member.
(6) Move the rack assembly forward as far as possible collecting any shims fitted between the right-hand mounting bracket and the front of the body cross-member. **It is important that these shims are preserved for refitting the rack assembly, if they are mislaid and their thickness has not been recorded the rack assembly must be realigned as described in Section Ja.3.**
(7) Remove the three toe-plate bolts.
(8) Slacken off the three steering-column upper fixing bolts and pull the column back sufficiently to disengage the column sleeve from the pinion.
(9) Remove the right-hand front road wheel and withdraw the rack assembly complete with mounting brackets.

Dismantling
(10) Carry out the operations detailed under 'Dismantling' in Section J.4.

Refitting
NOTE—**If a new rack assembly is being fitted it must be aligned as described under the appropriate heading in Section Ja.3.**
(11) Reverse the removing procedure in (1) to (9) noting the following points.
(a) Ensure that thickness of shims removed from between the rack assembly and the cross-member are refitted.
(b) When entering the pinion into steering-column sleeve ensure that both the column and the rack are in the dead-ahead position.

Section Ja.3
ALIGNMENT

When fitting new steering-column and steering gear:
(1) Fit both mounting brackets to the rack assembly and tighten the clamp bolts.
(2) Early cars:
(i) Slacken the clamp bolts on the pinion end bracket half a turn and the clamp bolts on the right-hand bracket one full turn.
(ii) Fit the rack assembly into the car.
(iii) Screw in and tighten the two front pinion end bracket securing bolts, then fit and tighten the top bolt.

Sprite and Midget. Issue 3. 82963

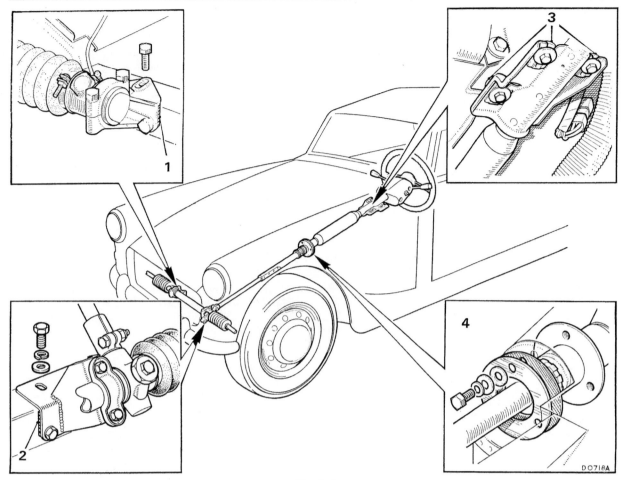

Fig. Ja.1

Steering alignment

1. Packing fitted behind right-hand mounting bracket—early cars.
2. Packing fitted behind left-hand mounting bracket—Midget Mk. III from Car No. G–AN5–114487.
3. Steering-column sleeve.
4. Packing washers fitted between column top fixing brackets.
5. Toe-plate fixings.

(3) Later Midget Mk. III cars from Car No. G–AN5–114487:
   (i) Slacken the clamp bolts one full turn.
   (ii) Fit the rack assembly into the car.
   (iii) Screw in the two front bolts and the top bolt securing the mounting bracket to the cross-member; do not tighten the mounting bracket securing bolts.

(4) Check that the rack is in the straight-ahead position with the pinch bolt flat on the pinion shaft uppermost.

(5) Fit the steering-column into the car, slide the fixing plate and sealing washer into the column.

(6) Turn the column to the straight-ahead position with the slot of the clamp uppermost.

(7) Slide the steering-column sleeve over the pinion shaft as far as it will go.

(8) Fit the two top bolts and nuts into the upper fixing brackets; tighten them by hand until the weight of the column is just taken and the column fixing flanges and body brackets are parallel to each other with the spaces between them equal at both

points; check that the column passes through the toe-plate approximately central of the hole.

(9) Measure the spaces between the column flanges and the brackets.

(10) Remove the two fixing bolts, fit packing washers equal in thickness to the spaces, refit the bolt tightening them by hand until the washers are just pinched.

(11) Fit the fixing ring and sealing washer then screw in and tighten the three toe-plate bolts.

(12) Fit and tighten the pinion pinch bolt.

(13) Turn the steering one complete turn to the left and back, then one complete turn to the right and back, noting any movement of the rack assembly in relation to the body cross-member; slowly turn the steering in both directions until the neutral point (i.e. where no movement of the rack assembly is visible) is found.

(14) Early cars:
   (i) Measure the gap between the right-hand rack mounting bracket and the front face of the body cross-member; fit packing to the thick-

Sprite and Midget. Issue 3. 82963   **Ja.3**

175

ness of the gap, then insert and tighten the two front fixing bolts.

    (ii) Fit and tighten the right-hand rack mounting bracket top fixing bolt.

(15) Midget Mk. III from Car No. G–AN5–114487:

    (i) Measure the gap between the left-hand rack mounting bracket and the front face of the body cross-member; fit packing to the thickness of the gap.

    (ii) Insert the two front bolts and the top bolt securing the mounting bracket to the cross-member.

    (iii) Tighten the mounting brackets top and front securing bolts to the torque figure given in **'GENERAL DATA'**.

(16) Fit and tighten the bracket top fixing bolt.

(17) Tighten the fixing bracket clamp bolts commencing with those on the pinion end bracket.

(18) Measure the gap between the upper column mounting flange and fixing bracket at the third bolt position, fit packing washers to the thickness of the gap then fit and tighten the bolt until the washers are just pinched.

(19) Remove the pinion pinch bolts and the three toe-plate bolts.

(20) Check, by pulling and pushing, that the steering-column slides reasonably freely up and down on the pinion; if the column is tight on the pinion the rack assembly alignment must be re-checked.

(21) If the steering-column alignment check in (17) is satisfactory, refit and tighten the three toe-plate bolts.

(22) Refit the pinion pinch bolt and tighten it to the figure given in **'GENERAL DATA'**.

(23) Tighten the three top fixing bolts to the figure given in **'GENERAL DATA'**.

When fitting a new rack assembly to an existing column

(24) Remove the rack assembly as described in Section Ja.2, (1) to (9) or Ja.4, (1) to (11).

(25) Carry out operations (2) and (3).

(26) Push the steering-column forward and enter the pinion into the column sleeve as far as it will go.

(27) Screw in and tighten the three toe-plate bolts.

(28) Tighten the three column upper securing bolts.

(29) Fit and tighten the pinion pinch bolt.

(30) Carry out operations (13) to (17) and (19) to (23).

When fitting a new column to an existing rack

(31) Carry out operations (4) to (12) and (19) to (23).

Steering-wheel

Refer to the instructions given in Section J.6 for removing and refitting the steering-wheel fitted to Midget Mk. III (GAN 5) cars.

Section Ja.4

STEERING RACK AND PINION
(Midget Mk. III from Car No. G–AN5–114487)

Removing

CAUTION.—Should a rubber bellows become damaged, with a subsequent loss of lubricant, it is necessary to remove the steering rack assembly for dismantling and inspection of the components as described in Section J.10. If a rubber bellows has been damaged in the workshop and dirt has not entered the steering rack assembly, a new bellows may be fitted and the bellows packed with a recommended grease (see Section J.9).

(1) Remove the radiator (Section C.5).

(2) Turn the steering to the straight-ahead position with the slot of the column clamp uppermost.

(3) Remove the road wheels.

(4) Remove the nuts from the tie-rod end assemblies.

(5) Using tool 18G 1063, detach the tie-rod end assemblies from the steering levers.

(6) Remove the steering-column pinch bolt.

(7) Remove the three toe-plate bolts.

(8) Slacken the three steering-column upper fixing bolts and pull the column back sufficiently to disengage the column sleeve from the pinion.

(9) Mark the steering rack housing in relation to the mounting bracket to assist when refitting.

(10) Remove the clamp bolts and clamps from the mounting brackets.

(11) Withdraw the steering rack assembly.

Dismantling, inspection, and assembling

(12) Carry out the operations detailed under **'Dismantling, Inspection, and Reassembling'** in Section J.10.

Refitting

CAUTION.—**If a new rack assembly or mounting brackets are being fitted the steering rack must be aligned as described under the appropriate heading in Section Ja.3.**

(13) Position the rack into the mounting brackets and fit the clamps but do not tighten the clamp fixing bolts.

(14) Check that the rack is in the straight-ahead position with the pinch bolt flat on the pinion shaft uppermost.

(15) Check that the column is in the straight-ahead position with the slot of the clamp uppermost.

(16) Slide the column over the pinion shaft as far as it will go.

(17) Tighten the steering-column upper fixing bolts.

(18) Fit and tighten the three toe-plate bolts.

(19) Turn the steering-wheel one complete turn to the left and back, then one complete turn to the right and back.

(20) Check that the marks made in (9) are aligned, and tighten the clamp bolts.

    CAUTION.—If the marks made in (9) are not aligned, the steering rack must be aligned as described under the appropriate heading in Section Ja.3.

(21) Tighten the steering-column pinch bolt to the torque figure given in **'GENERAL DATA'**.

(22) Reverse the removing procedure in (1) to (5) and:

    (*a*) Tighten the tie-rod end assembly ball joint nut to the torque figure given in **'GENERAL DATA'**.

    (*b*) Check the front wheel alignment (Section J.2).

SECTION K

THE FRONT SUSPENSION

THE FRONT SUSPENSION COMPONENTS

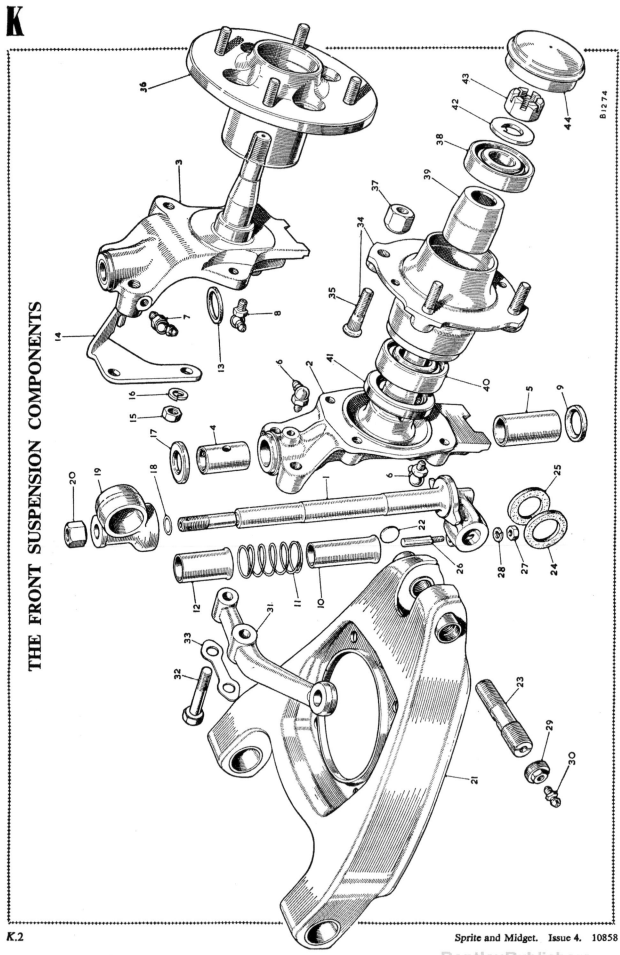

B1274

KEY TO THE FRONT SUSPENSION COMPONENTS

No.	Description	No.	Description	No.	Description
1.	Swivel pin.	16.	Spring washer.	31.	Steering lever.
2.	Swivel axle assembly.	17.	Thrust washer.	32.	Set screw.
3.	Swivel axle assembly.	18.	Adjustment washer.	33.	Lock washer.
4.	Bush (top).	19.	Suspension trunnion link.	34.	Hub assembly.
5.	Bush (bottom).	20.	Nut.	35.	Wheel stud.
6.	Lubricator.	21.	Lower link.	36.	Hub assembly.
7.	Lubricator.	22.	Plug.	37.	Nut.
8.	Lubricator.	23.	Fulcrum pin.	38.	Outer hub bearing.
9.	Sealing ring.	24.	Ring (large).	39.	Bearing distance piece.
10.	Dust excluder tube (bottom)	25.	Ring (small).	40.	Inner hub bearing.
11.	Dust excluder spring.	26.	Cotter pin.	41.	Oil seal.
12.	Dust excluder tube (top).	27.	Nut.	42.	Retaining washer.
13.	Sealing ring.	28.	Spring washer.	43.	Nut.
14.	Brake hose lock plate.	29.	Screwed plug.	44.	Cap.
15.	Nut.	30.	Lubricator.		

GENERAL DESCRIPTION

The independent suspension is of the 'wishbone' type. It consists of a single-armed, double-acting hydraulic damper bolted to its support bracket at its upper end. The single arm is towards the front of the car and is secured to the swivel pin trunnion link by a fulcrum pin

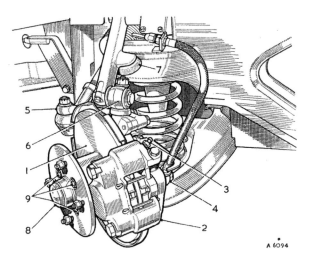

Fig. K.1

Front suspension (later cars)

1. Brake disc.	6. Suspension trunnion link.
2. Calliper assembly.	7. Rebound buffer.
3. Bleeder screw.	8. Retaining cap.
4. Calliper fluid connector.	9. Brake disc to hub securing bolts.
5. Steering lever.	

and Metalastik rubber bushes. The bottom end of the swivel pin is secured to the outer end of the lower links by a fulcrum which is cottered in position.

The inner arms of the lower links are fixed to brackets by Metalastik rubber bushes and fulcrum pins.

A rebound buffer is fitted to the bottom of the coil spring top bracket and a smaller rebound buffer under the damper arm.

A spring seat is secured to the lower links by bolts, flat washers, and self-locking nuts.

An anti-roll bar, mounted on the body underframe and connected to the suspension lower links, is fitted to later cars.

Section K.1

LUBRICATION

A lubricating gun filled with lubricant should be applied to each of the eight nipples and three or four strokes given at regular intervals. Nipples are provided on both lower arm joints where they meet the swivel axle housings and on the two tie-rod ball joints. There are two nipples on each swivel axle pin which are best lubricated when the weight of the car has been taken off the suspension with a jack or sling. This will allow the lubricant to penetrate around the bushes more effectively.

Section K.2

CASTOR, CAMBER, AND SWIVEL PIN ANGLES

The castor and camber angles and the swivel pin inclination are determined by machining and assembly of the components during manufacture, and are not adjustable.

Should the car suffer damage to the suspension, the angles (as given in 'GENERAL DATA') must be verified with a camber, castor, and swivel pin inclination gauge and new parts fitted as found necessary.

Section K.3

FRONT SUSPENSION ASSEMBLY

Removing

Raise the car and remove the wheel and coil spring (see Section K.4). Disconnect the steering side-tube from the steering-arm by withdrawing the split pin and removing the slotted nut. If the ball pin shank is tight in the steering-arm release the nut, but do not remove. Sharply tap the steering-arm at the side-tube end, when it will be found to come away quite easily on removing the nut. Disconnect the flexible hose. Withdraw the split pins, remove the nuts, tap the fulcrum pins through the lower link inner ends, and take away the two rubber bushes at the outer ends of the lower link inner brackets. Remove the bolts and nuts to release the anti-roll bar link bracket (later cars only) from the suspension lower link. The lower end of the suspension is now free.

At the upper end remove the clamp bolt and shakeproof washer in the hydraulic damper arm, withdraw the split pin, and release the slotted nut on the fulcrum pin. Tap off the fulcrum pin and retrieve the rubber bushes. The suspension unit is now free and can be lifted away.

Dismantling

Secure the suspension by clamping the web of the lower links between a dummy baseplate at the bottom and a solid metal disc and bolt at the top.

Remove the drum securing screw and withdraw the brake-drum (early cars). Remove the hub assembly as described in Section K.5 or K.6.

Detach the backplate by removing its securing bolts and washers.

Tap back the lock washers and remove the set screws to release the steering lever.

Extract the split pin and remove the slotted nut at the top of the swivel axle pin. Remove the trunnion and preserve the shims for use during assembly. Lift off the phosphor-bronze Oilite thrust washer and the swivel axle along with the dust excluder tubes and their spring, and the bevelled cork sealing ring at the bottom of the swivel axle pin.

Release the lower trunnion swivel pin cotter nut and knock the cotter loose. Remove the nut, spring washer, and cotter. Screw out the swivel pin lower trunnion oil nipple and its housing, which also serves to plug the lower trunnion.

Unscrew the swivel pin lower trunnion fulcrum pin, remove the swivel pin and cork sealing washers, and knock out the welch plug.

Sprite and Midget. Issue 3. 51576
MG Midget. AKM 2092/1

Reassembling

Reverse the sequence of operations detailed for dismantling, but note the following point. Place the phosphor-bronze thrust washer over the swivel axle. Put a ·008 in. shim (·008 in. [·2 mm.] and ·012 in. [·3 mm.] shims available) onto the swivel pin, followed by the trunnion with its bore towards the hub when it is fitted. Tighten the slotted nut. Resistance should be just felt when the swivel axle is moved from lock to lock and there should be no vertical movement of the swivel axle. Increase the thickness of the shims to loosen and decrease to tighten as required.

Refitting

Wet the spring rebound bumper and push it into its hole in the bottom of the hydraulic damper mounting plate, and the hydraulic damper arm rebound buffer in the top. Wet two of the large rubber bearings and position one from inside each lower link. Lift the two arms into position, insert the fulcrum pin from the inner end so that its washer registers, position the two remaining rubber bearings from outside the lower links, locate the special washer, tighten the slotted nuts, and insert and turn back the split pins.

With the block still under the hydraulic damper arm proceed to connect the top end.

Insert the two small rubber bearings in the upper trunnion eye, tap the fulcrum pin from the rear to go through the bearings and damper arm, and see that the notch in the fulcrum pin is to the top. Tighten the slotted nut till the notch is in line with the clamp bolt hole in the damper arm, split-pin the slotted nut, and tighten the clamp bolt onto its shakeproof washer.

Refit the coil spring (Section K.4). Replace the wheel and lower the car. The block can now be removed from under the hydraulic damper arm.

Section K.4

COIL SPRINGS

Removing

Place a hardwood or metal block 1·125 in. (28·57 mm). long under the hydraulic damper arm to keep the arm

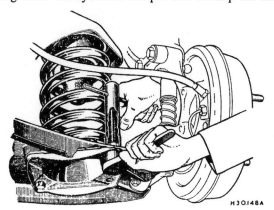

H30.148A.

Fig. K.2

Using a pair of slave bolts to remove or replace a coil spring

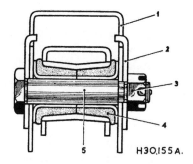

H30.155A.

Fig. K.3

Lower link mounting (inner end)

1. Mounting bracket.	3. Slotted nut.
2. Special washer.	4. Rubber bush (bearing).
	5. Fulcrum pin.

off its rubber rebound buffer when the car is in a raised position. With the vehicle raised to a workable height remove two diametrically opposite spring seat securing nuts and bolts. Using Service tool 18G 153 (or two slave bolts), compress the spring. Remove the remaining nuts and bolts from the spring seat and release the centre screw of the Service tool to allow the spring to expand.

Check the spring length against the figure given in **'GENERAL DATA'**, if not within the limits given, the spring must be renewed.

Refitting

Reverse the removal procedure when refitting, with attention being given to inserting two guide rods in diametrically opposite holes to bring the spring seat and wishbone lower links into line when in the process of compressing the spring.

Section K.5

FRONT HUBS
(Early Cars)

Removing

Raise the car and remove the wheel. Remove the brake-drum securing screw from the countersunk hole and withdraw the drum.

Remove the hub cap by levering with a screwdriver. Wipe away any excess grease and extract the split pin. Remove the slotted nut and washer. Withdraw the complete hub assembly from the swivel axle, using tool 18G 304 Z and adaptor 18G 304 F.

Should the inner bearing remain on the swivel axle, it should be carefully extracted, using Service tools 18G 8 and 18G 8 P. It is usually only the inner race of the inner bearing that is left behind, and removal will be found easier if the backplate is first removed.

With the hub removed, the outer bearing and distance piece can be tapped out, using Service tool 18G 260 together with 18G 260 A. Similarly, the inner bearing and oil seal can be detached by drifting them off from the other side of the hub, using Service tools 18G 260 and 18G 260 B.

Refitting

Pack the bearings and the cavity between them with grease.

Surplus grease must be removed after the hub has been fitted, to allow for expansion, and in no circumstances should grease be put into the retaining cap.

Reverse the removal procedure, with special attention being given to ensure that the inner and outer bearings are drifted on with their sides marked 'THRUST' towards the centre of the hub, using Service tool 18G 134 together with adaptors 18G 134 B and 18G 134 C.

Ensure also that the oil seal is pressed in with its lipped end towards the inner bearing.

Using Service tool 18G 7, refit the hub assembly on the swivel axle.

Fit the washer and nut. Tighten the nut to the torque wrench reading given in 'GENERAL DATA'.

Section K.6

FRONT HUBS
(Later Cars)

Removing
(1) Raise the front of the car and remove the wheel.
(2) Remove the brake calliper assembly as described in Section M.9 but do not disconnect the hydraulic hose; support the calliper assembly so that its weight is not taken by the hose.

Wire wheels
(3) Using tool 18G 363 withdraw the inner cap from the hub housing.
(4) Remove the split pin and nut.
(5) Using tool 18G 1032, withdraw the hub complete with brake disc.

Pressed wheels
(6) Remove the split pin and nut.
(7) Using tool 18G 304 Z with adaptor 18G 304 B, withdraw the hub complete with brake disc.

Dismantling
(8) Remove the brake disc retaining bolts and remove the disc.
(9) Remove the outer bearing and tapered spacer.
(10) Remove the inner bearing and oil seal.

Reassembling
(11) Reverse the dismantling procedure, noting the following points:
  (a) Pack the bearings with one of the recommended greases, allowing the grease to protrude slightly from the bearing.
  (b) Before fitting, dip the oil seal in light engine oil; take care not to damage the lip of the seal during fitting.
  (c) Ensure that the bearings are fitted with their thrust side adjacent to the bearing spacer.
  (d) After fitting the inner bearing and oil seal, pack the cavity between them with a recommended grease.

Refitting
(12) Reverse the removing procedure, noting the following points.
  (a) Before fitting the hub, inspect the oil seal journal on the stub axle for signs of damage.
  (b) After refitting the hub remove any surplus grease; the retaining cap should not be packed with grease before refitting.
  (c) After fitting, check the 'run out' at the outer periphery of the disc braking surface, if this exceeds ·006 in. (·152 mm.), remove and reposition the disc on the hub.

Section K.7

ANTI-ROLL BAR
(Later Cars)

Removing
(1) Raise the front of the car and position supports beneath the front suspension.
(2) Remove the four screws to release the anti-roll bar bearing straps from the underframe.
(3) Remove the two nuts to release the links from the anti-roll bar.
(4) Remove the four screws and nuts to release the end stops from the anti-roll bar.
(5) Withdraw the bearings from the anti-roll bar.
(6) Remove the two nuts to release the anti-roll bar links from the brackets on the suspension lower links.
(7) Remove the six bolts and nuts to release the link brackets from the suspension lower links.

Refitting
(8) Reverse the procedure in (1) to (7).

K.6

182

Sprite and Midget. Issue 6. 10858
MG Midget. AKM 2092/1

SECTION L

THE HYDRAULIC DAMPERS

GENERAL DESCRIPTION

The hydraulic dampers are of the double-acting piston type. All the working parts are submerged in oil. They are carefully set before dispatch and cannot be adjusted without special equipment. Any attempt to dismantle them will seriously affect their operation and performance. Should adjustment or repair be necessary, they must be returned to their makers.

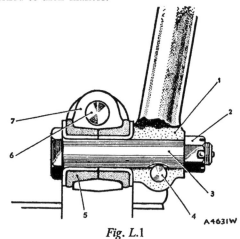

Fig. L.1
Trunnion link/damper arm assembly

1. Damper arm.	4. Clamp bolt.
2. Slotted nut.	5. Rubber bush (bearing).
3. Fulcrum pin.	6. Swivel axle pin.
	7. Trunnion link.

Section L.1

MAINTENANCE

The maintenance of the hydraulic dampers should include a periodical examination of their anchorages to the body frame. The fixing bolts must be tightened as necessary (25 to 30 lb. ft. or 3 to 4 kg. m.).

The cheese-headed screws securing the cover-plates must be kept fully tightened to prevent leakage of the fluid.

When checking the fluid level all road dirt must be carefully cleared away from the vicinity of the filler plugs before the plugs are removed. This is most important as it is absolutely vital that no dirt or foreign matter should enter the operating chamber.

The correct fluid level is just below the filler plug threads.

The use of Armstrong Super (Thin) Damper Oil is recommended. When this is not available any good-quality mineral oil to Specification S.A.E. 20/20W is acceptable. This alternative is not suitable for low-temperature operation.

Section L.2

FRONT DAMPERS

Removing

Jack up the car and place stands under the body in safe positions. Remove the road wheel, place a jack beneath

the outer end of the lower wishbone arm, and raise it until the damper is clear of its rebound rubber.

Remove the damper arm clamp bolt and its shakeproof washer. Remove the slotted nut on the fulcrum pin. Withdraw the fulcrum pin and retrieve the trunnion link rubber bushes. On removal of the assembly securing bolts the damper can be removed from the car.

NOTE.—The jack must be left in position under the suspension wishbone while the top link remains disconnected in order to keep the coil spring securely in position and to avoid straining the steering connections.

Refitting

Refitting is the reverse of the removal procedure.

NOTE.—The fulcrum pin bushes must be renewed if softening of the rubber or side-movement is evident.

Section L.3

REAR DAMPERS

Removing

Remove the nut and spring washer that secures the damper lever to the link arm. Withdraw the fixing bolts from the damper body and body frame and remove the damper assembly by threading the lever over the link arm bolt.

Refitting

The damper assembly may be refitted by simply reversing the removal procedure. However, when handling dampers that have been removed from their mountings, it is important to keep the assemblies upright as far as possible, otherwise air may enter the working chamber and cause erratic resistance.

NOTE.—The rubber bushes integral with both ends of the damper to axle connecting links cannot be renewed. When these bushes are worn renew the arm.

Fig. L.2
Rear spring mounting

1. Spring securing set bolts.	2. Damper nuts.
	3. 'U' bolt nuts.

SECTION M

THE BRAKING SYSTEM

185

THE FRONT BRAKE COMPONENTS

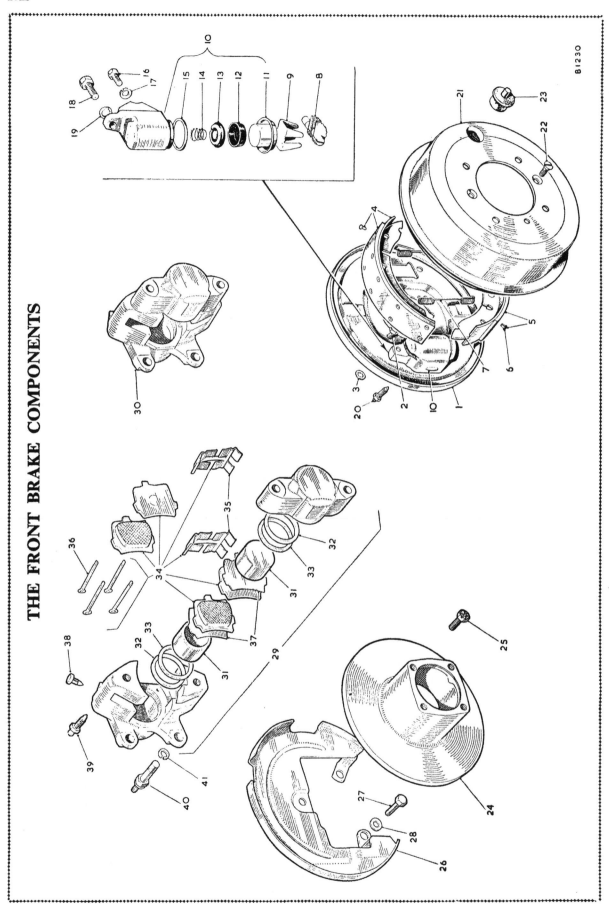

KEY TO THE FRONT BRAKE COMPONENTS

No.	Description		No.	Description		No.	Description	
1.	Brake-plate.		15.	Sealing ring.		29.	Calliper unit assembly—L.H.	
2.	Set screw.		16.	Set screw (small).		30.	Calliper—L.H.	
3.	Shakeproof washer		17.	Spring washer.		31.	Piston.	
4.	Brake-shoe assembly.		18.	Set screw (large).		32.	Inner seal.	
5.	Liner with rivets.		19.	Spring washer.		33.	Dust seal and retainer.	
6.	Rivet.		20.	Bleeder screw.		34.	Pad assembly.	Disc type.
7.	Pull-off spring.	Drum type.	21.	Brake-drum.	Drum type.	35.	Pad retaining spring.	
8.	Micram adjuster.		22.	Set screw.		36.	Split cotter pin.	
9.	Mask.		23.	Plug.		37.	Pad shim.	
10.	Wheel cylinder assembly.		24.	Brake disc.		38.	Plug.	
11.	Piston with dust cover.		25.	Set screw.		39.	Bleed screw.	
12.	Cup.		26.	Dust cover.	Disc type.	40.	Calliper mounting bolt.	
13.	Cup filler.		27.	Set screw.		41.	Spring washer.	
14.	Spring.		28.	Shakeproof washer.				

THE REAR BRAKE COMPONENTS

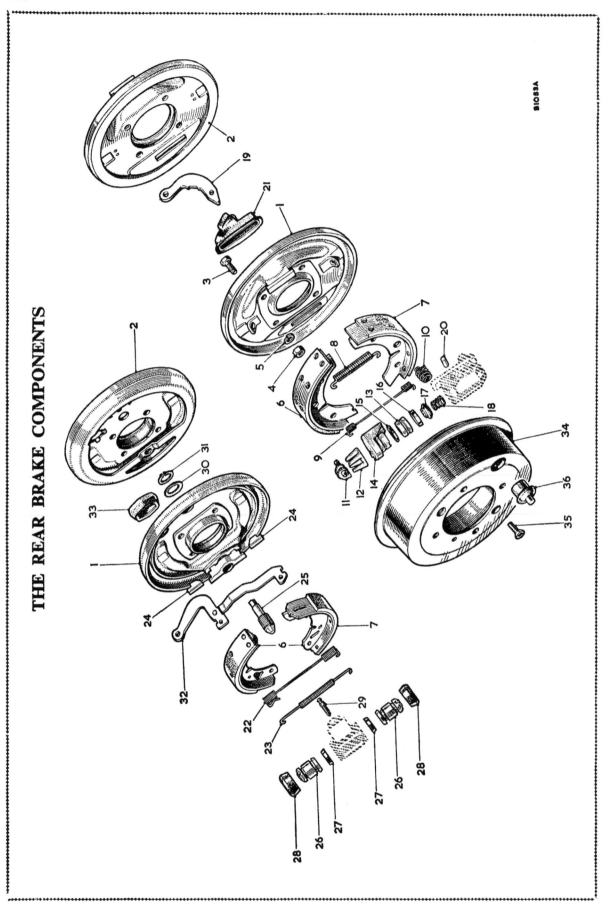

B1083A

KEY TO THE REAR BRAKE COMPONENTS

No.	Description	No.	Description	No.	Description
1.	Brake-plate—R.H.	13.	Piston.	25.	Wedge.
2.	Brake-plate—L.H.	14.	Piston with dust cover.	26.	Piston.
3.	Set screw.	15.	Seal.	27.	Seal.
4.	Nut.	16.	Cup.	28.	Boot.
5.	Spring washer.	17.	Cup filler.	29.	Bleeder screw.
6.	Brake-shoe assembly.	18.	Spring.	30.	Belleville washer.
7.	Liner with rivets.	19.	Hand brake lever.	31.	Circlip.
8.	Shoe return spring (abutment end).	20.	Pivot pin.	32.	Hand brake lever.
9.	Shoe return spring (cylinder end).	21.	Boot.	33.	Boot.
10.	Steady spring.	22.	Shoe return spring (cylinder end).	34.	Brake-drum.
11.	Adjuster assembly.	23.	Shoe return spring (adjuster end).	35.	Set screw.
12.	Mask adjuster.	24.	Tappet.	36.	Plug.

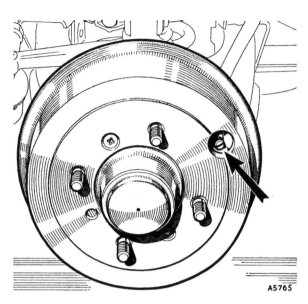

Fig. M.1
Showing a front brake-drum with one of the brake-shoe adjusters

Section M.1

MAINTENANCE

General

The fluid in the master cylinder reservoir must be maintained at a level $\frac{1}{4}$ in. (6·5 mm.) below the bottom of the filler neck. The necessity of frequent topping up is an indication of a leak in the system which must be traced and rectified.

IMPORTANT.—Serious consequences may result from the use of incorrect fluids, use only the recommended fluid given in 'GENERAL DATA'.

Excessive travel of the brake pedal is an indication that the brake-shoes require adjusting. For brake adjustments see Section M.2.

Disc brakes

In order to maintain peak braking efficiency and at the same time obtain maximum life from the front brake friction pads, the pads should be examined periodically, and if one pad is worn more than the other their operating positions should be changed over.

Lubrication

A lubricating nipple is provided on the hand brake balance lever, and on the hand brake cable. Both nipples should be charged with a recommended lubricant at the periods specified in the vehicle Driver's Handbook.

Preventive Maintenance

To safeguard against the possible effects of wear, or deterioration, it is recommended that:
(1) Disc brake pad, drum brake linings, hoses, and pipes should be examined at intervals no greater than those laid down in the Passport to Service.

(2) Brake fluid should be changed completely every 18 months or 24,000 miles (40000 km.) whichever is the sooner.
(3) All fluid seals in the hydraulic system and all flexible hoses should be examined and renewed if necessary every 3 years or 40,000 miles (65000 km.) whichever is the sooner. At the same time the working surface of the pistons and of the bores of the master cylinder, wheel cylinders, and other slave cylinders should be examined and new parts fitted where necessary.

Care must be taken always to observe the following points:
(*a*) At all times use the recommended brake fluid.
(*b*) Never leave fluid in unsealed containers. It absorbs moisture quickly and this can be dangerous.
(*c*) Fluid drained from the system or used for bleeding is best discarded.
(*d*) The necessity for absolute cleanliness throughout cannot be over-emphasized.

Section M.2

ADJUSTMENT

Front
Drum brakes
(1) Apply the hand brake, and jack up the car until the wheel is free to rotate.
(2) Remove the wheel disc, and the rubber plug in the drum.
(3) Rotate the wheel until one of the adjusters is accessible through the hole in the drum (see Fig. M.1).
(4) Using a screwdriver, turn the adjuster in a clockwise direction until the brake-shoe contacts the drum.
(5) Turn the adjuster back just sufficiently for the wheel to rotate without the brake-shoe rubbing the drum.

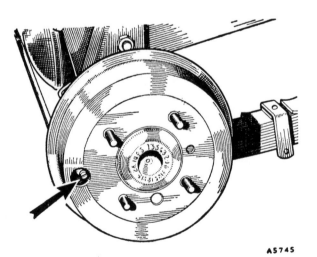

Fig. M.2
Showing rear brake-shoe adjuster

M.6

Sprite and Midget. Issue 5. 4780

(6) Turn the wheel until the other adjuster is accessible through the hole in the drum and repeat the operations in (4) and (5).

(7) Spin the wheel and apply the brakes hard, then recheck the adjustment.

(8) Refit the rubber plug and wheel disc.

(9) Repeat the operations in (1) to (8) for the other front brake.

Disc brakes

(10) Wear on the friction pads is automatically compensated during braking and therefore no manual adjustment is provided. If both friction pads are not worn the same amount change their operating positions (see Section M.1) or if the pads are worn down to the minimum thickness of $\frac{1}{16}$ in. (1·59 mm.) renew the pads (see Section M.9).

Rear

Early cars

(11) Block both front wheels, fully release the hand brake, and jack up the car until the wheel is free to rotate.

(12) Remove the wheel disc, and the rubber plug in the brake-drum.

(13) Rotate the wheel until the adjuster is accessible through the hole in the drum.

(14) Using a screwdriver turn the adjusters in a clockwise direction until the shoes lock the brake-drum.

(15) Turn the adjuster back just sufficiently for the wheel to rotate without the brake-shoes rubbing the drum.

(16) Repeat the operations in (11) to (15) for the other rear brake.

Later cars

(17) Block both front wheels, fully release the hand brake, and jack up the car until the wheel is free to rotate.

(18) Turn the adjuster, located on the back of the brake

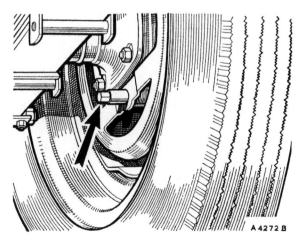

Fig. M.3

One square-headed brake adjusting bolt is provided on each rear brake-plate

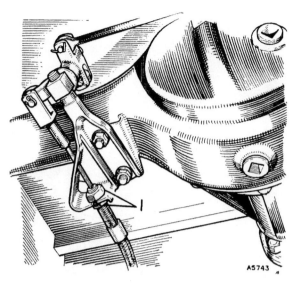

A5743

Fig. M.4

Shows location of hand brake cable adjuster (1) on the rear axle

backplate, in a clockwise direction until the shoes lock the brake-drum.

(19) Turn the adjuster back just sufficiently for the wheel to rotate without the brake-shoes rubbing.

(20) Repeat the operations in (17) to (19) for the other rear brake.

Hand brake

(21) Adjust the rear brake-shoes as detailed in (11) to (16) (early cars) or (17) to (20) (later cars).

(22) Block both front wheels and jack up the rear of the car.

(23) Apply the hand brake so that the pawl engages with the third notch on the ratchet.

(24) Adjust the hand brake cable, with the sleeve nut (Fig. M.4), until it is just possible to rotate each wheel by heavy hand pressure. Both wheels must offer equal resistance in order to get full braking power.

(25) Release the hand brake and check that both wheels rotate freely.

Section M.3

BRAKE PEDAL ADJUSTMENT

The correct amount of free movement of the master cylinder push-rod when the brake pedal is depressed is set during the vehicle assembly, and should only require adjustment if components have been renewed.

(1) Slacken the adjuster nut on the master cylinder push-rod.

(2) Set the length of the push-rod to give a free movement of the pedal pad of approximately $\frac{5}{32}$ in. (4 mm.) before the master cylinder piston begins to

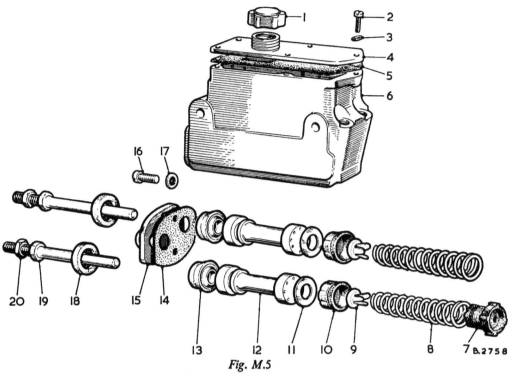

Fig. M.5

Master cylinder exploded

1. Filler cap.	8. Return spring.	15. Boot fixing plate.
2. Fixing screw.	9. Spring retainer.	16. Fixing screws.
3. Shakeproof washer.	10. Main cup.	17. Shakeproof washer.
4. Tank cover.	11. Piston washer.	18. Boot.
5. Tank cover gasket.	12. Piston.	19. Push-rod.
6. Cylinder barrel and tank.	13. Secondary cup.	20. Push-rod adjuster.
7. Valve (Brake bore only).	14. Gasket.	

move. The push-rod must have a minimum of $\frac{1}{32}$ in. (·8 mm.) free movement before the piston starts to move.

Section M.4

BLEEDING THE SYSTEM

The following procedure must be followed after any service operation or fault in the braking system which may have allowed air to enter the hydraulic system.

During the bleeding operation it is most important that the master cylinder reservoir is kept at least half-full to avoid drawing air into the system.

(1) Check that all connections are tightened and all bleed screws closed.

(2) Fill the reservoir with the recommended brake fluid (see 'GENERAL DATA').

(3) Remove the rubber cap from the rear bleed screw on the wheel cylinder farthest from the master cylinder, and fit a bleed tube to the screw.

(4) Immerse the free end of the tube in a clean glass containing a small quantity of brake fluid.

(5) Slacken the bleed screw and depress the brake pedal slowly through its full travel and allow it to return without assistance.

(6) Repeat the pedal pumping action with a slight pause before each depression of the pedal.

(7) When the fluid leaving the bleed tube is completely

free of air bubbles, hold the pedal down firmly and tighten the bleed screw.

(8) Repeat the operations in (3) to (7) on all the remaining wheel cylinders, finishing at the wheel nearest the master cylinder.

(9) Top up the reservoir to the correct level.

(10) Apply a normal work load to the brake pedal for a period of two or three minutes and examine the entire system for leaks.

Section M.5

MASTER CYLINDER

Removing

(1) Disconnect the electrical connections from the heater blower unit, remove the screws securing the blower unit to the bulkhead and remove the blower unit.

(2) Remove the screws securing the master cylinder mounting plate to the bulkhead.

(3) Disconnect the two hydraulic pipes from their unions on the master cylinder. Note which one of the pipes connects to the clutch slave cylinder.

(4) Withdraw the master cylinder upwards and at the same time manipulate the clutch and brake pedals through the hole in the bulkhead.

(5) Remove the spring clips, and withdraw the clevis pins from the push-rods to disconnect both pedals.

M.8

Sprite and Midget. Issue 3. 29459

(6) Unscrew the bolts securing the master cylinder to the mounting plate and remove the complete unit.

Dismantling

(7) Remove the filler cap and drain the fluid.

(8) Remove screws retaining the boot fixing plate to the master cylinder.

(9) Detach the fixing plate and remove the boots and push-rods.

(10) Withdraw the piston, piston washer, main cup, and return spring complete with spring retainer and valve assembly from the brake bore of the cylinder.

(11) Remove the secondary cup from the piston by stretching it over the end flange.

Inspection

(12) Clean all the parts thoroughly using the recommended brake fluid and dry them with a clean, non-fluffy cloth.

(13) Examine the metal parts for wear and damage, inspect the rubber cups for swelling, perishing, distortion, or any other signs of deterioration. Renew all worn, damaged, or suspect parts.

Reassembling

(14) Dip all the internal components in the recommended brake fluid and assemble them while wet.

(15) Stretch the secondary cup over the piston with the lip of the cup facing towards the head of the piston. When the cup is in its groove work round it with the fingers to ensure that it is correctly seated.

(16) Fit the spring retainer into the small diameter end of the spring and the valve assembly into the large diameter end.

(17) Insert the assembled spring into the body, valve assembly end first.

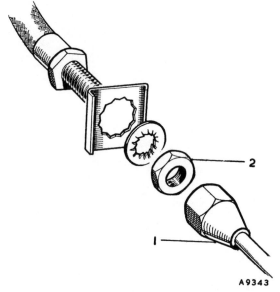

Fig. M.7

The union nut (1) is the one which must be first unscrewed to release the flexible hose from the pipeline. The attachment nut (2) can then be removed

(18) Fit the main cup, piston washer, and piston. When fitting the cups carefully enter the lip edge of the cups into the barrel first.

(19) Fit the boot fixing plate, boots, and push-rods. Each boot must be fitted with the vent hole at the bottom when the master cylinder is mounted in the car.

Refitting

(20) Reverse the removing procedure in (1) to (6) then bleed the system (Section M.4).

Section M.6

BRAKE PEDAL

Removing

(1) Raise the bonnet and remove the spring clips and clevis pins connecting the clutch and brake pedals to the master cylinder push-rods.

(2) From inside the car, detach the pedal return springs and remove the nut and spring washer retaining the pedal fulcrum pin.

(3) Withdraw the fulcrum pin and remove the pedals and distance piece.

Inspection

(4) Examine the pedal and fulcrum pin for excessive wear and renew the worn parts as necessary.

Refitting

(5) Reverse the removing procedure in (1) to (3) noting that the distance piece is fitted between the pedals.

Fig. M.6

Illustrating a rear brake bleed nipple

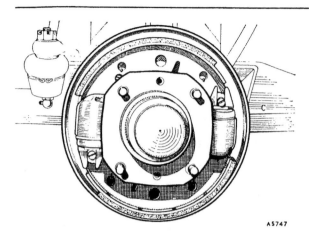

Fig. M.8

The front brake assembly

A5747

Section M.7

FLEXIBLE HOSES

Removing

(1) Unscrew the pipe union nut from its connection to the hose.

(2) Hold the hexagon on the flexible hose and remove the locknut and shakeproof washer securing the hose union to the bracket.

(3) Unscrew the flexible hose from the cylinder.

Refitting

(4) Reverse the removing procedure in (1) to (3).

Section M.8

FRONT BRAKE ASSEMBLIES—DRUM BRAKES

Removing

Brake-shoes

(1) Raise the front of the car and remove the road wheel.

(2) Remove the countersunk screw (disc wheels) or nuts (wire wheels) securing the brake-drum and withdraw the drum.

(3) Lift one brake-shoe, against the tension of the return springs, from its abutment with the closed end of one of the wheel cylinders, and slide the Micram mask off the piston cover of the other cylinder.

(4) With the return spring tension released detach the springs and remove both shoes.

Wheel cylinders

(5) Carry out the operations in (1) to (4).

(6) Disconnect the hydraulic bridge pipe from the wheel cylinders.

(7) Remove the bolts securing the wheel cylinder to the backplate and withdraw the cylinder from the backplate.

Backplate

(8) Carry out the operations in (1) and (2).

(9) Lever off the hub cap.

(10) Withdraw the split pin locking the hub retaining nut, and remove the nut and washer.

(11) Withdraw the hub assembly from the swivel axle using tool 18G 304 with adaptors 18G 304 F.

(12) Disconnect the hydraulic feed pipe from the backplate.

(13) Unscrew the bolts securing the backplate to the swivel axle and remove the backplate and brake assembly.

Dismantling

Wheel cylinder

(14) Withdraw the piston, complete with its cover, from the cylinder.

(15) Apply a gentle air pressure to the fluid connection and blow out the rubber cup, cup filler, and spring.

(16) Remove the sealing ring.

(17) Remove the bleed screw.

Inspection

Brake-shoes

(18) Clean the dust from the brake-shoes and linings using an air blast, examine the linings for wear. See Section M.11 for brake-shoe relining.

Wheel cylinders

(19) Clean the components thoroughly using the recommended brake fluid, and dry them with a clean, non-fluffy cloth.

(20) Examine the metal parts for wear and damage, inspect the rubber cup for swelling or signs of deterioration.

Renew all damaged, worn or suspect parts.

Reassembling

Wheel cylinders

(21) Dip the components in the recommended brake fluid and assemble them wet.

(22) Fit the cup filler into the small diameter end of the spring and insert the spring, large diameter end first, into the cylinder.

(23) Fit the cup, lip side first, into the cylinder.

(24) Fit the piston and piston cover.

Refitting

Backplate

(25) Reverse the removing procedure in (8) to (13) then bleed the system (Section M.4) and adjust the brake-shoes (Section M.2).

Wheel cylinders

(26) Reverse the removing procedure in (5) to (7), then bleed the system (Section M.4) and adjust the brake-shoes (Section M.2).

Brake-shoes

(27) Reverse the removing procedure in (1) to (4) then adjust the brake-shoes (Section M.2).

Section M.9

FRONT BRAKE ASSEMBLIES—DISC BRAKES

Removing

Friction pads

(1) Raise the front of the car and remove the road wheel.

(2) Depress the friction pad retaining spring and withdraw the split pins.

(3) Remove the retaining springs.

(4) Rotate the friction pads and anti-squeak shims slightly, and lift them from the calliper.

Calliper assembly

(5) Carry out the operations in (1) to (4).

(6) Disconnect the hydraulic supply hose.

(7) Remove the nuts securing the hose retaining plate to the calliper.

(8) Remove the studs securing the calliper to the stub axle and withdraw the calliper.

Brake discs

(9) Carry out the operations in (1) to (8).

(10) Remove the hub cap and withdraw the split pin locking the hub retaining nut.

(11) Remove the retaining nut and washer.

(12) Withdraw the hub complete with the brake disc from the swivel axle using tool 18G 304 with adaptors 18G 304 F (disc wheels) or tool 18G 363 (wire wheels—early cars) or 18G 1032 (wire wheels—later cars).

(13) Remove the bolts securing the brake disc to the hub, and remove the disc.

Calliper pistons and seals

(14) Carry out the operations in (1) to (8).

(15) Clean the outside of the calliper, ensuring that all dirt and cleaning fluid are completely removed.

(16) Note the position of the relieved portion of the piston face.

(17) Reconnect the hydraulic supply hose and support the calliper to avoid strain on the hose.

(18) Using tool 18G 590 clamp the piston in the mounting half of the calliper.

(19) Place a receptacle under the calliper and gently press the brake pedal until the piston in the rim half has emerged sufficiently for it to be removed by hand.

(20) Withdraw the piston.

(21) Gently prise the dust seal retainer from the mouth of the calliper bore and remove the dust seal taking care not to damage the seal groove.

(22) Remove the fluid seal from its groove in the calliper bore taking great care not to damage the bore of the calliper or the seal groove.

(23) Remove the clamping tool.

(24) To remove the mounting-half piston it is first necessary to refit the lip-half piston then repeat the procedure in (18) to (22) but with the lip-half piston clamped.

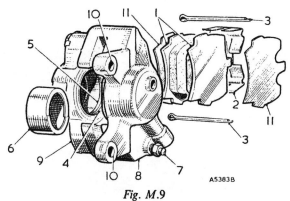

Fig. M.9

The front brake calliper components

1.	Friction pads.	6.	Piston.
2.	Pad retaining spring.	7.	Bleeder screw.
3.	Retaining pin.	8.	Calliper (mounting half).
4.	Piston dust seal.	9.	Calliper (rim half).
5.	Piston fluid seal.	10.	Calliper mounting point.
	11.	Anti-squeak shims.	

Dismantling

Calliper assembly

(25) Remove the bleeder screw.

NOTE.—Unless it is absolutely unavoidable the calliper should not be separated into two halves. In the event of separation becoming essential, the fluid channel seal, clamping bolts, and lock plates must be renewed when reassembling. Only bolts supplied by (Austin-Morris) Service division may be used. On assembly these must be tightened with a torque wrench set at between 33·5 and 37 lb. ft. (4·9 and 5·1 kg. m.).

Ensure that the calliper faces are clean and that the threaded bolt holes are thoroughly dry. Make certain that the new fluid seal is correctly located in the recessed face before assembling the two calliper halves.

Inspection

Friction pads

(26) Examine the lining material for wear, if the material is worn down to a maximum permissible thickness of $\frac{1}{16}$ in. (1·59 mm.) the friction pads must be renewed.

(27) Check that the friction pads move easily in the calliper recess, remove any high spots from the pad pressure plates by careful filing.

(28) Examine the pad retaining springs for damage or loss of tension, renew the springs as necessary.

Calliper assembly

(29) Clean any dirt or rust from the friction pad recesses. Thoroughly clean the exposed faces of the pistons or bores. Use only the recommended brake fluid or methylated spirit for cleaning, solvents must not be used.

(30) Blow the fluid passages clear with compressed air.

Reassembling

Calliper assembly

(31) Refit the bleeder screw.

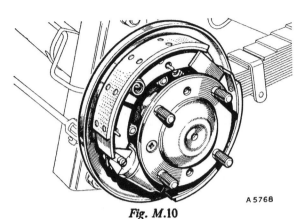

Fig. M.10

The rear brake assembly

Refitting

Brake disc

(32) Refit the brake disc to the hub.

(33) Fit the hub assembly to the stub axle.

(34) Check the maximum run-out of the brake disc at the periphery of the braking surface, if the run-out exceeds ·006 in. (·152 mm.) the components must be examined for damage and, if necessary, renewed.

Calliper pistons and seals

(35) Ensure that the new fluid seal is absolutely dry, and coat it with Lockheed Disc Brake Lubricant.

(36) Ease the seal into its groove in the calliper bore, then gently work round with the fingers until it is seating correctly.

(37) Slacken the bleeder screw one complete turn.

(38) Coat the piston with Lockheed Disc Brake Lubricant and locate the piston squarely in the mouth of the bore, with the cut-away portion of the piston face correctly positioned downwards.

(39) Press the piston into the bore until approximately $\frac{5}{16}$ in. (8 mm.) of the piston is protruding from the bore. Take great care to prevent the piston from lifting during this operation.

(40) Ensure that the new dust seal is absolutely dry, coat it with Lockheed Disc Brake Lubricant and fit the seal into its retainer.

(41) Position the seal assembly on the protruding portion of the piston with the seal innermost, ensuring that the assembly is square with the piston.

(42) Using tool 18G 590, press the piston and seal assembly home.

(43) Retighten the bleeder screw.

(44) Fit the seals and pistons into the mounting half of the calliper by the same procedure as in (34) to (42), noting that the hydraulic feed pipe must be disconnected to allow the clamping tool to be used.

Calliper assembly

(45) Reverse the removing procedure in (6) to (8), noting that the brake pedal must not be depressed.

Friction pads

(46) Check that the exposed surface of each piston is clean and the recesses in the calliper are free from rust and grit.

(47) Using tool 18G 590 press each piston fully back into the bore.

NOTE.—**During this operation, fluid displaced by the pistons will cause the fluid level in the master cylinder to rise, and it may be necessary to siphon off some of the fluid to prevent it from overflowing.**

(48) Check that the relieved face of each piston is correctly positioned downwards, and fit the friction pads into the calliper.

(49) Check that the friction pads are free to move easily in the calliper recesses and fit the anti-squeak shims between the pistons and friction pad pressure plates.

(50) Fit the pad retaining springs, press the spring down and insert the split pins.

(51) Bleed the system (Section M.4).

(52) Pump the brake pedal several times to adjust the friction pads and top up the master cylinder reservoir to the correct level.

Section M.10

REAR BRAKE ASSEMBLIES

Removing

Brake-shoes (early cars)

(1) Block both front wheels, fully release the hand brake, and raise the rear of the car.

(2) Remove the road wheel.

(3) Back off the brake-shoe adjuster and remove the brake-drum (see Section H.3).

(4) Depress each shoe steady spring, turn it, to release it from the backplate.

(5) Pull the trailing shoe, against the tension of the return springs, away from its abutment at either end.

(6) With the return spring tension released detach the springs and remove both shoes. The Micram adjuster will also come free when the shoes are removed.

Brake-shoes (later cars)

(7) Carry out the operations in (1) to (3) and (5).

(8) Remove the shoes and springs.

Wheel cylinder (early cars)

(9) Remove the brake-shoes as detailed in (1) to (6).

(10) Disconnect the hydraulic feed pipe at the wheel cylinder.

(11) Disconnect the hand brake rod at the wheel cylinder lever.

(12) Remove the rubber boot.

(13) Withdraw the piston and cover from the wheel cylinder.

(14) Swing the hand brake lever until the shoulder is clear of the backplate, and slide the cylinder assembly forward.

(15) Pivot the cylinder about its forward end and withdraw the rear end from the slot in the backplate.

(16) Move the cylinder rearwards and disengage the forward end from the backplate.

Wheel cylinder (later cars)

(17) Remove the brake-shoes as detailed in (7) and (8).

M.12

Sprite and Midget. Issue 4. 29459

(18) Disconnect the hydraulic feed pipe at the wheel cylinder.

(19) Disconnect the hand brake rod from the wheel cylinder lever and remove the rubber boot.

(20) Remove the bleed screw.

(21) Remove the circlip retaining the wheel cylinder to the backplate and withdraw the cylinder assembly.

Backplate

(22) Remove the wheel cylinder as detailed in (9) to (16) (early cars) or (17) to (21) (later cars).

(23) Remove the axle shaft (Section H.3).

(24) Remove the hub assembly (Section H.4).

(25) Unscrew the bolts securing the backplate to the hub, and remove the backplate.

Dismantling

Wheel cylinders (early cars)

(26) Withdraw the hand brake lever pivot pin and remove the lever.

(27) Apply a gentle air pressure to the fluid connection and blow out the hydraulic piston, rubber cup, cup filler, and spring.

(28) Remove the seal from the outer piston.

Wheel cylinders (later cars)

(29) Remove the dust seals from the ends of the cylinder.

(30) Withdraw both pistons complete with their seals.

(31) Withdraw the hand brake lever pivot pin and remove the lever.

(32) Remove the seals from the pistons.

Inspection

Brake-shoes

(33) Clean the dust from the brake-shoes and linings using an air blast, and examine the linings for wear. See Section M.11 for brake-shoe relining.

Wheel cylinders

(34) Clean the components thoroughly using the recommended brake fluid, and dry them with a clean, non-fluffy cloth.

(35) Examine the metal parts for wear and damage.

(36) Inspect the rubber cup and seals for swelling or signs of deterioration.

(37) Renew all damaged, worn, or suspect parts.

Reassembling

Wheel cylinders (early cars)

(38) Dip the internal components in the recommended brake fluid and assemble them wet.

(39) Fit the small diameter end of the spring into the cup filler and insert the spring, large diameter end first, into the cylinder.

(40) Fit the cup, lip side first, into the cylinder.

(41) Insert the hydraulic piston, aligning the slot in the piston with the slot in the cylinder.

(42) Fit the hand brake lever and pivot pin.

(43) Ease the seal into its groove in the outer piston.

(44) Fit the outer piston assembly.

Wheel cylinders (later cars)

(45) Dip the internal components in the recommended brake fluid and assemble them wet.

(46) Fit the seals to the pistons.

(47) Insert the pistons and fit the dust covers

(48) Fit the hand brake lever and pivot pin.

Refitting

Backplate

(49) Reverse the removing procedure in (22) to (25), bleed the system and adjust the brake-shoes.

Wheel cylinders (early cars)

(50) Reverse the removing procedure in (9) to (16), bleed the system and adjust the brake-shoes.

Wheel cylinders (later cars)

(51) Reverse the removing procedure in (17) to (21), bleed the system and adjust the brake-shoes.

Brake-shoes (early cars)

(52) Reverse the removing procedure in (1) to (6), noting the following.

    (a) Ensure that the Micram adjuster is in the slot in the leading shoe with the mask in position.

    (b) The interrupted return spring must be fitted on the wheel cylinder side and both springs must lie between the brake-shoes and backplate.

    (c) The shoes must be fitted with the unlined end of the leading shoe to the wheel cylinder, and the unlined end of the trailing shoe to the abutment block.

Brake-shoes (later cars)

(53) Reverse the removing procedure in (7) and (8), noting the following.

    (a) Ensure that the brake-shoes register correctly in the slots in the wheel cylinder pistons and on the adjuster tappets.

    (b) Ensure that the return springs are anchored in their correct holes in the shoe webs, with the interrupted spring fitted on the wheel cylinder side.

    (c) After refitting adjust the brake-shoes.

Section M.11

BRAKE-SHOE RELINING

It is not recommended that brake-shoes relining is undertaken unless all the special facilities necessary to carry out the work are available. Where the facilities are not available it is recommended that replacement brake-shoes are used.

When fitting new linings or replacement brake-shoes the following points must be observed.

(1) Only linings and replacement shoes with linings of the material specified in **'GENERAL DATA'** must be used.

(2) Shoes or linings must only be renewed in sets.

(3) After riveting new linings to the brake-shoes it is essential that any high-spots are removed before refitting the shoes to the backplate.

(4) When new brake-shoes or linings have been fitted the brake-shoe adjusters must be fully backed off and the hand brake fully released before attempting to fit the brake-drum over the new linings.

(5) Do not allow oil, grease, brake fluid, or paint to come into contact with the brake linings.

SECTION Ma

THE BRAKING SYSTEM

The information given in this Section refers specifically to the Sprite (Mk. IV) and Midget (Mk. III) and must be used in conjunction with Section M.

	Section
Master cylinder	Ma.1

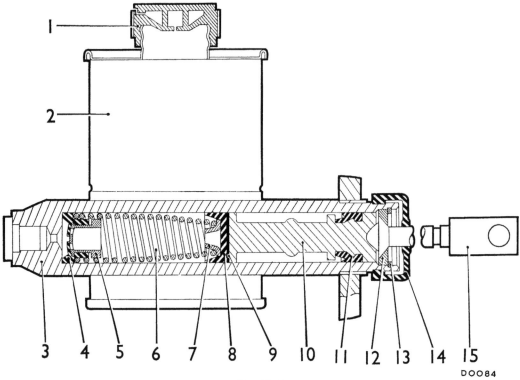

Fig. Ma.1

A section through the master cylinder

1. Filler cap.	5. Valve seat.	9. Piston washer.	13. Circlip.
2. Reservoir.	6. Spring.	10. Piston.	14. Rubber boot.
3. Body.	7. Spring retainer.	11. Secondary cup.	15. Push-rod.
4. Valve.	8. Main cup.	12. Dished washer.	

Section Ma.1

MASTER CYLINDER

Removing

(1) Raise the bonnet and remove the pedal box lid.

(2) Disconnect the hydraulic pipe from the brake master cylinder.

(3) Withdraw the split pin from the clevis pin connecting the push-rod to the brake pedal and remove the clevis pin.

(4) Unscrew the two bolts securing the master cylinder to the pedal box and remove the master cylinder.

Dismantling

(5) Remove the filler cap and drain the fluid.

(6) Detach the rubber boot from the body and slide it up the push-rod.

(7) Remove the circlip retaining the push-rod, and withdraw the push-rod complete with the rubber boot and dished washer.

(8) Withdraw the piston complete with the secondary cup.

(9) Remove the piston washer, main cup, and the spring complete with the spring retainer and valve.

(10) Remove the secondary cup from the piston by carefully stretching it over the end flange of the piston using only the fingers.

Inspection

(11) Clean all the parts thoroughly using the recom-

Ma.2

mended brake fluid and dry them with a clean non-fluffy cloth.

(12) Examine the metal parts for wear and damage, inspect the rubber components for swelling, perishing, distortion, or any other signs of deterioration. Renew all worn, damaged, or suspect parts.

Reassembling

(13) Dip all the internal components in the recommended brake fluid and assemble them while wet.

(14) Stretch the secondary cup over the piston with the lip of the cup facing towards the head of the piston. When the cup is in its groove, work round it gently with the fingers to ensure that it is correctly seated.

(15) Fit the spring retainer and the valve to the spring, and fit spring, valve end first, into the body.

(16) Fit the main cup, cup washer, piston and push-rod. When fitting the cups carefully enter the lip edge of the cup into the barrel first.

(17) Fit the circlip and rubber boot.

Refitting

(18) Reverse the removing procedure in (1) to (4) then fill the master cylinder with the recommended brake fluid (see 'GENERAL DATA') and bleed the system (Section M.4).

Section Mb

THE BRAKING SYSTEM (Tandem Master Cylinder)

The information given in this Section refers specifically to service operations on, or affected by equipment fitted to the Sprite Mk. IV and Midget Mk. III in conformity with local and territorial requirements, and must be used in conjunction with Section M and Section Ma.

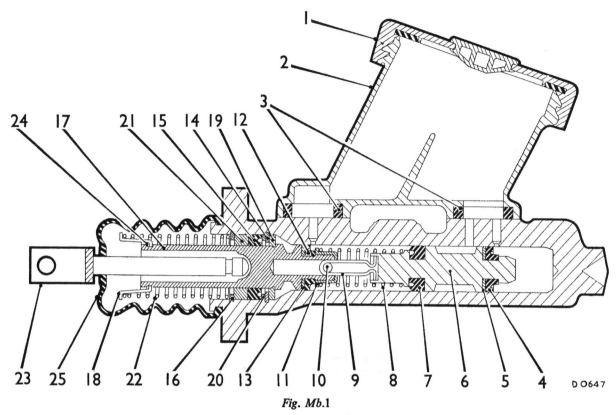

*Fig. Mb.*1

A section through the master cylinder

1. Filler cap.	7. Main cup.	13. Piston washer.	19. Stop washer.
2. Plastic reservoir.	8. Spring.	14. Circlip.	20. Washer.
3. Reservoir seals.	9. Piston link.	15. Cup.	21. Bearing.
4. Main cup.	10. Pin.	16. Circlip.	22. Spring.
5. Piston washer.	11. Pin retainer.	17. Piston.	23. Push-rod.
6. Piston.	12. Main cup.	18. Spring retainer.	24. 'Spirolox' ring.
	25. Rubber boot.		

Section Mb.1

PEDAL FREE MOVEMENT

A free movement of $\frac{1}{8}$ in. (3·2 mm.) measured at the pedal pad must be maintained on the brake pedal.

To adjust the free movement, slacken the stop light switch locknut, and turn the switch clockwise to decrease or anti-clockwise to increase the clearance. Tighten the switch locknut.

Section Mb.2

MASTER CYLINDER

Removing

(1) Unscrew the four retaining screws and remove the pedal box cover.

(2) Disconnect the hydraulic pipes from the master cylinder.

(3) Withdraw the split pin from the push-rod clevis pin and remove the clevis pin.

(4) Unscrew the two bolts securing the master cylinder to the pedal box and remove the master cylinder.

Dismantling

(5) Drain the fluid from the reservoir and refit the cap.

(6) Plug the pipe connections and thoroughly clean the exterior of the assembly.

(7) Detach the rubber boot and withdraw the push-rod.

(8) Grip the cylinder body in a soft-jawed vice with the mouth of the bore uppermost.

(9) Compress the return spring and remove the 'Spirolox' ring from its groove in the primary piston, taking care not to distort the coils of the ring or score the bore of the cylinder.

(10) Using tool 18G 1112 remove the piston retaining circlip. A slight radiusing of the sides of the tool may be necessary for ease of use on this master cylinder.

(11) Move the piston up and down in the bore to free the nylon guide bearing and cap seal, remove the guide bearing and seal.

(12) Remove the plain washer.

(13) Using tool 18G 1112 remove the inner circlip.

(14) Withdraw the primary and secondary piston assembly complete with stop washer.

*Mb.*2

Sprite and Midget. Issue 3. 80661

(15) Remove the stop washer.

(16) Compress the spring separating the two pistons and drive out the roll-pin retaining the piston link.

(17) Note the positions of the rubber caps by their moulded indentations and remove the cups and washers from the pistons.

(18) Unscrew the four bolts securing the plastic reservoir to the body and remove the reservoir.

(19) Remove the two reservoir sealing rings.

(20) Unscrew the connection adaptors, discard the copper gaskets, and remove the springs and trap valves.

Inspection

(21) Clean all the parts thoroughly using the recommended brake fluid and dry them with clean lint-free cloth.

(22) Examine the metal parts for wear and damage, inspect the rubber components for swelling, perishing, distortion, or any other signs of deterioration. Renew all worn, damaged, or suspect parts.

Reassembling

(23) Dip all the internal components in the recommended brake fluid and assemble them while wet.

(24) Locate the piston washer on the head of the secondary piston, convex surface first.

(25) Carefully ease the secondary main cup, lip last, over the end of the piston, using the fingers, and seat it correctly in the groove adjacent to the washer.

(26) Carry out the operations in (24) and (25) with the washer and main cup of the primary piston.

(27) Reverse the dismantling procedure in (5) to (16) and (18) to (20).

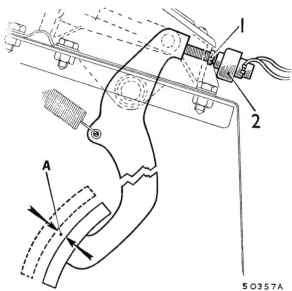

Fig Mb.2

Brake pedal adjustment.

1. Switch locknut. 2. Stop light switch.

A=⅛in. (3·2 mm.)

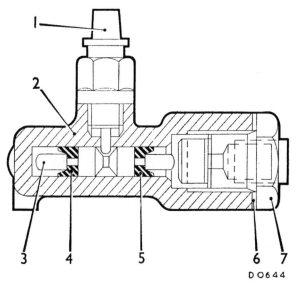

D 0644

Fig. Mb.3

A section through the pressure failure switch assembly

1. Nylon switch.
2. Switch body.
3. Shuttle valve piston.
4. Piston seal.
5. Piston seal.
6. Copper washer.
7. End plug.

Refitting

(28) Reverse the removing procedure in (1) to (4), fill the master cylinder with the recommended brake fluid (see 'GENERAL DATA') and bleed the system (see Section M.4) commencing with the rear brakes. Check, and, if necessary adjust the brake pedal free movement (Section Mb.1).

Section Mb.3

PRESSURE FAILURE SWITCH ASSEMBLY

Removing

(1) Disconnect the wiring from the switch.

(2) Clean the switch assembly and its adjacent surroundings particularly the pipe connections.

(3) Disconnect the plug and hydraulic pipes.

(4) Unscrew the retaining bolt and remove the assembly.

Dismantling

(5) Remove the end plug and discard the copper washer.

(6) Unscrew the nylon switch.

(7) Withdraw the shuttle valve piston assembly from the bore; use a low pressure air line to free the piston if necessary.

(8) Remove and discard the two piston seals.

Inspection

(9) Thoroughly clean all the components using Methylated Spirit (denatured alcohol) or the

Mb.3

recommended brake fluid, and dry with lint-free cloth.

(10) Inspect the bore of the casing for scoring and damage, the complete assembly must be renewed if the bore is not in a perfect condition.

(11) Reconnect the wiring to the switch and actuate the switch plunger, with the ignition switched on, to test the switch operation and warning light circuit.

Reassembling

(12) Fit two new seals, lips facing outwards, to the piston.

(13) Lubricate the piston assembly with Lockheed Disc Brake lubricant and fit the piston into the bore taking care that the lip of the leading seal is not turned back.

(14) Fit a new copper washer to the end plug, screw in and tighten the plug to the torque figure given in 'GENERAL DATA'.

(15) Screw in the switch and carefully tighten it to the torque figure given in 'GENERAL DATA'.

Refitting

(16) Reverse the removing procedure in (1) to (4), fill the master cylinder with the recommended brake fluid (see 'GENERAL DATA') and bleed the system (see Section M.4) commencing with the rear brakes.

SECTION N

THE ELECTRICAL SYSTEM

Sprite and Midget.   Issue 7.   82790   N.1

205

GENERAL DESCRIPTION

The 12-volt electrical equipment incorporates compensated voltage control for the charging circuit. The positive earth system of wiring is employed.

The battery is mounted on the dash under the bonnet and is readily accessible for examination and maintenance attention.

The dynamo is mounted on the right of the cylinder block and driven by an endless belt from the crankshaft pulley. A rotatable mounting enables the belt tension to be adjusted.

The voltage control unit adjustment is sealed and should not normally require attention. The fuses are carried in external holders mounted in an accessible position on the right-hand side of the engine compartment together with spare fuses.

The starter motor is mounted on the flywheel housing on the right-hand side of the engine unit and operates on the flywheel through the usual sliding pinion device.

The headlamps employ the double-filament dipping system. Both lamps are fitted with double-filament bulbs for Europe, and a sealed-beam unit is fitted for Home and U.S.A. markets, both types dipping according to the regulations existing in the countries concerned.

Section N.1

LUBRICATION

Dynamo

On early cars unscrew the lubricator with the felt pad and half-fill with lubricant at regular intervals. On later cars add two drops of lubricant at regular intervals in the lubricating hole in the centre of the rear end bearing plate.

Section N.2

BATTERY

The battery is a 12-volt lead-acid type, having six cells, each cell consisting of a group of positive and negative plates immersed in a solution of sulphuric acid (electrolyte).

The battery has three functions: to supply current for starting, ignition, and lighting; to provide a constant supply of current to the electrical equipment under normal operating conditions and when the consumption of the electrical equipment exceeds the output of the dynamo; and to control the voltage of the electrical supply system.

Adjustments in the vehicle

The purpose of the following operations is to maintain the performance of the battery at its maximum.

The battery and its surrounding parts should be kept dry and clean, particularly the tops of the cells, as any dampness could cause a leakage between the securing

strap and the battery negative terminal and result in a partially discharged battery. Clean off any corrosion from the battery bolts, strap, and tray with diluted ammonia, afterwards painting the affected parts with anti-sulphuric paint.

Remove the manifold and check it for cracks.

The electrolyte should be maintained just level with the tops of the separator guards by adding distilled water. Never add acid.

Check the terminal posts. If they are corroded remove the cables and clean with diluted ammonia. Smear the posts with petroleum jelly before remaking the connections and ensure that the cable terminal screws are secure.

Check the condition of the battery cells using a hydrometer. If the level of the electrolyte is too low for hydrometer readings to be taken, top up with distilled water and recharge the battery for at least 30 minutes before taking hydrometer readings.

The hydrometer readings and their indications are as follows:

For climates below 27° C. (80° F.)

Cell fully charged	1·270 to 1·290
Cell about half-discharged ..	1·190 to 1·210
Cell completely discharged.. ..	1·110 to 1·130

For climates above 27° C. (80° F.)

Cell fully charged	1·210 to 1·230
Cell about half-charged ..	1·130 to 1·150
Cell completely discharged.. ..	1·050 to 1·070

These figures are given assuming an electrolyte temperature of 16° C. (60° F.). If the temperature of the electrolyte exceeds this ·002 must be added to hydrometer readings for each 3° C. (5° F.) rise to give the true specific gravity. Similarly, ·002 must be subtracted from hydrometer readings for every 3° C. (5° F.) below 16° C. (60° F.).

The readings of all the cells should be approximately the same. If one cell gives a reading which differs from the remainder by 40 points (·040 S.G.) or more, an internal fault in that cell is indicated. The battery should then be checked by a battery specialist. Should the battery be in a low stage of charge, it should be recharged by taking the car for a long daytime run or by charging from an external source of D.C. supply at a current rate of 4·0 amps until the cells are gassing freely.

Removing

Disconnect both cables from the battery.
Release the battery clamp and lift out the battery.

Inspection

Place the battery on a lead-covered bench or on a wooden bench treated with anti-sulphuric paint.
Check the electrolyte levels.
Inspect the container for cracks, which may be indicated by external corrosion or extreme variation in the electrolyte levels.

Recharging from an external source

The length of time for a used battery to remain on charge before it can be accepted as fully charged depends entirely on the specific gravity before charging commences and the charging rate. The charging should continue at 4·0 amps. until all cells are gassing freely and evenly and the specific gravity in each of the six cells has reached a maximum, i.e. has shown no further rise in four hours. The specific gravity at the end of charging should be within the limits given and should not vary ·005 from the values given.

Do not allow the temperature of the electrolyte to exceed the maximum permissible temperature, i.e.

For climates below 27° C. (80° F.) ..	38° C. (100° F.)
For climates above 27° C. (80° F.) ..	49° C. (120° F.)

If this temperature is reached the charge should be suspended to allow the temperature to fall at least 6° C. (10° F.) otherwise the life of the battery will tend to be shortened.

NOTE:—Whenever booster charging of the battery or electrical welding of the body is carried out, the battery earth lead must be disconnected to prevent damage to the electrical system.

Refitting

The installation of the battery is a reversal of the procedure 'Removing'. Smear the terminal posts and cable connections with petroleum jelly and tighten the retaining screws sufficiently to prevent the cables from moving on the terminal posts when tested by hand, but do not overtighten.

Section N.3

PREPARING A DRY-CHARGED BATTERY FOR SERVICE

A dry-charged battery is supplied without electrolyte but with the plates in a charged condition. When it is required for service it is only necessary to fill each cell with sulphuric acid of the correct specific gravity. No initial charging is required.

Preparing electrolyte

The electrolyte is prepared by mixing together distilled water and concentrated sulphuric acid, taking the precautions given in Section N.4. The specific gravity of the filling electrolyte depends on the climate in which the battery is to be used.

Filling the battery

Remove the sealing tapes (when fitted) in the cell filling holes and fill each cell with electrolyte to the top

of the separator guards, **in one operation.** The temperature of the filling room, battery, and electrolyte should be maintained between 16 and 38° C. (60 and 100° F.). If the battery has been stored in a cool place it should be allowed to warm up to room temperature before filling.

Putting into use

Measure the temperature and specific gravity of the electrolyte in each of the cells. Allow to stand for 20 minutes and then re-check. The battery is ready for service unless the electrolyte temperature has risen by more than 5·5° C. (10° F.), or the specific gravity has fallen by more than 10 points (·010 S.G.). In this event, re-charge the battery at the normal re-charge rate until the specific gravity remains constant for three successive hourly readings and all cells are gassing freely. During the charge the electrolyte must be kept level with the top of the separator guards by the addition of distilled water.

Section N.4

PREPARING A NEW, UNFILLED, UNCHARGED BATTERY FOR SERVICE

Preparing electrolyte

A battery should not be filled with acid until required for initial charging. Electrolyte is prepared by mixing distilled water and concentrated sulphuric acid, usually of 1·840 S.G. The mixing must be carried out either in a lead-lined tank or in suitable glass or earthenware vessels. Slowly add the acid to the water, stirring with a glass rod. **Never add the water to the acid,** as the resulting chemical reaction causes violent and dangerous spurting of the concentrated acid. The approximate proportions of acid and water are indicated in the following table:

	To obtain specific gravity (corrected to 16° C. [60° F.])	*Add 1 vol. of acid of 1·840 S.G. (corrected to 16° C. [60° F.])*
For climates	*of*	*to*
Below 27° C. (80° F.)	1·260	3·2 volumes of water
Above 27° C. (80° F.)	1·210	4·3 volumes of water

Heat is produced by mixing acid and water, and the electrolyte should be allowed to cool before taking hydrometer readings—unless a thermometer is used to measure the actual temperature and a correction applied to the readings before pouring the electrolyte into the battery.

Filling the battery

The temperature of the filling room, battery, and electrolyte should be maintained between 16 and 38° C. (60 and 100° F.).

Carefully break the seals in the filling holes and **half-fill** each cell with electrolyte of the appropriate specific gravity. Allow the battery to stand for at least six hours in order to dissipate the heat generated by the chemical action of the acid on the plates and separators, and then add sufficient electrolyte to fill each cell to the top of the separators. Allow to stand for a further two hours and then proceed with the initial charge.

Initial charge

The initial charging rate is 2·5 amperes. Charge at this rate until the voltage and specific gravity readings show no increase over five successive hourly readings. This will take from 48 to 80 hours, depending on the length of time the battery has been stored before charging.

Keep the current constant by varying the series resistance of the circuit or the generator output. **This charge should not be broken by long rest periods.** If, however, the temperature of any cell rises above the permissible maximum, i.e.

For climates below 27° C. (80° F.) .. 38° C. (100° F.),
For climates above 27° C. (80° F.) .. 49° C. (120° F.),

the charge must be interrupted until the temperature has fallen at least 5·5° C. (10° F.) below that figure. Throughout the charge the electrolyte must be kept level with the top of the separators by addition of acid solution of the same specific gravity as the original filling-in acid until specific gravity and charge readings have remained constant for five successive hourly readings. If the charge is continued beyond that point, top up with distilled water.

At the end of the charge carefully check the specific gravity in each cell to ensure that, when corrected to 16° C. (60° F.) it lies between the specified limits. If any cell requires adjustment some of the electrolyte must be siphoned off and replaced either by distilled water or by acid of strength originally used for filling in, depending on whether the specific gravity is too high or too low. Continue the charge for an hour or so to ensure adequate mixing of the electrolyte and again check the specific gravity readings. If necessary, repeat the adjustment process until the desired reading is obtained in each cell. Finally, allow the battery to cool, and siphon off any electrolyte over the tops of the separators.

Section N.5

DYNAMO

Testing on vehicle when dynamo is not charging

Make sure that belt slip is not the cause of the trouble. It should be possible to deflect the belt approximately ½ in. (13 mm.) with moderate hand pressure at the centre of its longest run between two pulleys. If the belt is too slack tightening is effected by slackening the two dynamo suspension bolts and then the bolt of the slotted adjustment link. A gentle pull on the dynamo outwards will enable the correct tension to be applied to the belt and all three bolts should then be tightened firmly.

Check that the dynamo and control box are connected correctly. The dynamo terminal 'D' should be connected to the control box terminal 'D' and the dynamo terminal 'F' connected to the control box terminal 'F'.

After switching off all lights and accessories disconnect the cables from the dynamo terminals marked 'D' and 'F' respectively.

Connect the two terminals with a short length of wire.

Start the engine and set to run at normal idling speed.

Clip the negative lead of a moving coil-type voltmeter calibrated 0–20 volts to one dynamo terminal and the other lead to a good earthing point on the dynamo yoke.

Gradually increase the engine speed: the voltmeter reading should rise rapidly and without fluctuation. Do not allow the voltmeter reading to reach 20 volts. Do not race the engine in an attempt to increase the voltage. It is sufficient to run the dynamo up to a speed of 1,000 r.p.m.

If there is no reading check the brush gear.

If the reading is low (approximately ½ to 1 volt) the field winding may be faulty.

If the reading is approximately 4 to 5 volts the armature winding may be faulty.

If the dynamo is in good order leave the temporary link in position between the terminals and restore the original connections, taking care to connect the dynamo terminal 'D' to the control box terminal 'D' and the dynamo terminal 'F' to the control box terminal 'F'. Remove the lead from the 'D' terminal on the control box and connect the voltmeter between this cable and a good earthing point on the vehicle. Run the engine as before. The reading should be the same as that measured directly on the dynamo. No reading on the voltmeter indicates a break in the cable to the dynamo. Carry out the same procedure for the 'F' terminal, connecting the voltmeter between cable and earth. Finally, remove the link from the dynamo. If the reading is correct test the control box (Section N.6).

Removing

To remove the dynamo disconnect the dynamo leads from the dynamo terminals.

Slacken all four attachment bolts and pivot the dynamo towards the cylinder block to enable the fan belt to be removed from the dynamo pulley. The dynamo can then be removed by withdrawing the two upper and one lower attachment bolts.

Dismantling

Remove the securing nut and take off the drive pulley.

Remove the Woodruff key from the commutator shaft.

Unscrew and remove the two through-bolts and take off the commutator end bracket. The driving end bracket, together with the armature and its ball bearing, can now be lifted out of the yoke. Unless the ball bearing is damaged or requires attention it need not be removed from the armature. Should it be necessary to remove the bearing, the armature must be separated from the end bracket by means of a hand press.

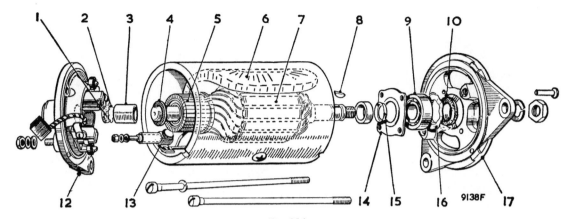

Fig. N.1

The windowless yoke dynamo (C39 type)

1. Felt pad.
2. Aluminium disc.
3. Bronze bush.
4. Fibre washer.
5. Commutator.
6. Field coils.
7. Armature.
8. Shaft key.
9. Bearing.
10. Felt washer.
12. Commutator end bracket.
13. Field terminal post.
14. Bearing retaining plate.
15. Cup washer.
16. Corrugated washer.
17. Driving end bracket.

Servicing

Brushes

Lift the brushes up in the brush boxes and secure them in that position by positioning each brush spring at the side of the brush. Fit the commutator end bracket over the commutator and release the brushes. Hold back each of the brush springs and move the brush by pulling gently on its flexible connector. If the movement is sluggish, remove the brush from its holder and ease the sides by lightly polishing it on a smooth file. Always refit the brushes in their original positions. If the brushes are badly worn, new brushes must be fitted and bedded to the commutator. The minimum permissible length of brush is $\frac{11}{32}$ in. (8·8 mm.) (C39 type), $\frac{1}{4}$ in. (6 mm.) (C40/1 type).

Test the brush spring tension, using a spring scale. The tension of the springs when new is 18 to 26 oz. (510 to 737 grs.) (C39 type), 22 to 25 oz. (624 to 709 grs.) (C40/1 type). In service it is permissible for this value to fall to 15 oz. (425 grs.) before performance may be affected. Fit new springs if the tension is low.

Commutator (See Editor's note at end of Section N.)

A commutator in good condition will be smooth and free from pits or burned spots. Clean the commutator with a cloth moistened with fuel. If this is ineffective carefully polish with a strip of fine glass-paper while rotating the armature. To remedy a badly worn commutator mount the armature (with or without the drive end bracket) in a lathe, rotate at high speed, and take a light cut with a very sharp tool. Do not remove more metal than is necessary. Polish the commutator with very fine glass-paper. Undercut the mica insulation between the segments to a depth of $\frac{1}{32}$ in. (·8 mm.) with a hacksaw blade ground down to the thickness of the mica.

Some commutators fitted to the C40/1 dynamos are of the moulded type and may be re-skimmed to a minimum diameter of 1·45 in. (36·8 mm.).

The undercut must conform to the following dimensions:

Width	·040 in. (1·016 mm.).
Depth	·020 in. (·508 mm.).

It is important that the sides of the undercut clear the moulding material by a minimum of ·015 in. (·381 mm.).

The most common armature faults are usually confined to open- or short-circuited windings. Indications of an open-circuited armature winding is given by burnt commutator segments. A short-circuited armature winding is easily identified by discoloration of the overheated windings and badly burnt commutator segments.

Field coils

Test the field coils with an ohmmeter without removing them from the dynamo yoke. The reading on the ohmmeter should be between 6·0 and 6·3 ohms. If this is not available connect a 12-volt D.C. supply with an ammeter in series between the field terminal and the dynamo yoke. The ammeter reading should be approximately 2 amps. If no reading is indicated the field coils are open-circuited and must be renewed.

If the current reading is much more than 2 amps. or the ohmmeter reading much below 6 ohms it is an indication that the insulation of one of the fields coil has broken down.

In either case, unless a substitute dynamo is available, the field coils must be renewed. To do this carry out the procedure outlined below.

Drill out the rivet securing the field coil terminal assembly to the yoke and unsolder the field coil connections.

Remove the insulation piece which is provided to prevent the junction of the field coils from contacting the yoke.

Mark the yoke and pole-shoes in order that they can be refitted in their original positions.

Unscrew the two pole-shoe retaining screws by means of a wheel-operated screwdriver.

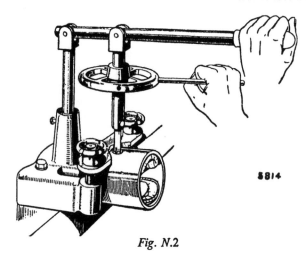

Fig. N.2

Using a wheel-operated screwdriver to remove the pole-shoe screws

Draw the pole-shoes and coils out of the yoke and lift off the coils.

Fit the new field coils over the pole-shoes and place them in position inside the yoke. Take care that the taping of the field coils is not trapped between the pole-shoes and the yoke.

Locate the pole-shoes and field coils by lightly tightening the fixing screw.

Fully tighten the screws by means of a wheel-operated screwdriver and lock them by caulking.

Replace the insulation piece between the field coil connections and the yoke.

Resolder the field coil connections to the field coil terminal tags and rerivet the terminal assembly to the yoke.

Armature

The testing of the armature winding requires the use of a voltage drop-test and growler. If these are not available the armature should be checked by substitution. No attempt should be made to machine the armature core or to true a distorted armature shaft.

Bearings

Bearings which are worn to such an extent that they will allow side-movement of the armature shaft must be renewed.

To renew the bearing bush in a commutator end bracket proceed as follows.

Remove the old bearing bush from the end bracket. The bearing can be withdrawn with a suitable extractor or by screwing a $\frac{5}{8}$ in. (15·87 mm.) tap into the bush for a few turns and pulling out the bush with the tap. Screw the tap squarely into the bush to avoid damaging the bracket.

Press the new bearing bush into the end bracket, using a shouldered, highly polished mandrel of the same diameter as the shaft which is to be fitted in the bearing, until the visible end of the bearing is flush with the inner face of the bracket. Porous bronze bushes should not be opened out after fitting or the porosity of the bush may be impaired.

N.6

NOTE.—Before fitting the new bearing bush it should be allowed to stand for 24 hours completely immersed in thin (S.A.E. 20) engine oil; this will allow the pores of the bush to be filled with lubricant. In cases of extreme urgency this period may be shortened by heating the oil to 100° C. (212° F.) for two hours, then allowing it to cool before removing the bearing bush.

The ball bearing is renewed as follows.

Drill out the rivets which secure the bearing retaining plate to the end bracket and remove the plate. Press the bearing out of the end bracket and remove the corrugated washer, felt washer, and oil-retaining washer.

Before fitting the replacement bearing see that it is clean and pack it with high-melting-point grease.

Place the oil-retaining washer (C39 type only), felt washer, and corrugated washer in the bearing housing in the end bracket.

Press the bearing into the housing. The outer bearing journal is a light push-fit in the bearing housing.

Refit the bearing retaining plate, using rivets having the same dimensions as those originally fitted.

NOTE.—When fitting a drive end bracket to the armature shaft the inner journal of the bearing MUST be supported by a mild-steel tube—do not use the drive end bracket.

Reassembling

The reassembly of the dynamo is a reversal of the dismantling sequence.

If the end bracket has been removed from the armature in dismantling, press the bearing end bracket onto the armature shaft, taking care to avoid damaging the end plate and armature winding. When assembling the commutator end bracket the brushes must first be held clear of the commutator by partially withdrawing them from their boxes until each brush is trapped in position by the side pressure of its spring. The brushes can be released onto the commutator by a small screwdriver or

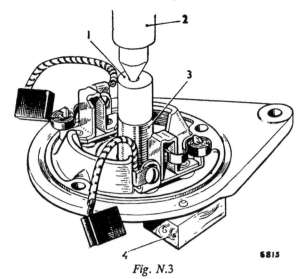

Fig. N.3

The method of pressing in the commutator end bracket bush

1. Shouldered mandrel.	3. Bearing bush.
2. Hand press.	4. Support block.

Sprite and Midget. Issue 3. 65317

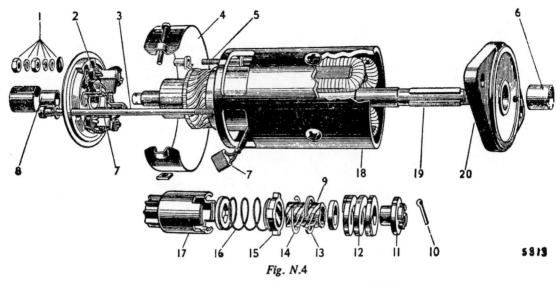

Fig. N.4

An exploded view of the starter motor and drive

1. Terminal nuts and washers.	8. Bearing bush.	15. Control nut.
2. Brush spring.	9. Sleeve.	16. Restraining spring.
3. Through-bolt.	10. Split pin.	17. Pinion and barrel.
4. Band cover.	11. Shaft nut.	18. Yoke.
5. Terminal post.	12. Main spring.	19. Armature shaft.
6. Bearing bush.	13. Retaining ring.	20. Driving end bracket.
7. Brushes.	14. Washer.	

similar tool when the end bracket is assembled to within about $\frac{1}{2}$ in. (12·7 mm.) of the yoke. Before closing the gap between the end bracket and the yoke see that the springs are in correct contact with the brushes.

Refitting

Reverse the removal procedure, noting that on later models plain washers are fitted under the heads of the two upper fixing bolts.

Section N.6

STARTER

Testing on vehicle when starter is not operating

In the following test it is assumed that the battery is in a charged condition.

Switch on the lamps and operate the starter control. If the lights go dim, but the starter is not heard to operate, an indication is given that the current is flowing through the starter motor windings but that for some reason the armature is not rotating; possibly the starter pinion is meshed permanently with the geared ring on the flywheel. This could be caused by the starter being operated while the engine is still moving. In this case the starter motor must be removed from the engine for examination.

Should the lamps retain their full brilliance when the starter switch is operated, check that the switch is functioning. Next, if the switch is in order, examine the connections at the battery and starter switch, and also examine the wiring joining these units. Continued failure of the starter to operate indicates an internal fault in the starter, which must be removed for examination.

Sluggish action of the starter is usually caused by a poor connection in the wiring which causes a high resistance in the starter circuit. Check the wiring as described above.

Removing

Remove the distributor as described in Section B.

Release the starter cable from the terminal and unscrew the top starter securing bolt.

Working beneath the vehicle, release and withdraw the dirt deflector situated under the starter motor and unscrew the bottom starter securing bolt.

Manœuvre the starter forward and lift clear of the engine.

Examination of commutator and brush gear

Remove the starter cover band and examine the brushes and commutator.

Hold back each of the brush springs and move the brush by pulling gently on its flexible connector. If the movement is sluggish remove the brush from its holder and ease the sides by lightly polishing with a smooth file. Always replace brushes in their original positions. If the brushes are worn so that they no longer bear on the commutator, or if the brush flexible lead has become exposed on the running face, they must be renewed.

If the commutator is blackened or dirty, clean it by holding a fuel-moistened cloth against it while the armature is rotated.

Secure the body of the starter in a vice and test by connecting it with heavy-gauge cables to a 12-volt battery. One cable must be connected to the starter terminal, the other held against the starter body or end bracket. Under these light load conditions the starter should run at a very high speed.

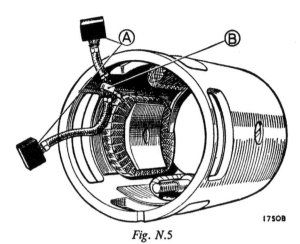

Fig. N.5

The starter brush connections

A. Brushes.　　　　B. Tapping on field coils.

If the operation of the starter is still unsatisfactory, it should be dismantled for detailed inspection and testing.

Dismantling

Hold back the brush springs and take out the brushes.

Remove the terminal nuts and washers from the terminal post on the commutator end bracket.

Unscrew and withdraw the two through-bolts and take off the commutator end bracket.

Remove the driving end bracket complete with armature and drive assembly.

Servicing

Brushes

Test the brush springs with a spring balance. The correct tension is 25 to 15 oz. (709 to 425 gm.). Fit a new spring if the tension is low.

If the brushes are worn so that they no longer bear on the commutator, or if the flexible connector has become exposed on the running face, they must be renewed. Two of the brushes are connected to terminal eyelets attached to the brush boxes on the commutator end bracket. The other two brushes are connected to tappings on the field coils.

The flexible connectors must be removed by unsoldering and the connectors of the new brushes secured in their place by soldering. The brushes are preformed so that bedding of the working face to the commutator is unnecessary.

Drive

If the pinion is tight on the screwed sleeve, wash away any dirt with paraffin (kerosene).

If any parts are worn or damaged they must be renewed.

On earlier cars remove the split pin, unscrew the nut (R.H. thread), and take off the main springs.

On later cars compress the spring and extract the circlip.

The complete drive can now be removed from the splined shaft by pulling it off with a rotary movement. Unscrew the screwed sleeve from the barrel assembly.

N.8

Further dismantling of the barrel assembly is carried out by removing the large retaining ring.

NOTE.—If the screwed sleeve is worn or damaged it is essential that it is renewed together with the control nut.

Reassemble by reversing the above procedure.

Commutator

A commutator in good condition will be smooth and free from pits and burnt spots. Clean the commutator with a cloth moistened with fuel. If this is ineffective, carefully polish with a strip of fine glass-paper while rotating the armature. To remedy a badly worn commutator, dismantle the starter drive as described above and remove the armature from the end bracket. Now mount the armature on a lathe, rotate it at high speed, and take a light cut with a very sharp tool. Do not remove any more metal than is absolutely necessary, and finally polish with very fine glass-paper.

The mica on the starter commutator **must not be undercut.**

Field coils

The field coils can be tested for an open circuit by connecting a 12-volt battery having a 12-volt bulb in one of the leads to the tapping-point of the field coils to which the brushes are connected and the field terminal post. If the bulb does not light there is an open circuit in the wiring of the field coils.

Lighting of the bulb does not necessarily mean that the field coils are in order, as it is possible that one of them may be earthed to a pole-shoe or to the yoke. This may be checked by removing the lead from the brush connector and holding it on a clean part of the starter yoke. Should the bulb now light, it indicates that the field coils are earthed.

Should the above tests indicate that the fault lies in the field coils, they must be renewed. When renewing the field coils carry out the procedure detailed in the dynamo section.

Armature

Examination of the armature will in many cases reveal the cause of failure, e.g. conductors lifted from the

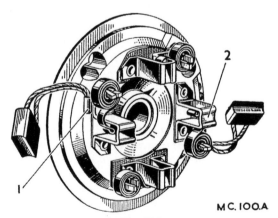

Fig. N.6

Commutator end bracket

1. Terminal eyelet.　　　　2. Brush holder.

Sprite and Midget. Issue 4. 29459

commutator due to the starter being engaged while the engine is running and causing the armature to be rotated at an excessive speed. A damaged armature must in all cases be renewed—no attempt should be made to machine the armature core or to true a distorted armature shaft.

Bearings

Bearings which are worn to such an extent that they will allow excessive side-play of the armature shaft must be renewed. To renew the bearing bush proceed as follows.

Press the new bearing bush into the end bracket, using a shouldered mandrel of the same diameter as the shaft which is to fit into the bearing.

NOTE.—The bearing bush is of the porous phosphor-bronze type, and before fitting, new bushes should be allowed to stand completely immersed for 24 hours in thin engine oil in order to fill the pores of the bush with lubricant.

Reassembling

The reassembly of the starter is a reversal of the operations described in this section.

Refitting

Refitting is a reversal of the removal procedure.

Section N.7

CONTROL BOX

This unit contains the cut-out and voltage regulator. The regulator controls the dynamo output in accordance with the load on the battery and its state of charge. When the battery is discharged the dynamo gives a high

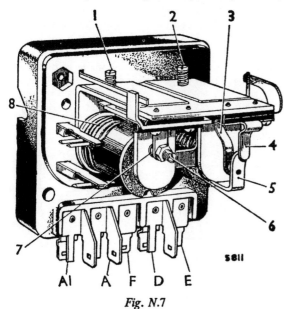

Fig. N.7

The control box

1. Regulator adjusting screw.
2. Cut-out adjusting screw.
3. Fixed contact blade.
4. Stop arm.
5. Armature tongue and moving contact.
6. Regulator fixed contact screw.
7. Regulator moving contact.
8. Regulator series windings.

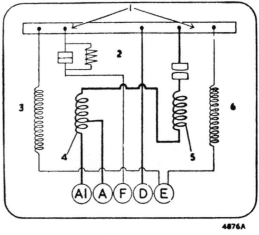

Fig. N.8

The control box (regulator and cut-out) internal connections

1. Regulator and cut-out frame.
2. Field resistance.
3. Shunt coil.
4. Tapped series coil.
5. Series coil.
6. Shunt coil.

output, so that the battery receives a quick recharge which brings it back to its normal state in the minimum time.

On the other hand, if the battery is fully charged the dynamo is controlled to give only a trickle charge, which is sufficient to keep it in good condition without any possibility of causing damage to the battery by over-charging.

The regulator also causes the dynamo to give a controlled boosting charge immediately after starting up, which quickly restores to the battery the energy taken from it when starting. After about 30 minutes' running, the output of the dynamo has fallen to a steady rate best suited to the particular state of charge of the battery.

The cut-out is an automatic switch for connecting and disconnecting the battery with the dynamo. This is necessary because the battery would otherwise discharge through the dynamo when the engine is stopped or running at a low speed.

Regulator adjustment

The regulator is carefully set to suit the normal requirements of the standard equipment before leaving the Works, and in general it should not be necessary to alter it. If, however, the battery does not keep in a charged condition, or if the dynamo output does not fall when the battery is fully charged, it may be advisable to check the setting and, if necessary, to readjust.

It is important, before altering the regulator setting when the battery is in a low state of charge, to check that its condition is not due to a battery defect or to the dynamo belt slipping.

Checking and adjusting the electrical setting

The regulator setting can be checked without removing the cover of the control box.

Withdraw the cables from the terminals marked 'A' and 'A1' at the control box and join them together.

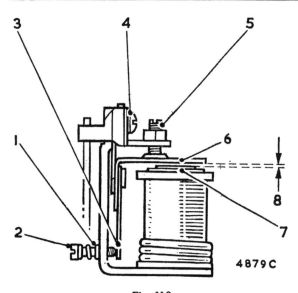

Fig. N.9

Mechanical setting of the regulator

1. Spring.
2. Voltage adjusting screw.
3. Armature tension spring.
4. Armature securing screws.
5. Fixed contact adjustment screw.
6. Armature.
7. Core face and shim.
8. ·015 in. (·38 mm.).

Connect the negative lead of a moving-coil voltmeter (0 to 20 volts full scale reading) to the 'D' terminal on the dynamo and connect the other lead from the meter to a convenient chassis earth.

Slowly increase the speed of the engine until the voltmeter needle 'flicks' and then steadies; this should occur at a voltmeter reading between the limits given for the appropriate temperature of the regulator.

If the voltage at which the reading becomes steady occurs outside these limits, the regulator must be adjusted.

Shut off the engine, remove the control box cover, and turn the adjusting screw (2) (Fig. N.9) in a clockwise direction to raise the setting or in an anti-clockwise direction to lower the setting. Turn the adjustment screw a fraction of a turn at a time until the setting is correct.

When adjusting, do not run the engine up to more than half-throttle because, while the dynamo is in open circuit, it will build up to a high voltage if run at a high speed and in consequence a false voltmeter reading will be obtained.

Electrical settings of the regulator must be made as quickly as possible because of the temperature rise effects.

Mechanical setting

The mechanical settings of the regulator are accurately adjusted before leaving the Factory, and provided that the armature carrying the moving contact is not removed, these settings should not be tampered with. If, however, the armature has been removed, the regulator will have to be reset. To do this proceed as follows.

Slacken the fixed contact locknut and unscrew the contact until it is well clear of the armature moving contact. Slacken the two armature assembly securing **screws.**

N.10

Slacken the voltage adjusting screw until it is well clear of the armature tension spring.

Insert a ·015 in. (·4 mm.) feeler gauge between the armature and core shim. Take care not to turn up or damage the end of the shim. Press the armature squarely down against the gauge and retighten the two armature assembly securing screws.

With the gauge still in position, screw the adjustable contact down until it just touches the armature contact. Tighten the locknut and remove the feeler gauge. Reset the voltage adjusting screw as described under '**Electrical setting**'.

Cleaning regulator contacts

After periods of long service it may be found necessary to clean the regulator contacts. Fine carborundum stone or fine emery-cloth may be used. Carefully wipe away all traces of dust or other foreign matter, using a clean, fluffless cloth moistened with methylated spirits.

Cut-out electrical setting

If the regulator is correctly set but the battery is still not being charged, the cut-out may be out of adjustment. To check the voltage at which the cut-out operates remove the control box cover and connect the voltmeter between the terminals 'D' and 'E'. Start the engine and slowly increase its speed until the cut-out contacts are seen to close, noting the voltage at which this occurs. This should be 12·7 to 13·3 volts.

If operation of the cut-out takes place outside these limits it will be necessary to adjust. To do this, turn the cut-out adjusting screw (2) (Fig. N.7) in a clockwise direction to raise the voltage setting or in an anti-clockwise direction to reduce the setting. Turn the screw a fraction at a time. Test after each adjustment by increasing the engine speed and noting the voltmeter readings at the instant of contact closure. Electrical settings of the cut-out, like the regulator, must be made as quickly as possible because of temperature rise effects.

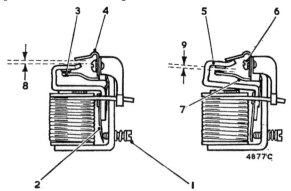

Fig. N.10

Mechanical setting of the cut-out

1. Cut-out adjusting screw.
2. Armature tension spring.
3. Follow through'—·010 to ·020 in. (·254 to ·508 mm.).
4. Stop arm.
5. Armature tongue and moving contact.
6. Armature securing screws.
7. Fixed contact blade.
8. ·025 to ·040 in. (·63 to 1·01 mm.).
9. ·010 in. to ·020 in. (·254 to ·508 mm.).

Sprite (Mks. II and III) and Midget (Mks. I and II). **Issue 3.** 51576

Adjustment of the drop-off voltage is effected by carefully bending the fixed contact blade. If the cut-out does not operate there may be an open circuit in the wiring of the cut-out and regulator unit, in which case the unit should be removed for examination or renewal.

Cut-out mechanical setting

If for any reason the cut-out armature has to be removed from the frame, care must be taken to obtain the correct air gap settings on reassembly. These can be obtained as follows.

Turn the adjusting screw until it is well clear of the armature tension spring. Slacken the two armature assembly securing screws (Fig. N.10). Press the armature firmly down against the copper-sprayed core face and retighten the two armature assembly securing screws.

Using a pair of round-nosed pliers, adjust the gap between the armature stop-arm and armature tongue by bending the stop-arm. The gap must be ·025 to ·040 in. (·6 to 1·0 mm.) when the armature is pressed squarely down on the core face.

Similarly, the insulated contact blade must be bent so that when the armature is pressed squarely down against the core face there is a 'follow through' or contact deflection of ·010 to ·020 in. (·25 to ·50 mm.). Reset the cut-out adjusting screw as described under 'Cut-out electrical setting'.

Cleaning cut-out contacts

If the contacts appear rough or burnt place a strip of fine glass-paper between them, close them by hand, and draw the paper through. This should be done two or three times with the abrasive side towards each contact. Wipe away all dust or other foreign matter, using a clean, fluffless cloth moistened with methylated spirits.

Do not use emery-cloth or carborundum stone for cleaning the cut-out contacts.

Section N.8

FUSE UNIT

Description

The fuse unit, which is located on the right-hand side of the engine compartment, is an open, insulated moulding carrying two single-pole 35-amp. cartridge-type fuses which are held in spring clips between the Lucar connectors. Two spare fuses are carried in recesses in the fuse unit box and are positioned by retaining springs. The fuse which bridges the terminal blocks 'A1'—'A2' is to protect general auxiliary circuits, e.g. the horn, which is independent of the ignition switch. The other fuse, bridging terminal blocks 'A3'—'A4', is to protect the ignition and auxiliary circuits, e.g. the fuel gauge, windshield wiper motor, and flasher indicators, which only operate when the ignition is switched on.

Section N.9

LOCATION AND REMEDY OF FAULTS

Although every precaution is taken to eliminate possible causes of trouble, failure may occasionally

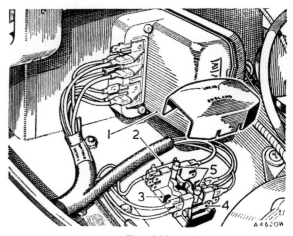

Fig. N.11

Regulator and fuse unit

1. Regulator cover.
2. AUX. IGN. fuse (35-amp.).
3. Fuse block.
4. AUX fuse (35-amp.).
5. Spare fuses.

develop through lack of attention to the equipment or damage to the wiring. The following pages set out the recommended procedure for a systematic examination to locate and remedy the causes of some of the more usual faults encountered.

The sources of trouble are by no means always obvious, and in some cases a considerable amount of deduction from the symptoms is needed before the cause is disclosed.

For instance, the engine might not respond to the starter switch; a hasty inference would be that the starter motor is at fault. However, as the motor is dependent on the battery it may be that the battery is exhausted.

This in turn may be due to the dynamo failing to charge the battery, and the final cause of the trouble may be, perhaps, a loose connection in some part of the charging circuit.

If, after carrying out an examination, the cause of the trouble is not found the equipment should be checked.

CHARGING CIRCUIT

1. Battery in low state of charge

(a) This state will be shown by lack of power when starting, poor light from the lamps, and the hydrometer readings below 1·200. It may be due to the dynamo not charging or giving low or intermittent output. The ignition warning light will not go out if the dynamo fails to charge, or will flicker on and off in the event of intermittent output.

(b) Examine the charging and field circuit wiring, tighten any loose connections, or renew any broken cables. Pay particular attention to the battery connections.

(c) Examine the dynamo driving belt; take up any undue slackness by swinging the dynamo outwards on its mounting after slackening the attachment bolts.

(d) Check the regulator setting, and adjust if necessary.

(e) If, after carrying out the above, the trouble is still not cured, have the equipment examined.

2. Battery overcharged

This will be indicated by burnt-out bulbs, very frequent need for topping up the battery, and high hydrometer readings. Check the charge reading with an ammeter when the car is running. It should be of the order of only 3 to 4 amps.

If the ammeter reading is in excess of this value it is advisable to check the regulator setting, and adjust if necessary.

STARTER MOTOR

1. Starter motor lacks power or fails to turn engine

(a) See if the engine can be turned over by hand. If not, the cause of the stiffness in the engine must be located and remedied.

(b) If the engine can be turned by hand first check that the trouble is not due to a discharged battery.

(c) Examine the connections to the battery, starter, and starter switch, making sure that they are tight and that the cables connecting these units are not damaged.

(d) It is also possible that the starter pinion may have jammed in mesh with the flywheel, although this is by no means a common occurrence. To disengage the pinion rotate the squared end of the starter shaft by means of a spanner.

2. Starter operates but does not crank the engine

This fault will occur if the pinion of the starter drive is not allowed to move along the screwed sleeve into engagement with the flywheel, due to dirt having collected on the screwed sleeve. Remove the starter and clean the sleeve carefully with paraffin (kerosene).

3. Starter pinion will not disengage from flywheel when engine is running

Stop the engine and see if the starter pinion is jammed in mesh with the flywheel, releasing it if necessary by rotation of the squared end of the starter shaft. If the pinion persists in sticking in mesh have the equipment examined. Serious damage may result to the starter if it is driven by the flywheel.

LIGHTING CIRCUITS

1. Lamps give insufficient illumination

(a) Test the state of charge of the battery, recharging it if necessary from an independent electrical supply.

(b) Check the setting of the lamps.

(c) If the bulbs are discoloured as the result of long service they should be renewed.

2. Lamps light when switched on but gradually fade out

As paragraph 1 (a).

3. Brilliance varies with speed of car

(a) As paragraph 1 (a).

(b) Examine the battery connections, making sure that they are tight, and renew any faulty cables.

Section N.10

FLASHER UNIT

Description

The unit is contained in a small cylindrical metal container, one end of which is rolled over onto an insulated plate carrying the mechanism and three terminals. The unit depends for its operation on the linear expansion of a length of wire which becomes heated by an electric current flowing through it. This actuating wire controls the movement of a spring-loaded armature attached to a central steel core and carrying a moving contact—the sequence of operation being as follows.

When the direction indicator switch is turned either to the left or right, current flows through the actuating wire, ballast resistor, and coil wound on the central core and hence to earth via the flasher lamp filaments. This current is limited by the ballast resistor to a value which will ensure that the flasher lamp filaments do not light at this stage. The actuating wire increases in length under the heating influence of the current and allows the armature to move inwards to its alternative position, thereby closing a pair of contacts in the supply circuit to the flasher lamps and at the same time short-circuiting the actuating wire. The increased electro-magnetic attraction of the armature to the core, due to the full lamp current now flowing through the coils, serves to hold the closed contacts firmly together. At the same time a secondary spring-loaded armature is attracted to the core and closes a pilot warning lamp circuit so that now both flasher lamps and warning lamp are illuminated.

Since, however, heating current no longer flows through the short-circuited actuating wire, the latter cools and consequently contracts in length. The main armature is therefore pulled away from the core, the contacts opened, and the light signals extinguished. The consequent reduction of electro-magnetism in the core allows the secondary armature to return to its original position and so extinguish the pilot warning light. The above sequence of operations continues to be repeated until the indicator switch is returned to the 'off' position.

Functions of warning lamp

The warning lamp not only serves to indicate that the flasher unit is functioning correctly but also gives a warning of any bulb failure occurring in the external direction indicator lamps—since a reduction in bulb current flowing through the coil reduces the electro-magnetic effect acting on the secondary armature and so prevents closure of the pilot light contacts.

N.12

Sprite and Midget. Issue 4. 4780

Checking faulty operation

In the event of trouble occurring with a flashing light direction indicator system, the following procedure should be followed.

Check the bulbs for broken filaments.

Refer to the vehicle wiring diagram and check all flasher circuit connections.

Check the appropriate fuse.

Switch on the ignition.

Check with a voltmeter between the flasher unit terminal 'B' (or '+') and earth that battery voltage is present.

Connect together flasher unit terminals 'B' (or '+') and 'L' and operate the direction indicator switch. If the flasher lamps now light, the flasher unit is defective and must be renewed.

Maintenance

Flasher units cannot be dismantled for subsequent reassembly. A defective unit must therefore be renewed, care being taken to connect as the original.

Renewing flasher unit

When renewing a flasher unit or installing a flashing light system it is advisable to test the circuits before connections to flasher terminals are made. When testing join the cables normally connected to those terminals (green, green with brown, and light green) together and operate the direction indicator switch. In the event of a wrong connection having been made, the ignition auxiliaries fuse will blow but no damage will be done to the flasher unit.

Section N.11

WINDSHIELD WIPERS

Maintenance

Inspect the rubber wiping elements, which after long service become worn and should be renewed.

Lubricate the rubber grommet or washer around the wheelbox spindle with a few drops of glycerine.

Methylated spirits (denatured alcohol) should be used to remove oil, tar spots, and other stains from the windshield. It has been found that the use of some silicone- and wax-based polishes for this purpose can be detrimental to the rubber wiper blades.

The gearbox and cable rack are packed with grease during manufacture and need no further lubrication.

Checking switching mechanism

If the wiper fails to park or parks unsatisfactorily, the limit switch in the gearbox cover should be checked. Unless the limit switch is correctly set, it is possible for the wiper motor to overrun the open-circuit position and continue to draw current.

Resetting the limit switch

Slacken the four screws securing the gearbox cover and observe the projection near the rim of the limit switch. Position the projection in line with the groove in the gearbox cover. Turn the limit switch 25° in an anti-clockwise direction and tighten the four securing screws. If the wiping blades are required to park on the opposite side of the windshield, the limit switch should be turned back 180° in a clockwise direction.

Checking current consumption

If the wiper fails to operate, or operates unsatisfactorily, switch on the wiper and note the current being supplied to the motor. The normal running current should be 2·3 to 3·1 amps. Use a 0 to 15 amps. moving-coil ammeter connected in the wiper circuit, then proceed as follows.

Wiper takes no current

Examine the fuse protecting the wiper circuit. If the fuse has blown, examine the wiring of the motor circuit and of all other circuits protected by that fuse. Renew, if necessary, any cables which are badly worn or chafed, fitting protective sleeving over the cables to prevent a recurrence of the fault.

If the external wiring is found to be in order, replace the fuse with one of the recommended rating. Then proceed as for the wiper taking an abnormally high current.

If the fuse is intact, examine the wiring of the motor circuit for breaks, and ensure that the wiper control switch is operating correctly.

When a current-operated thermostat is fitted test it by connecting an ohmmeter across its terminals in place of the two cables. If a closed circuit is indicated the thermostat is in order and the cables must be refitted. An open circuit means that the thermostat has operated but not reset. Check the thermostat by substitution. Adjustment of the thermostat must not be attempted.

If the thermostat is in order, proceed as for the wiper taking an abnormally high current.

Wiper takes abnormally low current

Check that the battery is fully charged. The performance of the motor is dependent on the condition of the battery.

Remove the commutator end bracket and examine the brush gear, ensuring that it bears firmly on the commutator. The tension spring must be renewed if the brushes do not bear firmly on the commutator. Brush levers must move freely on the pivots. If these levers are stiff they should be freed by working them backwards and forwards by hand.

Examine the commutator and, if necessary, clean with a fuel-moistened cloth. A suspected armature should be checked by substitution.

Wiper takes abnormally high current

If an abnormally high current is shown on the ammeter, this may be due to excessive load on the driving shaft. The stall current of the motor when cold is 14 amps. and when hot is 8 amps.

If there is no obvious reason for this, such as a sticking wiper blade, a check should be made at the gearbox.

Remove the gearbox cover and examine the gear assembly, checking that a blow on the gearbox end bracket has not reduced the armature end-float. The armature end-float adjusting screw must be set to give an armature end-play of ·008 to ·012 in. (·20 to ·30 mm.).

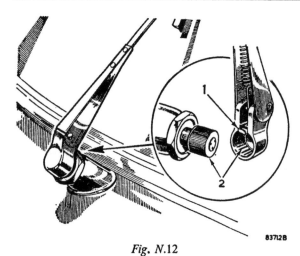

Fig. N.12

Removal and replacement of the windshield wiper arm

1. Retaining clip.	2. Splined drive.

Sluggish operation with excessive current consumption may be caused through frictional losses in badly positioned or defective connecting tubes. The connecting tubes can be checked, using a cable gauge. (Details of this gauge can be obtained from any Lucas Agent.) The gauge cable is similar in appearance to the driving rack but is ·010 in. (·25 mm.) larger in diameter and is less flexible. The gauge will not easily pass through connecting tubes having less than the minimum permissible curvature.

To check the tubing, using the gauge, it is necessary to remove the inner rack. Insert the gauge into the connecting tube as far as the first wheelbox and then withdraw it. Remove the tubing connecting the wheelboxes. Insert and withdraw the gauge. If the gauge moves freely the tubing is correctly installed. If the gauge does not move freely the tubing must be checked for sharp bends and obstructions. Check the wheelboxes for alignment and then reassemble.

Removing the motor, gearbox, and wheelboxes

The motor and gearbox is located beneath the passenger's side of the fascia panel and is mounted on a bracket secured to the bulkhead panel by three set screws and nuts.

The cable rack connected to the cross-head in the gearbox passes through outer casings which connect the gearbox to the first wheelbox and the first wheelbox to the second wheelbox.

Remove the fascia panel, Section R and Ra.

Disconnect the wiper arms, the electrical connections from the motor, and the outer cable from the gearbox housing. Remove the three nuts securing the motor to the bulkhead panel and withdraw the motor, and cable rack.

Slacken the cover screws in each wheelbox and remove the cable rack outer casings.

Remove the nut, front bush, and washer from the front of each wheelbox and remove the wheelbox together with the rear bush and spindle tube from beneath the fascia panel.

Replacement is a reversal of the removal sequence, but ensure that the wheelboxes are correctly lined up and that the cable rack engages the gear and spindle assemblies.

Dismantling the motor

Withdraw the four screws securing the gearbox cover and remove the cover.

Withdraw the connectors and through-bolts at the commutator end bracket.

Remove the commutator end bracket clear of the yoke.

The brush gear can be removed by lifting it clear of the commutator and withdrawing it as a unit. Care should be taken at this point to note the particular side occupied by each brush so that each may be replaced in its original setting on the commutator.

Access to the armature and field coils can be gained by withdrawing the yoke.

If it is necessary to remove the field coil, unscrew the two screws securing the pole-piece to the yoke. These screws should be marked so that they can be returned to their original holes.

Press out the pole-piece complete with field coil, marking the pole-piece so that it can be replaced in its correct position inside the yoke. The pole-piece can now be pressed out of the field coil.

Pieces of carbon short-circuiting adjacent segments of the commutator will also cause excessive current consumption. The resistance between adjacent commutator segments should be ·34 to ·41 ohm. Cleaning the commutator and brush gear removes this fault. When dismantling, check the internal wiring of the motor for evidence of short-circuiting due to chafed or charred insulation. Slip a new piece of sleeving over any charred connections, and arrange them so that they do not rub against sharp edges.

While the motor is dismantled check the value of the field resistance. If it is found to be lower than 12·8 to 14 ohms, a short-circuit in the windings is indicated and a new field coil must be fitted. Other evidence of a short-circuit will be given by charred leads from the field coil.

Dismantling the gearbox unit

Remove the circlip and washer from the cross-head connecting link pin and lift off the cross-head and cable rack assembly. Then remove the circlip and washer from the final gear shaft located underneath the gearbox unit. Remove any burr from the circlip groove before lifting out the final gear. The armature and worm drive can now be withdrawn from the gearbox. All gear teeth should be examined for signs of damage or wear and, if necessary, new gears fitted.

Reassembling

Reassembly is a reversal of the above procedures. When reassembling, the following components should be lubricated.

Armature bearings

These should be lubricated with S.A.E. 20 engine oil—the self-aligning bearing being immersed in this for 24 hours before assembly.

Armature shaft (commutator end)

Apply S.A.E. 20 engine oil.

Felt lubricator in gearbox

Apply S.A.E. 20 engine oil.

N.14

Worm wheel bearings, cross-head, guide channel, connecting rod, crankpin, worm, and final gear shaft
Grease liberally.

Cable rack and wheelboxes
Grease liberally.

Testing

Switch on the ignition and the wiper control. The two wiper areas should be approximately symmetrical on the windshield.

Fitting a blade to a wiper arm

Pull the wiper arm away from the windshield and insert the curved 'wrist' of the arm into the slotted spring fastening of the blade. Swivel the two components into engagement.

Fitting a wiper arm to the driving spindle

First ensure that the wiper spindles are in the correct parking position by switching on the ignition and turning the wiper control on and then off.

To fit the arms, press the headpieces onto the spindles at the correct parking angle until the retaining clip is heard to snap over the end of the spindle drum.

Operate the wiper control to ensure that the arms come to rest in the correct parking position.

Adjusting

Correct operation can be obtained by adjusting the position of the arms relative to the spindles. If necessary, the position of the arms may be adjusted by removing and re-engaging them with the splined driving spindles, the angular pitch of the splines being 5°.

Do not attempt to turn the arms whilst in position, but press back the retaining clip (Fig. N.12) in the headpieces and withdraw the arms from the driving spindles. Refit in the desired position. The above adjustment may affect the self-parking position. If so, it may be corrected by adjustment of the limit switch position as described previously.

Fig. N.13

The side and direction indicator lamp

1. Sidelamp bulb.
2. Direction indicator bulb.
3. Amber direction indicator bulb cover.

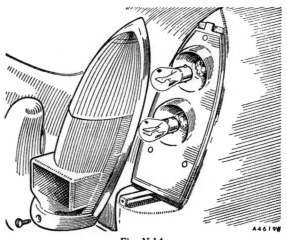

Fig. N.14

The tail, stop, and direction indicator lamps

If the arms and blades are required to come to rest on the opposite side, the limit switch should be turned through 180°. It should be noted that the switch cover is designed for turning through a sector only and not through 360°. This feature prevents unnecessary twisting of the external flexible connections.

Section N.12

PILOT AND FLASHING DIRECTION INDICATOR LAMPS

Remove the two securing screws and lift away the plated rim and glass. An amber cover is fitted over the direction indicator bulb when the vehicle is operating in countries where the lighting regulations require amber flashing indicators.

Refitting is a direct reversal of the removal procedure.

Section N.13

TAIL AND STOP AND DIRECTION INDICATOR LAMPS

The tail lamp bulbs are of the double-filament type, the second filament giving a marked increase in brilliance when the brakes are applied.

Access to the bulbs is gained by extracting the securing screws from the outer face of the lamp lens to release the lens.

The tail and stop lamp bulbs must be fitted one way only; offset retaining pegs ensure that they are replaced correctly.

The lamp body can be removed when the lens is taken off as indicated in Fig. N.14 and the three screws located in the lamp body withdrawn. When refitting the glass to the body make certain that it is seating correctly over the sealing rubber.

Section N.14

PANEL AND WARNING LAMPS

Access to the warning lamps for the ignition and headlamp beam is effected from under the fascia by withdrawing the push-in-type holders from the rear of the fascia panel.

A list of the correct types of bulbs for replacement purposes and their part numbers appears in Section N.19.

Section N.15

NUMBER-PLATE ILLUMINATION LAMP

The number-plate is illuminated by a separate lamp with twin bulbs.

The cover is removed by unscrewing the single attachment screw, which enables it to be withdrawn, giving easy access to the bulbs.

Section N.16

HEADLAMPS

The two types of headlamp fitted have sealed-beam units or, alternatively, replaceable bulb light units.

Variations within the two basic types cater for the local lighting regulations existing in the country for which the car was produced. The method of retaining and adjusting the light unit together with the type of lens and bulb used are subject to territorial variation. Fig. N.15 shows the alternative methods of retaining and adjusting the light unit and Fig. N.16 the different types of bulb fittings used.

Removing a light unit

Removable-type retaining screw (1) *Fig. N.15*
(1) Unscrew the outer rim retaining screw from the bottom of the rim, and withdraw the rim.
(2) Remove the rubber dust excluder (if fitted).
(3) Remove the three screws securing the light unit retaining plate and withdraw the light unit from the lamp body.

Combined adjusting/retaining screw (2) *Fig. N.15*
(4) Carry out the operations detailed in (1) and (2).
(5) Press the light unit inwards against the tension of the springs and turn it in an anti-clockwise direction until the heads of the screws can pass through the enlarged ends of the slots in the retaining plate, then withdraw the light unit.

Captive-type retaining screw (3) *Fig. N.15*
(6) Carry out the operations detailed in (1) and (2).
(7) Slacken the three retaining screws and turn the light unit retaining plate in an anti-clockwise direction until the heads of the screws can pass through the enlarged ends of the slots in the retaining plate, then withdraw the retaining plate and light unit.

Bulb replacement
Cap-type holder (1) *Fig. N.16*
(8) Press and turn the cap anti-clockwise, lift off the cap and withdraw the bulb.
(9) Fit the bulb into the reflector ensuring that the notch in the bulb flange locates on the ridge in the reflector.
(10) Engage the cap lugs in the reflector slots, press and turn the cap clockwise.

Spring clip type (2) *Fig. N.16*
(11) Withdraw the three-pin socket.
(12) Disengage the spring clip from the reflector lugs, swing the clip up and withdraw the bulb.
(13) Fit the bulb into the reflector ensuring that the pip on the bulb flange engages the slot in the reflector.

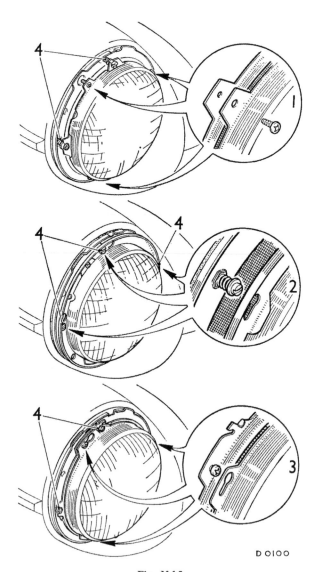

D 0100

Fig. N.15

Light unit retaining screws

1. Removable screw.	3. Captive retaining screw.
2. Combined adjusting/ retaining screw.	4. Beam-setting adjusting screws.

(14) Swing the spring clip back, ensure that the coils in the clip are resting on the base of the bulb, and engage the legs of the spring clip under the reflector lugs.

Headlamp pilot lamp (3) Fig. N.16

(15) Withdraw the holder from the reflector.

(16) Press and turn the bulb anti-clockwise and withdraw the bulb.

(17) Locate the pins of the bulb in the grooves in the holder, press and turn the bulb clockwise.

(18) Press the holder into its hole in the reflector.

Refitting a light unit

(19) Reverse the removing procedure.

Beam setting

The headlamps must be set so that the main driving beams are parallel with the road surface or in accordance with local regulations.

Section N.17

HORN AND HORN-PUSH

Removing the horn

Remove the horn bracket to body securing nuts, spring washers, and set screws. Disconnect the horn leads and remove the horn assembly.

Maintenance

If the horn fails to operate, or operates unsatisfactorily, first carry out the following external checks.

Examine the cables of the horn circuit, renewing any that are badly worn or chafed. Ensure that all connections are clean and tight and that the connecting nipples are firmly soldered to the cables.

Check that the bolts securing the horn brackets are tight and that the horn body does not foul any other fixtures.

Check the current consumption which should be 3 to 3½ amps. when the horn is operating correctly.

After making a thorough external check remove the horn cover and examine the cable connections inside the horn. Examine the contact breaker contacts. If they are burnt or blackened clean them with a fine file, then wipe with a petrol-moistened cloth.

Refitting

Refitting is a reversal of the removal procedure.

Removing the horn-push

When removing the horn-push it is a simple operation of levering the complete assembly out of the steering-wheel with a screwdriver. Take care not to damage the bakelite surround.

Refitting

When refitting ensure that the brass contact strip is in line with the live contact in the steering-wheel assembly.

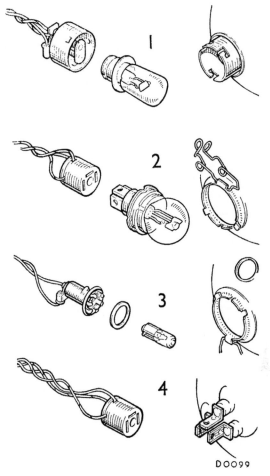

D0099

Fig. N.16

Bulb holders and fixings

1.	Cap-type holder.	3. Headlamp pilot lamp.
2.	Spring clip type.	4. Sealed-beam unit.

Section N.18

SWITCHES

NOTE.—In all cases when removing switches the battery terminals should be disconnected.

Lighting, direction indicator, and windshield wiper

Removing

In all of the above cases disconnect the Lucar connectors, unscrew the fixing nut, and remove the switch assembly complete with its 'D'-shaped locking washer.

Refitting

Refitting is a reversal of the removal procedure.

Ignition

Removing

Disconnect the Lucar connectors, unscrew the fixing nut, and remove the switch assembly complete with its 'D'-shaped locking washer.

Dismantling

To remove the locking barrel from the switch body insert the key and turn the switch to the 'ignition on' position to align the barrel-retaining plunger with the small hole in the switch body. Using an awl, depress the plunger and withdraw the barrel complete with key.

Reassembling and refitting

Reverse the dismantling and removing procedure.

Starter

Removing

Disconnect the battery leads from the switch terminals.

Remove the switch-operating cable by slackening the lock screw on the connecting sleeve and pulling the wire out of the sleeve. Remove the locknut from the threaded sleeve of the switch and withdraw the switch assembly from its mounting bracket.

Refitting

Refitting is a reversal of the removal procedure.

Headlight dipper

Removing

Remove the dipping switch to bracket securing screws and withdraw the switch assembly.

Disconnect the cables from the switch connectors and remove the switch assembly. Switches are serviced as complete units only.

Refitting

Reverse the removal procedure.

Panel

Removing

Remove the securing screws and withdraw the switch assembly.

Disconnect the cables from the switch connectors and remove the switch assembly.

Refitting

Reverse the removal procedure.

Section N.19

REPLACEMENT BULBS

	Volts	Watts	BMC Part No.
Headlamps—L.H.D. except North America and Europe .. ·	12	50/40	BFS 415
Headlamps—Europe except France	12	45/40	BFS 410
Headlamps—France only	12	45/40	BFS 411
Sidelamps	12	6	BFS 989
Sidelamps, direction indicator lamps—North America and Italy	12	6/21	BFS 380
Direction indicator lamps (front)	12	21	BFS 382
Direction indicator lamps (rear)	12	21	BFS 382
Tail and stop lamps	12	6/21	BFS 380
Number-plate illumination lamp	12	6	BFS 989
Panel and warning lights	12	2·2	BFS 9874
Reverse lamps	12	21	27H 881

THE WINDSHIELD WIPER COMPONENTS

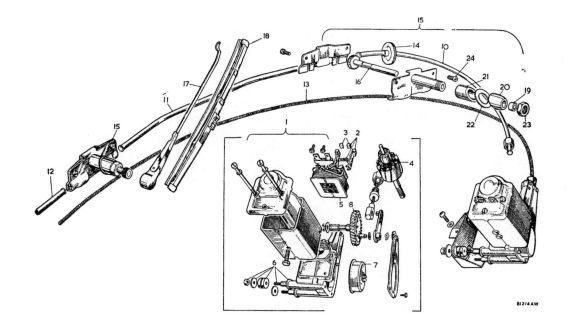

No.	Description	No.	Description
1.	Windshield wiper motor.	13.	Cross-head and rack assembly.
2.	Brush gear.	14.	Grommet.
3.	Brush.	15.	Wheelbox.
4.	Armature.	16.	Spindle and gear.
5.	Field coil.	17.	Wiper arm.
6.	Fixing parts.	18.	Wiper blade.
7.	Parking switch.	19.	Rubber tube spindle.
8.	Gear and shaft.	20.	Front bush.
10.	Motor to wheelbox outer casing.	21.	Rear bush.
11.	Wheelbox to wheelbox outer casing.	22.	Rubber washer.
12.	Wheelbox extension outer casing.	23.	Nut.
		24.	Cover screw.

WIRING DIAGRAM

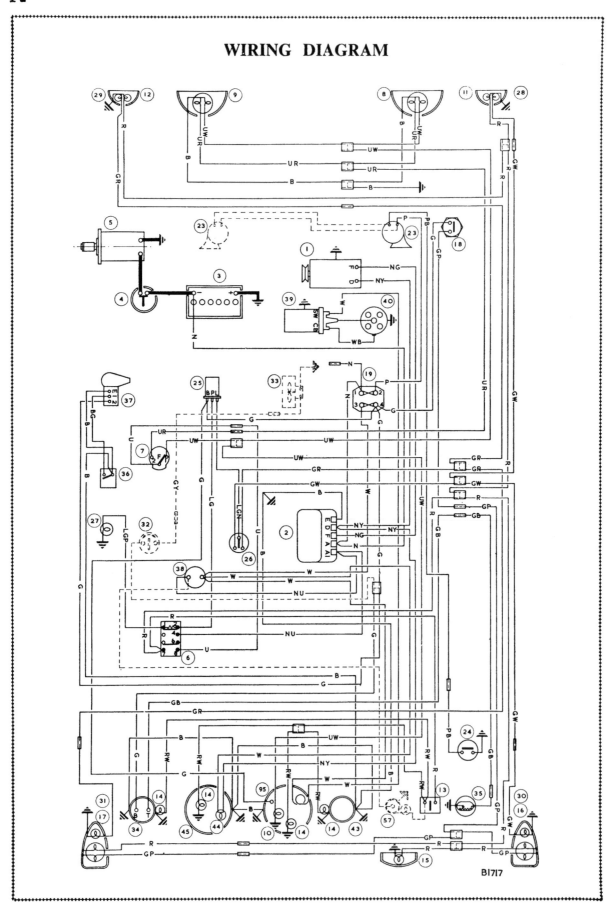

B1717

KEY TO THE WIRING DIAGRAM

No.	Description	No.	Description
1.	Dynamo.	25.	Flasher unit.
2.	Control box.	26.	Direction indicator switch.
3.	Battery—12-volt.	27.	Direction indicator warning lamp.
4.	Starter switch.	28.	Front flasher lamp—R.H.
5.	Starter motor.	29.	Front flasher lamp—L.H.
6.	Lighting switch.	30.	Rear flasher lamp—R.H.
7.	Headlamp dip switch.	31.	Rear flasher lamp—L.H.
8.	Headlamp—R.H.	32.	Heater or fresh-air motor switch (when fitted).
9.	Headlamp—L.H.	33.	Heater or fresh-air motor (when fitted).
10.	Main-beam warning lamp.	34.	Fuel gauge.
11.	Sidelamp—R.H.	35.	Fuel gauge tank unit.
12.	Sidelamp—L.H.	36.	Windscreen wiper switch.
13.	Panel lamps switch.	37.	Windscreen wiper motor.
14.	Panel lamps.	38.	Ignition switch.
15.	Number-plate illumination lamp.	39.	Ignition coil.
16.	Stop and tail lamp—R.H.	40.	Distributor.
17.	Stop and tail lamp—L.H.	43.	Oil pressure gauge.
18.	Stop lamp switch.	44.	Ignition warning lamp.
19.	Fuse unit.	45.	Speedometer.
23.	Horn (twin horns when fitted).	57.	Cigar-lighter (when fitted).
24.	Horn-push.	95.	Tachometer (impulse) (later cars).

CABLE COLOUR CODE

N. Brown. P. Purple. W. White.
U. Blue. G. Green. Y. Yellow.
R. Red. LG. Light Green. B. Black.

When a cable has two colour code letters the first denotes the main colour and the second denotes the tracer colour.

EDITOR'S NOTES

N. The Electrical System

Dynamo-commutator
Polish the commutator with fine glass paper (sandpaper).
Do not use emery paper.

Section Na

THE ELECTRICAL SYSTEM

The information given in this Section refers specifically to the Sprite (Mk. III and IV) and Midget (Mk. II and III) and must be used in conjunction with Section N

Section Na.1

SWITCHES

Direction indicator switch

Removing

Disconnect the battery. Remove the set screws securing the two halves of the cover and disconnect the snap connections beneath the column. Remove the set screws securing the switch to the column and lift away the assembly.

Refitting

Reverse the removal procedure.

Horn switch (Early cars)

Removing

Disconnect the battery. Press the horn switch and turn anti-clockwise to remove.

Refitting

Reverse the removal procedure.

Ignition and starter switch

Removing

Disconnect the battery. Remove the bezel ring with Service tool 18G 671. Disconnect the leads and pull the switch from the rear of the instrument panel.

Refitting

Reverse the removal procedure.

D0097

Fig. Na.2

The cigar lighter components

1. Pop-out heater unit.
2. Switch base.
3. Glow ring.
4. Shell.
5. Lamp cover.
6. Bulb.
7. Bulb holder.

Section Na.2

CIGAR-LIGHTER

Removing

(1) Disconnect the cigar-lighter feed wire from the ignition switch terminal.

(2) Disconnect the earth wire from the cigar-lighter.

(3) Press in the sides of the illumination lamp cover and withdraw the lamp unit from the lighter shell.

(4) Unscrew the lighter shell from the switch base.

(5) Withdraw the switch base and glow ring from the front of the fascia panel.

Refitting

(6) Reverse the removing procedure in (1) to (5).

Section Na.3

TACHOMETER—IMPULSE TYPE

The equipment consists of an indicator head and pulse lead. The pulse lead is connected in series between the ignition switch and the ignition coil, and transmits voltage pulses to the indicator head.

Faulty operation

Check wiring connections to the indicator head and continuity of the circuit. Poor connections may result in faulty readings.

The pulse lead should form a symmetrical loop and not tight against the plastic forms (inset Fig. Na.1).

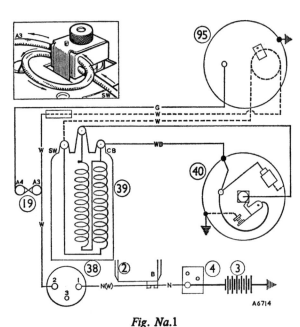

Fig. Na.1

Impulse tachometer circuit

2. Control box.
3. Batteries (12-volt).
4. Starter solenoid.
19. Fuse—A3–A4.
38. Ignition switch.
39. Ignition coil.
40. Distributor.
95. Tachometer.

Inset: symmetrical loop of pulse lead

Sprite and Midget. Issue 7. 82790

Section Na.4

REVERSE LAMPS

Bulb replacement

(1) Remove the screws securing the reverse lamp to the rear panel.

(2) Withdraw the lens.

(3) Press the bulb down towards the lower contact and withdraw it from the lamp.

(4) Fit one end of the bulb into the hole in the lower contact, then press the top of the bulb until the point on the bulb cap engages in the hole in the upper contact.

(5) Refit the lens and securing screws.

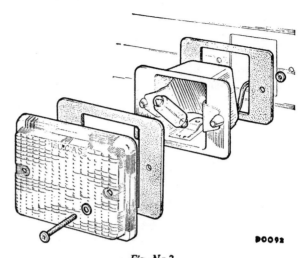

Fig. Na.3

The reverse lamp

Section Na. 5

WINDSHIELD WIPERS
(Later cars)

Removing

Wiper arms

Slacken the screw securing the wiper arm to the wheelbox spindle. Tap the screw head to release the splined locking wedge and withdraw the wiper arm.

Motor and gearbox assembly

(1) Disconnect the battery.

(2) Disconnect the wiring from the motor terminals.

(3) Remove the wiper arms.

(4) Remove the two motor securing nuts and bolts.

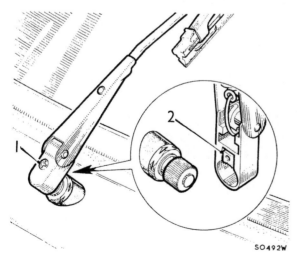

Fig. Na.4

Removal and replacement of the windshield wiper arms

1. Screw.	2. Splined locking wedge.

(5) Withdraw the motor and gearbox assembly complete with the inner drive cable. The inner cable will rotate the wiper spindles as it is withdrawn.

Dismantling

Motor and gearbox assembly

(6) Unscrew the four gearbox cover retaining screws and remove the cover.

(7) Remove the circlip and flat washer securing the connecting rod to the crankpin.

(8) Withdraw the connecting rod, taking care not to lose the flat washer fitted under it.

(9) Remove the circlip and washer securing the shaft and gear.

(10) Clean any burrs from the gear shaft and withdraw the gear, taking care not to lose the dished washer fitted under it.

(11) Mark the yoke and gearbox for reassembly.

(12) Unscrew the two fixing bolts from the motor yoke and remove the yoke assembly and armature. The yoke must be kept clear of metallic particles which will be attracted to the pole piece.

(13) Remove the screws securing the brushgear and the terminal and switch assembly, and remove both assemblies.

Inspection

Motor and gearbox assembly

(14) Examine the brushes for excessive wear; if the brushes are worn to $\frac{3}{16}$ in. (4·8 mm.) the brush gear assembly must be renewed.

(15) Check the brush spring pressure with a push-type gauge, the gauge reading should be 5 to 7 oz. (140 to 200 gm.) when the bottom of the brush is level with the bottom of the slot in the brush box. The brush gear assembly must be renewed if the springs are not satisfactory.

(16) Test the armature for insulation and open or short circuits; renew the armature if faulty.

(17) Examine the gear wheel for damage or excessive wear; renew if necessary.

Reassembling

Motor and gearbox assembly

(18) Reverse the dismantling procedure in (6) to (13) noting the following points:

(a) Use Ragosine Histate Grease to lubricate the gear wheel teeth and cam, armature shaft worm gear, connecting rod and connecting pin, cross-head slide, cable rack, and wheelbox gear wheels.

(b) Use Shell Turbo 41 oil to lubricate the bearing bushes, armature shaft bearing journals (sparingly), gear wheel shaft and crankpin, felt washer in the yoke bearing (thoroughly soak), and the wheelbox spindles.

(c) Tighten the yoke fixing bolts to a torque figure of 20 lb. in. (·23 kg. m.).

(d) If a replacement armature is being fitted, slacken the thrust screw to provide end-float for fitting the yoke.

(e) Fit the thrust disc inside the yoke bearing with its concave side towards the end face of the bearing.

(f) Fit the dished washer beneath the gear wheel with its concave side towards the gear wheel.

(g) When fitting the connecting rod to the crankpin ensure that the larger of the two flat washers is fitted under the connecting rod with the smaller one on top beneath the circlip.

(h) With the thrust screw fully tightened against the gearbox casting, an end-float of ·004 to ·008 in. (·1 to ·21 mm.) should exist on the armature. Adjustment of the armature end float can be achieved by adjustment of the thrust screw.

Refitting

Motor and gearbox assembly

Reverse the removing procedure in (1) to (5) ensuring that the inner cable engages correctly with the wheelbox gear teeth.

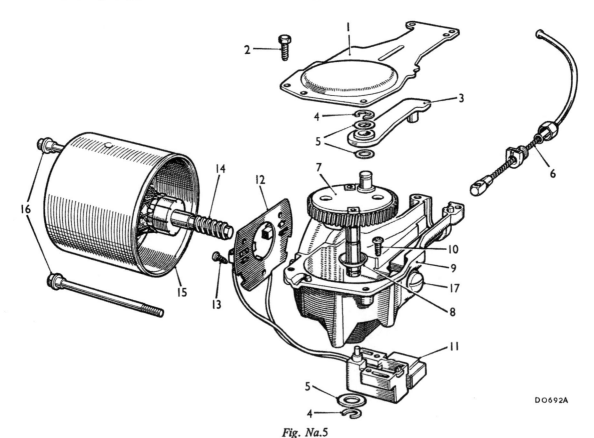

Fig. Na.5

The windshield wiper motor components

1. Gearbox cover.	7. Shaft and gear.	13. Screw for brush gear.
2. Screw for cover.	8. Dished washer.	14. Armature.
3. Connecting rod.	9. Gearbox.	15. Yoke assembly.
4. Circlip.	10. Screw for limit switch.	16. Yoke bolts.
5. Plain washer.	11. Limit switch assembly.	17. Armature adjusting screw.
6. Cable assembly.	12. Brush gear.	

Section Na.6

LAMPS

Stop, tail and direction indicator

Bulb replacement

(1) Remove the two screws securing the lamp lens and remove the lens. When refitting, ensure that the lens seal is correctly positioned.

Lamp unit removing

(2) Disconnect the battery.

(3) Remove the nuts and washers retaining the lamp unit.

(4) Disconnect the electrical leads at the harness connectors.

(5) Remove the lamp.

Number-plate lamp

Bulb replacement

(6) Remove the two securing screws and lift off the lamp hood and lens. Remove the bulb.

(7) When reassembling, ensure that the lamp lens seal is correctly positioned. Tighten the screws evenly and progressively to compress the seal.

Lamp unit removing

(8) Remove the two nuts and washers retaining the lamp to the mounting bracket; alternatively, remove the lamp complete with the bracket.

(9) Disconnect the electrical leads at the harness connectors inside the boot. Remove the lamp unit.

    NOTE.—The lamp mounting brackets are handed left- and right-hand.

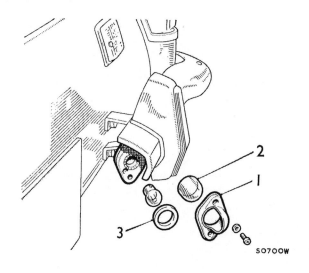

Fig. Na.7

The number-plate lamp

Interior courtesy lamp

Bulb replacement

(10) Remove the two screws securing the lamp lens and withdraw the festoon-type bulb from the retaining clips.

Lamp unit removing

(11) Remove the two screws, nuts and washers retaining the lamp to the mounting bracket.

(12) Disconnect the electric leads behind the mounting bracket. Remove the lamp unit.

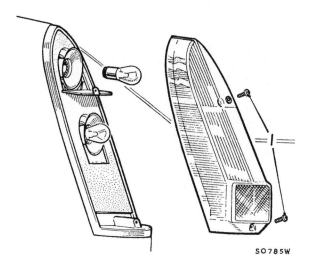

Fig. Na.6

The stop tail and direction indicator lamp

Sprite and Midget. Issue 4. 80661

Na.5

Section Na. 7

CONTROL BOX (Model RB340)

General description

The RB340 control box operates on the current–voltage system of dynamo output regulation. Three units are housed in the control-box: two separate, vibrating armature-type, single-contact regulators, and a cut-out relay. One regulator is responsive to changes in current and the other to changes in voltage.

The voltage regulator and cut-out relay are temperature- and voltage-compensated. The effect of temperature fluctuation is further minimized by a swamp resistor connected in series with the shunt coils of the voltage regulator and cut-out relay.

Voltage and current adjustments are made by turning toothed cams with a suitable tool; a special tool is available from Joseph Lucas Ltd.

Testing and adjusting

Equipment: Hydrometer; 0–20 volt moving-coil voltmeter; 0–40 amp. moving-coil ammeter.

IMPORTANT.—Check and adjust as rapidly as possible to avoid errors due to heating of the operating coil. Aim for nominal setting when making electrical and mechanical adjustments. Before attempting to adjust the control box settings, the following preliminary checks must be made.

(1) Check the state of the battery with a hydrometer.
(2) Check the dynamo output (Section N.5).
(3) Check the charging circuit wiring between the dynamo, control box, and ignition switch for insulation and continuity.
(4) Check the earth connections, particularly the control box.

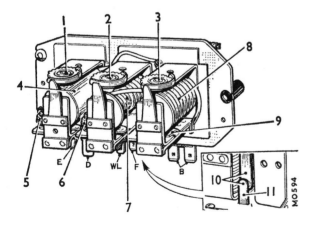

Fig. Na.8

Control box (RB340)

1. Adjustment cam—voltage.
2. Adjustment cam—current.
3. Adjustment cam—cut-out.
4. Voltage regulator.
5. Voltage contacts.
6. Current contacts.
7. Current regulator.
8. Cut-out relay.
9. Armature back stop.
10. Cut-out contacts.
11. Fixed contact bracket.

Na.6

Voltage regulator

(5) Withdraw the cables from the control box terminals 'B' and bridge the disconnected cables.
(6) Withdraw the cable from the control box terminal 'WL' and connect the voltmeter between the terminal blade and a good earth point on the car.
(7) Start the engine and run the dynamo at 3,000 r.p.m.
(8) A steady voltmeter reading should be registered within the limits given according to the ambient temperature.

Ambient temperature	Voltage regulator checking limits	Voltage regulator setting limits
10° C. (50° F.)	14·5 to 15·8 volts	14·9 to 15·5 volts
20° C. (68° F.)	14·4 to 15·6 volts	14·7 15·3 volts
30° C. (86° F.)	14·3 to 15·3 volts	14·5 to 15·1 volts
40° C. (104° F.)	14·9 to 15·1 volts	14·3 to 14·9 volts

(9) If the reading obtained is within the limits but fluctuates more than ±3 volts, check for dirty contacts or foreign matter in the air gaps.
(10) If the reading is steady but falls outside the appropriate limits, carry out the adjustment in (11) to (15).
(11) Stop the engine and remove the control box cover.
(12) Start the engine and run the dynamo at 3,000 r.p.m.
(13) Turn the voltage adjustment cam clockwise to raise the voltage setting or anti-clockwise to lower it, until the correct setting within the appropriate setting limits given is obtained.
(14) Check the setting by stopping the engine, re-starting it, and running the dynamo at 3,000 r.p.m.
(15) Stop the engine, refit the cover and restore the original connections.

Current regulator

(16) Remove the control box cover.
(17) Short out (clip together) the voltage regulator contacts to enable the dynamo to develop its maximum rated output.
(18) Withdraw the cables from the control box terminals 'B' and bridge the disconnected cables.
(19) Connect the ammeter between the bridged cables and the 'B' terminal blades.
(20) Check that no other loads are taken from the control box side of the ammeter.
(21) Start the engine, switch on the headlamps and run the dynamo at 4,500 r.p.m.
(22) Note the ammeter, which should register a steady reading equal to the maximum rated output of the dynamo.
(23) If this is correct but fluctuates more than ±1 amp., check for dirty contacts or foreign matter in the air gap.

Sprite and Midget. Issue 4. 80661

(24) If the reading is steady but falls outside the limits, carry out the adjustment in (25) to (26).

(25) Turn the current adjustment cam, clockwise to raise the current setting or anti-clockwise to lower it, until the correct setting is obtained.

(26) Stop the engine, refit the cover and restore the original connections.

Cut-out relay—contacts closing
Cut-in voltage

(27) Withdraw the cable from the control box terminal 'WL' and connect the voltmeter between the terminal blade and a good earth on the car.

(28) Switch on the headlamps.

(29) Start the engine and slowly increase its speed and observe the voltmeter.

(30) The voltmeter reading should rise steadily as the engine speed is increased and then drop back slightly when the cut-out contacts close. The cut-in voltage is that which is indicated immediately before the voltmeter reading drops back and should be within the limits given.

(31) If the reading falls outside the limits, carry out the adjustments in (32) to (35).

(32) Remove the control box cover.

(33) Reduce the engine speed so that the cut-out contacts re-open.

(34) Turn the cut-out relay adjustment cam, clockwise to raise the setting or anti-clockwise to lower it, until the correct setting is obtained.

(35) Stop the engine, refit the cover, and restore the original connections.

Cut-out relay—contacts opening

NOTE.—The contact opening setting may be checked by using a voltmeter to check the '*Drop-off voltage*', or using an ammeter to check the '*Reverse current*'; both are given.

Drop-off voltage

(36) Withdraw the cables from the control box terminals 'B' and bridge the disconnected cables.

(37) Connect the voltmeter between the terminal blades 'B' and a good earth on the car.

(38) Start the engine and run the dynamo at 3,000 r.p.m.

(39) Slowly decelerate, noting the voltmeter reading. Opening of the contacts is indicated by the voltmeter reading dropping to zero, which should occur between the limits given.

(40) If the reading falls outside the limits, carry out the adjustments in (41) to (44).

(41) Stop the engine and remove the control box cover.

(42) Adjust the cut-out contact gap by carefully bending the fixed contact bracket; reducing the gap will raise the drop-off voltage setting and increasing the gap will lower the setting.

(43) Repeat the test in (38) and (39) and, if necessary, re-adjust until the correct setting is obtained.

(44) Stop the engine, refit the cover and restore the original connections.

Reverse current

(45) Withdraw the cables from the control box terminals 'B' and bridge the disconnected cables.

(46) Connect the ammeter between the control box terminals 'B' and the bridged cables.

(47) Start the engine and increase the speed until the ammeter registers a charge.

(48) Slowly decelerate, noting the ammeter reading, which should fall momentarily to show a reverse current flow within the limits given.

(49) If the reverse current reading falls outside the limits given, carry out the adjustments in (50) to (53).

(50) Stop the engine and remove the control box cover.

(51) Adjust the cut-out contact gap by carefully bending the fixed contact bracket; reducing the gap will reduce the reverse current and increasing the gap will raise it.

(52) Repeat the test in (47) and (48) and, if necessary, re-adjust until the correct setting is obtained.

(53) Stop the engine, refit the cover and restore the original connections.

Air-gap settings

The electrical settings of the regulators must be checked after the air-gaps have been adjusted.

Voltage and current regulators

(54) Withdraw the cables from the control box terminals 'B' and remove the cover.

(55) Turn the adjustment cam clockwise to the point giving minimum lift to the armature spring.

(56) Slacken the locknut and unscrew the contact.

(57) Insert a ·054 in. (1·37 mm.) feeler gauge between the armature and the copper separation on the core face, as far back as the rivet heads on the armature.

(58) Screw the contact in until the feeler gauge is just trapped (i.e. light resistance to removal).

(59) Tighten the back nut.

(60) Check that the narrowest part of the back gap between the back face of the armature is between ·030 to ·040 in. (·76 to 1·02 mm.) with a maximum taper of ·010 in. (·25 mm.) on the current regulator.

(61) Repeat the adjustment in (55) to (59) for the other regulators.

(62) Check the electrical setting of the voltage regulator. The current regulator setting must be checked after the cut-out has been checked and adjusted electrically and mechanically.

Cut-out relay

(63) Carry out (54) and (55).

(64) Press the armature squarely down against the copper separation on the core face.

(65) Check that a gap of ·030 to ·040 in. (·76 to 1·02 mm.) exists between the back face of the armature and the frame on both sides of the armature.

(66) Insert a ·015 in. (·38 mm.) feeler gauge between the head of the core and the armature using the nearest rivet as a datum.

(67) Press the armature down and bend the fixed contact bracket until the contacts just touch.

(68) With the feeler gauge still in position, adjust the armature back stop until it just touches the armature.

(69) Using the nearest rivet as a datum, check that the top gap is from ·035 to ·045 in. (·9 to 1·14 mm.).

(70) Check the electrical settings of the cut-out.

(71) Check the electrical setting of the current regulator.

Cleaning the contacts

Regulators

(72) Use a fine carborundum stone or silicon carbide paper.

Cut-out

(73) Use fine glass-paper only, never carborundum or emery cloth.

(74) Use a cloth moistened with methylated spirit (denatured alcohol) to wipe away foreign matter.

Section Na.8

BATTERY

(Types A9, AZ9, A11, AZ11)

The electrolyte levels are visible through the translucent battery case or may be checked by fully raising the vent cover and tilting it to one side. The electrolyte level in each cell must be maintained so that the separator plates are just covered. To avoid flooding, the battery must not be topped up within half an hour of it having been charged from any source other than the generating system fitted to the car.

To top up the levels, raise the vent cover and pour distilled water into the trough until all the rectangular filling slots are full and the bottom of the trough is just covered. Wipe the cover seating grooves dry and press the cover firmly into position; the correct quantity of distilled water will automatically be distributed to each cell. In extremely cold conditions, run the engine immediately after topping-up to mix the electrolyte.

The manifold must be in position at all times except during the filling or topping-up operation.

Na.8

Charging the battery with the manifold raised will cause flooding of the electrolyte. Normal charging procedure should be followed, however, when fast charging, the manifold must still remain closed and this precludes the use of a thermostat. Fast charging may be carried out at a current in amps. not greater than the capacity in ampere-hours (20-hour rate) of the battery. The limit time for fast charging is 1 to 1½ hours.

The 'A'-type battery does not have accessible inter-cell connectors and the battery case must not in any circumstances be drilled. Twin cadmium testing probes should be used. A cell comparison test can be made with a hydrometer in the usual way.

Section Na.9

FUSE UNIT

(Type 7FJ)

The fuses are housed in a fuseblock (1) mounted in the engine compartment body adjacent to the battery.

Fuses 2 and 3 protect the side and tail lamps.

Fuse 4 protects the circuits which operate only when the ignition switch is on, viz., heater blower, stop lamps, reverse lamps.

Fuse 5 protects the equipment which operates independently of the ignition switch, viz., horns, interior lamp, cigar-lighter.

Two spare fuses (6) are provided and it is important to use the correct replacement fuse. The fusing value, current rated 17 amp. (35 amp. blow rated), is marked on a coloured slip of paper inside the glass tube of the fuse.

Removing

(1) Disconnect the battery.

(2) Disconnect the electrical connections at the fuse unit.

(3) Remove the two self-tapping screws retaining the fuse unit.

When refitting, refer to the Wiring Diagram to ensure that the correct connections are made to the fuse unit.

Line fuse

A line fuse (7) situated above the main fuse block protects the heater blower motor and the windscreen wiper.

NOTE.—The heater blower motor was originally fused through Fuse 4 of the fuse unit.

Sprite and Midget. Issue 3. 80661

Section Na.10

STARTER
(Type M35J)
(Inertia drive)

Dismantling

(1) Remove the screws securing the drive-end bracket.

(2) Withdraw the drive-end bracket complete with the armature and drive.

(3) Remove the thrust washer from the commutator end of the armature.

(4) Remove the screws securing the commutator end bracket.

(5) Detach the bracket from the yoke, disengage the field brushes from the brush gear and remove the bracket.

(6) If necessary, the drive assembly can be removed by compressing the spring, removing the jump ring and withdrawing the drive from the shaft.

Inspection

Brush gear

(7) Check the brush spring tension; fit a new brush into each holder in turn, press on top of the brush with a push-type spring gauge until the brush protrudes approximately $\frac{1}{16}$ in. (1·5 mm.) from the holder. At this point check the gauge reading against the figure given. If the spring pressures vary considerably from the figure given the commutator-end bracket assembly must be renewed.

(8) Check the brushes for wear; renew any brush worn to, or approaching, the minimum length.

(9) To renew the end bracket brushes, cut the brush leads from the terminal post, slot the head of the post sufficiently deep to accommodate the new brush leads and solder the new leads to the posts.

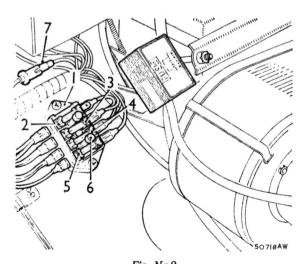

Fig. Na.9

The fuse unit type 7FJ

(10) To renew the field winding brushes, cut the brush leads approximately $\frac{1}{4}$ in. (6·4 mm.) from the field winding junction, solder the new brush leads to the stumps of the old ones ensuring that the insulation sleeves provide adequate coverage.

Commutator

(11) Clean the commutator with a cloth moistened with fuel and examine it for burns, pitting, and excessive wear; **provided that the amount of metal removed does not reduce the thickness of the commutator beyond the minimum thickness,** the commutator may be reconditioned as follows:

(a) Turn the commutator at high speed and using a very sharp tool remove the minimum amount of metal necessary to restore the surface.

(b) Polish the commutator with very fine sandpaper.

(c) Using an air blast, clean any copper residue from the armature.

IMPORTANT.—The commutator segment insulators must not be undercut.

Armature

(12) Test the insulation of the armature windings with a 110-volt A.C., 15-watt test lamp connected between the armature shaft and the commutator; if the lamp lights the armature must be renewed.

(13) Check the windings at their connections with the commutator for signs of melted solder or lifted conductors.

(14) Check the shaft for distortion; if the shaft is bent or distorted the armature must be renewed. Do not attempt to straighten the shaft or machine the armature core laminations.

Field windings

(15) Connect a 12-volt battery-operated test lamp between each of the field brushes and a clean part of the yoke; the lamp will light if continuity is satisfactory between the brushes, windings, and yoke connection.

(16) Disconnect the field windings from their riveted connection with the yoke. Using a 110-volt A.C., 15-watt test lamp connected between each of the brushes in turn and the yoke, check the insulation of the field windings. If the lamp lights the windings must be renewed.

(17) The field windings may be renewed as follows:

(a) Disconnect the windings from the connection with the yoke.

(b) Slacken the pole-shoe retaining screw using a wheel-operated screwdriver.

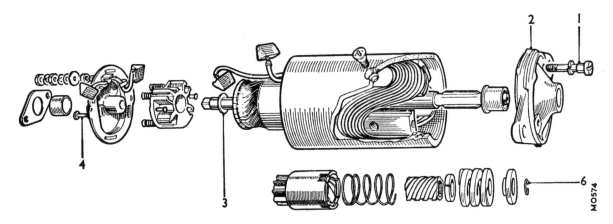

*Fig. Na.*10

The starter motor type M35J

(c) Remove the retaining screws from one pair of diametrically opposite pole-shoes and remove the pole-shoes from the yoke.

(d) Slide the windings from beneath the remaining pole-shoes and withdraw them from the yoke.

(e) Clean the inside of the yoke, the pole-shoes and insulation piece.

(f) Loosely fit the new windings and the pole-shoes and position the insulation piece between the yoke and the brush connections to the windings.

(g) Tighten the pole-shoe screws evenly using a wheel-operated screwdriver.

(h) Re-connect the winding junction connector to the yoke.

Commutator end bracket

(18) Check the insulation of the brush springs and terminal post by connecting a 110-volt A.C., 15-watt test lamp between each spring and the terminal and a clean part of the end bracket; the lamp will light if the insulation is not satisfactory.

Bearings

(19) If a bearing is worn sufficiently to allow excessive side-play of the armature shaft, the bearing bush must be renewed as follows.

Commutator-end bracket

(a) Drill out the rivets securing the brush box moulding, remove the moulding, bearing seal retaining plate and felt washer seal.

(b) Screw a ½ in. tap a few turns into the bush and withdraw the bush with the tap.

Drive-end bracket

(c) Support the bracket and press out the bush.
  NOTE.—New bushes must be immersed in S.A.E. 30/40 engine oil for 24 hours or in oil heated to 100° C. (212° F.) for two hours prior to fitting. The bushes must not be reamed after fitting.

(d) Using a polished, shouldered mandrel, the same diameter as the shaft bearing journal, press the new bushes into the brackets.

Drive

(20) Wash the drive with paraffin (kerosene) and dry using an air blast.

(21) Check the components for damage and excessive wear; renew worn or damaged parts.

Reassembling

(22) Reverse (1) to (6).

Bench testing

Light running current

(23) Clamp the starter firmly in a vice.

(24) Connect a starter switch, a 0–600 amp. ammeter and a 12-volt battery, in series, to the starter, using the lug as the earth connection.

(25) Connect a voltmeter between the starter terminal and the yoke.

(26) Operate the switch and check the speed of the motor with a tachometer while noting the voltmeter and ammeter readings.

(27) Check the readings obtained in 26 against the figures given in 'GENERAL DATA' for light running speed, current, and voltage.

Lock torque and current

(28) With the starter connected and clamped as for the light running check, secure an arm to the driving pinion.

(29) Connect a spring balance to the free end of the arm.

(30) Operate the switch and note the ammeter, voltmeter, and spring balance readings. Calculate the lock torque by multiplying the reading of the spring balance in pounds by the length of the arm in feet.

(31) Check the readings obtained in 30 against the figures given in 'GENERAL DATA' for lock torque, and voltage.

NOTE.—If a constant-voltage supply is used for this test, a higher voltage may be registered on the voltmeter than the figure given. If this should occur, a variable resistance must be added to the circuit and adjusted to give the required reading and the test repeated.

*Na.*10

Sprite and Midget. Issue 3. 80661

Section Na.11

REPLACEMENT BULBS

	Volts	Watts	Part No.
Headlamp—Home and R.H.D. Export (English sealed beam)	12	60/45	GLU 101
Headlamp—North America (American sealed beam)	12	50/40	
Headlamp—Europe (except France) (European sealed beam)	12	60/50	
Headlamp—France (bulb type 411 yellow)	12	45/40	BFS 411
Sidelamp—all markets except North America and Italy	12	6	GLB 989
Sidelamp (with flasher)—North America and Italy	12	5/21	GLB 380
Stop, tail—all markets	12	5/21	GLB 380
Reverse—all markets except France	12	18	BFS 273
Reverse—France	12	15	BFS 267
Number-plate lamp	12	6	GLB 989
Direction indicator	12	21	GLB 382
Side-marker lamp—front and rear	14	4	BFS 222
Ignition warning—all markets except North America, Sweden and West Germany	12	2·2	GLB 987
Ignition warning—North America, Sweden and West Germany	12	2	GLB 281
Main beam—all markets except North America, Sweden and West Germany	12	2·2	GLB 987
Main beam—North America, Sweden and West Germany	12	2	GLB 281
Direction indicator warning lamp	12	2·2	GLB 987
Brake warning lamp—North America, Sweden and West Germany	12	1·5	GLB 280
Panel illumination lamp	12	2·2	GLB 987
Cigar-lighter illumination	12	2·2	BFS 643
Luggage compartment lamp	12	6	GLB 254
Interior courtesy lamp	12	6	GLB 254
Hazard warning lamp—North America	12	2·2	GLB 987
Seat belt warning lamp—North America	12	2	GLB 281

Section Na.12

SWITCHES
(Midget Mk. III from Car No. G–AN5–105501)

Removing

CAUTION: Disconnect the battery before attempting to remove any of the switches.

Panel and wiper switches

(1) Disconnect the wiring from the switches.

(2) Remove the switches, using 18G 1201.

Light switch

(3) Depress the pin in the heater knob and remove the knob.

(4) Unscrew the heater switch bezel and remove the heater switch.

(5) Disconnect the wiring from the light switch.

(6) Remove the switch, using 18G 1201.

Hazard warning switch (if fitted)

(7) Compress the switch retaining tags, using tool 18G 1201, and push the switch rearwards out of the fascia.

(8) Pull the wiring harness plug off the back of the switch.

Refitting

Panel and wiper switches

(9) Reverse the removing procedure in (1) and (2).

(10) Re-connect the battery.

Light switch

(11) Reverse the removing procedure in (3) to (6).

(12) Re-connect the battery.

Hazard warning switch

(13) Reverse the removing procedure in (7) and (8).

Section Na.13

DIRECTION INDICATOR/HEADLIGHT FLASHER/ LOW-HIGH BEAM SWITCH
(Midget Mk. III from Car No. G–AN5–105501)

Removing

(1) Disconnect the battery.

(2) Unscrew the four switch cowl retaining screws and remove the cowl.

(3) Disconnect the switch wiring from the multi-snap connector and from the clip around the steering-column.

(4) Remove the two screws retaining the direction indicator/headlight flasher/low-high beam switch, and remove the switch and retaining clip.

Refitting

(5) Reverse the procedure in (1) to (4), ensuring that the small tongue on the switch engages in the cutaway of the outer steering-column.

Section Na.14

IGNITION SWITCH
(Midget Mk. III from Car No. G–AN5–105501)

Removing

(1) Disconnect the battery.

(2) Turn the key to position 'O'.

(3) Disconnect the wiring from the switch.

(4) Remove the two screws retaining the switch to the steering lock.

(5) Withdraw the switch.

Refitting

(6) Reverse the removing procedure in (1) to (5).

Sprite and Midget. Issue 3. 82790
MG Midget. AKM 2092/1

Section Nb

THE ELECTRICAL SYSTEM

The information given in this Section refers specifically to service operations on, or affected by, equipment fitted to the Sprite Mk. IV and Midget Mk. III in conformity with local and territorial requirements, and must be used in conjunction with Section N and Section Na.

THE SWITCHES

No.	Description
1.	Heater blower switch.
2.	Brake pressure—warning light/test push.
3.	Retaining clip.
4.	Lighting switch.
5.	Retaining clip.
6.	Panel light switch.
7.	Hazard warning switch.

No.	Description
8.	Ignition switch.
9.	Screw for switch.
10.	Steering-column switch cowl.
11.	Direction indicator/headlight flasher/low-high beam/horn switch.
12.	Windshield washer/wiper switch.
13.	Audible warning door switch.

Section Nb.1

INSTRUMENTS AND SWITCHES

Removing

IMPORTANT.—Disconnect the battery before attempting to remove any of the switches or instruments.

Tachometer

(1) Unscrew the two knurled retaining nuts, disconnect the earth cable and remove the retaining brackets.

(2) Withdraw the instrument from the fascia, and disconnect the wiring.

Speedometer

(3) Remove the console (Section Rb.1).

(4) Unscrew the trip recorder reset retaining nut and disengage the reset from its bracket.

(5) Disconnect the speedometer drive cable from the instrument.

(6) Unscrew the two knurled retaining nuts, disconnect the earth cable and remove the retaining brackets.

(7) Withdraw the instrument from the fascia and detach the illumination lamp.

Fuel gauge

(8) Remove the speedometer as in (3) to (7).

(9) Remove the knurled retaining nut and disconnect the earth cable.

(10) Remove the retaining bracket, withdraw the instrument from the fascia and disconnect the wiring.

Brake failure warning lamp assembly

(11) Remove the speedometer as in (3) to (7).

(12) Remove the fuel gauge as in (8) to (10).

(13) Disconnect the wiring from the back of the switch.

(14) Disengage the spring retaining clip and withdraw the switch.

Lighting switch

(15) Remove the console (Section Rb.1).

(16) Disconnect the wiring from the back of the switch.

(17) Using a short, wide-bladed screwdriver or similar tool carefully press in the two lugs on the interior of the switch and withdraw the interior from the switch case.

(18) Disengage the spring retaining clip from the switch case and withdraw the case.

Heater blower switch

(19) Remove the tachometer as in (1) and (2).

(20) Disconnect the wiring from the back of the switch.

(21) Carry out operations (17) and (18) as for the lighting switch.

Air control

(22) Press in the knob retaining button located behind the lettering 'ON'.

(23) Unscrew the control retaining nut and disengage the control from the fascia.

(24) Disconnect the control inner cable from the heater air valve.

(25) Detach the outer cable from its clip on the heater unit.

(26) Attach a piece of cord to the inner cable to assist refitting and draw the cable through the bulkhead from the inside of the car.

Hazard warning switch

(27) Remove the console (Section Rb.1).

(28) Disconnect the wiring from the switch.

(29) Press in the four retaining lugs on the switch outer case and withdraw the switch.

Direction indicator/horn switch

(30) Remove the steering column pinch bolt.

(31) Remove the three toe-plate to column securing bolts.

(32) Note the location, quantity and thickness of the packing washers fitted between the column upper fixing flanges and the body brackets, remove the three securing bolts and nuts and collect the packing washers. **If the packing washers are mislaid or their fitting positions are not recorded the steering column must be aligned as described in Section Ja.3 when refitted.**

(33) Pull the steering column back sufficiently for the switch cowl to clear the fascia.

(34) Unscrew the four switch cowl retaining screws and remove the cowl.

(35) Remove the two screws securing the direction indicator/horn switch to the steering column.

(36) Disconnect the switch wiring at the multi-snap connector below the fascia and remove the switch complete with its wiring.

Windshield wiper/washer switch

(37) Carry out operations (30) to (34).

(38) Remove the two screws securing the windshield wiper/washer switch to the steering column.

(39) Disconnect the switch wiring at the multi-snap connector below the fascia and remove the switch complete with its wiring.

Ignition switch

(40) Carry out operations (30) to (34).

(41) Unscrew the four screws securing the switch retaining saddle and remove the saddle.

(42) Disconnect the switch wiring at the snap connectors below the fascia and remove the switch complete with its wiring.

Panel light switch

(43) Carry out operations (30) to (34).

(44) Remove the switch retaining nut.

(45) Disconnect the switch wiring at the snap connectors below the fascia and remove the switch complete with its wiring.

Refitting

Tachometer

(46) Reverse the removing procedure in (1) and (2).

Speedometer

(47) Reverse the removing procedure in (3) to (7).

Fuel gauge
(48) Reverse the removing procedure in (3) to (10).

Brake failure warning lamp assembly
(49) Reverse the removing procedure in (3) to (14).

Lighting switch
(50) Reverse the removing procedure in (15) to (18).

Heater blower switch
(51) Attach the end of the control cable to the end of the cord pulled through the bulkhead when removing and carefully pull the cable through to the heater unit.
(52) Reverse the removing procedure in (22) to (25).

Hazard warning switch
(53) Reverse the removing procedure in (27) to (29).

Direction indicator/horn switch
(54) Reverse the removing procedure in (34) to (36).
(55) Enter the steering gear pinion into the steering column sleeve as far as it will go.
(56) Fit the packing washers in their original positions between the column fixing flanges and the body brackets; fit the three securing bolts and nuts tightening them by hand until the packing washers are just pinched.
(57) Screw in and tighten the three toe-plate to column securing bolts.
(58) Tighten the three column upper fixing bolts to the torque figure given in 'GENERAL DATA'.
(59) Fit and tighten the pinion pinch bolt to the torque figure given in 'GENERAL DATA'.

Windshield wiper/washer switch
(60) Reverse the removing procedure in (34), (38), and (39).
(61) Carry out the operations in (55) to (59).

Ignition switch
(62) Reverse the removing procedure in (34), (41), and (42).
(63) Carry out the operations in (55) to (59).

Panel light switch
(64) Reverse the removing procedure in (34), (44), and (45).
(65) Carry out the operations in (55) to (59).

Section Nb.2

WINDSHIELD WASHER MOTOR

Removing
(1) Disconnect the battery.
(2) Disconnect the wiring from the pump.
(3) Disconnect the water tubes from the pump.
(4) Unscrew the two pump mounting screws and remove the pump.

Refitting
(5) Reverse the removing procedure in (1) to (4).

Nb.4

Section Nb.3

WINDSHIELD WIPERS

Removing
Motor and gearbox assembly
(1) Disconnect the battery.
(2) Disconnect the wiring from the motor terminals.
(3) Remove the wiper arms.
(4) Remove the two motor securing nuts and bolts.
(5) Withdraw the motor and gearbox assembly complete with the inner drive cable. The inner cable will rotate the wiper spindles as it is withdrawn.

Right-hand wheelbox
(6) Remove the fascia (Section Rb.2).
(7) Remove the right-hand demister duct.
(8) Remove the wheelbox cover plate and slide the outer cable from the inner.
(9) Remove the spindle housing securing nut.
(10) Slide the wheelbox from the inner cable.

Left-hand wheelbox
(11) Remove the motor and gearbox as in (1) to (5).
(12) Remove the fascia (Section Rb.2).
(13) Remove the left-hand demister duct.
(14) Remove the wheelbox cover plate and detach the outer cable.
(15) Remove the spindle housing retaining nut.
(16) Withdraw the wheelbox.

Dismantling
Motor and gearbox assembly
(17) Unscrew the four gearbox cover retaining screws and remove the cover.
(18) Remove the circlip and flat washer securing the connecting rod to the crankpin.
(19) Withdraw the connecting rod, taking care not to lose the flat washer fitted under it.
(20) Remove the circlip and washer securing the shaft and gear.
(21) Clean any burrs from the gear shaft and withdraw the gear, taking care not to lose the dished washer fitted under it.
(22) Mark the yoke and gearbox for reassembly.
(23) Unscrew the two fixing bolts from the motor yoke and remove the yoke assembly and armature. The yoke must be kept clear of metallic particles which will be attracted to the pole piece.
(24) Remove the screws securing the brushgear and the terminal and switch assembly, and remove both assemblies.

Inspection
Motor and gearbox assembly
(25) Examine the brushes for excessive wear, if the main brushes (diametrically opposite) are worn to $\frac{3}{16}$ in. (4·8 mm.) or if the narrow section of the third brush is worn to the full width of the brush the brush gear assembly must be renewed.

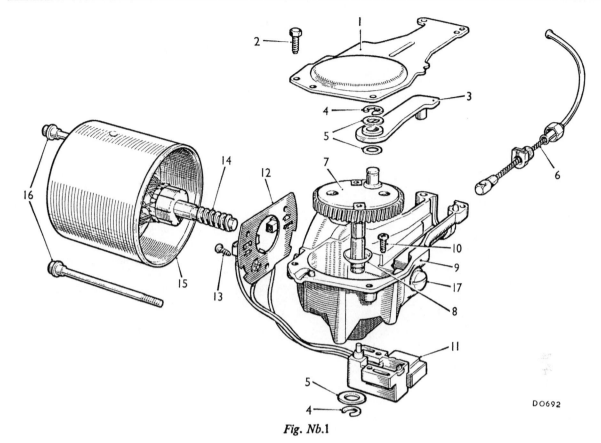

*Fig. Nb.*1

The two-speed windshield wiper motor components

1.	Gearbox cover.	9.	Gearbox.
2.	Screw for cover.	10.	Screw for limit switch.
3.	Connecting rod.	11.	Limit switch assembly.
4.	Circlip.	12.	Brush gear.
5.	Plain washer.	13.	Screw for brush gear.
6.	Cable assembly.	14.	Armature.
7.	Shaft and gear.	15.	Yoke assembly.
8.	Dished washer.	16.	Yoke bolts.
		17.	Armature adjusting screw.

(26) Check the brush spring pressure with a push-type gauge, the gauge reading should be 5 to 7 oz. (140 to 200 gm.) when the bottom of the brush is level with the bottom of the slot in the brush box. The brush gear assembly must be renewed if the springs are not satisfactory.

(27) Test the armature for insulation and open or short circuits, renew the armature if faulty.

(28) Examine the gear wheel for damage or excessive wear; renew if necessary.

Reassembling

Motor and gearbox assembly

(29) Reverse the dismantling procedure in (17) to (24) noting the following points:

    (*a*) Use Ragosine Histate Grease to lubricate the gear wheel teeth and cam, armature shaft worm gear, connecting rod and connecting pin, cross-head slide, cable rack, and wheelbox gearwheels.

    (*b*) Use Shell Turbo 41 oil to lubricate the bearing bushes, armature shaft bearing journals (sparingly), gear wheel shaft and crankpin, felt washer in the yoke bearing (thoroughly soak), and the wheelbox spindles.

    (*c*) Tighten the yoke fixing bolts to a torque figure of 20 lb. in. (·23 kg. m.).

    (*d*) If a replacement armature is being fitted, slacken the thrust screw to provide end-float for fitting the yoke.

    (*e*) Fit the thrust disc inside the yoke bearing with its concave side towards the end face of the bearing.

    (*f*) Fit the dished washer beneath the gear wheel with its concave side towards the gear wheel.

    (*g*) When fitting the connecting rod to the crankpin ensure that the larger of the two flat washers is fitted under the connecting rod with the smaller one on top beneath the circlip.

(h) With the thrust screw fully tightened against the gearbox casting, an end-float of ·004 to ·008 in. (·1 to ·21 mm.) should exist on the armature. Adjustment of the armature end float can be achieved by adjustment of the thrust screw.

Refitting
Right-hand wheelbox

(30) Reverse the removing procedure in (6) to (10).

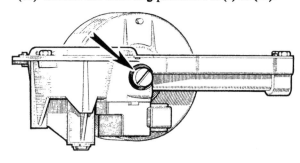

Fig. Nb.2 DO668

The armature end-float adjusting screw

Left-hand wheelbox

(31) Reverse the removing procedure in (11) to (16) ensuring that the inner cable engages correctly with the wheelbox gear teeth.

Motor and gearbox assembly

(32) Reverse the removing procedure in (1) to (5) ensuring that the inner cable engages correctly with the wheelbox gear teeth.

Section Nb.4

WINDSHIELD WIPERS
(Later cars)

Later cars have a three-blade wiper system; the additional wheelbox is fitted in the centre position.

Removing
Centre-position wheelbox

(33) Remove the fascia (Section Rb.2).
(34) Remove the wheelbox cover-plate and slide the outer cable from the inner.
(35) Remove the spindle housing securing nut.
(36) Withdraw the wheelbox.

Refitting

(37) Reverse the removal procedure.

Section Nb.5

LAMPS
Front and rear side-marker lamps
Removing

(1) Disconnect the battery.

(2) Remove the two nuts, and four washers securing the lamp.

(3) Partially remove the lamp and disconnect the electrical leads at the harness connectors.

Bulb replacement

Front (amber). To renew a bulb, remove the securing screw (1) and lift off the lamp lens, noting that one end is secured by a locating tab (2). When refitting, ensure that the sealing rubber is positioned correctly and that the lens tab (2) is located beneath the lamp body rim before refitting the securing screw.

Rear (red). To gain access to the bulb (3), the rubber lips retaining the chrome bezel and lamp lens should be eased open with a screwdriver and the bezel (1), and lens (2), removed. When refitting ensure that the thick end of the wedge-shaped lens faces rearwards.

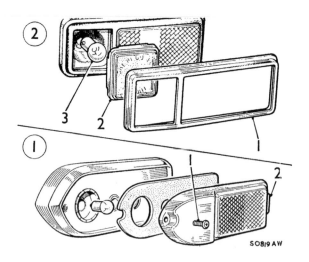

SO819 AW

Fig. Nb.3

The front (1) and rear (2) side-marker lamps

Section Nb.6

ALTERNATOR—Lucas Type 16ACR
(Midget Mk. III from Car No. G–AN5–105501)

Service precautions

Polarity

Ensure that correct battery polarity is maintained at all times; reversed battery or charger connections will damage the alternator rectifiers.

Battery connections

Do not disconnect the battery while the engine is running.

Testing semi-conductor devices

Never use an ohmmeter of the type incorporating a hand-driven generator for checking the rectifiers or transistors.

Testing the charging circuit

Test conditions

Alternator drive belt adjusted correctly, battery terminals clean and tight, battery in good condition (electrolyte specific gravity readings consistent), and cables and terminal connections in the charging circuit in good condition.

Test	Procedure	Remarks
1. To check that battery voltage is reaching the alternator	Remove the cable connector from the alternator. Connect the negative side of a voltmeter to earth. Switch on the ignition. Connect the positive side of the voltmeter to each of the alternator cable connectors in turn.	(a) If battery voltage is not available at the 'IND' cable connector, check the no-charge warning lamp bulb and the warning lamp circuit for continuity. (b) If battery voltage is not available at the main charging cable connector, check the circuit between the battery and the alternator for continuity. (c) If battery voltage is available at the cable connectors mentioned in (a) and (b) proceed with test 2.
2. Alternator test	Reconnect the cable connector to the alternator. Disconnect the brown cable with eyelet from the terminal on the starter motor solenoid. Connect an ammeter between the brown cable and the terminal on the starter motor solenoid. Connect a voltmeter across the battery terminals. Run the engine at 6,000 alternator rev/min and wait until the ammeter reading is stable.	(a) If a zero ammeter reading is obtained, remove the end cover and disconnect the surge protection device lead from its terminal on the alternator. If the alternator output is normal, renew the surge protection device. If the reading is still zero, remove and overhaul the alternator. (b) If an ammeter reading below 10 amps. and a voltmeter reading between 13·6 and 14·4 volts is obtained, and the battery is in a low state of charge, check the alternator performance on a test bench. The alternator output should be 34 amperes at 14 volts, at 6,000 r.p.m.

Sprite and Midget. Issue 1. 82790
MG Midget. AKM 2092/1

245

Nb.7

Testing the charging circuit (*continued*)

		(*c*) If an ammeter reading below 10 amps. and a voltmeter reading below 13·6 volts is obtained, remove the alternator and renew the voltage regulator.
		(*d*) If an ammeter reading above 10 amps. and a voltmeter reading above 14·4 volts is obtained, remove the alternator and renew the voltage regulator.

Removing

(1) Disconnect the battery.

(2) Unclip and withdraw the wiring harness plug from the alternator.

(3) Detach the temperature gauge capillary tube from the clip mounted on the alternator rear pivot bolt.

(4) Remove the alternator adjusting link nut.

(5) Remove the alternator pivot bolts and nuts, noting the temperature gauge capillary tube clip.

(6) Detach the drive belt from the alternator pulley and withdraw the alternator.

(7) Remove the set bolt to release the adjusting link from the alternator.

Dismantling

(8) Remove the two screws to release the end cover from the alternator.

(9) Detach the leads from the terminal blades on the rectifier plates.

(10) Remove the four screws to release the two brush assemblies and the leads from the brush holder, noting the leaf spring fitted at the side of the inner brush.

(11) Remove the screw to release the surge protection device lead from the brush holder.

(12) Alternator type 23717 and 23750: Remove the bolt securing the regulator to the slip-ring end bracket.

(13) Remove the two bolts to release the brush holder complete with regulator from the slip-ring end bracket.

(14) Remove the screw to release the regulator from the brush holder, noting the connector link and the distance piece fitted to alternator type 23795.

(15) Remove the set bolt securing the surge protection device to the slip-ring end bracket.

(16) Remove the set bolt securing the rectifier earthing link to the slip-ring end bracket.

(17) Using a pair of pliers as a thermal shunt to avoid overheating the diodes, unsolder each of the three stator cables in turn from the rectifier.

(18) Slacken the nut to release the rectifier assembly from the clip-ring end bracket.

(19) Mark the drive-end bracket, the stator lamination pack, and the slip-ring end bracket 'to assist re-assembly.

(20) Remove the three through-bolts and withdraw the slip-ring end bracket and the stator lamination pack.

(21) Remove the 'O' ring from inside the slip-ring end bracket.

(22) Remove the nut and withdraw the pulley and fan from the rotor shaft.

(23) Remove the pulley key and withdraw the distance piece from the rotor shaft.

(24) Press the rotor out of the drive-end bracket bearing.

(25) Withdraw the distance piece from the drive end of the rotor.

(26) Remove the circlip to release the bearing, bearing cover-plates, 'O' ring, and felt washer from the drive-end bracket.

Inspection

(27) Check the bearings for wear and roughness; if necessary, repack the bearings with Shell Alvania RA grease. To renew the slip-ring end bearing, unsolder the two field connections from the slip-ring and withdraw the slip-ring and the bearing from the rotor shaft. Reassemble ensuring that the shielded side of the bearing faces the slip-ring assembly. Use Fry's H.T. 3 solder to remake the field connections to the slip-ring.

(28) Clean the surfaces of the slip-ring, removing any evidence of burning using very fine glass paper.

Nb.8

246

Sprite and Midget. Issue 1. 82790
MG Midget. AKM 2092/1

THE ALTERNATOR COMPONENTS

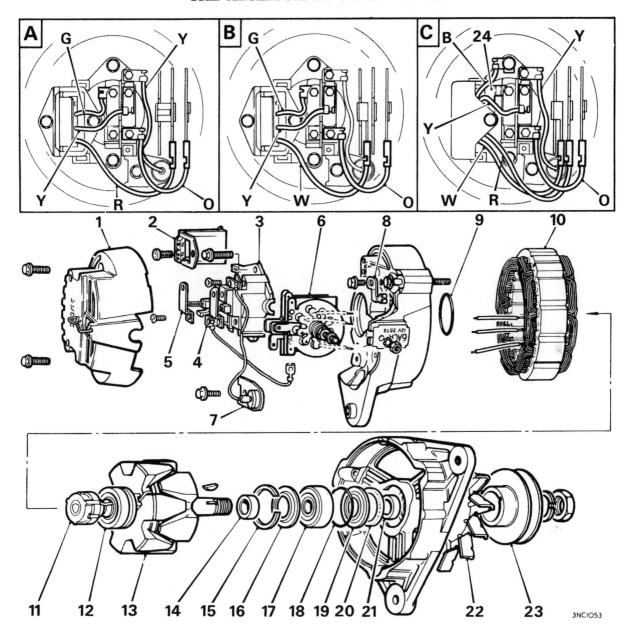

3NCIO53

No.	Description	No.	Description	No.	Description
1.	End cover.	9.	'O' ring.	17.	Bearing.
2.	Regulator.	10.	Stator lamination pack.	18.	'O' ring.
3.	Brush holder.	11.	Slip-ring.	19.	Cover plate.
4.	Outer brush.	12.	Bearing.	20.	Felt washer.
5.	Inner brush.	13.	Rotor.	21.	Distance piece.
6.	Rectifier.	14.	Distance piece.	22.	Fan.
7.	Surge protection device.	15.	Circlip.	23.	Pulley.
8.	Earthing link.	16.	Cover plate.	24.	Metal connector link.

Rectifier, brush holder and regulator arrangement
A = Alternator type 23717.   B = Alternator type 23750.   C = Alternator type 23795.

CABLE COLOUR CODE

B.	Black.	W.	White.	R.	Red.
Y.	Yellow.	G.	Green.	O.	Orange.

Sprite and Midget.   Issue 1.   82790
MG Midget.   AKM 2092/1

(29) Check the field winding insulation, connecting the test equipment (see **'GENERAL DATA'**) between one of the slip-rings and a rotor lobe.

(30) Check the field windings against the specification given in **'GENERAL DATA'**, connecting the test equipment between the slip-rings.

(31) Check the stator windings for continuity, connecting the test equipment (see **'GENERAL DATA'**) between any two of the stator cables, then repeating the test using the third cable in place of one of the first two.

(32) Check the stator winding insulation, connecting the test equipment (see **'GENERAL DATA'**) between any one of the three stator cables and the stator lamination pack.

(33) Check the nine rectifying diodes, connecting the test equipment (see **'GENERAL DATA'**) between each diode pin and its associated heatsink in the rectifier pack in turn, and then reverse the test equipment connections. Current should flow in one direction only. Renew the rectifier assembly if a diode is faulty.

(34) Check the brush spring pressure and the brush length against the specification given in **'GENERAL DATA'**.

Reassembling

(35) Reverse the procedure in (8) to (26), noting:

(*a*) Support the inner track of the bearing when refitting the rotor to the drive-end bracket.

(*b*) Use 'M' grade 45–55 tin–lead solder to re-make the stator to rectifier pack connections, using a pair of pliers as a thermal shunt to avoid overheating of the diodes.

(*c*) Tighten the alternator pulley nut to 25 lb. ft. (3·46 kg. m.).

(*d*) Refer to the illustration on page Na.14 when

reconnecting the regulator and surge protection device leads to the rectifiers and the brushes.

Refitting

(36) Reverse the procedure in (1) to (7), applying leverage to the alternator drive-end bracket only when tensioning the drive belt. A correctly tensioned drive belt can be deflected a total of $\frac{1}{2}$ in. (13 mm.) by hand pressure at the middle of the belt's longest run.

Section Nb. 7

AUDIBLE WARNING BUZZER

Removing

The audible warning buzzer is positioned under the fascia behind the air-flow rotary control.

(1) Disconnect the battery.

(2) Disconnect the wiring from the buzzer.

(3) Remove the screw retaining the buzzer.

Refitting

(4) Reverse the removing procedure in (1) to (3).

Section Nb. 8

HAZARD WARNING FLASHER UNIT

Removing

(1) Disconnect the battery.

(2) Remove the centre console—Section Rb.1.

(3) Withdraw the flasher unit from its retaining clip.

(4) Disconnect the wiring plug from the flasher unit.

Refitting

(5) Reverse the removing procedure in (1) to (4).

Sprite and Midget. Issue 3. 85737
MG Midget. AKM 2092/1

WIRING DIAGRAMS

Key to wiring diagrams page Nc.2

Midget Mk. III, positive earth (up to 1967) .. .. ⎫
Sprite Mk. IV, positive earth (up to 1967) .. .. ⎬ Diagram 1
⎭

Midget Mk. III, negative earth
    Car Nos. G–AN4–60460 to 74885 (1967–69) .. .. ⎫
Sprite Mk. IV, negative earth ⎬ Diagram 2
    Car Nos. H–AN9–72041 to 85286 (1967–69) .. .. ⎭

Midget Mk. III, negative earth
    Car Nos. G–AN5–74886 to 89514* (1969–70) .. .. ⎫
Sprite Mk. IV, negative earth ⎬ Diagram 3
    Car Nos. H–AN10–85287 to 86302 (1969–70) .. .. ⎭

Midget Mk. III, negative earth
    Car Nos. G–AN5–89515 to 105500 (1970–71) .. .. ⎫
Sprite Mk. IV, negative earth ⎬ Diagram 4
    Car No. H–AN10–86303 onwards (1970–71) .. .. ⎭

Midget Mk. III, negative earth
    Car Nos. G–AN5–105501 to 128262 (1971–73) .. .. **Diagram 9**
    Car Nos. G–AN5–128263 to 138800 (1973) .. .. **Diagram 11****
    Car No. G–AN5–138801 onwards (1973–74) .. .. **Diagram 12****

The following wiring diagrams are for Midget and Sprite cars fitted with electrical equipment in conformity with various local and territorial motor vehicle regulations.

Midget Mk. III, North America, negative earth
    Car Nos. G–AN4–60460 to 66225 (1967–68) .. .. ⎫
Sprite Mk. IV, North America, negative earth ⎬ Diagram 5
    Car Nos. H–AN9–72041 to 77590 (1967–68) .. .. ⎭

Midget Mk. III North America, negative earth
    Car Nos. G–AN4–66226 to 74885 (1968–69) .. .. ⎫
Sprite Mk. IV, North America, negative earth ⎬ Diagram 6
    Car No. H–AN9–77591 onwards (1968–69) .. .. ⎭

Midget Mk. III, North America, negative earth
    Car Nos. G–AN5–74886 to 89514* (1969–70) .. .. **Diagram 7**
    Car Nos. G–AN5–89515 to 105500 (1970–71) .. .. **Diagram 8**
    Car Nos. G–AN5–105501 to 123730 (1971–72) .. .. **Diagram 10**
    Car Nos. G–AN5–123731 to 138800 (1972–73) .. .. **Diagram 13****
    Car No. G–AN5–138801 onwards (1973–74) .. .. **Diagram 14****

* 74901–74947 ⎱ Midget Mk. III
  75701–75735 ⎰ G–AN4 cars.

**These diagrams appear in the Appendix, beginning on page 373.

KEY TO THE WIRING DIAGRAMS

Use the one key to identify components on these wiring diagrams.

Refer to the appropriate wiring diagram, and disregard any additional numbered items appearing in the key and not on a particular diagram.

1. Dynamo/alternator.
2. Control box.
3. Battery.
4. Starter solenoid.
5. Starter motor.
6. Lighting switch.
7. Headlamp dip switch.
8. R.H. headlamp.
9. L.H. headlamp.
10. High-beam warning lamp.
11. R.H. parking lamp.
12. L.H. parking lamp.
13. Panel lamp switch.
14. Panel lamps.
15. Number-plate illumination lamp.
16. R.H. stop and tail lamp.
17. L.H. stop and tail lamp.
18. Stop lamp switch.
19. Fuse unit.
20. Interior courtesy lamp.
21. R.H. door switch.
22. L.H. door switch.
23. Horns.
24. Horn-push.
25. Flasher unit.
26. Combined direction indicator/headlamp flasher.
   or
26. Combined direction indicator/headlamp flasher/headlamp high-glow beam/hornpush switch.
26. Combined direction indicator/headlamp flasher/headlamp high-low beam switch
27. Direction indicator warning lamp.
28. R.H. front flasher lamp.
29. L.H. front flasher lamp.
30. R.H. rear flasher lamp.
31. L.H. rear flasher lamp.
32. Heater or fresh-air motor switch.
33. Heater or fresh-air motor.
34. Fuel gauge.
35. Fuel gauge tank unit.

36. Windscreen wiper switch.
37. Windscreen wiper motor.
38. Ignition/starter switch.
39. Ignition coil.
40. Distributor.
41. Fuel pump.
43. Oil pressure gauge.
44. Ignition warning lamp.
45. Speedometer.
46. Coolant temperature gauge.
49. Reverse lamp switch.
50. Reverse lamp.
57. Cigar-lighter—illuminated.
60. Radio.
64. Bi-metal instrument voltage stabilizer.
65. Luggage compartment lamp switch.
66. Luggage compartment lamp.
67. Line fuse.
77. Windscreen washer pump.
94. Oil filter switch.
95. Tachometer.
105. Oil filter warning lamp.
118. Combined windscreen washer and wiper switch.
152. Hazard warning lamp.
153. Hazard warning switch.
154. Hazard warning flasher unit.
159. Brake pressure warning lamp and lamp test push.
160. Brake pressure failure switch.
168. Ignition key audible warning buzzer.
169. Ignition key audible warning door switch.
170. R.H. front side-marker lamp.
171. L.H. front side-marker lamp.
172. R.H. rear side-marker lamp.
173. L.H. rear side-marker lamp.
198. Driver's seat belt buckle switch.
199. Passenger's seat belt buckle switch.
200. Passenger seat switch.
201. Seat belt warning gearbox switch.
202. 'Fasten belts' warning light.
203. Line diode.

CABLE COLOUR CODE

N. Brown.	P. Purple.	W. White.	K. Pink.
U. Blue.	G. Green.	Y. Yellow.	O. Orange.
R. Red.	L.G. Light Green.	B. Black.	

When a cable has two colour code letters the first denotes the main colour and the second denotes the tracer colour

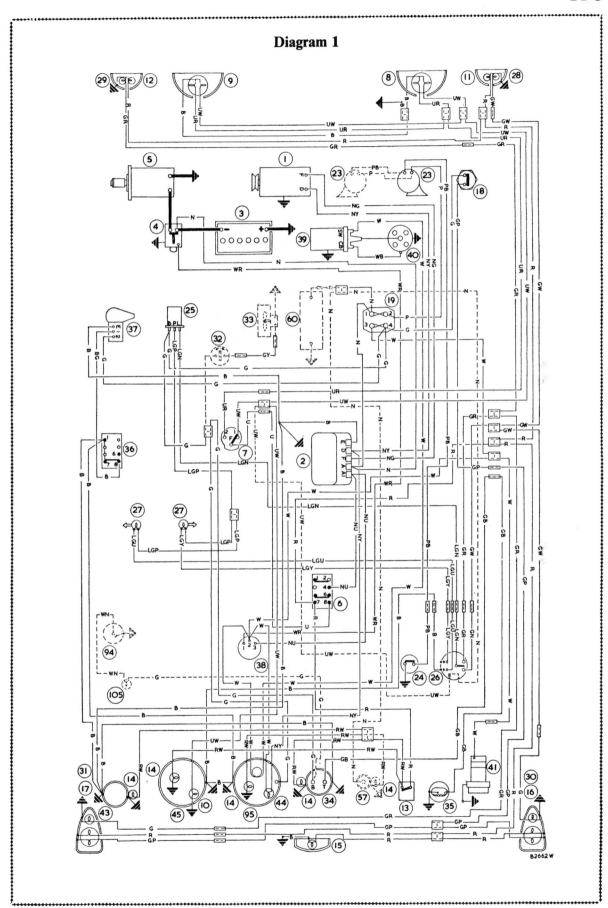

Diagram 1

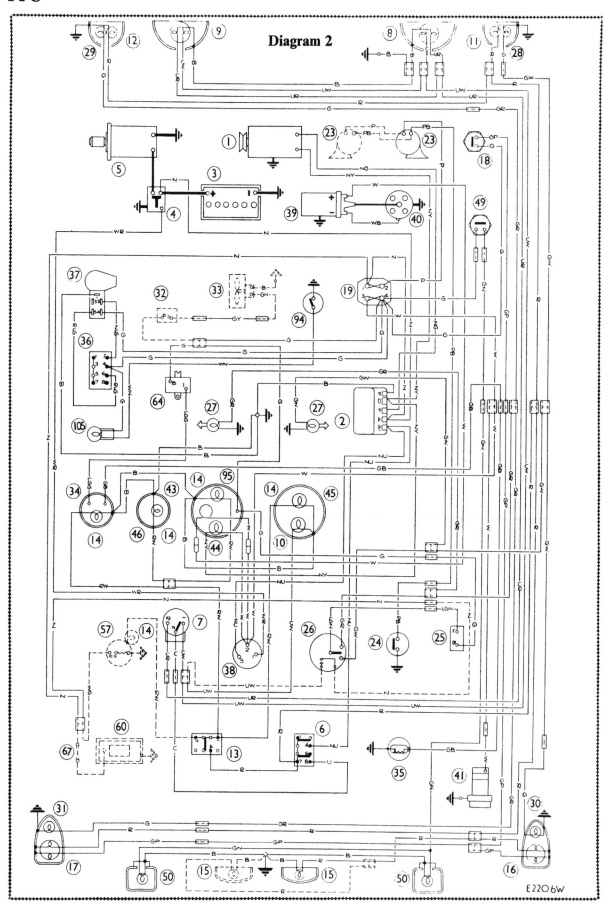

Diagram 2

E 2206W

Sprite and Midget. Issue 1. 82790

Diagram 3

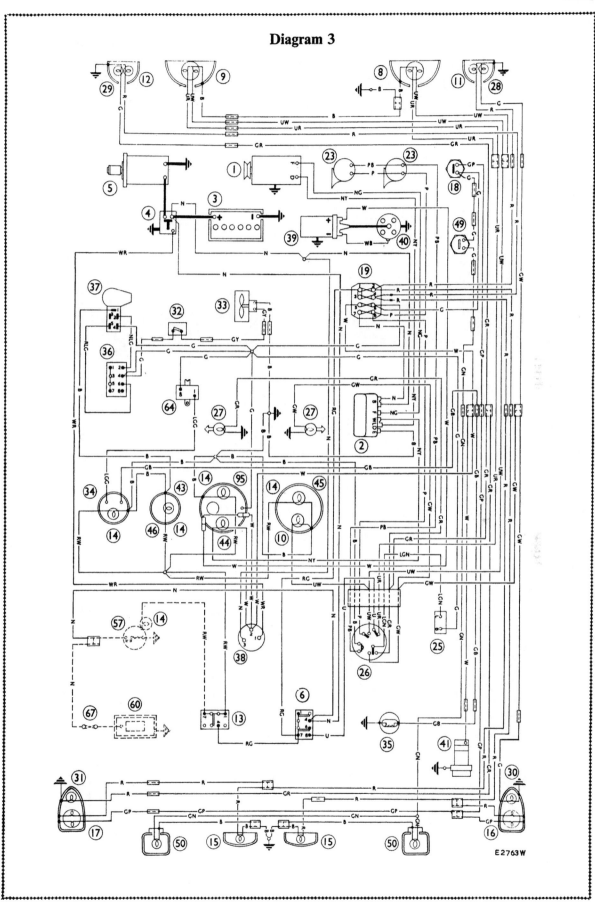

Diagram 4

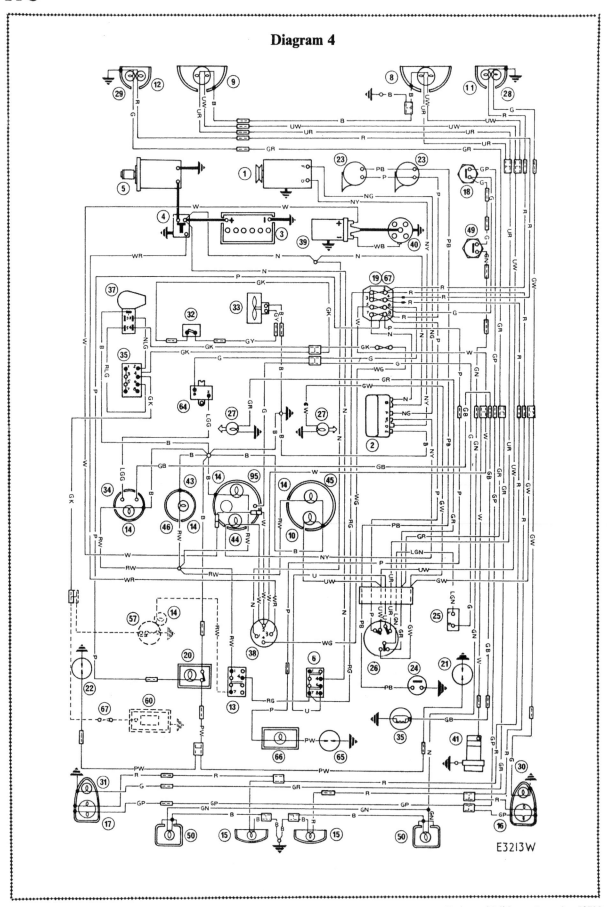

E3213W

Sprite and Midget. Issue 1. 82790

254

Diagram 5

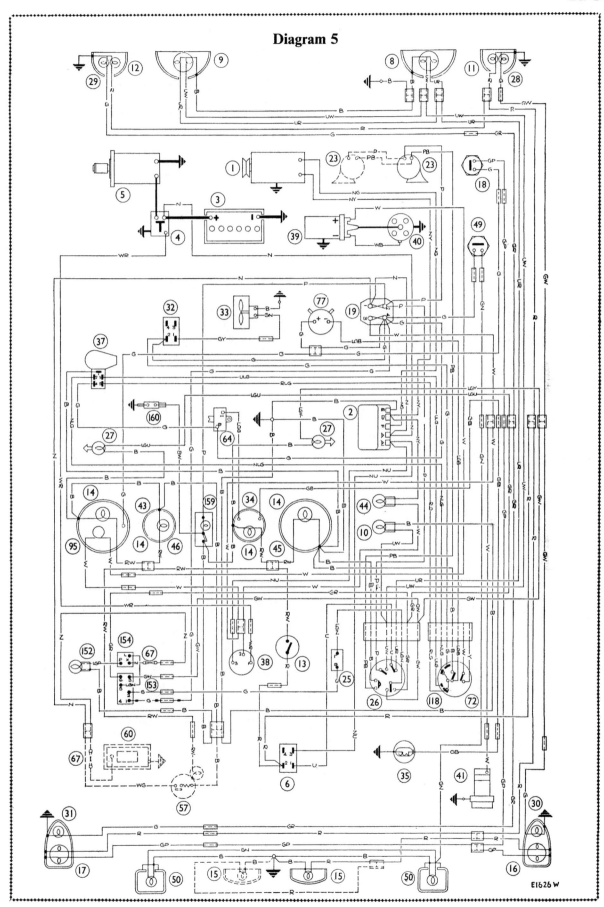

E1626W

Diagram 6

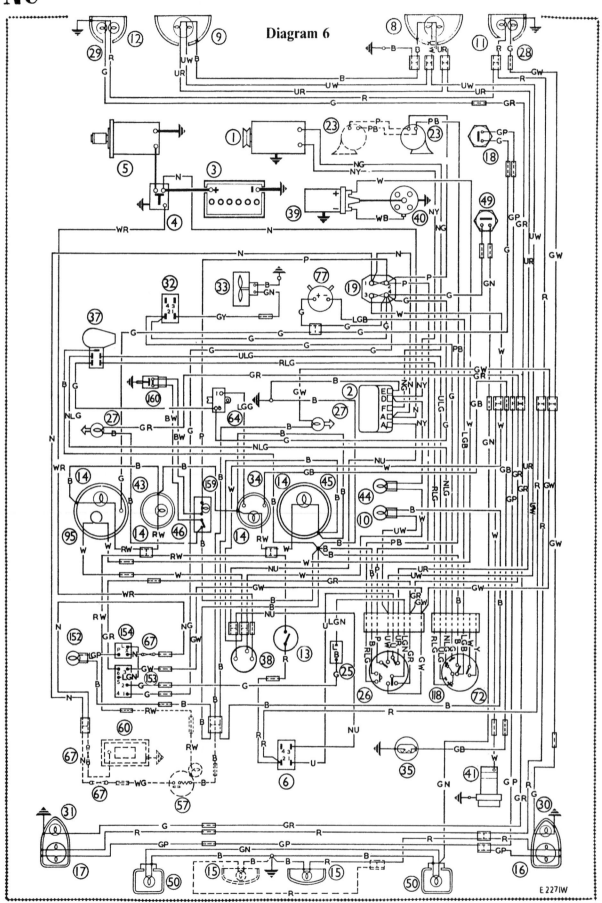

Sprite and Midget. Issue 1. 82790

E 2271W

Diagram 7

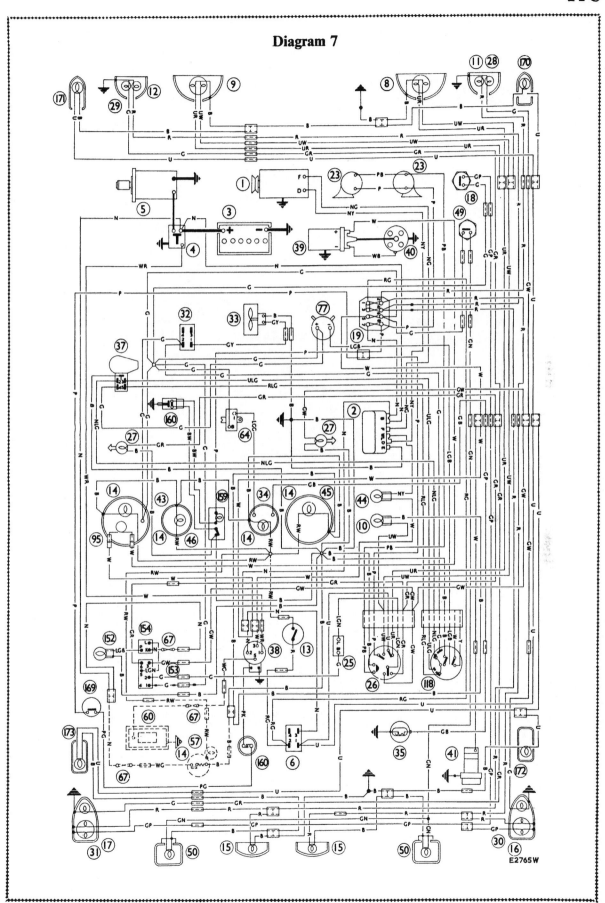

E2765W

Diagram 8

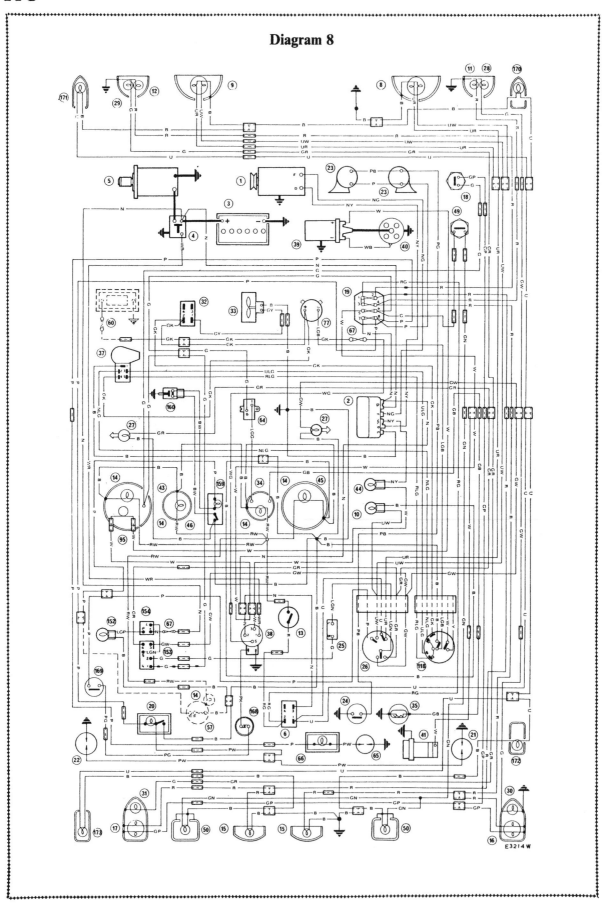

E3214 W

258

Diagram 9

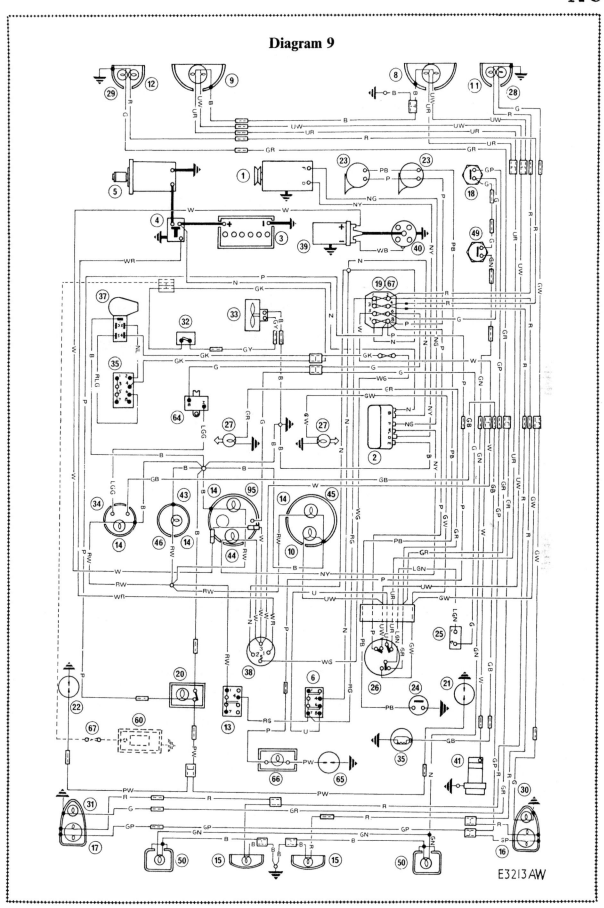

E3213AW

Diagram 10

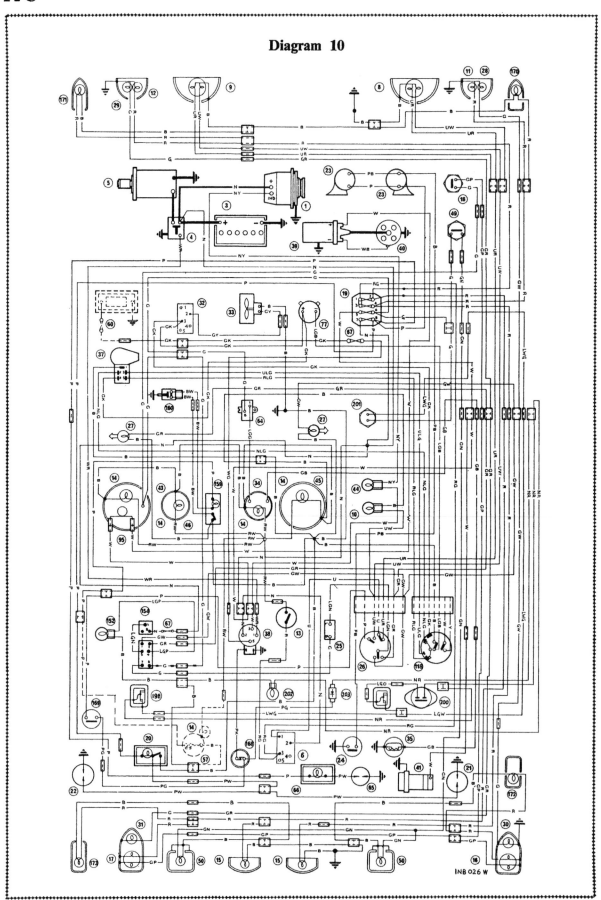

INB 026 W

SECTION O

THE WHEELS AND TYRES

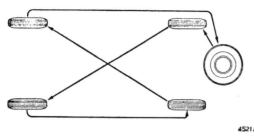

4521A

Fig. O.1

Interchange the road wheels diagonally, bringing the spare wheel into use

Section O.1

TYRE MAINTENANCE

IMPORTANT. The insertion of a plug to repair a puncture in a tubeless tyre must be regarded as a temporary repair only and a permanent vulcanized repair must be made as soon as possible.

(1) Maintain the tyres, including the spare at the recommended pressures given in 'GENERAL DATA'.

(2) Occasionally change the wheels round diagonally and bring the spare into use. See 'TYRE REPLACEMENT'.

(3) Keep the treads free from grit and stones.

(4) Remove oil and grease with petrol (fuel) and wipe dry.

(5) Inspect the tyres for rapid or uneven wear; if present, check the front wheel alignment (Section J.2.).

Section O.2

TYRE REPLACEMENT

Radial-ply tyres (SP)

Radial-ply tyres (SP) should only be fitted in sets of four, although in certain circumstances it is permissible

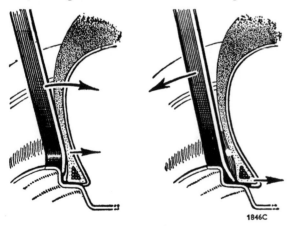

1846C

Fig. O.2

The tyres have wired edges and no attempt must be made to stretch them. If the cover fits tightly on the rim seating it should be freed by using the tyre levers as indicated

to fit a pair on the rear wheels; tyres of different construction must not be used on the same axle. A pair must never be fitted to the front wheels with conventional tyres at the rear. Consult your Distributor or Dealer before changing to radial-ply tyres.

The positional changing of wheels must not be undertaken if radial-ply tyres have been fitted to the rear wheels only. (See Editor's note at end of Section O.)

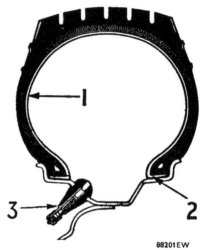

88201EW

Fig. O.3

A section through a tubeless tyre

1. Air-retaining liner.   2. Rubber air seal.
3. Rubber-sealed valve.

Section O.3

JACKING UP

The jack is designed to lift one side of the car at a time, a jacking socket is provided in each door sill panel.

(1) Apply the hand brake, and place a wedge against each side of one of the wheels on the opposite side of the car to the one being jacked.

(2) Remove the rubber plug from the jacking socket and insert the jack lifting arm, ensure that the arm is pushed fully home into the socket and that the top of the jack leans slightly outwards.

(3) Operate the jack handle until the car is raised to the desired height.

NOTE.—Do not work under the car with the jack as the sole support.

Section O.4

Removing   **WHEELS**
Pressed type

(1) Insert the wheel disc lever into the recess provided in the road wheel and lever off the disc, using a sideways motion.

(2) Slacken the wheel nuts.

(3) Jack up the car until the wheel is clear of the ground.

(4) Remove the nuts and withdraw the wheel.

Wire type

(5) Slacken the hub nut using the mallet (winged nuts) or the spanner (octagonal nuts), the nuts are marked with the word 'UNDO' and an arrow.

(6) Jack up the car until the wheel is clear of the ground.

(7) Remove the hub nut and withdraw the wheel from the hub splines.

Inspection

Pressed type

(8) Clean the wheel rim with a wire brush and remove all traces of corrosion.

(9) Examine the rim and the welds or rivets securing the rim to the wheel centre. Damage to the rim may be repaired provided it is confined to the flange lip area.

(10) Inspect the wheel centre for cracks or fractures.

Fig. O.4

A simple tool for fitting tubeless tyre valves

Wire type

(11) Carry out the operations in (8).

(12) Examine the rim and wheel centre. Damage to the rim may be repaired provided it is confined to the flange tip area.

(13) Check the spokes and nipples for security and damage.

(14) Examine the splines in the wheel centre for wear, if the splines are worn, renew the hub centre.

Refitting

Pressed type

(15) Reverse the removing procedure in (1) to (4) noting that the wheel nuts must be fitted with their tapered side towards the wheel and tightened to the torque figure given in 'GENERAL DATA'.

Fig. O.5

Valve for a tubeless tyre

Wire type

(16) Wipe the threads and splines of the hub and wheel and lightly coat them with grease.

(17) Reverse the removing procedure in (5) to (7) and hammer the hub nut tight with the mallet.

Section O.5

VALVES
(Tubeless tyres)

The valves used on tubeless tyres are secured and sealed to the wheel by a stepped flange on the rubber body of the valve and by the air pressure inside the tyre.

A simple but effective tool (see Fig. O.4) for fitting the valves can be made by soldering a valve cap into the end of a short length of steel tube.

To fit a new valve:

(1) Liberally coat the valve body and the perimeter of the valve hole in the wheel with soapy water.

(2) Insert the valve into the hole and screw on the tool.

(3) Pull the tool sharply so that the valve is seated correctly in the wheel.

(4) Fit and inflate the tyre, and check the valve for air-tightness.

Section O.6

WHEEL AND TYRE BALANCE

Unbalance in wheel and tyre assemblies may be responsible for various effects such as wheel wobble, abnormal wear of tyres and suspension parts, vibration in the steering or, in extreme cases, in the whole car, If any of these faults develop, for which no other cause can be found, wheel and tyre balance should be checked and corrected according to instructions supplied by the manufacturer of the balancing machine.

When wheels are to be re-balanced it is essential that the weight of the car be removed from the tyres as soon as possible after a run so that temporary flat spots do not form on the tyres. Nylon tyres are particularly prone to this and re-balancing with the tyres in this condition is pointless.

EDITOR'S NOTES

O. The Wheels and Tires

Removing and Refitting tires

Almost any service station has tire changing equipment which not only does a better job than can be done by hand (in terms of tire damage), but also requires less effort.

SECTION R

THE BODY

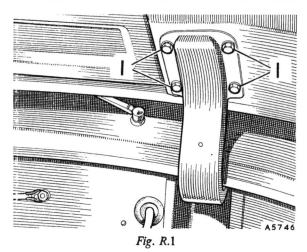

Fig. R.1

The bonnet to hinge securing set screws are shown at (1)

Section R.1

BODYWORK

Coachwork

Regular care of the body finish is necessary if the new appearance of the car exterior is to be maintained against the effects of air pollution, rain, and mud.

Wash the bodywork frequently, using a soft sponge and plenty of water containing a mild detergent. Large deposits of mud must be softened with water before using the sponge. Smears should be removed by a second wash in clean water, and with the sponge if necessary. When dry, clean the surface of the car with a damp chamois-leather. In addition to the regular maintenance, special attention is required if the car is driven in extreme conditions such as sea spray, or on salted roads. In these conditions and with other forms of severe contamination an additional washing operation is necessary, which should include underbody hosing. Any damaged areas should be immediately covered with paint and a complete repair effected as soon as possible. Before touching-in light scratches and abrasions with paint thoroughly clean the surface. Use petrol/white spirit (gasoline/hydro-carbon solvent) to remove spots of tar or grease.

The application of BMC Car Polish is all that is required to remove traffic film and to ensure the retention of the new appearance.

Bright trim

Never use an abrasive on stainless, chromium, aluminium, or plastic bright parts and on no account clean them with metal polish. Remove spots of grease or tar with petrol/white spirit (gasoline/hydrocarbon solvent) and wash frequently with water containing a mild detergent. When the dirt has been removed polish with a clean dry cloth or chamois-leather until bright. Any slight tarnish found on stainless or plated parts which have not received regular washing may be removed with BMC Chrome Cleaner. An occasional application of mineral light oil or grease will help to preserve the finish, particularly during winter, when salt may be used on the roads, but these protectives must not be applied to plastic finishes.

Windshield

If windshield smearing has occurred it can be removed with BMC Screen Cleaner.

Interior

Clean the carpets with a stiff brush or vacuum cleaner, preferably before washing the outside of the car. To thoroughly clean the carpets, apply BMC 2-way Cleaner with a semi-stiff brush, brush vigorously, and remove the surplus with a damp cloth or sponge. Carpets must not be cleaned by the 'dry-clean' process. The upholstery may be cleaned with BMC 2-way Cleaner applied with a damp cloth and a light rubbing action.

Coachwork repairs

The specially designed body jack 18G 308 B is an essential item when rectifying any misalignment of the body construction.

With the addition of a suitable oxy-acetylene outfit any type of mono-construction repair can be effected.

Preservative on Export cars

Certain cars leaving the factory are sprayed with a wax preservative to safeguard their body finish. The wax can be removed by the following procedure. Wash the waxed surfaces liberally with water to remove dirt. To soften the wax apply white spirit, either by using a spray and wiping off with mutton-cloth, or by using the cloth dipped in white spirit.

Polish the body with clean dry mutton cloth.

Cleaning the hood

To clean the hood it is only necessary to use soap and water, with a soft brush to remove any ingrained dirt. Frequent washing with soap and water considerably improves the appearance and wearing qualities of the hood, and it should be washed at least as often as the rest of the car.

Do not use caustic soaps, detergents, or spirit cleaners to clean the hood or the hood back-light.

Section R.2

BONNET

Removing

Remove the set screws securing each hinge to the under side of the bonnet and lift the bonnet complete with the bonnet prop clear of the vehicle.

To assist when refitting, as the fit of the bonnet will be disturbed during removal, it is advisable to mark the position of the hinges on their mounting brackets on the bonnet; this is best carried out by outlining the profile of the hinge levers where they contact the mounting brackets on the bonnet.

Refitting

Reverse the removal procedure.

Section R.3

RADIATOR GRILLE

Removing

The top bolts and nuts securing the radiator grille to the front body section are easily accessible when the bonnet is raised or removed. Working beneath the car, remove the lower grille securing bolts and lift the grille assembly away from the vehicle.

Refitting

Refitting is a reversal of the removal procedure.

Section R.4

BUMPERS

Front

Removing

The front bumper, when fitted, can be lifted away from the vehicle after the securing nuts and washers have been removed.

Refitting

Reverse the removal procedure.

Rear

Removing

Remove the rear bumper bracket securing set screws and remove the bumper, together with its brackets.

Refitting

Reverse the removal procedure.

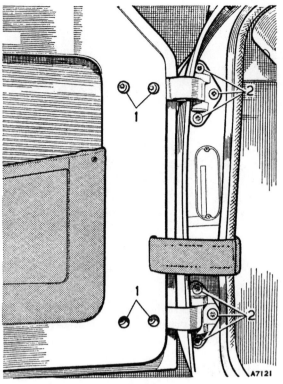

Fig. R.3

Hinge screws

1. Door to hinge screws.   2. Hinge to pillar screws.

Section R.5

WINDSHIELD AND SIDESCREENS

Windshield

Removing

Remove the Phillips screws securing the windshield to the side pillars and slide the windshield out of the pillars. The pillars themselves are attached to the scuttle by one Phillips screw and one bolt, the nut of which is accessible when the door is open.

Refitting

Reverse the removal procedure.

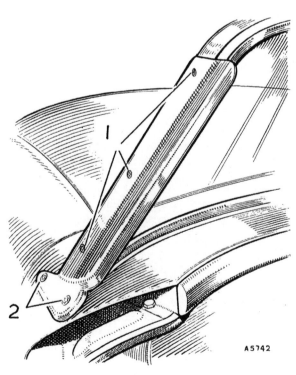

Fig. R.2

Windshield pillar

1. Pillar to body screws.   2. Windshield to pillar screws.

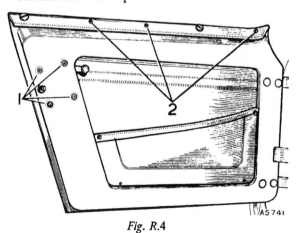

Fig. R.4

The door lock (1) and top moulding fixings (2)

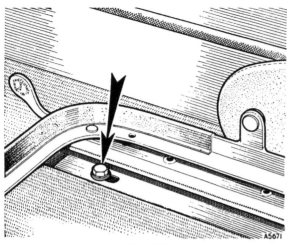

Fig. R.5
Seat frame securing points

Sidescreens

Each sidescreen has two clamping brackets at its base which are held by two large-headed set screws at the door top moulding.

Section R.6

DOORS

Door and hinges
Removing

Both the upper and lower hinge of each door is secured to the door pillar by three Phillips screws. At the door frame each hinge is secured by two Phillips screws.

There is a check strap fitted to each door which must be released when removing a door from the body. This can be done by withdrawing the two set screws from the coupling bracket on the inside of the door pillar. With the door wide open, the hinges can readily be uncoupled from the door pillar and the door and hinges removed.

Refitting

When refitting, reverse the removal procedure.

Door catch and operating handle
Removing

The catch and operating handle complete may be withdrawn by removing the securing set screws positioned inside the door.

Refitting

Reverse the removal procedure.

Section R.7

FASCIA PANEL AND COCKPIT MOULDINGS

Fascia panel
Removing

Remove the steering-wheel as described in Section J. Remove the securing nuts and bolts along the top edge of the fascia.

Remove the Phillips screws securing the fascia at the bottom edge together with the set screws behind the steering-column surround.

Remove the speedometer and tachometer drives at their instrument unions and disconnect the oil pressure pipe from behind the combined oil pressure and water temperature gauge. It is advisable to withdraw the water thermal element from its connection with the radiator.

Release the starter and choke cables. The fascia can then be brought forward into the cockpit, giving access to the rear of each instrument.

Refitting

Reverse the removal procedure.

Cockpit moulding
Removing

The front and rear cockpit mouldings can readily be lifted away from the vehicle after removing the Phillips securing screws.

The door top mouldings are secured in a similar manner.

Refitting

Refitting in each case is a reversal of the removal procedure.

Section R.8

SEATS

Passenger's seat
Removing

Lift out the seat cushion and remove the seat frame securing nuts.

Seat adjustment can be made by releasing the seat frame bracket securing set screws.

Refitting

Refitting is a reversal of the removal procedure.

Driver's seat
Removing

Lift out the seat cushion and remove the frame to runner securing nuts. Remove the bolts and nuts securing the runners to the body floor and lift out the runners.

Refitting

Reverse the removal procedure, ensuring that the seat runner packing pieces are fitted correctly.

An adjustable seat is provided for the driver; it can be moved forwards or rearwards by pushing the lever beneath the seat towards the runner and then moving the seat to the required position and releasing the lever.

Section R.9

HEATER UNIT

Description

The heating and demisting system is designed to provide heated fresh air to the car interior at floor level and to the windshield for demisting and defrosting.

A valve controlling the flow of hot water through the heater unit is fitted at the rear of the cylinder head. The valve is opened by turning in an anti-clockwise direction when heating is required or shut off by turning clockwise when the system is to be used for cool air ventilation.

R.4

Sprite and Midget. Issue 4. 4780

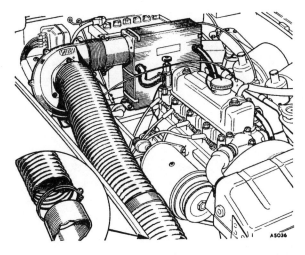

Fig. R.6

Showing the correct location of the heater and inset is the heater blower induction pipe connection at the radiator wing valance

Air is drawn into the system through a forward-facing intake, and the ram effect caused by the car's motion will provide a sufficient quantity of air for the heater's requirements at speeds above 25 m.p.h. (40 km.p.h.). A blower motor is provided for use at lower speeds or when a greater quantity of air is required. The blower is switched on by **turning** the control on the fascia (marked 'H') in a clockwise direction.

A shut-off valve is incorporated in the air intake to prevent fumes entering the car in traffic and is operated by **pulling out** the control marked 'H'. The blower motor must be switched off before the valve is closed and cannot be switched on again until the valve is returned to the open position.

Two doors located forward at either side of the engine scuttle control distribution of air between screen and car interior. For heating, open the doors. For defrosting (i.e. boosting flow of hot air to shield), close the doors.

Fitting

Drain the cooling system (see Section C) and disconnect the battery.

Remove the blanking plate from the battery shelf. Place the heater seal in position over the aperture and fit the heater unit. Secure the blower unit to the right-hand bulkhead and fit the earth tag below to any fixing screw. Connect the blower to the heater with the air hose and secure the intake plate and tube to the radiator wing valance support bracket. Connect the intake tube to the blower and fasten the hose to the inner wheel arch, using the air hose securing clip.

Remove the blanking grommets from either side of the engine scuttle and fit the elbow assemblies. Fit the demisting nozzles and connect the elbows to the demisting nozzles with two lengths of air hose.

When fitting the heater control connections a hole will be found in the fascia panel to the right-hand side of the direction indicator switch; cut a corresponding hole in

the rexine covering and assemble the push-and-turn switch through the hole.

Push the control cable and one lead through the blind grommet provided in the bulkhead on the right-hand side behind the battery. Connect the other lead to the green lead with the brown tracer issuing from the harness below the fascia. Fit the trunnion to the forked lever below the heater intake tube, pull the control knob out to its fullest extent, and rotate the forked lever towards the rear of the car. Press the lever firmly in position, pass the cable inner wire through the trunnion, and tighten the trunnion screw and the cable clamp on the outer casing. Connect the snap connector from the blower to the push-and-turn switch lead, using the connector tube provided. Before fitting the water connections remove the blanking plate from the rear of the cylinder head and fit the water control valve adaptor. Screw the water control valve into the adaptor and ensure that, when tight, it faces the right-hand side of the car. Connect the water control valve to the heater lower radiator pipe with the moulded hose and secure with hose clips. Bore a hole in the engine-to-radiator return hose with a hose cutter and fit the universal hose connector. Secure the copper heater return pipe to the manifold studs, using the existing fittings. Connect the upper heater radiator pipe to the copper tube with rubber hose, and connect the copper pipe to the universal hose connector with a short length of rubber hose. Secure all connections with hose clips and fasten a caution label in a prominent position to one of the water hoses.

Reconnect the battery and refill the cooling system, run the engine at a fast tick-over, and switch on the heater.

NOTE.—If the water return hose does not warm up in a few minutes an air lock may be present in the system, and to clear it the procedure is as follows.

Switch off the engine, remove the hose from the universal connector, and extend by temporary hose so that the water will flow back into the radiator via the filler cap; temporarily plug the lower union.

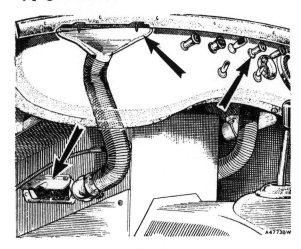

Fig. R.7

The heater blower control on the fascia, the interior heating control doors and the demisting duct

Start the engine and note the water flow into the radiator; when this is smooth and bubble-free, remake the hose-to-union connections and tighten as quickly as possible.

When draining the cooling system the heater may not be completely emptied: therefore, in cold weather only anti-freeze of the ethylene glycol type incorporating the correct type of corrosion inhibitor is suitable, and owners are recommended to use Bluecol Anti-freeze. We also approve the use of any anti-freeze which conforms to Specification B.S.3151 or B.S.3152.

Removing

Removing is a reversal of the fitting procedure.

Section R.10

BODY ALIGNMENT CHECKING JIG

Before checking the body alignment it is most important that the body is raised to a workable height on a level plane. This is done to facilitate body jig checking with the aid of a straight-edge, or with a stout cord stretched from one point to another to obtain measurements between jig components. These measurements should then be checked against the correct dimensions provided in Fig. R.8.

This tool 18G 603 is intended to be used solely as a checking fixture and not as a welding jig. No welding whatsoever is to be undertaken with the body jig in position.

The left-hand inset in Fig. R.8 shows the front section of the jig mounted in position, while the right-hand inset shows the correct method of fitting the rear section to the rear spring mountings.

NOTE.—All jig sections are marked 'FORWARD' to enable easy and correct positioning.

Section R.11

BMC SEAT BELTS

Fitting

Rear wheel arch

Remove the domed nuts and plain washers. Fit the belt bracket, spring washers, and domed nuts in position on the wheel arch mounting studs.

Sill

It will be found necessary to cut the sill trim board covering to expose the 1 in. (25.4 mm.) dia. hole. Assemble the belt bracket, anti-rattle washer (concave face to

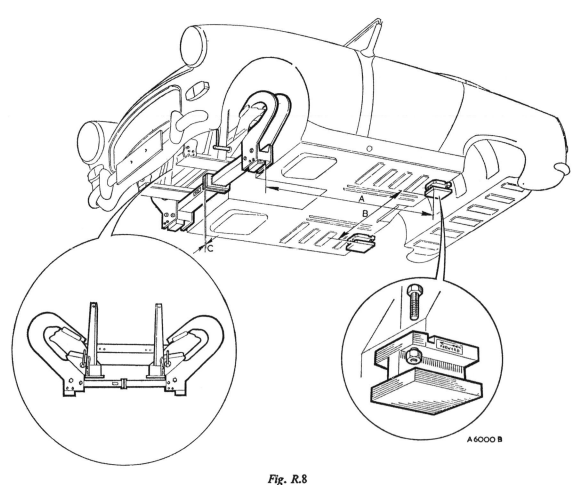

Fig. R.8

A. 63.250 in. (1606.55 mm.).   B. 31.75 in. (806.45 mm.).   C. .250 ± .0625 in. (6.34 ± 1.59 mm.).

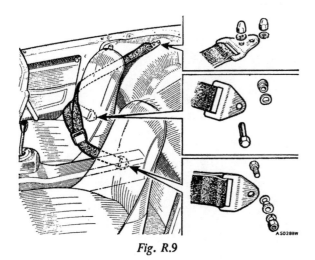

Fig. R.9

The seat belt attachment points and fittings

bracket), and distance piece (shouldered end towards the sill) on to the set screw. Assemble to the sill fixing, ensuring that the belt bracket faces forward along the centre-line of the car.

Propeller shaft tunnel

Remove the rubber plug and cut a 1 in. (25 mm.) dia. hole in the carpet to coincide with the hole in the tunnel. Assemble the belt bracket, anti-rattle washer (concave face to bracket), and distance piece (shouldered end towards the tunnel).

Assemble to the tunnel fixing, ensuring that the belt bracket faces rearwards along the centre-line of the car. Position the spring washer and nut on the inside of the tunnel.

Removing

When removing the seat belt reverse completely the fitting instructions.

Section R.12

STRIKERS

Removing

Mark the position of the striker on the door pillar to assist when refitting. Remove the set screws securing the striker to the door pillar and lift away the assembly.

Refitting

Reverse the removal procedure.

Section R.13

LUGGAGE COMPARTMENT LID

Removing

Remove the set screws securing the hinges to the lid and lift off the assembly.

Refitting

Reverse the removal procedure.

Section R.14

LUGGAGE COMPARTMENT LOCK

Removing

Remove the nuts securing the lid handle to the lid and the set screws and nuts securing the locking plate to the lid and lift away the assembly.

Refitting

Reverse the removal procedure.

(*For* 'PAINT REFINISHING INSTRUCTIONS' *see page* R.8)

PAINT REFINISHING INSTRUCTIONS

Operation	Material	Thinning	Drying times	Application	Instructions
Stripping original paint	Water-soluble paint remover, e.g. Sunbeam Anti-corrosives 'Stripolene 799'	—	—	Brush	Remove the original finish with a scraper after allowing paint-strip 10 minutes to react (repeat if necessary). Wash off thoroughly with cold water, rubbing with wire wool. Dry. Blow out crevices with compressed air. Strip a small area at a time to enable correct neutralizing of the stripper
Metal abrading	Emery-cloth, e.g. Howarth Blue Twill, grade 1½ M	—	—	Hand or disc	Paper thoroughly to ensure satisfactory key. Wipe with cleaner solvent or white spirits
Acid etching	Apply Deoxidine 125 (I.C.I.)	1 part Deoxidine, 1 part water	—	Brush	Apply solution generously and rub in with wire wool. Do not allow Deoxidine solution to dry off before the wash-off operation. Allow approximately five minutes to complete reaction. Wash thoroughly with cold water to remove all traces of Deoxidine solution, followed by a hot rinse. Thoroughly dry surfaces with a clean cloth and blow out crevices with compressed air
Priming	Synthetic primer G.I.P. No. S3178 or	6 to 1 with Z1048	½-hour to 4 hours	Spray	Apply one thin coat of synthetic primer (recommended for superior adhesion) or one thin coat of cellulose primer (recommended for good adhesion). The use of a primer coat enhances adhesion and gives the system a much greater safety factor
	Grey cellulose primer G.I.P. C3971 MOD	50/50 with 2045M	½-hour	Spray	
Applying stopper	Stopper Grey G.I.P. 824D or Stopper Brown G.I.P. 1543	—	6–8 hours, or overnight if possible	Glazing knife	Apply stopper in thin layers, allowing 15–20 minutes' drying between applications. Heavy layers result in insufficient drying, with subsequent risk of cracking
Filling	Primer Filler Grey G.I.P. C3663M	50/50 with 2045M	3–4 hours	Spray	Apply two or three full coats, allowing 15–25 minutes' drying time between coats

Operation	Material	Thinners	Flash off	Method	Remarks
Wet-sanding	Abrasive paper 280 grade	—	—	—	Rub down wet until smooth; a guide coat (a weak contrasting colour) may be used to ensure that the whole surface is rubbed level. Wash off thoroughly with water, sponge all sludge, wash off, dry with clean sponge. Dry off. Minimum of paint should be removed consistent with a satisfactory surface. Film thickness after rubbing should be ·0025 in. (·06 mm.) min.
Applying sealer or undercoat	Sealer Grey or Sealer White or Red undercoat (see BMC Paint Scheme schedule)	50/50 with 2045M	15–20 minutes	Spray	Apply one coat, flash off
Dry-sanding or de-nibbing as required	320 grade paper	—	—	—	De-nib or dry-sand with 320 paper. Clean with white spirit. The grade of paper quoted is from the 3M Company (Minnesota Mining and Mfg. Co. Ltd.); the grade of paper may vary according to manufacture
Applying colour coats	BMC body finishes (see BMC Paint Scheme schedule)	50/50 with 2045M	5–10 minutes' flash between coats. Overnight dry	Spray	Apply two double coats with a 5–10-minute flash between coats. Overnight dry
Flatting colour coat	320 or 400 paper (dependent on conditions)	—	—	Hand	Flat with 320 or 400 paper, dependent on conditions
Applying final colour coat	BMC body finishes (see BMC Paint Scheme schedule)	50/50 with 2045M	Overnight dry	Spray	Spray final double colour coat
Polishing	Cut and polish (see BMC Paint Scheme schedule)	—	—	Hand or machine	The colour coat must be thoroughly dry before polishing. After cutting, burnish to a high gloss with a clean mop, and finally clean with a liquid polish, e.g. Apollo liquid polish

NOTE.—(1) For faster drying of undercoats or local repairs G.I.P. thinners 1523 may be used.
(2) Under extreme circumstances of heat and/or humidity retarder G.I.P. Z1694 can be used added to the 2045M thinners.

THE BODY SHELL COMPONENTS

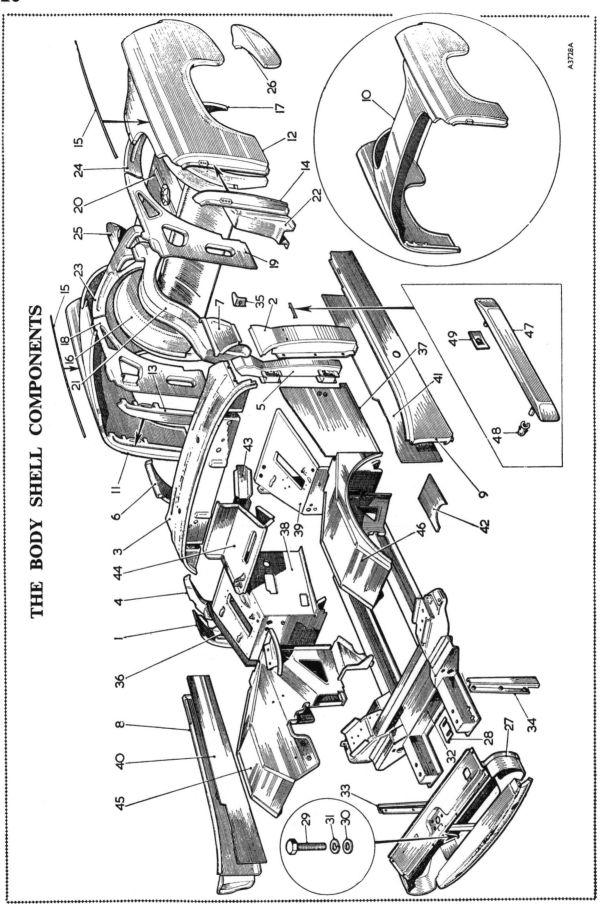

A3728A

KEY TO THE BODY SHELL COMPONENTS

No.	Description
1.	Shroud side panel assembly—R.H.
2.	Shroud side panel assembly—L.H.
3.	Shroud and dash top panel assembly.
4.	'A' post assembly—R.H.
5.	'A' post assembly—L.H.
6.	'A' post to scuttle extension—R.H.
7.	'A' post to scuttle extension—L.H.
8.	Outer sill panel—R.H.
9.	Outer sill panel—L.H.
10.	Rear panel assembly.
11.	Rear wing assembly—R.H.
12.	Rear wing assembly—L.H.
13.	'B' post assembly—R.H.
14.	'B' post assembly—L.H.
15.	Rear wing to panel moulding.
16.	Rear wheel arch panel assembly—R.H.
17.	Rear wheel arch panel assembly—L.H.

No.	Description
18.	Reinforcement assembly—R.H.
19.	Reinforcement assembly—L.H.
20.	Luggage floor panel assembly.
21.	Wheel arch to luggage floor reinforcement member—R.H.
22.	Wheel arch to luggage floor reinforcement member—L.H.
23.	Wheel arch to luggage floor gusset—R.H.
24.	Wheel arch to luggage floor gusset—L.H.
25.	Luggage floor rear extension—R.H.
26.	Luggage floor rear extension—L.H.
27.	Front end assembly.
28.	Front end to underframe shim.
29.	Front end to underframe screw.
30.	Plain washer.
31.	Spring washer.
32.	Front suspension and main beam assembly.
33.	Radiator mounting bracket assembly—R.H.

No.	Description
34.	Radiator mounting bracket assembly—L.H.
35.	Hand brake abutment bracket.
36.	Foot-well outer panel assembly—R.H.
37.	Foot-well outer panel assembly—L.H.
38.	Foot-well front and inner side panel assembly—R.H.
39.	Foot-well front and inner side panel assembly—L.H.
40.	Sill side plate—R.H.
41.	Sill side plate—L.H.
42.	Splash plate—L.H.
43.	Heater support platform.
44.	Heater platform assembly.
45.	Front wheel arch assembly—R.H.
46.	Front wheel arch assembly—L.H.
47.	Shroud moulding.
48.	Speed clip.
49.	Push-on fix.

THE WING COMPONENTS

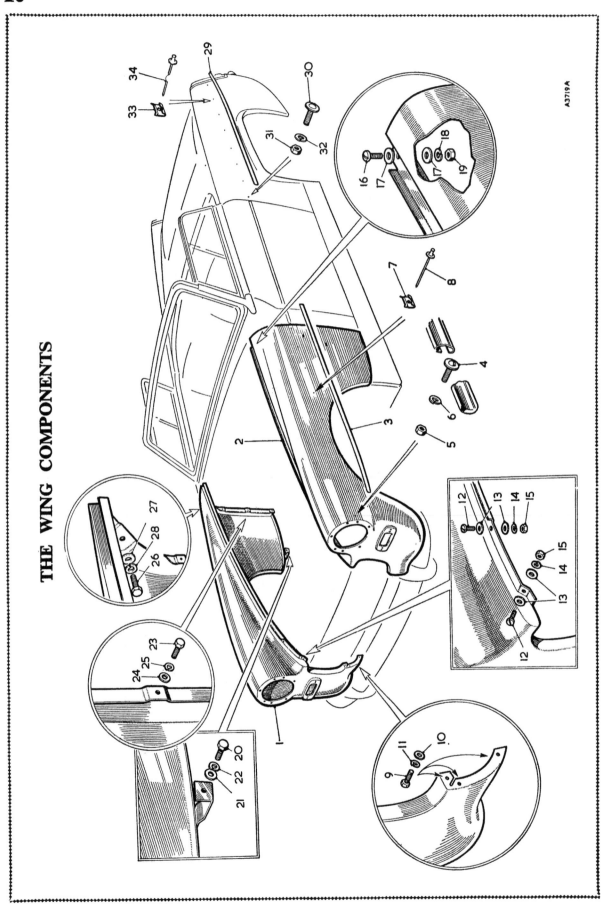

Sprite and Midget. Issue 2. 51576

KEY TO THE WING COMPONENTS

No.	Description
1.	Wing assembly—R.H.
2.	Wing assembly—L.H.
3.	Front wing moulding.
4.	Moulding stud plate.
5.	Nut.
6.	Spring washer.
7.	Moulding clip.
8.	Fixing clip rivet.
9.	Screw.
10.	Washer.
11.	Spring washer.
12.	Screw.

No.	Description
13.	Washer.
14.	Spring washer.
15.	Nut.
16.	Screw.
17.	Washer.
18.	Spring washer.
19.	Nut.
20.	Screw.
21.	Washer.
22.	Spring washer.
23.	Screw.

No.	Description
24.	Washer.
25.	Spring washer.
26.	Screw.
27.	Washer.
28.	Spring washer.
29.	Rear wing moulding.
30.	Moulding stud plate.
31.	Nut.
32.	Spring washer.
33.	Moulding clip.
34.	Fixing clip rivet.

Sprite and Midget. Issue 2. 51576   R.13

277

THE BONNET ASSEMBLY COMPONENTS

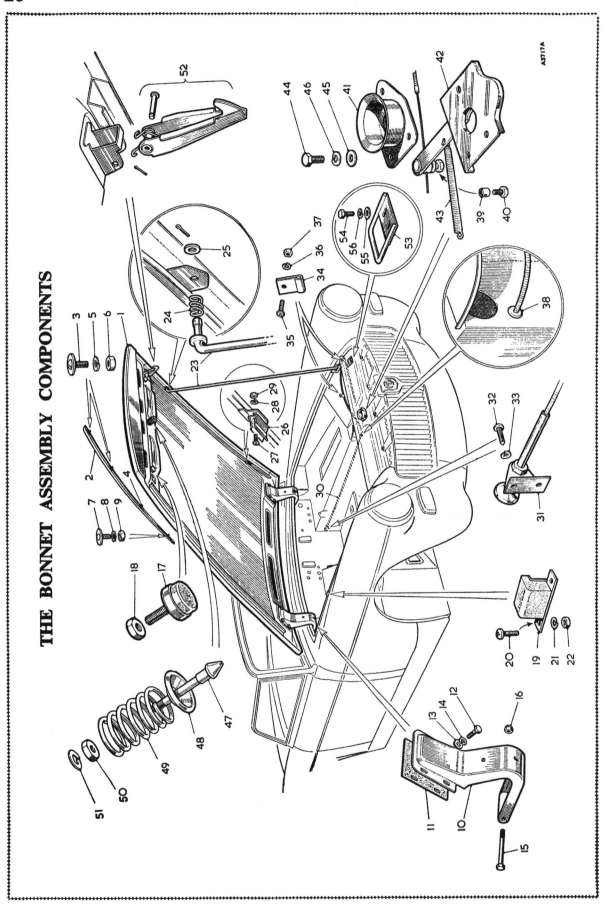

A3717A

KEY TO THE BONNET ASSEMBLY COMPONENTS

No.	Description	No.	Description	No.	Description
1.	Bonnet top assembly.	20.	Drain channel screw.	39.	Cable clamp.
2.	Centre moulding.	21.	Spring washer.	40.	Clamp screw.
3.	Front moulding plate stud.	22.	Nut.	41.	Lock locating cup.
4.	Centre moulding plate stud.	23.	Prop rod.	42.	Catch plate.
5.	Spring washer.	24.	Prop rod spring.	43.	Catch plate spring.
6.	Nut.	25.	Washer.	44.	Cup to locking platform screw.
7.	Rear moulding plate stud.	26.	Prop rod clip.	45.	Washer.
8.	Spring washer.	27.	Clip screw.	46.	Spring washer.
9.	Nut.	28.	Spring washer.	47.	Bonnet lock pin.
10.	Hinge.	29.	Nut.	48.	Bonnet lock thimble.
11.	Hinge packing.	30.	Bonnet release cable.	49.	Bonnet lock spring.
12.	Bonnet to hinge screw.	31.	Bracket.	50.	Pin to bonnet locknut.
13.	Plain washer.	32.	Screw.	51.	Spring washer.
14.	Spring washer.	33.	Spring washer.	52.	Safety catch assembly.
15.	Bulkhead to hinge bolt.	34.	Cable clip.	53.	Safety catch bracket.
16.	Nut.	35.	Clip screw.	54.	Bracket fixing screw.
17.	Bonnet buffer.	36.	Spring washer.	55.	Washer.
18.	Buffer to bonnet locknut.	37.	Nut.	56.	Spring washer.
19.	Side buffer.	38.	Cable grommet.		

Sprite and Midget. Issue 2. 51576 R.15

279

THE BOOT LID COMPONENTS

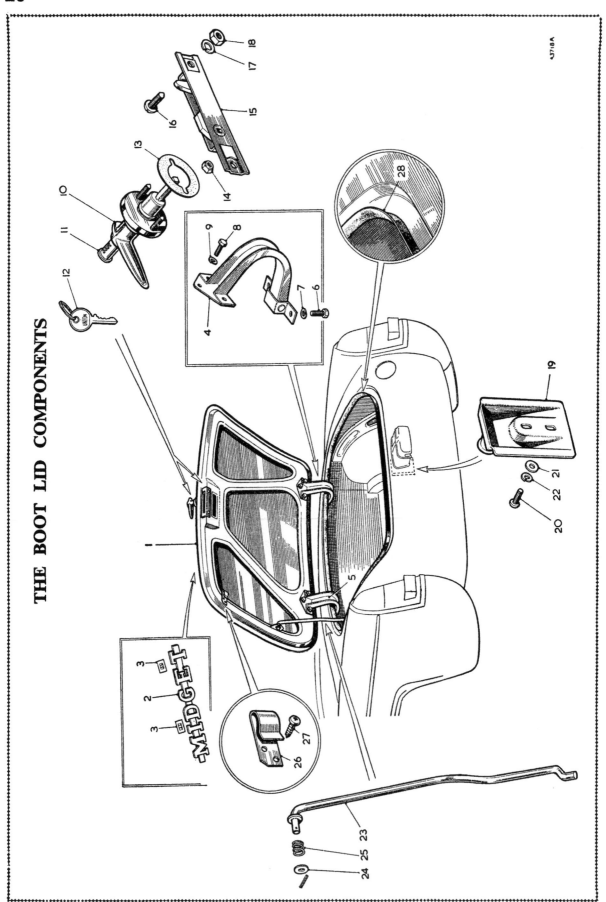

Sprite and Midget. Issue 2. 51576

KEY TO THE BOOT LID COMPONENTS

No.	Description
1.	Boot lid assembly.
2.	'Midget' or 'Sprite' motif.
3.	Push-on fix.
4.	Boot lid hinge—R.H.
5.	Boot lid hinge—L.H.
6.	Hinge screw.
7.	Spring washer.
8.	Hinge to boot lid screw.
9.	Spring washer.
10.	Locking handle assembly.

No.	Description
11.	Barrel lock.
12.	Key.
13.	Handle seating washer.
14.	Handle to boot lid nut.
15.	Lock assembly.
16.	Screw.
17.	Spring washer.
18.	Nut.
19.	Striker plate.

No.	Description
20.	Screw.
21.	Plain washer.
22.	Spring washer.
23.	Prop rod.
24.	Plain washer.
25.	Spring.
26.	Prop rod clip.
27.	Screw.
28.	Boot lid sealing rubber.

Section R.16

HORIZONTAL ALIGNMENT CHECK

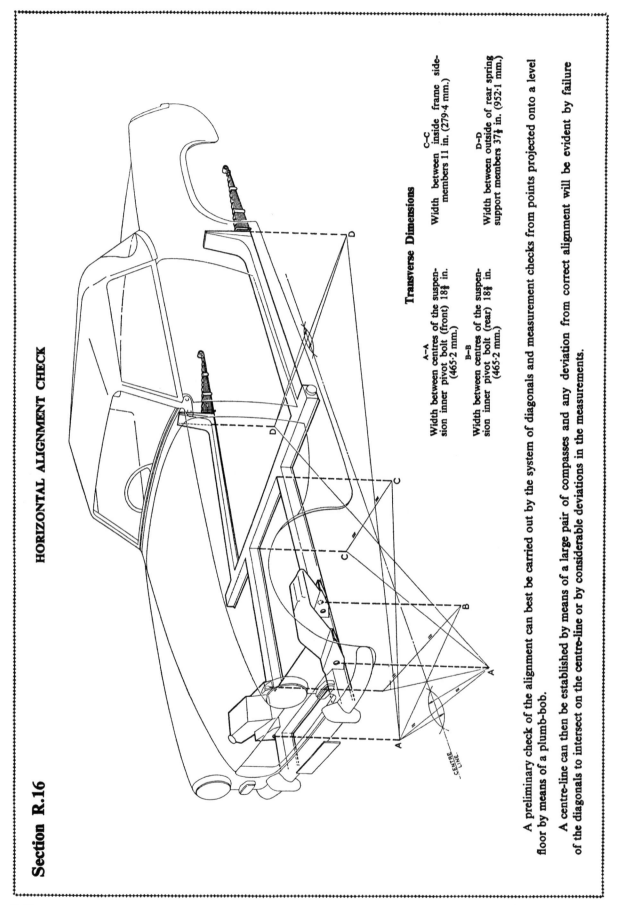

Transverse Dimensions

A–A
Width between centres of the suspension inner pivot bolt (front) 18⅜ in. (465·2 mm.)

B–B
Width between centres of the suspension inner pivot bolt (rear) 18⅜ in. (465·2 mm.)

C–C
Width between inside frame side-members 11 in. (279·4 mm.)

D–D
Width between outside of rear spring support members 37⅝ in. (952·1 mm.)

A preliminary check of the alignment can best be carried out by the system of diagonals and measurement checks from points projected onto a level floor by means of a plumb-bob.

A centre-line can then be established by means of a large pair of compasses and any deviation from correct alignment will be evident by failure of the diagonals to intersect on the centre-line or by considerable deviations in the measurements.

Section Ra

THE BODY

The information given in this Section refers specifically to the Sprite (Mk. III and IV) and Midget (Mk. II and III) and must be used in conjunction with Section R

	Section
Crash rail	Ra.2
Doors	
Glass	Ra.4
Glass regulators	Ra.7
Interior handles and window regulators	Ra.8
Lock and remote control	Ra.10
Outer handles	Ra.9
Striker	Ra.11
Trim pad	Ra.6
Fascia..	Ra.1
Heater	Ra.15
Radiator grille	Ra.14
Seat belts	Ra.12
Seats	Ra.13
Ventilator	Ra.5
Windshield	Ra.3

Section Ra.1

FASCIA

Removing

Remove the set screws at the far ends of the fascia panel. Remove the steady bracket securing set screws. Disconnect and lower the steering-column (Section J). Remove the fascia securing set screws beneath the crash rail and lower the panel to disconnect the instruments and switches. Remove the panel assembly.

Refitting

Reverse the removal procedure.

Section Ra.2

CRASH RAIL

Removing

Remove the fascia (Section Ra.1). Remove the crash rail securing nuts and drive screws and lift off the assembly.

Refitting

Reverse the removal procedure.

Section Ra.3

WINDSHIELD

Removing

Remove the fascia (Section Ra.1). Remove the windshield to 'A' post securing set screws and the centre stay securing set screws. Lift off the windshield assembly.

Refitting

Reverse the removal procedure, ensuring that the packing washers are replaced in their original positions.

Section Ra.4

DOOR WINDOW GLASS

Removing

Remove the door-pull, internal door handle, and window regulator handle (Section Ra.8). Remove the door trim pad (Section Ra.6) and the drive screws securing the backing panel to the door.

Remove the inner door cappings and the set screws securing the rear glass guide channel to the door.

Remove the set screws and nuts securing the top of the ventilator to the door. Remove the front channel set screws and the ventilator steady set screw. Remove the glass stop at the bottom of the front channel and the glass stop in the bottom of the door. Remove the regulator securing set screws and the regulator extension set screws. Lower the window and remove the ventilator assembly. Lift out the glass.

Refitting

Reverse the removal procedure.

Section Ra.5

VENTILATOR

Removing

Remove the trim pad, door handles, and window regulator handle (see Section Ra.8). Remove the set screws and nuts securing the ventilator top to the door. Remove the ventilator steady set screw and the set screws securing the front window channel to the bottom of the door. Remove the front door channel, and window stop and lift out the ventilator assembly.

Refitting

Reverse the removal procedure.

Section Ra.6

TRIM PAD

Removing

Remove the interior door handle, door-pull, and window regulator handle (Section Ra.8). Lever the door trim pad away from the door panel and withdraw the trim pad from the padded sill roll.

Refitting

Reverse the removal procedure.

Section Ra.7

WINDOW REGULATORS

Removing

Remove the interior door handle, door-pull, and window regulator handle (Section Ra.8). Remove the door trim pad assembly (Section Ra.6).

Remove the regulator securing screws and the regulator bracket securing screws. Release the window regulator arc from the bottom of the window glass. Lift the window glass up to clear the regulator and remove the regulator and bracket assembly.

Refitting

Reverse the removal procedure when refitting.

Section Ra.8

WINDOW REGULATOR AND INTERIOR DOOR HANDLES

Removing

Window regulator handle
(1) Close the window.
(2) Press the spring cup into the escutcheon plate.
(3) Remove handle retaining pin and withdraw the handle.

Pull handle
(4) Prise off the end caps covering the pull handle screws (Midget Mk. III from Car No. G–AN5–105501).
(5) Remove the screws securing the pull handle to the door and lift off the handle.

Ra.2

Sprite and Midget. Issue 5. 82790

284

Door opening handle

(6) Remove the screw securing the handle to the lock, and withdraw the handle.

Escutcheon plate

(7) Remove the door opening handle (6)

(8) Remove the two screws securing the escutcheon plate and withdraw the plate. The escutcheon plate is removed complete with the locking catch.

Refitting

Window regulator handle

(9) Reverse the removing procedure in (1) to (3).

Pull handle

(10) Reverse the removing procedure in (4) and (5) as applicable.

Escutcheon plate

(11) Reverse the removing procedure in (7) to (8) noting that the locking catch on the escutcheon plate must be engaged in the square hole in the lock linkage.

Door opening handle

(12) Reverse the removing procedure in (6.)

Section Ra.9

OUTER DOOR HANDLE

Removing

(1) Close the window.

(2) Remove the door trim pad (Section Ra.6).

(3) Remove the nut and washers from the handle securing stud.

(4) Remove the screw and washers retaining the push button end of the handle.

(5) Withdraw the handle from the door.

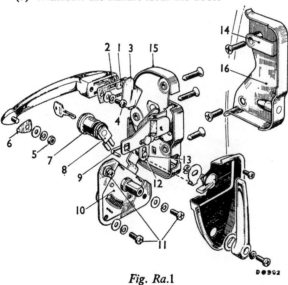

Fig. Ra.1

The lock assembly

1.	Plunger bolt.	9.	Locking lever.
2.	Locknut.	10.	Remote control.
3.	Lock contactor.	11.	Securing screws.
4.	Handle retaining screw.	12.	Stud.
5.	Stud nut.	13.	Operating lever.
6.	Seating washer.	14.	Anti-burst strap.
7.	Spring collar.	15.	Lock assembly.
8.	Lock fork.	16.	Striker.

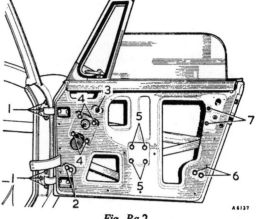

Fig. Ra.2

The door assembly

1. Door hinge securing set screws.
2. Ventilator securing set screws.
3. Regulator arm stop.
4. Regulator securing set screws.
5. Regulator extension securing set screws.
6. Rear door glass guide channel securing set screws.
7. Door lock remote control securing set screws.

Refitting

(6) Position the handle on the door with its seating washers correctly located.

(7) Check the clearance between the plunger bolt and the lock contactor from inside the door. The clearance must be a minimum of $\frac{1}{32}$ in. (·79 mm.), slacken the locknut and adjust the length of the plunger bolt to obtain the correct clearance.

(8) Reverse the removal procedure in (1) to (5), and check for correct functioning.

Section Ra.10

DOOR LOCK AND REMOTE CONTROL

NOTE. Before attempting to remove any part of the door lock mechanism because of faulty operation, first check that the unserviceability is not caused by incorrect adjustment or installation.

Removing

Remote control

(1) Remove the door trim pad (Section Ra.6).

(2) Remove the remote control securing screws.

(3) Move the remote control inwards, to disengage the stud from the slot in the lock operating lever, then withdraw the assembly.

Lock

(4) Remove the lock securing screws and withdraw the assembly.

Refitting

Lock

(5) Depress the lock contactor so that the latch is in the open position.

(6) Position the assembly in the door ensuring that the locking lever engages in the private lock operating fork.

(7) Screw in and tighten the lock securing screws, noting that the short screw is fitted in the lower hole.

Remote control

(8) Position the assembly in the door so that the stud engages in the slot in the lock operating lever.

(9) Fit, but do not tighten the securing screws.

(10) Move the remote control towards the lock until the lock operating lever is up against its stop.

(11) Refit the trim pad, and check the door lock for correct functioning.

Section Ra.11

STRIKER

Removing

(1) Remove the securing screws and lift off the striker and any shims fitted behind it.

Refitting

(2) Position the striker and shims.

(3) Screw in, but do not fully tighten the securing screws.

(4) Close the door and check the clearance between the face of the striker and the lock face. The clearance must be between $\frac{1}{32}$ in. ($\cdot$79 mm.) and $\frac{1}{16}$ in. (1$\cdot$59 mm.), adjust the clearance by increasing or decreasing the thickness of the shims fitted behind the striker.

(5) When the correct clearance in (4) has been obtained, tighten the securing screws and check that the door closes easily without rattling, lifting, or dropping.

NOTE.—The striker must be retained in the horizontal plane relative to the door axis.

(6) Check the door lock for correct functioning.

Section Ra.12

SEAT BELTS

The following instructions refer to fitting the approved 'Kangol Magnet' seat belt to the fixing points incorporated in the body structure.

Rear wheel arch

Sprite Mk. III and Midget Mk. II

(1) Remove the two domed nuts and plain washers from the fixing studs.

(2) Fit the bracket on the studs and secure it using plain washers, spring washers, and the domed nuts.

Sprite Mk. IV and Midget Mk. III

(3) Remove the plastic cap from the fixing boss.

First type seat belt

(4) Fit a spring washer to the short $\frac{7}{16}$ in. bolt, pass the bolt through the centre of the three holes in the belt bracket, and secure the bracket to the fixing boss.

Second type seat belt

(5) Fit the belt bracket on the short $\frac{7}{16}$ in. bolt, followed by a waved washer and a distance piece, with the small diameter end of the distance piece towards the bolt head.

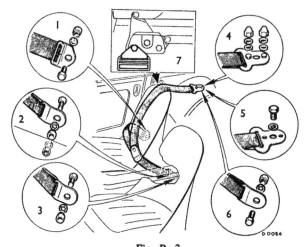

Fig. Ra.3

Seat belt fixings

1. Sill (all models).
2. Drive shaft tunnel (Sprite Mk. III; Midget Mk. II).
3. Drive shaft tunnel (Sprite Mk. IV; Midget Mk. III).
4. Wheel arch (Sprite Mk. III; Midget Mk. II).
5. Wheel arch, first type belt (Sprite Mk. IV; Midget Mk. III).
6. Wheel arch, second type belt (Sprite Mk. IV; Midget Mk. III).
7. Stowage clip, second type belt.

(6) Secure the assembled bracket to the fixing boss.

Sill

(7) Locate the fixing point (its position can be felt through the trim) and cut the trim to expose the fixing hole.

(8) Fit the belt bracket to one of the $\frac{7}{16}$ in. bolts, followed by a waved washer and a distance piece (small diameter end towards the bolt head).

(9) Screw the assembled bracket to the sill.

Drive shaft tunnel

Sprite Mk. III and Midget Mk. II

(10) Remove the plug from the fixing point on the same side of the tunnel as the seat for which the belt is being fitted.

(11) Cut a 1 in. (25$\cdot$4 mm.) diameter hole in the covering over the fixing point.

(12) Fit the bracket of the short belt to the remaining $\frac{7}{16}$ in. bolt followed by a waved washer and a distance piece (small diameter end towards the bolt head.)

(13) Secure the assembled bracket with the spring washer and nut fitted from inside the tunnel.

Sprite Mk. IV and Midget Mk. III

(14) Fit the belt bracket of the short belt to the remaining $\frac{7}{16}$ in. bolt followed by a waved washer and a distance piece (smaller diameter end towards the head of the bolt).

(15) Secure the assembled bracket to the exposed fixing boss on the same side of the tunnel as the seat to which the belt is being fitted.

Stowage clip second type belt

(16) Fit the stowage clip under the head of the front hood bracket securing screw.

Sprite and Midget. Issue 4. 82790

Section Ra.13

SEATS
(Later cars)

Removing

(1) Move the seat forward and remove the screw, spring washer and plain washer securing the rear of the seat runner to the body.

(2) Under the body of the car, remove the nut, spring and plain washers securing the front of the seat runner to the body.

(3) Remove the seat.

Refitting

(4) Reverse the removal procedure. Ensure the carpet is correctly positioned before finally tightening the runner securing nuts and bolts.

Section Ra.14

RADIATOR GRILLE

Removing

(1) Remove the four screws securing the grille to the bonnet lock platform.

(2) From each side of the grille remove the three self-tapping screws.

(3) From below the car, just behind the bumper, remove the two self-tapping screws and washers.

(4) Remove the grille assembly.

Refitting

Reverse sequence (1) to (4).

Section Ra.15

HEATER
(Midget Mk. III from Body No. GBE–100651 and Sprite Mk. IV from Body No. GUN–151301)

NOTE.—To remove the blower motor only, carry out operations 1, 2, 10 and 11.

Removing

(1) Disconnect and remove the battery and the battery tray.

(2) Disconnect the blower motor cables from the wiring harness at the snap connectors.

(3) Remove the bolt to release the heater control cable from the bracket on the heater air intake tube.

(4) Slacken the set bolt and release the heater control inner cable from the lever on the heater air intake flap valve spindle.

(5) Disconnect the air hose from the heater air intake tube.

(6) Slacken the clips and detach the two water hoses from the heater unit.

(7) Remove the six screws to release the heater unit from its platform on the dash bulkhead.

Dismantling

(8) Detach the four spring clips to release the heater cover complete with blower motor from the heater body.

(9) Withdraw the matrix from the heater body.

(10) Remove the three screws and withdraw the blower motor complete with fan from the heater unit cover.

(11) Drive the motor spindle out of the fan to release the fan from the motor.

(12) Remove the three screws to release the air intake tube from the heater unit.

(13) Remove the two screws and withdraw the spindle to release the air intake valve from the intake tube.

Reassembling

(14) Reverse the procedure in (8) to (13) ensuring that the air intake valve lever is on the heater body side of the valve spindle.

Refitting

(15) Reverse the procedure in (1) to (7), but before connecting the air hose to the heater air intake tube, check the operation of the air intake valve. If necessary, adjust the positions of the control inner and outer cables to give full opening and closing of the valve.

Sprite and Midget. Issue 2. 29459
MG Midget. AKM 2092/1

287

*Ra.*5

Section Rb

THE BODY

The information given in this Section refers specifically to service operations on, or affected by equipment fitted to the Sprite Mk. IV and Midget Mk. III in conformity with local and territorial requirements, and must be used in conjunction with Section R and Section Ra.

Section Rb.1

CONSOLE

Removing

(1) Disconnect the battery.

(2) Remove the screw securing the left-hand front end of the parcel shelf.

(3) Remove the console retaining screws.

(4) Withdraw the console rearwards, tilting the top forward slightly to clear the under edge of the fascia.

(5) Disconnect the console electrical wiring from the snap connectors.

(6) Remove the console complete with switches and fittings.

Refitting

(7) Reverse the removing procedure in (1) to (6).

Section Rb.2

FASCIA

Removing

(1) Disconnect the battery.

(2) Drain the cooling system (Section Ca.1).

(3) Remove the retaining gland nut and withdraw the temperature gauge sensing bulb from the cylinder head.

(4) Remove the clips retaining the oil pressure and temperature gauge pipes.

(5) Disconnect the oil pressure gauge pipe at the flexible pipe connection on the bulkhead.

(6) Disconnect the choke control cable from the carburetters.

(7) Remove the console (Section Rb.1).

(8) Disconnect the speedometer cable from the back of the instrument, and remove the speedometer.

(9) Withdraw the heater air control knob, and remove the control retaining nut.

(10) Remove the four nuts securing the upper edge of the fascia and the four screws securing the fascia lower fixing brackets.

(11) Pull the fascia away from the body, disconnect the electric wiring from the instruments and switches, and withdraw the warning and panel lamp holders.

(12) Raise the left-hand end of the fascia sufficiently to clear the steering column switch cowl, tilt the top of the fascia forward slightly and withdraw it, at the same time ease the choke cable, temperature and oil pressure gauge pipes from their grommets in the bulkhead.

Refitting

(13) Reverse the removing procedure in (1) to (12).

Section Rb.3

CUBBY BOX ASSEMBLY
(Midget Mk. III from Car No. G–AN5–105501)

Removing

Cubby box

(1) Remove the two screws retaining the cubby box lid stay to the trim pad.

(2) Remove the seven retaining screws.

(3) Carefully withdraw the cubby box.

Cubby box lid lock

(4) Unscrew the lock bezel.

(5) Remove the two screws and the retainer.

(6) Withdraw the lock.

Refitting

Cubby box

(7) Reverse the removing procedure in (1) to (3).

Cubby box lid lock

(8) Reverse the removing procedure in (4) to (6).

SECTION S

SERVICE TOOLS

All Service tools mentioned in this Manual are only obtainable from the tool manufacturer:
Messrs. V. L. Churchill & Co. Ltd.,
P.O. Box No. 3,
London Road, Daventry,
Northants, England.

Operation	Tool No.	Page No.
ENGINE		
Camshaft liner reaming	18G 123 A	S.6
	18G 123 AQ	S.6
	18G 123 AT	S.6
	18G 123 BA	S.6
	18G 123 BB	S.6
	18G 123 BC	S.6
	18G 123 AN	S.6
	18G 123 AP	S.6
	18G 123 B	S.6
	18G 123 AL	S.6
Camshaft liner, removing and replacing	18G 124 A	S.6
	18G 124 K	S.6
	18G 124 B	S.6
	18G 124 M	S.6
Crankshaft gear and pulley, removing	18G 2	S.4
Starting nut spanner	18G 98 A	S.5
Gudgeon pin, removing and replacing (1275 cc)	18G 587	S.12
	18G 1002	S.13
Oil pump relief valve seat, grinding	18G 69	S.5
Piston refitting	18G 55 A	S.5
Timing cover and oil seal, replacing:	18G 134	S.6
	18G 134 BD	S.7
with external seal	18G 138	S.7
with internal seal	18G 1044	S.13
Torque spanners	18G 372	S.11
	18G 537	S.12
	18G 587	S.12
Valve rocker bush, removing and replacing	18G 226	S.9
	18G 226 A	S.9
Valve seat cutting	18G 27	S.4
	18G 167	S.8
	18G 167 A	S.8
	18G 167 B	S.8
	18G 167 C	S.8
	18G 167 D	S.8

	Operation							Tool No.	Page No.
Valve seat grinding	..	..	..	..	..	..	..	18G 29	S.4
								18G 29 B	S.4
Valves, removing and refitting	..	..	..	..	..	..	18G 45	S.5

CLUTCH

Dismantling and reassembling (coil spring type)	..	..	..	18G 99 A	S.5
Refitting	..	..	..	..	..	..	..	..	18G 139	S.7

GEARBOX

Layshaft, replacing	..	..	..	..	..	..	..	18G 194	S.9
								18G 471	S.11
Oil seal, removing and replacing	..	..	..	..	..	..	18G 134	S.6
								18G 134 L	S.7
								18G 389	S.11
								18G 389 A	S.11
								18G 488	S.12
Synchromesh unit, reassembly	..	..	..	..	..	..	18G 144	S.7

PROPELLER SHAFT

Flange, removing and replacing	..	..	..	..	..	18G 2	S.4
						18G 138	S.7

REAR AXLE AND REAR SUSPENSION

Bevel pinion bearing inner race, removing and replacing	..	..	18G 285	S.10
Bevel pinion bearing outer race, removing and replacing	..	..	18G 264	S.10
			18G 264 D	S.10
			18G 264 E	S.10
Bevel pinion bearing preload gauge	..	..	..	..	..	18G 207	S.9
Bevel pinion and differential bearing setting gauge	..	..	..	18G 191	S.9
				18G 191 A	S.9
Bevel pinion flange wrench..	..	..	..	..	..	..	18G 34 A	S.4
Differential bearing removing and replacing	..	..	..	..	18G 47 C	S.5
					18G 47 M	S.5
					18G 134	S.6
					18G 134 Q	S.7
Hub removing—disc wheels	..	..	..	..	..	..	18G 304	S.10
							18G 304 Z	S.10
							18G 304 F	S.10
							18G 304 H	S.10
Hub removing—wire wheels (12 T.P.I.)	..	..	..	..	18G 363	S.11
(8 T.P.I.)	..	..	..	..	..	18G 1032	S.13

S.2   Sprite and Midget. Issue 3. 82790

292

Operation	Tool No.	Page No.
Hub dismantling—wire and disc wheels	18G 4	S.4
	18G 14	S.4
	18G 134	S.6
	18G 134 Q	S.7
	18G 152	S.7

STEERING GEAR

Operation	Tool No.	Page No.
Steering tie-rod ball housing, dismantling	18G 312	S.11
	18G 313	S.11
Steering arm and swivel hub ball pin, removing..	18G 1063	S.14
Steering-wheel, removing	18G 562	S.12
Steering-wheel, hub removing	18G 1181	S.14

FRONT SUSPENSION

Operation	Tool No.	Page No.
Coil spring compressor	18G 153	S.8
Hub bearing inner race, removing	18G 2	S.4
	18G 705	S.13
	18G 705 G	S.13
Hub bearing outer race, removing	18G 260	S.9
	18G 260 A	S.9
	18G 260 B	S.9
Hub inner and outer bearing, removing and replacing	18G 134	S.6
	18G 134 B	S.6
	18G 134 C	S.7
Hub, removing—disc wheels	18G 304	S.10
	18G 304 F	S.10
Hub removing—wire wheels (12 T.P.I.)	18G 363	S.11
(8 T.P.I.)	18G 1032	S.13
Swivel axle bush, broaching	18G 155	S.8
	18G 155 A	S.8
Swivel axle bush reaming	18G 1006 A	S.13
Swivel axle bush, removing and replacing: early cars	18G 154 A	S.8
later cars	18G 1006	S.13

MISCELLANEOUS

Operation	Tool No.	Page No.
Switch bezel nut, removing and replacing	18G 671	S.13
Petrol gauge tank attachment lock ring spanner	18G 1001	S.14
Rocker type switch and bezel removing	18G 1145	S.15
Rocker type switch (slim type) removing	18G 1201	S.15

Operation							Tool No.	Page No.
BRAKING SYSTEM								
Disc brake piston, resetting	..	..	..	..	..	..	18G 590	S.12
Drum brake, adjusting	..	..	..	..	..	..	18G 619 A	S.13
Master cylinder (tandem) circlip removing		..	..	..	..	18G 1112	S.14

Sprite and Midget. Issue 1. 82790

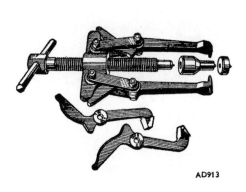

AD913

18G 2. Crankshaft Gear, Pulley, and Propeller Shaft Flange Remover

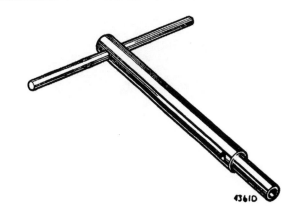

43610

18G 27. Valve Seat Cutter and Pilot Handle

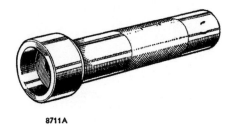

8711A

18G 4. Rear Hub Bearing Replacer

18G 29. Valve Grinding-in Tool

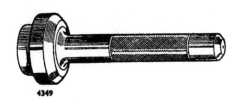

4349

18G 14. Rear Hub Oil Seal Replacer

Sprite and Midget.   Issue 3.   82790

8710

18G 34 A. Bevel Pinion Flange Wrench

S.5

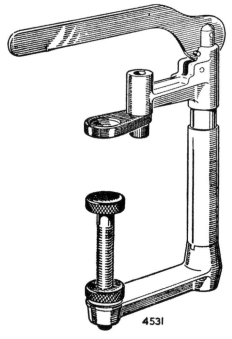

18G 45. Valve Spring Compressor

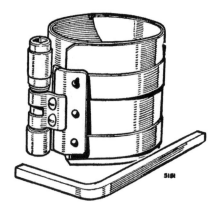

18G 55 A. Piston Ring Clamp

18G 69. Oil Pump Relief Valve Grinding-in Tool

18G 47 C. Differential Bearing Remover (basic tool)

18G 98 A. Starting Nut Spanner

18G 47 M. Differential Bearing Remover Adaptor

*S.*6

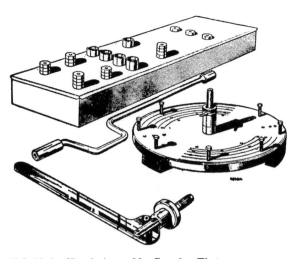

18G 99 A. Clutch Assembly Gauging Fixture

Sprite and Midget.   Issue 3.   82790

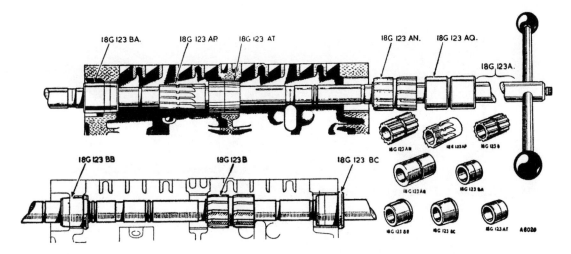

18G 123 A. Camshaft Liner Reamer

CUTTERS
18G 123 AN, 18G 123 AP,
18G 123 B

PILOTS
18G 123 AQ, 18G 123 AT,
18G 123 BA, 18G 123 BB,
18G 123 BC

18G 124 K, 18G 124 B, and 18G 124 M. Camshaft Liner Remover Adaptors

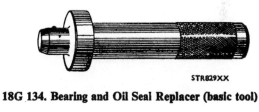

STR829XX

18G 134. Bearing and Oil Seal Replacer (basic tool)

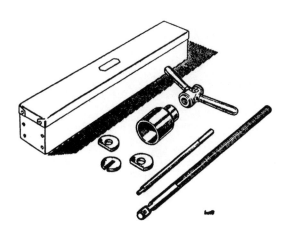

18G 124 A. Camshaft Liner Remover and Replacer (basic tool)

4345F

18G 134 B. Front Hub Outer Bearing Replacer Adaptor

Sprite and Midget.   Issue 2.   82790

18G 134 BD. Timing Case Oil Seal Replacer Adaptor

18G 138. Crankshaft Gear, Pulley, and Propeller Shaft Flange Replacer

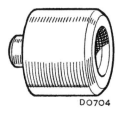

18G 134 C. Front Hub Inner Bearing Replacer Adaptor

18G 139. Clutch Centralizer

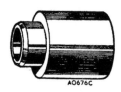

18G 134 L. Gearbox Rear Oil Seal Replacer Adaptor

18G 144. Synchromesh Assembly Ring

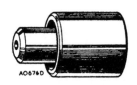

18G 134 Q. Rear Hub Replacer and Adaptor

*S.*8

18G 152. Rear Hub Nut Spanner

Sprite and Midget.   Issue 2.   82790

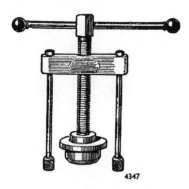

18G 153. Front Suspension Spring Compressor

18G 167. Valve Seat Finishing Cutter

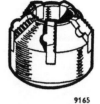

18G 167 A. Valve Seat Glaze Breaker

18G 154 A. Swivel Axle Bush Remover and Replacer

18G 167 B. Valve Seat Narrowing Cutter—Top

18G 155. Swivel Axle Bush Broaching Equipment

18G 167 C. Valve Seat Narrowing Cutter—Bottom

18G 155 A. Swivel Axle Bush Broach Guide

Sprite and Midget.   Issue 3.   82790

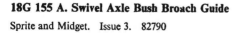

18G 167 D. Valve Seat Cutter Pilot

*S.*9

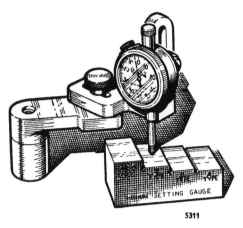

18G 191. Bevel Pinion Setting Gauge

18G 226 and 18G 226A. Valve Rocker Bush Remover and Replacer

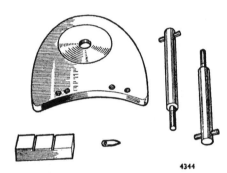

18G 191 A. Differential Bearing Gauge

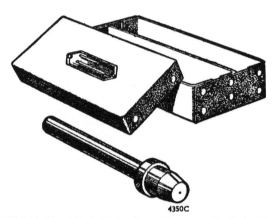

18G 260. Front Hub Outer Race Remover (basic tool)

18G 194. Needle-roller Bearing Replacer

18G 260 A. Front Hub Bearing Outer Race Remover Adaptor

18G 207. Bevel Pinion Bearing Preload Gauge

*S.*10

18G 260 B. Front Hub Bearing Outer Race Remover Adaptor

Sprite and Midget. Issue 3. 82790

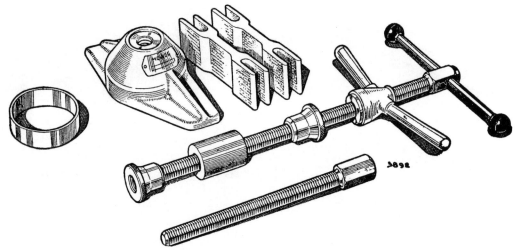

18G 264. Bevel Pinion Bearing Outer Race Remover (basic tool)

A1045

18G 264 D. Bevel Pinion Bearing Outer Race Remover Adaptor

8251F

18G 304. Front and Rear Hub Remover (basic tool)

9154A

18G 264 E. Bevel Pinion Bearing Outer Race Remover Adaptor

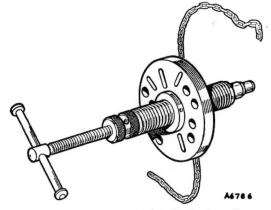

A6786

18G 304 Z. Hub Remover—Hydraulic (basic tool)

8251E

18G 304 F. Bolt Adaptor—$\frac{3}{8}$ in. UNF

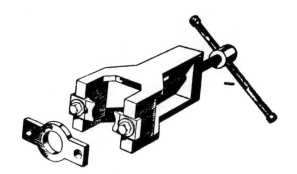

18G 285. Bevel Pinion Bearing Inner Race Remover and Replacer

8251G

18G 304 H. Hub Remover Thrust Pad

Sprite and Midget.   Issue 2.   82790

S.11

18G 312. Steering Tie-rod Pin Spanner

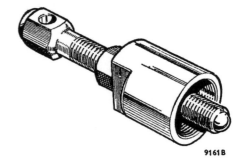

9161B

18G 389. Gearbox Rear Oil Seal Remover (basic tool)

18G 313. Steering Tie-rod 'C' Spanner

9168

18G 389 A. Gearbox Rear Oil Seal Remover Adaptor

8327W

18G 363 Hub Remover—Wire Wheels (12 T.P.I.)

3869

18G 372. Torque Wrench—30 to 140 lb. ft. (4·15 to 19·4 kg. m.)

18G 471. Dummy Layshaft

*S.*12

18G 488. Gearbox Oil Seal Clinching Tool

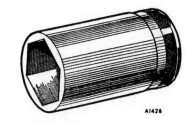

18G 587. Spanner

18G 537 Torque wrench—10 to 50 lb. ft. (2 to 7 kg. m.)

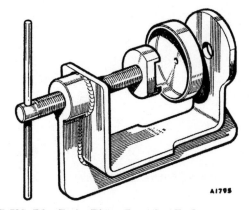

18G 590. Disc Brake Piston Resetting Tool

18G 562. Steering-wheel Nut Spanner

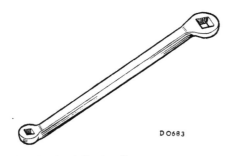

18G 619 A. Brake Adjusting Spanner

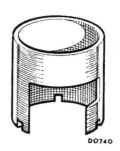

18G 1001. Gauge Locking Ring

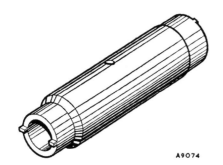

18G 671. Switch Bezel Nut Spanner

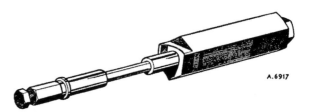

18G 1002. Gudgeon Pin Removing and Replacing Tool
(Use later type 18G 1150 if available)

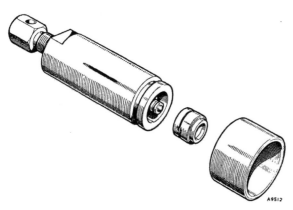

18G 705. Bearing Centre Race Remover

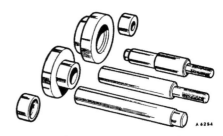

18G 1006. Swivel Axle Remover and Replacer

18G 1006 A. Swivel Axle Bush Reamer

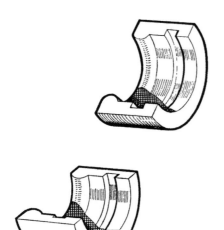

18G 705 G. Bearing Centre Race Remover Adaptor

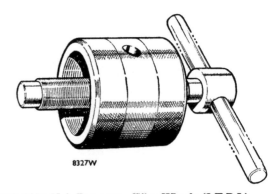

18G 1032 Hub Remover—Wire Wheels (8 T.P.I.)

*S.*14

Sprite and Midget.   Issue 4.   82790

304

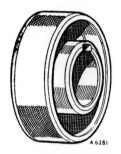

18G 1044. Engine Front Cover Centralizer

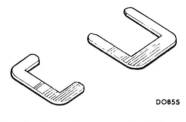

18G 1145. Rocker Type Switch and Bezel Remover

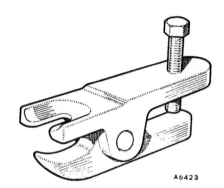

18G 1063. Steering Arm and Swivel Hub Ball Pin Remover

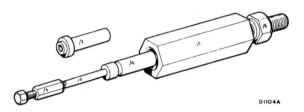

18G 1150. Gudgeon Pin Removing and Replacing Tool

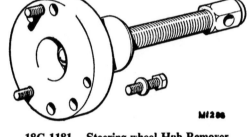

18G 1181. Steering-wheel Hub Remover

18G 1112. Circlip Pliers

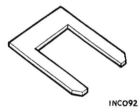

18G 1201. Rocker-type Switch (Slim Type) Remover

RECOMMENDED LUBRICANTS

RECOMMENDED LUBRICANTS

Component	Engine, Synchromesh Gearbox, Carburetter, Distributor and Oilcan			Rear Axle and Steering Gear		Grease Points	Upper Cylinder Lubrication
Climatic conditions	All temperatures above —10° C. (10° F.)	Temperatures —15° to —5° C. (0° to 20° F.)	All temperatures below —15° C. (0° F.)	All temperatures above —10° C. (10° F.)	All temperatures below —5° C. (20° F.)	All conditions	All conditions
Viscosity requirement	S.A.E. 10W/50 S.A.E. 10W/40 S.A.E. 20W/50 or S.A.E. 20W/40	S.A.E. 10W/50 S.A.E. 10W/40 or S.A.E. 10W/30	S.A.E. 5W/30 or S.A.E. 5W/20	S.A.E. 90 Hypoid	S.A.E. 80 Hypoid	—	—
Minimum performance level	MIL-L-2104B	MIL-L-2104B	MIL-L-2104B	MIL-L-2105B	MIL-L-2105B		
ESSO	Uniflo or Esso Extra Motor Oil 20W/50	Uniflo or Esso Extra Motor Oil 10W/30	Esso Extra Motor Oil 5W/20	U.K.: Gear Oil G.X. 90/140 Overseas; Gear Oil G.X. 90	Esso Gear Oil G.X. 80	Esso Multipurpose Grease H	Esso Upper Cylinder Lubricant
MOBIL	Mobiloil Special 20W/50 or Super 10W/50	Mobiloil Super 10W/50	Mobiloil 5W/20	Mobilube H.D. 90	Mobilube H.D. 80	Mobilgrease M.P.	Mobil Upperlube
BP	BP Super Visco-Static	BP Super Visco-Static	BP Super Visco-Static	BP Hypogear 90 E.P.	BP Hypogear 80 E.P.	BP Energrease MP* Energrease L.2	BP Powerlube* BP Upper Cylinder Lubricant
SHELL	Shell Super Motor Oil	Shell Super Motor Oil	Shell Super Motor Oil	Shell Spirax Heavy Duty 90	Shell Spirax Heavy Duty 80	Shell Darina AX* Shell Retinax A	Shell Upper Cylinder Lubricant
FILTRATE	Filtrate Super 20W/50	Filtrate Super 10W/30	Filtrate Super 5W/20	Filtrate Epex 90	Filtrate Epex 80	Filtrate Super Lithium Grease	Filtrate Petroyle
STERNOL	Sternol Super W.W. Motor Oil	Sternol W.W. Multigrade 10W/40	Sternol W.W. Multigrade 5W/20	Sternol Ambroleum H.D. 90	Sternol Ambroleum H.D. 80	Sternol Ambroline Grease L.H.T. 2	Sternol Magikoyl
DUCKHAMS	Duckhams Q. 20-50	Duckhams Q. 5500	Duckhams Q. 5-30	Duckhams Hypoid 90S	Duckhams Hypoid 80S	Duckhams L.B. 10 Grease	Duckhams Adcoid Liquid
CASTROL	Castrol GTX or Castrol XL (20/50)	Castrolite or Castrol Super	Castrol CRI 5W/20	Castrol Hypoy B. 90	Castrol Hypoy B. 80	Castrol L.M. Grease	Castrollo

* AMERICA ONLY

MG Midget.   AKM 2092/1

308

Sprite/Midget

Workshop Manual Supplement
on
Engine Emission Control

Part 3

FOREWORD

This supplement provides service operatives with the information necessary to carry out the maintenance, servicing, and testing of engine emission and fuel evaporative loss control systems fitted to vehicles manufactured by the **BRITISH MOTOR CORPORATION** for which a certificate has been issued in accordance with the **UNITED STATES CLEAN AIR ACTS** and any applicable State Legislation.

Distributors and Dealers are advised to familiarize themselves with the legal requirements, in particular those concerning minimum standards of facilities, personnel, and servicing equipment.

Service operations in Workshop Manuals, where applicable, which may affect the efficiency of the emission or evaporative loss control equipment carry the following symbol, denoting that the control system must be checked on completion of the operation

Engine Emission. Issue 3. 24062

INDEX

SECTION 1

EQUIPMENT AND SERVICING

Section 1-A

EQUIPMENT

The recommended equipment for servicing should include at least the following:

Ignition Analyser Oscilloscope	Cam Angle Dwell Meter
Ohmmeter	Ignition Timing Light
Voltmeter	Engine Exhaust Combustion Analyser
Tachometer	Cylinder Leak Tester
Vacuum Gauge	Distributor Advance Tester
Pressure Gauge (0–10 lb./sq. in.)	Carburetter Piston Loading Tool
Carburetter Balance Meter	

The following equipment covers most of the requirements for engine testing and tuning vehicles fitted with exhaust emission control devices.

Equipment	Type/Model	Manufacturer
Oscilloscope Engine Tuning Set and Exhaust Gas Analyser	1020 or 720	Sun Electric Corp.
Engine Analyser	40–162	Marquette
Exhaust Gas Analyser	42–141	Marquette

Equipment made by other suppliers may also be adequate.

It is important that your test equipment has regular maintenance and calibration.

Section 1-B

SERVICING

General

The efficient operation of the exhaust emission control system is dependent on the engine being in good mechanical condition and correctly tuned to the settings given in **'TUNING DATA'**.

Tuning and test procedure for the carburetters, ignition system, and engine are given at the end of the manual. These procedures are the quickest and surest way of locating engine faults or maladjustments and are the only methods that should be used for engine tuning.

Fault diagnosis

After tuning the engine to the correct settings, check for indications of the following symptoms:

Symptons	Causes	Cure
	1. Leak in exhaust system	Locate and rectify leak
	2. Leaks in hoses or connections to gulp valve, vacuum sensing pipe or other inlet manifold joint	Locate and rectify leak
Backfire in exhaust system	3. Faulty gulp valve	Test gulp valve, and renew if faulty
	4. Leak in intake system	Locate and rectify leak
	5. High inlet manifold depression on over-run—faulty carburetter limit valve	Fit new throttle disc and limit valve assembly

Symptons	Causes	Cure
Hesitation to accelerate after sudden throttle closure	1. Low carburetter damper oil	Top up to correct level
	2. Leaks in hoses or connections to gulp valve, vacuum sensing pipe or other inlet manifold joint	Locate and rectify leak
	3. Faulty gulp valve	Test gulp valve, and renew if faulty
	4. Leak in intake system	Locate and rectify leak
Engine surges (erratic operation at varying throttle openings)	1. Leaks in hoses or connections to gulp valve, vacuum sensing pipe or other inlet manifold joint	Locate and rectify leak
	2. Faulty gulp valve	Test gulp valve, and renew if faulty
	3. Air supply to adsorption canister restricted	Check air filter pad, vent pipe, and canister for obstruction
Erratic idling or stalling	1. Carburetter damper oil low	Top up to correct level.
	2. Leaks in hoses or connections to gulp valve or vacuum sensing pipe or other inlet manifold joint	Locate and rectify leak
	3. Faulty gulp valve	Test gulp valve, and renew if faulty
	4. Incorrect carburetter settings	Reset to **TUNING DATA**
	5. Carburetter limit valve not seating	Fit new throttle disc and limit valve assembly
	6. Carburetter suction chamber damaged	Replace carburetter or components
Burned or baked hose between air pump and check valve	1. Faulty check valve	Test check valve, and renew if faulty
	2. Air pump not pumping	Test air pump; service or renew if faulty
Noisy air pump	1. Incorrect belt tension	Adjust belt tension
	2. Pulleys damaged, loose or misaligned	Tighten loose pulleys, renew damaged pulleys
	3. Air pump failing or seizing	Test air pump; service or renew if faulty
Excessive exhaust system temperature	1. Incorrect ignition timing	Recheck timing against 'TUNING DATA'
	2. Choke control system not fully returned	Check choke mechanism for correct operation; instruct driver on correct usage
	3. Fast idle speed too high	Reset fast idle speed—see 'TUNING DATA'
	4. Air injector missing	Remove air manifold and check injectors
	5. Air pump relief valve inoperative	Test relief valve, and renew if faulty

Symptons	Causes	Cure
Mixture requires excessive enriching to obtain correct exhaust emission readings	1. Air leak into crankcase	Locate and rectify leak
	2. Early cars—Diaphragm of crankcase control valve perforated or not correctly seated	Locate and rectify leak or control valve
	Later cars—Crankcase breather hose or connections to carburetter leaking	Locate and rectify leak
Fuel leakage	1. Fracture in fuel pipe or fuel vapour ventilation system	Locate and rectify leak
	2. Fuel filler cap not sealing	Check condition of cap and filler seal
	3. Leak on fuel filler tube or tank unit	Locate and rectify leak
Engine stops after short running periods (i.e. fuel starvation)	1. Obstructed vapour line between fuel tank and adsorption canister	Locate and clear obstruction
	2. Air supply to adsorption canister restricted	Check air filter pad, vent pipe and canister for obstruction
	3. Faulty fuel pump	Check operation and rectify fault
Engine runs after ignition is switched off	1. Fuel grade too low	Refill with correct grade fuel
	2. Ignition retarded	Reset timing to 'TUNING DATA'
	3. Idle speed too high	Reset to 'TUNING DATA'
	4. Fuel mixture too weak	Tune carburetter(s)

Engine Emission. Issue 5. 82454

SECTION 2

CRANKCASE EMISSION CONTROL

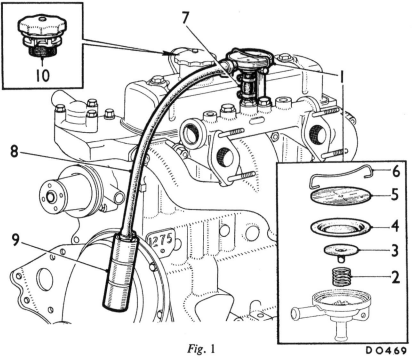

Fig. 1

A typical crankcase emission valve control system

1. Emission control valve.	5. Cover plate.	8. Breather hose.
2. Valve spring.	6. Spring clip.	9. Oil separator.
3. Metering valve.	7. Manifold connection.	10. Filtered filler cap.
4. Diaphragm.		

Section 2-A

VALVE CONTROL SYSTEM—General description

The system consists of a diaphragm control valve connected by hoses between the inlet manifold and the engine crankcase. The crankcase outlet connection incorporates an oil separator to prevent oil being pulled over with the vapours leaving the crankcase. On four-cylinder engines a filtered, restricted orifice ($\frac{9}{64}$ in. diameter) in the oil filler cap provides a supply of fresh air into the crankcase as vapours are withdrawn by inlet manifold depression. Six-cylinder engines are fitted with a standard oil filler cap and a tube connected between the rocker cover oil filler tube and the air intake filter provides the supply of fresh air to the engine. The control valve diaphragm varies the opening to the inlet manifold according to the depression or pressure acting on it. With a decrease in manifold depression or when the crankcase obtains a positive pressure the diaphragm opens the valve allowing the crankcase vapours to be drawn into the inlet manifold. During conditions of high manifold depression, e.g. low engine speeds or loads, the diaphragm closes the valve and restricts the flow into the inlet manifold, thus preventing a leaning-off of the air/fuel mixture to the cylinders.

Section 2-B

VALVE CONTROL SYSTEM—Testing

(1) Warm up the engine to normal operating temperature.

(2) With the engine running at idling speed remove the oil filler cap.

   (a) A rise in engine speed, the change being audibly noticeable, indicates that the control valve is functioning correctly.

   (b) No rise in speed, service the control valve.

Section 2-C

VALVE CONTROL SYSTEM—Servicing

Oil filler cap (*four-cylinder engines only*)

(1) Renew every 12,000 miles or 12 months.

Control valve

(2) Disconnect the hoses and renew the valve assembly, or clean as follows:

   (a) Remove the spring clip and withdraw the cover plate, diaphragm, metering valve and spring.

   (b) Clean all metal parts with a solvent (trichlorethylene, fuel, etc.). **Do not use an abrasive.** If deposits are difficult to remove, immerse in boiling water before applying the solvent.

   (c) Clean the diaphragm with a detergent or methylated spirit (denatured alcohol).

   (d) Examine the parts thoroughly for wear or damage, and renew where necessary.

   (e) Reassemble the valve ensuring that the metering valve fits correctly in its guides and the diaphragm is correctly seated.

   (f) Refit the valve and check its operation.

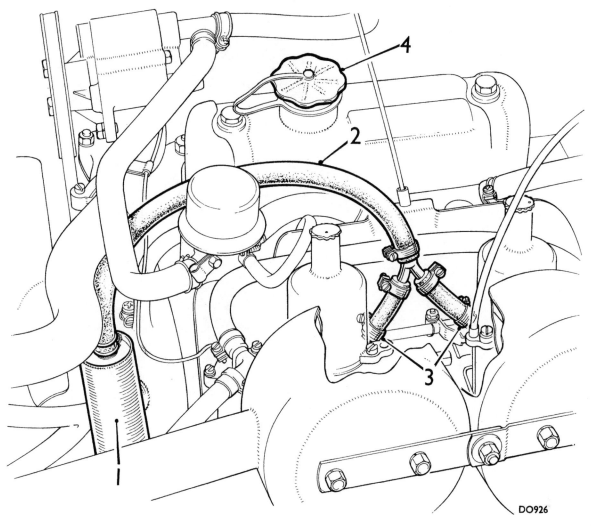

Fig. 2
Carburetter control system

1. Oil separator.   3. Carburetter chamber connection.
2. Breather hose.   4. Filtered filler cap.

Section 2-D

CARBURETTER CONTROL SYSTEM

Description

With this system the engine breather outlet is connected by hoses to the controlled depression chamber; the chamber between the piston and the throttle disc valve, of the carburetter(s). Engine fumes and blow-by gases are drawn from the crankcase by the depression in this chamber, through an oil separator incorporated in the engine outlet connection, and from there to the inlet manifold. Fresh air is supplied to the engine through the combined oil filler cap and filter (four-cylinder engines) or through the air intake filter (six-cylinder engines).

Servicing

The oil filler cap (four-cylinder engines only) must be renewed every 12,000 miles (20000 km.) or 12 months; no other service is required.

If a failure of the system is suspected, check the hoses and connections for leaks and obstructions. An indication of a failure is loss of crankcase depression.

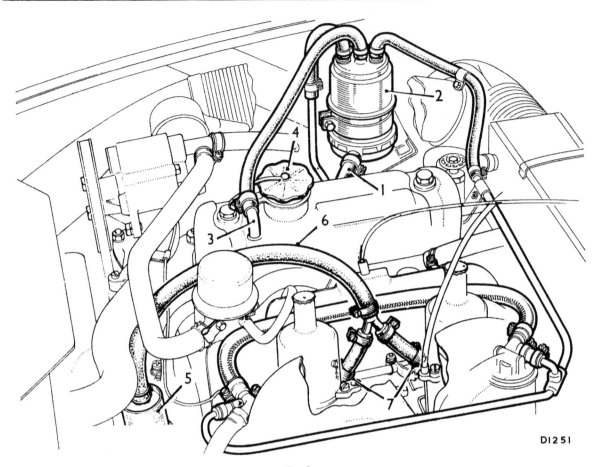

Fig. 3

A carburetter control system with fuel evaporative loss control

1. Ventilation air intake.
2. Absorption canister.
3. Restricted connection to rocker cover.
4. Sealed oil filler cap.
5. Oil separator.
6. Breather hose.
7. Carburetter chamber connections.

Section 2-E

CARBURETTER CONTROL SYSTEM—
with evaporative loss control

This system incorporates most of the components of the carburetter control system, with the exception of the combined oil filler cap and filtered air intake. Its operation differs in that air for engine breathing is drawn through the filtered adsorption canister of the evaporative loss control system into the engine valve rocker cover. A restrictor in the rocker cover connection reduces the air flow to ensure crankcase depression under all conditions.

Engine fumes and blow-by gases are drawn from the crankcase, through an oil separator, into the inlet manifold by the controlled depression chamber of the carburetter.

Servicing

No direct servicing of the system is required. The air intake filter pad in the absorption canister is renewed at the intervals required by the fuel evaporative loss control.

If a failure of the system is suspected, check the hoses and connections for leaks and obstruction. An indication of a failure is loss of crankcase depression.

SECTION 3

EXHAUST EMISSION CONTROL
(Exhaust Port Air Injection)

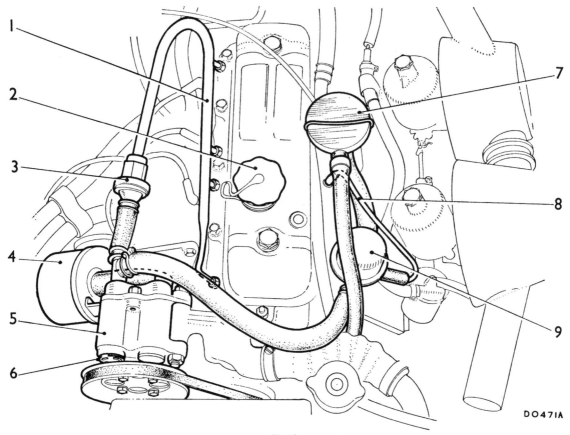

Fig. 1

A typical engine emission control system layout

1. Air manifold.	4. Emission air cleaner.	7. Crankcase emission valve.
2. Filtered oil filler cap.	5. Air pump.	8. Vacuum sensing tube.
3. Check valve.	6. Relief valve.	9. Gulp valve.

Section 3-A

GENERAL DESCRIPTION

Air is pressure-fed from an air pump via an injection manifold to the cylinder head exhaust port of each cylinder. A check valve in the air delivery pipe prevents blow-back from high pressure exhaust gases. The pump also supplies air through a gulp valve to the inlet manifold to provide air during conditions of deceleration and engine over-run.

IMPORTANT. The efficient operation of the system is dependent on the engine being correctly tuned. The ignition and spark plug settings, valve clearances, and carburetter adjustments given for a particular engine (see 'TUNING DATA') must be strictly adhered to at all times.

Air pump

The rotary vane type air pump is mounted on the front of the cylinder head and is belt driven from the water pump pulley. Provision is made for tensioning the belt.

Air is drawn into the pump through a dry-type renewable element filter. A relief valve in the pump

discharge port allows excessive air pressure at high engine speeds to discharge to the atmosphere.

Check valve

The check valve, fitted in the pump discharge line to the injection manifold, protects the pump from the back-flow of exhaust gases.

The valve shuts if the air pressure ceases while the engine is running; for example, if the pump drive belt should break.

Gulp valve

The gulp valve, fitted in the pump discharge line to the inlet manifold, controls the flow of air for leaning-off the rich air/fuel mixture present in the inlet manifold immediately following throttle closure after running at full throttle opening (i.e. engine over-run).

A sensing pipe connected between the inlet manifold and the gulp valve maintains manifold depression directly to the underside of the diaphragm and through a bleed hole to the upper side. Sudden increases in manifold depression which occur immediately following throttle closure act on the underside of the diaphragm which opens the valve and admits air to the inlet manifold. The

3-2

Engine Emission. Issue 3. 12383

bleed hole allows the differences in depression acting on the diaphragm to equalize and the valve closes.

On some engines a restrictor is fitted in the air pump discharge connection to the gulp valve, to prevent surging when the gulp valve is operating.

Carburetter

The carburetters are manufactured to a special exhaust emission control specification and are tuned to give optimum engine performance with maximum emission control.

A limit valve is incorporated in the carburetter throttle disc which limits the inlet manifold depression ensuring that under conditions of high inlet-manifold depression the mixture entering the cylinders is at a combustible ratio.

Section 3-B

AIR PUMP (four-cylinder engines)

Drive belt tension

When correctly tensioned, a total deflection of $\frac{1}{2}$ in., under moderate hand pressure, should be possible at the midway point of the longest belt run between the pulleys.

To tension the belt:

(1) Slacken the air pump mounting bolt and adjusting link bolts (see Fig. 3).

(2) Using hand pressure only, move the pump in the required direction until the correct tension is obtained.

(3) Tighten the mounting and adjusting bolts to a torque figure of 10 lb. ft.

Testing

(1) Check the drive belt for correct tensioning.

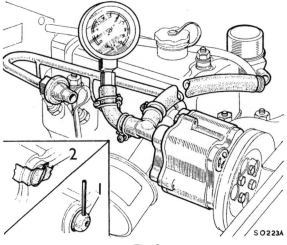

Fig. 2

The pressure gauge connected (four-cylinder engines)

   1. Relief valve test tool.   2. Tape used to duct air.

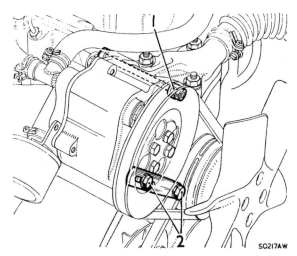

Fig. 3

Air pump (four-cylinder engines)

   1. Pump mounting bolt.   2. Adjusting link bolts.

(2) Connect a tachometer to the engine in accordance with the instrument-maker's instructions.

(3) Disconnect the gulp valve air supply hose at the gulp valve and securely plug the hose.

(4) Disconnect the air manifold supply hose at the check valve, and connect a pressure gauge to the hose (see Fig. 2).

(5) Run the engine at the air pump test speed given in 'TUNING DATA': a gauge reading of not less than 2·75 lb./sq. in. should be registered.

   (*a*) If a lower reading is obtained, remove, dismantle and clean the pump air cleaner. Reassemble using a new element, refit the air cleaner and repeat the test.

   (*b*) If the reading is still unsatisfactory, temporarily blank off the relief valve and repeat the test; if the reading is now correct, renew the relief valve.

   (*c*) If a satisfactory reading is still unobtainable, remove and service the air pump.

(6) Stop the engine and fit a temporary air duct over the face of the relief valve. Two methods of doing this are shown in Fig. 2. The tool (1) may be fabricated from grommet (Part No. 1B 1735) and a short length of metal brake tube, or (2) by using a piece of adhesive tape to form the duct.

DO NOT ATTEMPT TO CHECK AIR FLOW FROM THE RELIEF VALVE BY PLACING A FINGER BETWEEN THE VALVE AND THE DRIVING PULLEY.

   (*a*) Start the engine and slowly increase the speed until air flow from the relief valve duct is detected, when a gauge reading of 4·5 to 6·5 lb./sq. in. should be registered.

   (*b*) If the relief valve fails to operate correctly, remove the pump and renew the valve.

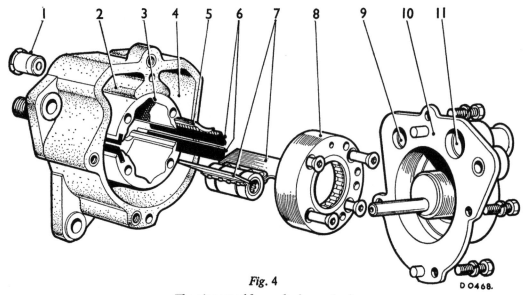

Fig. 4

The air pump (four-cylinder engines)

1. Relief valve.
2. Inlet chamber.
3. Rotor.
4. Outlet chamber.
5. Spring.
6. Carbons.
7. Vane assemblies.
8. Rotor bearing end plate.
9. Outlet port.
10. Port-end cover.
11. Inlet port.

Removing

(1) Disconnect the air hoses from the pump connections and remove the air cleaner.
(2) Slacken the mounting and adjusting link bolts and slip the drive belt from the pump pulley.
(3) Remove the top adjusting link bolt and the nut securing the pump mounting bolt.
(4) Support the pump, withdraw the mounting bolt and lift the pump from the engine.

Dismantling

(1) Remove the four port-end cover retaining bolts and withdraw the cover.
(2) Remove the four screws securing the rotor bearing end plate to the rotor and remove the end plate.
(3) Lift out the vane assemblies.
(4) Remove the carbon and spring assemblies from the rotor.

Servicing

(1) Wipe the interior and components of the pump clean, using a lint-free cloth.

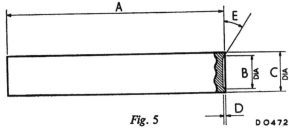

Fig. 5

The dimensions of the relief valve replacing tool

A = 5 in.   B = ·986 in.   C = 1·062 in.
D = ·05 in.   E = 30°.

(2) Clean the vane carrier roller bearings and the rotor end plate bearing and repack the bearings with Esso 'Andok' 260 lubricant.
(3) Inspect the vane assemblies for signs of having fouled the pump wall, and for grooving in area of contact with the carbons. Renew worn or damaged vanes.
(4) Fit new carbons (the original springs may be re-used if serviceable). Note that the slots which carry the carbon and springs are the deeper ones, and the carbons are all fitted with the chamfered edge to the inside.

Reassembling

(1) Reassemble the pump by reversing the dismantling procedure and noting that the underside of the heads of the rotor bearing end plate screws must be smeared with 'Locktite' before tightening.

Refitting

(1) Position the pump in the mounting bracket and fit, but do not tighten, the pump mounting bolt.
(2) Screw in, but do not tighten, the adjusting link bolt.
(3) Fit and tension the drive belt.
(4) Reconnect the hoses and refit the air cleaner.

Relief valve—replacing

(1) Remove the air pump.
(2) Remove the pump pulley.
(3) Pass a ½-in. diameter soft metal drift through the pump discharge connection so that it registers against the relief valve, and drive the valve from the pump.

3-4

Engine Emission. Issue 3. 12383

(4) Fit a new copper seating washer to the new relief valve and enter the valve into the pump body.

(5) Using a tool made to the dimensions shown in Fig. 5, drive the valve into the pump until the copper seating washer is held firmly, but not compressed, between the valve and the pump.

(6) Refit the pulley and refit the air pump.

Section 3-C

AIR PUMP (six-cylinder engines)

Drive belt tension

When correctly tensioned, a total deflection of $\frac{1}{2}$ in., under moderate hand pressure should be possible at the midway point of the longest belt run between the pulleys.

To tension the belt:

(1) Slacken the air pump mounting bolt and adjusting link bolts (see Fig. 6).

(2) Using hand pressure only, move the pump in the required direction until the correct tension is obtained.

(3) Tighten the mounting and adjusting link bolts to a torque figure of 10 lb. ft.

Testing

Faulty operation of the air pump is indicated by excessive pump noise. If excessive noise is present and the air pump is suspected, remove the air pump drive belt and run the engine to check that the noise is not from another source. If this check shows that the air pump is excessively noisy renew the air pump assembly or proceed as follows:

(1) Check the drive belt for correct tensioning.

(2) Run the engine at idle speed and check the air

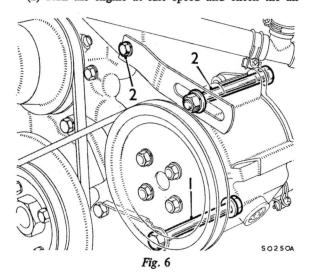

Fig. 6

Air pump (six-cylinder engines)

1. Pump mounting bolt.   2. Adjusting link bolts.

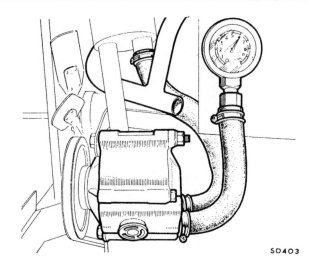

SO403

Fig. 7

The pressure gauge connected (six-cylinder engines)

supply hoses and connections for leaks and for intermittent contact with other parts of the vehicle.

(3) Connect a tachometer to the engine in accordance with the instrument maker's instructions.

(4) Disconnect the air supply hose tee connection from its connection with the air pump discharge hose.

(5) Connect a pressure gauge to the air pump discharge hose (see Fig. 7).

(6) Run the engine at the air pump test speed given in 'TUNING DATA'. A gauge reading of not less than 2·75 lb./sq. in. should be registered.

   (a) If a lower reading is obtained, remove, dismantle, and clean the pump air cleaner. Reassemble using a new element, refit the air cleaner, and repeat the test.

   (b) If the reading is still unsatisfactory, temporarily blank off the relief valve and repeat the test; if the reading is now correct, renew the relief valve.

   (c) If a satisfactory reading is still unobtainable the air pump assembly must be replaced.

   (d) From idling speed, slowly increase the engine speed until air flow from the relief valve is detected, this should occur before the gauge reading exceeds 10 lb./sq. in.

   (e) If the relief valve fails to operate correctly, remove the pump and renew the valve.

(7) If the foregoing tests fail to remedy or locate the cause of the air pump noise renew the air pump assembly.

Removing

(1) Disconnect the hoses from the pump connections and remove the air cleaner.

(2) Slacken the mounting and adjusting link bolts and slip the drive belt from the pump pulley.

(3) Remove the nut from the adjusting link bolt, support the pump and withdraw the bolt.

(4) Unscrew the mounting bolt and remove the pump.

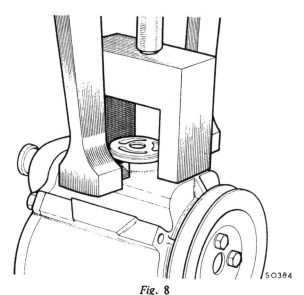

Fig. 8
Removing the relief valve (six-cylinder engines)

Relief valve—replacing

(1) Remove the air pump.

(2) Using a gear puller and a fabricated bridge as shown in Fig. 8, withdraw the relief valve from the pump body.
DO NOT HOLD THE PUMP BY CLAMPING IT IN A VICE.

(3) Enter the new relief valve into the pump body.

(4) With a protective plate over the valve, carefully drive the valve into the pump until its flange registers lightly on the pump body.

(5) Insert the pressure setting plug into the relief valve, using a suitable tool, apply pressure to the centre of the plug until the legs of the plug lock under the relief valve cage.

Section 3-D

CHECK VALVE

Removing

(1) Disconnect the air supply hose from the check valve connection.

(2) Hold the air manifold connection to prevent it twisting and unscrew the check valve.

Testing

(1) Blow through the valve, orally, in turn from each connection. Air should only pass through the valve when blown from the air supply hose connection. If air passes through when blown from the air manifold connection, renew the check valve.
On no account may an air blast be used for this test.

Refitting

(1) Hold the air manifold connection to prevent it twisting, screw in and tighten the check valve.

(2) Reconnect the air supply hose to the check valve.

Section 3-E

AIR MANIFOLD AND INJECTORS

Testing

(1) Disconnect the air manifold from the cylinder head connections.

(2) Slacken the air supply hose clip at the check valve connection.

(3) Rotate the manifold about its connection axis until the injector connections are accessible.

(4) Tighten the air supply hose clip.

(5) Run the engine at idle speed and observe the flow of air from each of the manifold connection tubes. Should the flow of air from any of the connections be restricted, remove the manifold and clear the obstruction using an air blast.

(6) With the engine running at idle speed, check that exhaust gases blow from each of the cylinder head injectors.

IMPORTANT.—The injectors may be free in the cylinder head and care must be taken to ensure that they are not displaced during this test.

To clear a restricted injector:

(a) Crank engine until the exhaust valve below the injector is closed.

(b) Using a hand drill (not power-driven), pass a $\frac{1}{8}$-in. drill through the injector bore, taking care that the drill does not contact the exhaust valve stem after passing through the injector. Damage may result if a power-driven drill is used.

(c) Insert an air-blast nozzle into the injector connection to clear carbon dust from the exhaust port.

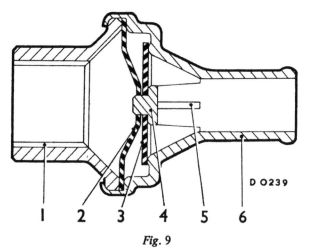

Fig. 9
A section through the check valve

1. Air manifold connection.	4. Valve pilot.
2. Diaphragm.	5. Guides.
3. Valve.	6. Air supply connection.

Section 3-F

GULP VALVE

Testing

(1) Disconnect the gulp valve air supply hose from the air pump connection.

(2) Connect a vacuum gauge, with a tee connection to the disconnected end of the gulp valve air hose.

(3) Start the engine and run it at idle speed.

(4) Temporarily seal the open connection on the gauge tee and check that a zero gauge reading is maintained for approximately 15 seconds; if a vacuum is registered, renew the gulp valve. It is most important that the engine speed is not increased above idling during this test.

(5) With the gauge tee connection temporarily sealed, operate the throttle rapidly from closed to open; the gauge should then register a vacuum. Repeat the test several times, temporarily unsealing the tee piece connection to destroy the vacuum before each operation of the throttle. If the gauge fails to register a vacuum, renew the gulp valve.

Removing

(1) Disconnect the air hoses.

(2) Unscrew the mounting screw and remove the gulp valve.

Fig. 10

The vacuum gauge connected for testing the gulp valve

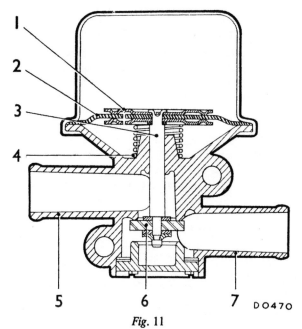

Fig. 11

A section through the gulp valve

1. Metering balance orifice.
2. Diaphragm.
3. Valve spindle.
4. Return spring.
5. Inlet manifold hose connection.
6. Valve.
7. Air pump hose connection.

Refitting

(1) Reverse the removing procedure.

Section 3-G

LIMIT VALVE (INLET MANIFOLD DEPRESSION)

Testing

(1) Disconnect the gulp valve sensing pipe from the inlet manifold.

(2) Connect a vacuum gauge to the sensing pipe connection on the inlet manifold.

(3) Connect a tachometer in accordance with the instrument maker's instructions.

(4) Warm the engine at fast idle speed until normal operating temperature is reached.

(5) Increase the engine speed to 3,000 r.p.m. then release the throttle quickly; the vacuum gauge reading should immediately rise to between 20·5 and 22 in. Hg. If the gauge reading falls outside these limits the carburetter must be removed and the throttle disc and limit valve assembly renewed. After refitting, the carburetter must be tuned as described in Section 4-A.

Section 3-H
RUNNING ON CONTROL VALVE

The solenoid operated valve is connected by hoses between the adsorption canister ventilation connection of the evaporative loss control system and the inlet manifold. A third hose connected to the valve is open to atmosphere for canister ventilation while the engine is running normally. The electrical circuit of the solenoid is connected through the ignition switch and an oil pressure operated switch.

The valve is fitted to prevent prolonged running on (dieseling) which may occur when using low octane fuels.

Operation

When the ignition is switched off the solenoid is energized through an oil pressure switch and the valve closes, shutting off the ventilation connection and opening the connection to the inlet manifold. Inlet manifold depression then acts on the fuel in the carburetter float chamber(s) to prevent fuel flow and the engine is stopped by fuel starvation.

Testing

If the running on valve is suspected of being faulty the control electrical circuit and operation of the valve should be checked as follows:

(1) Check the control valve line fuse.
(2) Turn the ignition switch to the off position.
(3) Disconnect the control valve electrical lead at the oil pressure switch.
(4) Touch the disconnected lead to a good earth point on the vehicle. If the control electrical circuit and valve are satisfactory, the valve will be heard to operate as the control lead is earthed.

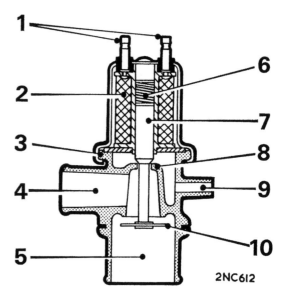

2NC612

Fig. 12
A section through the running on control valve

1. Electrical terminals.
2. Solenoid.
3. Valve body.
4. Adsorption canister hose connection.
5. Air vent hose connection.
6. Spring.
7. Valve spindle.
8. Primary valve.
9. Inlet manifold hose connection.
10. Secondary valve.

SECTION 3A

EXHAUST EMISSION CONTROL
(Engine Modifications System)

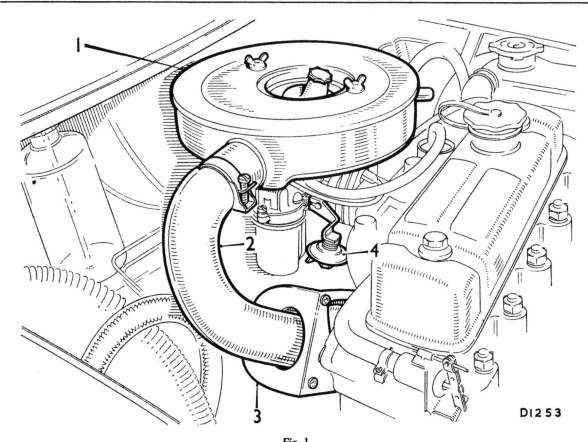

Fig. 1
An engine modification exhaust emission control system showing the air intake tube in the low ambient temperature operating position

1. Air cleaner.
2. Air intake tube.
3. Manifold shroud.
4. Throttle damper.

Section 3A-A

GENERAL DESCRIPTION

This system incorporates modifications to a high compression ratio engine and using a carburetter manufactured to a special exhaust emission control specification.

IMPORTANT. The efficient operation of the system is dependent on the engine being correctly tuned. The settings given for a particular engine (see 'TUNING DATA') must be strictly adhered to at all times.

Carburetter

The carburetter is tuned to give optimum engine performance with maximum exhaust emission control.

A limit valve is incorporated in the carburetter throttle disc which limits the inlet manifold depression ensuring that under conditions of high inlet-manifold depression the air/fuel mixture entering the cylinders is at a combustible ratio.

Throttle damper

A damper is fitted to act on the throttle lever as it returns to the closed position ensuring a gradual closing of the throttle valve giving smooth deceleration. Provision

is made for adjusting the damping effect; the correct setting is given in 'TUNING DATA'.

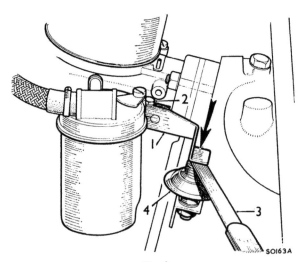

Fig. 2
Adjusting the throttle damper setting

1. Throttle lever.
2. Clamp screw
3. Feeler gauge.
4. Throttle damper.

Engine Emission. Issue 2. 82454

Air intake

In low ambient temperature conditions the intake tube of the air cleaner is positioned in a shroud formed over a section of the exhaust manifold. Air drawn through the cleaner to the carburetter is warmed by heat given off by the manifold.

In high ambient temperature conditions the air intake tube is positioned away from the manifold and air entering the carburetter is drawn into the air cleaner from the engine compartment at ambient temperature.

Section 3A-B

THROTTLE DAMPER

Adjusting

(1) Slacken the clamp nut on the damper operating lever.

(2) Insert a feeler gauge (see 'TUNING DATA') between the damper plunger and the operating arm.

(3) With the carburetter throttle disc valve in the fully closed position, press the operating lever down until the plunger is fully depressed.

(4) Hold the lever in this position and tighten the clamp nut.

(5) Remove the feeler gauge.

Section 3A-C

AIR INTAKE

Repositioning

(1) Slacken the intake tube securing clip.

(2) Slacken the air cleaner wing nuts.

(3) Withdraw the intake tube from the air cleaner and manifold shroud.

(4) Refit the intake tube with its entry positioned adjacent to the end of the rocker cover.

(5) Tighten the wing nuts and securing clip.

Section 3A-D

AIR BLEED COMPENSATOR

Description

An air bleed temperature compensator is fitted to some engines equipped with twin type HS carburetters required to conform with European E.C.E. or E.E.C. exhaust emission control regulations.

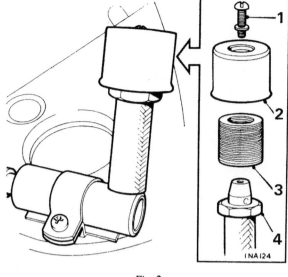

Fig. 3

The air bleed temperature compensator (showing the cap type air filter components)

1. Cap retaining screw.   3. Filter element.
2. Filter cap.   4. Filter base.

The air bleed temperature compensator is fixed to the underside of the carburetter air cleaner and consists of a bi-metal air control valve and an air filter. It is connected by hoses to the constant depression chambers, between the piston and the throttle disc valve, of the carburetters.

With an increase in engine or engine compartment air temperature, the valve will open and allow air at ambient temperature to be drawn through the air filter and into the carburetter constant depression chambers.

The controlled admission of air into the carburetter chambers reduces the velocity and volume of air passing the needles of the carburetters, causing the pistons to fall and subsequently reduce the amount of fuel supplied, thus giving a constant air/fuel mixture ratio.

Servicing

The air bleed temperature compensator air filter must be renewed every 12,000 miles (20000 km.) or 12 months.

(1) Disconnect the air cleaner to carburetter hoses.

(2) Remove the air cleaner.

(3) *Push-on type filters:* withdraw and discard the filter. *Cap type filters:* unscrew the filter cover retaining screw, remove the cover, and discard the filter element. Clean the base and cover of the filter, fit a new element, refit the cover and retaining screw.

(4) Refit the air cleaner and reconnect the hoses.

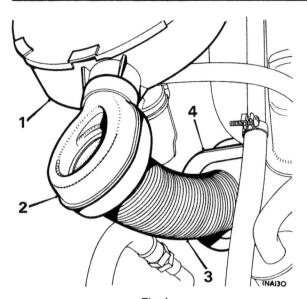

Fig. 4

The air intake temperature control

1. Air cleaner.
2. Air intake temperature control.
3. Air intake tube.
4. Exhaust manifold shroud.

Section 3A-E

AIR INTAKE TEMPERATURE CONTROL

An air intake temperature control is fitted to some engines equipped with single Type H.S. carburetters required to conform with European E.C.E. or E.C.C. exhaust emission control regulations.

The control consists of a bi-metal operated valve, fitted in the air intake of the carburetter air cleaner, and is designed to maintain the temperature of the ingoing air within predetermined limits.

When the engine is cold, air is drawn into the air cleaner from the shrouded area adjacent to the exhaust manifold. As the temperature of the air entering the air cleaner rises, the valve opens and admits cooler air at ambient temperature to mix with the hot air and maintain a constant temperature.

SECTION 4

CARBURETTERS

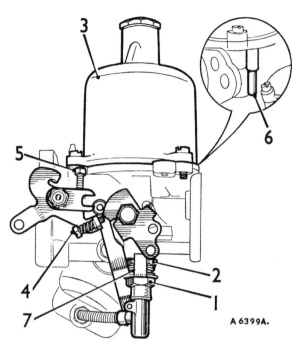

The type HS carburetter

1. Jet adjusting nut.
2. Jet locking nut.
3. Piston suction chamber.
4. Fast-idle adjusting screw.
5. Throttle adjusting screw.
6. Piston lifting pin.
7. Jet adjustment restrictor.

Section 4-A

CARBURETTER TUNING—BASIC

GENERAL

The carburetters fitted to cars equipped with engine emission control systems are balanced to provide maximum performance with maximum pollution control. Under no circumstances may they be interchanged, or parts substituted.

Tuning must be carried out with the engine emission control equipment connected and operating, and is confined to the following procedure. If the required settings cannot be obtained, the service procedure detailed under 'CARBURETTER SERVICING' must be carried out and then the carburetter tuned in accordance with the procedure given in 'CARBURETTER TUNING —COMPLETE'.

Tuning conditions

To ensure that the engine temperature and mixture requirements are stabilized, tuning must be carried out in accordance with the following setting cycle.

(1) Connect a tachometer in accordance with the instrument-maker's instructions.

(2) Warm the engine at a fast idle to normal operating temperature, preferably with the car standing in an ambient temperature of between 16 and 27° C. (60 to 80° F.). Run the engine for at least five minutes after the thermostat has opened; the

thermostat opening point can be detected by the sudden rise in temperature of the radiator header tank.

(3) Set the engine speed at 2,500 r.p.m., at no load, and run for one minute.

(4) Tuning operations may now be commenced and must be carried out in the shortest possible time. If the time for settings exceeds a three-minute period, open the throttle and run the engine at 2,500 r.p.m. for one minute then resume tuning. Repeat this clearing operation if further periods of three minutes are exceeded.

SINGLE CARBURETTERS

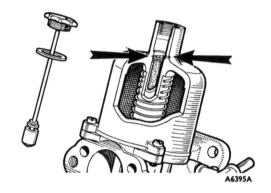

NOTE.—In no case should the jet adjustment restrictor be removed or repositioned. Only mixture adjustments within the limits of the restrictor are available for tuning. If satisfactory adjustment is not obtainable within the limits of the jet adjustment restrictor refer to 'CARBURETTER SERVICING'.

(1) Top up the piston damper with the recommended engine oil until the level is $\frac{1}{2}$-in. above the top of the hollow piston rod.

NOTE.—On dust-proofed carburetters, identified by a transverse hole drilled in the neck of the suction chambers and no vent hole in the damper cap, the oil level must be $\frac{1}{2}$-in. below the top of the hollow piston rod.

(2) Check throttle control action for signs of sticking.

(3) Check the idling speed (Tachometer) against the figure given in 'TUNING DATA'.

(a) If the reading is correct and the engine runs smoothly, proceed to operations (7) and (8).

(b) If the reading is not correct, adjust the speed by turning the throttle adjusting screw in the required direction until the correct speed consistent with smooth running is obtained, then proceed to operations (7) and (8).

(c) If a smooth idle at the correct speed is not obtainable by turning the throttle adjusting screw, carry out operations (4) to (8).

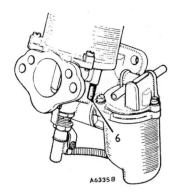

A6335B

(4) With the engine stopped, check that the piston falls freely onto the bridge, indicated by a distinct metallic click, when the lifting pin (6) is released. If not refer to **'CARBURETTER SERVICING'.**

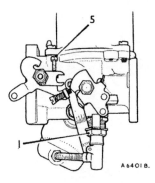

A6401B.

(5) Turn the jet adjusting nut (1) to cover the full range of adjustment available within the limits of the restrictor, selecting the setting where maximum speed is recorded on the tachometer consistent with smooth running.

(6) Readjust the throttle adjusting screw (5) to give the correct idling speed if necessary.

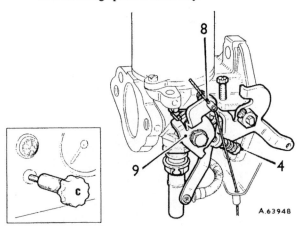

A.6394B

(7) Check, and if necessary adjust, the mixture control wire (8) to give a free movement of approximately $\frac{1}{16}$-in. before it starts to pull on the jet lever (9).

(8) Pull the mixture control knob until the linkage is about to move the carburetter jet and adjust the fast-idle screw (4) to give the engine fast-idle speed (Tachometer) given in **'TUNING DATA'.**

TWIN CARBURETTERS

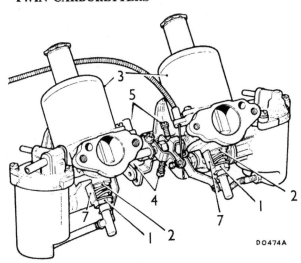

DO474A

A twin-carburetter installation

1. Jet adjusting nuts.
2. Jet locking nuts.
3. Piston/suction chambers.
4. Fast-idle adjusting screws.
5. Throttle adjusting screws.
7. Jet adjustment restrictors.

NOTE.—In no case should the jet adjustment restrictor be removed or repositioned. Only mixture adjustments within the limits of the restrictor are available for tuning. Balancing of twin carburetters must only be carried out with the use of an approved balancing meter. If satisfactory adjustment or balancing is not obtainable within the limits of the jet adjustment restrictor, refer to **'CARBU-RETTER SERVICING'.**

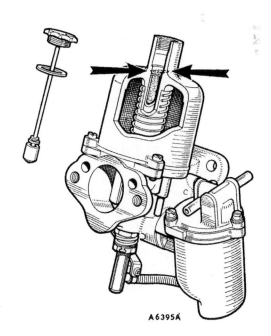

A6395A

(1) Top up the piston damper with the recommended engine oil until the level is $\frac{1}{2}$-in. above the top of the hollow piston rod.

NOTE.—On dust-proofed carburetters, identified by a transverse hole drilled in the neck of the suction chambers and ño vent hole in the damper cap, the oil level must be $\frac{1}{2}$-in. below the top of the hollow piston rod.

(2) Check the throttle control action for signs of sticking.

(3) Check the idling speed (Tachometer) against the figure given in 'TUNING DATA'.

    (a) If the reading is correct and the engine runs smoothly, proceed with operations (11) to (17).

    (b) If the reading is not correct, carry out operations (4) to (17).

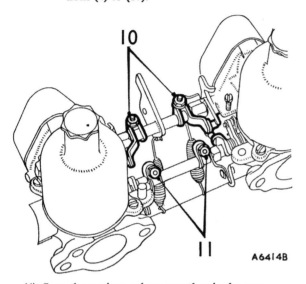

A6414B

(4) Stop the engine and remove the air cleaners.

(5) Slacken both of the clamping bolts (10) on the throttle spindle interconnections.

(6) Disconnect the jet control interconnection by slackening the clamping bolts (11).

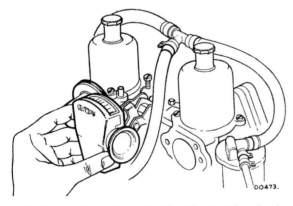

OO473.

(7) Restart the engine and adjust the throttle adjusting screws on **both** carburetters to give the correct idling speed as registered by the tachometer.

(8) Using an approved balancing meter in accordance with the maker's instructions, balance the carburetters by altering the throttle adjusting screws; the idling speed obtained during this operation must be as given in 'TUNING DATA'.

(a) If after this operation the balance is satisfactory and consistent with smooth running at the correct idle speed, proceed with operations (14) to (17).

(b) If correct balance cannot be obtained, check the intake system for leaks (i.e. brake servos, engine emission control equipment); if still unsatisfactory, refer to 'CARBURETTER SERVICING'.

(c) If with the carburetters correctly balanced the idling is still erratic, carry out operations (9) to (17).

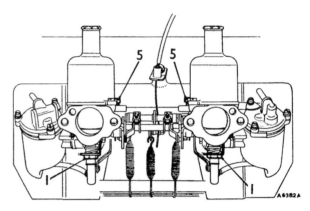

A6382A

(9) Turn the jet adjusting nut (1) on both carburetters to cover the full range of adjustment available within the limits of the restrictor, selecting the setting where maximum speed is recorded on the tachometer consistent with smooth running.

(10) Readjust the throttle adjusting screws (5) to give the correct idling speed (see 'TUNING DATA') if necessary, ensuring that both carburetters are adjusted by an equal amount.

    If the correct idling speed consistent with smooth running cannot be obtained, refer to 'CARBU-RETTER SERVICING'.

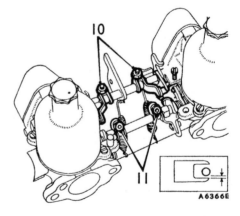

A6366E

(11) Set the throttle interconnection clamping levers (10) so that the link pin is ·012 in. away from the lower edge of the fork (see inset). Tighten the clamp bolts ensuring that there is approximately $\frac{1}{32}$ in. end-float on the interconnection rod.

4-4

Engine Emission. Issue 3. 12383

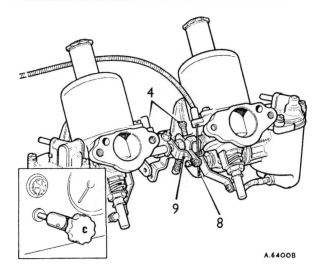

A.6400B

(12) With both jet levers at their lowest position, set the jet interconnection lever clamp bolts (11) so that both jets commence to move simultaneously.

(13) Run the engine at 1,500 r.p.m. and, using the balance meter, check that the carburetters are balanced. If they are not balanced, reset the levers, rebalance at idle speed, then recheck at 1,500 r.p.m.

(14) Check, and if necessary adjust, the mixture control wire (1) to give approximately $\frac{1}{16}$ in. free movement before it starts to pull on the jet levers (9).

(15) Pull the mixture control knob until the linkage is about to move the carburetter jets.

(16) Using the carburetter balancing meter to ensure equal adjustment, turn the fast idle adjusting screws (4) to give the correct fast idling speed (see 'TUNING DATA').

(17) Refit the air cleaners.

Section 4-B
CARBURETTER SERVICING

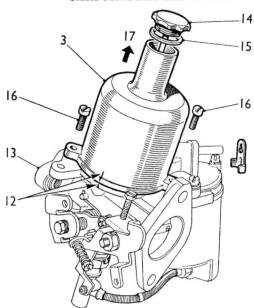

A6699B

Dismantling

Carburetters—all types

(1) Thoroughly clean the outside of the carburetter.

(2) Mark the relative position (12) of the suction chamber (3) and the carburetter body (13).

(3) Remove the damper (14) and its washer (15). Unscrew the chamber retaining screws (16).

(4) Lift off the chamber in the direction of arrow (17) without tilting.

(5) Remove the piston spring (18).

(6) Carefully lift out the piston assembly (19) and empty the damper oil from the piston rod (20).

Carburetters—fixed needle type

(7) Remove the needle locking screw (21) and withdraw the needle (22). If it cannot easily be removed, tap the needle inwards first and then pull outwards. Do not bend the needle.

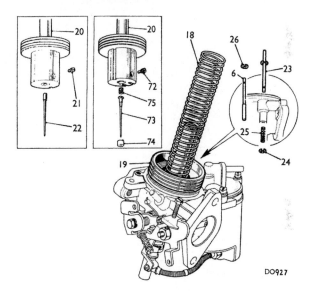

DO927

Carburetters—spring-loaded needle type

(8) Remove the guide locking screw (72), withdraw the needle assembly (73), needle support guide (74) and spring (75), taking care not to bend the needle.

(9) Withdraw the needle from the guide and remove the spring from the needle assembly.

Carburetters—all types

(10) If a piston lifting pin (23) with an external spring is fitted, remove the spring retaining circlip (24) and spring (25), then push the lifting pin upwards to remove it from its guide. With the concealed spring type (6) press the pin upwards, detach the circlip (26) from its upper end, and withdraw the pin and spring downwards.

(11) Support the moulded base of the jet (26) and slacken the screw (27) retaining the jet pick-up link (28).

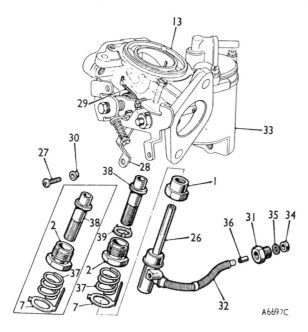

A6697C

(12) Relieve the tension of the pick-up lever return spring (29) from the screw and remove screw and brass bush (30) (when fitted).

(13) Unscrew the brass sleeve nut (31) retaining the flexible jet tube (32) to the float-chamber (33) and withdraw the jet assembly (26) from the carburetter body (13). Note the gland (34), washer (35), and ferrule (36) at the end of the jet tube.

(14) Bend back the small tag on the restrictor (7) to clear the jet adjusting nut, and remove the jet adjusting nut (1), restrictor (7), and spring (37). Unscrew the jet locking nut (2) and detach the nut

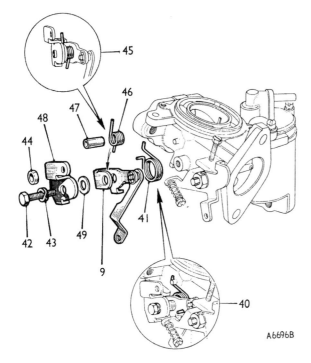

A6696B

and jet bearing (38). Withdraw the bearing from the nut, noting, on fixed needle carburetters only, the locking washer (39) under the shoulder of the bearing.

(15) Note the location points (see inset, 40) of the two ends of the pick-up lever return spring (41). Unscrew the lever pivot bolt (42) together with its double-coil spring washer (43), or spacer (44). Detach the lever assembly (9) and return spring.

(16) Note the location (see inset, 45) of the two ends of the cam lever spring (46) and push out the pivot bolt tube (47) (or tubes), taking care not to lose the spring. Lift off the cam lever (48), noting the skid washer (49) between the two levers.

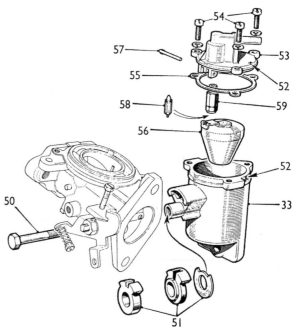

A6695B

(17) Slacken and remove the bolt (50) retaining the float-chamber (33) to the carburetter body. Note the component sequence of the flexibly mounted chambers (33) and (51).

(18) Mark (52) the location of the float-chamber lid (53). Unscrew the lid retaining screws (54) and detach the lid and its gasket (55) complete with float assembly (56).

(19) Push out the float hinge pin (57) from the end opposite its serrations and detach the float.

(20) Extract the float needle (58) from its seating (59) and unscrew the seating from the lid, using a wrench ·338 in. across the flats. Do not distort the seating.

(21) Close the throttle and mark (60) the relative positions of the throttle disc (61) and the carburetter flange (62). **Do not mark the throttle disc in the vicinity of the limit valve (63).**

4-6

Engine Emission. Issue 3. 16939

(22) Unscrew the two disc retaining screws (64). Open the throttle and ease out the disc from its slot in the throttle spindle (65). The disc is oval and will jam if care is not taken; store the disc in a safe place until required for reassembly.

(23) Tap back the tabs of the tab washer (66) securing the spindle nut (67). Note the location of the lever arm (68) in relation to the spindle and carburetter body; remove the nut and detach the arm.

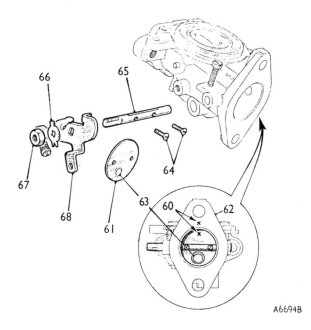

A6694B

Reassembling

Carburetters—all types

NOTE.—Before reassembling, examine all components for wear and damage. Renew unserviceable components, ensuring that only parts to the correct specification (see **'TUNING DATA'**) are used.

(1) Examine the throttle spindle and its bearings in the carburetter body. Check for excessive play. Renew parts as necessary.

(2) Refit the spindle to the body. Assemble the operating lever with tab washer and spindle nut, to the spindle. Ensure that when the stop on the lever is against the abutment on the carburetter body (i.e. throttle closed position) the countersunk ends of the holes in the spindle face outwards. Tighten the spindle nut and lock with the tab washer.

(3) Insert the throttle disc in the slot in the spindle in its original position as marked. Manœuvre the disc in its slot until the throttle can be closed, snap the throttle open and shut to centralize it in the bore of the carburetter, taking care not to damage the throttle limit valve. When assembled, the valve must be positioned at the bottom of the disc with the head of the valve towards the engine. Fit two new disc retaining screws but do not fully tighten. Check visually that the disc closes fully, and adjust

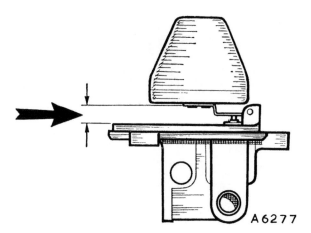

A6277

its position as necessary. With the throttle closed there must be clearance between the throttle lever and the carburetter body. Tighten the screws fully and spread their split ends just enough to prevent turning.

(4) Examine the float needle and seating for damage. Check that the spring-loaded plunger in the end of the plastic-bodied needle operates freely.

(5) Screw the seating into the float-chamber carefully. Do not overtighten. Replace the needle in the seating, coned end first. Test the assembly for leakage with air pressure.

(6) Refit the float and lever to the lid and insert the hinge pin and invert the float-chamber lid. With the needle valve held in the shut-off position by the weight of the float only, there should be a $\frac{1}{8}$ to $\frac{3}{16}$ in. gap (arrowed) between the float lever and the rim of the float-chamber lid.

(7) Examine the lid gasket for re-use. Assemble the gasket on the lid and refit the lid to the float-chamber in the position marked on dismantling. Tighten the securing screws evenly.

(8) Refit the float-chamber assembly to the carburetter body and tighten the retaining bolt fully, making sure that the registers on the body and the chamber engage correctly.

(9) Refit the piston lifting pin, spring and circlip.

(10) Examine the piston assembly for damage on the piston rod and the outside surface of the piston. The piston assembly must be scrupulously clean. Use gasoline or methylated spirit (denatured alcohol) as a cleaning agent. **Do not use abrasives.** Wipe dry, using a clean dry cloth.

(11) Clean inside the suction chamber and piston rod guide using gasoline or methylated spirit (denatured alcohol) and wipe dry. Refit the damper and washer. Temporarily plug the piston transfer holes (69) and fit the piston into the suction chamber. Fit a nut and screw, with a large flat washer under the head of the screw into one of the suction

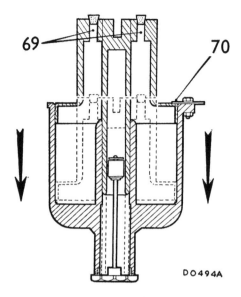

D0494A

chamber fixing holes, positioning the washer (70) so that it overlaps the suction chamber bore (see illustration). Check that the piston is fully home in the suction chamber and invert the assembly to allow the chamber to fall away from the piston until the piston contacts the flat washer. Check the time taken for the suction chamber to fall the full extent of the piston travel. For HS2-type carburetters of $1\frac{1}{4}$ in. bore the time taken should be 3 to 5 seconds, and for larger carburetters 5 to 7 seconds. If these times are exceeded check the piston and suction chamber for cleanliness and mechanical damage. If after rechecking the time taken is still not within these limits, renew the suction chamber and piston assembly.

Carburetters—fixed needle type

(12) Refit the needle to the piston assembly (19). The lower edge of the needle shoulder (22) must be level with the bottom face of the piston rod (20).

(13) Fit a new needle locking screw (21) and tighten. Invert the suction chamber and spin the piston assembly inside it to check for concentricity of the needle.

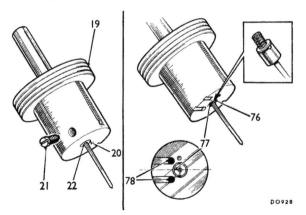

D0928

(14) Check the piston key for security in the carburetter body. Refit the piston assembly to the body and replace the piston spring over the piston rod.

(15) Fit the suction chamber and retaining screws, taking care not to wind up the spring; tighten the securing screws evenly.

(16) Refit the jet bearing, a new locking washer, and the locking nut; do not tighten the nut.

(17) Centralize the jet as follows:

   (a) Enter the end of the nylon feed tube into the base of the float-chamber, without the gland or washer fitted. Loosely secure with the retaining nut.

   (b) Feed the jet into the jet bearing; do not fit the jet nut spring, jet adjustment restrictor, or adjusting nut at this stage.

   (c) With the carburetter positioned with its inlet flange downwards, insert the piston loading tool into damper tube at the top of the suction chamber and screw in until fully home. Screw the tool back until the arrow, on the tool, points towards the inlet flange of the carburetter. **The tool and carburetter must remain in this position throughout the centering operation.**

   (d) With the piston at the bottom of its travel (on the bridge), and the jet hard up against the jet bearing, slowly tighten the jet locking nut. During the tightening process ensure that the jet is not binding in its bearing when drawn in and out. If any tightness between the jet and bearing is detected, the jet locking nut must be slackened and the process repeated.

   (e) Remove the jet loading tool.

(18) Withdraw the jet and tube; refit the spring, restrictor and jet adjusting nut. Fit the gland and washer to the flexible tube. The end of the tube should project a minimum of $\frac{3}{16}$ in. beyond the gland. Refit the jet and tube. Tighten the sleeve nut until the neoprene gland is compressed. Overtightening can cause leakage.

Carburetters—spring-loaded needle type

(19) Refit the jet bearing, fit and tighten the jet locking nut. No jet centering is required with the spring-loaded type jet needle.

(20) Fit the jet nut spring and adjustment restrictor. Fit the jet adjusting nut and screw it up as far as possible.

(21) Feed the jet into the jet bearing. Fit the sleeve nut, washer and gland to the end of the flexible tube. The tube must project a minimum of $\frac{3}{16}$ in. (4·8 mm.) beyond the gland. Tighten the sleeve nut until the gland is compressed. Overtightening can cause leakage.

Engine Emission. Issue 3. 16939

(22) Refit the spring to the jet needle assembly, ensuring that it locates completely in the groove of the needle support.

(23) **IMPORTANT.** Spring-loaded needles are supplied complete with shouldered spring seats; no attempt should be made to alter the position of the spring seat or convert a fixed-type needle to spring-loaded application. The raised 'pip' formed in the needle guide ensures that the needle is correctly centralized. Under no circumstances must the 'pip' be removed or repositioned.

Fit the needle assembly into its guide and fit the assembly into the piston. The lower edge of the guide (76) must be flush with the face of the piston and the guide positioned so that the etched locating mark (77) on its lower face is adjacent to and in line with the midway point between the two piston transfer holes as illustrated.

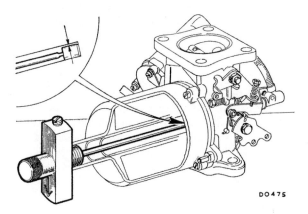

DO475

Alternative needle guides have a flat machined on the guide which must be positioned so that the guide locking screw tightens down onto the flat. If the guide is incorrectly positioned so that the locking screw has not tightened down on the flat, the head of the screw will protrude from the piston.

(24) Fit a new guide locking screw. **NOTE.**—Guide locking screws for spring-loaded needles are shorter than the needle locking screws used with fixed needles.

(25) Check the piston key for security in the carburetter body. Refit the piston assembly to the body and place the piston spring over the piston rod.

(26) Fit the suction chamber and retaining screws, taking care not to wind up the spring; tighten the securing screws evenly.

Carburetters—all types

(27) Refit the damper and washer.

(28) Reassemble the pick-up lever, cam lever, cam lever spring, skid washer, and pivot bolt tube or tubes in the positions noted on dismantling.

(29) Place the pick-up lever return spring in position over its boss and secure the lever assembly to the carburetter body with the pivot bolt. Ensure that the double-coil spring washer or spacer fits over the projecting end of the pivot bolt tube.

(30) Register the angled end of the return spring in the groove in the pick-up lever, and hook the other end of the spring around the moulded peg on the carburetter body.

(31) Fit the brass ferrule to the hole in the end of the pick-up link. Relieve the tension of the return spring and fit the link to the jet with its retaining screw. When finally tightening the screw, support the moulded end of the jet.

(32) Without removing the suction chamber, screw the jet adjusting nut until the top face of the jet is flush with the bridge of the carburetter.

(33) Turn down the jet adjusting nut to the initial jet setting given in **'TUNING DATA'.**

(34) Refit the carburetter(s) to the engine, following the instructions given in the relevant vehicle Workshop Manual.

Tune the carburetters in accordance with the instructions given in **'CARBURETTER TUNING —COMPLETE'.**

Section 4-C

CARBURETTER TUNING—COMPLETE

The following instructions apply only to new carburetters or carburetters which have been serviced as described in **'CARBURETTER SERVICING'**.

The tuning must be carried out with the engine emission control equipment connected and operating.

SINGLE CARBURETTERS

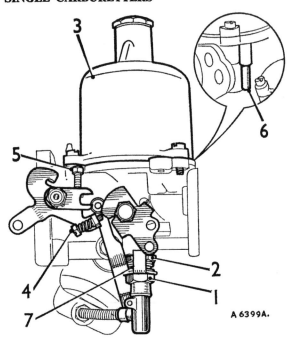

The type HS carburetter

1. Jet adjusting nut.
2. Jet locking nut.
3. Piston suction chamber.
4. Fast-idle adjusting screw.
5. Throttle adjusting screw.
6. Piston lifting pin.
7. Jet adjustment restrictor.

Initial setting

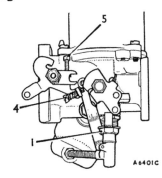

(1) Disconnect the mixture control (choke) wire if fitted.

(2) Unscrew the fast-idle screw (4) until it is well clear of the cam.

(3) Unscrew the throttle adjusting screw (5) until it is just clear of its stop and the throttle is closed.

(4) Set the throttle adjusting screw one full turn open.

(5) The jet adjusting nut must not be altered at this stage as it will be initially set to a datum setting at the factory or during the carburetter servicing procedure.

Tuning conditions

To ensure that the engine temperature and mixture requirements are stabilized, tuning must be carried out in accordance with the following setting cycle.

(1) Connect the tachometer and an approved exhaust gas analyser in accordance with the instrument-maker's instructions.

(2) Warm the engine at a fast idle to normal operating temperature preferably with the car standing in an ambient temperature of between 16 and 27° C. (60 to 80° F.). Run the engine for at least five minutes after the thermostat has opened; the thermostat opening point can be detected by the sudden rise in temperature of the radiator header tank.

(3) Set the engine speed at 2,500 r.p.m., at no load, and run for one minute.

(4) Tuning operations may now be commenced and must be carried out in the shortest possible time. If the time for settings exceeds a three-minute period, open the throttle and run the engine at 2,500 r.p.m. for one minute then resume tuning. Repeat this clearing operation if further periods of three minutes are exceeded.

Tuning procedure

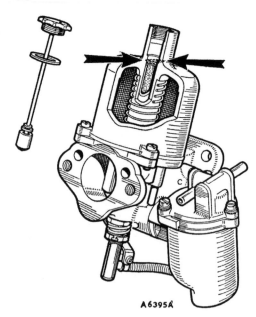

(1) Top up the piston damper with the recommended engine oil until the level is ½ in. above the top of the hollow piston rod.

4-10

Engine Emission. Issue 4. 18959

NOTE.—On dust-proofed carburetters, identified by a transverse hole drilled in the neck of the suction chambers and no vent hole in the damper cap, the oil level must be $\frac{1}{2}$ in. below the top of the hollow piston rod.

(2) Warm up the engine as described in **'Tuning conditions'**.

Turn the throttle adjusting screw until the idling speed given in **'TUNING DATA'** is obtained.

(3) During the following procedure, just before the readings of the tachometer and exhaust gas analyser are taken gently tap the neck of the suction chamber with a light non-metallic instrument (e.g. a screwdriver handle).

Turn the jet adjusting nut up to weaken, down to richen, until the fastest speed is recorded on the tachometer. Turn the jet adjusting nut very slowly up (weaken) until the engine speed just commences to fall, then turn the nut one flat down (rich). Check the idling speed against the figure given in **'TUNING DATA'**, and adjust if necessary using the throttle adjusting screw.

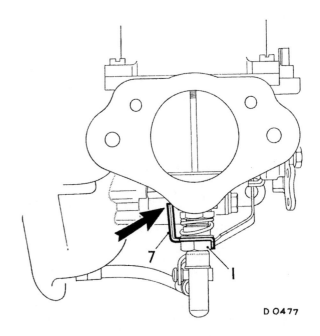

D 0477

(5) Hold the jet adjusting nut (1) to prevent it turning, and rotate the adjustment restrictor (7) round the nut until the vertical tag contacts the carburetter body on the left-hand side when viewed from the air cleaner flange (see illustration). In this position, bend the small tag on the adjustment restrictor down so that the restrictor locks to the nut and will follow its movements.

(6) Paint the small tag of the jet adjusting nut restrictor and the adjacent flat of the jet nut to identify the locking position.

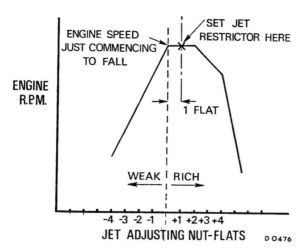

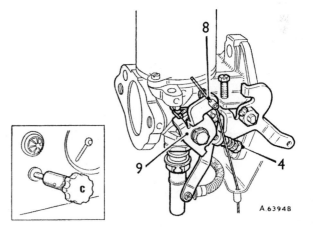

A 6394B

(4) Using the exhaust gas analyser, check that the percentage CO reading is within the limits given in **'TUNING DATA'**.

If the reading falls outside the limits given, reset the jet adjusting nut by the minimum amount necessary to bring the reading just within the limits. If an adjustment exceeding two flats is required to achieve this the test equipment should be checked for correct calibration.

(7) Reconnect the mixture control wire (8) with approximately $\frac{1}{16}$ in. free movement before it starts to pull on the jet lever (9).

(8) Pull the mixture control knob until the linkage is about to move the carburetter jet and adjust the fast-idle screw (4) to give the engine fast-idle speed.

(9) Check and if necessary adjust the throttle damper setting—if fitted (see **'TUNING DATA'**).

TWIN CARBURETTERS

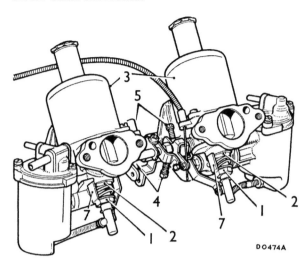

A twin-carburetter installation

1. Jet adjusting nuts.
2. Jet locking nuts.
3. Piston/suction chambers.
4. Fast-idle adjusting screws.
5. Throttle adjusting screws.
7. Jet adjustment restrictors.

Initial settings

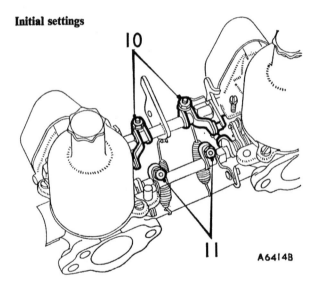

(1) Slacken both clamping bolts (10) on the throttle spindle interconnections.
(2) Disconnect the jet control interconnection by slackening the clamping bolts (11).
(3) Disconnect the mixture control wire if fitted.

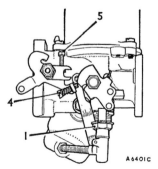

(4) Unscrew the fast-idle screw (4) on both carburetters until they are well clear of the cams.
(5) Unscrew the throttle adjusting screw (5) on both carburetters until they are just clear of their stops and the throttles are closed.
(6) Set the throttle adjustment screws on both carburetters half a turn open.
(7) The jet adjusting nuts must not be altered at this stage as they will be initially set to a datum setting either at the factory or during the carburetter servicing procedure.

Tuning conditions

To ensure that the engine temperature and mixture requirements are stabilized, tuning must be carried out in accordance with the following setting cycle.

(1) Connect a tachometer and an approved exhaust gas analyser in accordance with the instrument-maker's instructions.
(2) Warm the engine at a fast idle to normal operating temperature preferably with the car standing in an ambient temperature of between 16 and 27° C. (60 to 80° F.). Run the engine for at least five minutes after the thermostat has opened; the thermostat opening point can be detected by the sudden rise in temperature of the radiator header tank.
(3) Set the engine speed at 2,500 r.p.m., at no load, and run for one minute.
(4) Tuning operations may now be commenced and must be carried out in the shortest possible time. If the time for settings exceeds a three-minute period, open the throttle and run the engine at 2,500 r.p.m. for one minute then resume tuning. Repeat this clearing operation if further periods of three minutes are exceeded.

Tuning procedure

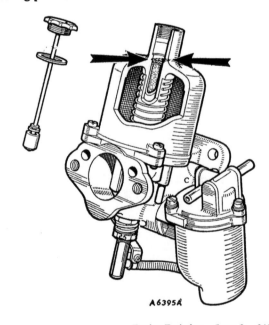

(1) Top up the piston damper with the recommended engine oil until the level is ½ in. above the top of the hollow piston rod.

NOTE.—On dust-proofed carburetters, identified by a transverse hole drilled in the neck of the suction chambers and no vent hole in the damper cap, the oil level must be ½ in. below the top of the hollow piston rod.

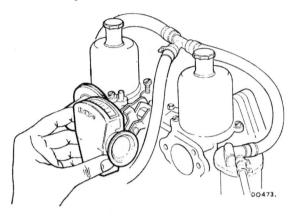

(2) Warm up the engine as described in 'TUNING CONDITIONS.'

(3) Turn the throttle adjusting screw on both carburetters until the idling speed given in 'TUNING DATA' is obtained.

(4) Using an approved balancing meter in accordance with the maker's instructions, balance the carburetters by altering the throttle adjusting screws; the idling speed obtained during this operation must be as given in 'TUNING DATA'.

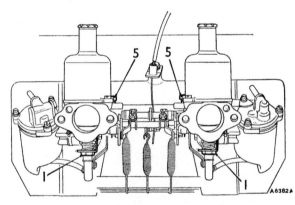

(5) During the following procedure, just before the readings of the tachometer and exhaust gas analyser are taken, gently tap the neck of each suction chamber with a light non-metallic instrument (e.g. a screwdriver handle).

Turn the jet adjusting nut (1) on both carburetters up to weaken, down to richen, the same amount until the fastest speed is recorded on the tachometer.

Turn both adjusting nuts very slowly up (weaken) until the engine speed just commences to fall, then turn both adjusting nuts one flat down (rich).

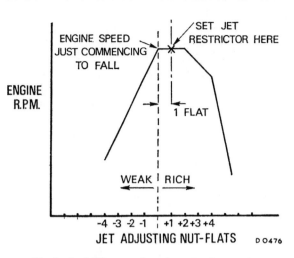

JET ADJUSTING NUT-FLATS

Check the idling speed against the figure given in **'TUNING DATA'**, and adjust if necessary by altering both throttle adjusting screws, each by the same amount. Using the balancing meter, check that the carburetters are balanced.

(6) Using the exhaust gas analyser, check that the percentage CO reading is within the limits given in **'TUNING DATA'**.

If the reading falls outside the limits given, reset both jet adjusting nuts by the minimum amount necessary to bring the reading just within the limits. If an adjustment exceeding two flats is required to achieve this the test equipment should be checked for correct calibration.

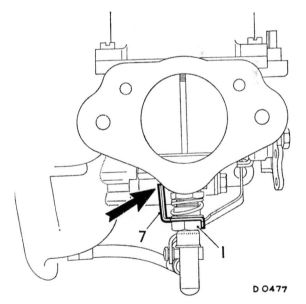

(7) Hold the jet adjusting nut (1) on each carburetter, to prevent it turning, and rotate the adjustment restrictor (7) round the nut until the vertical tag contacts the carburetter body on the left-hand side when viewed from the air cleaner flange (see illustration). In this position, bend the small tag on the adjustment restrictor down so that the restrictor locks to the nut and will follow its movements.

(8) Paint the small tag of the jet adjusting nut restrictor and the adjacent flat of the jet nut to identify the locking position.

(9) Set the throttle interconnection clamping levers (10) in accordance with the instructions given in the relevant vehicle Workshop Manual, so that a clearance exists between the link pin and the lower edge of the fork (see inset). Tighten the clamp bolts ensuring that there is approximately $\frac{1}{32}$ in. end float on the interconnection rod.

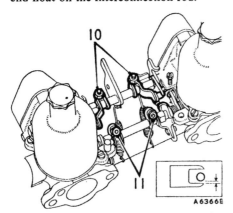

(10) With both jet levers at their lowest position, set the jet interconnection lever clamp bolts (11) so that both jets commence to move simultaneously.

Run the engine at 1,500 r.p.m. and, using the balance meter, check that the carburetters are balanced.

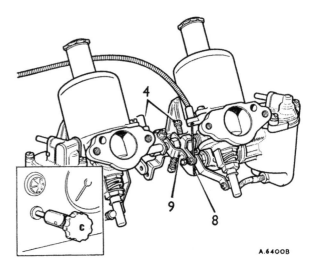

A.6400B

(11) Reconnect the mixture control wire (8) with approximately $\frac{1}{16}$ in. free movement before it starts to pull on the jet levers (9).

(12) Pull the mixture control knob until the linkage is about to move the carburetter jets.

(13) Using the carburetter balancing meter to ensure equal adjustment, turn the fast-idle adjusting screws (4) to give the correct fast idling speed (see 'TUNING DATA').

(14) Refit the air cleaners.

Section 4-D

TYPE HIF CARBURETTERS—TUNING
(Fitted to MGB from 1972 Model Year)

General

The carburetters fitted to cars equipped with engine emission control systems are balanced to provide engine performance with pollution control. Under no circumstances may they or their components be interchanged or substituted with normal carburetters.

Tuning must be carried out with the engine emission control equipment connected and operating.

IMPORTANT.—Before servicing or tuning a carburetter in an endeavour to rectify poor engine performance, make sure that the maladjustment or fault is not from another source by checking the following:

Valve clearance
Spark plug condition
Contact breaker (dwell angle)
Ignition timing and advance
Presence of air leaks into the induction system

Single and twin carburetters

(1) Remove the air cleaner(s).
(2) Check the throttle for correct operation and signs of sticking.
(3) Unscrew the throttle adjusting screw (both screws on twin carburetters) until it is just clear of the throttle lever, with the throttle closed, then turn the screw clockwise two full turns.
(4) Raise the piston of each carburetter with the lifting pin and check that it falls freely onto the bridge when the pin is released. If the piston shows any tendency to stick, the carburetter must be serviced.
(5) Lift and support the piston clear of the bridge so that the jet is visible; if this is not possible due to the installed position of the carburetter, remove the suction piston chamber.
(6) Turn the jet adjusting screw anti-clockwise until the jet is flush with the bridge or as high as possible without exceeding the bridge height. Ensure that both jets on twin carburetters are in the same relative position to the bridge of their respective carburetters.
(7) Check that the needle guide(s) is flush with the bottom of the piston groove.
(8) Turn the jet adjusting screw two turns clockwise (both screws on twin carburetters).
(9) Turn the fast idle adjusting screw anti-clockwise (both screws on twin carburetters) until it is well clear of the cam.
(10) Refit the suction piston chamber if it has been removed and, using the lifting pin, check that the piston falls freely onto the bridge.
(11) Top up the piston damper reservoir(s) with a recommended oil until the level is $\frac{1}{2}$ in. (13 mm.) above the top of the hollow piston rod.

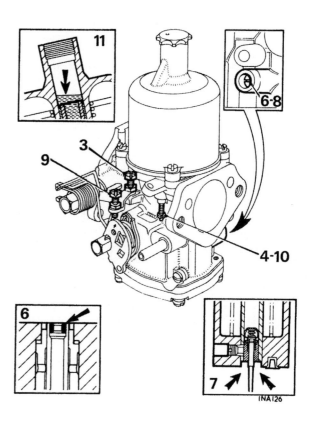

INA126

(12) Connect a reliable tachometer to the engine in accordance with the instrument manufacturer's instructions.

(13) Start the engine and run it at a fast idle speed until it attains normal running temperature, then run it for a further five minutes.

(14) Increase the engine speed to 2,500 r.p.m. for thirty seconds.

(15) Connect an approved exhaust gas analyser to the engine in accordance with the instrument manufacturer's instructions.

NOTE.—Tuning can now commence. If the correct setting cannot be obtained within three minutes, increase the engine speed to 2,500 r.p.m. for thirty seconds and then recommence tuning. Repeat this clearing operation at three-minute intervals until tuning is completed.

Single carburetters

(16) Adjust the throttle adjusting screw until the correct idle speed (see **'TUNING DATA'** and/or Vehicle Emission Control Information Label) is obtained.

NOTE.—During the following procedure, just before the readings of the tachometer and exhaust gas analyser are taken, gently tap the neck of the suction chamber with a light-metallic instrument (e.g. a screwdriver handle).

(17) Turn the jet adjusting screw, clockwise to enrich or anti-clockwise to weaken, until the fastest speed is indicated on the tachometer; turn the screw anti-clockwise until the engine speed just commences to fall. Turn the screw clockwise very slowly the minimum amount until the maximum speed is regained.

(18) Check the idle speed, and re-adjust it as necessary with the throttle adjusting screw to obtain the correct setting.

(19) Using the exhaust gas analyser, check that the percentage CO reading is within the limits given in **'TUNING DATA'** and/or Vehicle Emission Control Information Label. If the reading falls outside the limits given, reset the jet adjusting screw by the minimum amount necessary to bring the reading just within the limits. If an adjustment exceeding half a turn of the adjusting screw is required to achieve this, the carburetter must be removed and overhauled.

(20) With the fast idle cam against its return stop, check that a $\frac{1}{16}$ in. (1·5 mm.) free movement of the mixture control (choke) cable exists before the cable moves the cam.

(21) Pull out the mixture control (choke) until the arrow marked on the cam is positioned under the fast idle adjusting screw.

(22) Turn the fast idle adjusting screw clockwise until the correct fast idle speed (see **'TUNING DATA'** and/or Vehicle Emission Control Information Label) is obtained.

(23) Refit the air cleaner.

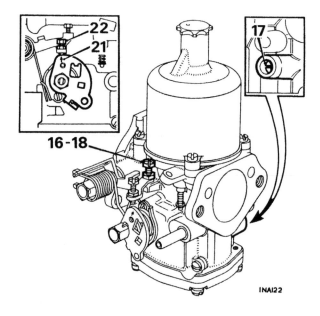

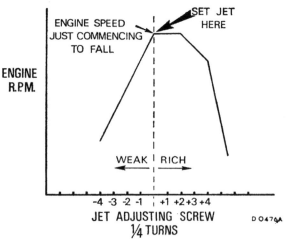

4-16

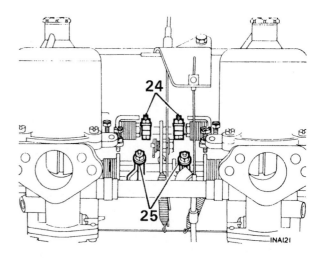

Twin carburetters

(24) Slacken both clamping bolts on the throttle spindle interconnections.

(25) Slacken both clamping bolts on the cold start interconnections.

(26) Using an approved balancing meter in accordance with the maker's instructions, balance the carburetters by altering the throttle adjusting screws until the correct idle speed and balance is achieved.

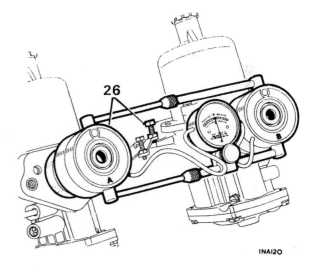

NOTE.—During the following procedure, just before reading the tachometer and exhaust gas analyser, gently tap the neck of each suction chamber with a non-metallic instrument (e.g. a screwdriver handle).

(27) Turn the jet adjusting screw on both carburetters clockwise to enrich or anti-clockwise to weaken, by the same amount until the fastest speed is registered on the tachometer; turn both screws anti-clockwise until the engine speed just commences to fall. Turn both screws very slowly clockwise by the minimum amount until the maximum speed is regained.

(28) Using the exhaust gas analyser, check that the percentage CO reading is within the limits given in **'TUNING DATA'** and/or Vehicle Emission Control Information Label. If the reading falls outside the limits given, reset both jet adjusting screws by the minimum amount necessary to bring the readings just within the limits. If an adjustment exceeding half a turn is required to achieve this the carburetters must be removed and overhauled.

(29) Set the throttle interconnection clamping levers, in accordance with the instructions given in the relevant vehicle Workshop Manual, so that a clearance exists between the link pin and the lower edge of the fork. Tighten the clamp bolts, ensuring that there is approximately $\frac{1}{32}$ in. end-float on the interconnection rod.

(30) Run the engine at 1,500 r.p.m. and check the throttle linkage for correct connection by re-checking the carburetter balance.

(31) With the fast idle cams of both carburetters against their respective stops, set the cold start interconnections so that both cams begin to move simultaneously.

(32) With the fast idle cams against their stops check that a $\frac{1}{16}$ in. (1·5 mm.) free movement of the mixture control (choke) cable exists before the cable moves the cams.

(33) Pull out the mixture control (choke) until the arrow marked on the cam is positioned under the fast idle adjusting screw of each carburetter.

(34) Using the balancing meter to ensure equal adjustment, turn the fast idle adjusting screws to give the correct fast idle speed (see **'TUNING DATA'** and/ or Vehicle Emission Control Information Label).

(35) Refit the air cleaners.

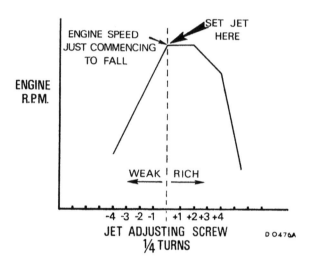

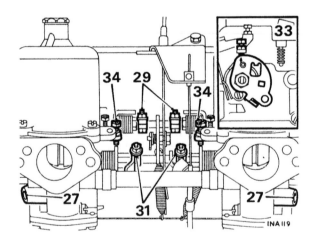

Section 4-E

TYPE HIF CARBURETTERS—OVERHAULING
(Fitted to MGB from 1972 Model Year)

Dismantling

(1) Thoroughly clean the outside of the carburetter.

(2) Remove the piston damper and its washer.

(3) Unscrew the suction piston chamber retaining screws and remove the identity tag.

(4) Lift the chamber vertically from the body without tilting it.

(5) Remove the piston spring, lift out the piston assembly and empty the oil from the piston rod.

(6) Unscrew the needle guide locking screw.

(7) Withdraw the needle, guide and spring.

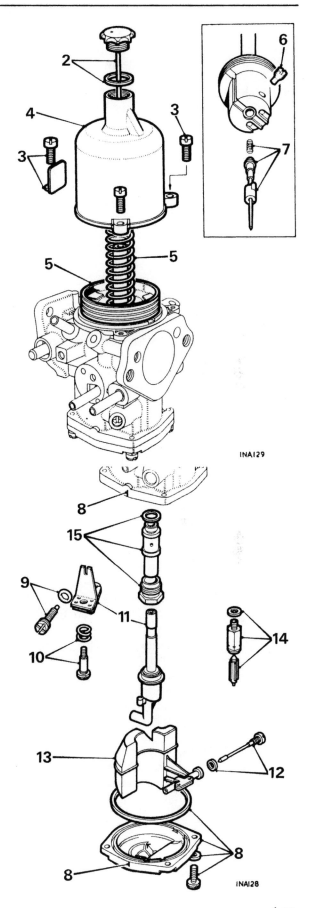

INA129

(8) Mark the bottom cover-plate and body to ensure correct reassembly, unscrew the retaining screws and remove the cover complete with sealing ring.

(9) Remove the jet adjusting screw complete with 'O' ring.

(10) Remove the jet adjusting lever retaining screw and spring.

(11) Withdraw the jet complete with adjusting lever and disengage the lever.

(12) Remove the float pivot spindle and fibre washer.

(13) Withdraw the float.

(14) Remove the needle valve and unscrew the valve seat.

(15) Unscrew the jet bearing locking nut and withdraw the bearing complete with fibre washer.

INA128

(16) Note the location of the ends of the fast idle cam lever return spring.

(17) Unlock and remove the cam lever retaining nut and locking washer.

(18) With the return spring held towards the carburetter body, prise off the cam lever and remove the return spring.

(19) Unscrew the starter unit retaining screws and remove the cover-plate.

(20) Withdraw the starter unit assembly and remove its gasket.

(21) Withdraw the valve spindle and remove the 'O' ring, seals and dust cap.

(22) Note the location and loading of the ends of the throttle lever return spring and remove the spring.

(23) Unlock and remove the nut and tab washer retaining the throttle levers.

(24) Remove the throttle lever and throttle actuating lever.

(25) Remove the throttle disc retaining screws.

(26) Open the throttle; note that the throttle disc is oval, and carefully withdraw the disc from the throttle spindle. Do not damage the over-run valve.

(27) Withdraw the throttle spindle and remove its seals.

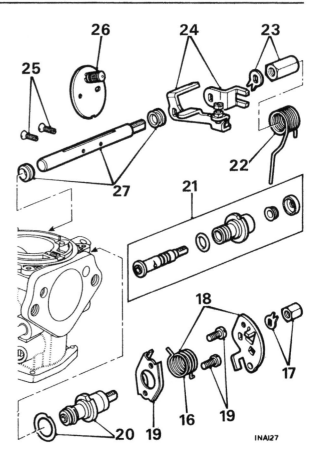

INSPECTION

(28) Examine the throttle spindle and its bearings in the carburetter body; check for excessive play, and renew parts as necessary.

(29) Examine the float needle and seating for damage and excessive wear; renew if necessary.

(30) Examine all rubber seals and 'O' rings for damage deterioration; renew as necessary. The cover-plate sealing ring must be renewed.

(31) Check condition of all fibre washers and gaskets renew as necessary.

(32) Clean the inside of the suction chamber and piston rod guide with fuel or methylated spirit (denatured alcohol) and wipe dry. Abrasives must not be used.

(33) Examine the carburetter body for cracks and damage and for security of the brass connections and the piston key.

    NOTE.—It is only necessary to carry out the following timing check if the cause of the carburetter malfunction which necessitated the dismantling has not been located.

(34) Temporarily plug the piston transfer holes.

(35) Fit the piston into the chamber without its spring.

(36) Fit a nut and screw, with a large flat washer under the screw head, into one of the suction chamber fixing holes, positioning the washer so that it overlaps the chamber bore.

(37) Fit the damper and washer.

(38) Check that the piston is fully home in the chamber, invert the assembly to allow the chamber to fall away until the piston contacts the washer.

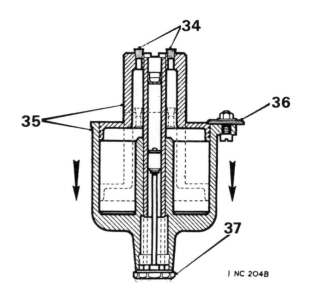

4-20

(39) Check the time taken for the chamber to fall the full extent of the piston travel. For HIF carburetters 1½ in. (38 mm.) bore the time taken should be 4 to 6 seconds; for HIF6 1¾ in. (44·5 mm.) bore the time taken should be 5 to 7 seconds.

(40) If the times are exceeded, check the piston and chamber for cleanliness and damage. If after re-checking the time is still not within these limits, renew the chamber and piston assembly.

Reassembling

(41) Reverse the procedure in 1 to 28, noting the following:

(a) The throttle spindle must be fitted with the threaded end at the piston lifting pin side of the body.

(b) Fit the throttle disc so that the over-run valve is at the top of the bore and its spring towards the inside when the throttle is closed.

(c) New throttle disc retaining screws must be used when refitting the disc. Ensure that the throttle disc is correctly positioned and closes correctly before tightening and locking the retaining screw.

(d) Position the throttle spindle end seals just below the spindle housing flange.

(e) The starter unit valve is fitted with the cut-out towards the top retaining screw hole, and its retaining plate is positioned with the slotted flange towards the throttle spindle.

(f) After fitting the float and valve, invert the carburetter so that the needle valve is held in the shut position by the weight of the float only. Check that the point indicated on the float (see illustration) is 0·04±0·02 in. (1·0 ±·5 mm.) below the level of the float chamber face. Adjust the float position by carefully bending the arm.

(g) Check that the small diameter of the jet adjusting screw engages the slot in the adjusting lever and set the jet flush with the bridge of the body.

(h) Use a new retaining screw when refitting the needle and ensure that the needle guide etch mark aligns correctly with the piston transfer holes (see illustration). After fitting the needle assembly, check that the shoulder of the needle aligns the full face of the piston.

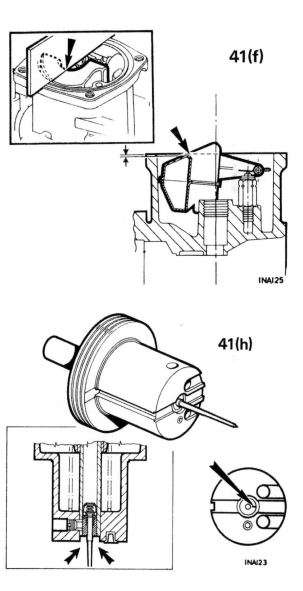

41(f)

INA125

41(h)

INA123

ENGINE SPEED	TEST	COMPONENT CONDITION	READ/OBSERVE	READINGS	CHECK SEQUENCE—FAULT LOCATION
START (cranking)	Cranking voltage	Battery; starting system	Voltmeter	9·6 volts minimum at the battery	Battery—connections/cables—starter motor—dynamo/alternator—regulator
	Cranking coil output	Coil and ignition circuit	Scope trace	17 KV. minimum	Ignition coil
	Positive crankcase ventilation/cranking vacuum	Crankcase emission equipment	Vacuum gauge	6—10 in. Hg (crankcase ventilation operating) 8—15 in. Hg (crankcase ventilation blanked)	Hoses and connections—Oil filler cap—Valve rocker clearance—Emission valve—Gulp valve—Oil separator—Servo (if fitted)—Inlet manifold leaks—Valves or seats—Piston rings—Any air leak to crankcase
IDLING (see 'TUNING DATA')	Idle speed	Carburetter idle setting	Tachometer	See 'TUNING DATA'	Carburetter adjustment—Hoses and connections—Gulp valve—Servo (if fitted)—Carburetter limit valve or mechanical condition
	Dwell	Distributor/drive; points	Dwell meter; scope	4-cyl.: 57 to 63° See Pattern 1 (see inset A)	Breaker points—Distributor and drive mechanical condition
	Initial timing	Spark timing setting	Timing light	See 'TUNING DATA'	Distributor adjustment
	Fuel mixture	Carburetter setting	Exhaust gas analyser	See 'TUNING DATA'	Carburetter adjustment—Hoses and connections—Gulp valve—Crankcase emission valve—Servo (if fitted)—Carburetter limit valve or mechanical condition—Air pump—Check valve—Spark plugs
	Manifold vacuum	Engine idle efficiency	Vacuum gauge	12 in. Hg minimum (engine fully run in)	Hoses and connections—Gulp valve—Inlet manifold leaks—carburetter limit valve—Valves or seats—Piston rings
	Dwell variation	Distributor mechanical	Dwell meter	Variation of 2° maximum	Distributor and drive mechanical condition
	Coil polarity	Ignition circuit polarity	Scope trace	See Pattern 2 (Trace inverted)	Ignition circuit connections—Ignition coil
	Cam lobe accuracy	Distributor cam	Scope trace	3° max. variation. See Pattern 3 (inset A correct; inset B—overlap indicates cam error)	Distributor mechanical condition (cam)
FAST IDLE (see 'TUNING DATA')	Secondary circuit	Plugs; leads; cap; rotor	Scope trace	Standard pattern	Spark plugs and leads—Breaker points—Carburetter adjustment—Hoses and connections—Gulp valve—Servo (if fitted)
	Coil and condenser condition	Coil windings; condenser	Scope trace	See Pattern 4 (lack of oscillations indicate fault)	Ignition coil—Condenser
	Breaker point condition	Points closing/opening/bounce	Scope trace	See Pattern 1 (inset B)	Breaker points—Condenser
	Spark plug firing voltage	Fuel mixture; compression; plug/rotor gaps	Scope trace	See Pattern 5; voltage 6—9 kV	Spark plugs and leads—Distributor cap and rotor—Carburetter adjustment (multi-carburetters)
ACCELERATE—DECELERATE	Spark plugs under load	Spark plugs	Scope trace	See Pattern 6; acceptable voltage rise 6 to 10 kV	Spark plugs and leads
	Carburetter open/close action	Carburetter	Exhaust gas analyser and vacuum gauge	Initial rich, lean off at throttle closure	Carburetter limit valve and mechanical condition—Hoses and connections—Gulp valve—Air pump
TURNPIKE (Maximum ignition advance speed see 'TUNING DATA')	Timing advance	Distributor mech./vacuum advance	Timing light/advance meter	See 'TUNING DATA'	Distributor mechanical condition, vacuum unit, centrifugal weights and springs
	Maximum coil output	Coil; condenser; ignition primary	Scope trace	Standard pattern; minimum reserve ⅓ more than requirement	Ignition coil—H.T. circuit insulation
	Secondary circuit insulation	H.T. cables, cap, rotor	Scope trace	Standard pattern	H.T. leads—Distributor cap and rotor
	Charging voltage	Regulator; cut-out	Voltmeter	14·5 volts; steady reading	Cut-out—Voltage regulator—Dynamo/Alternator
	Fuel mixture	Air cleaner, carburetter	Exhaust gas analyser	Leaning off following peak when test speed is reached	Hoses and connections—Carburetter adjustment—Air cleaners—Gulp valve—Air pump—Check valve—Injectors
	Exhaust restriction	Exhaust system	Vacuum gauge	No variation in reading at constant speed for 10 sec.	Exhaust system

Pattern 1 (4 CYL.) — POINTS CLOSED / POINTS OPEN / 60°

Pattern 2

Pattern 3

Pattern 4 — FAULT

Pattern 5 — WIDE GAP / KV / 10 / 5

Pattern 6 — NO ACCEPTABLE VOLTAGE RISE / KV / 10 / 5

354

SECTION 5

EVAPORATIVE LOSS CONTROL

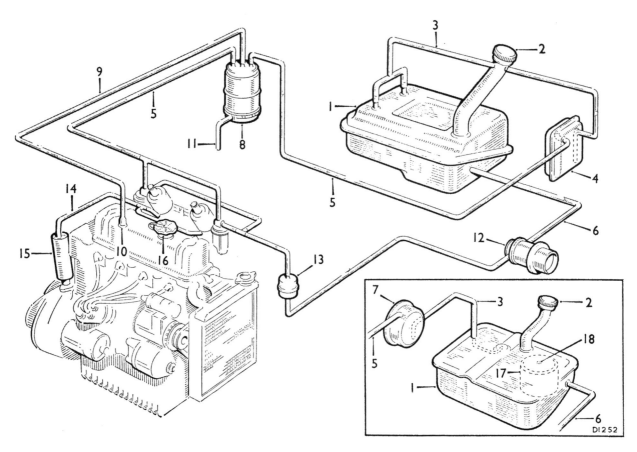

Fig. 1

A typical evaporative loss control system, with inset showing the arrangement of a separation tank and capacity-limiting fuel tank

1. Fuel tank.	7. Separation tank.	13. Fuel line filter.
2. Sealed fuel filler cap.	8. Adsorption canister.	14. Breather pipe.
3. Expansion/vapour line.	9. Purge line.	15. Oil separator.
4. Expansion tank.	10. Restricted connection.	16. Sealed oil filler cap.
5. Vapour pipe.	11. Air vent.	17. Capacity limiting tank.
6. Fuel pipe.	12. Fuel pump.	18. Air lock bleed.

Section 5-A

GENERAL DESCRIPTION

The system is designed to collect fuel vapour evaporated from the fuel in the fuel tank, and on some twin carburetter cars from the fuel in the carburetter float-chambers. The vapour is stored in an adsorption canister while the engine is stopped, and then after the engine is restarted, passed through the crankcase emission control system to the combustion chambers. While the car is being driven the vapours are drawn directly to the crankcase emission control system.

Ventilation tubes on the fuel tank ensure that vapours are vented through the control system when the car is parked on other than a level surface.

To prevent spillage of fuel by displacement due to expansion, sufficient capacity is provided in the expansion tank to accommodate the amount of fuel from a full tank which would be displaced by a high temperature rise.

By the positioning of the expansion tank connections, or by the inclusion of a small separation tank in the vapour line, liquid fuel is prevented from being carried with the vapour to the storage canister.

IMPORTANT. The fuel and oil filler caps seal the system, and it is essential for its efficient function that they are correctly refitted after removal.

Adsorption canister

The adsorption or vapour storage canister mounted in the engine compartment contains activated charcoal (carbon) granules. Filter pads are fitted at both sides of the charcoal to filter incoming ventilating air and to prevent the granules from leaving the canister through the purge line. Provision is made for renewing the ventilation air filter pad. Vapour tubes from the fuel tank and carburetter float-chambers and the purge line from the engine breather system are connected to the ports on the

Engine Emission. Issue 4. 24062

top of the canister. The port on the bottom section provides a connection for the ventilating air tube.

Fuel vapour entering the canister through the vapour tubes is adsorbed and held by the charcoal. When the engine is started, air is drawn by the crankcase emission control system, through the ventilation tube and into the canister. As the air passes over the charcoal granules the vapours are given up and are carried with the air through the crankcase emission system to the combustion chambers.

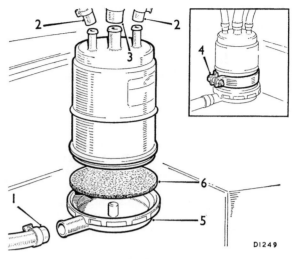

Fig. 2

The adsorption canister air filter pad

1. Air vent tube.
2. Vapour pipes.
3. Purge pipe.
4. Canister securing clip.
5. End cap.
6. Air filter pad.

Fuel line filter

On some models an additional renewable filter is fitted in the main fuel line as an added safeguard against foreign matter causing the setting of the carburetter float-chamber level to be exceeded.

Mixture temperature compensator

On some applications a small temperature-sensitive valve is fitted adjacent to the carburetter. The valve is connected between the air cleaner and the controlled depression chamber of the carburetter.

Under conditions where fuel is entering the carburetter at high temperature, i.e. prolonged idling in high ambient temperatures, the valve opens and allows a small quantity of air to pass into the carburetter, bypassing the jet. The air leans off the mixture which has been enriched by vapours from the evaporative loss control system and by

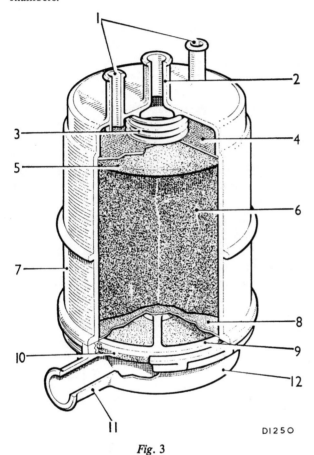

Fig. 3

The adsorption canister

1. Vapour pipe connections.
2. Purge pipe connection.
3. Spring.
4. Gauze.
5. Filter pad.
6. Charcoal granules.
7. Canister.
8. Gauze.
9. Retainer.
10. Filter pad.
11. Air vent connection.
12. End cap.

Fuel expansion

Two methods are used to ensure that sufficient space is available to accommodate fuel displaced by expansion due to high ambient temperatures. The method used on the Austin America is by fitting an additional tank into which the displaced fuel flows when the volume of the fuel exceeds that of the fuel tank. The MGB and MG Midget use an air lock chamber in the fuel tank which prevents the tank being completely filled with fuel, thereby ensuring that sufficient space is always available for expansion.

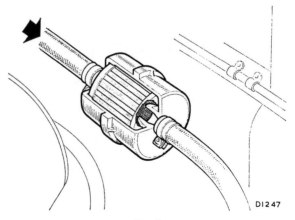

Fig. 4

The fuel line filter

the increase in fuel flow through the carburetter due to the high fuel temperature.

Section 5-B

ADSORPTION CANISTER

Renewing

The air filter fitted in the bottom section of the canister must be renewed every 12,000 miles (20000 km.) or more frequently in dusty operating conditions. The complete canister must be renewed every 50,000 miles (80000 km.) or if at any time it should inadvertently become saturated with liquid fuel.

WARNING. Do not attempt to recover a saturated canister by passing compressed air through the charcoal.

(1) Disconnect the air vent tube from the bottom of the canister.

(2) Disconnect the vapour and purge pipes from the top of the canister.

(3) Unscrew the securing clip screw and lift out the canister.

(4) If the air filter pad only is being renewed:
  (a) Unscrew the lower end cap of the canister.
  (b) Remove and discard the filter pad.
  (c) Clean any dirt from the cap.
  (d) Fit the new filter pad and refit the cap.

(5) Fit the canister ensuring that the purge pipe (from the engine rocker cover) is connected to the large centre connection on the top of the canister.

Section 5-C

FUEL LINE FILTER

Renewing

The fuel line filter must be renewed every 12,000 miles (20000 km.).

(1) Check that the ignition is switched off.

(2) Disconnect and discard the filter.

(3) Connect the new filter.

(4) Switch on the ignition and check the filter connections for fuel leakage.

(5) Start the engine and recheck for fuel leakage.

Section 5-D

LEAK TESTING

NOTE. As a preliminary check for leaks on the induction and evaporative loss control systems on cars fitted with running on control valves, temporarily block the air vent pipe of the valve while the engine is idling. If no air leaks exist in the systems the engine will stop almost immediately; if the engine continues to run an air leak is indicated.

If a fault in the operation is suspected or components of the system other than the filters or canister have been removed and refitted, the evaporative loss control system must be pressure-tested for leaks as follows:

(1) Check that there is at least one gallon of fuel in the fuel tank.

(2) Switch on the ignition for one minute to prime the fuel system.

(3) Switch off the ignition and disconnect the fuel tank ventilation pipe from its connection on the adsorption canister.

(4) Connect a 0 to 10 lb./sq. in. pressure gauge, a Schrader valve, and a low-pressure air supply (i.e. a tyre pump) to the disconnected pipe.

(5) Pressurize the system until 1 lb./sq. in. is registered on the gauge. **DO NOT EXCEED THIS PRESSURE AT ANY TIME.**

(6) Check that the gauge reading is maintained for 10 seconds without falling more than ·5 lb./sq. in. If the reading is not maintained, check the system for leaks commencing with the fuel filler cap and seal.

(7) Make a visual check for fuel leakage from the tank and its connections.

(8) Remove the fuel filler cap and check that the gauge falls to zero.

(9) Remove the test equipment and re-make the connections.

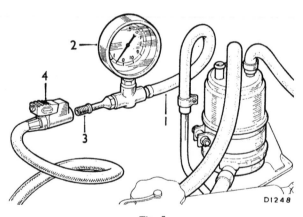

Fig. 5

Leak-testing the control system

1. Fuel tank ventilation pipe.
2. Pressure gauge.
3. Schrader valve.
4. Low-pressure air supply.

SECTION 6

TUNING DATA

MODEL: SPRITE (Mk. IV)/MIDGET (Mk. III) Up to 1972

ENGINE

Type	12CD or 12CJ
Firing order	1, 3, 4, 2
Capacity	1274·86 c.c. (77·8 cu. in.)
Compression ratio	8·8 : 1
Compression pressure	120 lb./sq. in. (8·44 kg./cm.²)
Idle speed	1,000 r.p.m.
Fast idle speed	1,100 r.p.m. to 1,200 r.p.m.
Valve rocker clearance	·012 in. (·305 mm.) set cold
Stroboscopic ignition timing*	10° B.T.D.C. at 1,000 r.p.m.
Static ignition timing	4° B.T.D.C.
Timing mark location	Pointer on timing case, notch on crankshaft pulley

DISTRIBUTOR

Make	Lucas
Type	25D4
Serial number	41229 to 1971; 41271 from 1971 on
Contact breaker gap	·014 to ·016 in. (·35 to ·40 mm.)
Rotation of rotor	Anti-clockwise
Dwell angle	57° to 63°
Condenser capacity	·18 to ·24 mF
Centrifugal advance	
Crankshaft degrees*	4° at 500 to 700 r.p.m.
	19° at 2,300 to 2,500 r.p.m.
	30° ± 2° at 4,300 r.p.m.
Vacuum advance	
Starts	5 in. Hg
Finishes	8 in. Hg
Total crankshaft degrees	6° ± 2°

SPARKING PLUGS

Make	Champion
Type	N-9Y
Gap	·024 to ·026 in. (·625 to ·660 mm.)

IGNITION COIL

Make	Lucas
Type	11C12
Resistance—primary	3 to 3·4 ohms at 20° C. (68° F.)
Consumption	
Ignition on—standing	3·5 to 4 amps.
at 2,000 r.p.m.	1 amp.

CARBURETTER(S)

Make	S.U.
Type	Twin HS2
Specification—fixed needle type	AUD 266
—spring-loaded needle type ..	AUD 328 to 1971; AUD 404 from 1971 on
Choke diameter	1¼ in. (31·75 mm.)
Jet size	·090 in. (2·28 mm.)
Needle—fixed type	AN
—spring-loaded type	AAC
Piston spring	Blue
Initial jet adjustment	11 flats from bridge

EXHAUST EMISSION

Exhaust gas analyser reading:	
At engine idle speed	2·5% CO (maximum)
Air pump test speed	1,200 r.p.m. (engine)

* Vacuum pipe disconnected.

MODEL: M.G. MIDGET (Mk. III) from 1972 on

ENGINE

Type	12V
Firing order	1, 3, 4, 2
Capacity	1274·86 c.c. (77·8 cu. in.)
Compression ratio	8 : 1
Compression pressure	120 lb./sq. in. (8·44 kg./cm.²)
Idle speed	1,000 r.p.m.
Fast idle speed	1,100 r.p.m. to 1,200 r.p.m.
Valve rocker clearance	·012 in. (·305 mm.) set cold
Stroboscopic ignition timing*	9° B.T.D.C. at 1,500 r.p.m.
Static ignition timing	T.D.C.
Timing mark location	Pointer on timing case, notch on crankshaft pulley

DISTRIBUTOR

Make	Lucas
Type	25D4
Serial number	1972—41369; from 1973—41400
Contact breaker gap	·014 to ·016 in. (·35 to ·40 mm.)
Rotation of rotor	Anti-clockwise
Dwell angle	57° to 63°
Condenser capacity	·18 to ·24 mF

Centrifugal advance

Crankshaft degrees*	15° at 1,800 to 2,000 r.p.m.	
	24° at 2,700 to 3,100 r.p.m.	
	36°±2° at 4,200 r.p.m.	
	Serial No.	*Serial No.*
Vacuum advance	41369 (1972)	41400 (1973)
Starts	4 in. Hg	10 in. Hg
Finishes	9 in. Hg	15 in. Hg
Total crankshaft degrees	16°±2°	10°±2°

SPARKING PLUGS

Make	Champion
Type	N–9Y
Gap	·024 to ·026 in. (·625 to ·660 mm.)

IGNITION COIL

Make	Lucas
Type	11C12
Resistance—primary	3 to 3·4 ohms at 20° C. (68° F.)

Consumption

Ignition on—standing	3·5 to 4 amps.
at 2,000 r.p.m. ..	1 amp.

CARBURETTER(S)

Make	S.U.
Type	Twin HS2
Specification	1972—AUD 502; from 1973—AUD 549
Choke diameter	1¼ in. (31·75 mm.)
Jet size	·090 in. (2·28 mm.)
Needle	1972—AAT; from 1973—ABC
Piston spring	Blue
Initial jet adjustment	11 flats from bridge

EXHAUST EMISSION

Exhaust gas analyser reading:

At engine idle speed	1972—3% CO (maximum); from 1973, 2·5% CO (maximum)
Air pump test speed	1,200 r.p.m. (engine)

* Vacuum pipe disconnected.

Engine Emission. Issue 4. 83919

Section Da.4

CARBURETTERS

(Engine Type 12V 778F)

Tuning

Before tuning the carburetters in an endeavour to rectify poor engine performance, check the following items to ensure that the maladjustment or fault is not from another source.

(a) Valve clearance.

(b) Spark plug condition.

(c) Contact breaker (dwell angle).

(d) Ignition timing and advance.

(e) Presence of air leaks in the induction system.

(f) Operation of engine controls.

Carburetter tuning is confined to setting the idle and fast idle speeds, and mixture at idle speed. To achieve the best results, a reliable tachometer, a balancing meter and an exhaust gas analyser (CO meter of the infra-red non-dispersive type or equivalent) are required.

(1) Remove the air cleaners as detailed in Section D.6.

(2) Check the throttle for correct operation and signs of sticking.

(3) Unscrew each throttle adjusting screw until it is just clear of the throttle lever stop when the throttle is closed, then turn each screw one turn in a clockwise direction.

(4) Raise the piston of each carburetter, using the lifting pin, and check that the piston falls freely onto the bridge in the carburetter body when the lifting pin is released. If the piston tends to stick, the carburetter must be serviced.

(5) Lift and support the piston of each carburetter clear of the bridge in the carburetter body so that each carburetter jet is visible.

(6) Turn the jet adjusting nut of each carburetter upwards until each jet is flush with the bridge in the carburetter body or as high as possible without exceeding the bridge height. Ensure that both jets are in the same relative position to the bridge of their respective carburetter.

(7) Check that the shank of each needle is flush with the underside of its respective piston.

(8) Turn the jet adjusting nut of each carburetter two turns downwards.

(9) Turn the fast idle adjusting screw of each carburetter in an anti-clockwise direction until it is well clear of its fast idle cam.

(10) Unscrew and withdraw the piston dampers from the suction chambers. Top up with new engine oil (preferably S.A.E. 20) until the level is ½ in.

13 mm.) above the top of each hollow piston rod. Refit the damper assemblies.

(11) Connect the tachometer of tool 18G 677 Z to the engine.

(12) Start the engine and run it at a fast idle until it attains normal running temperature, then run it for a further five minutes.

(13) Increase the engine speed to 2,500 r.p.m. for 30 seconds.

(14) Connect an exhaust gas analyser to the engine in accordance with the instrument manufacturer's instructions.

Setting can now commence. If the correct setting cannot be obtained within three minutes, increase the engine speed to 2,500 r.p.m. for 30 seconds and then recommence tuning. Repeat this clearing operation at three-minute intervals until tuning is completed.

(15) Slacken the two throttle inter-connecting rod lever clamping bolts.

(16) Slacken the two jet inter-connecting rod lever clamping bolts.

(17) Using a balance meter in accordance with the manufacturer's instructions, balance the carburetters, altering the throttle adjusting screws until the correct idle speed (see 'ENGINE TUNING DATA') and balance is achieved. Alternatively, use a 'listening tube' to compare the intensity of the intake hiss from both carburetters and alter the throttle adjusting screws until the hiss from both carburetters is the same at idling speed.

(18) Turn the jet adjusting nut of each carburetter by the same amount, downwards to enrich or upwards to weaken, until the fastest engine speed is indicated on the tachometer; turn each nut upwards by the same amount until the engine speed just commences to fall. Turn each nut very slowly downwards by the minimum but same amount until the maximum engine speed is regained.

(19) Check the engine idling speed and re-adjust it as necessary, turning each throttle adjusting screw by the same amount.

(20) Using the exhaust gas analyser, check that the carbon monoxide percentage is within the limits given in 'ENGINE TUNING DATA'. If the reading falls outside the limits, reset both jet adjusting nuts by the same minimum amount necessary to bring the reading just within the limits. If an adjustment exceeding three flats of the jet adjusting nuts is required to achieve this, the carburetters must be removed and serviced.

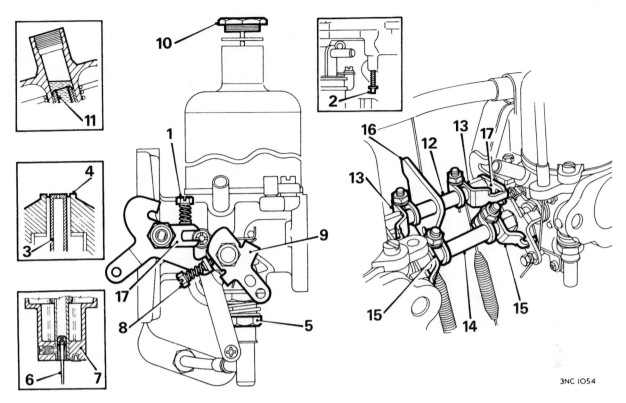

Fig. Da.9

Carburetter tuning

1. Throttle adjusting screw.	7. Piston.	13. Throttle inter-connection rod lever.
2. Piston lifting pin.	8. Fast idle adjusting screw.	14. Jet inter-connecting rod.
3. Jet.	9. Fast idle cam lever.	15. Jet inter-connecting rod lever.
4. Bridge.	10. Piston damper.	16. Throttle inter-connecting rod stop lever.
5. Jet adjusting nut.	11. Piston rod.	17. Throttle lever.
6. Jet needle.	12. Throttle inter-connecting rod.	

(21) Stop the engine and set the throttle inter-connecting rod levers so that a clearance of 0·012 in. (0·31 mm.) exists between each lever link pin and the lower arm of its respective throttle lever fork.

   (*a*) Insert a 0·012 in. (0·31 mm.) feeler gauge between the throttle inter-connecting rod stop lever and the carburetter heat shield.

   (*b*) Move each throttle inter-connector lever downwards until each lever link pin rests on the lower arm of its respective throttle lever fork. Tighten the throttle inter-connecting rod lever clamp bolts, ensuring that the throttle inter-connecting rod has an end-float of approximately $\frac{1}{32}$ in. (0·8 mm.). Remove the feeler gauge.

(22) Run the engine at 1,500 r.p.m. and re-check the carburetter balance to ensure that the throttle linkage is connected correctly.

(23) Ensure that the fast idle cam lever of each carburetter is against its respective stop and tighten the jet inter-connecting rod lever clamp bolts so that both cam levers begin to move simultaneously when the mixture control is operated.

(24) Ensure that the fast idle cam lever of each carburetter is against its respective stop and check that the mixture control cable has $\frac{1}{16}$ in (1·5 mm.) free movement before it commences to operate the cam levers.

(25) Pull the mixture control out until the jet linkage is about to move both jets downwards.

(26) Run the engine and using the balance meter or 'listening tube' to ensure equal adjustment, turn the fast idle adjusting screws to set the engine fast idling to the speed given in '**ENGINE TUNING DATA**'.

(27) Refit the air cleaners.

Section Db.5

FUEL PUMP
(S.U. Type AUF 305)

Removing and refitting

(1) Disconnect the battery earth lead.

(2) Drain the fuel from the tank, or plug the pump inlet hose after disconnecting it from the fuel pump.

(3) Disconnect the fuel inlet and outlet hoses from the unions on the pump body.

(4) Remove the two strap securing bolts and nuts to release the pump from its mounting bracket on the underside of the luggage boot.

(5) Disconnect the supply and earth leads from the terminals on the pump.

(6) Disconnect the vent pipes from the connections on the pump coil housing and the vent valve on the pump end-cover.

(7) Remove the mounting rubber from the pump.

(8) Refitting is a reversal of the foregoing procedure.

Dismantling

Contact breaker

(1) Follow the instructions given in Section Da.1.

Coil housing and diaphragm

(2) Follow the instructions given in Section Da.1, noting the joint washer between the diaphragm and the pump body.

Pedestal and rocker

(3) Follow the instructions given in Section Da.1, noting that the contact blade screw secures one of the condenser tags together with one of the coil tags, and that one of the pedestal screws secures the other tag of the condenser together with the earthing tag.

Body and valves

(4) Remove the two screws securing the inlet and outlet valve clamp plate and withdraw the valve caps, valves, valve seating washers and the fuel filter from the pump body.

(5) Unscrew the four screws to release the flow-smoothing device cover and withdraw the 'O' ring, diaphragm, and sealing washer from the pump body.

(6) Remove the screw to release the inlet air bottle cover and its joint washer from the pump body.

Inspection

(7) Follow the instructions given in Section Da.1, with the following additions.

(*a*) Examine the components of the delivery flow-smoothing device for damage. If the condition of the diaphragm is doubtful it must be renewed.

(*b*) Examine the inlet air bottle cover and its joint washer for damage.

Reassembly

Pedestal and rocker

(8) Follow the instructions given in Section Da.1, noting that the pedestal to coil housing screw spring washer is dispensed with and is replaced by one of the condenser leads.

Diaphragm assembly

(9) Follow the instructions given in Section Da.1.

Body components

(10) Fit the outlet valve joint washer, the outlet valve with its tongue side downwards and the valve cap, into the shallower of the two recesses in the pump body.

(11) Fit the inlet valve components into the deeper of the two recesses in the pump body, in the following order: joint washer, fuel filter with its domed side downwards, joint washer, inlet valve with its tongue side upwards, and valve cap.

(12) Ensure that both valve assemblies are properly seated in their recesses, and refit the valve clamp plate and screws.

(13) Refit the inlet air bottle cover components.

(14) Fit the delivery flow-smoothing device sealing washer followed by the diaphragm with its concave side uppermost, 'O' ring and cover.

Body attachment

(15) Fit the pumping diaphragm joint washer to the pump body, align the screw holes then follow the instructions given in Section Da.1.

Contact blade

(16) Follow the instructions given in Section Da.1, noting that the screw securing the coil lead secures one of the condenser leads.

Contact gap setting

(17) Follow the instructions given in Section Da.1.

End-cover

(18) Follow the instructions given in Section Da.1.

Testing on a test stand

(19) Follow the instructions given in Section Da.1, noting that the pump minimum delivery is 120 pints (144 U.S. pts., 68 litres) per hour.

MG Midget. AKM 2092/1

364

THE FUEL PUMP COMPONENTS
(S.U. Type AUF 305)

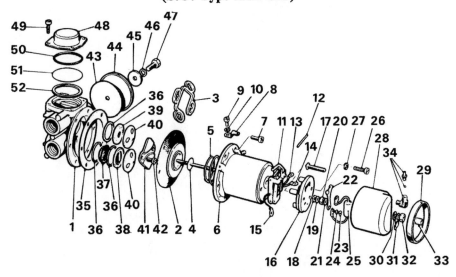

3NC 691A

No.	Description	No.	Description	No.	Description
1.	Pump body.	19.	Lead washer.	36.	Sealing washer.
2.	Diaphragm and spindle assembly.	20.	Terminal nut—2 B.A.	37.	Inlet filter.
3.	Armature guide plate.	21.	Sealing washer—end cover.	38.	Inlet valve.
4.	Impact washer.	22.	Contact blade.	39.	Outlet valve.
5.	Armature spring.	23.	Screw—5 B.A.	40.	Valve cap.
6.	Coil housing.	24.	Washer.	41.	Clamp plate.
7.	Screw—housing to body—2 B.A.	25.	Condenser.	42.	Screw—plate to body.
8.	Connector—earth.	26.	Screw—pedestal to housing—2 B.A.	43.	Joint—inlet air bottle.
9.	Screw—4 B.A.	27.	Spring washer.	44.	Cover—inlet air bottle.
10.	Spring washer.	28.	End cover.	45.	Dished washer.
11.	Rocker mechanism.	29.	Sealing band.	46.	Spring washer.
12.	Rocker pivot pin.	30.	Shakeproof washer.	47.	Screw—cover to body.
13.	Terminal tag—5 B.A.	31.	Connector—feed.	48.	Cover—flow smoothing device.
14.	Terminal tag—2 B.A.	32.	Nut—2 B.A.	49.	Screw—cover to body.
15.	Earth tag—2 B.A.	33.	Insulating sleeve.	50.	'O' ring seal.
16.	Pedestal.	34.	One-way vent valve.	51.	Diaphragm.
17.	Terminal stud.	35.	Gasket—diaphragm to body.	52.	Sealing washer.
18.	Spring washer.				

Section Nb. 9

SWITCHES, WARNING LAMPS AND CONTROLS
(Midget Mk. III from Car No. G–AN5–123731)

NOTE.—Refer to Section Nb.1 for the removal and refitting of the instruments and steering-column switches.

Removing

IMPORTANT.—Disconnect the battery before attempting to remove any of the switches, warning lamps or controls.

Heater blower switch
(1) Remove the bulb holder from the switch retainer.
(2) Disconnect the wiring from the switch.
(3) Remove the retainer from the switch and withdraw the switch from the fascia.

Lighting switch
(4) Remove the centre console—Section Rb.1.
(5) Remove the bulb holder from the switch retainer.
(6) Disconnect the wiring from the switch.
(7) Remove the retainer from the switch and withdraw the switch from the fascia.

MG Midget.   AKM 2092/1

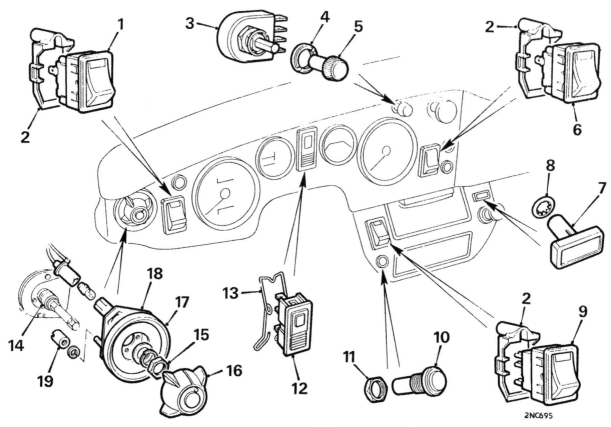

Fig. Nb.5

The switches, lamps and controls (Midget Mk. III from Car No. 123731)

1. Heater blower switch.
2. Retainer for switch.
3. Panel lamp rheostat switch.
4. Retainer for rheostat switch.
5. Knob for panel lamp rheostat switch.
6. Lighting switch.
7. Seat belt warning lamp.
8. Retainer for seat belt warning lamp.
9. Hazard warning switch.
10. Hazard warning lamp.
11. Retainer for hazard warning lamp.
12. Brake pressure—warning light test-push.
13. Retaining clip.
14. Rotary control.
15. Retaining nut.
16. Rotary control knob.
17. Dial assembly.
18. Light box.
19. Retaining nut.

Hazard warning switch

(8) Remove the centre console—Rb.1.

(9) Withdraw the bulb holder from the switch retainer.

(10) Disconnect the wiring plug from the switch.

(11) Remove the retainer from the switch and withdraw the switch from the console.

Panel lamp rheostat switch

(12) Remove the centre console—Section Rb.1.

(13) Disconnect the wiring from the switch.

(14) Depress the pin in the switch knob and withdraw the knob from the switch.

(15) Unscrew the switch retainer and remove the switch from the fascia.

Seat belt warning lamp

(16) Remove the centre console—Section Rb.1.

(17) Remove the bulb holder from the warning lamp.

(18) Remove the warning lamp clip retainer and push the warning lamp out of the centre console.

Hazard warning lamp

(19) Remove the centre console—Section Rb.1.

(20) Remove the bulb holder from the warning lamp.

(21) Unscrew the warning lamp retainer and remove the warning lamp from the centre console.

Air-flow rotary control

(22) Depress the pin in the rotary control knob and withdraw the knob from the spindle.

(23) Remove the bulb holder from the rotary control light box.

(24) Unscrew the nut retaining the rotary control to the fascia and remove the spring and plain washer.

(25) Remove the rotary control from the fascia.

(26) Unscrew the three nuts and remove the three spring and plain washers to release the light box from the dial assembly.

(27) Remove the dial assembly from the fascia.

Sprite and Midget.   Issue 2.   85737

*Nb.*11

Audible warning and courtesy light door switch
   (28) Remove the retaining screw and withdraw the switch.
   (29) Disconnect the wiring from the switch.

Refitting
Heater blower switch
   (30) Reverse the removing procedure in (1) to (3).

Lighting switch
   (31) Reverse the removing procedure in (5) to (7).
   (32) Refit the centre console—Section Rb.1.

Hazard warning switch
   (33) Reverse the removing procedure in (9) to (11).
   (34) Refit the centre console—Section Rb.1.

Panel lamp rheostat switch
   (35) Reverse the removing procedure in (13) to (15).
   (36) Refit the centre console—Section Rb.1.

Seat belt warning lamp
   (37) Reverse the removing procedure in (17) and (18).
   (38) Refit the centre console—Section Rb.1.

Hazard warning lamp
   (39) Reverse the removing procedure in (20) and (21).
   (40) Refit the centre console—Section Rb.1.

Air-flow rotary control
   (41) Reverse the removing procedure in (22) to (27).

Audible warning and courtesy light door switch
   (42) Reverse the removing procedure in (28) and (29).

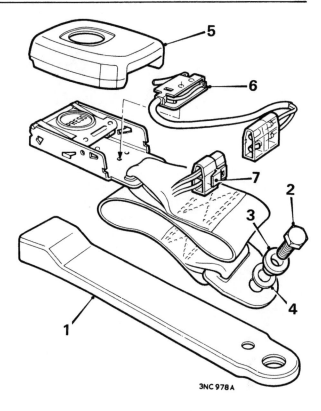

3NC 978A

Fig. Nb.6

Seat belt warning lamp and buzzer—seat belt switch

1. Sleeve.	5. Switch and buckle cover.
2. Retaining bolt.	6. Switch.
3. Spacer.	7. Plug and socket retainers.
4. Bowed spring washer.	

Section Nb.10

SEAT BELT WARNING LAMP AND BUZZER—SEAT BELT SWITCH

Removing
   (1) Disconnect the battery.
   (2) Remove the bolt to release the seat belt buckle assembly from the floor tunnel.
   (3) Compress the retainers and disconnect the belt switch plug from the wiring harness socket.
   (4) Withdraw the sleeve from the buckle until the sleeve is clear of the belt switch cover.
   (5) Prise the sides of the belt switch cover, at its lower end, away from the buckle and withdraw the switch cover.
   (6) Remove the rivets to release the switch from the seat buckle.
   (7) Unsolder the cables from the switch.

Refitting
   (8) Reverse the procedure in 1 to 7.

Section Nb.11

SEAT BELT WARNING LAMP AND BUZZER—SEAT SWITCH

Removing
   (1) Disconnect the battery.
   (2) Remove the two screws securing the rear of the seat runners to the floor and from beneath the car remove the two nuts securing the front of the seat runners to the floor.
   (3) Compress the retainers and disconnect the seat switch plug from the wiring harness socket. Remove the seat from the car.
   (4) Remove the clips to release the seat cover from the rear and one side of the seat frame.
   (5) Detach the seat strapping and frame from the front, rear and one side of the seat frame.
   (6) Detach the hessian cover from the underside of the seat cushion and withdraw the seat switch.

Refitting
   (7) Reverse the procedure in 1 to 6.

*Nb.*12

Sprite and Midget. Issue 2. 85737

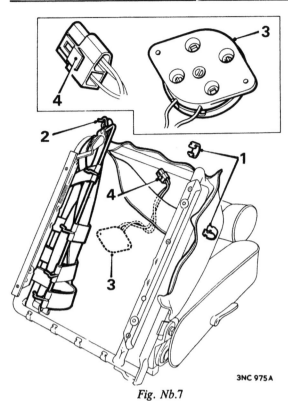

3NC 975A

Fig. Nb.7

Seat belt warning lamp and buzzer—seat switch

1. Seat cover clip.   2. Seat strapping and frame.
3. Switch.   4. Plug and socket retainers.

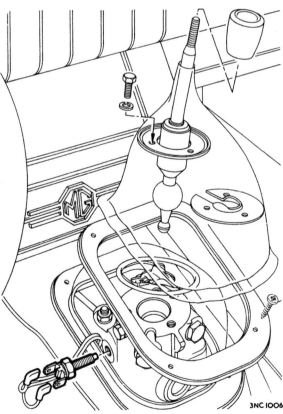

3NC 1006

Fig. Nb.8

Seat belt warning lamp and buzzer—gearbox switch

Section Nb.12

SEAT BELT WARNING LAMP AND BUZZER—GEARBOX SWITCH

Removing

(1) Disconnect the battery.

(2) Remove the tunnel front carpet.

(3) Unscrew the gear lever knob.

(4) Remove the four screws to release the gaiter retainer from the tunnel and withdraw the fabric gaiter.

(5) Remove the three bolts to release the gear lever complete with rubber gaiter from the gearbox.

(6) Disconnect the wiring harness from the two terminal blades on the gearbox switch.

(7) Partially unscrew the switch from the gearbox, secure the switch with a piece of twine to prevent it falling into the propeller shaft tunnel and completely unscrew the switch from the gearbox.

Refitting

(8) Reverse the procedure in 1 to 7.

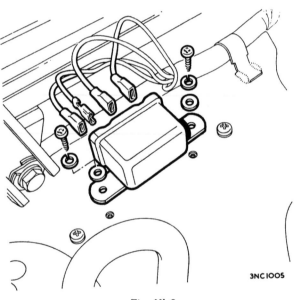

3NC1005

Fig. Nb.9

Sequential seat belt system—starter motor relay

Section Nb.13

SEQUENTIAL SEAT BELT SYSTEM— STARTER MOTOR RELAY

Removing

(1) Disconnect the battery.

(2) Disconnect the wiring harness from the terminal blades on the starter motor relay.

(3) Remove the two screws to release the starter motor relay from the right hand side of the dash bulkhead panel.

Testing

(4) Connect a 12-volt direct current supply between the relay terminals 'W1' and 'W2', and a 12-volt, 2·2-watt test lamp in circuit with a 12-volt direct current supply between terminals 'C1' and 'C2'.

   (*a*) If the testlamp fails to light, check the relay winding resistance, using an ohmmeter connected between terminals 'W1' and 'W2'. Renew the relay if a reading of 76 ohms is not obtained.

   (*b*) If the winding resistance is correct, faulty contact adjustment is indicated which may be corrected as follows:

     (i) Remove the cover from the relay.

     (ii) Check the air gap between the relay bobbin core and the underside of the armature. The air gap should be 0·030± 0·005 in. (0·76±0·13 mm.) when the contact points are open, and 0·010±0·003 in. (0·25±0·08 mm.) when the points are closed. Bend the fixed contact post as necessary.

(5) After any adjustment to the air gap, check the relay cut-in and drop-off voltages as follows:

   (*a*) Connect a variable direct current supply between the relay terminals 'W1' and 'W2' and a 12-volt direct current supply in circuit with a test lamp between terminals 'C1' and 'C2'.

   (*b*) Raise the voltage slowly from zero to 15 volts and check that the test lamp lights at 4·0 to 7·5 volts.

   (*c*) Reduce the voltage slowly from 15 to zero volts and check that the test lamp goes out at 5 volts maximum.

   (*d*) Repeat operation 4 as necessary, and re-check the relay cut-in and drop-off voltages.

(6) Refit the relay cover and crimp the cover lip at the points provided.

Refitting

(7) Reverse the procedure in 1 to 3.

Section Nb.14

SEQUENTIAL SEAT BELT SYSTEM CONTROL UNIT

Removing

(1) Disconnect the battery.

(2) Disconnect the demister hose from the right-hand demister duct and the heater.

(3) Through the aperture in the top of the cubby box, compress the two retaining tags and withdraw the wiring harness plug from the sequential seat belt system control unit.

(4) Remove the two screws to release the control unit from the dash bulkhead panel.

Refitting

(5) Reverse the procedure in 1 to 4.

Nb.14

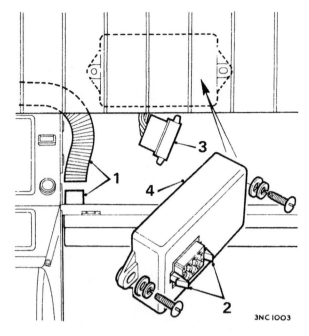

*Fig. Nb.*10

Sequential seat belt system control unit

1. Demister hose.   3. Wiring harness plug.
2. Retaining tags.   4. Control unit.

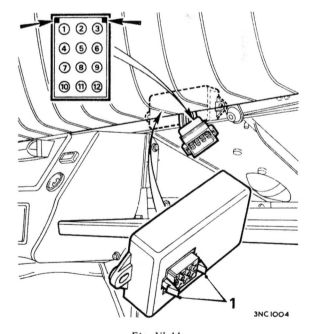

*Fig. Nb.*11

Sequential seat belt system control unit wiring harness plug pin identification numbers. The arrows indicate the plug polarizing keys. Compress the two retaining tags (1) to withdraw the plug from the control unit

Sprite and Midget. Issue 1. 85737

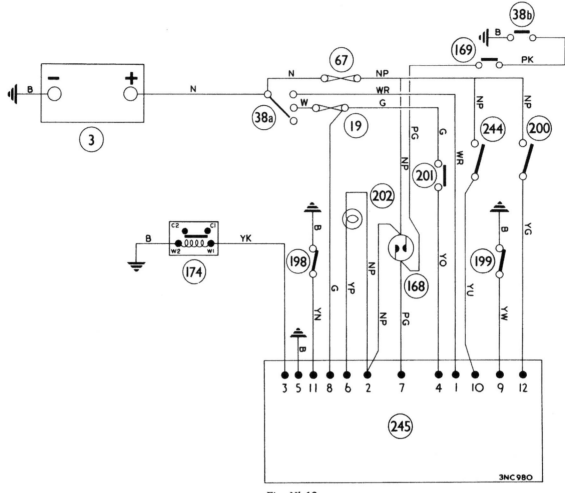

*Fig. Nb.*12

Sequential seat belt system circuit wiring diagram

3. Battery.	174. Starter motor relay.
19. Fuse—35 amp. (connecting fuse box terminals 5 and 6).	198. Driver's seat belt switch (normally closed).
	199. Passenger's seat belt switch (normally closed).
38a. Ignition/starter switch.	200. Passenger's seat switch (normally open).
38b. Ignition key switch.	201. Gearbox switch (closed in gear).
67. Line fuse (500 milliamp.)	202. 'Fasten belts' warning lamp.
168. Warning buzzer.	244. Driver's seat switch (normally open).
169. Warning buzzer door switch.	245. System control unit.

CABLE COLOUR CODE

B. Black.	N. Brown.	U. Blue.
G. Green.	O. Orange.	W. White.
K. Pink.	P. Purple.	Y. Yellow.
	R. Red.	

When a cable has two colour code letters, the first denotes the main colour
and the second denotes the tracer colour.

Section Nb.15

TESTING THE SEQUENTIAL SEAT BELT SYSTEM

Test conditions

1. Battery in good condition.
2. 500 milliamp. line fuse and the 35 amp. fuse connecting fusebox terminals '5' and '6' in good condition.
3. Gear lever in the neutral position.
4. Hand brake applied.
5. Detach the demister hose from the right-hand demister duct and the heater unit.

6. Compress the two retaining tags (see Fig. Nb.11) on the seat belt system control unit and disconnect the wiring plug from the control unit.

Control unit

Prove the control unit by substitution.

Switches and circuit wiring

Referring to Figs. Nb.11 and Nb.12 for circuit diagram and wiring harness plug pin identification numbers, carry out the following test procedure using a 12-volt 2·2-watt test lamp and a length of insulated cable.

Sprite and Midget.   Issue 1.   85737

Test	Procedure		Circuit	Requirements	Remarks
	Using test lamp to bridge plug pins	Using cable only to bridge plug pins			
1. Supply from battery	2 and 5	—	Positive battery feed to earth	Test lamp ON	If the test lamp does not operate, the circuit is faulty.
2. Driver's seat belt switch	2 and 11	—	Positive battery feed via belt switch to earth	(a) Test lamp ON— seat belt unfastened (b) Test lamp OFF— seat belt fastened	If the test lamp does not operate in (a) or lights in (b) either the seat belt switch or the circuit wiring is faulty.
3. Driver's seat switch	5 and 10	—	Positive battery feed via driver's seat switch to earth	(c) Test lamp ON— driver seated (d) Test lamp OFF— driver unseated	If the test lamp does not operate in (c) or lights in (d), either the seat switch or the circuit wiring is faulty.
4. Passenger's seat belt switch	2 and 9	—	Positive battery feed via belt switch to earth	(e) Test lamp ON— seat belt unfastened (f) Test lamp OFF— seat belt fastened	If the test lamp does not operate in (e) or lights in (f), either the seat belt switch or the circuit wiring is faulty.
5. Passenger's seat switch	5 and 12	—	Positive battery feed via passenger's seat switch to earth	(g) Test lamp ON— passenger seated (h) Test lamp OFF— passenger unseated	If the test lamp does not operate in (g) or lights in (h), either the seat switch or the circuit wiring is faulty.
6. Gearbox switch	4 and 5 (ignition on)	—	Positive battery feed via ignition and gearbox switches to earth	Test lamp ON— gear engaged	If the test lamp does not operate when a gear is engaged, either the ignition or the gearbox switch, or the circuit wiring is faulty. If the test lamp lights when the gear lever is in neutral, the gearbox switch is faulty.

Nb.16

Sprite and Midget. Issue 1. 85737

371

Test	Procedure		Circuit	Requirements	Remarks
	Using test lamp to bridge plug pins	Using cable only to bridge plug pins			
7. Steering-column lock, ignition/starter switch	1 and 5	—	Positive battery feed via starter switch to earth	(j) Test lamp ON—switch in position 'III' (k) Test lamp OFF—switch in position 'O' or 'I' or 'II'	If the test lamp does not operate in (j), either the steering column lock, ignition/starter switch or the circuit wiring is faulty. If the test lamp lights in (k), the steering-column lock, ignition/starter switch is faulty.
8. Starter relay	—	2 and 3	Positive battery feed via starter relay to earth	Starter motor operates	If the starter motor does not operate, either the starter relay or its circuit wiring or the starter or its circuit wiring is faulty.
9. Seat belt warning lamp	—	5 and 6	Positive battery feed via warning lamp to earth	Warning lamp ON	If the warning lamp does not operate, either the warning lamp bulb or the circuit wiring is faulty.
10. Warning buzzer	—	5 and 7	Positive battery feed via warning buzzer to earth	(l) Warning buzzer operates—ignition key removed (m) Warning buzzer does not operate—ignition key in switch, driver's door closed, and bridging cable disconnected from pins 5 and 7.	If the warning buzzer does not operate in (l), either the warning buzzer or the circuit wiring is faulty. If the warning buzzer operates in (m), either the driver's door switch or the circuit wiring between the warning buzzer and the door switch is faulty.

Sprite and Midget.   Issue 1.   85737

Nb.17

KEY TO THE WIRING DIAGRAMS

Use the one key to identify components on these wiring diagrams.

Refer to the appropriate wiring diagram, and disregard any additional numbered items appearing
in the key and not on a particular diagram.

[NOTE:—The diagrams on the four following pages apply to
the car models listed on page 249.]

1.	Dynamo/alternator.	40.	Distributor.
2.	Control box.	41.	Fuel pump.
3.	Battery.	43.	Oil pressure gauge.
4.	Starter solenoid.	44.	Ignition warning lamp.
5.	Starter motor.	45.	Headlamp flasher switch.
6.	Lighting switch.	46.	Coolant temperature gauge.
7.	Headlamp dip switch.	49.	Reverse lamp switch.
8.	Headlamp dip-beam.	50.	Reverse lamp.
9.	Headlamp main beam.	57.	Cigar-lighter—illuminated.
10.	Headlamp main-beam warning lamp.	60.	Radio.
11.	R.H. parking lamp.	64.	Bi-metal instrument voltage stabilizer.
12.	L.H. parking lamp.	65.	Luggage compartment lamp switch.
13.	Panel lamp switch.	66.	Luggage compartment lamp.
14.	Panel lamps.	67.	Line fuse.
15.	Number-plate illumination lamp.	77.	Windscreen washer pump.
16.	Stop lamp.	82.	Switch illumination lamp.
17.	R.H. tail lamp.	94.	Oil filter switch.
18.	Stop lamp switch.	95.	Tachometer.
19.	Fuse unit.	105.	Oil filter warning lamp.
20.	Interior courtesy lamp.	118.	Combined windscreen washer and wiper switch.
21.	Interior courtesy lamp door switch.	152.	Hazard warning lamp.
22.	L.H. tail lamp.	153.	Hazard warning switch.
23.	Horns.	154.	Hazard warning flasher unit.
24.	Horn-push.	159.	Brake pressure warning lamp and lamp test push.
25.	Flasher unit.	160.	Brake pressure failure switch.
26.	Direction indicator switch.	168.	Ignition key audible warning buzzer.
27.	Direction indicator warning lamp.	169.	Ignition key audible warning door switch.
28.	R.H. front flasher lamp.	170.	R.H. front side-marker lamp.
29.	L.H. front flasher lamp.	171.	L.H. front side-marker lamp.
30.	R.H. rear flasher lamp.	172.	R.H. rear side-marker lamp.
31.	L.H. rear flasher lamp.	173.	L.H. rear side-marker lamp.
32.	Heater or fresh-air motor switch.	198.	Driver's seat belt buckle switch.
33.	Heater or fresh-air motor.	199.	Passenger's seat belt buckle switch.
34.	Fuel gauge.	200.	Passenger seat switch.
35.	Fuel gauge tank unit.	201.	Seat belt warning gearbox switch.
36.	Windscreen wiper switch.	202.	'Fasten belts' warning light.
37.	Windscreen wiper motor.	203.	Line diode.
38.	Ignition/starter switch.	211.	Heater control illumination bulb.
39.	Ignition coil.		

CABLE COLOUR CODE

N.	Brown.	P.	Purple.	W.	White.	K.	Pink.
U.	Blue.	G.	Green.	Y.	Yellow.	O.	Orange.
R.	Red.	L.G.	Light Green.s	B.	Black.		

When a cable has two colour-code letters the first denotes the main
colour and the second denotes the tracer colour

Diagram 11
(Refer to page 373 for the key)

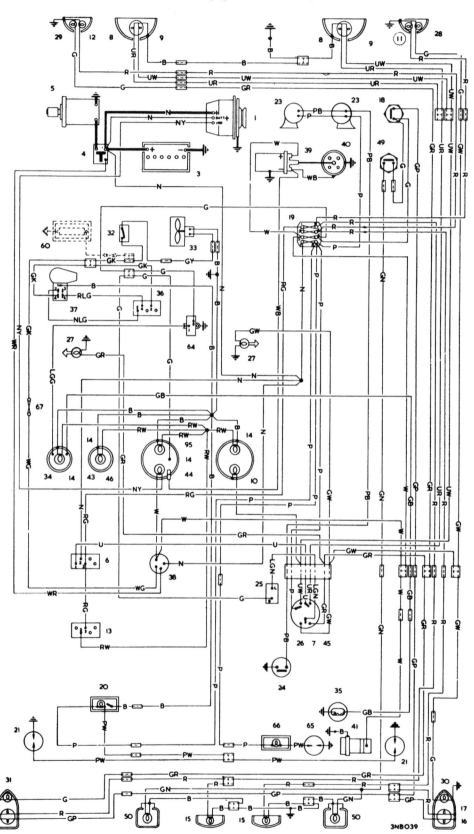

3NBO39

Diagram 12
(Refer to page 373 for the key)

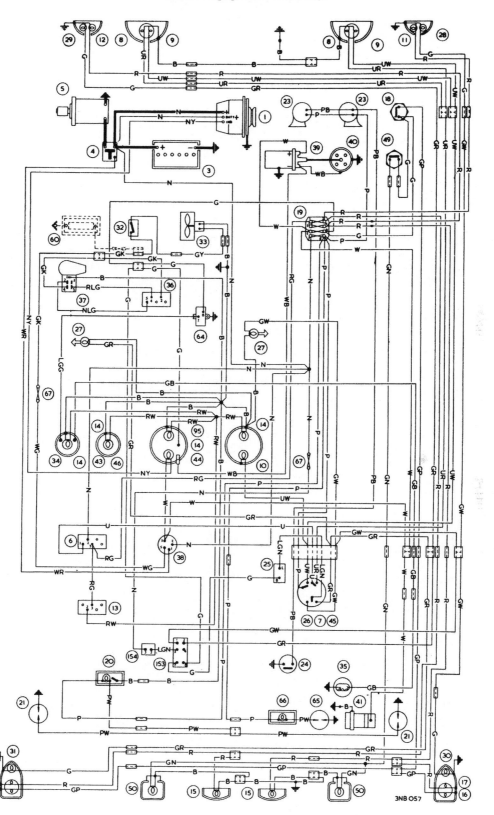

3NB 057

MG Midget.   AKM 2092/1

Diagram 13
(Refer to page 373 for the key)

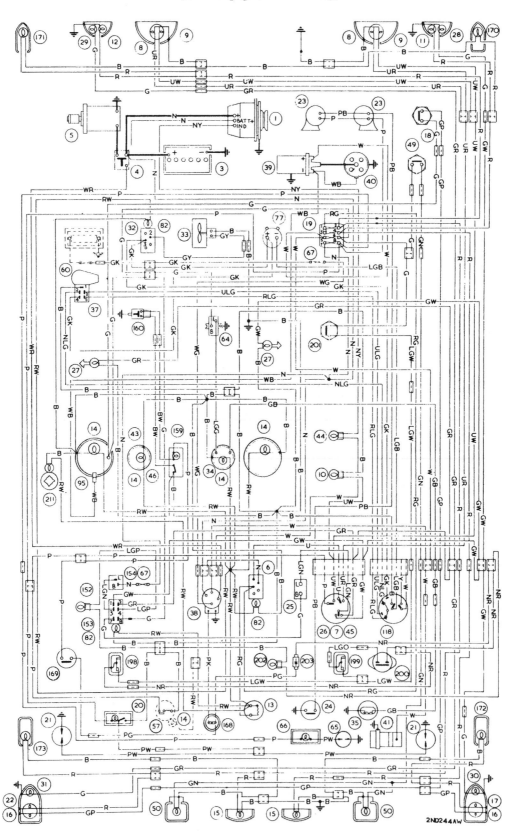

2ND244AW

MG Midget. AKM 2092/1

Diagram 14

(Refer to page 373 for the key)

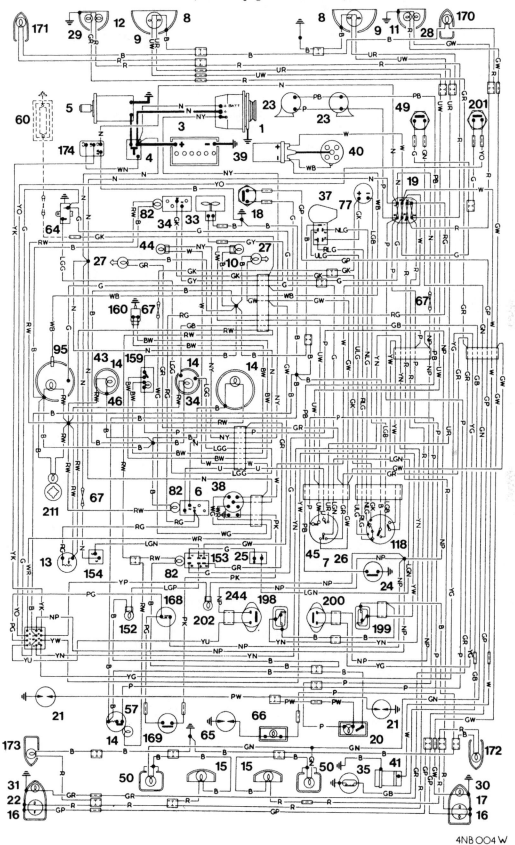

4NB 004 W

MG Midget.   AKM 2092/1

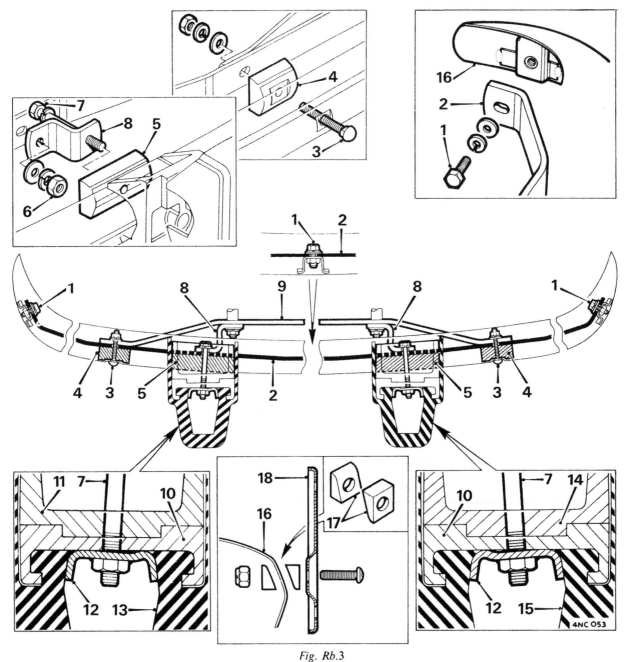

Fig. Rb.3

The front bumper assembly (Midget Mk. III from Car No. G–AN5–143355)

1. Bumper bar securing bolt.
2. Main spring.
3. Dome head bolt.
4. Small spacer.
5. Large spacer.
6. Bumper assembly securing nut.
7. Over-rider assembly securing bolt.
8. Reinforcement bracket.
9. Support spring.
10. Over-rider mounting bracket.
11. Right-hand support casting.
12. Over-rider clamping bracket.
13. Right-hand over-rider.
14. Left-hand support casting.
15. Left-hand over-rider.
16. Bumper bar.
17. Spacers.
18. Number-plate.

Section Rb.6

THE FRONT BUMPER AND OVER-RIDERS

(Midget Mk. III from Car No. G–AN5–143355)

Removing

(1) Remove the two nuts to release the front bumper assembly from the mounting brackets.

(2) Remove the nuts from the dome headed bolts, withdraw the bolts and detach the support spring from the main spring, noting the small spacers fitted between the main spring and the bumper bar.

(3) Remove the small bolts securing the centre and each end of the bumper bar to the main spring.

(4) Remove each over-rider assembly retaining bolt and detach the over-riders, support castings, bumper bar, main spring, and reinforcement bracket, noting the large spacer fitted between the bumper bar and the main spring.

(5) Remove the nuts, bolts, and spacers to release the number-plate from the bumper.

(6) To dismantle the over-rider assembly proceed as follows:

   (*a*) Mark the over-rider clamping bracket and mounting bracket at the top to assist re-assembling.

   (*b*) Remove the clamping bracket securing screws and remove the clamping bracket.

   (*c*) Slide the mounting bracket from the over-rider.

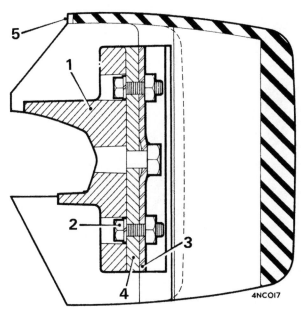

Fig. Rb.4

The over-rider assembly and support casting
(Midget Mk. III from Car. No. G–AN5–143355)

1. Support casting.
2. Clamping bracket securing bolt.
3. Clamping bracket.
4. Mounting bracket.
5. Over-rider.

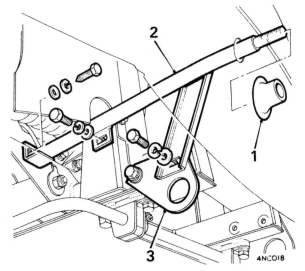

Fig. Rb.5

The front bumper mounting bracket
(Midget Mk. III from Car No. G–AN5–143355)

1. Grommet.
2. Towing eye.
3. Front bumper mounting bracket

Refitting

(7) Reverse the procedure in 1 to 6, referring to Fig. Rb.3 and noting:

   (*a*) Ensure that the clamping bracket is correctly fitted.

   (*b*) The over-rider assemblies are handed.

   (*c*) The fitted position of the over-rider assembly retaining bolt is at an angle; take care not to damage the thread.

   (*d*) Ensure that the bumper spacers and number-plate spacers are correctly fitted, noting that the flat face of the bumper spacers are lower-most.

Section Rb.7

THE FRONT BUMPER MOUNTING BRACKET

(Midget Mk. III from Car No. G–AN5–143355)

Removing

(1) Remove the two nuts securing the bumper assembly to release the front bumper assembly.

(2) Remove the grommet from the front mounting bracket.

(3) Slacken the towing eye rearmost securing bolt.

(4) Remove the three bolts securing the mounting bracket.

(5) Swing the long support of the mounting bracket towards the road wheel and manœuvre the mounting bracket down and then rearwards.

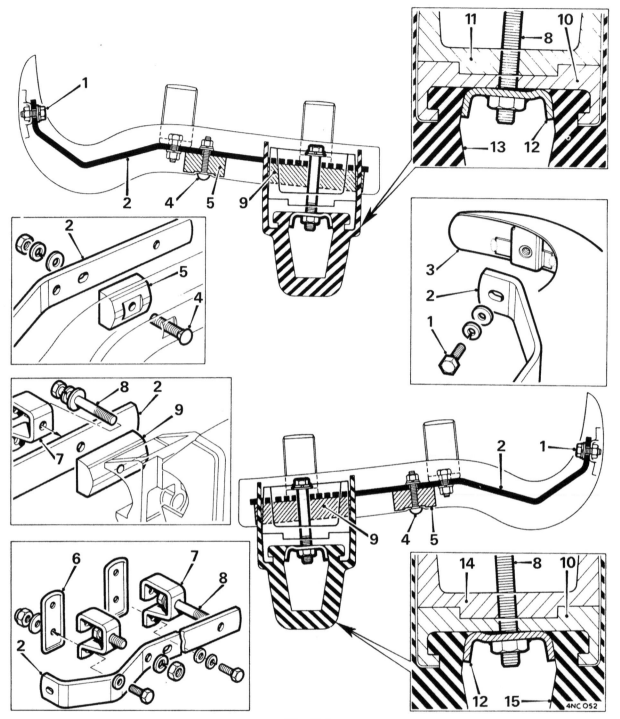

Fig. Rb.6

The rear bumper assembly (*Midget Mk. III from Car No. G–AN5–143355*)

1. Bumper bar securing bolt.
2. Main spring.
3. Bumper bar.
4. Dome head bolt.
5. Small spacer.
6. Gasket.
7. Mounting bracket.
8. Over-rider assembly securing bolt.
9. Large spacer.
10. Over-rider mounting bracket.
11. Left-hand over-rider support casting.
12. Over-rider clamping bracket.
13. Left-hand over-rider.
14. Right-hand over-rider support casting.
15. Right-hand over-rider.

MG Midget.   AKM 2092/1

Refitting

(6) Reverse the procedure in 1 to 5, noting:

    (*a*) The towing eye bracket is fitted between the mounting bracket support and the longitudinal member.

    (*b*) Fit the mounting bracket securing bolts finger tight, tightening them only when the bumper assembly is secured to the brackets.

Section Rb.8

THE REAR BUMPER AND OVER-RIDERS

(Midget Mk. III from Car No. G–AN5–143355)

Removing

(1) Remove the mounting bracket securing nuts and bolts to release one half of the rear bumper assembly from the body together with the gaskets.

(2) Remove the nut and bolt to release the outer mounting bracket from the main spring.

(3) Unscrew the nut and remove the dome headed bolt, noting the small spacer fitted between the bumper bar and the main spring. Remove the small bolt securing the end of the bumper to the main spring.

(4) Remove the over-rider assembly retaining bolt to remove the over-rider assembly, support casting and inner mounting bracket from the bumper bar and main spring, noting the large spacer fitted between the bumper bar and main spring.

(5) To dismantle the over-rider assembly proceed as follows:

    (*a*) Mark the clamping bracket and the mounting bracket at the top to assist reassembling.

    (*b*) Remove the clamping bracket securing screws and remove the clamping bracket.

    (*c*) Slide the mounting bracket from the over-rider.

(6) Repeat procedures 1 to 5 for the other rear bumper assembly.

Refitting

(7) Reverse the procedure in 1 to 6, referring to Fig. Rb.6 and noting the following:

    (*a*) Ensure that the clamping bracket is correctly fitted to the over-rider.

    (*b*) The over-rider assemblies are handed.

    (*c*) The fitted position of the over-rider assembly retaining bolt is at an angle; take care not to damage the thread.

APPENDIX

R.H.D. and L.H.D. EXCEPT NORTH AMERICA

SERVICE OPERATIONS—SUMMARY

After Sales Service = 1,000 miles (1500 km)
A   Every 6,000 miles (10 000 km) or 6 months
B   Every 12,000 miles (20 000 km) or 12 months
Items included in the 3,000 miles (5000 km) or 3 months interval Optional Inspection Check are indicated in **column C**

After Sales	A	B	C	ACTION ● OPERATION X **Leycare Service**	
●	●	●	●	Fit seat cover	
	X	X	X	Check condition and security of seats and seat belts	
●	●	●	●	Drive on lift; stop engine	
X	X	X	X	Check operation of lamps	
X	X	X	X	Check operation of horns	
X	X	X	X	Check operation of warning indicators	
X	X	X	X	Check/adjust operation of windscreen washers	
X	X	X	X	Check operation of windscreen wipers	
X	X	X	X	Check operation of hand brake; release fully after checking	
	X	X	X	Check rear view mirrors for cracks and crazing	
X				Check operation of window controls	
●	●	●	●	Open bonnet, fit wing covers. Raise lift to convenient working height with wheels free to rotate	
●	●	●	●	Remove hub cap	
	●	●		Mark stud to wheel relationship, remove road wheel	⎫
	X	X	X	Check tyre complies with manufacturer's specification	
	X	X	X	Check tyre for tread depth	
X	X	X	X	Check tyre visually for external cuts in fabric	
X	X	X	X	Check tyre visually for external exposure of ply or cord	
X	X	X	X	Check tyre visually for external lumps and bulges	
X	X	X	X	Check/adjust tyre pressures	
	X	X		Inspect brake pads for wear and discs for condition	Starting at the
X	X	X	X	Check for oil leaks from steering and fluid leaks from shock absorbers	right-hand front wheel, complete
X	X	X	X	Check condition and security of steering unit, joints and gaiters	these operations at each wheel
		X		Remove brake-drum, wipe out dust, inspect shoes for wear and drum for condition, refit drum	
X	X	X	X	Adjust brakes	
X	X	X		Lubricate all grease points (excluding hubs)	
	●	●		Refit road wheel in original position	
X	X	X	X	Check tightness of road wheel nuts	
●	●	●	●	Refit hub cap	⎭
●	●	●	●	Raise lift to full height	
X	X	X		Drain engine oil	
X				Drain gearbox oil	
X		X	X	Check/top up rear axle oil	
	X	X		Lubricate hand brake mechanical linkage and cables	
X	X	X	X	Check visually brake pipes and unions for chafing, leaks and corrosion	
X	X	X	X	Check visually fuel and clutch pipes for chafing, leaks and corrosion	
	X	X	X	Check exhaust system for leakage and security	
X				Check security of accessible engine mountings	
X				Check security of suspension fixings	
	X	X		Renew engine oil filter element	
●	●	●		Refit engine drain plug	
●				Refit gearbox drain plug	
●	●	●		Clean/paint timing marks	
●	●	●	●	Lower lift	

MG Midget. AKM 2092/1

R.H.D. and L.H.D. except North America—continued

After Sales	A	B	C	ACTION ● OPERATION X
●	●	●		Fit exhaust extractor pipe
	X	X		Check/top up gearbox oil
X				Fill gearbox with oil
X	X	X		Lubricate front end of the propshaft (early models only)
	X	X		Lubricate steering rack and pinion (early models only)
X				Check/adjust torque of cylinder head nuts
X				Check/adjust torque of rocker shaft nuts
X				Check/adjust torque of manifold nuts
X		X		Check/adjust valve clearances
X	X	X		Fill engine with oil
			X	Check/top up engine oil
		X		Lubricate water pump (early models only)
	X	X		Lubricate dynamo bearing (early models only)
X	X	X		Top up carburetter piston dampers
X	X	X		Lubricate accelerator control, linkage and pedal pivot
		X		Renew air cleaner elements
X				Check security of accessible engine mountings
X	X	X	X	Check driving belts, adjust or renew
	X			Clean/adjust spark plugs
		X		Renew spark plugs
X	X	X	X	Check/top up battery electrolyte
	X	X		Clean and grease battery connections
X	X	X	X	Check/top up clutch fluid reservoir
X	X	X	X	Check/top up brake fluid reservoir
X	X	X	X	Check/top up windscreen washer reservoir
X	X	X	X	Check/top up cooling system
X	X	X		Check cooling and heater system for leaks
		X		Clean and test crankcase breather valve
		X		Renew engine breather filter (oil filler cap)
	●	●		Run engine and check sealing of oil filter, stop engine
X	X	X		Recheck/top up engine oil
●	●	●		Connect electronic instruments
X	X	X		Check visually distributor points, renew if necessary
X	X	X		Check for volt drop between coil CB and earth
X	X	X		Lubricate distributor
●	●	●		Run engine
X	X	X		Disconnect vacuum pipe, check dwell angle, adjust points as necessary
X	X	X		Check stroboscopic ignition timing
X	X	X		Check distributor automatic advance
X	X	X		Check advance increase as vacuum pipe is reconnected
X	X	X		Check throttle operation, set to fast idle until engine reaches normal running temperature
X	X	X		Lubricate all locks and hinges (not steering lock)
	X	X	X	Check and if necessary renew windscreen wiper blades
X	X	X		Check/adjust engine idle speed and carburetter mixture setting
●	●	●		Stop engine, disconnect instruments
●	●	●	●	Remove wing covers
	●	●		Fill in details and fix appropriate Unipart underbonnet stickers
●	●	●	●	Close bonnet
●	●	●		Remove exhaust extractor pipe
●	●	●	●	Remove spare wheel
	X	X	X	Check spare tyre complies with manufacturer's specification
	X	X	X	Check depth of tread

Refer to Data Card *(brackets rows: Disconnect vacuum pipe … Check advance increase as vacuum pipe is reconnected)*

MG Midget. AKM 2092/1

R.H.D. and L.H.D. except North America—continued

After Sales	A	B	C	ACTION ● OPERATION X
X	X	X	X	Check visually for external cuts in tyre fabric
X	X	X	X	Check visually for external exposure of ply or cord
X	X	X	X	Check visually for external lumps or bulges
X	X	X	X	Check/adjust tyre pressures
●	●	●	●	Refit spare wheel. Drive car off lift
X	X	X	X	Check/adjust headlamp alignment
X	X	X		Check/adjust front wheel alignment
X	X	X		Carry out road or roller test and check function of all instrumentation
X	X	X	X	Report any additional work required
X	X	X	X	Ensure cleanliness of controls, door handles, steering-wheel, etc.
●	●	●	●	Remove seat cover

This Maintenance Summary was produced from Leycare Supplementary Job Sheet AKD 8495 (1st Edition). Job sheets used by British Leyland Distributors and Dealers operating Leycare Service are updated as modifications affecting routine maintenance are introduced, and the content of this maintenance summary may differ from that currently used by Leycare Service operatives.

APPENDIX

NORTH AMERICA

Basic engine tuning data will be found on the Vehicle Emission Control Information label, located in the engine compartment.

The following items should be checked weekly by the driver:

Engine oil level
Brake fluid level
Radiator coolant level
Battery electrolyte level
Windshield washer reservoir fluid level
All tyre pressures
All lights for operation
Horn operation
Windshield wipers operation

MAINTENANCE INTERVALS

†**These items are emission related**

Carry out the services indicated by **X** in column

The Lubrication Service at **3,000-mile or 3 month** intervals
A at **6,000-mile or 6-month** intervals
B at **12,000-mile or 12-month** intervals
*Specified otherwise

	Lubrication Service	A	B
LUBRICATION			
Lubricate all points	X	X	X
Check level of all fluid reservoirs, brake, clutch, battery, rear axle, transmission, cooling system and windshield washer	X	X	X
Renew engine oil	X	X	X
Renew engine oil filter		X	X
ENGINE			
†Check all drive belts; adjust if necessary			X
†Check all hoses, vacuum, air and water, for condition and tightness			X
†Renew all air filter cleaner elements (air pump and carburetter)			X
†Check restrictor in rocker cover purge line for obstruction			X
†Adjust valve rocker clearances		X	X
†Check gulp valve operation (renew if necessary)			X
FUEL SYSTEM			
†Renew fuel line filter			X
†Check condition of fuel filler cap seal			X
†Check fuel pipes and unions for chafing, corrosion and leaks			X
†Top up carburetter piston dampers		X	X
OSCILLOSCOPE AND COMBUSTION CHECK			
†Check distributor points, resistance and dwell		X	X
†Renew distributor points			X
†Check ignition timing and distributor advance or retard characteristics		X	X
†Check spark plugs (cruise and unload condition)		X	X
†Renew spark plugs			X
†Check distributor cap and wires		X	X
Check charging system output		X	X
†Power check, engine cylinder comparison			X
†Check engine idle speed		X	X
†Check choke and carburetter fast idle setting		X	X
†Check exhaust emission (CO HC) at idle		X	X

MG Midget. AKM 2092/1

North America—continued

	A	B
SAFETY		
Check/adjust front wheel alignment		X
Check visually hydraulic pipes, unions for chafing, leaks and corrosion		X
Check/adjust hand brake operation	X	X
Inspect brake pads for wear and discs for condition	X	
Inspect brake linings and pads for wear, drums and discs for condition		X
Check/adjust headlights	X	X
Check tyres visually and report depth of tread, cuts in fabric, exposure of ply or cord structure, lumps or bulges	X	X
Check operation of all door locks and window controls		X
Check condition, operation and security of seats and seat belts/interlock		X
Check wiper blades for condition		X
ROAD TEST		
Ensure that operation of vehicle is satisfactory and report all items requiring attention	X	X

*24,000 miles or 24-month intervals

*†Renew all drive belts
*†Check air pump (correct or renew if necessary)
*†Renew adsorption canister
*†Renew distributor cap and wires

*36,000 miles or 36-month intervals

*Renew all hydraulic brake seals

The maintenance summary on this and the preceding pages is the minimum service required to maintain your vehicle under normal driving conditions. For other than normal driving conditions and those caused by seasonal changes, we recommend that you consult your Dealer.

MG Midget.   AKM 2092/1

R.H.D. and L.H.D. EXCEPT NORTH AMERICA

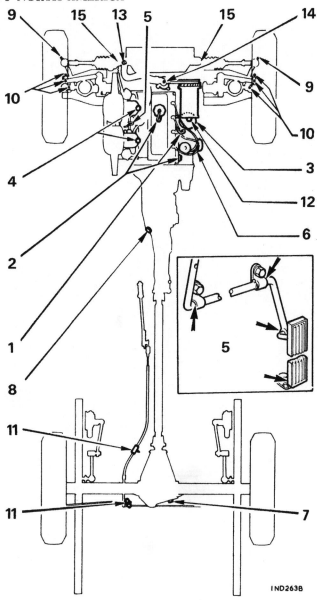

IND263B

NOTE.—Ensure that the vehicle is standing on a level surface when checking the oil levels.

Weekly
(1) ENGINE. Check oil level and top up if necessary.

Every 6,000 miles (10 000 km) or 6 months
(2) ENGINE. Drain and refill with new oil.
(3) ENGINE OIL FILTER. Remove disposable cartridge, fit new. Early cars: Drain filter, wash filter bowl in fuel and fit new element.
(4) CARBURETTERS. Top up carburetter piston dampers.
(5) ACCELERATOR. Lubricate accelerator control linkage, cable and pedal fulcrum.
(6) DISTRIBUTOR. Lubricate all parts as necessary.
(7) REAR AXLE. Check oil level, and top up if necessary.
(8) GEARBOX. Check oil level and top up if necessary.
(9) STEERING TIE-ROD BALL JOINT (2 nipples)
(10) FRONT SUSPENSION (6 nipples)
(11) HAND BRAKE CABLE (1 nipple) and mechanical linkage

Give three or four strokes with a grease gun.

(12) DYNAMO (*Early cars only*). Add a few drops of oil through the oil hole in the commutator end bearing.

Every 12,000 miles (20 000 km) or 12 months
(13) STEERING RACK (*Early cars*—with an oil nipple fitted). give 10 strokes with an oil gun.
(14) WATER PUMP (*Early cars only*). Remove the plug and add grease; do not overgrease.

Every 30,000 miles (50 000 km) or 36 months
(15) STEERING RACK (*Later cars*—from Car No. G-AN5-114643). Lubricate steering rack.—It is advisable that this work is entrusted to your Distributor or Dealer.

Optional lubrication at 3,000 miles (5000 km) or 3 months
(1) ENGINE. Check oil level and top up if necessary.

MG Midget. AKM 2092/1

NORTH AMERICA

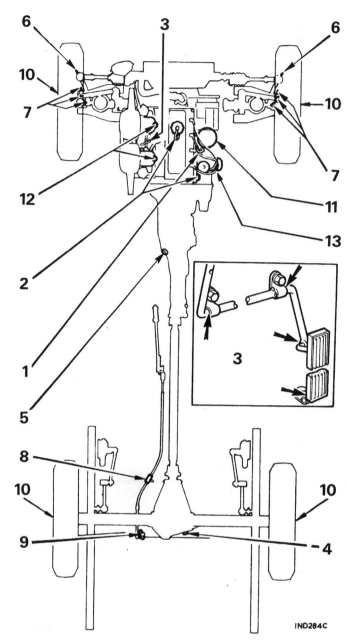

IND284C

NOTE.—Ensure that the vehicle is standing on a level surface when checking the oil levels.

Weekly
(1) ENGINE. Check oil level, and top up if necessary.

Lubrication service every 3,000 miles or 3 months
(2) ENGINE. Drain and refill with new oil.
(3) THROTTLE AND CHOKE. Lubricate throttle and choke control linkages, cables, and accelerator pedal fulcrum.
(4) REAR AXLE. Check oil level, and top up if necessary.
(5) GEARBOX. Check oil level, and top up if necessary.
(6) STEERING TIE-ROD BALL JOINT (2 nipples)
(7) FRONT SUSPENSION (6 nipples)
(8) HAND BRAKE CABLE (1 nipple)
(9) HAND BRAKE COMPENSATING LEVER (1 nipple)

} Give three or four strokes with a grease gun

(10) WHEELS AND HUBS. Lubricate wire wheel and hub splines.
LOCKS, HINGES AND LINKAGES. Lubricate all door, bonnet and boot locks and hinges; and the hand brake mechanical linkage.
FRICTION POINTS. Spray lubricant on all friction points.

'A' service every 6,000 miles or 6 months; AND 'B' service every 12,000 miles or 12 months
(11) ENGINE OIL FILTER. Remove disposable cartridge, fit new.
(12) CARBURETTERS. Top up carburetter piston dampers.
(13) DISTRIBUTOR. Lubricate all parts as necessary.

MG Midget. AKM 2092/1